MASTER VISUALLY®

eBay® Business Kit

by Sherry Kinkoph and Mike Wooldridge

From

maranGraphics®

&

Wiley Publishing, Inc.

Master VISUALLY® eBay® Business Kit

Published by
Wiley Publishing, Inc.
111 River Street
Hoboken, NJ 07030-5774

Published simultaneously in Canada

maranGraphics, Inc.
5755 Coopers Avenue
Mississauga, Ontario, Canada
L4Z 1R9

Library of Congress Control Number: 2004102591

ISBN: 0-7645-6816-7

Manufactured in the United States of America

10 9 8 7 6 5 4 3 2 1

1V/SQ/QX/QU/IN

Trademark Acknowledgments

Important Numbers

For U.S. corporate orders, please call maranGraphics at 800-469-6616 or fax 905-890-9434.

For general information on our other products and services or to obtain technical support please contact our Customer Care Department within the U.S. at 800-762-2974, outside the U.S. at 317-572-3993 or fax 317-572-4002.

Permissions

maranGraphics

Certain text and illustrations by maranGraphics, Inc., used with maranGraphics' permission.

Permissions Granted

SquareTrade

U.S. Corporate Sales

Contact maranGraphics
at (800) 469-6616 or
fax (905) 890-9434.

U.S. Trade Sales

Contact Wiley
at (800) 762-2974 or
fax (317) 572-4002.

Praise for Visual books...

"If you have to see it to believe it, this is the book for you!"
–PC World

"A master tutorial/reference – from the leaders in visual learning!"
–Infoworld

"A publishing concept whose time has come!"
–The Globe and Mail

"Just wanted to say THANK YOU to your company for providing books which make learning fast, easy, and exciting! I learn visually so your books have helped me greatly – from Windows instruction to Web page development. I'm looking forward to using more of your Master VISUALLY series in the future, as I am now a computer support specialist. Best wishes for continued success."
–Angela J. Barker (Springfield, MO)

"I have over the last 10-15 years purchased thousands of dollars worth of computer books but find your books the most easily read, best set out, and most helpful and easily understood books on software and computers I have ever read. Please keep up the good work."
–John Gatt (Adamstown Heights, Australia)

"I am an avid fan of your Visual books. If I need to learn anything, I just buy one of your books and learn the topic in no time. Wonders! I have even trained my friends to give me Visual books as gifts."
–Illona Bergstrom (Aventura, FL)

"The Greatest. This whole series is the best computer-learning tool of any kind I've ever seen."
–Joe Orr (Brooklyn, NY)

"What fantastic teaching books you have produced! Congratulations to you and your staff."
–Bruno Tonon (Melbourne, Australia)

"I have quite a few of your Visual books and have been very pleased with all of them. I love the way the lessons are presented!"
–Mary Jane Newman (Yorba Linda, CA)

"Like a lot of other people, I understand things best when I see them visually. Your books really make learning easy and life more fun."
–John T. Frey (Cadillac, MI)

"Your Visual books have been a great help to me. I now have a number of your books and they are all great. My friends always ask to borrow my Visual books - trouble is, I always have to ask for them back!"
–John Robson (Brampton, Ontario, Canada)

"I would like to take this time to compliment maranGraphics on creating such great books. I work for a leading manufacturer of office products, and sometimes they tend to NOT give you the meat and potatoes of certain subjects, which causes great confusion. Thank you for making it clear. Keep up the good work."
–Kirk Santoro (Burbank, CA)

"I write to extend my thanks and appreciation for your books. They are clear, easy to follow, and straight to the point. Keep up the good work! I bought several of your books and they are just right! No regrets! I will always buy your books because they are the best."
–Seward Kollie (Dakar, Senegal)

"You're marvelous! I am greatly in your debt."
–Patrick Baird (Lacey, WA)

Dec 02

maranGraphics is a family-run business located near Toronto, Canada.

At maranGraphics, we believe in producing great computer books – one book at a time.

maranGraphics has been producing high-technology products for over 25 years, which enables us to offer the computer book community a unique communication process.

Our computer books use an integrated communication process, which is very different from the approach used in other computer books. Each spread is, in essence, a flow chart – the text and screen shots are totally incorporated into the layout of the spread. Introductory text and helpful tips complete the learning experience.

maranGraphics' approach encourages the left and right sides of the brain to work together – resulting in faster orientation and greater memory retention.

Above all, we are very proud of the handcrafted nature of our books. Our carefully-chosen writers are experts in their fields, and spend countless hours researching and organizing the content for each topic. Our artists rebuild every screen shot to provide the best clarity possible, making our screen shots the most precise and easiest to read in the industry. We strive for perfection, and believe that the time spent handcrafting each element results in the best computer books money can buy.

Thank you for purchasing this book. We hope you enjoy it!

Sincerely,

Robert Maran
President
maranGraphics

Rob@maran.com
www.maran.com

CREDITS

Project Editor
Sarah Hellert

Acquisitions Editor
Jody Lefevere

Product Development Manager
Lindsay Sandman

Copy Editor
Kim Heusel

Technical Editor
Kerwin McKenzie

Editorial Manager
Robyn Siesky

Permissions Editor
Laura Moss

Media Development Specialist
Kit Malone

Manufacturing
Allan Conley
Linda Cook
Paul Gilchrist
Jennifer Guynn

Project Coordinator
Maridee V. Ennis

Book Design
maranGraphics®

Layout
Beth Brooks
Sean Decker
Carrie Foster
Jennifer Heleine
Heather Pope
Kristin McMullan

Screen Artist
Jill A. Proll

Illustrators
Ronda David-Burroughs
David E. Gregory

Proofreader
Laura L. Bowman

Quality Control
Susan Moritz
Charles Spencer
Brian Walls

Indexer
Sherry Massey

Vice President and Executive Group Publisher
Richard Swadley

Vice President and Publisher
Barry Pruett

Composition Director
Debbie Stailey

ABOUT THE AUTHORS

Sherry Willard Kinkoph is a freelance author and a fan of all things computer related. She has written over 50 books over the past 10 years covering a variety of computer topics ranging from hardware to software, from Microsoft Office programs to the Internet. Some of her recent titles include *Easy Quicken 2004, Master VISUALLY Dreamweaver MX and Flash MX,* and *Teach Yourself VISUALLY Restoration and Retouching with Photoshop Elements 2*. Sherry's on-going quest is to help users of all levels master the ever-changing computer technologies.

Mike Wooldridge is a Web developer, author, and eBay seller living in the San Francisco Bay Area. This is his twelfth Visual book.

AUTHORS' ACKNOWLEDGMENTS

Sherry Kinkoph: Special thanks go out to publisher, Barry Pruett, and to acquisitions editor Jody Lefevere, for allowing us the opportunity to tackle this exciting project; to project editor Sarah Hellert, for her dedication and patience in guiding this project from start to finish; to copy editor Kim Heusel, for ensuring that all the i's were dotted and t's were crossed; to technical editor Kerwin McKenzie, for skillfully checking each step and offering valuable input along the way; and finally to the production team at Wiley for their able efforts in creating such a visual masterpiece. A very special thanks to all the wonderful bidders and buyers who populate eBay for making my auction experiences so enjoyable.

Mike Wooldridge: Thanks to Sarah Hellert, Jody Lefevere, and all the other talented people at Wiley who worked on this book.

To my nephews, Jacob and Joshua Cannon, future eBay enthusiasts.
— Sherry Kinkoph

To Dr. Jablons, Dr. Sherman, Sean, and my running buddies Storn, Kim, and Frank.
— Mike Wooldridge.

EBAY BUSINESS KIT

I EXPLORING EBAY

1) Introduction to eBay
2) Finding Anything on eBay

II START SELLING ON EBAY NOW!

3) Creating an eBay Seller Account
4) Preparing for Your First Listing
5) Create an eBay Auction

III MANAGING AND PROMOTING YOUR AUCTION

6) Using My eBay
7) Monitoring and Managing Your Auctions
8) Bringing in the Bidders

WHAT'S INSIDE

IV AFTER THE AUCTION ENDS

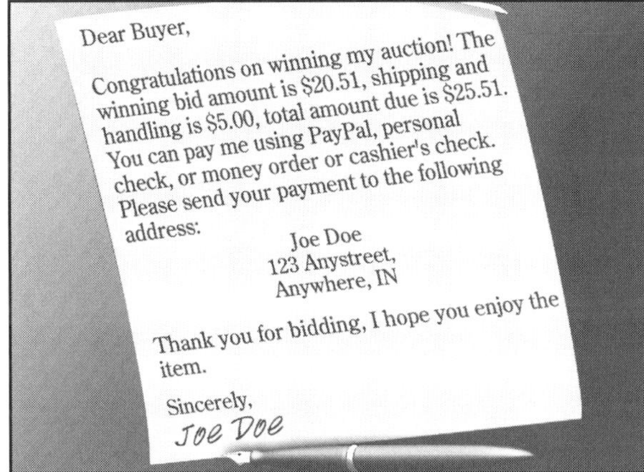

Dear Buyer,

Congratulations on winning my auction! The winning bid amount is $20.51, shipping and handling is $5.00, total amount due is $25.51. You can pay me using PayPal, personal check, or money order or cashier's check. Please send your payment to the following address:

Joe Doe
123 Anystreet,
Anywhere, IN

Thank you for bidding, I hope you enjoy the item.

Sincerely,
Joe Doe

V TAKING ADVANTAGE OF EBAY SERVICES AND RESOURCES

VI ADVANCED TECHNIQUES: AUCTION TOOLS, PHOTO EDITING, AND HTML

VII YOUR OWN EBAY STORE

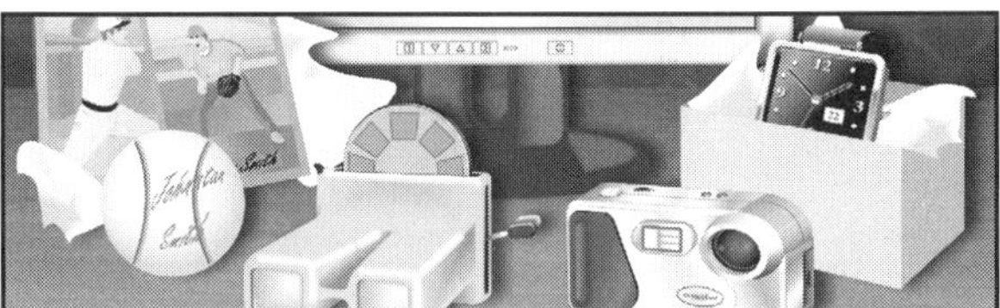

VIII APPENDIXES

1 EXPLORING EBAY

1) INTRODUCTION TO EBAY

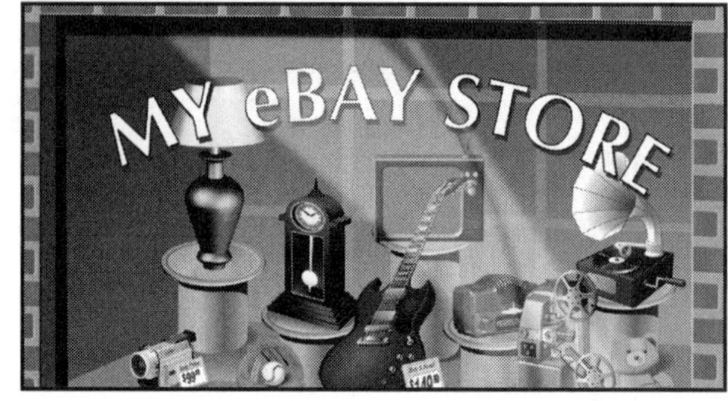

2) FINDING ANYTHING ON EBAY

2 START SELLING ON EBAY NOW!

3) CREATING AN EBAY SELLER ACCOUNT

USER NAME JonBee13
PASSWORD *******

TABLE OF CONTENTS

4) PREPARING FOR YOUR FIRST LISTING

5) CREATE AN EBAY AUCTION

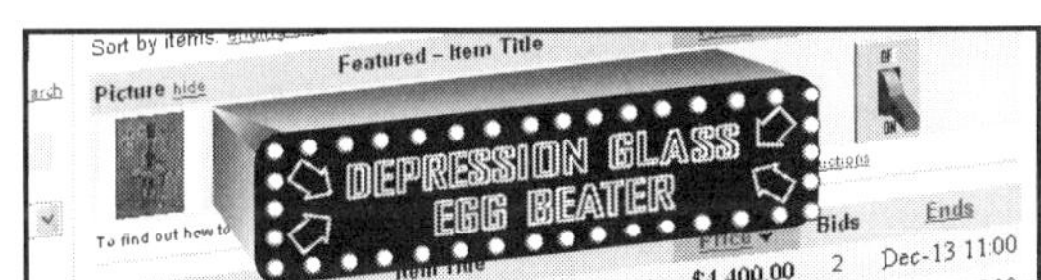

3 MANAGING AND PROMOTING YOUR AUCTION

6) USING MY EBAY

7) MONITORING AND MANAGING YOUR AUCTIONS

8) BRINGING IN THE BIDDERS

4 AFTER THE AUCTION ENDS

9) FINALIZING THE SALE

Dear Buyer,

Congratulations on winning my auction! Th
winning bid amount is $20.51, shipping an
handling is $5.00, total amount due is $25.
You can pay me using PayPal, personal

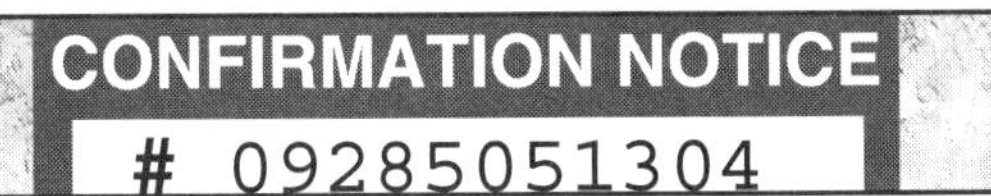

10) USE PAYPAL WITH AUCTIONS

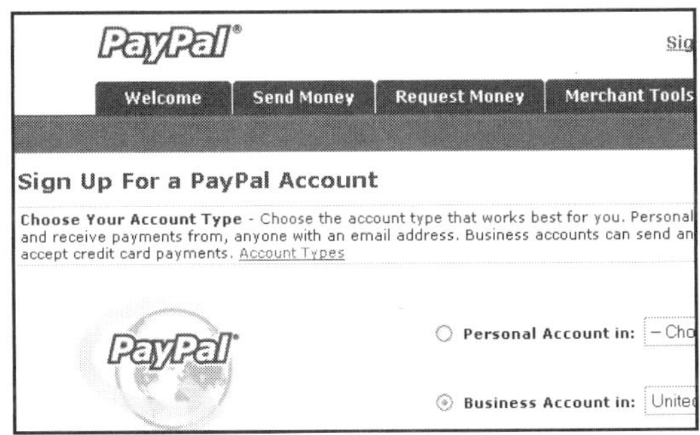

11) KEEPING TRACK OF FEEDBACK

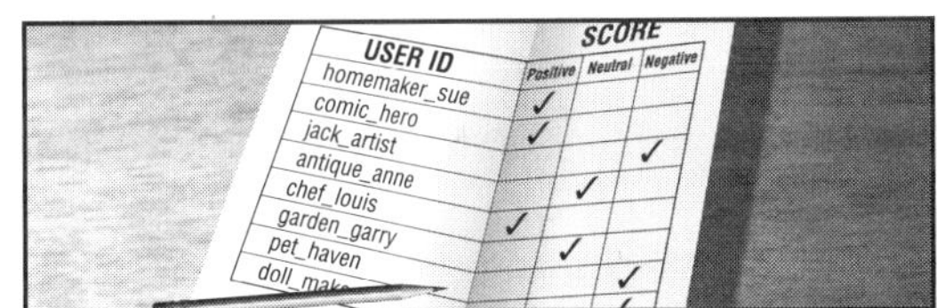

12) WHEN GOOD AUCTIONS GO BAD

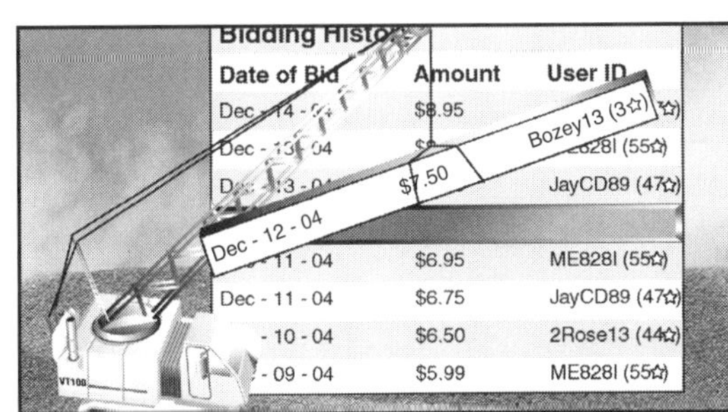

5 TAKING ADVANTAGE OF EBAY SERVICES AND RESOURCES

13) FINDING HELP WITH EBAY

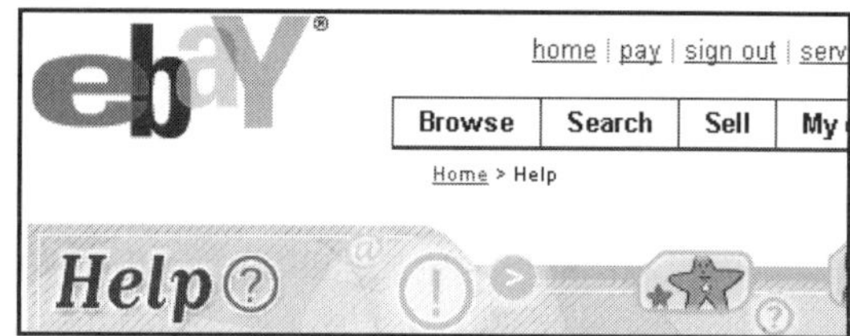

14) USING EBAY COMMUNITY RESOURCES

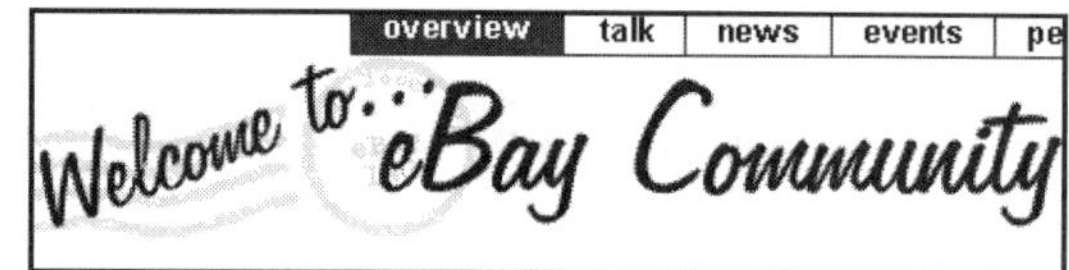

15) SELLING HIGH-PRICED ITEMS ON EBAY

16) GETTING SELLING HELP

News & Updates
Don't miss out--sign up for eBay email today and get advance notice of upcoming events, promotions, and your monthly Seller Newsflash!

17) USING EBAY GROUPS

6 ADVANCED TECHNIQUES: AUCTION TOOLS, PHOTO EDITING, AND HTML

18) LIST ITEMS AUTOMATICALLY WITH TURBO LISTER

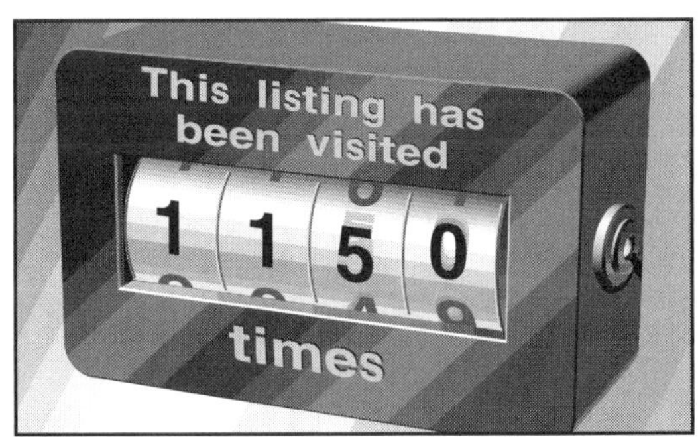
This listing has been visited
1 1 5 0
times

19) USING SELLER'S ASSISTANT AND SELLING MANAGER

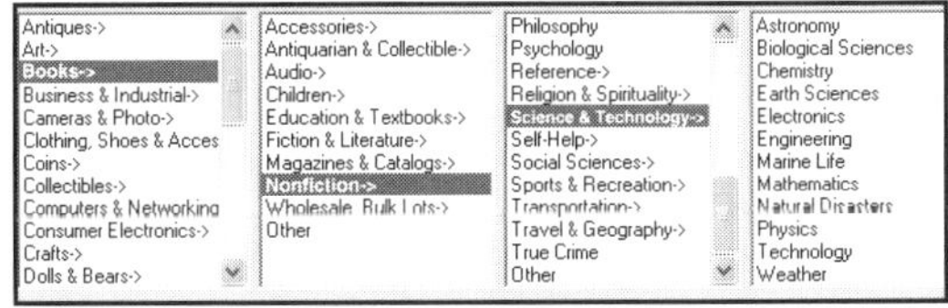

Sold Listings
Keep track of sold listings by customizing and sending sales records ( ) to your buyers.
9 sold listings.

20) MAKE BEST USE OF PHOTOS

eBAY PICTURE
SERVICES

21) USING HTML IN EBAY LISTINGS

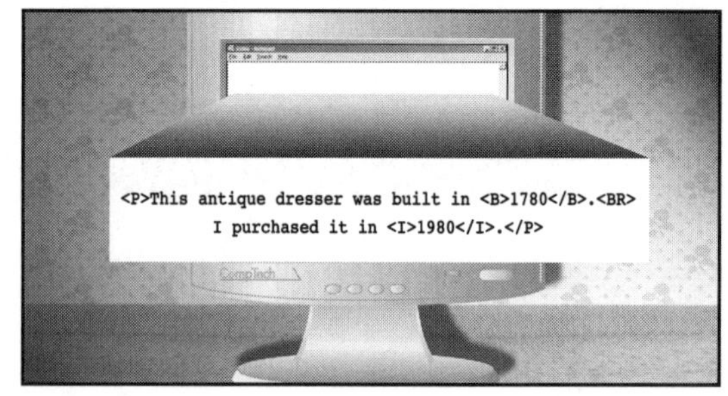

<P>This antique dresser was built in <B>1780</B>.
I purchased it in <I>1980</I>.</P>

22) THIRD-PARTY AUCTION SOFTWARE

Feedback	FB	Comment	Date	Item #
4	POS	GREAT TRANSACTION. WOULD DO BUSINESS WITH AGAIN. A++++++++++	04/03/2004	359770368
63	POS	FAST DELVIERY, PRODUCT AS PROMISED! A+++	03/09/2004	359056087
1	POS	EXCELLENT!!! SUPER FAST DELIVERY.	03/03/2004	359056087

7 YOUR OWN EBAY STORE

23) SET UP AN EBAY STORE

24) MARKET YOUR EBAY STORE

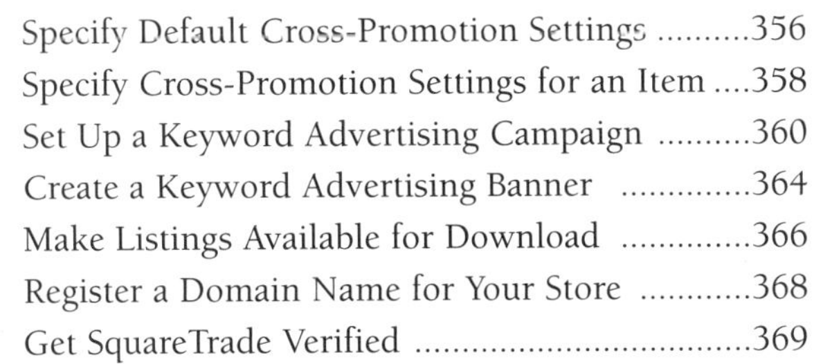

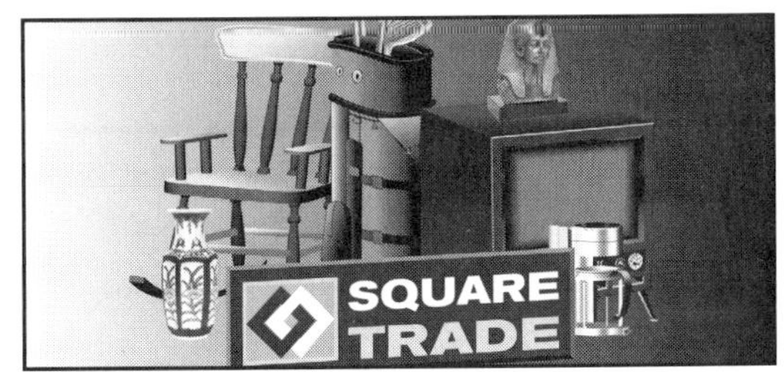

25) A STORE ALTERNATIVE: HALF.COM

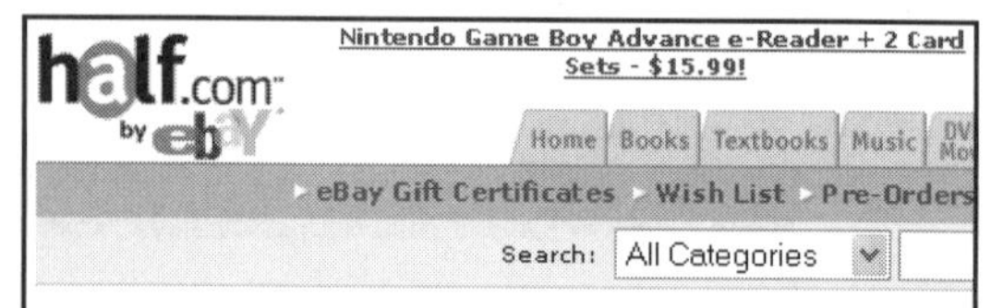

8 APPENDIXES

A) EBAY SELLER RESOURCES

B) EBAY TIME ZONES

C) HTML TAGS REFERENCE

D) WHAT'S ON THE CD-ROM

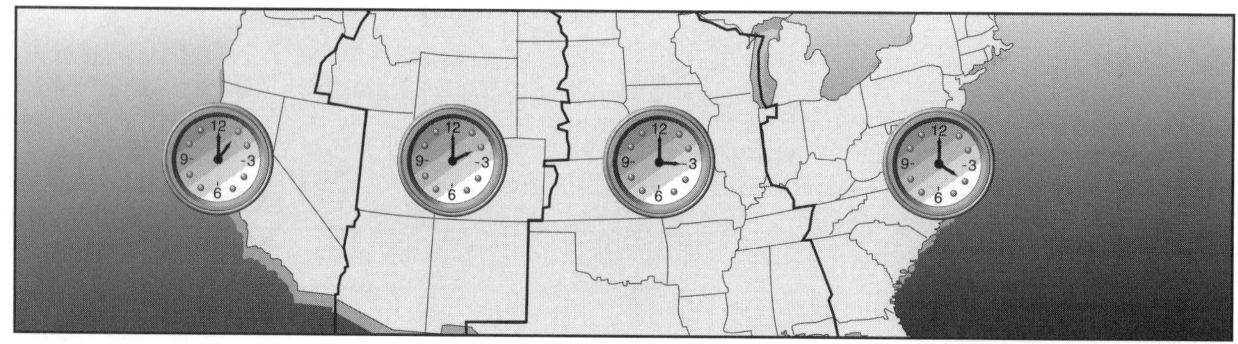

TABLE OF CONTENTS

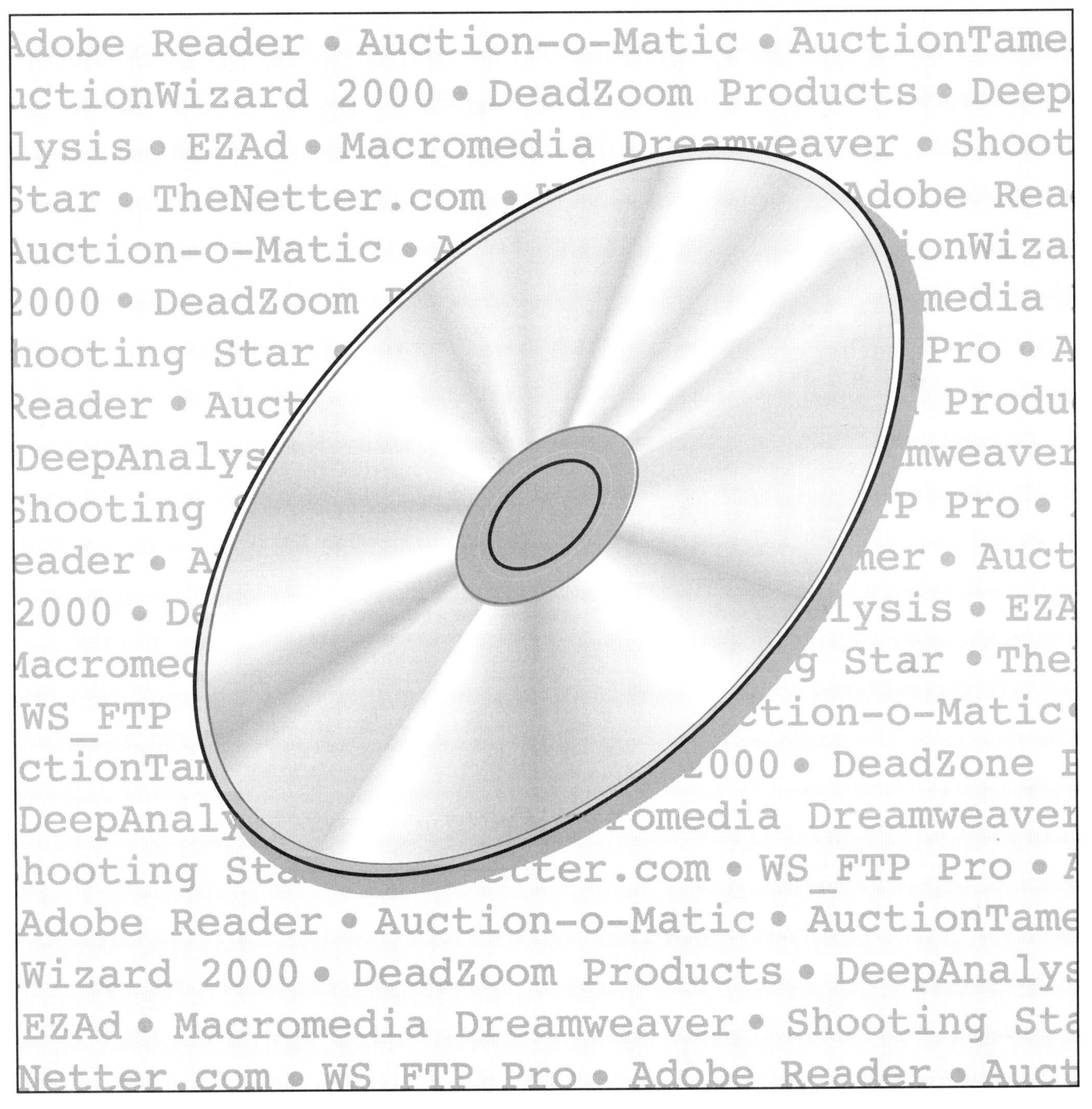

EBAY BUSINESS KIT

Master VISUALLY eBay Business Kit contains straightforward examples to teach you how to sell and market your items in auctions and eBay stores. Learn everything it takes to start and run your own eBay business, from auction creation to leaving feedback after the sale is over. Discover how to write appealing descriptions and promote your auctions to potential bidders. Find out how to manage your auctions, handle transaction problems, and tap into eBay's seller tools.

The accompanying CD includes third-party programs, HTML templates, and other useful tools that sellers can use to streamline their eBay selling, improve the appearance of their listings, and boost their eBay profits.

This book is designed to help a reader receive quick access to any area of question. You can simply look up a subject within the Table of Contents or Index and go immediately to the task of concern. A *section* is a set of self-contained units that walks you through a computer operation step-by-step. That is, with rare exception, all the information you need regarding an area of interest is contained within a section.

Note that in some examples, e-mail addresses, eBay user IDs, and other personal information has been blurred to protect the privacy of buyers and sellers on eBay. eBay is constantly changing and improving its Web site, and in some cases your eBay Web pages may appear differently than those shown in this book.

The Organization of Each Chapter

Each section contains an introduction, a set of screen shots with steps, and, if the steps go beyond one page, a set of tips. The introduction tells why you want to perform the steps, the advantages and disadvantages of performing the steps, a general explanation of any procedures, and references to other related tasks in the book. The screens, located on the bottom half of each page, show a series of steps that you must complete to perform a given task. The tip section gives you an opportunity to further understand the task at hand, to learn about other related tasks in other areas of the book, or to apply more complicated or alternative methods.

A chapter may also contain an illustrated group of pages that gives you background information that you need to understand the tasks in a chapter.

The General Organization of This Book

Master VISUALLY eBay Business Kit has 25 chapters and 4 appendices and is divided into 7 parts.

Section I: This section explores the various ways you can prepare for an eBay business. Learn how eBay auctions work and the necessities needed to sell items on eBay. This section also shows you how to navigate the Web site and use practical ways to search for items, whether you are looking for items to buy, or researching items you plan to sell.

Section II: This section shows you how to start a seller's account, pull together an auction listing and post it on eBay. Find out how eBay categories work, types of auctions you can run, and how to create your own promotional page. This section also teaches you how to define your terms of sale, including payment options, shipping and handling.

Section III: In this section, you discover ways to manage your auctions, attract bidders, and keep track of your eBay accounts. Find out how to cancel bids, revise your listings, and communicate with bidders.

Section IV: This section examines the tasks after an auction. Learn about eBay's checkout feature, how to invoice your buyers, and how to pay your eBay fees. Find out how to use PayPal to make purchases or receive payments, and how to use eBay's feedback system to rate transactions. This section also covers ways to handle auction problems.

Section V: This section describes how to take advantage of the various help-related areas of eBay — including the discussion boards and eBay Groups — to find answers to questions. It also looks at the challenges sellers face when selling high-priced items on eBay.

Section VI: This section focuses on extra tools that sellers can use to make their eBay business more efficient. These tools include subscription-based eBay features such as Selling Manager, free eBay programs such as Turbo Lister, and third-party programs. The section also looks at how to use photos and HTML effectively in your listings.

Section VII: This section looks at eBay Stores, which are sets of customizable Web pages that sellers can use to market their items at fixed prices. The section also looks at Half.com, eBay's sister Web site, where sellers can also market their goods.

Who This Book is For

This book is for the beginner, who is unfamiliar with how to use the eBay Web site and related programs to buy and sell online. It is also for more computer-literate individuals who want to expand their knowledge of the different features that eBay has to offer.

What You Need to Use This Book

To access the eBay Web site, readers need an Internet-connected PC or Macintosh computer running a Web browser such as Microsoft Internet Explorer or Netscape Navigator.

To run the Turbo Lister software, (Chapter 18), readers need a PC running Microsoft Windows 98/ME/2000/XP/NT, 64MB (Win 98/ME128) or 128MB (Win 2000/XP/NT) of RAM, and 30MB free hard-disk space. Turbo Lister does not run on Macintosh.

To run the Seller's Assistant software, (Chapter 19), readers need a PC running Microsoft Windows 95/98/ME/2000/XP/NT, 64MB RAM, and 40MB free hard-disk space. Seller's Assistant does not run on Macintosh.

To run Adobe Photoshop Elements, (Chapter 20), PC users need Microsoft Windows 98/ME/2000/XP, 128MB of RAM, and 150MB of free hard-disk space. Macintosh users need Mac OS 9.1/9.2/X, 128MB of RAM, and 350MB of free hard-disk space. System requirements for the third-party programs included on the CD and described in Chapter 22 vary. See the user documentation for each program for details.

Conventions When Using the Mouse

This book uses the following conventions to describe the actions you perform when using the mouse:

Click
Press and release the left mouse button. You use a click to select an item on the screen.

Double-click
Quickly press and release the left mouse button twice. You use a double-click to open a document or start a program.

Right-click
Press and release the right mouse button. You use a right-click to display a shortcut menu, a list of commands specifically related to the selected item.

Click and Drag, and Release the Mouse
Position the mouse pointer over an item on the screen and then press and hold down the left mouse button. Still holding down the button, move the mouse to where you want to place the item and then release the button. Dragging and dropping makes it easy to move an item to a new location.

The Conventions in This Book

A number of typographic and layout styles have been used throughout *Master VISUALLY eBay Business Kit* to distinguish different types of information.

Bold
Indicates the information that you must type into a dialog box.

Italics
Indicates a new term being introduced.

Numbered Steps
Indicate that you must perform these steps in order to successfully perform the task.

Bulleted Steps
Give you alternative methods, explain various options, or present what a program will do in response to the numbered steps.

Notes
Give you additional information to help you complete a task. The purpose of a note is three-fold: It can explain special conditions that may occur during the course of the task, warn you of potentially dangerous situations, or refer you to tasks in the same, or a different chapter. References to tasks within the chapter are indicated by the phrase "See the section..." followed by the name of the task. References to in other chapters are indicated by "See Chapter . . ." followed by the chapter number.

Icons
Icons in the steps indicate a button that you must press.

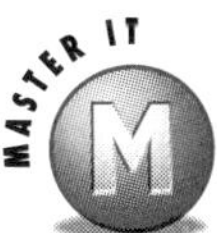

Most of the sections in this book are supplemented with a section called Master It. These are tips, hints, and tricks that extend your use of the section beyond what you learned by performing the steps in the section.

SECTION I

1) INTRODUCTION TO EBAY

2) FINDING ANYTHING ON EBAY

EXPLORING EBAY

EXPLORE EBAY'S BUSINESS OPPORTUNITIES

eBay is a 24-hour-a-day, 7-day-a-week marketplace that reaches online computer users all over the world. With over 85.5 million registered users and growing, eBay offers a variety of unique business opportunities for everyone from the casual seller to the full-time seller. If you are serious about making the most of an eBay business, this book can help you find your way through the many nuances of starting and maintaining an online business.

Founded in 1995, eBay has far surpassed the status of a big electronic flea market to become one of the fastest-growing global marketplaces today for new and used goods. Millions of items are listed each day on eBay spanning thousands of categories. No longer a place for finding collectibles and garage sale discards, eBay now sells everything from office supplies to real estate and automobiles.

Explaining eBay's success is simple. Unlike a local market that only reaches a select number of buyers, eBay auction listings have the potential to reach millions of people, providing the best deals for buyers and sellers alike. Market values are established quickly through eBay's auction feature. As a result, sellers often sell for higher prices than in a local market, and buyers often pay lower prices than in a local market.

What Is So Special about eBay?

Auctions are the heart of eBay, allowing potential buyers the chance to find bargains, and allowing sellers to reach an expanded market and sell at the highest price. eBay auction listings advertise your wares to exactly the people to whom you want to sell. Every item up for sale on eBay has its own market, and only those buyers interested in your item will look at your auction, so your potential buyers are essentially self-selected.

Unlike regular forms of business in which marketing and selling costs typically consume about 50 percent of the product price, your marketing costs on eBay are the insertion and final value fees you pay for your auctions. In essence, eBay puts you on a level playing field with every other individual or company, allowing you to compete without having to spend large amounts on advertising, marketing, and salespeople. In eBay's environment, manufacturers, wholesalers, and retailers do not have an advantage over the single seller. In addition, eBay provides a solid framework of rules and feedback in which you can operate your online business. All participants must operate under the same system of feedback, rules, and guidelines that help keep eBay's registered users honest and aboveboard.

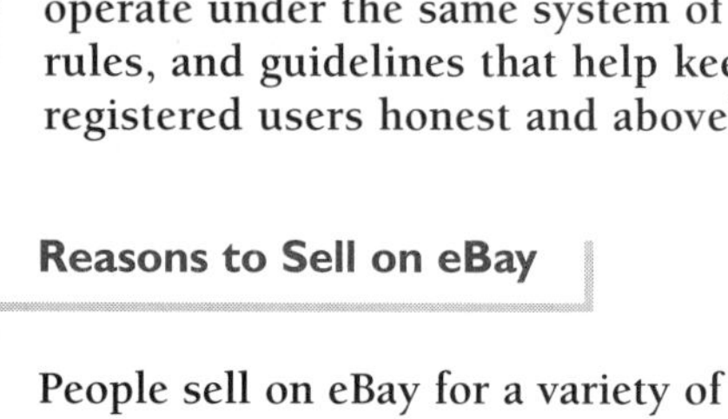

Reasons to Sell on eBay

People sell on eBay for a variety of reasons. For example, many individuals use eBay to generate an extra source of income for paying bills, to save for college expenses or vacations, or just to support an ongoing hobby. Collectors enjoy trading on eBay to find rare pieces to add to their collections or to dispose of pieces that no longer interest them. Retailers, for example, might sell on eBay to keep current with competition or to find a wider audience. Many retailers sell on eBay as well as an e-commerce Web site.

You may find yourself selling items on eBay to clear out an attic or garage, or you may be ready to part with collectible items. Perhaps you find yourself with duplicate items and you want to sell the second item online. Rather than set up a garage sale and invite strangers to stop by, you can sell unwanted items from the comfort of your own home.

The old adage, "One man's trash is another man's treasure," certainly holds true on eBay. Odd and quirky items that may not draw much interest at your local garage sale may very well attract a number of interested parties online. In fact, many people frequent garage sales and estate sales throughout the year to look for items to auction off on eBay. Regardless of your reason to sell, eBay provides plenty of opportunities to list your wares and find potential buyers.

Part-Time Sellers

A good way to get started selling on eBay is to try your hand at selling part time. Part-time sellers typically have full-time jobs and sell items on eBay on the side. As a part-time seller, you can decide how much time and effort you want to put into listing items for sale. As you become more successful, you can invest more time as needed to keep up with auctions and shipping tasks.

Part-time sellers list anywhere from five to 100 or more items for auction each week, depending on how much work they want to put into the effort.

Full-Time Sellers

After you establish that you can sell successfully on eBay, you may consider turning it into a full-time job. This option is ideal for people who want to work from their own homes, work their own hours, and control their own destinies. Discipline and staying on schedule, handling customer questions, and finalizing sales and shipping are the keys to keeping up with online listings.

Building an eBay business can be very fulfilling and rewarding, but it takes a lot of hard work and dedication. Finding the right items to sell on eBay also takes a lot of experimentation and patience. As with other full-time jobs, a full-time eBay seller can spend long hours finding items to sell, preparing auction listings, e-mailing, collecting payments, and shipping items. If full-time selling is your dream, you need a lot of dedication to keep a regular source of income flowing in.

eBay Stores

If you build up enough feedback, you can create an eBay store. eBay stores are actually Web pages where you can list items at fixed prices for 30 days. You might use your eBay store to sell overstock or unload items that did not sell the first time. An eBay store is a good way to advertise your business or items, and serves as a place where returning customers can find and contact you regularly.

AREAS TO SELL ON EBAY

eBay offers several places online in which to sell your merchandise. The most common area to sell is to list among eBay's many auction categories. For example, you can sell your DVD movie collection in the Entertainment; DVDs & Movies category. eBay has hundreds of categories to organize the wide variety of auctions that appear each day. By placing an auction in a particular category, you can advertise your auction to buyers who are specifically interested in your item. Potential buyers can find your item by looking through the categories listed on eBay's home page as well as by conducting a search.

But what if you want to sell something bigger than a DVD movie collection, such as a car or a plot of land? Perhaps you want to auction a specialized service instead of an actual item? eBay has designated areas for just such types of items. You can navigate to each of these areas through eBay's main Web page.

eBay Motors

Buying and selling used cars and trucks is fast becoming a booming business on eBay. Just about any vehicle with two or more wheels can be found for sale online. Ordinarily, you may not think to look for a vehicle online. You would probably focus on finding one locally because it is easier to view and test drive the car. However, the vehicle you want may not be available in the local market, and the perfect vehicle may be found more easily somewhere else. Here again, eBay's larger market makes it a good place to sell and buy cars.

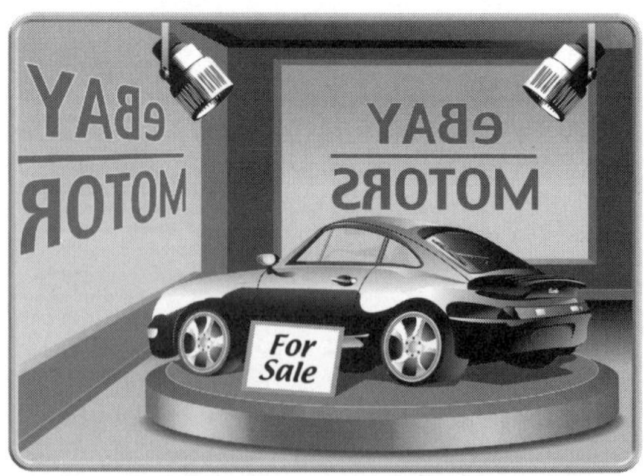

In 2002, 300,000 vehicles were sold on eBay, making up 23 percent of eBay's total sales for the year. You can buy a car within 1,000 miles of your area, hop on a plane for a relatively inexpensive fare, and drive the car home over a weekend. You can also have vehicles shipped for less than $1,000. Buying and selling a large-ticket item such as a car may not turn out to be as expensive as you think.

Real Estate Auctions

Although real estate is a growing category in eBay, real estate auctions are not always legally binding because eBay is not licensed to sell real estate online for all states. This makes real estate auctions mostly an advertising forum for now. You can probably count on more states allowing eBay real estate auctions in the years to come.

You can list homes and acreage, or commercial real estate, in an eBay auction. Real estate auctions allow you to search for properties by state. Timeshares are also a popular real estate item on eBay. You can list real estate ads for 30 or 90 days in eBay's Real Estate section.

B2B

Business-to-business auctions, called B2B for short, allow businesses to auction new and used goods to other businesses through the Business & Industrial category on eBay. The service is particularly appealing to small businesses that want to trade items such as supplies and equipment with other companies. For example, if your company needs to sell some older equipment to make room for new equipment, or reduce your supply of materials, the Business & Industrial area may be just the place to auction those items.

Half.com

If you prefer to sell without haggling over price, Half.com is the place for you. Half.com started out as an area in which registered users could sell new and used books. The site has expanded to include music and movies, computer equipment, games, and other items. Unlike other eBay areas, buyers do not bid on items, but pay a set price established by the seller.

Half.com listings do not end at a scheduled time. Instead, your items are grouped with other similar items on the same page. For example, you may sell a used textbook that five other people are also offering. When a potential buyer views the listing, he or she can also view the other books and compare prices and details.

A big difference between regular eBay and Half.com is how the buyer pays a seller. Rather than pay the seller directly, the buyer pays Half.com, which then pays the seller after deducting fees. This can save you the hassle of dealing with bounced checks and other types of payment fraud that can happen with regular eBay auctions.

Live Auctions

eBay's live auctions allow you to bid in real time on items from auction houses and in auctions conducted by live auctioneers. Live auctions typically feature art and art objects, antiques, and high-end collectibles. To participate in a live auction, you must register and be verified. You can access live auctions through the Live Auctions link, which is located near the bottom of the Categories column on the left side of eBay's home page. The Live Auctions page lists upcoming live auction schedules in a variety of categories, as well as featuring items up for auction.

eBay recently partnered with the famous Southeby's auction house to allow buyers to utilize eBay's live auction technology to bid on art items during live auctions taking place at the auction house.

Elance

eBay also offers an area in which you can sell your professional services. Called Elance, a merge of the words *electronic* and *freelance*, the service provides companies with a way to outsource projects and service providers to sell their talents. Employers can post projects that require specialized services, such as freelance writing or graphic design work, and qualified individuals can bid on the projects. You can find the Elance area through eBay's Professional Services link on the home page. As with other eBay selling areas, you must register separately to utilize the service. See Chapter 23 for more about Elance.

HOW EBAY AUCTIONS WORK

Auction listings are the most popular aspect of eBay and offer the most fun and excitement for bidders and sellers alike. Auctions allow buyers to bid for items they want, and they allow sellers to sell items for the best possible price. As a bidder, searching for a good bargain and bidding against others can take some skill. Likewise, the art of selling requires some finesse in knowing in which category to place an item, what price to start the bidding, how long to list the item, and how to write a description of the item.

To best understand how eBay auctions work, you must understand the steps involved in posting an auction as well as how the auction is handled when the bidding is complete.

Create an Auction Listing

The first step to selling an item is to create an auction listing. An auction listing is your advertisement for the item. A listing describes in detail the item for sale. Listings typically show at least one photo of the item. Your listing information should also include terms of sale that describe payment options, shipping and handling costs, and return policy.

After you register as a seller on eBay, you can use the online seller's form for your listing details. You can complete the form in several steps, starting with choosing the category in which you want to post your auction. Auctions are posted into categories to help keep the thousands of items available for sale organized and easy to find. eBay offers hundreds of categories, ranging from collectible items — such as stamps and coins — to home decorating items. Knowing in which category to place your item can make a huge difference in helping people find your item.

After specifying a category, you can write a descriptive heading, set a starting price and auction length, describe the item, and determine payment and shipping methods. You can choose a picture to accompany your listing.

The online seller's form offers you extra options you can add, such as posting in more than one category, setting up a special auction type, or adding extra photos. Extra items often require additional listing fees. You can also use third-party software to create and post auction listings.

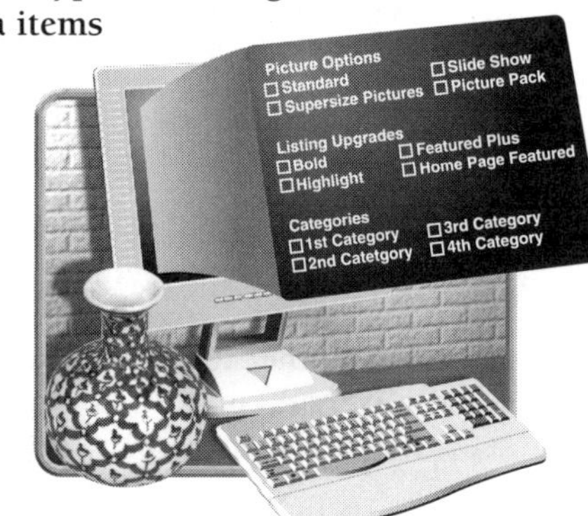

Let the Bidding Commence

After you complete your auction listing, you can post the auction on eBay. When potential buyers find your auction, they can read your description and place bids on the item for as long as the auction is listed. During this time, you may receive e-mails from potential bidders requesting additional information about the item you have for sale. As a seller, it is up to you to respond promptly and professionally to any queries. Your customer service reputation begins with good communication skills.

During the bidding process, it is not uncommon to see a flurry of last-minute activity. Often, your item may have no bids until the last few minutes before the auction closes. Last-minute bidding is an effective method for experienced eBayers to win an item at the best price.

End of Auction

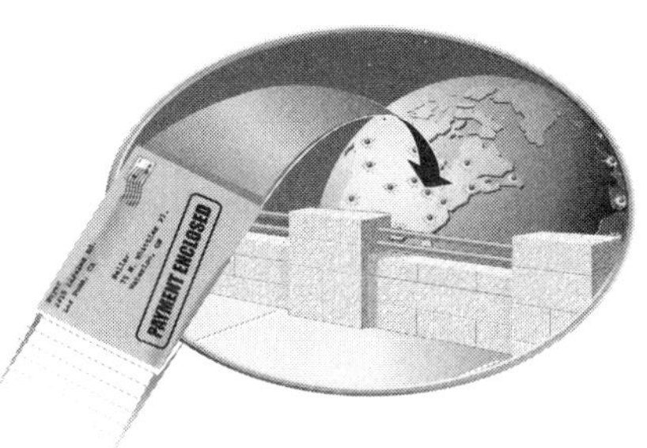

At the end of the auction, the highest bidder is declared the winner. In the case of Buy It Now auctions, the buyer simply clicks a button and purchases the item for the designated price. The seller sends out an invoice, and the buyer pays for the item based on the final price and any shipping and handling fees determined by the seller.

In some instances, the buyer may pay immediately after winning an auction. In such situations, it is not unusual to have no communication at all between seller and buyer, and you do not need to send out an invoice.

For most auctions, however, an invoice alerting the buyer to his or her winning bid and final price, or a personal e-mail congratulating the buyer on their win, is an accepted courtesy. eBay's policy suggests contacting your buyer within three days after the end of the auction.

Ship the Item

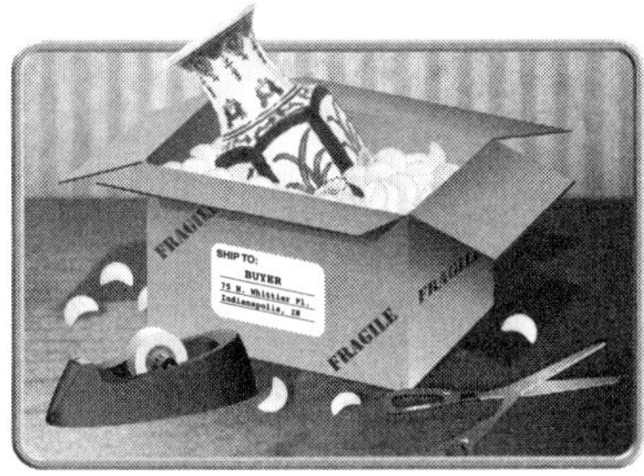

As soon as the item is paid for, you can ship it to the winning bidder. Shipping may seem like a last-minute task; however, for best customer service results, it is up to the seller to ship the item as carefully as possible. Until the item is in the physical hands of the buyer, it is the seller's responsibility to make sure the item arrives safely. If the buyer fails to receive the item, it is your responsibility to refund the price paid for the item or send a duplicate item.

Pay eBay Fees

After you sell an item on eBay, you must pay fees to eBay. Sellers are responsible for two main fees — the *insertion fee*, also called the listing fee; and the *final value fee*. You pay the insertion fee regardless of whether the item sells or not. The final value fee is a percentage of the final price for the item.

Post Feedback

The last phase of the auction process is to leave feedback. Feedback sums up the transaction experience. Others can look at your feedback and determine if you paid in time, were easy to communicate with, or shipped the items quickly. Sellers leave feedback for buyers and buyers leave feedback for sellers. Feedback is a voluntary system on eBay, but it figures mightily into the success of any eBayer's online business. The more positive feedback you acquire as a seller, the more buyers trust you and your auction listings, and the more likely they are to bid on your items.

DETERMINE WHAT TO SELL

Every item has a market. As a seller, it is your challenge to match the right item to the right market. Although eBay has a reputation for being a marketplace for odd or unusual items, mainstream products are the bulk of online sales. Your goal as an eBay business seller is to find items on which eBay users are going to bid and buy consistently.

Like other commercial markets, eBay follows the law of supply and demand. If you are one of the few sellers who are auctioning off a popular item, you can expect to sell the item for a higher price. If you are one among many sellers who are auctioning a popular item, you can expect the item price to go down. An overcrowded market is a buyer's market.

Plenty of eBayers sell used items successfully. These can include mistaken purchases and duplicates, items from around the house, items found at estate sales and garage and tag sales. Many other eBayers sell retail items on eBay and new goods at a deep discount. These items can come from closeout sales, wholesalers, and discount clubs. To keep a steady flow of either type of product, however, sellers must keep looking for more inventory.

Research the Market

What do you want to sell on eBay? Research is important in determining what items to list in an auction. Most eBay businesses sell more than one type of item. Some eBay sellers sell related items; others find success selling disparate items.

A savvy eBayer knows his or her market. Take time to investigate other auction categories and listings. Find out which items receive bids and which ones do not. Study the listings, and compare successful auctions to not-so-successful auctions. Research can go a long way in helping you figure out what items sell well on eBay. If you do not know the market for the goods you plan to sell, you cannot achieve ongoing success on eBay.

Sell Items You Like

When determining what to sell, a good place to start is with items with which you are already familiar and about which you have some knowledge. Selling something you know and love is much easier than selling something with which you are completely unfamiliar.

For example, if you have no experience with antiques, trying to sell them on eBay may result in problems regarding authenticity and evaluation standards. As an inexperienced seller, you can also encounter problems in using the correct terminology to describe the antiques in your auction listings. On the other hand, if you have been collecting coins for years, you probably already know a few things about the value, condition, and lingo of coin trading.

Find a Niche

Most users experience retailing success on eBay when they find a niche market. A niche, or specialty area, targets a group of buyers that are looking for the items you are selling. For example, collectible items are a common niche on eBay. Any type of item that people collect, such as trading cards, movies, figurines, toys, stamps, coins, and memorabilia, has a niche market on eBay. If you happen to be a collector, too, you can find an instant market with your fellow collectors.

With some types of collectible items, you do not necessarily have to select a particular item. If your specialty is nostalgic memorabilia from the 1960s, for example, the items you collect for sale can vary. You can sell anything from clothing items to household bric-a-brac. When specializing in a niche area, you must be knowledgeable in the items you pick, and learn to recognize which items are authentic and which are not. The more knowledgeable you are, the more likely you can identify items of value.

You can find niche items through a variety of venues such as garage sales, secondhand stores, and other auctions.

Locating Inventory

If you decide to sell new goods on eBay, you can acquire inventory through venues such as trade shows, wholesalers, and craftspeople. Going-out-of-business sales, surplus stores, and dollar stores are also good sources for building an inventory. A common practice is to buy off-season when bargains are easily found, and then sell for a profit during the proper season. For example, you can purchase holiday-related items for a lot less in July than in November.

Before you purchase large quantities of any item to resell on eBay, do your homework and find out if there is a market for the item. If the market is saturated, you may need to find another category in which to sell the item or move on to another item entirely. It is good practice to experiment with a few auctions first to make sure there is a market for your product.

In a best-case scenario, you may find exclusive products to sell on eBay for a profit. Such scenarios are rather rare, however. For many eBay sellers, a niche might be profitable for a while, but then the market becomes crowded or suddenly declines. You need to be prepared with ideas for other items to sell in case your niche does not offer long-term sales results.

Among all the places you shop for inventory, eBay is also a good place to check. You can find everything from discounted office supplies to wholesale lots online.

GATHER ESSENTIAL EQUIPMENT

To build a serious online business, you need to acquire all the necessary equipment. You can operate a successful eBay business from your own home, and unlike brick-and-mortar stores, you do not need to worry about overhead or renting office space. All you really need to create in an office environment is some space for your equipment, good lighting, a comfortable chair and adequate desk, and plenty of electrical outlets and a phone jack nearby.

After designating a space for your business, the next step is gathering the necessary equipment to run your business. Thankfully, you do not need a lot of equipment or supplies to run an eBay business, just a few essentials.

A Computer

Naturally, one of the key components for an eBay business is a computer system. It is not necessary to run out and buy a state-of-the-art computer system to sell items on eBay, but an up-to-date operating system can certainly help. Older machines tend to be slow when running today's programs, and older hardware can be unreliable. If your computer seems sluggish when you view Web pages, you may want to look into an upgrade.

While buying and selling on eBay does not require a super-fast computer with all the latest features, you can certainly benefit from a system with plenty of random access memory (RAM). Reasonably fast computers today require processor speeds of at least 300 or 400MHz. A minimum of 128MB of RAM is necessary for memory-intensive jobs on your computer, such as running photo-editing software or viewing Web graphics. Slower systems can affect the way in which you interact with eBay by slowing the process for posting multiple auctions, tracking listings, and handling e-mail correspondence. Slower systems can also affect the timely submission of bids during auctions.

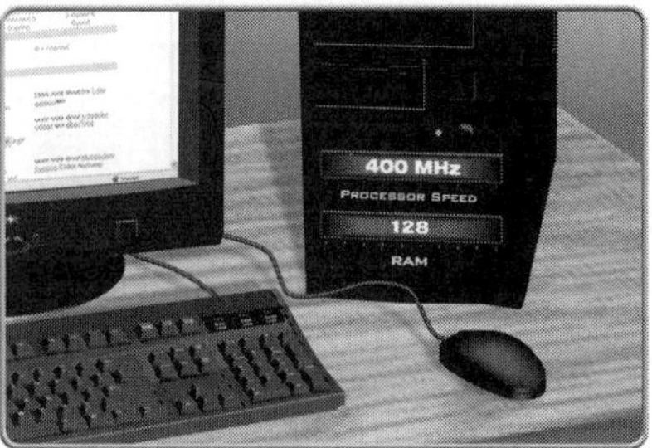

If your computer runs Windows 2000 or later, you are in good shape for running an online business. If you own an older computer, however, upgrading may not be as expensive as you think. You can find good deals on new and used computers these days, even on eBay.

An Internet Connection

Reliable Internet access is essential to any online business. You must be able to go online at numerous times of the day to post auctions, handle e-mail queries, manage your auctions, send invoices, and more.

Internet access comes in several flavors. The most common is direct dial-up in which you connect to the Internet through a modem and an Internet Service Provider. Prices for dial-up connections typically hover around a range of $20 per month.

The drawback, however, is a slower connection speed. 56 kilobits per second is as fast as you can go. ISDN dial-ups run a bit faster and cost a bit more. DSL connections run through telephone lines at a top speed of 1500 kilobits per second and average $50 per month.

You can get the fastest connections from Broadband DSL, cable, or satellite Internet connections at the highest cost. The benefits, however, are huge. Because these types of connections are direct lines to the Internet, you and your computer are always connected without tying up a phone line, and browsing Web pages is an almost instantaneous experience. With a direct connection, however, you need to install protection from hackers. You can find many good free or low-cost firewall programs on the Internet.

Software

An important part of every computer system is software. The main software for your eBay business is your Web browser and e-mail program. Your browser program needs to display images and support security levels, such as encryption and secure transactions. If you have not updated your browser program in awhile, it is a good idea to do so before launching your eBay business. Your e-mail program needs to support file attachments for times when you need to send a bidder additional pictures or invoices.

As you grow your business, you may need to invest in some auction software. Auction management software, such as eBay's own Seller's Assistant or Virtual Auction Ad Pro by Virtual Notions, can help you create and upload auction listings, track bidding, and manage your sales. Auction management software often can include functions found in other office programs, such as spreadsheet, database, and accounting features. If you already own business software, such as Microsoft Excel or Access, you can use it to help you with spreadsheet or database functions.

A Camera

Because you need to include photos of the items you want to sell in your eBay auction listings, a camera is an essential piece of equipment to include in your eBay business. There are several ways you can create digital images. If you want to import your photos directly into your computer, you need a digital camera capable of capturing sharp pictures. Digital cameras are a hot item today and are capable of taking good close-up shots. Two-megapixel cameras are fine for eBay photos, and you can find numerous models at affordable prices online as well as at your local camera or electronics retailer. If you need to take a lot of close-up shots of items such as jewelry, consider choosing a camera that includes a zoom lens capable of macro photography.

When purchasing a digital camera, you must also consider how to transfer the images from the camera to your computer. Many digital cameras use USB cables and bundled software to transfer images. Memory cards are another way to transfer images. If your digital camera has a SmartCard or Compact Flash card, you can simply pop out the card and place it in a card reader that you can connect to your computer through a USB cable.

If you do not own a digital camera, you can use a regular camera, have the film developed into prints at a photo shop, and then scan the images using a scanner. You can also have the photo shop place the images on a CD and import the image files into your computer.

After you import or transfer your photos, a photo-editing program can help you edit your pictures to their best advantage. For example, you can crop out unwanted areas of the image, brighten a dark image, or fine-tune the image contrast. There are numerous, inexpensive image-editing software programs available today, including programs like Adobe Photoshop Elements and Paint Shop Pro by Jasc Software.

PREPARE FOR AN EBAY BUSINESS

Before you jump in and start selling on eBay, it is a smart idea to spend some time preparing and setting things up for a successful online business. There are many misconceptions about operating an eBay business, and numerous unfounded stories and advertisements commonly purport instant wealth for little effort. The exact opposite of these misconceptions is the norm. Selling items takes a lot of research, drive, and motivation. Success does not happen overnight, and it does not come without a lot of hard work, but good preparation can make your efforts flow much easier.

For starters, establish some goals and objectives. Like any other business, a well-developed business plan can help you keep on track. Your plan should include some basic questions to ask yourself: What do I want to sell? Is there a market for the items I want to sell? How much time do I want to devote to selling? After answering basic questions such as these, you can start with practical steps and setup.

Organize Your Items

As you prepare to sell on eBay, you must take some practical steps for handling your items. The more you sell, the more you must buy to keep selling. Where will you store your items while waiting for them to be auctioned? Planning ahead for storage can be helpful, especially as your sales increase. A spare room in your home or apartment can really come in handy. If space is already at a premium, you may need to apply some creative approaches for storage such as renting space or enlisting spare rooms in the homes of friends or relatives.

Along with storage, you must take time to photograph the items you want to auction. If you plan to sell many items online each week, you need to set aside time for in-home photo shoots. If you plan on using a regular camera to photograph your items, you must also schedule time to take the film in for developing and plan for the time needed to scan the prints.

Make Plans for Shipping

Shipping is another major part of running an eBay business. Shipping and handling is often a source of contention for buyers and sellers alike, especially when some eBayers overcharge for their services and shipping materials. No one likes to be overcharged for shipping, and as a seller, it is up to you to find the best and most reasonable methods for shipping the items you sell.

Be sure to shop around for the best rates, and compare costs among all major shippers. The United States Postal Service (USPS), United Parcel Service (UPS), and Federal Express (FedEx) are the three big shipping services commonly used by eBay sellers. Each service has pros and cons. Take time to gather shipping rates for a variety of weights, and keep them on hand for comparison. Find out the best location for shipping with each of these services. Driving distance can factor in to which service you choose. Each of the big services has Web sites you can peruse for additional information.

Also, be sure to check the prices on all the extra features offered by shipping companies, such as insurance, delivery confirmation, delivery receipts, and so on. It is in your best interest to always pay for delivery confirmation so there is no mistake an item has been delivered to its destination.

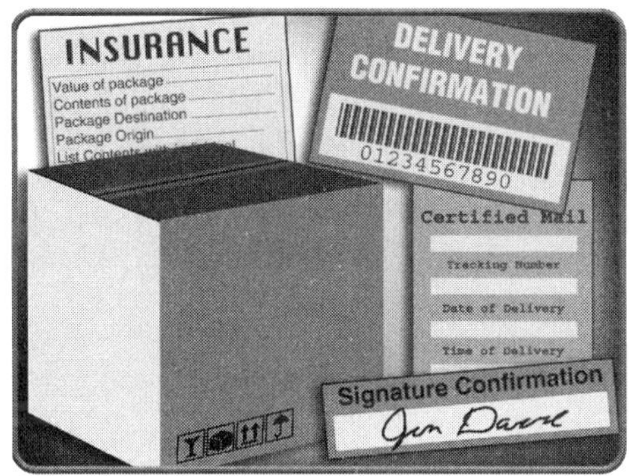

Start stocking up on shipping and packing items such as different sizes of boxes, bubble wrap and foam peanuts, packing tape, bubble envelopes, and labels. You can often find shipping materials at a discount on eBay. How well you pack an item figures greatly into your customer feedback. Do not risk negative feedback by skimping on your packing materials. Keeping an accurate scale on hand can help you determine shipping weights.

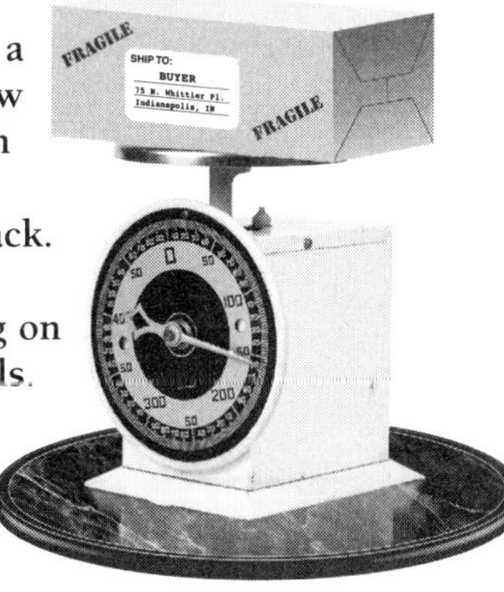

Explore Payment Methods

Another essential element of online selling is preparing for how you want buyers to pay for the items they purchase on eBay. Common ways to pay for eBay purchases include personal checks, money orders, cashier's checks, bank account transfers, and credit card payments. Payment services, such as eBay's PayPal and BidPay, enable instant payments through credit cards and bank accounts. PayPal is the most widely used payment method on eBay.

When evaluating payment methods, consider convenience and safety. If you choose to offer just one payment method, you may close the door to potential bidders. For example, if you decide to only take money orders as payment for your auctions, bidders may see the method as a major inconvenience if they have to drive to a store or bank, wait in line to purchase the money order, and then send the money order.

Take time to investigate the various payment options available. Communicate with other eBayers, and choose a method that allows the easiest transfer of funds between your buyers and you.

EXPLORE EBAY

As you explore the eBay Web site, you can find yourself visiting some parts of the site more than others. You can traverse the eBay Web site using the links at the top of any eBay Web page, but you may end up frequenting a few select pages most often.

eBay's home page lists links to auction categories, specialty sites, and featured auctions. Although eBay's home page is a good place to start viewing auction categories and listings, the Site Map page gives you quick access to every area on eBay, including pages of interest to sellers. The Site Map page is literally a map listing all the links to services and areas on eBay. Many eBay users find the site map the fastest way to link to other areas on the Web site. Rather than wade through several pages to find the area you want, you can link to the area faster using the Site Map page.

The My eBay page is bound to be your most-used page on eBay. You can use the page to watch auction items, place bids, track items you buy and sell, keep track of feedback, and save your favorite searches. The My eBay page, a one-stop-shop for all your eBay tasks, is set up to load automatically after you log on to the eBay Web site if you are a registered eBay user.

EXPLORE EBAY

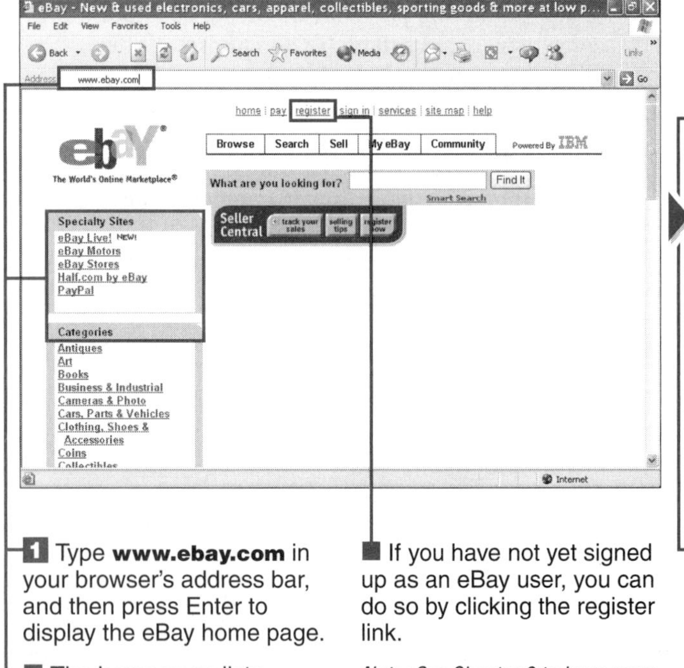

1 Type **www.ebay.com** in your browser's address bar, and then press Enter to display the eBay home page.

■ The home page lists popular parts of eBay, including specialty sites and auction listing categories.

■ If you have not yet signed up as an eBay user, you can do so by clicking the register link.

Note: See Chapter 3 to learn more about registering.

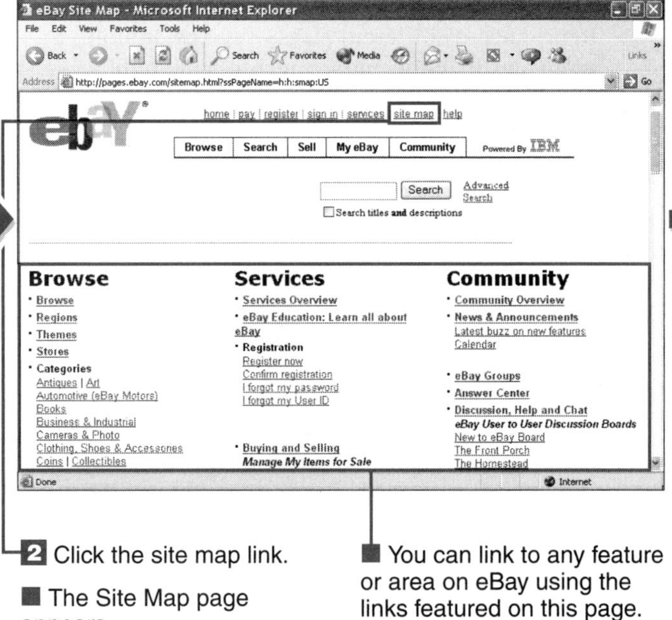

2 Click the site map link.

■ The Site Map page appears.

■ You can link to any feature or area on eBay using the links featured on this page.

I already signed in to eBay. Does eBay always start with the My eBay page after signing in?

✔ Yes. As soon as you sign up as a registered eBay user, your My eBay page is created and becomes your starting point every time you log on to the Web site. You can change which My eBay page appears by default on your page by setting another preference. See Chapter 6 to learn more. Also, as you access various parts of the site, eBay may ask you to sign in again. For example, for security purposes you may need to reauthenticate your ID if you are inactive for a certain amount of time while logged on to the eBay Web site. Simply type your password again to log back on, and continue viewing the page you requested.

How safe is eBay?

✔ eBay has several checks and balances in place to keep the Web site secure. First, your password is automatically encrypted during sign-in. eBay's feedback reporting system is also another way to keep transactions reputable. In addition, every eBay transaction is covered by the eBay Fraud Protection Program, which provides resources if you pay for an item that you never receive. If you sell on eBay Motors, additional insurance coverage is part of your account. In addition, using a credit card to pay for your purchases through a service like PayPal can also help you keep your purchases secure.

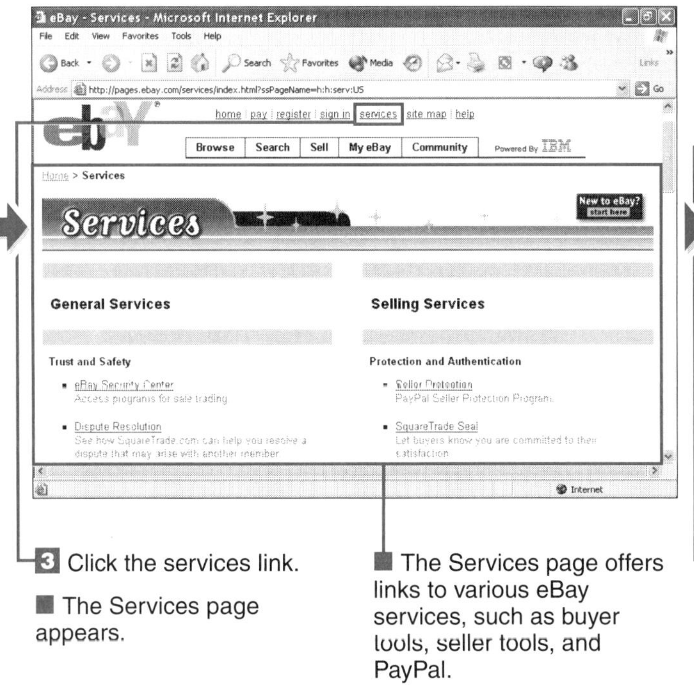

3 Click the services link.

■ The Services page appears.

■ The Services page offers links to various eBay services, such as buyer tools, seller tools, and PayPal.

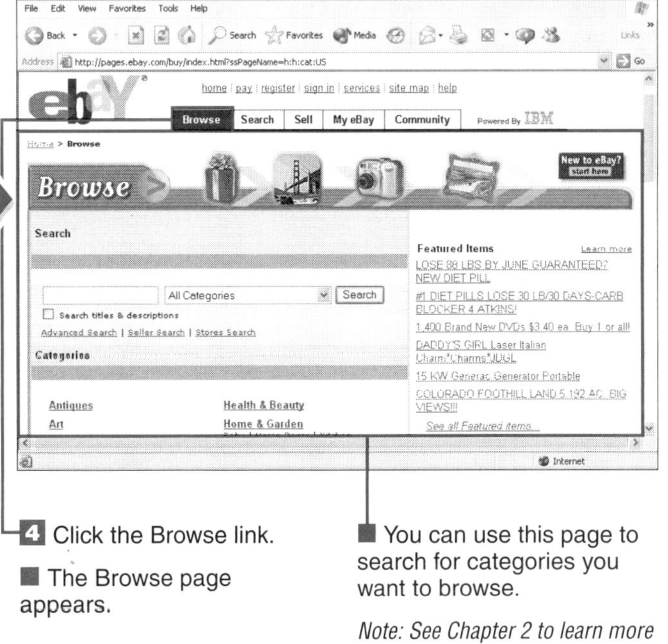

4 Click the Browse link.

■ The Browse page appears.

■ You can use this page to search for categories you want to browse.

Note: See Chapter 2 to learn more about searching for auctions on eBay.

VIEW EBAY POLICIES

Do not post your first auction listing without visiting eBay's Policies pages to find out what types of items you can sell on the site. Some items, such as firearms, are absolutely prohibited. Other items may require some clarification before listing them in an auction. The eBay Web site features a variety of guidelines you can consult regarding items you plan to sell.

Some of the eBay item restrictions are fairly obvious — you cannot sell hazardous materials, fireworks, or weapons. Items such as autographed memorabilia require certificates of authenticity. Because such items are easily forged, offering your buyers a certificate of authenticity can help reassure them that the item is legitimate.

If you end up selling an item that is not allowed on eBay, you can be reported for a listing violation. eBay can revoke your selling status if you accumulate several violations. Violations are the quickest way to end your eBay business. If you have any doubts about whether the item you want to sell is acceptable or not, consult the Prohibited and Restrictive Items list. You should check the list from time to time to view any changes in eBay policies.

VIEW EBAY POLICIES

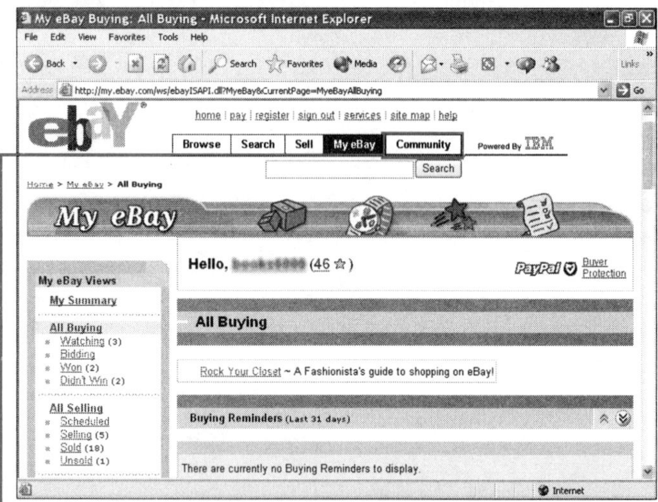

1 From any eBay page, click the Community link.

Note: The Community link is available at the top of the main eBay pages throughout the Web site.

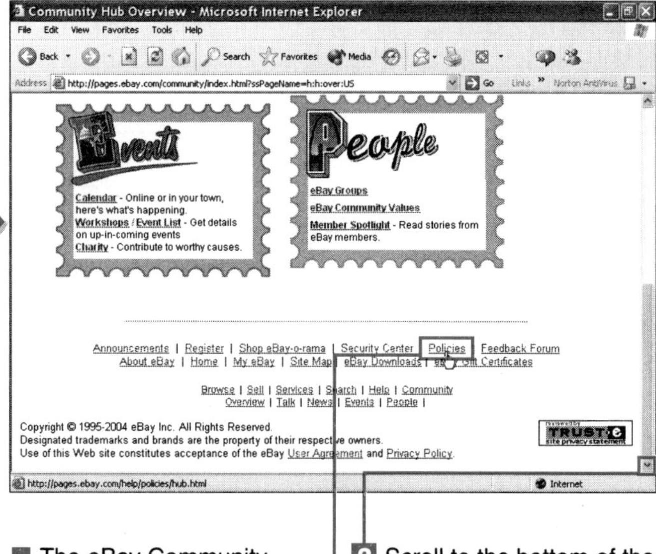

■ The eBay Community page appears.

2 Scroll to the bottom of the page.

3 Click the Policies link.

What other offenses can I commit besides selling illegal items?

✔ Selling offenses can include everything from shill bidding, which is using another ID to raise the bidding on your own item, to fee avoidance tactics, such as pulling your auction at the last minute, or conducting auction business off eBay. Buying offenses include contacting fellow bidders, or habitually submitting winning bids without completing the transaction. Feedback offenses include threatening to leave negative feedback to demand an undeserved action from another user, or offering to buy or trade feedback. The Policies page has links for finding eBay rules of conduct for both buyers and sellers.

How do I report listing violations I find with other sellers' auctions?

✔ You can report any auction listing you suspect of violating eBay rules and policies. To do so, click the help link at the top of any eBay page, and then click the Contact Us link on the Help page. This opens a form you can use to specify the type of problem you want to report. If you are reporting a particular auction listing, be sure to copy the auction number to include with your report. After filling out the report details, you can submit the report via e-mail to eBay's support team to investigate the problem. Depending on the type of problem, you may or may not hear back from eBay.

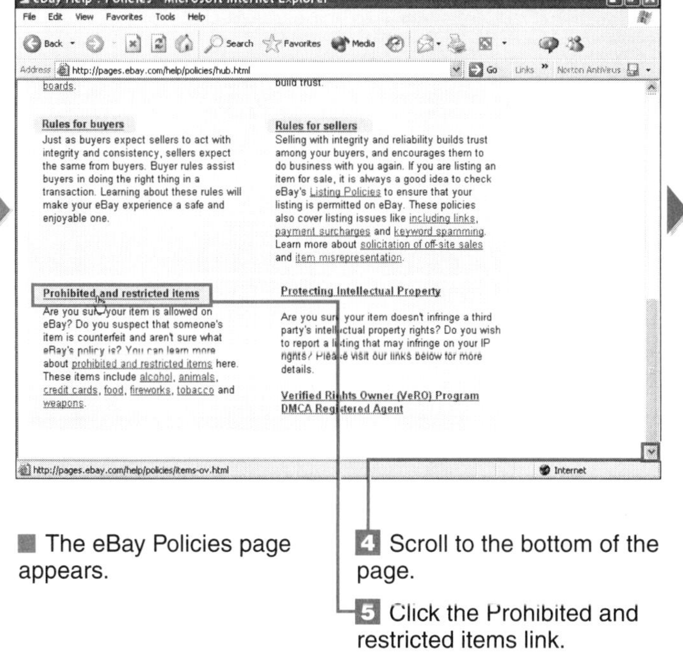

■ The eBay Policies page appears.

4 Scroll to the bottom of the page.

5 Click the Prohibited and restricted items link.

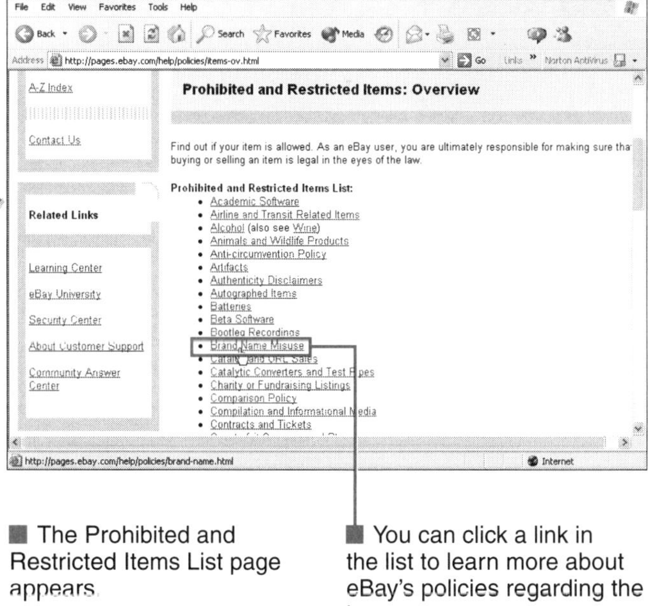

■ The Prohibited and Restricted Items List page appears.

■ You can click a link in the list to learn more about eBay's policies regarding the item category.

CONDUCT A BASIC SEARCH

eBay's Search tool is one of the site's most important features. Without it, you could not search through the thousands of auctions posted each day. You can conduct a basic keyword search to look through the auction listings for a particular item. When you conduct a basic search, eBay's search tool looks through the auction headers, or titles, for words that match the keyword you specify. You can also choose to include the description text in your search. For example, if you want to find auction listings for fireplace screens, you can simply type the keywords *fireplace screen*.

eBay searches are not case sensitive, so it does not matter whether you type your search keywords in capital letters, initial caps, or all lowercase letters. If your search includes more than one keyword and you want to make sure the search returns matches on all the keywords in a certain order, be sure to enclose the keywords in quotation marks, such as "*iron fireplace screen*". The search produces results containing all three words in the order specified.

You can conduct a basic search using the Search box at the top of the home page. You can also use the Basic Search box that appears at the top of any category listings page or search results page. You can also use the Search page to search for items; see the next section for details.

CONDUCT A BASIC SEARCH

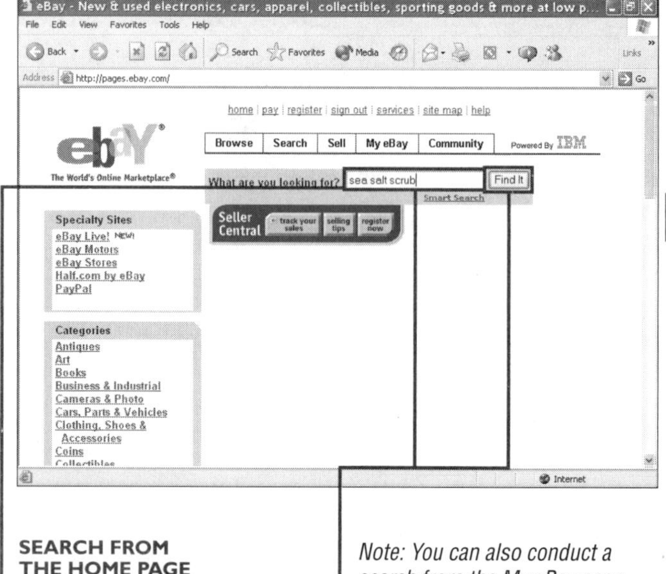

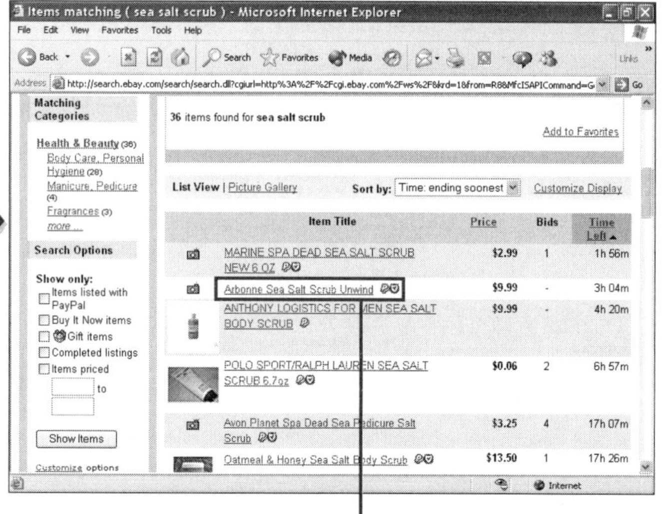

SEARCH FROM THE HOME PAGE

1 Click inside the Search text box at the top of the home page.

Note: See Chapter 1 to learn how to display the home page.

Note: You can also conduct a search from the My eBay page. See Chapter 3 to learn how to register for an account and display the My eBay page.

2 Type your keyword or keywords.

3 Click Find It.

■ Results matching the keyword or keywords that you typed appear.

■ You can click an item to view the listing.

How can I exclude certain word matches from my search results?

✔ To exclude words from your search matches, type a minus sign (-) before the word. For example, if you want the search results to return matches for dishes, but not red dishes, you can type *dishes -red*, including a space between dishes and the minus sign. To exclude a list of words, use the minus sign and surround the list with parentheses, separating each word with a comma, but no spaces. For example, to exclude your search results from showing any green, blue, or yellow dishes, type the keywords *dishes -(green,blue,yellow)*.

Do I need to use conjunctions or articles in my keyword searches?

✔ No. You can leave out conjunctions, such as *or* or *and* when typing your search text. You can also leave out articles such as *a*, *an*, and *the*. You should also leave out extra punctuation, unless you expect to find it in the auction title.

My search results did not reveal much. How do I try again?

✔ If your initial search does not produce the results you are looking for, you can immediately type another keyword or words into the Search text box in the Basic Search box and search again. Try using a different, yet similar, keyword.

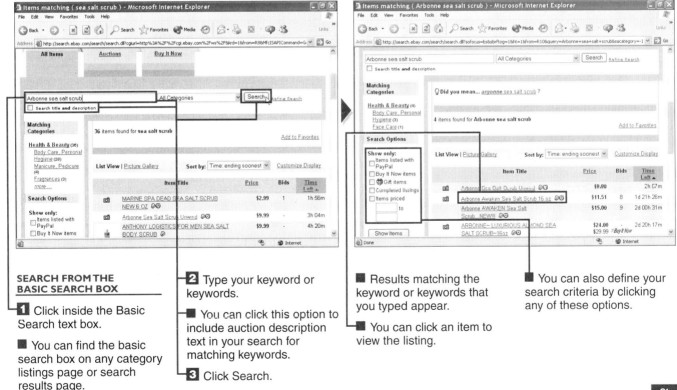

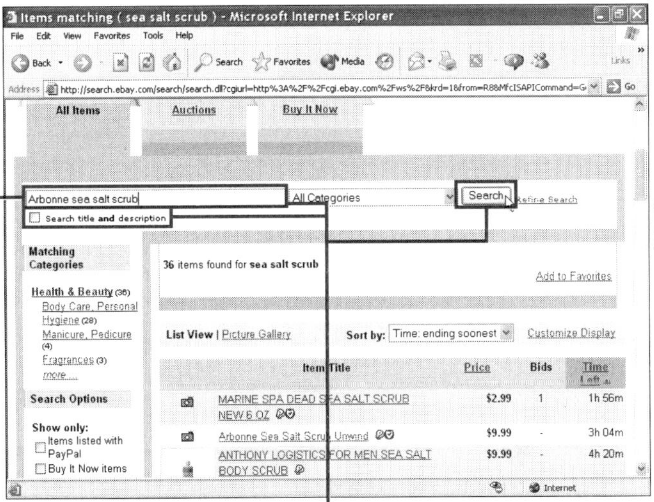

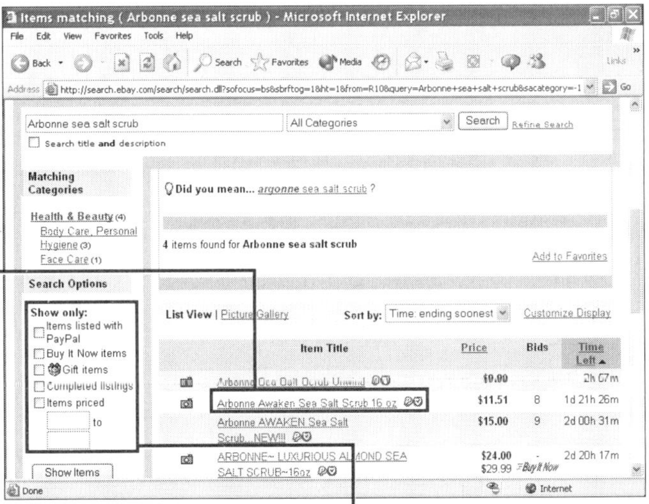

SEARCH FROM THE BASIC SEARCH BOX

1 Click inside the Basic Search text box.

■ You can find the basic search box on any category listings page or search results page.

2 Type your keyword or keywords.

■ You can click this option to include auction description text in your search for matching keywords.

3 Click Search.

■ Results matching the keyword or keywords that you typed appear.

■ You can click an item to view the listing.

■ You can also define your search criteria by clicking any of these options.

USE EBAY ADVANCED SEARCH TECHNIQUES

You can use the Search page on eBay to utilize more advanced search techniques. The Search page offers five different ways to conduct a search, including a more detailed basic search as well as an advanced search. Any time you want to conduct a search by specifying certain criteria, be sure to utilize the Search page.

Unlike the regular search text box that appears on the home page or your My eBay page, the Basic Search on the Search page allows you to specify more details about the search. For example, you can type words to exclude from the matching results, or you can choose to search a particular category instead of the entire Web site. You can instruct the search engine to search all of the eBay site, or just certain regions, such as the Miami, Florida region. You can also specify how you want the search matches to appear, such as listing lowest prices first or newly listed items first.

To perform an advanced search, you can use the Advance Search options on the Search page. These options include settings for controlling types of items, locations, display, and payment method.

You can learn how to search by bidder or seller, or conduct a search through the eBay stores in the sections following this task.

USE EBAY ADVANCED SEARCH TECHNIQUES

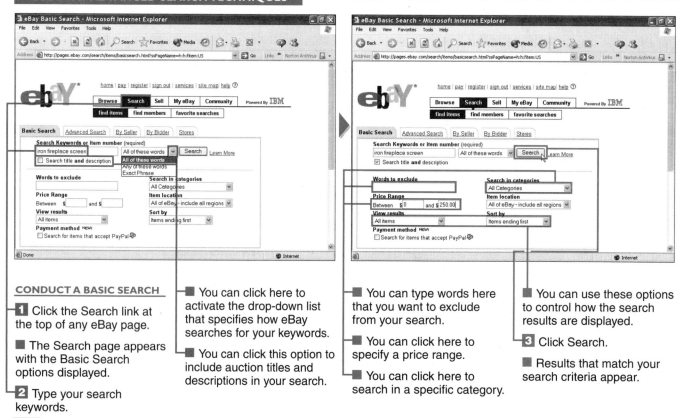

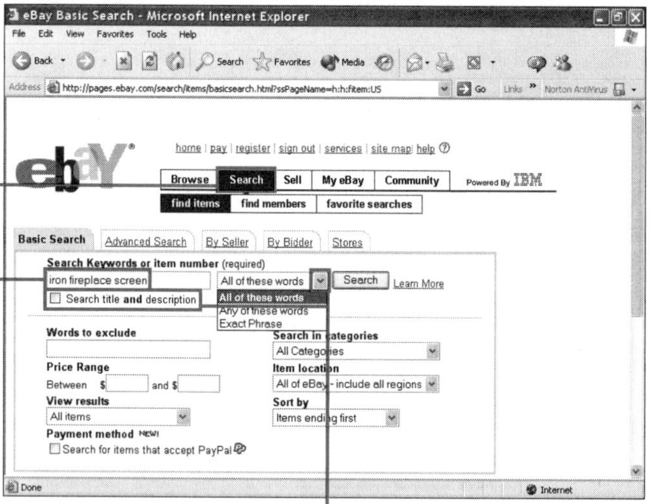

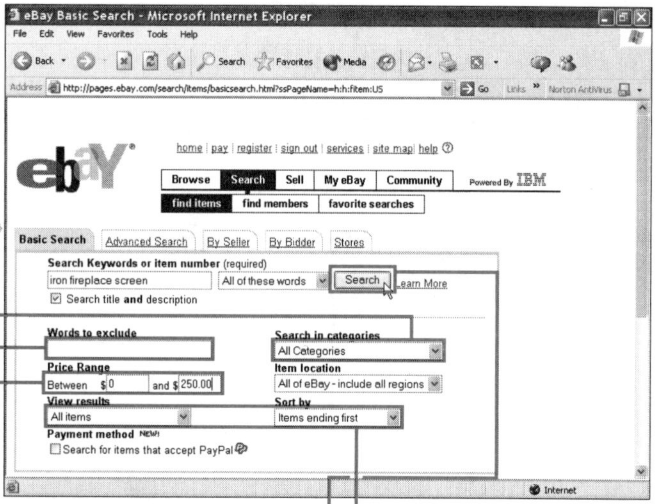

CONDUCT A BASIC SEARCH

1 Click the Search link at the top of any eBay page.

■ The Search page appears with the Basic Search options displayed.

2 Type your search keywords.

■ You can click here to activate the drop-down list that specifies how eBay searches for your keywords.

■ You can click this option to include auction titles and descriptions in your search.

■ You can type words here that you want to exclude from your search.

■ You can click here to specify a price range.

■ You can click here to search in a specific category.

■ You can use these options to control how the search results are displayed.

3 Click Search.

■ Results that match your search criteria appear.

How do I search for an expired auction listing?

✔ Expired auction listings are called *completed items* on eBay. You can search for completed items using the Advanced Search tab on the eBay Search page. You can search for completed items to find prices paid for items similar to those you are listing. To search for completed items, click the Completed Items only option (☐ changes to ☑) on the Advanced Search tab.

Can I save a search on eBay?

✔ Yes. You can save your favorite searches and revisit them again to see new listings matching your search criteria. See the section "Save Your Favorite Searches" to learn more.

What does the Payment method search option do?

✔ Because PayPal is the most widely used payment method on eBay, a new feature added to the Search tool allows you to specify only search results that include PayPal as a payment method. You can click the Search for items that accept PayPal option (☐ changes to ☑) to activate the feature.

My search does not produce many results. Why not?

✔ There are many different words people use to describe an item. Try using a different but similar word for the same thing, or try using one word instead of two. If you used a plural keyword, you can try dropping the *s* to see how that affects the search results.

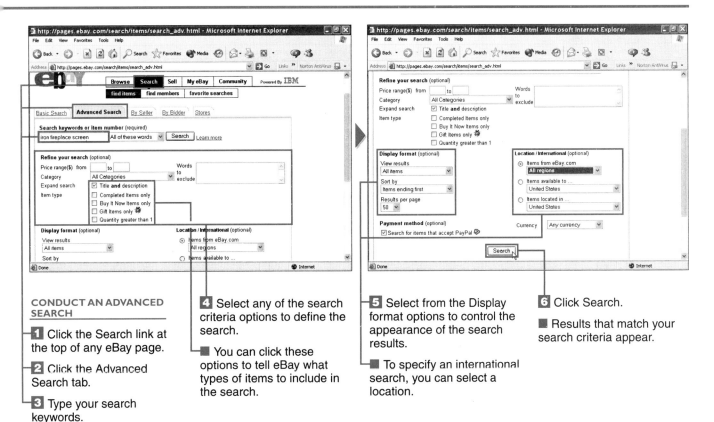

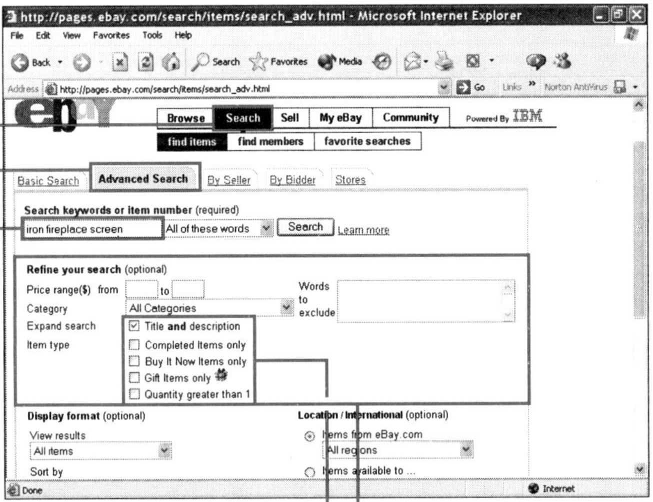

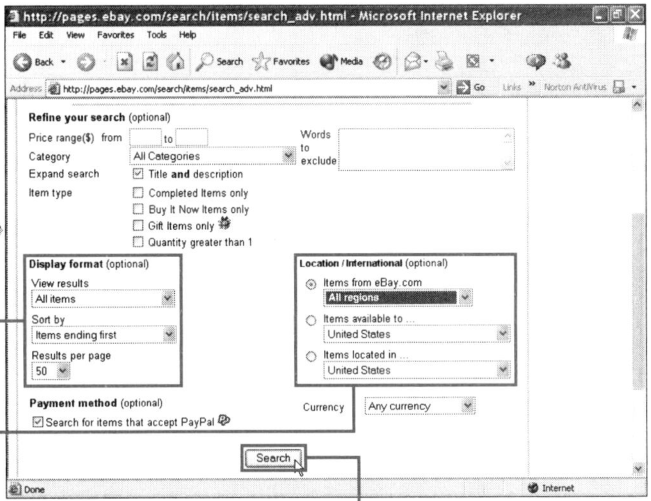

CONDUCT AN ADVANCED SEARCH

1 Click the Search link at the top of any eBay page.

2 Click the Advanced Search tab.

3 Type your search keywords.

4 Select any of the search criteria options to define the search.

■ You can click these options to tell eBay what types of items to include in the search.

5 Select from the Display format options to control the appearance of the search results.

■ To specify an international search, you can select a location.

6 Click Search.

■ Results that match your search criteria appear.

SEARCH BY SELLER OR BIDDER

You can search for sellers or buyers on eBay. eBay offers a more detailed search option that allows you to search the site for other members. To search eBay for a buyer or seller, you must use the detailed Search page instead of the regular Search text box. The Search page includes two tabs for looking up a bidder or a seller.

As a seller, you may want to look up a buyer's recent bidding history or find out which items the buyer has won in past auctions. You can look up a bidder as long as you know the bidder's ID.

As a buyer, perhaps you discovered a favorite seller you like to work with and want to check his or her auctions on a weekly basis. You can search the eBay Web site for any auction listings posted by your favorite seller, but only if you know the seller's User ID.

You can also search for more than one seller for any given item. Using the Search page options, you can expand your search to include auction listings from two or more sellers, or you can exclude any matches from sellers for which you do not want to view listings.

SEARCH BY SELLER OR BIDDER

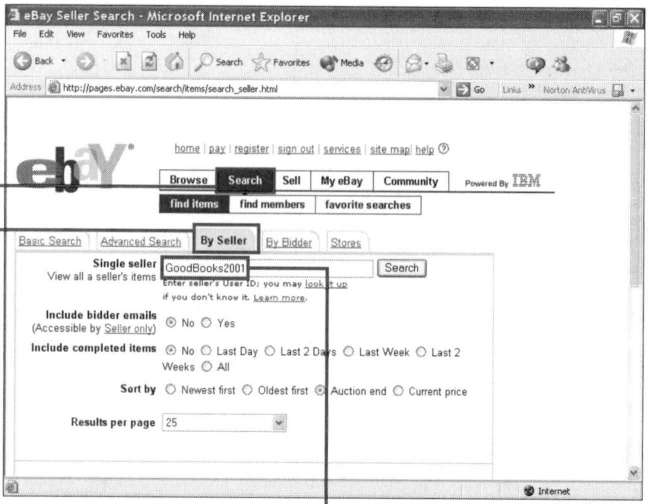

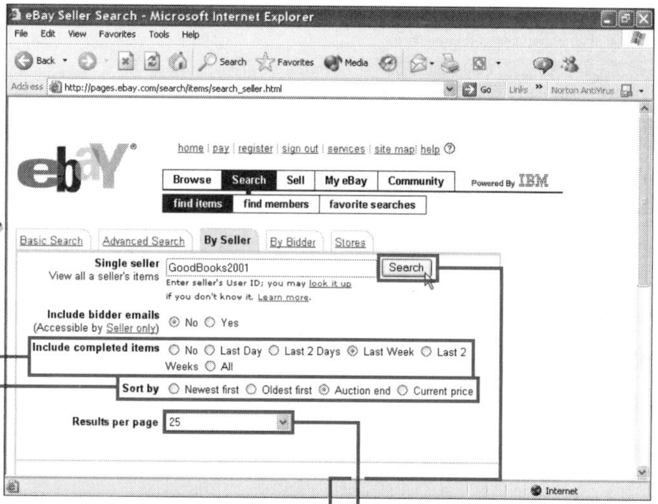

SEARCH BY SELLER

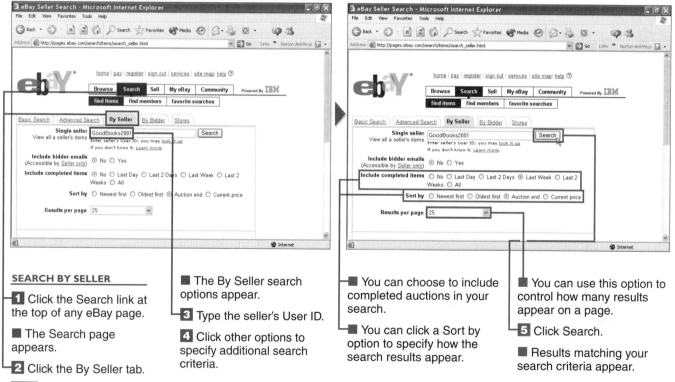

1 Click the Search link at the top of any eBay page.

■ The Search page appears.

2 Click the By Seller tab.

■ The By Seller search options appear.

3 Type the seller's User ID.

4 Click other options to specify additional search criteria.

■ You can choose to include completed auctions in your search.

■ You can click a Sort by option to specify how the search results appear.

■ You can use this option to control how many results appear on a page.

5 Click Search.

■ Results matching your search criteria appear.

How do I find a seller's ID?

✔ If you previously won an auction from the seller and he or she left feedback for you, you can find the seller's ID listed on your Feedback page. From the My eBay page, click the Feedback link to view all the auctions you won. Locate the auction listing for the seller you want to look up, and then copy the seller's User ID. You can then paste the ID number into the Search text box on the Search page.

Can I use the By Seller option to track my competitors' auctions?

✔ Yes. You can use the By Seller search options on the Search page to track the sales of similar items by other sellers. Below the Single seller options on the By Seller tab, you can find options for conducting a multiple seller search. In the Search Title text box, type the keywords for which you want to search. Click the Multiple Sellers text box and type the sellers' names, separating each with a comma. Leave the Find items from these sellers option selected. Click the Search button to begin the search.

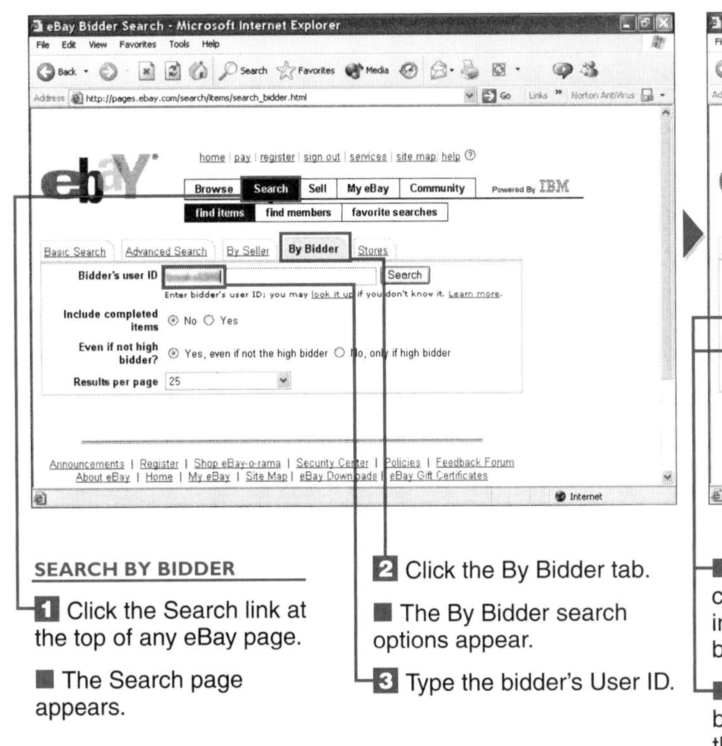

SEARCH BY BIDDER

1 Click the Search link at the top of any eBay page.

■ The Search page appears.

2 Click the By Bidder tab.

■ The By Bidder search options appear.

3 Type the bidder's User ID.

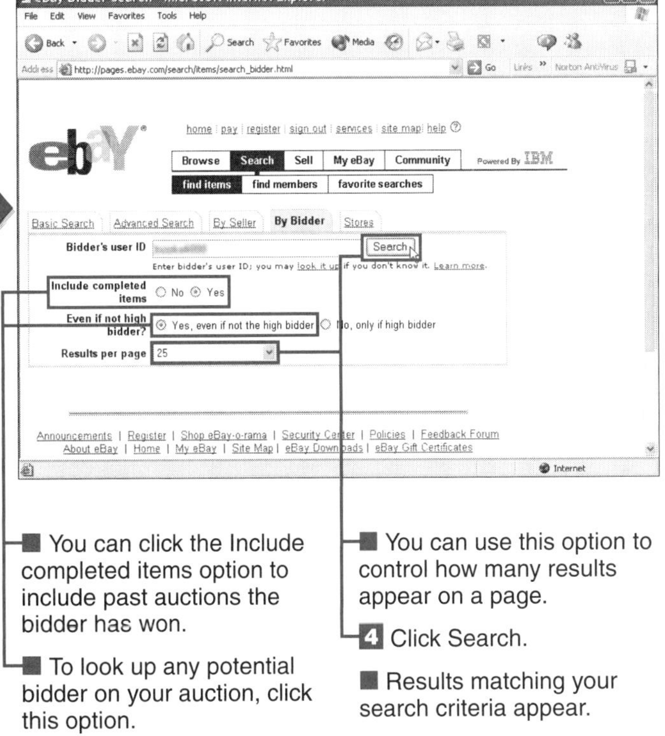

■ You can click the Include completed items option to include past auctions the bidder has won.

■ To look up any potential bidder on your auction, click this option.

■ You can use this option to control how many results appear on a page.

4 Click Search.

■ Results matching your search criteria appear.

SEARCH EBAY STORES

You can use the eBay Search page to search for items among the various eBay stores. Unlike regular auction listings that allow users to bid on items, eBay stores allow sellers to sell items at a fixed price, also called a Buy It Now price. Sellers can list items in an eBay store for lower listing fees, so you can often find fixed-price items at really good prices. Also, by searching eBay stores, you can access additional items you might not normally view in regular auction listings.

By default, when you conduct a search of eBay stores, the search results list all the matches from the sellers, including their regular auction listings as well as their fixed-price listings. For example, if you have a favorite seller who operates an eBay store, you can browse all the items the seller has for sale, both in auction format and fixed-price format.

Like the other search options found on the Search page tabs, you can specify exactly how you want to conduct a search of eBay stores. For example, you can choose to search just the store inventory and exclude the auction listings from the search.

SEARCH EBAY STORES

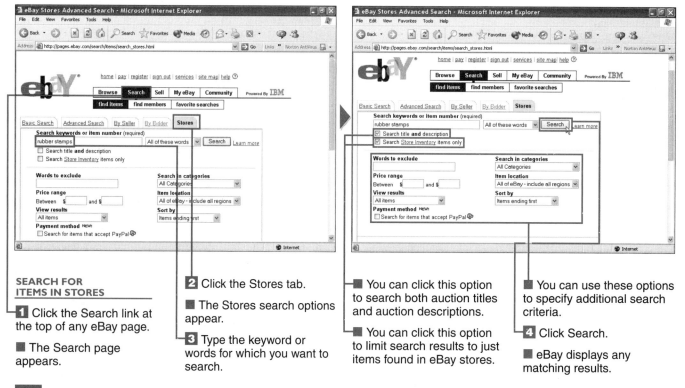

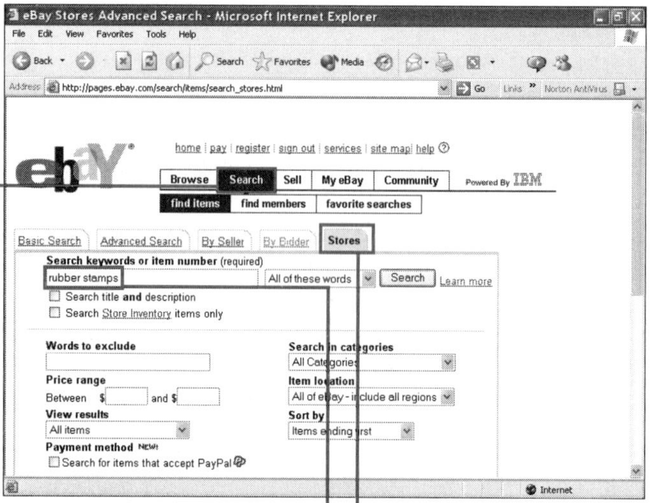

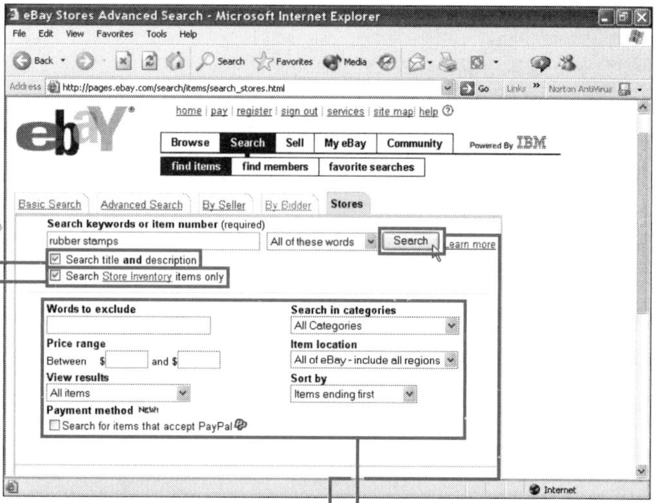

SEARCH FOR ITEMS IN STORES

1 Click the Search link at the top of any eBay page.

■ The Search page appears.

2 Click the Stores tab.

■ The Stores search options appear.

3 Type the keyword or words for which you want to search.

■ You can click this option to search both auction titles and auction descriptions.

■ You can click this option to limit search results to just items found in eBay stores.

■ You can use these options to specify additional search criteria.

4 Click Search.

■ eBay displays any matching results.

Is there an easier way to revisit my favorite stores?

✔ Yes. You can keep a running list of your favorite stores on the Favorites section of your My eBay page. When you display listings from your favorite store, a special link appears at the top of the page to save the search. Click the Add to My Favorite Stores link and eBay adds the store to your Favorites section. You can click the link in the Favorites section to quickly display the current listings for the store. To learn more about saving your favorite searches, see the next section.

How can I tell which store listing is a fixed-price item or an item open for bidding?

✔ Look in the Time Left column at the far right side of the store's listing page to view whether items are auctions or not. If you see a time next to the item, the item is an auction listing, which means it is open for bids. If you do not see a time listed in the Time Left column, the item is a fixed-price item, and you can purchase it using the Buy It Now option.

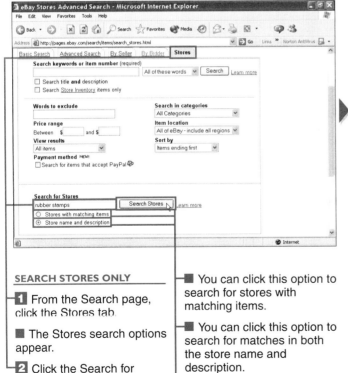

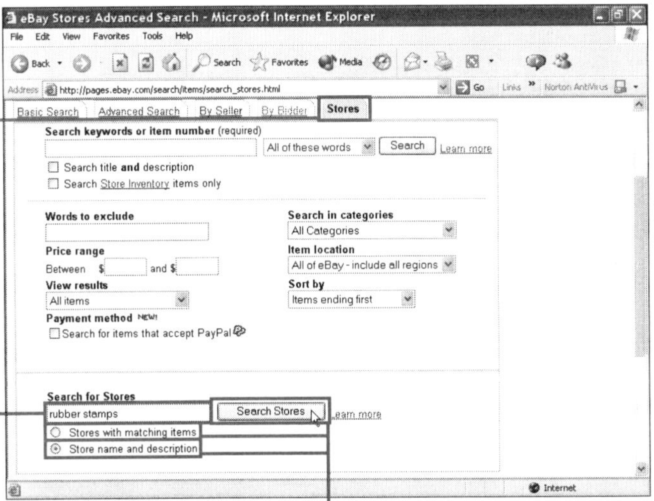

SEARCH STORES ONLY

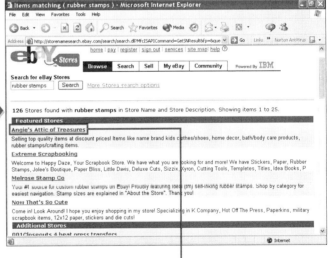

1 From the Search page, click the Stores tab.

■ The Stores search options appear.

2 Click the Search for Stores text box, and type your search keyword.

■ You can click this option to search for stores with matching items.

■ You can click this option to search for matches in both the store name and description.

3 Click Search Stores.

■ Results matching your search criteria appear.

■ You can click a store name link to view the matching listings.

SAVE YOUR FAVORITE SEARCHES

If you repeatedly search eBay for the same item each day or week, you can save your search criteria as a favorite search. For example, if you check for new auctions each day looking for a special collectible item, you can set up your search so it launches with a click of a link. This can eliminate the time spent retyping your keywords and specifying search criteria each time.

eBay stores your favorite searches on the Favorites section of the My eBay page. You can save a maximum of 100 searches. You can revisit a search at any time and display the latest matches for your search criteria. You can add any search to your Favorite Searches list. You can edit your list of favorites to remove old searches you no longer use, or edit existing searches to change the search criteria. You can also set up your favorite searches to send new search results to your e-mail address.

You can save searches conducted with the basic Search text box or searches conducted from the eBay official Search page. To save a search, you must first perform the search and list potential matches. The save feature is not available unless you display search results.

SAVE YOUR FAVORITE SEARCHES

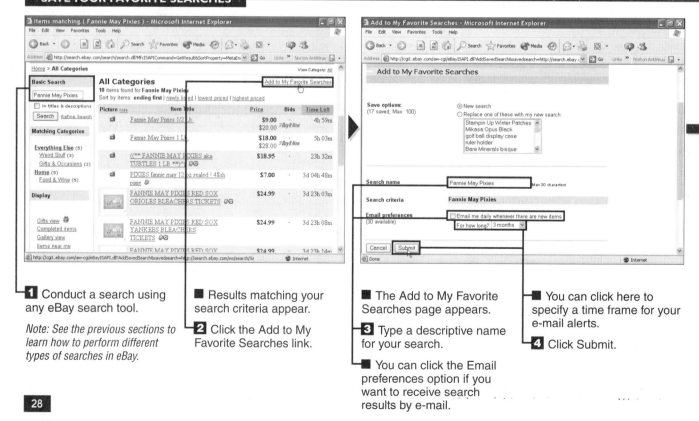

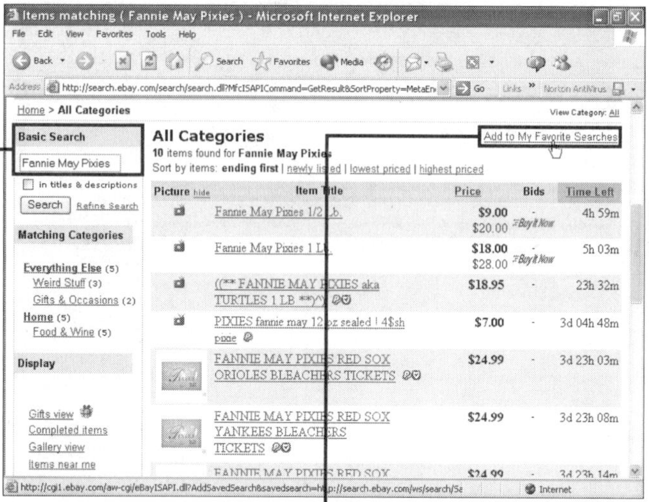

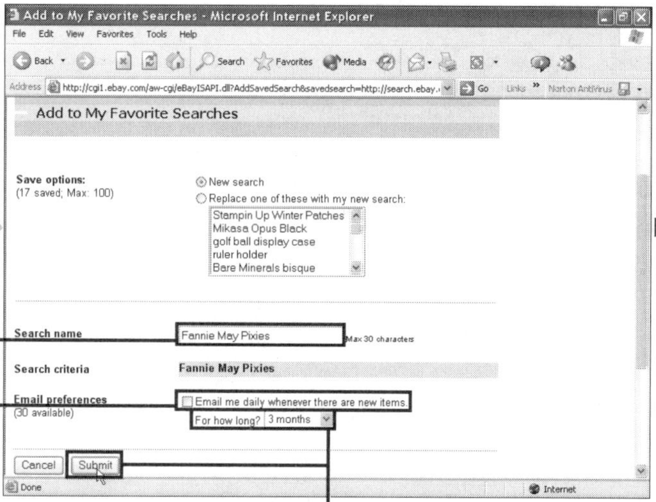

1 Conduct a search using any eBay search tool.

Note: See the previous sections to learn how to perform different types of searches in eBay.

■ Results matching your search criteria appear.

2 Click the Add to My Favorite Searches link.

■ The Add to My Favorite Searches page appears.

3 Type a descriptive name for your search.

■ You can click the Email preferences option if you want to receive search results by e-mail.

■ You can click here to specify a time frame for your e-mail alerts.

4 Click Submit.

How do I edit the criteria for a favorite search?

✔ Return to the My eBay page and click the Favorites link to view your list of favorite categories, searches, and stores. To edit a favorite search, click the Refine link next to the search name. This opens the Search page along with the search criteria options. You can make changes to your search criteria.

Can I change my search e-mail settings?

✔ Yes. Click the Preferences link next to the favorite search listed in the Favorites section to open a page where you can change the search name and e-mail preferences.

How do I remove a search I no longer want to save?

✔ Display the Favorites section on your My eBay page, and then click the favorite search item option (☑ changes to ☐) you want to remove from your list. You can then click the Delete button to permanently remove the search.

What happens if I save more than 100 searches?

✔ If you save more than 100 searches, you must delete searches you no longer want to keep to make room for new searches. The Add to My Favorite Searches page offers an option for replacing an existing search with a new search.

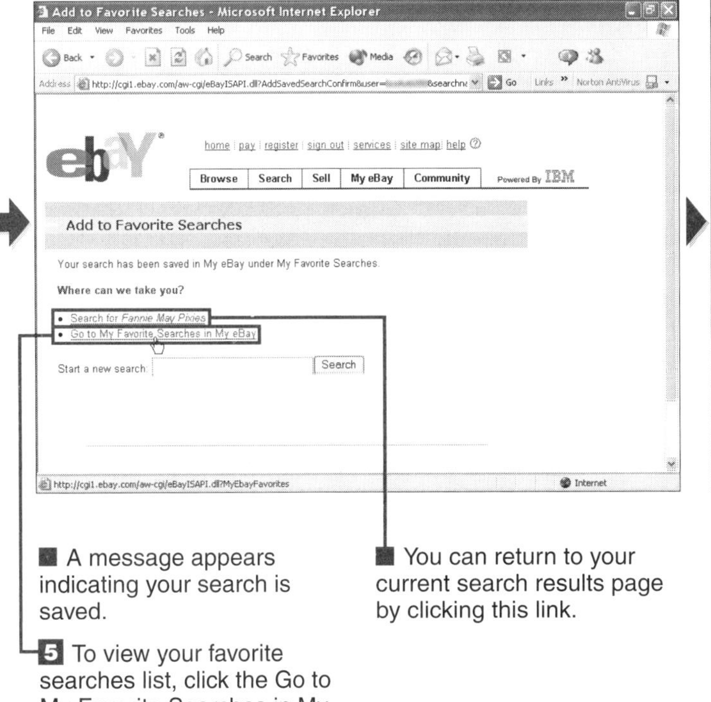

■ A message appears indicating your search is saved.

■ You can return to your current search results page by clicking this link.

5 To view your favorite searches list, click the Go to My Favorite Searches in My eBay link.

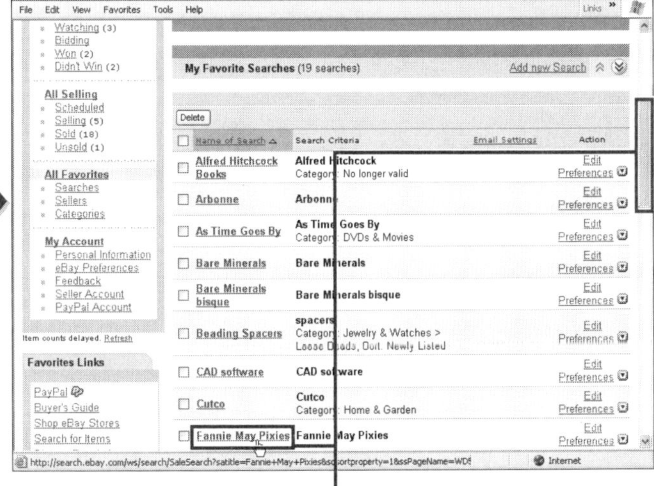

■ The Favorites section on your My eBay page appears.

■ You can scroll down the page to see the new search that you listed.

■ You can click a favorite link to conduct a search.

BROWSE EBAY CATEGORIES

If you are not looking for anything in particular, you can simply browse eBay's many categories and view auction listings for items of interest. Although browsing may not be the most focused way to find things on eBay, it is a pleasurable pastime for many bidders, and you never know what exciting bargain you may find.

You can use the Browse link at the top of any eBay page to view a list of main categories. The Browse page lists a variety of main categories, such as Antiques and Computers. Within each main category are numerous subcategories with groups of related subcategories narrowing down the category focus.

For example, if you browse the Books category, you can find subcategories for different book classifications such as fiction, nonfiction, and children's books. Some subcategories include additional subcategories. The number of categories offered by eBay changes frequently, so browsing from time to time may reveal a new category for you to explore.

When you find a category you like, you can open it to view its auction listings. By default, eBay lists the soon-to-expire auctions first, and the newly-posted auctions last.

BROWSE EBAY CATEGORIES

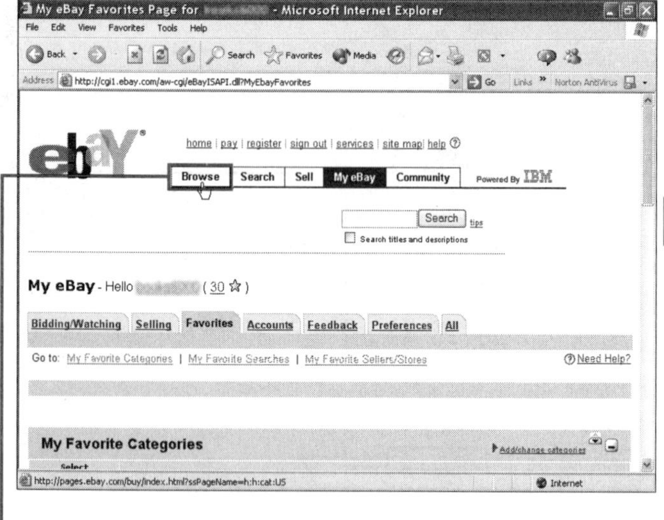

1 Click the Browse link at the top of any eBay page.

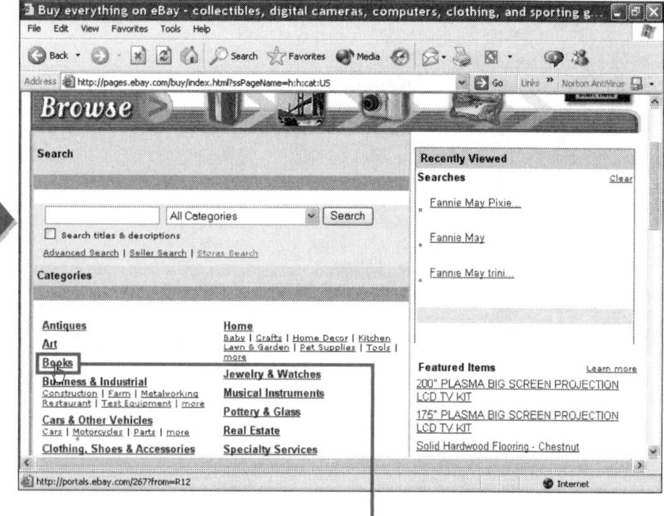

■ The Browse page appears.

2 Click a category.

How do I search within a category?

✔ After browsing to a particular category, the Search area on the left side of the page displays a check box for searching only in the current category. Type your search keyword in the Basic Search text box, and then click the Only In option (☐ changes to ☑). eBay searches only in the current category rather than searching throughout the entire site. See the section "Conduct a Basic Search" to learn more about using the Search area next to the auction listings.

Can I save categories in my Favorites list?

✔ Yes. You can save your favorite categories and revisit them with a simple click from your My eBay page. You can save a category by clicking the Add/change categories link in the Favorites page. You can find the link next to the My Favorite Categories section of the page. The Add or Modify Your Favorite Categories page appears, and you can select from the list of categories. You can select up to four categories to save. Click the Submit button at the bottom of the page to save the category to your list of favorites.

■ The listing page for the category you clicked appears.

3 Click a subcategory.

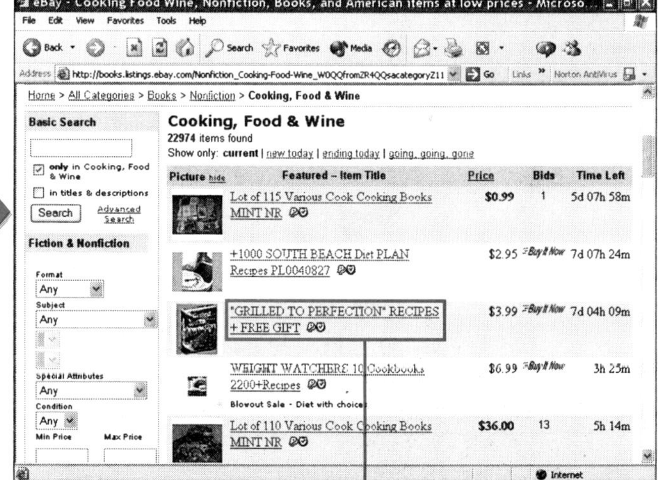

■ A list of available auctions appears.

■ To view an auction listing, click on the auction title.

SECTION II

START SELLING ON EBAY NOW!

VINTAGE JUKEBOX - PERFECT CONDITION!!
Starting bid:
Time Left:
History
High bidde
Item Locatior
You are bidding on a vintag
capacity with a visible roller
and picks the record. Only
rare, and very few exist. Th
up restaurant that had beer
that time, it works as well a
sound, etc., is in perfect co
for 5 cents,
button on the side
Will ship anywher

REGISTER AS AN EBAY USER

Before you can start buying or selling on eBay, you must first register with the Web site and create an account. eBay's registration is very straightforward. The process consists of three stages: providing information, agreeing to eBay's terms of use, and confirming your e-mail address.

To create an account, you must provide your personal information, including your name, address, phone number, and e-mail address. The contact information must be current. If you type the wrong information, eBay can cancel your account. In addition, you must create a User ID that identifies you and is unique from all the other eBay users.

When creating a User ID for an eBay business, take time to think about how you want to be identified by your customers on eBay. For example, you may want to use your business name as an ID to help create recognition. You may also consider an ID that reflects your type of business or specialty.

You must also create a password to use to access the account. As soon as you complete the basic information form, the registration process takes you to the next stage.

REGISTER AS AN EBAY USER

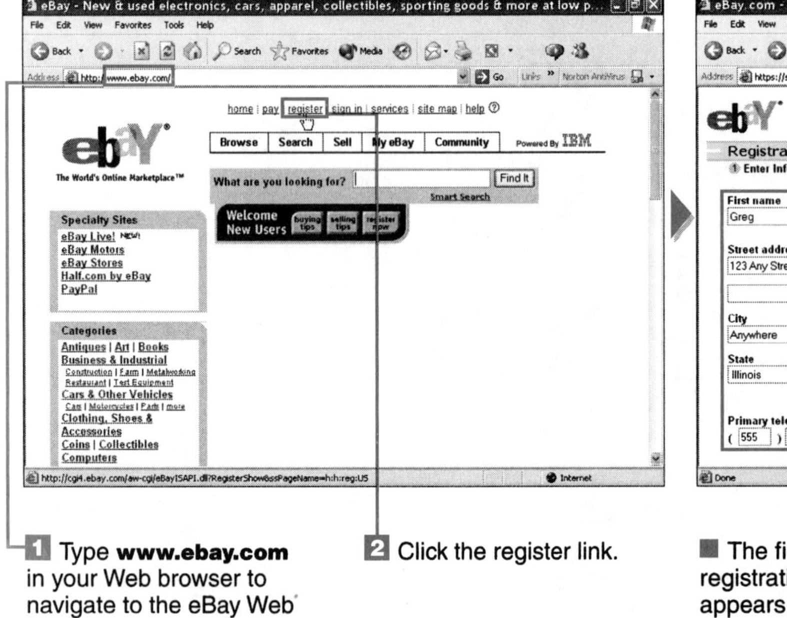

1 Type **www.ebay.com** in your Web browser to navigate to the eBay Web site.

2 Click the register link.

■ The first page of the registration process appears.

3 In the appropriate text boxes, type your name, address, and phone number.

Can I use my e-mail address as my User ID?

✔ No. eBay does not allow users to utilize their e-mail address as a User ID. You also cannot use your Web address, or URL, as an ID. That practice was common on eBay in the past, but eBay no longer accepts it. One of the reasons for the change is the proliferation of junk e-mail. Spammers could easily spot your e-mail identification and start sending you junk e-mail. eBay users who need to contact you can do so by clicking the Ask seller a question link.

I already have a User ID. Can I change it to something else?

✔ Yes. You can change your User ID and still keep your accumulated feedback score. Click the Preferences link on your My eBay page to change your User ID. See Chapter 11 to learn more about feedback on eBay. See Chapter 6 for more about the My eBay page.

Are there any rules to eBay User IDs?

✔ Yes. You cannot use the @ or & symbols in your ID name. You can use other characters, such as numbers and symbols. Do not use blank spaces. If you do need to separate two words, use a single underscore character.

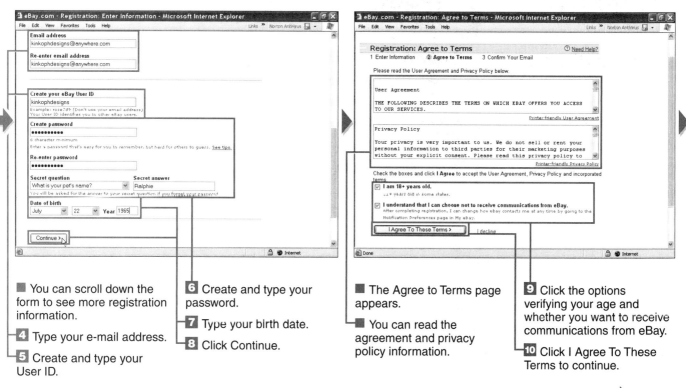

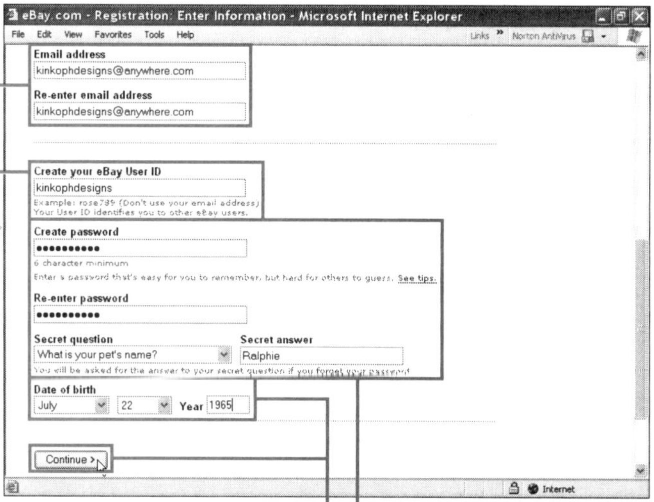

■ You can scroll down the form to see more registration information.

4 Type your e-mail address.

5 Create and type your User ID.

6 Create and type your password.

7 Type your birth date.

8 Click Continue.

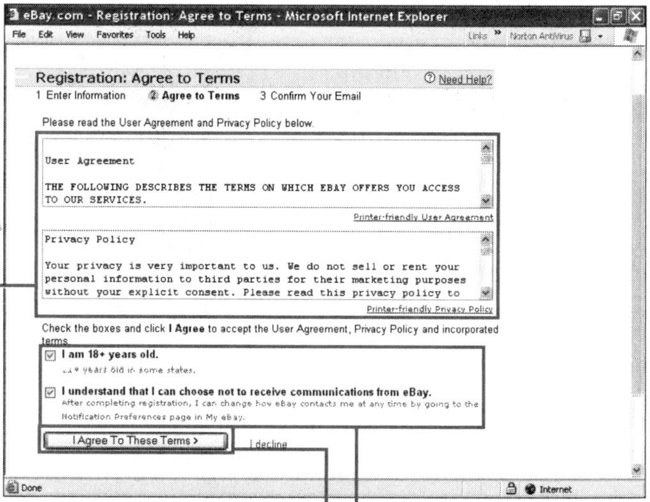

■ The Agree to Terms page appears.

■ You can read the agreement and privacy policy information.

9 Click the options verifying your age and whether you want to receive communications from eBay.

10 Click I Agree To These Terms to continue.

CONTINUED

REGISTER AS AN EBAY USER (CONTINUED)

Another important part of registering as an eBay user is to create a secure password. If you follow a few basic principles, you can improve your eBay security. A good rule of thumb is to create a password that uses between six and nine characters, mixing both numbers and upper- and lowercase letters. Refrain from using words or short passwords. If someone does gain access to your password, he or she can wreak havoc on your eBay account as well as with your financial information set up to use your account.

After you provide your personal information, create a User ID and password, read the eBay user agreement, and agree to the eBay policies, you can enter the final phase of the registration process. As a final step, eBay asks you to confirm your e-mail address. The site does this to make sure you are a legitimate user. After you activate the agreement phase, eBay e-mails you a confirmation message containing a link to return to the site using your new ID.

When you activate the e-mail message link, eBay confirms your User ID, and you can start using the Web site to view auction listings, bid on items, and more.

REGISTER AS AN EBAY USER (CONTINUED)

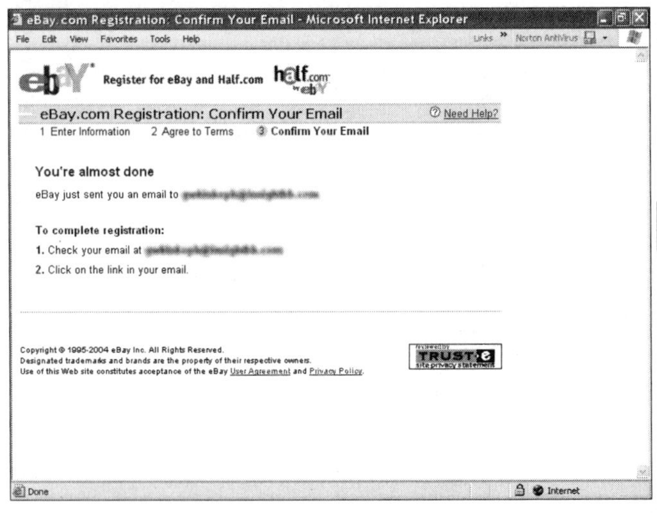

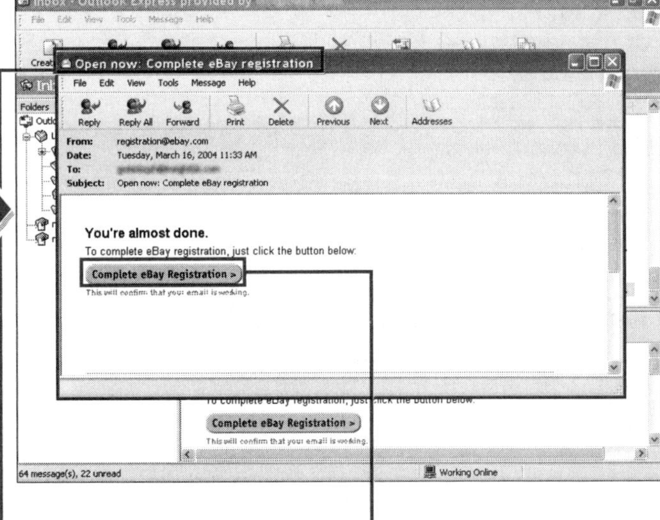

■ The Confirm Your Email page appears.

■ The last phase of the registration process directs you to check your e-mail.

11 Open your e-mail program and the e-mail message received from eBay.

12 Click the Complete eBay Registration link within the e-mail.

How do I sign up to pay for items I bid on?

✔ Auctions vary in their payment policies. Some accept personal checks and money orders, others accept credit card payments and bank account transfers. The most widely used method for payment online is PayPal. You can sign up for the service and pay for auctions using your credit card or bank account funds. As a seller, it is in your best interest to offer a payment method that reaches the largest number of users. To learn more about using PayPal, see Chapter 10. Before you do sign up for a PayPal account, be sure to read about PayPal guidelines, policies, and fees.

I want to start selling right away. Do I need to set up a different account?

✔ You can use your current User ID to set up a seller's account on eBay. To establish yourself as a seller, you must fill out an additional online form. See the section "Sign Up for an eBay Seller Account," later in this chapter, to learn more.

What information does the user agreement contain?

✔ The eBay user agreement outlines the relationship between you and eBay, and spells out the site's privacy principles. You can reread the agreement at any time at the following Web address: http://pages.ebay.com/help/policies/user-agreement.html.

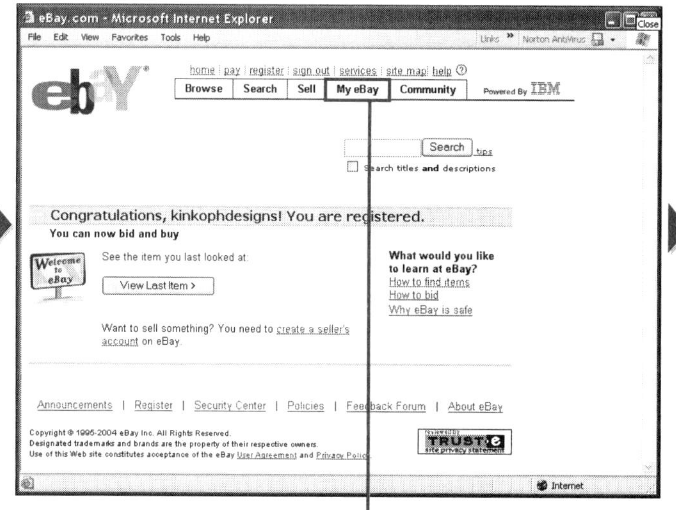

■ A new page appears in your Web browser connecting you to your new eBay account.

13 Click the My eBay link.

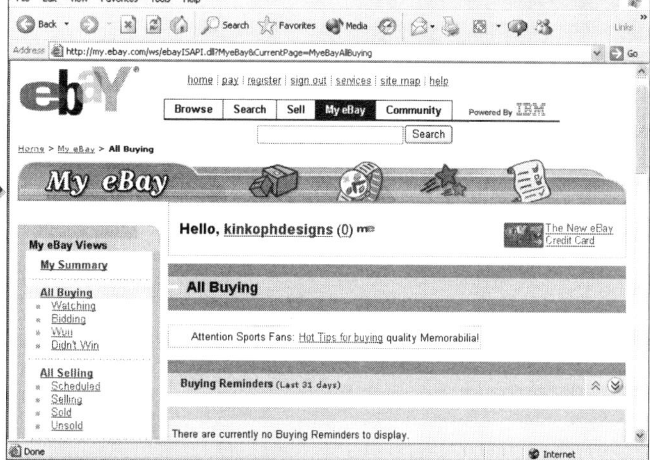

■ Your new My eBay page appears, displaying your new User ID.

SIGN IN TO EBAY

When you sign up to be a registered user on eBay, you can use the Sign In procedure to log onto your eBay account. You must be logged on in order to bid on an auction, post a new auction listing, or check on existing auctions currently running. The sign-in process involves logging onto the Web site using your User ID and your password, which you created when you started your new account. The Sign In page includes a link for registering for a new account.

The Sign In page includes some help links that you can use in case you forget your User ID or your password. For example, if you forget your password, you can activate the Forgot your password link and eBay e-mails you a password reminder. The Sign In page also features an option to keep you signed in for as long as you use your computer, until you turn it off or sign off of the Web site.

When you finish using your eBay account, you can simply close the browser window to exit your account. If you share your computer with other users, you can activate the Sign Out feature and log off of your account without shutting down the browser window.

SIGN IN TO EBAY

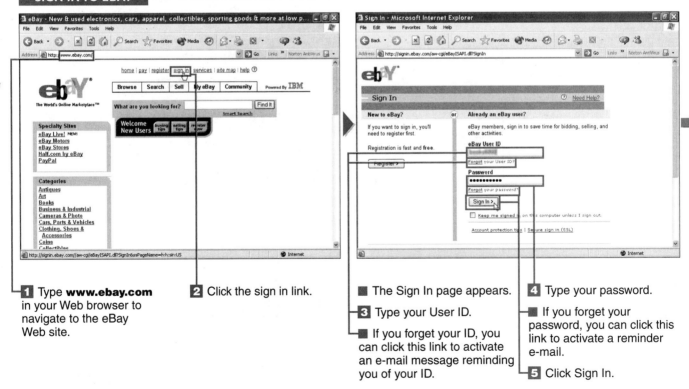

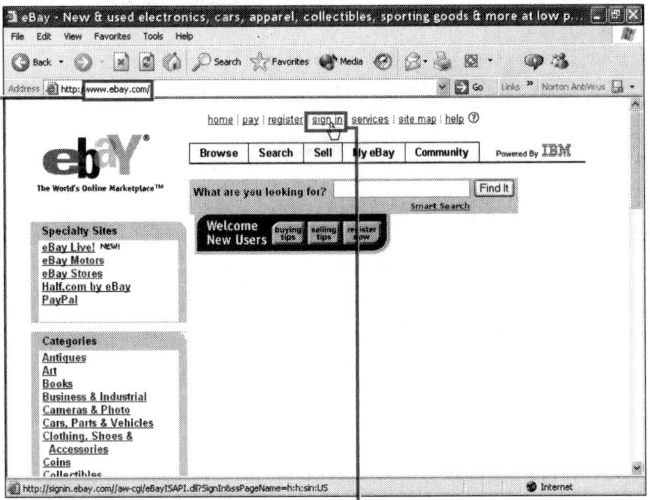

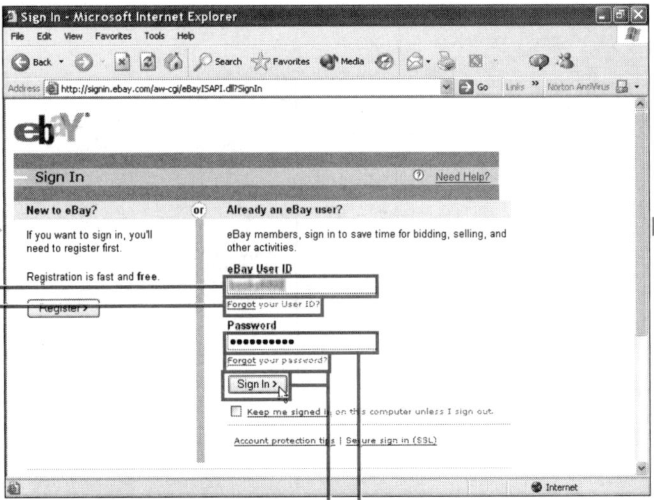

1 Type **www.ebay.com** in your Web browser to navigate to the eBay Web site.

2 Click the sign in link.

■ The Sign In page appears.

3 Type your User ID.

■ If you forget your ID, you can click this link to activate an e-mail message reminding you of your ID.

4 Type your password.

■ If you forget your password, you can click this link to activate a reminder e-mail.

5 Click Sign In.

When I try to log on, I receive an error message that says the browser I am using is rejecting cookies. What do I do?

✔ To utilize the eBay Web site, your browser program must be set to accept cookies, which are small bits of data that store your Web preferences. Turn on your browser's cookie acceptance feature. Check your browser's help features to learn more about setting cookie options. If the cookies feature is already active, consider deleting old cookies from your computer and try again. Be sure to use the newest version of your browser program.

I keep having to log back on. Why?

✔ If you are inactive for a period of time, your eBay session expires automatically and you need to log back on again.

How do I make a shortcut to the Sign In page?

✔ If you use Internet Explorer and Windows, you can quickly create a shortcut icon on your desktop that leads you to the Sign In page. First, display the Sign In page. Choose File, Send, and then Shortcut to Desktop. Windows immediately places a shortcut icon for the Web page on your desktop. The next time you want to log on, click the shortcut icon to open the browser and the Sign In page.

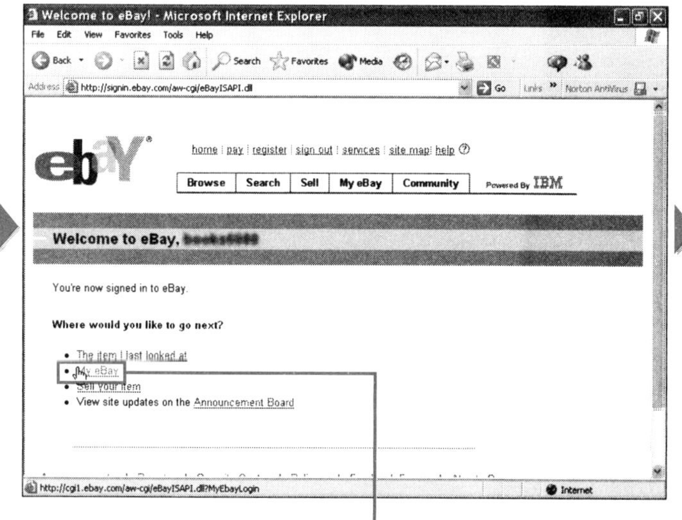

■ A Welcome to eBay page appears.

6 Click the link for the page you want to view.

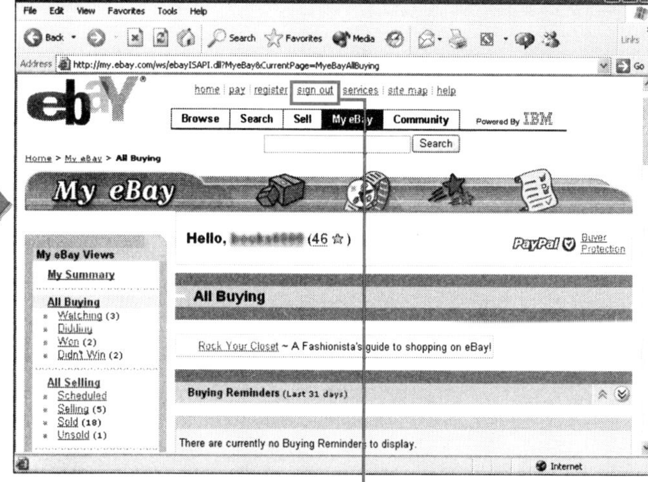

■ The page you selected appears.

■ In this example, the My eBay page appears.

■ To sign out, you can click the sign out link at the top of any eBay page.

SIGN UP FOR AN EBAY SELLER ACCOUNT

The first step to becoming an eBay seller is to establish a seller account. When you add a seller account, you are simply upgrading your current account to establish selling privileges. Creating a seller account involves two steps. In the first step, eBay asks you to verify your current information. This is the information you provided when you created your account and User ID.

The second step is to specify how you want to pay your seller fees.

eBay makes its money from fees it charges to sellers for listing auctions and selling items to buyers. Any time you create an auction listing and post it on eBay, eBay charges an initial listing fee. After someone wins your auction, eBay charges you a final value fee. You can arrange for eBay to charge those fees to a credit card or bank debit card account, or take the fees directly from a checking account. eBay bills you each month for fees you accumulate with your auctions.

Your credit card and checking account information essentially establishes your identity and helps to ensure that you are a legal and legitimate businessperson. The process also helps protect eBayers from fraudulent sellers.

SIGN UP FOR AN EBAY SELLER ACCOUNT

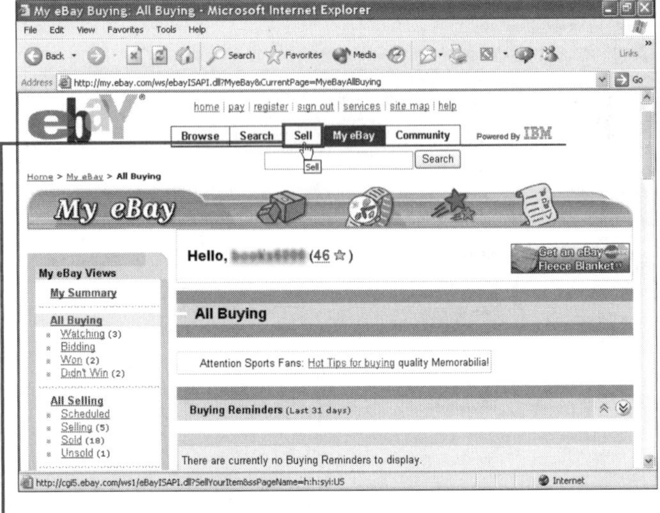

1 Click the Sell link at the top of any eBay page.

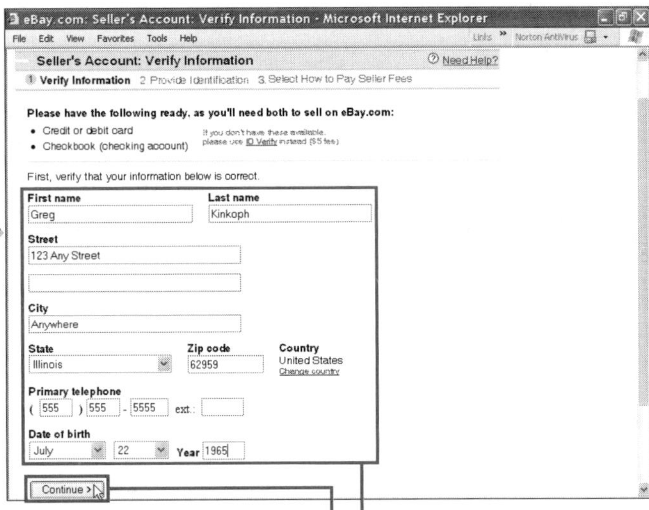

■ The Seller's Account: Verify Information page appears.

2 Type the information in the appropriate fields to verify your name, address, phone number, and birth date.

3 Click Continue.

Are there other fees involved with selling on eBay?

✔ It does not cost anything to create a buyer's account, also called a regular or normal account, or a seller's account. Other than the two types of fees eBay charges before and after the auction, you may incur additional fees if you opt for auction listing extras, such as additional photos, bold heading type, gift icons, and more. To learn more about extra listing fees, see Chapter 5. The only time eBay charges you fees is if you use your selling account to list auctions. If you do not use the account, no fees are incurred.

What if I do not have a credit card or checking account?

✔ The purpose of the financial information you provide during the signup process is to verify your identity. These steps are for your own safety as well as the safety of other eBay users. If you do not want to use a credit card for your seller's account or do not want to list a checking account, you can use eBay's ID Verify feature for a fee of $5. The feature establishes proof of your identity by cross-checking your financial and personal information against consumer and business databases.

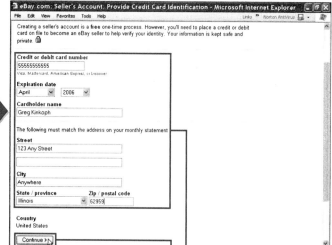

■ The Seller's Account: Provide Check Identification page appears.

■ eBay asks you to provide two sources of identification, starting with a checking account.

4 In the appropriate text fields, type your checking account information.

5 Click Continue.

■ The Seller's Account: Provide Credit Card Information page appears.

6 In the appropriate text fields, type your credit card information.

7 Click Continue.

CONTINUED

SIGN UP FOR AN EBAY SELLER ACCOUNT (CONTINUED)

In addition to verifying your identity with both a credit or debit card and a banking account, eBay also asks you to select an account from which to pay your seller fees. The account you select depends on your financial situation. For example, if your checking account varies daily in the amount of available funds, you may want to specify a charge account to pay your fees instead. This saves you the risk of overdrawing on your bank account.

On the other hand, if your credit card is already heavily used, yet your checking account funds remain fairly stable, you may prefer to have eBay withdraw its fees from your checking account directly. If it turns out either account has insufficient funds at the time of your monthly fee collection, eBay uses the alternative account listed.

Depending on which account type you select, the remainder of the signup process may vary. At the end of the signup procedure, eBay informs you that the process is complete. After you finish signing up, you can immediately start listing auctions on eBay.

SIGN UP FOR AN EBAY SELLER ACCOUNT (CONTINUED)

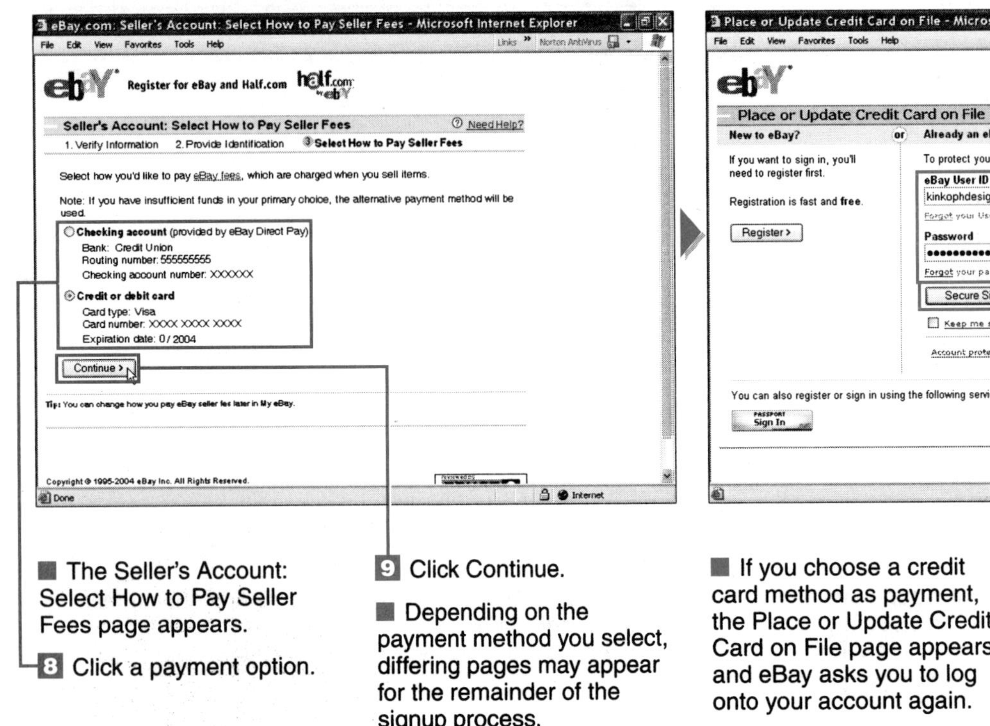

■ The Seller's Account: Select How to Pay Seller Fees page appears.

8 Click a payment option.

9 Click Continue.

■ Depending on the payment method you select, differing pages may appear for the remainder of the signup process.

■ If you choose a credit card method as payment, the Place or Update Credit Card on File page appears, and eBay asks you to log onto your account again.

10 Type your User ID and password.

11 Click Secure Sign In.

How do I change my information at a later time?

✔ You can update your account information using the Preferences link on your My eBay page. For example, you may want to change your billing to another credit card or bank account. It is very important that you always keep your contact information current with your eBay seller accounts. If a bidder or buyer cannot contact you with the information on file, eBay can remove your account entirely. See the section "Change or Update Your eBay Registration Info," later in this chapter, to learn more about updating your personal or financial information.

How do I know the information I provide to eBay is safe?

✔ eBay keeps all of your personal and financial information secure and private. eBay also works very hard to keep its servers safe from hackers and other criminals. You can learn more about eBay's Privacy Policy by clicking the Policies link at the bottom of any page. If you have any questions about eBay's security features, visit the Security Center pages, found within eBay's Help area. To learn more about using the online help pages and features, see Chapter 13.

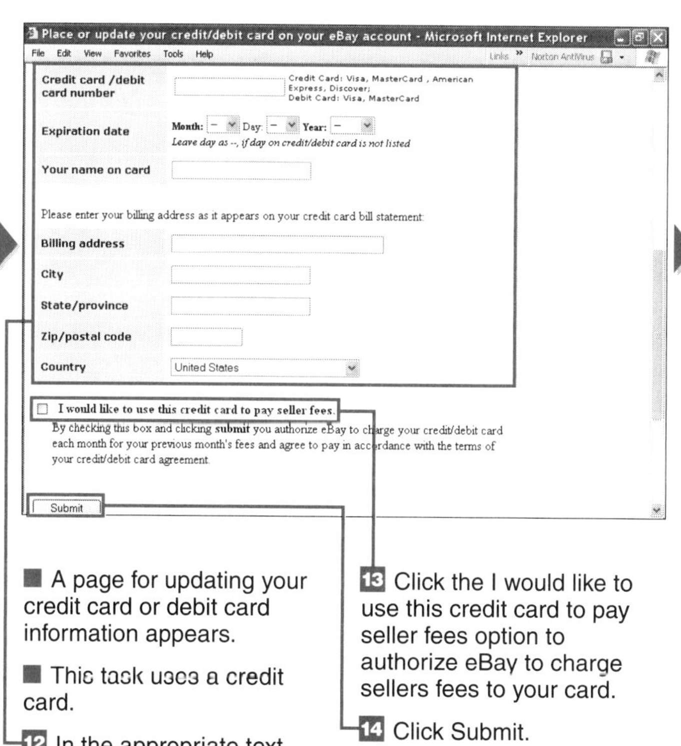

■ A page for updating your credit card or debit card information appears.

■ This task uses a credit card.

12 In the appropriate text fields, type the required credit card and billing information.

13 Click the I would like to use this credit card to pay seller fees option to authorize eBay to charge sellers fees to your card.

14 Click Submit.

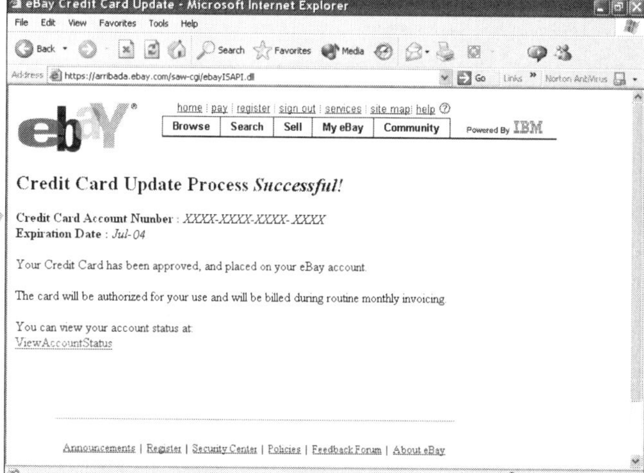

■ The Credit Card Update page appears and verifies the process.

■ You can now use your seller's account to sell items on eBay.

CREATE AN ABOUT ME PAGE

One of the most valuable tools you can use to assist your eBay business is the About Me page. Sadly, new sellers often overlook this feature. The About Me page gives you a chance to tell other eBayers about yourself, your business, your interests, and what draws you to sell items on eBay. Your About Me page can help you connect to the larger eBay community and build a sense of trust with other users.

The About Me page is simply a Web page stored on the eBay servers. When you create an auction, a special link to your page appears with your listing that allows bidders to learn more about you. When bidders are deciding whether to participate in your auction, allowing them to read more about who you are can help give them confidence about your reputation and authenticity.

You do not need any special skills to create an About Me page, just some advance thinking about what information you want the page to contain. Before you begin, take time to explore other users' About Me pages to get a feel for what sort of content they contain.

CREATE AN ABOUT ME PAGE

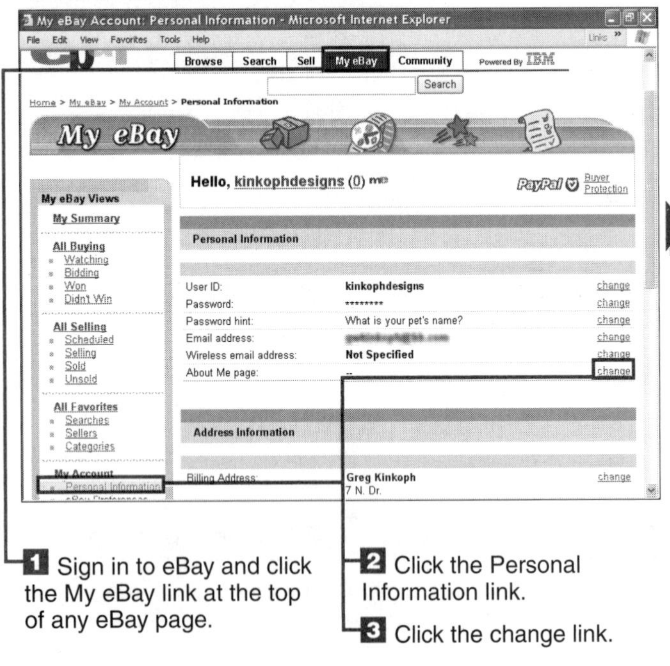

1 Sign in to eBay and click the My eBay link at the top of any eBay page.

2 Click the Personal Information link.

3 Click the change link.

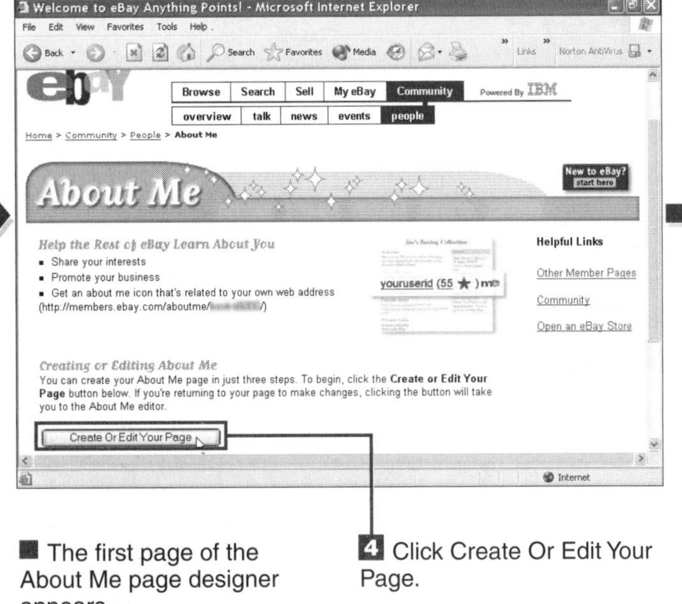

■ The first page of the About Me page designer appears.

4 Click Create Or Edit Your Page.

How do I view other users' About Me pages?

✔ If you see a ME icon next to a user's name, you can click the icon to quickly view the person's About Me page. You can also use this same technique to view your own page.

Should I prepare my text content in advance?

✔ If you foresee a need to change your About Me page from time to time, such as updating the information, consider saving your text as a separate document file and copying and pasting it into the About Me design form to update or start over with a new page and layout.

Which layout works best?

✔ The layout you choose depends on the type of information you want to convey. For example, you may choose the two-column layout to address different subjects of interest. The multicolumn format works well to present a variety of information across three columns. The centered layout is perfect for a page that uses a smaller amount of content. If you do not like the layout you choose, you can click the Back button to return to the layout page and choose another.

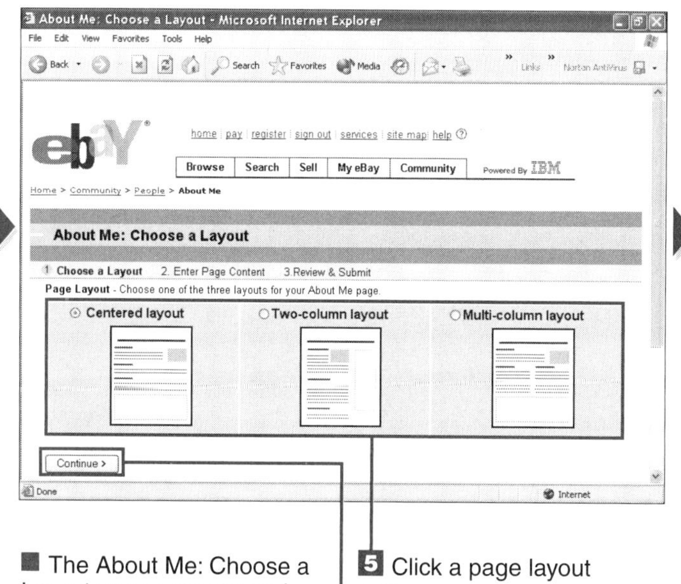

■ The About Me: Choose a Layout page appears and prompts you to choose a layout.

Note: If you already created an About Me page, eBay may ask if you want to create a new page.

5 Click a page layout option.

6 Click Continue.

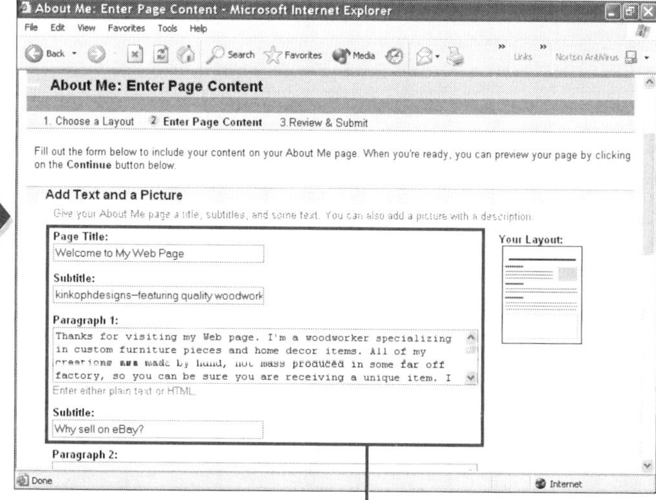

■ The About Me: Enter Page Content page appears.

7 In the appropriate text fields, type information you want to convey about your Web page and yourself.

CONTINUED

CREATE AN ABOUT ME PAGE (CONTINUED)

eBay makes it easy to create your own Web page. All it takes is three steps: choosing a layout, typing your text, and then reviewing and submitting the page to eBay. When creating your page content, spend some time thinking about the amount of detail you want to provide. For example, larger eBay businesses may include a mission statement or selling points that make their items unique. More personal pages may include information about hobbies, background, and information about the types of items you sell.

Along with promotional and personal information, About Me pages allow you to post feedback information others have written about you, current auctions you are running, and links to other Web pages or Web sites. Although you can add a link to your own Web site, you cannot use the About Me page to promote business off of eBay or to sell items prohibited by eBay's policies.

The About Me page also features a place to add pictures. To use the picture option, you must have your picture stored on a Web server and know the URL to retrieve the image file.

After you create and preview your page, eBay displays a URL, or address, that you can copy to share the page with others.

CREATE AN ABOUT ME PAGE (CONTINUED)

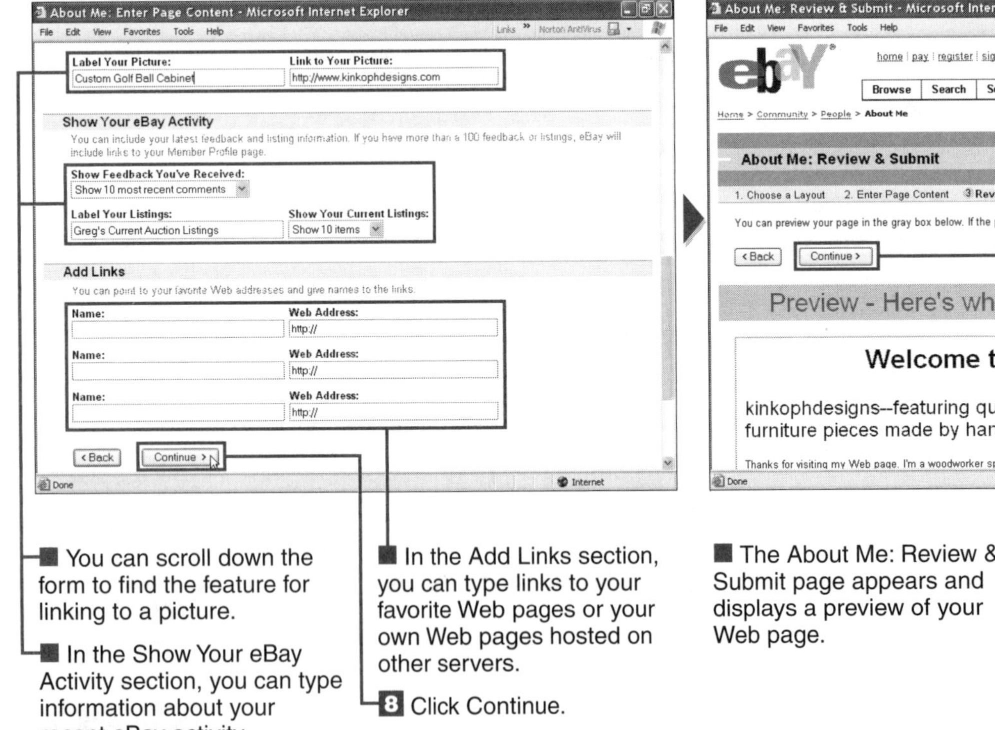

■ You can scroll down the form to find the feature for linking to a picture.

■ In the Show Your eBay Activity section, you can type information about your recent eBay activity.

■ In the Add Links section, you can type links to your favorite Web pages or your own Web pages hosted on other servers.

8 Click Continue.

■ The About Me: Review & Submit page appears and displays a preview of your Web page.

9 Click Continue.

How do I edit my About Me page?

✔ Follow the steps at the beginning of this section to open the first About Me page. An Edit Your HTML button appears. You can click the button and make changes to your content by editing the current HTML used to create the page. Editing HTML is a bit trickier than entering straightforward text into the About Me page designer form. You must edit your text without affecting any HTML tags surrounding the text. If the task proves too daunting, you can choose to create a new About Me page instead. For more information about using HTML tags, see Appendix C at the back of this book.

Can I view my About Me page from outside the eBay Web site?

✔ As long as you know your page's URL, which eBay assigns at the end of the design process, you can type the URL into any browser program and view your page. A URL is simply the Web address to a particular page on the Internet. You can share the URL with others to let them view your page as well.

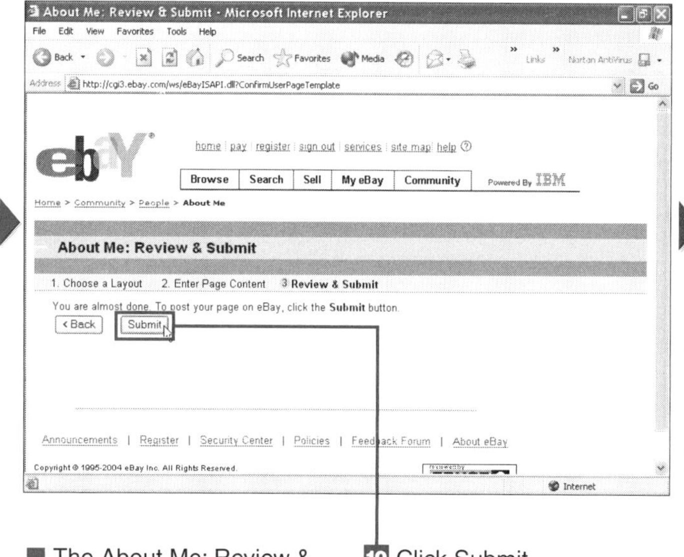

■ The About Me: Review & Submit page appears.

10 Click Submit.

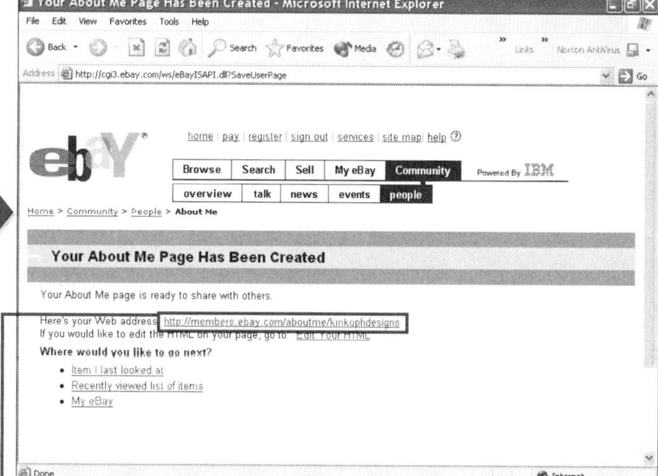

■ The Your About Me Page Has Been Created page appears.

■ To view the page again, click the Here's your Web address link.

■ You can view your new About Me page by clicking the URL.

CHANGE OR UPDATE YOUR EBAY REGISTRATION INFO

You can change or update your eBay information at any time. For example, you may need to change your password, your User ID, or your e-mail address. You can use the My Account section of your My eBay page to make changes to different types of personal information, including the contact information you gave eBay when first establishing your account.

If you change your contact information, such as phone number or e-mail address, you must let eBay know. Keeping your contact information up to date is a critical part of maintaining your eBay account. This is particularly true for sellers. Bidders and auction winners must know how to contact you with questions. If your contact information is obsolete or unverified, and detected as invalid by another user, it can be reported to eBay. Invalid contact information is a violation of eBay policy, and your account can be suspended.

Depending on which type of information you want to edit, the eBay forms may vary in appearance. In most cases, eBay prompts you to reenter your logon information before making any new changes to your account.

CHANGE OR UPDATE YOUR EBAY REGISTRATION INFO

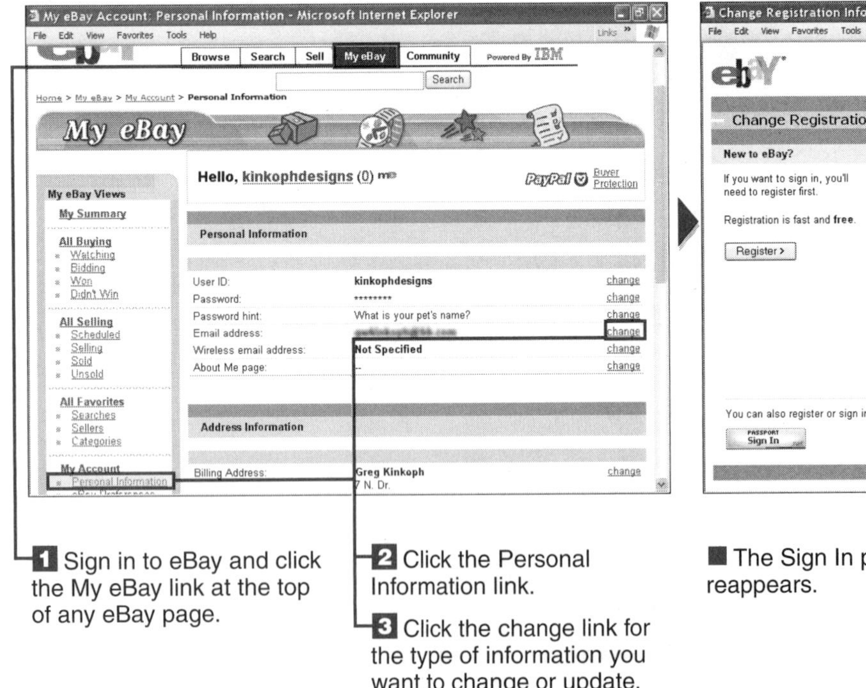

1 Sign in to eBay and click the My eBay link at the top of any eBay page.

2 Click the Personal Information link.

3 Click the change link for the type of information you want to change or update.

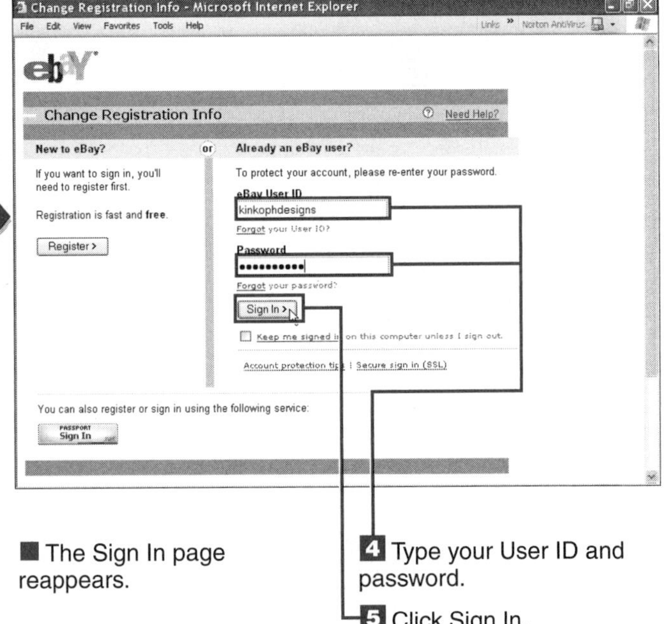

■ The Sign In page reappears.

4 Type your User ID and password.

5 Click Sign In.

What are seller preferences?

✔ If you sign up for a seller account, your eBay Preferences page includes links for changing seller preferences. You can click the eBay Preferences link to view all of your account preferences, including seller preferences. Seller preferences include seller-related setup options such as changing your Web hosting service for pictures, setting up new payment preferences, and changing your credit card information. To access the seller-related links, look for the Seller Preferences heading on the eBay Preferences page.

What do the other preferences do?

✔ In addition to Personal Information preference settings, the links under the My Account section also include a section for changing eBay preferences. For example, you can change which tab appears by default whenever you open your My eBay page. You can make changes to the way in which you sign in to your eBay account. You can learn more about customizing your My eBay page in Chapter 6.

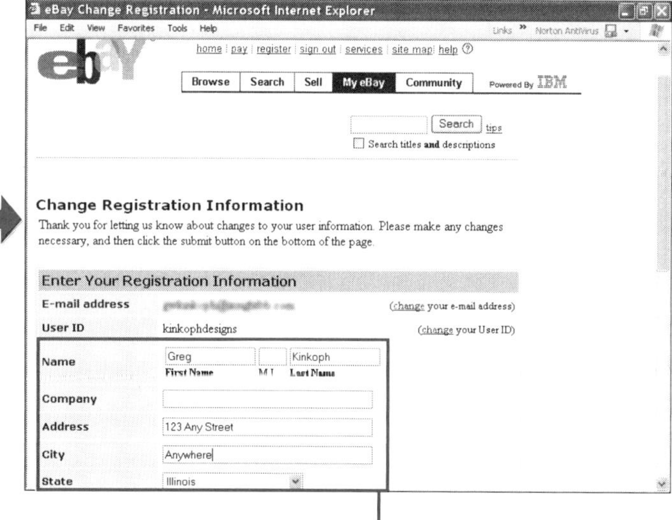

■ The appropriate page for making changes to your info appears.

6 In the appropriate text fields, type any changes you want to make.

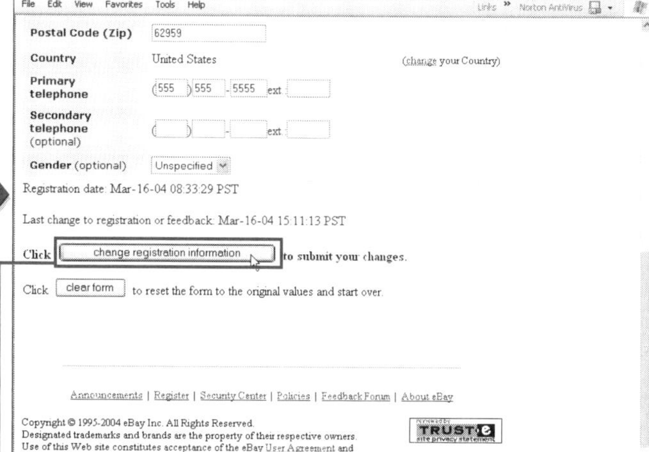

7 At the bottom of the page, click here to submit your changes.

■ In this example, the registration information is updated, and the submission button is labeled change registration information.

■ Your information is changed or updated.

ELEMENTS OF AN AUCTION LISTING

Whether you are an experienced eBay user or just getting started, it is important to understand the basic elements that go into creating an auction listing page. An auction listing is your primary selling tool. Regardless of whether you use the straightforward eBay seller's form to create an auction listing, write your own HTML for an auction page, or use an auction listing program such as Turbo Lister, all eBay auctions consist of several key elements.

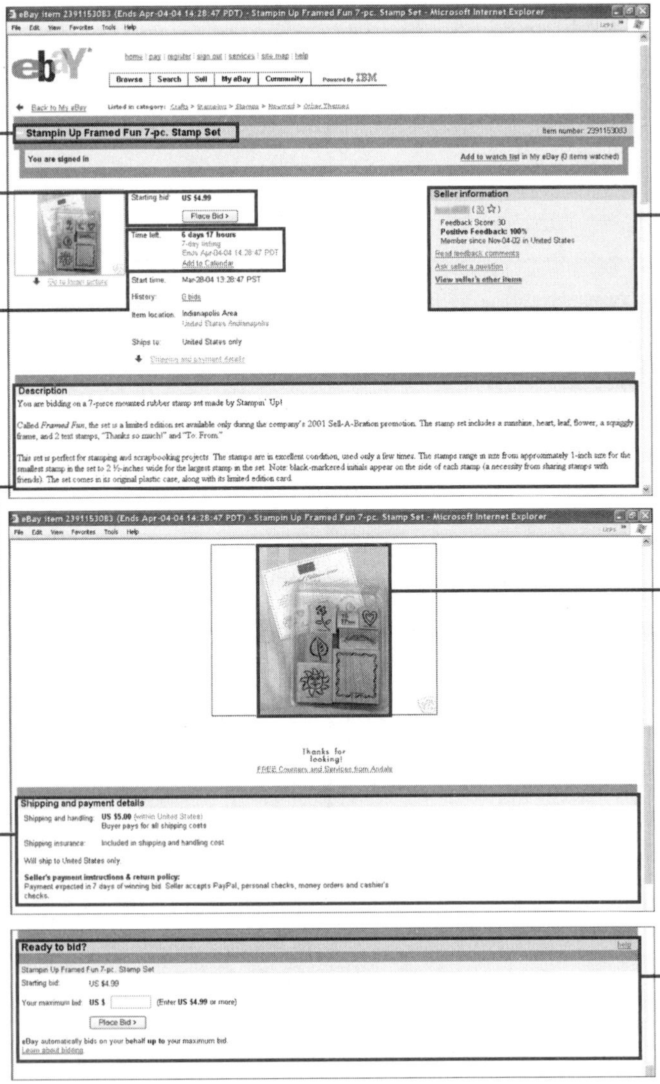

Auction Title

A brief heading describing the auction item's keywords.

Starting or Current Bid

Information about the starting bid amount or the current bid amount.

Time

The amount of time left for the auction.

Description

Text describing the auction item in detail.

Terms of Sale

Information about shipping and handling costs and available payment methods.

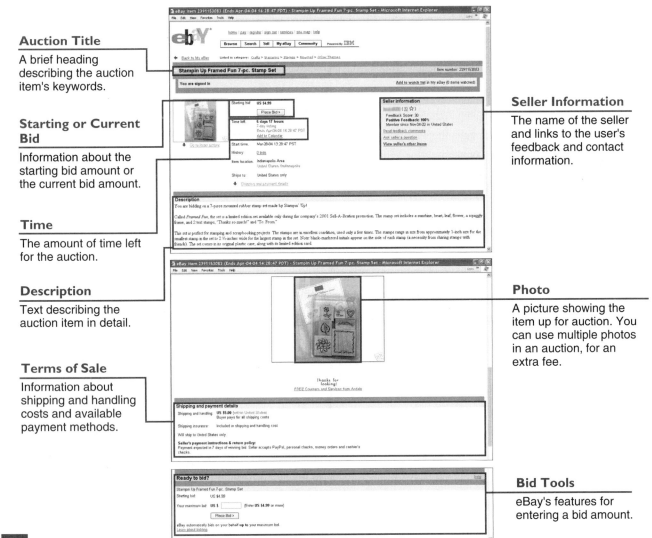

Seller Information

The name of the seller and links to the user's feedback and contact information.

Photo

A picture showing the item up for auction. You can use multiple photos in an auction, for an extra fee.

Bid Tools

eBay's features for entering a bid amount.

Auction Title

At the top of every auction listing is the title. When other eBayers conduct a search for the item, eBay's search tool looks through your title information for matching keywords. The title needs to include keywords that others might use in a search. To learn more about making the best use of title space, see the section "Create Better Auction Titles and Descriptions," later in this chapter.

Description

The description area is the place to write the text describing the item, its condition, and any extra information you want to convey to potential buyers. A good description goes a long way in selling your item, and unlike regular print ads in magazines or newspapers, eBay does not charge by word. The more information the better in an eBay auction ad. You can use your description area to generate excitement about the item, suggesting possible uses, describing its history, and disclosing any flaws. See the section "Create Better Auction Titles and Descriptions" to learn tips and tricks for writing auction ads.

Photo

Every eBay auction ad can include one photo of an item without added cost. The single photo is stored on eBay's Web server. You can include additional snapshots showing different angles or magnifications of the item for an extra fee.

If multiple photos are important to your auction ads, you may also consider using a Web storage service to store your photos for auction listings. Some photo hosting services are free; others offer storage for a small fee. To learn more about ways to use photos in your auction ads, see the section "Understanding Photo Options," later in this chapter.

Terms of Sale

Beneath the description area on an auction ad is the seller's terms of sale. This area lists important information regarding shipping and handling costs, as well as descriptions of what payment methods the seller accepts, such as PayPal or personal check. For an eBay business, establishing terms of sale is an important part of doing business online.

As you study other auction listings, you may notice some users add details about return policies, shipping policies, payment policies, and other statements to help clarify the terms of the auction.

Bid Status, Time, and Seller Information

As soon as you post your auction ad, eBay automatically adds several pieces of information directly below the auction title. Some of this information is gleaned from your ad's seller form, such as the starting bid price and the seller's physical location. As your auction progresses, eBay keeps track of the number of bids, the highest bidder, and the current bid price in this area of the listing page.

To the right of the bid status information, eBay automatically displays seller information, including links to the seller's feedback report, other items the seller is auctioning, and a link for asking the seller a question.

Bid Tools

eBay automatically adds a text box for entering a bid and a button to submit the bid to the bottom of the page when you post an auction. You cannot change or add to the information in this area.

TYPES OF EBAY AUCTIONS

The most familiar auction format on eBay is a traditional auction in which potential bidders view a listing ad and place bids. However, eBay offers a variety of auction formats you can pursue, based on the type of item or items you want to sell. Before you sit down and fill out the seller's form or use an auction listing program to create an ad, first determine what type of auction you want to present. Consider all the auction formats available, and choose an auction type that best meets your sales goals.

Traditional Auction

The traditional auction format, also called a regular or normal online auction, makes up the vast majority of auction types on eBay. Traditional auctions can run for a variety of set time lengths, ranging from one day to 10 days. At any point during the auction, potential buyers can view the auction, place bids, and ask questions. At the end of the auction, the highest bidder wins. Traditional auctions are the heart and soul of eBay, and offer both bidders and sellers the most excitement as they watch to see how high the bids go.

A traditional auction starts with an opening bid price, also called the starting bid price. Determining an opening bid can take some experimentation. If you set the price too high, you might scare off bidders or overstate the market value for the item. If you set the price too low, you might attract inexperienced bidders. Be sure to research similar items on sale to help you determine the fair market value. A good rule of thumb is to set the starting price at the lowest amount for which you are willing to sell the item.

When you use a traditional auction listing, eBay collects a listing fee and a final value fee for the auction.

Reserve Auction

You can use a reserve auction if you want to protect an item from selling for less than it is worth. A reserve amount is really just a secret minimum bid amount you want the item to achieve. The reserve amount is not displayed in the listing ad. Instead, a line of notation text appears in the auction ad, telling potential bidders a reserve is set for the item. As soon as a reserve is met, eBay displays a notation saying so on the listing ad.

For example, if you set a reserve of $50, you are not obligated to sell to the highest bidder unless the reserve price is met. If the high bid is $50 or more, your reserve is met and the highest bidder wins. If the highest bid turns out to be less than the reserve, you do not have to complete the sale and the winning bidder is not obligated to purchase the item.

Some bidders do not like bidding on reserve auctions because they do not know if the reserve price is reasonable or not. Many sellers prefer to set the minimum bid amount as their reserve amount instead of setting up a reserve auction. This is mainly because a reserve auction incurs an additional reserve price listing fee based on the reserve price, as well as a basic listing fee and final value fee.

Buy It Now Auction

A Buy It Now auction allows you to sell an item immediately for a specific price, called a Buy It Now price. This allows users the option of purchasing your item without bidding. When you create a Buy It Now auction, eBay adds a Buy It Now button to the auction ad. If bidders come along who prefer to bid on the item instead, they can do so and the Buy It Now option disappears from the auction ad. The Buy It Now option is only available until someone chooses to buy it for the set price, or places a lower bid amount. As soon as a bid is placed, the set price is no longer available. Keep in mind that a Buy It Now auction incurs an additional auction listing fee.

Fixed-Price Auction

You can also choose to create a fixed-price auction. Like the Buy It Now feature, a fixed-price auction offers an item at a set price, but without any bidding allowed. A buyer can simply purchase the item at the fixed price.

When you create a fixed-price auction, eBay adds a Buy It Now button to the listing ad. The Buy It Now button remains in the ad for as long as the listing is active. You can use a fixed-price auction to provide your buyers a quick and easy way to make a purchase, attract new buyers to a bargain price, or help sell a quantity of items at a set price.

When you designate a fixed-price auction, an additional listing fee is charged. You can only use the fixed-price format if you have a minimum feedback rating of ten or more, or are ID verified.

Dutch Auction

If you have identical items to sell at the same time, you can use a Dutch auction, also called a multiple-item listing. A Dutch auction allows more than one bidder to win an item. When bidders bid on your auction, they offer a bid price as well as a quantity. For example, if you sell five staplers in a Dutch auction, a bidder can choose to bid on more than one stapler.

What makes Dutch auctions a bit confusing is the final price. All the winning bidders pay the same price, which is the lowest successful bid. If eight people place bids on your five items, only the top bids win, yet the lowest bid amount of the top bids is the price everyone pays.

You can only use the Dutch auction format if you have a feedback rating of 30 or more and have been registered for at least 14 days.

Private Auction

You can use the private auction format if you want all of the User IDs of your bidders to remain unknown. The only time you know a bidder's ID is if he or she wins the auction. There really is not much use for a private auction unless you simply do not want bidders to know the names of other bidders.

WORK WITH EBAY CATEGORIES

An essential step in creating any auction listing in eBay is knowing in what category to list the item. Categories are eBay's way of organizing the millions of ads users post on the Web site. eBay's home page lists all the major categories, and as you browse each main category, you encounter numerous lower-level categories. eBay calls the main categories *top-level categories* and the lower-level categories *subcategories*. There are literally thousands of subcategories on eBay, and the number changes frequently as eBay adds new categories to suit the ever-changing marketplace.

Top-Level Categories

You can quickly view the top-level categories from eBay's home page. eBay offers over 30 top-level categories. Some categories are a bit broader than others. For example, the Stamps category covers items related to the hobby of stamp collecting, while the Home & Garden category covers everything from home décor items, such as pillows and prints, to furniture and garden tools. When determining which category your item fits into, start by establishing a top-level category.

For example, perhaps you have an old toy you want to sell. Does the item fit better in the Antiques category or in the Toys & Hobbies category? Where is the first place an interested buyer might look for the item? Some research into similar items available on eBay can help you decide which main category best represents the type of item you want to sell.

Subcategories

eBay's subcategories help to further organize the millions of auction items appearing daily. Rather than overwhelm a user with thousands of auctions for the general Antiques category, the category's subcategories organize auctions into specialty areas such as Antiquities, Architectural & Garden, Books & Manuscripts, Decorative Arts, Furniture, and more.

You can drill down into subcategories located within each top-level category to find which area to list your item. For example, if you want to sell a used music CD, start with the Music top-level category and work your way down until you find just the right music genre in which to list your auction. Not only must you determine a music medium, such as cassette or CD, you must also select a genre, such as Country Western or Jazz.

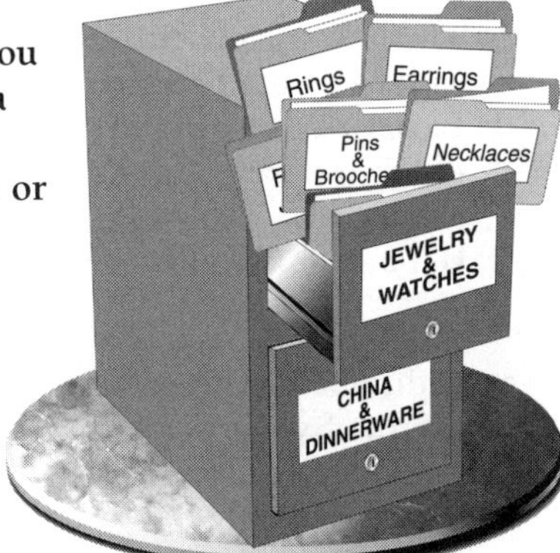

Category Placement

Category placement is a crucial part of selling on eBay and making sure your business targets the buyers you want to reach. Choosing the wrong category can result in missed sales opportunities. If your target audience cannot find your item, you may have trouble finding competitive bids. If you place your item in the wrong category, eBay may pull the auction or move it to the appropriate category. If you continue to list auctions improperly, eBay can cancel your account. It is up to you, as the seller, to list your item in the proper category. To make sure you do, take time to do your research.

A good place to start is to examine where other users list items similar to yours. For example, if you want to sell a set of dishes, conduct an eBay search for dishes and take note of the categories listed at the top of the ads. Do your dishes fit in Dinner & Serving Pieces, a subcategory in Home & Garden, or do they fit better in the Pottery & Glass category in a subcategory such as China & Dinnerware? Check out the auctions you find in these categories and compare them to your item.

Research may show your item may fit in more than one category. You may opt to pay for a second category listing, or you may just need to narrow your options to the best choice. This may take some experimentation. You can try running the auction in one category; then, if you do not receive any results, you can try the other category.

As you research potential categories, also think about what category keywords others might use to locate your item. Is the buyer likely to type china or dinnerware when looking for a set of dishes? Try conducting category keyword searches yourself to see what types of auctions appear in the results list. To learn more about searching for items on eBay, see Chapter 2.

Seller Form Categories

When you are ready to create your auction ad, one of the first areas you encounter in the eBay seller's form is the Select Category page. This page requires you to specify your item's categories. You can use three methods to assign a category. You can assign a recently used category, browse through the categories, or ask eBay to recommend a category.

As with browsing through categories on the home page, the seller's form allows you to start with a top-level category and limit your selection to a specific subcategory. When you create an auction listing, you can choose to list your ad in one category as part of the overall listing fee. If you feel your item would do better listed in two categories, you can add a second category for an additional fee.

If you experience any trouble in knowing where to categorize your listing, you can tell eBay to assist you with suggested categories. You can type the keywords best describing your item, and then eBay opens a separate window offering category suggestions.

CREATE BETTER AUCTION TITLES AND DESCRIPTIONS

To help your auctions stand out from all the rest, take time to prepare and present your auctions using proven tips and techniques. Paying attention to details can make a big difference in how others perceive your auction listings and can help you develop your eBay business. Buying and selling on eBay is built on trust, and one way to begin building a good reputation is to take time to be accurate and polished in your ads.

Title Tips

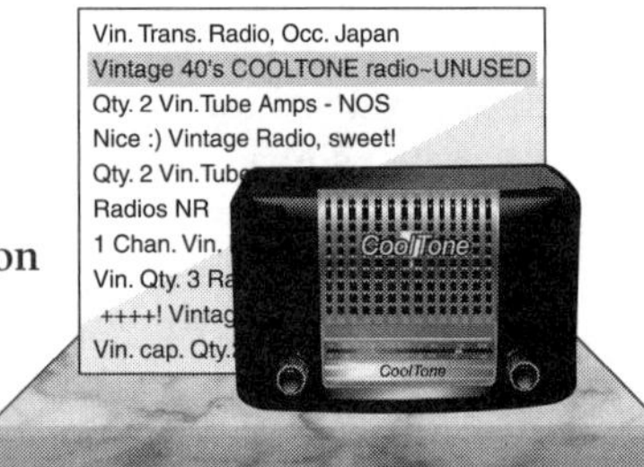

The first thing a potential bidder sees is your auction title. The title, or heading, appears on the search results page when a bidder searches eBay, as well as at the top of your auction listing page when a bidder opens your ad. Make sure your auction titles include the necessary keywords to help potential buyers find your items. You are limited to 55 characters in a title, with no quotes or asterisks, so keep your titles simple. The title is not the place to add cute phrases, or special characters or symbols, but rather, identify the item you have for sale. Avoid using abbreviations, if possible, because you cannot anticipate how others may search for your item. The auction title is not the place to market your item; leave that job to your listing's description area.

Your auction title must also be easy to read. Remember, potential bidders skim the list of similar auctions, so make sure your auction title adheres to basic typesetting rules. Some of these rules may seem to contradict popular marketing ideas, but typesetting standards are time-tested.

One rule to keep in mind is to avoid typing your title in all capital letters. Although this may seem like a good way to get your title noticed, using all caps impairs reading. If someone is interested in bidding on your Minolta digital camera, for example, putting the name in all caps is not going to make any difference in whether the person reads your ad or not. A user who is interested in a Minolta camera will look at your ad with or without the title in caps.

Some people are convinced that bold and color type attract attention to title text. eBay even assists in these misconceptions by offering these extra touches for a small fee. For example, for an extra fee, you can choose to make your auction title bold when it appears on the search results page. However, bold text can also slow down the reader, making him more likely to skip bold text. The extra cost is simply not worth it. Try quickly reading a search results page yourself to see the difference. Take note of what titles are jarring as you skim through the results, and which are easier to read.

Description Text Tips

The description area of your listing ad is your opportunity to sell the item. Present your information about the item in an easy-to-read fashion. Use good grammar and complete sentences, and break up your text into paragraphs. Do not rely on abbreviations and acronyms, particularly eBay acronyms, such as NIB (New In Box) or NIP (New In Package). Half of your potential bidders do not know what the acronyms mean.

Start by specifically identifying the type of item you are selling. The text at the top of the description area should identify the exact model number, make, or manufacturer. Presenting this information up front can help prevent any confusion on the part of potential bidders.

Next, clearly state the condition of the item. Is the item new, in mint condition, or gently used? Let the potential buyer know the history of the item, if possible. Describe any wear and tear, and be sure to back up your condition description with good photos. If the item has a flaw or defect of any kind, disclose the information in your description.

Thirdly, offer any benefits for owning or using the item, "selling points" for the item. Think of what uses might draw a potential bidder to the item. For example, if you are selling a state-of-the-art blender, mention the various ways to use the appliance, and point out any differences or improvements over other blenders.

After covering the basics, you can then use the remainder of the description area to give more details about the item, such as product information from the box, or to express your personal opinions about the product. Always try to be positive about the item, and if you cannot, do not express an opinion. Try to avoid making your ad text too long, but do give your potential buyers all the information they need in order to determine whether they want to bid or not.

Ads that thoroughly explain a product sell for much higher amounts and receive more bids than those with scant information. As a buyer, however, it is easier to find a bargain when you run across ads in which the seller does not take time to describe the item; these listings attract fewer bids and go for lower prices. Bottom line: As a seller, it pays to give buyers all the information they need, if not more.

Text Formatting Tips

The same typesetting rules you apply to your auction titles apply to your description text as well. For example, stick with browser default fonts such as Times New Roman, Times, Arial, and Helvetica, because such fonts are readable in nearly any browser window. Other fonts may cause problems for the reader based on what the browser can handle.

For best results, use at least 12-point type in your ads; larger type is more difficult to read. Only use italics for emphasis; using bold in the middle of a sentence is jarring to the reader. Keep your paragraph text aligned flush left; center and right alignments are not as easy to read. Use caution when indulging in color type; what you might consider cool and engaging may be unattractive to someone else. Users do not base their decision to bid on your item on fancy formatting or color additions to an ad. They base their decision on how well you convey information about the item.

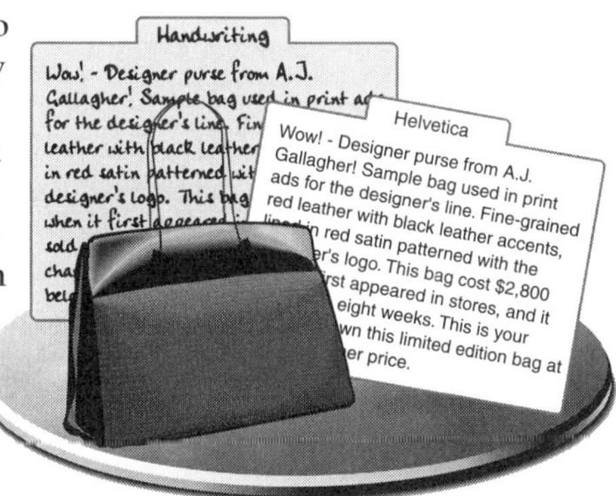

Check Your Spelling

Last, before you ever post your listing online, stop and check it for spelling and punctuation mistakes. Spelling errors say a lot about the seller's level of professionalism and attention to detail. If a seller cannot manage to spell the product name correctly, the buyer may question whether the product is even authentic.

UNDERSTANDING PHOTO OPTIONS

Photos are an important part of selling items on eBay, and essential to any eBay business. A good photo speaks volumes about the condition of an item. If you are serious about conducting an eBay business, it is worth your while to invest in a good digital camera capable of taking quality photos, including close-ups. You can then transfer your item images to your computer, usually with a USB cable. By storing the images on your computer, you can quickly add them to any auction listing you create on eBay.

If a digital camera is not in your budget right now, you can always use a regular camera, develop the images at a photo shop, and either have them placed on a CD or scan the images yourself using a scanner. After taking a picture, you can use an image-editing program to make any changes to the image, such as cropping or adjusting the lighting. You can learn more about taking and editing pictures for your listings in Chapter 20.

Whether you take a photo with a digital camera or take a photo with a regular camera and scan it, you must upload the image to appear with your auction listing. eBay allows you to insert one photo into every listing and stores the photo on its Web server. This service is part of your regular listing fee. However, some items require more than one photo. For example, some collectible items may need a photo showing each side of the object. Or if an item has a flaw, additional photos can show the defect and illustrate the full nature of the flaw in relation to the rest of the object. Extra photos can result in extra listing fees.

eBay Picture Services

eBay offers its own picture hosting service, called eBay Picture Services. For additional fees, you can add multiple pictures to a listing. You can use the seller's form to indicate how many extra pictures to add to the listing. Each extra picture adds an extra cost. If you plan on selling hundreds of items a month with multiple pictures, the service could easily start costing you more than you realize. On the plus side, storing both your ad listing and photos on the same Web site is convenient, and you know the site is operable at all times. You can simply specify which image files to include by indicating the location on your computer where the images are stored, and then upload them onto eBay's Web servers.

eBay Picture Services also offers extra enhancements for your photos, such as displaying your images as a slide show on the auction listing ad, or displaying photos as supersized images. These enhancements can also increase the cost of your listing.

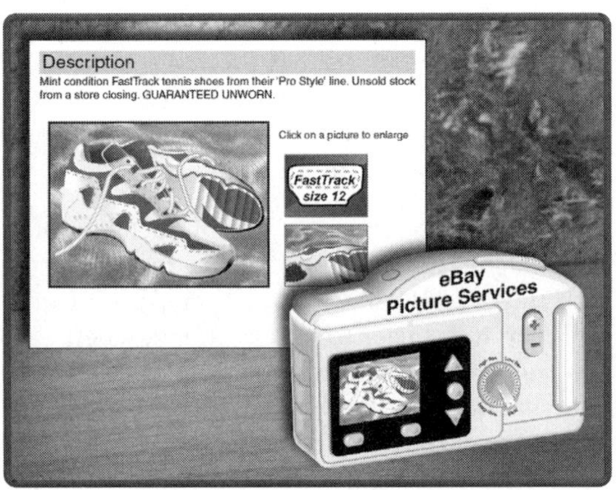

Image Hosting Sites

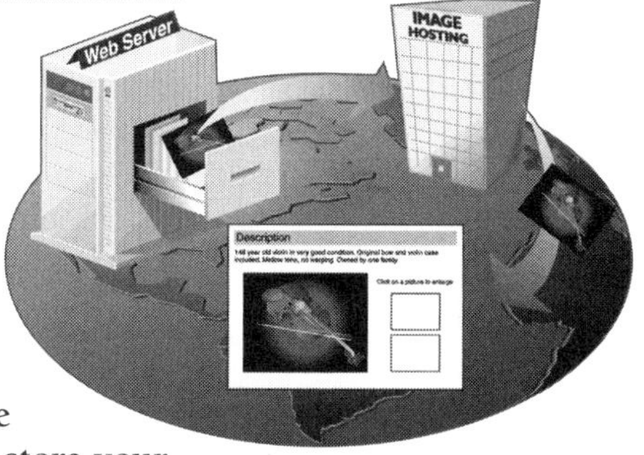

Another option you can pursue for handling your listing photos is an image hosting service. Some sites offer to store your images online for free, while others charge a minimal fee. There are numerous dedicated Web hosting sites on the Internet. Conduct a simple Web search on the keywords "image hosting" to find plenty of choices. For example, the site www.MyAuctionPhotos.com can host up to 500 images on a private FTP site for a flat monthly rate of $26.95 or you can choose to pay by the image. The site keeps your photos on hand for up to 60 days. Similar sites, like ImageMagician.com (www.imagemagician.com), Boomspeed.com (www.boomspeed.com), and Hosting4Less (www.hosting4less.com), offer a variety of features and customer support.

Depending on the site, you may need to use a special software program for transferring the image files from your computer to the hosting site. File transfer programs, or FTP software, help your computer send files to another computer. Most sites give you detailed instructions on how to upload image files.

With an image hosting site, you can upload your pictures to the site and link to them when you fill out the eBay seller's form. Image hosting sites are a good investment if you find yourself using the same images over and over again.

With a little research, you may also find some free hosting sites for image storage. Sites like Village Photos (www.villagephotos.com), MyImages.com (www.myimages.com), and Walagata (www.walagata.com) are among those that you can check out.

Auction Management Sites

Many auction management services also offer image hosting. Auction management services are Web sites dedicated to helping online auctioneers build, list, and manage auction ads. Management services like Andale (www.andale.com), Auction Hawk (www.auctionhawk.com), and HammerTap (www.hammertap.com) operate online, which means you access their features and services from their Web sites.

When you fill out the eBay seller's form, you can enter the link to your images stored on the auction management site's server.

Your Own ISP Service

You can also tap into hosting services from your own Internet Service Provider (ISP). Most ISPs allow you a set amount of Web storage. You can use it to set up a Web site to store your eBay auction pictures. For example, your local ISP might allow 5 to 10MB of free space for each e-mail account you or your family uses. Be sure to contact your provider to learn more about this amenity.

If you use a commercial service such as America Online, you can use 2MB of Web server space for each username on the account, which is quite adequate for auction pictures.

An added bonus to using your own ISP space is most providers include the necessary software to help users upload files. After uploading the images, you can link to them from the eBay seller's form.

DETERMINE PAYMENT METHODS

Taking payment for your auctions is as important as creating auction listings. Naturally, as a seller, receiving payment is a crucial part of your eBay auctions, but you may be surprised to know payment methods are often even more important to buyers. Buyers look for auctions that offer their favorite method of payment. Although every customer is different, many choose to participate in only one type of payment. As a seller, if you do not offer the method of choice, you lose a potential customer.

Some eBay sellers balk at offering all possible payment methods. For example, some sellers may refuse to take personal checks because they take a few extra days to clear, or refuse to take credit card payments because the payment service charges fees for every transaction. Some users think certain payment types are riskier than others. The fact is, all payment methods include the risk of fraud, just as there are fraudulent sellers and fraudulent buyers. The same is true off of eBay as well. If you are serious about good customer service and increasing your online sales, it is essential that you try to make your auction items as easy for buyers to purchase as possible.

It is entirely your choice regarding whether you want to take one or two types of payments, and perhaps your situation dictates just one method. Just remember, however, limiting the payment methods you accept limits your bidders. If you are not interested in reaching the widest possible audience for your ads, then being selective about payment methods may work for you.

Keep in mind that buyers look for payment methods based on convenience and safety. Because eBay transactions are based on trust, buyers depend on payment methods they can count on as safe, secure, and easy to handle.

As you prepare for your first auction listing, you must take time to figure out what payment methods you want to accept from your buyers. The most common methods employed in eBay ads today include personal check, money order, cashier's check, or credit card. Take time to examine the pros and cons of each.

Checks

American customers like to pay by personal checks, so a popular way to pay for purchases on eBay is by check. As a seller, it is good practice to allow seven to 10 days for a check to clear the bank, so be sure to specify this in your auction's terms of sale. Most buyers paying by personal check are well aware of this processing requirement and willingly wait patiently.

Although the vast majority of personal check payments clear without any problem, you may eventually encounter one that does bounce. Rather than avoid the possibility entirely by refusing to take checks, try the method for a while and see if your buyers are trustworthy.

With today's technology, you are not limited to receiving checks by mail for payments. You can also accept electronic check payments. Services such as Billpoint and PayPal allow electronic funds transfer.

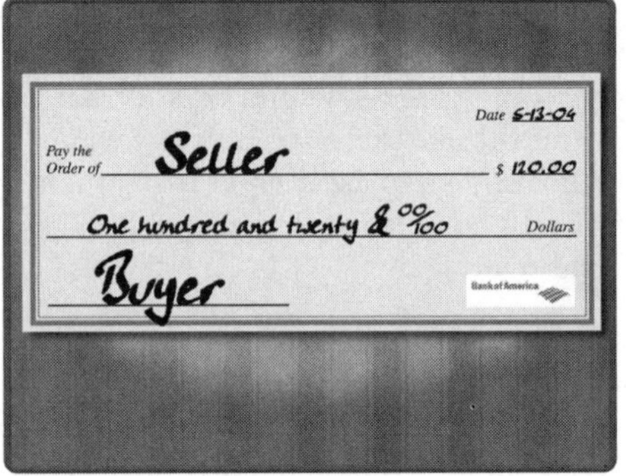

Money Orders and Cashier's Checks

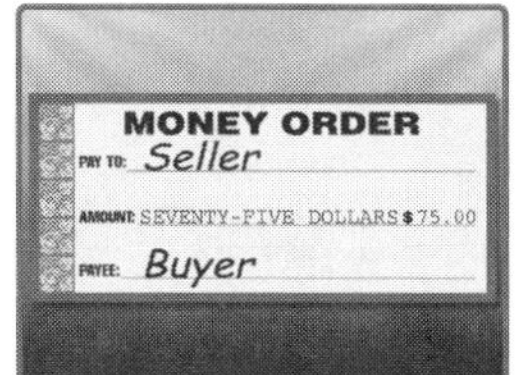

Money orders and cashier's checks are another common payment method for eBay auctions. A money order is simply a paper order for the payment of a specified amount of money. A money order can be purchased at a variety of places such as grocery stores, banks, and the post office. Most places charge a small service fee. For overseas customers, money orders are often the only way to pay for items purchased abroad and are easy to purchase at post offices around the world.

Cashier's checks are secured from a banking service. The amount is deducted from the user's account immediately, so you do not need to wait for the check to clear when it arrives to you by mail. Cashier's checks carry larger service fees than money orders, often $3 to $5.

The disadvantage of money orders and cashier's checks to the buyer is that he or she must physically visit a place, such as a bank or store, that issues money orders or cashier's checks, and then mail the order to you. The disadvantage to you as the seller is that you, too, must also physically deposit or cash the order or check. You can deposit such payments to your bank account just as you do regular checks.

Credit Cards

Credit card payments are the preferred payment method on eBay. Payment services, like PayPal and BidPay, can help you accept credit card payments from your buyers. You might also qualify for a merchant credit card account through your bank or a wholesale store like Costco. Payment services and merchant credit card accounts act like middlemen between the buyer and seller. They accept payment from the buyer's credit card issuer and pass it along to the seller's account. With any payment service or merchant credit card account, you can expect to pay fees on the transactions processed.

There are many advantages to accepting credit card payments. There is no guesswork in determining if someone receives payment or not, because the transaction is instantaneous. In addition, purchases are covered by the issuing credit card's protection policies. Disadvantages hinge around the fees for taking credit card payments.

eBay's own payment service, PayPal, is the number one payment method on eBay. The service costs nothing for buyers, but charges fees for every transaction to the seller. To accept credit card payments through PayPal, you must sign up for a Premier/Business account. If you sell $1,000 or more each month, you can qualify for merchant rate fees. Check the PayPal Web site for the current fee schedule. See Chapter 10 to learn more about PayPal.

Other Payment Options

From time to time, buyers may ask you to make exceptions to your payment methods and take cash on delivery (COD) or cash in general. It is not a good idea to take cash payments, because it leaves no proof of payment for the seller or buyer, and is easily lost in transit. COD is practiced among mail-order merchants, but is not necessarily a good practice for eBay sellers. COD orders are heftier in shipping prices, and risky if the buyer does not pay.

If you plan to sell high-priced items, $1,000 or more, consider an escrow account. For a fee, eBay's Escrow.com service (www.escrow.com) collects the money from the buyer, holds the money until the buyer and seller reach an agreement, and then releases the money to the seller based on the instructions agreed upon by both parties.

DETERMINE SHIPPING AND HANDLING OPTIONS

Although shipping seems like one of the last tasks to tackle for any auction, your auction's terms of sale (TOS) need to alert the buyer to your shipping and handling fees. Your TOS lets potential bidders know up front what charges to expect to deliver the item to their door. Shipping and handling costs can often factor in with a buyer's decision to bid or not. Charge too much, and you lose a customer.

Some sellers prefer to wait until they know the winning zip code of the buyer before determining shipping costs. These days, however, sellers can place automatic shipping calculators into their ads to allow buyers to determine costs based on location. Other sellers wait until a bidder contacts them for shipping information. To give your buyers good customer service, it can be helpful to determine shipping and handling costs before you post your auction, if possible. Leaving the costs open until after a winning bid can bring confusion and dismay to both the buyer and the seller.

Handling Charges

The handling portion of the term "shipping and handling" refers to the seller's time and materials used to ship an item. These costs are completely separate from the actual shipping charge the carrier charges to send the item to the buyer.

The subject of shipping and handling charges is a common source of contention between buyers and sellers online. Buyers often disregard the cost of materials to pack an item properly. These materials, ranging from bubble wrap and boxes to packing tape, cost the seller money. More often than not, buyers simply look at the printed shipping cost and wonder why it is lower than the ad's quoted shipping and handling charges. They fail to take into account the added cost of shipping materials. Handling includes everything from materials to the time and cost to drive to a shipping carrier, stand in line, and purchase additional shipping features, such as insurance and delivery confirmation.

On the other hand, some sellers try to sneak eBay listing fees and PayPal fees into the handling category to help cover auction expenses. This is not what handling charges refer to. If you want to cover auction expenses, add those costs to the starting bid amount, not to the shipping and handling charges.

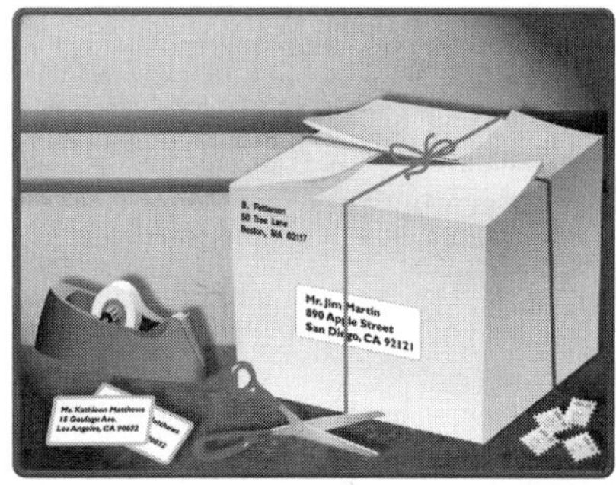

Shipping Charges

Shipping charges typically refer to the actual costs the shipping carrier charges you to deliver the item to the buyer. You can easily get an idea of what the carrier will charge by knowing the weight of the item you want to ship, along with the weight of the packing materials. All of the big shipping carriers offer charts on their Web sites to help customers determine shipping costs. For example, if your item weighs one and a half pounds when packaged, and you plan to ship it via the United States Postal Service (USPS), you can log onto the USPS Web site and estimate the cost to ship the item anywhere in the United States or overseas.

eBay encourages sellers to be reasonable about the shipping and handling fees they charge. To avoid misconceptions and misunderstandings with your buyers, take time to investigate the major shipping carriers in your area, compare rates and convenience, and determine a method that works best for you. Be fair about your charges.

In case a dispute arises, do your best to work out an agreement with the buyer. Failing to do so may result in a negative feedback rating on your report and affect your online reputation.

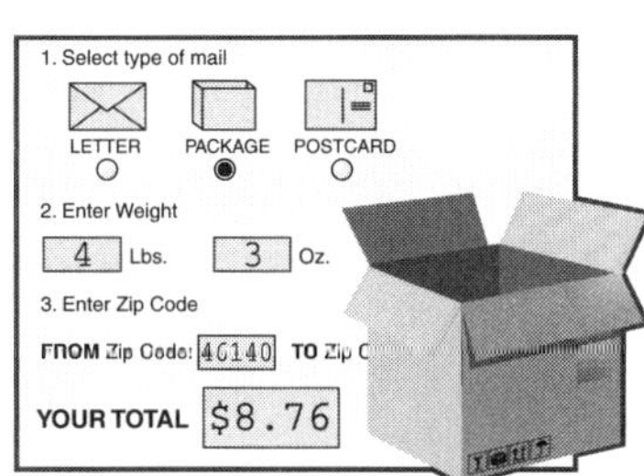

The Post Office

Your local post office is the most popular shipping carrier for eBay purchases. Most post offices are convenient to get to, and you do not need to set up a special account to start shipping. Many sellers use Priority Mail, not only because items only take a couple of days to arrive, but the USPS gives out free shipping supplies to people who use this service. Priority Mail is a good choice for packages weighing one or two pounds. Tracking numbers and delivery confirmation cost extra, and you can track the shipment using the USPS Web site. To keep yourself safe from shipping problems, consider adding delivery confirmation to all your shipments. You can add the cost to your auction ad's shipping and handling charges.

The USPS also offers a great way to ship books, videos, DVDs, and CDs using Media Mail. Shipping time is longer than the Priority Mail service, but the cost is less. For heavier packages, you must use Parcel Post rates, which can be more expensive than UPS or FedEx ground rates. To check out current rates, visit www.usps.com.

Other Delivery Services

Aside from regular mail, you can choose from several delivery services to ship your eBay auction items. Federal Express (FedEx) and United Parcel Service (UPS) are two of the most popular delivery services. Many regard FedEx as more expensive, but the company's recent purchase of Roadway Package Service (RPS) added a cost-effective ground shipment service to the company. You can set up a shipping account with FedEx using its Web site at www.fedex.com. You can use its handy Ship Manager software to help you print out shipping labels.

UPS has now established shipping locations all over the world, and more than likely, there is a local shipping store in your neighborhood. You can drop off packages at these sites without needing to open a shipping account. Or, for an extra charge, the UPS driver can stop by your doorstep to pick up packages. You can also establish your own account using the UPS Web site, www.ups.com, and print your own labels.

Both FedEx and UPS provide free tracking services and delivery confirmation.

UNDERSTANDING AUCTION VIOLATIONS

As you begin selling items on eBay, it is important to understand what is and what is not allowed in your auction listings. Before you start creating your auction listing, especially for the first time or for an item you are new at selling, familiarize yourself with eBay policies and guidelines. A little knowledge up front can help you stay out of trouble with both eBay and other eBay users.

For starters, as a seller, it is your responsibility to make sure the items you sell are legal on eBay. You can do this by frequently checking the prohibited items list. See Chapter 1 to learn more about viewing eBay policies.

In addition to keeping your auctions safe by selling only legal items, it is also important not to violate eBay policies regarding the words you use and the pictures you show in your auction listings. For example, you are not allowed to copy another user's text or photos. If a fellow eBayer catches you copying an ad, the violation is reported and eBay can pull your ad. If you generate enough violations, eBay can suspend your account.

Keyword Spamming

Keyword spamming is an auction violation. Keyword spamming is any intentional use of auction title keywords to misdirect bidders to your listing. For example, comparing your item to brand X manipulates the eBay search system to include your listing along with all the legitimate listings for brand X items. Users end up wasting time looking at your ad thinking it is brand X when it is not.

Other common keyword spamming violations include listing superfluous brand names in your title or description text, lists of words added to your title or description text simply to make the eBay search engine attract bidders, or hidden HTML text that remains readable by the search engine, but does not appear on the auction page. You should always be careful of trademark and copyright infringement as well.

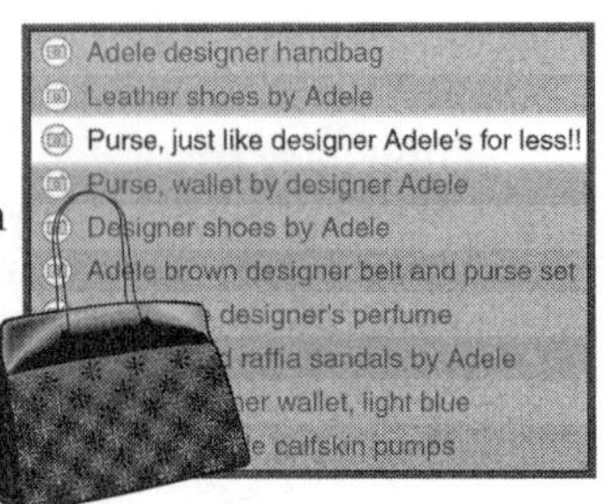

Links

There are restrictions to using links to other pages on your listing page. You are allowed to link to a page describing your product in more detail, such as a manufacturer's Web site, but you cannot link to another page selling your item. You can add links to photos and your e-mail address, as well as to your eBay store and About Me page. You cannot link to other auction services outside of eBay, or to Web pages selling items not allowed on eBay. For a full list of link information, visit eBay's Links Policy page in the Help area.

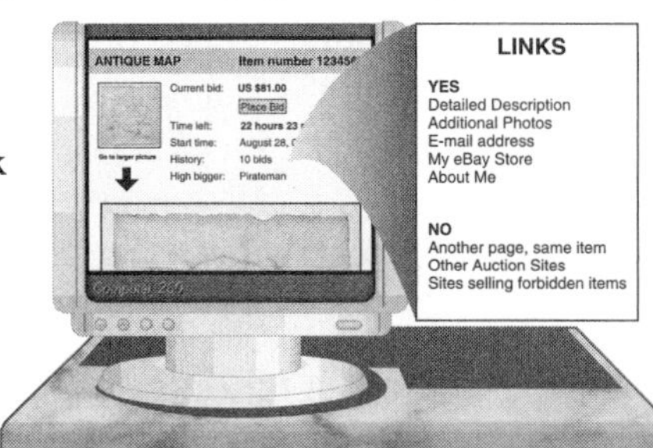

Bidding Offenses

Shill bidding is the practice of bidding up your own auction items to increase the price, usually by using other user names or inviting other users to do so. This form of auction manipulation is not only an eBay violation, but a federal crime.

In a similar vein, bid shielding is also a bidding offense. Bid shielding is the practice of using two IDs to win an auction, by placing a proxy bid with the first ID, bidding up the auction beyond the first proxy bid with a second ID, and then withdrawing the high bid to leave the lower bid as the winning bid. This practice artificially inflates the price of the item, and is also used to drive bidders away from competitor's listings.

Any bidding manipulation to attempt to put an item at 30 bids, which is considered a hot category item on eBay, is another type of bidding offense. eBay notes hot items with a flaming match to draw the attention of more bidders. More bids presumably mean a better price for the seller.

Transaction Interference

Transaction interference can include several types of actions intended to disrupt an auction. Transaction interference includes unsolicited e-mail to other users. Any attempt to lure bidders from another user's item to your own item is transaction interference. For example, you may bid on an item and then get an e-mail from another seller directing you to his or her item at a lower price. This is transaction interference.

Users are not allowed to solicit sales outside of eBay, either. If someone contacts you inviting you to buy an item off of eBay, this is a violation; plus, if you pursue the offer, your purchase is not covered by eBay's protection.

Another transaction interference ploy is to pretend to be the seller and contact a winning bidder to collect payment.

Transaction interference also can happen with disgruntled buyers and sellers who try to undermine another user's auction out of spite, such as e-mailing bidders and warning them of the seller's supposed bad business practices. As a good eBay citizen, you should report transaction interference violations to eBay.

Fee Avoidance

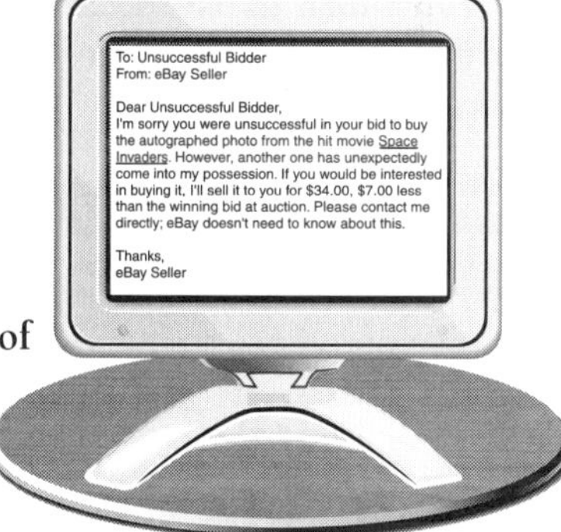

Fee avoidance is any attempt to evade paying eBay fees by circumventing the system. Fee avoidance can include a variety of violations, some of which you may not even be aware of as violations. For example, someone may e-mail you with an offer to buy your item, leading you to cancel the auction early to accept the offer. This is considered fee avoidance, because you do not hand over a final value fee for the item to eBay. A similar prohibited transaction is to make arrangements with a buyer to sell an item at a higher price than the current bid price by canceling the auction early and canceling all the current bids.

In another scenario, perhaps your reserve was not met on an auction at closing. If you contact another bidder after the auction is closed to sell the item, it is considered fee avoidance.

Fee avoidance also includes any attempts to sell an item off of eBay, offering duplicates of your item to the unsuccessful bidders of your auction, or simply ending an auction

CREATE AN AUCTION LISTING

An auction listing page is your main tool for selling an item on eBay. After you register as a seller, you can use the eBay seller's form to create and post your auction listing online. The seller's form walks you through each step for creating your auction ad, starting with choosing a category in which to list the ad. The form consists of five main pages: Category, Title & Description, Pictures & Details, Payment & Shipping, and Review & Submit.

Each page includes sections to help you add details to your ad, such as description text and terms of sale information. Terms of sale include information you want potential bidders to know about shipping, handling, payment, return policies, and other information about your auction.

To make the process as smooth as possible, take time to prepare the information you want to convey in your auction ad in advance. You may prefer to type it in a word processing program, and then copy and paste the text into the description area of the seller's form. Preparing ahead of time can help you move through the seller's form more quickly.

CREATE AN AUCTION LISTING

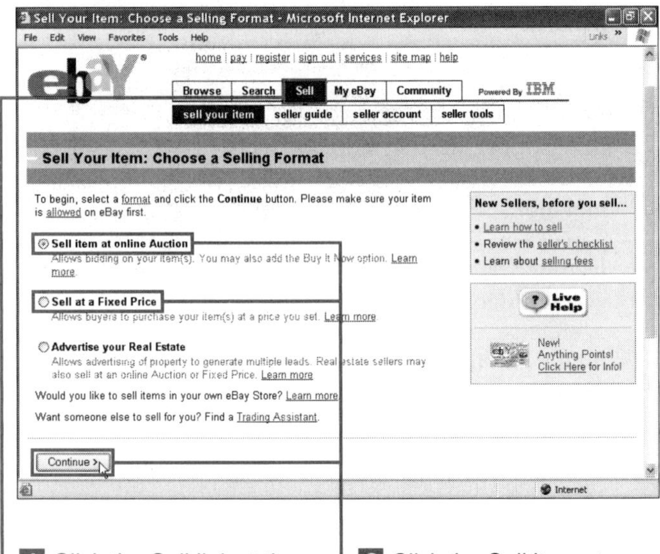

1 Click the Sell link at the top of any eBay page.

Note: You must first register as a seller before you can utilize the seller's form. See Chapter 3 to learn how.

■ The opening page of the seller's form appears.

2 Click the Sell item at online Auction option.

■ If you want to sell the item at a fixed price rather than let users bid for the item, you can click this option.

3 Click Continue.

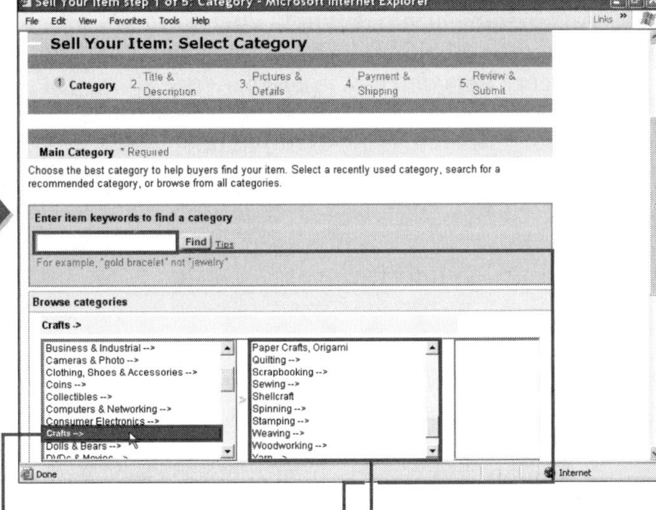

■ The Category page, the first step of the seller's form, appears.

4 Select a category for your item.

■ You can click a category, and then refine your selection in the Browse categories list boxes.

■ If you need help choosing a category, type your item keywords here and eBay can assist you.

How can eBay help me choose a category for my ad?

✔ From the Category page of the seller's form, you can type title keywords into the Enter item keywords to find a category text box, and eBay opens another window with related suggestions. Depending on your Internet connection speed, the process may take a few moments. The Find Suggested Categories window then displays a list of suggestions and a ranking of that category's usage by other users selling similar items. You can make a selection from eBay's suggestions window and return to the seller's form to continue creating your ad.

Is there a way to reuse a category I previously entered?

✔ Yes. After you post your first auction, eBay adds a Select a Previously Used Category drop-down list box to the seller's form. You can click the box and quickly select a category you previously set up for an auction. This can save you from having to reenter category information each time you create an ad.

Can I return to a page I previously filled out in the seller's form?

✔ Yes. You can use your browser window's Back and Forward buttons to move between the seller's form pages. For example, you may need to return to a previous page to make a change to your entry.

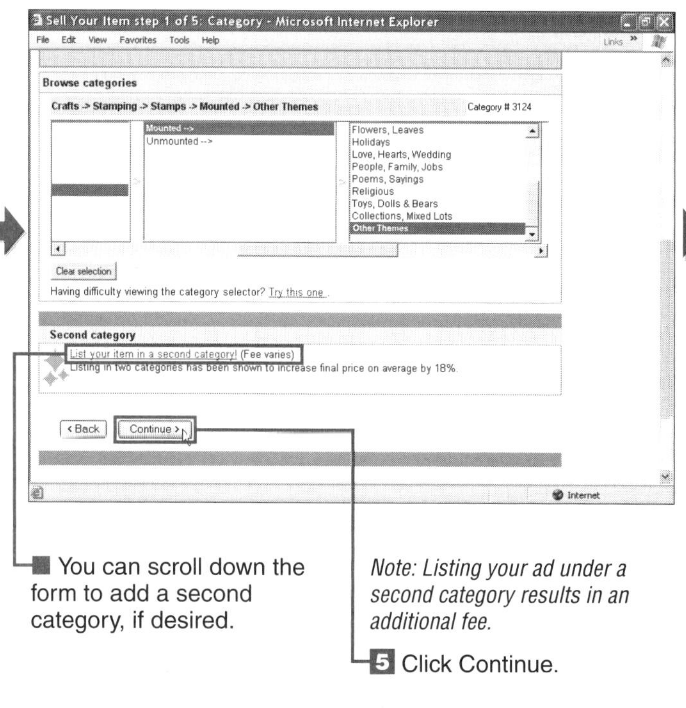

■ You can scroll down the form to add a second category, if desired.

Note: Listing your ad under a second category results in an additional fee.

5 Click Continue.

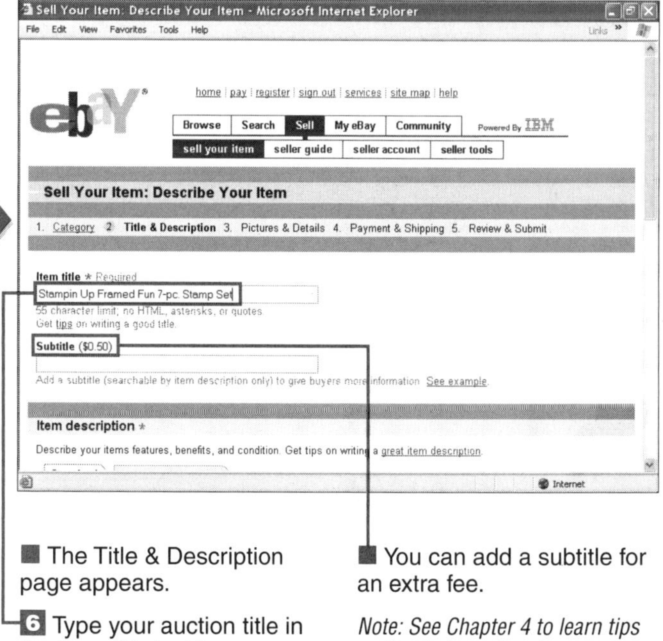

■ The Title & Description page appears.

6 Type your auction title in the Item title text box.

■ You can add a subtitle for an extra fee.

Note: See Chapter 4 to learn tips and techniques for eBay auction titles.

CONTINUED

CREATE AN AUCTION LISTING (CONTINUED)

The Title & Description page includes a text box you can use to type your ad's title text and description text. The page also includes several formatting tools you can use to add formatting elements to your description text. For example, you can change the font, font size, and font color using the tools. You can also specify bold, italics, and underlining; control the alignment of your text on the page layout; and set indents, bullets, and numbered items.

Use the formatting commands wisely. Your description text needs to be legible to anyone browsing your ad. If you use too many formatting attributes, you can overpower the reader and completely distract from your information. Always employ tried and true typesetting rules to your auction text. To learn more about typesetting tips and techniques, see Chapter 4.

After creating your description text, you can move on to setting up the auction price and duration. You can use the price options to determine a type of auction, such as a Buy It Now auction, a reserve auction, or a regular auction. To learn more about auction types, see Chapter 4.

CREATE AN AUCTION LISTING (CONTINUED)

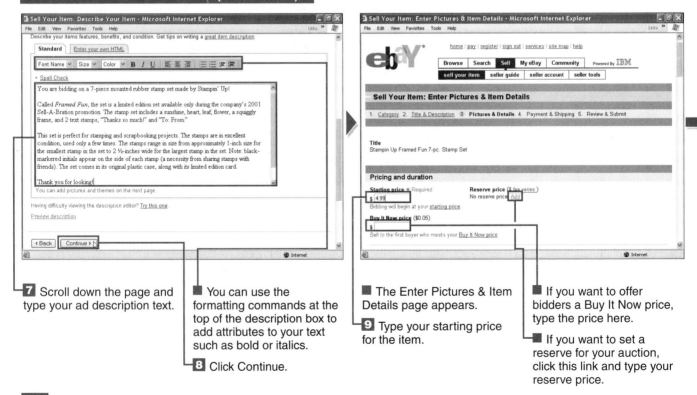

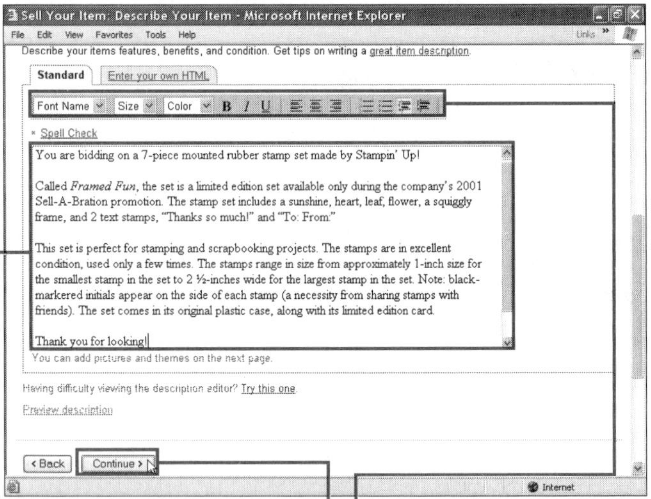

7 Scroll down the page and type your ad description text.

■ You can use the formatting commands at the top of the description box to add attributes to your text such as bold or italics.

8 Click Continue.

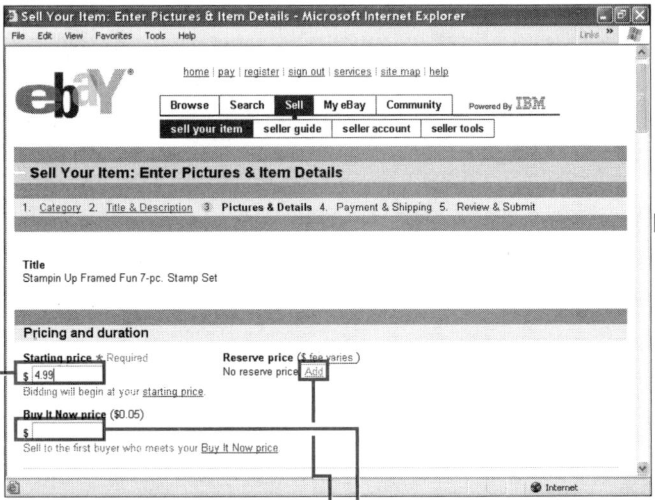

■ The Enter Pictures & Item Details page appears.

9 Type your starting price for the item.

■ If you want to offer bidders a Buy It Now price, type the price here.

■ If you want to set a reserve for your auction, click this link and type your reserve price.

Can I use HTML to write my ad?

✔ Yes. You can click the Enter your own HTML tab of the description text box to type HTML. If you are familiar with writing HTML, you can use it to create background colors for your ads, and insert additional text formatting not available through the formatting tools found on the seller's form. To learn more about using HTML to create your auction ads, see Chapter 21.

When would I use a one-day auction?

✔ You may use a one-day auction for an item you must sell right away, such as a ticket to an upcoming concert, or an airline ticket.

How do I create a fixed-price auction?

✔ A fixed-price auction allows you to sell an item for a specified price, without allowing others to bid on it. Buyers purchase the item by clicking a Buy It Now button in the ad. You can create a fixed-price auction by clicking the Sell at a Fixed Price option (○ changes to ◉) on the first page of the seller's form. See Chapter 4 to learn more about auction types.

Do I have to type my city and state in the seller's form?

✔ Yes. Any fields you see in the form that have an asterisk next to the field name are required.

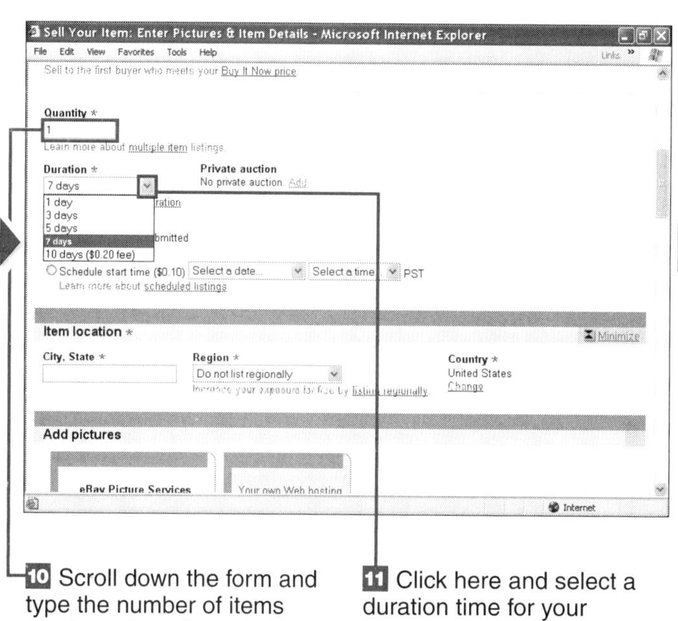

10 Scroll down the form and type the number of items you have for sale.

Note: Leave this number set at 1 unless you are listing a Dutch auction.

11 Click here and select a duration time for your auction.

■ You can run an auction from 1 day to 7 days, or for an extra fee, you can run your auction for 10 days.

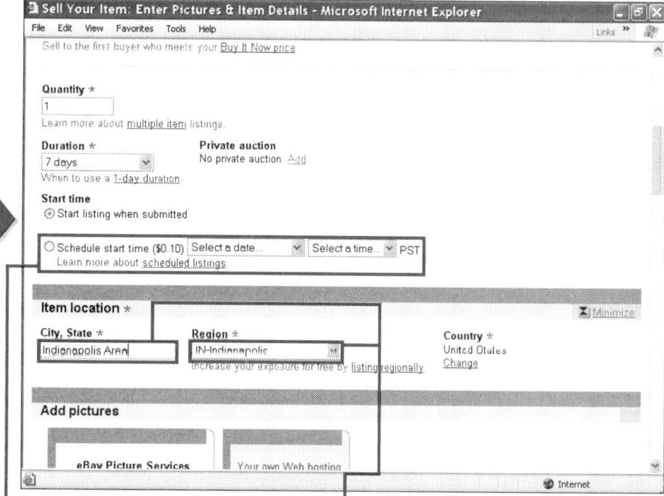

■ For an extra fee, you can click this option to schedule a specific time for the auction to start.

Note: eBay starts your auction as soon as you post it online, unless you specify otherwise.

12 Type a location.

13 Select a region.

CONTINUED

CREATE AN AUCTION LISTING (CONTINUED)

The Enter Pictures & Item Details page is one of the longest pages of the eBay seller's form. In addition to helping you to establish an auction price, duration, and location, the page also features options for adding photos to your ad. eBay allows one photo posted with an ad as part of your listing fee. If you want to include more than one photo, you can add them for an additional cost.

To add a photo to your listing, you must tell eBay where to find the file to upload to its server. To keep photos easy to find, consider storing them in a specially marked folder in your default My Pictures folder. After you designate the image file to use, eBay uploads it for you and places a thumbnail image of the photo on the seller's form page. If you prefer to use a Web hosting service instead of eBay's servers, you can click a link and type a URL to your images.

Along with adding a photo, eBay offers a variety of listing options you can use to increase your item's visibility. You can click links next to some of the options to see examples of the feature at work. Just remember that each option adds an additional cost to your listing fee. You can learn more about listing options in the section "Increase Your Item's Visibility," later in this chapter.

CREATE AN AUCTION LISTING (CONTINUED)

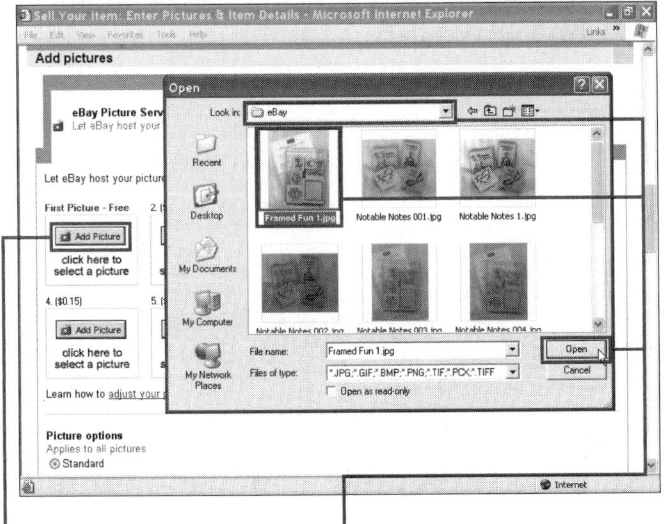

14 Scroll down the form page and click Add Picture.

Note: You can add one picture to your ad as part of your listing fee.

■ The Open dialog box appears.

15 Navigate to the folder containing the picture file you want to post in the ad.

16 Click the filename.

17 Click Open.

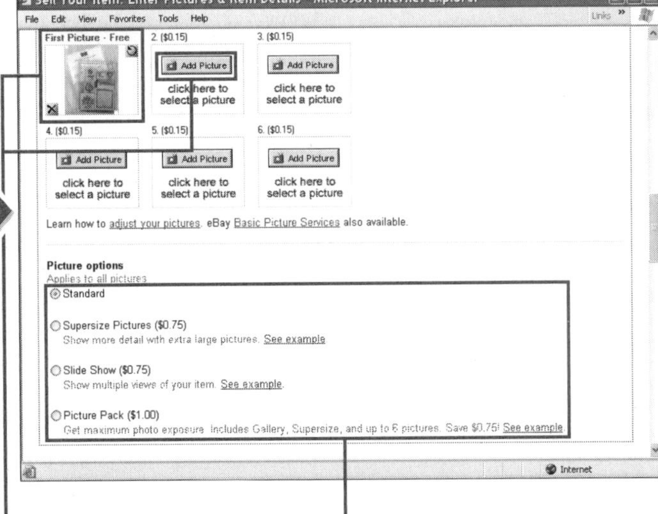

■ Your picture appears on the form.

■ You can add more pictures by clicking the remaining Add Picture buttons.

Note: You can add up to six pictures, but each additional image you upload adds to the cost of your listing.

■ You can also select several picture display options, again for an additional fee. To forego extra options, leave the Standard option selected.

How do I tell eBay to get photos from a Web hosting service?

✔ If you store your auction photos on another Web site, you can designate a Web hosting site on the Enter Pictures & Item Details page of the eBay seller's form. Just above the buttons for adding pictures to your listing is a link for using your own Web hosting service. Click the link and follow the directions for linking to photos on another Web server. To learn more about photo hosting options, see Chapter 4.

Do I really need to try some of the optional picture features?

✔ The default picture option places a standard-size picture in your auction listing. Other options include supersizing your photo and turning multiple photos into a slide show on the listing page. The slide show option simply allows bidders to see multiple views of your photos. You can click the link next to each picture option to see an example of the feature. You can also invest in the Picture Pack option, which combines several picture options along with a Gallery photo, which simply places your photo next to your auction title on a search results page.

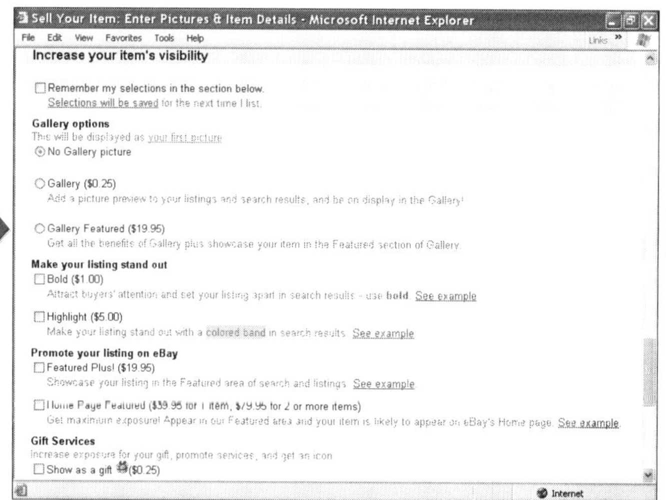

■ Scroll down the form to find fee-based upgrade options to help you increase your listing's visibility.

Note: See the section "Enhance Your Auction with Listing Designer" to learn about Listing designer.

Note: See the section "Increase Your Item's Visibility," later in this chapter, to learn about upgrade features.

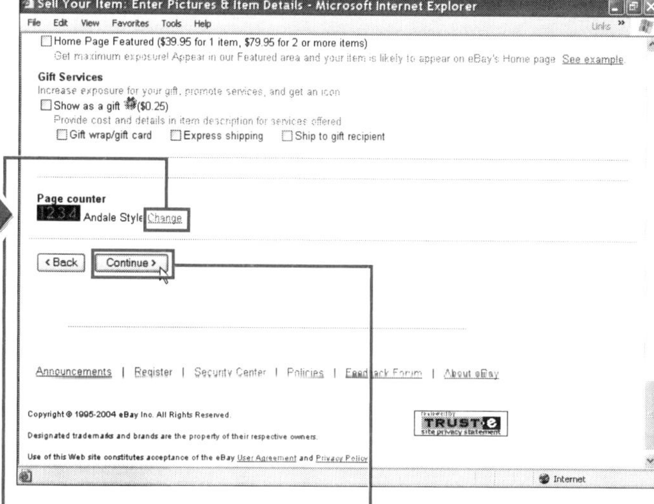

■ If you want to add a counter to your listing to count how many people visit your ad, click this link and choose a counter style.

Note: If you do not want a counter on the page, click the Change link and click No Counter.

18 Scroll to the bottom of the form and click Continue.

■ eBay uploads any photo files from your computer to the eBay Web servers.

CONTINUED

CREATE AN AUCTION LISTING (CONTINUED)

The Payment & Shipping page of the seller's form gives you the opportunity to note payment and shipping information on your ad. Also called the terms of sale, or TOS, this information alerts potential buyers to what types of payment you accept, your shipping terms, and any other relevant terms of sale, such as a return policy or other special instructions.

It is a good idea to determine your payment and shipping information before you ever begin creating your ad. This can save you time later as you enter your ad information. The payment methods section of the page lets you specify which types of payments you accept from your winning bidders. The shipping costs area of the page helps you to establish shipping and handling costs. The section also includes handy links to several shipping carriers so you can check out current rates for your item.

The payment instructions area of the page provides a spot for clarifying your terms of sale, such as a return policy, or offering combined-item shipping incentives if a buyer purchases other auction items from you. The bottom of the page displays your payment address information and a section for specifying to which parts of the world you are willing to ship your items.

CREATE AN AUCTION LISTING (CONTINUED)

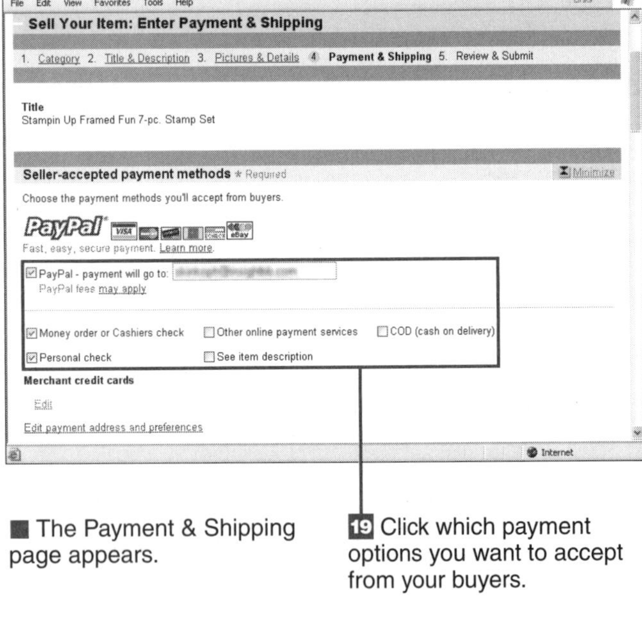

■ The Payment & Shipping page appears.

19 Click which payment options you want to accept from your buyers.

20 Scroll down the page and type a shipping and handling cost.

■ If you prefer to wait until after the auction to determine shipping costs, click this option.

■ Optionally, if you want to specify how shipping insurance is applied, click here and make a selection.

■ If you need to collect sales tax for your auction, you can specify tax information using this option.

Can I select the PayPal payment method if I do not want to take credit card payments?

✔ No. Do not click the PayPal option if you do not want to accept credit card payments through PayPal. If you leave this option selected, eBay adds credit card logos along with the PayPal logo. Any time you display credit card logos in your listing, even if you say you only take bank account transfers through PayPal, you are obligated to accept credit card payments. If you refuse to do so, and continue to display the credit card logos in your ad, the buyer can report you to eBay and PayPal as a non-selling seller because you falsely advertised your payment methods.

How do I calculate international shipping costs?

✔ You can click any of the shipping carrier links on the Payment & Shipping page to find more information about international rates. Some eBayers hesitate to ship items to other countries, but the process is not much more difficult than shipping items within the United States.

Do I have to specify shipping and handling costs?

✔ No. You can click the Don't provide shipping costs option (○ changes to ◉), and eBay adds a note to your ad instructing bidders to contact you for shipping information. Remember, providing shipping and handling information up front can give your buyers more confidence in knowing there are no hidden fees you can charge them later.

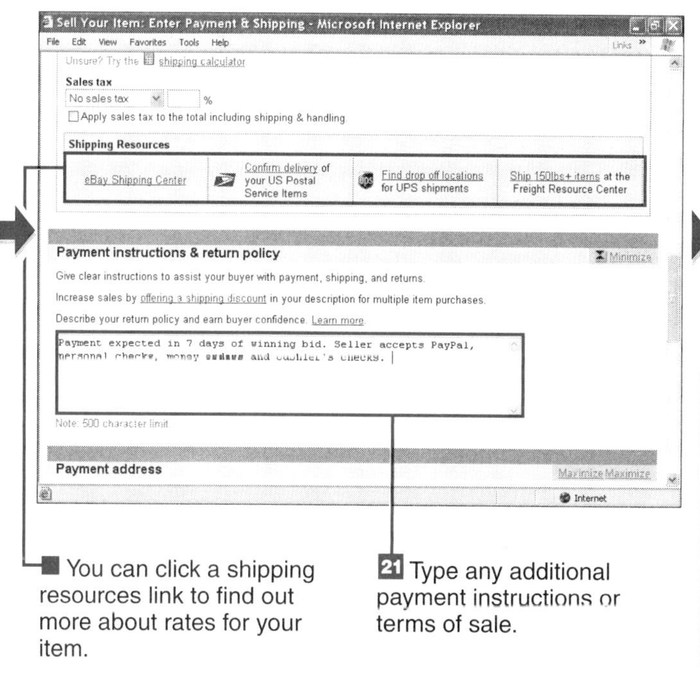

■ You can click a shipping resources link to find out more about rates for your item.

21 Type any additional payment instructions or terms of sale.

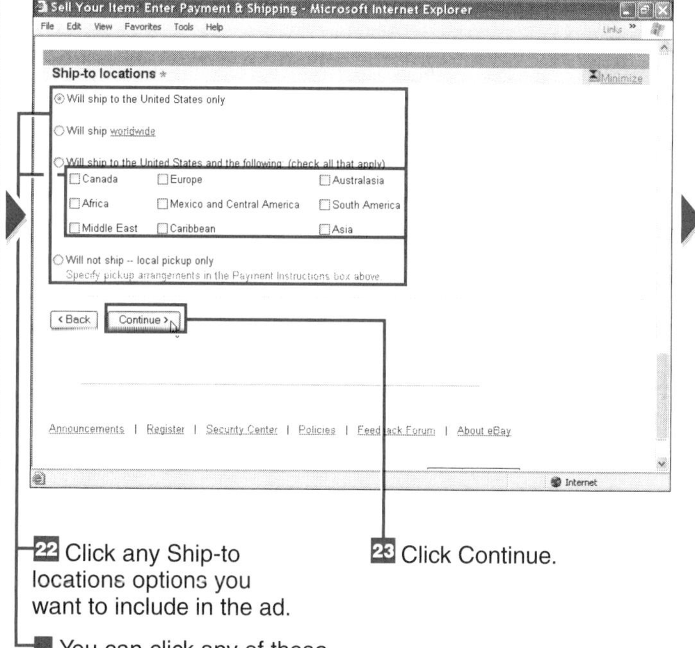

22 Click any Ship-to locations options you want to include in the ad.

■ You can click any of these options if you are willing to ship to locations outside the United States.

23 Click Continue.

CONTINUED

CREATE AN AUCTION LISTING (CONTINUED)

The last page of the seller's form allows you to check all of your work completed thus far in creating the ad. Carefully read your text, checking for spelling and grammar problems. Check your photo to make sure it matches your item description. Finally, review your payment and shipping instructions, and any additional information concerning your ad.

If you find an error, you can click the corresponding link and make changes to the information. You can also click the Back button on your browser window to revisit the seller's form pages.

Take time to be thorough in your review. As soon as you post your ad, your listing is final. Although you can make some revisions, depending on whether your ad has bids, your information stands as is. If you find an error after others place bids on the item, you cannot change the auction. Instead, you must cancel the bids and end the auction early, which frustrates your bidders immensely.

After you review and submit your ad, eBay offers to help you start another auction. eBay also sends you an e-mail confirming your listing. To learn more about viewing your posted auctions, see the section "View Your Listing" later in this chapter.

CREATE AN AUCTION LISTING (CONTINUED)

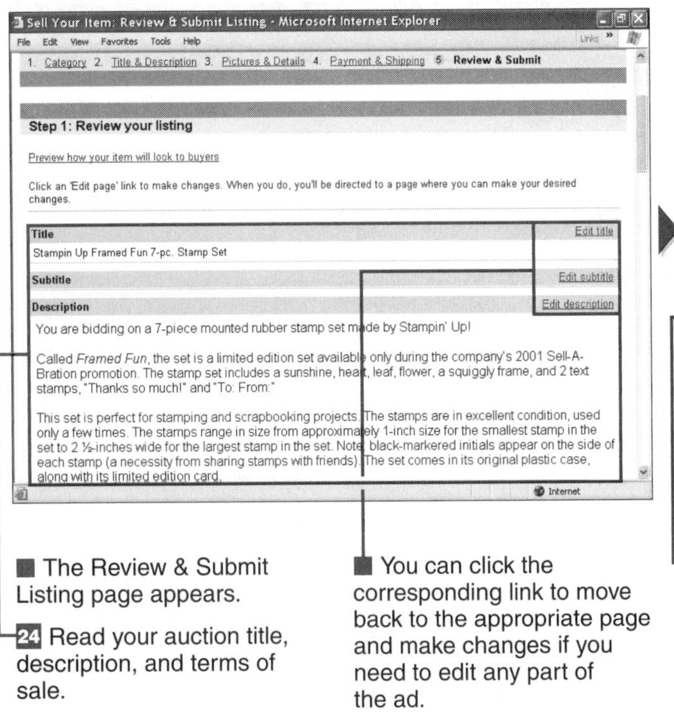

■ The Review & Submit Listing page appears.

24 Read your auction title, description, and terms of sale.

■ You can click the corresponding link to move back to the appropriate page and make changes if you need to edit any part of the ad.

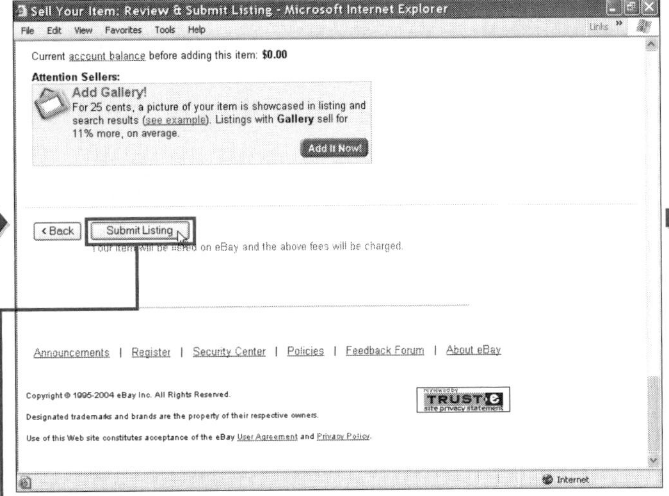

25 Scroll to the bottom of the page and click Submit Listing.

Note: As soon as you activate this command, eBay posts your auction.

How do I keep track of my posted auctions?

✔ You can use the My eBay page to track your auctions online. To learn more about this feature, see Chapter 6. You can also use auction management services and programs to manage your listings. See Chapters 19 and 22 to learn more.

Does eBay include a spell checker I can use?

✔ Yes. You can find a Spell Check link above the description box on the Title & Description page. Although the spell checker is a nice feature, it is good practice to read all of your material yourself to double-check for errors the spell checker cannot catch.

Is there an offline program I can use to create my auctions and then post them later?

✔ Yes. You can download and install eBay's own Turbo Lister program and create all your ads offline. This allows you to take all the time you need to make your ads. Then you can log on to eBay and post all the ads at the same time. See Chapter 18 to learn more about Turbo Lister. You can also use auction management software and services to help you generate ads and post them on eBay. See Part VI of this book to learn about other ways to create auction listings.

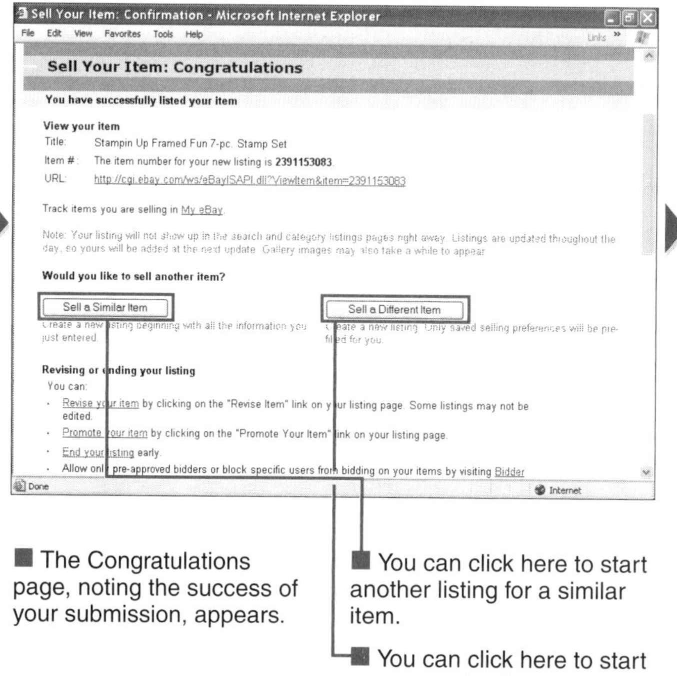

■ The Congratulations page, noting the success of your submission, appears.

■ You can click here to start another listing for a similar item.

■ You can click here to start a new auction for a different item.

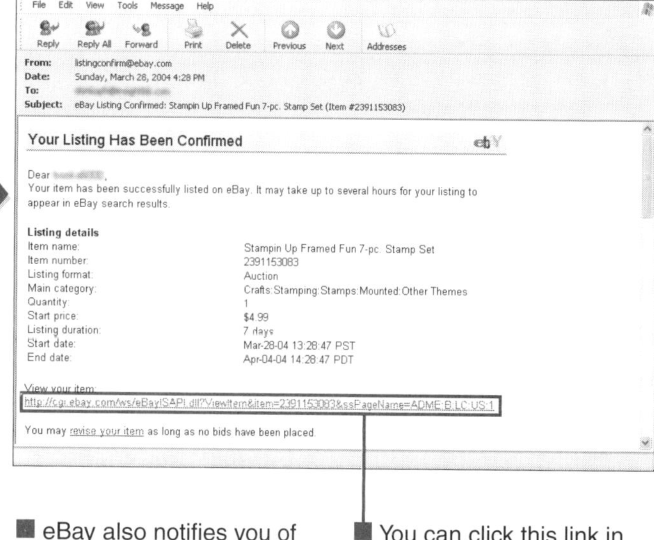

■ eBay also notifies you of your posted auction with a listing confirmation e-mail similar to the one shown in this example.

■ You can click this link in the e-mail message to view your listing.

INCREASE YOUR ITEM'S VISIBILITY

The eBay's seller's form includes upgrade features you can elect to add to your listing in an effort to increase your ad's visibility online. Whether any of the upgrade features work or not is a matter of opinion. The real consideration is the cost. Each upgrade adds an additional fee to your overall listing fee. If you are not careful and start adding upgrade features haphazardly, you may end up spending more than you want on your auction listing.

Many of the upgrade features are tempting, but you really need to ask yourself if the cost justifies the application. For example, is highlighting your auction title in a swath of color on a search results page really worth $5? Is featuring your ad in the Featured section of the Gallery worth $19.95? And most important, will any of the upgrades induce a buyer to bid on your ad? To help you discern your options, take a moment and examine what each upgrade option offers.

Gallery Options

The Gallery is another way in which you can bring extra attention to your auction listing. You can view Gallery Listings browsing categories or viewing search results pages. When users conduct a search and display a list of matching auction results, listings that feature the Gallery upgrade display thumbnail images of their items to the left of the auction titles. Listings without Gallery photos display icons of a camera instead, indicating the item does have a picture, but you must open the ad to view the image. Listings with no camera icon do not feature any photos in the ad at all.

To add your own ad's photo to the Gallery Listings, you must pay an extra 25 cents. If you want your auction title and thumbnail picture featured even more prominently, you can pay an extra $19.95 and eBay places it automatically at the top of the search results page in a featured section of the Gallery Listings.

When determining whether to use the Gallery upgrade or not, consider the intent of the buyer. If a buyer is interested in viewing your ad, he or she will still open the ad to learn more about the item, regardless of whether a thumbnail photo appears or not. On the other hand, some users insist the Gallery Listings are a great way to skim listings to see if a listed item is remotely like the item for which they are looking.

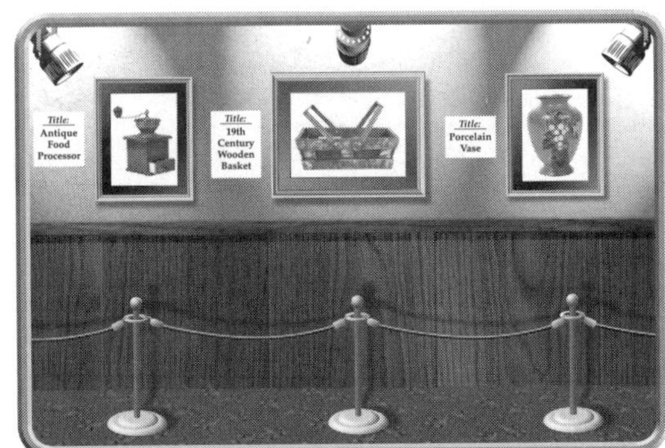

Auction Title Upgrades

Another way to make your listing titles stand out on the category pages and the search results pages is to add bold to the title or to bathe the title with background color. The bold upgrade, theoretically designed to make your title stand out from the rest, costs an additional $1. However, time-tested typesetting rules prove that reading bold lines of type amidst regular lines of type can be jarring for the reader. This is especially true on eBay when you skim down a list of auctions trying to read each title.

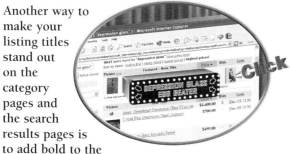

For an extra $5, you can choose to add a color highlight behind your auction text, further drawing attention to the listing. Again, you must ask yourself whether a color highlight is the key to bringing buyers to your ad: Formulating a good auction title is a better, and cheaper, approach.

Featured Promotions

You can add the Featured Plus! upgrade for $19.95 to make your auction listing appear featured at the top of any category listing or search results page. This means your ad appears not only at the top of the page, but also in its natural position among the regular listings, giving you twice the exposure. Unless you are selling a high-priced item, the price tag of this upgrade is probably cost prohibitive.

For an extra $39.95, you can have your ad featured on the eBay home page, the first page many users see when they log on to the site or start to browse categories. Your ad is rotated on the featured item area along with other featured ads. On the downside, the rotation sequence may not give you as much exposure as you like. You must also keep in mind that many users never visit the home page, preferring to launch their searches from their My eBay pages. Again, this upgrade may not pay off in

Gift Services

If you think your item is perfect as a gift, you can elect to add a special gift icon to your listing title. In addition, you can offer your buyers extra features such as gift wrap, a gift card, express shipping, and shipment to the gift recipient instead of the buyer. This upgrade may enhance your listing around special holidays, but for an extra 25 cents, you may not find the feature worthwhile.

Picture Options

eBay also offers upgrades for the photos you choose to include in your ads. You can supersize a photo for 75 cents, allowing bidders to see more details in the image. The actual size of the supersize photo is up to 11 inches by 8 inches, or 800 pixels wide by 600 pixels high. You can also turn multiple pictures into a slide show on your ad for an additional 75 cents. The show can run by itself, or the bidder can interact with the show using navigational buttons.

You can also elect to upgrade to the Picture Pack service, which includes up to six supersize photos and a Gallery Listing, all for just $1.

If you do feel a need to upgrade your listings, be sure to experiment and take note of the results. If you see improved traffic to your ads, you might consider other upgrade features. If not, you know to save your money.

ENHANCE YOUR AUCTION WITH LISTING DESIGNER

Within the eBay seller's form pages is an upgrade feature, called Listing designer, that allows you to enhance your ads with graphics, colors, and backgrounds. For a small fee, you can add a theme to your ad to improve the overall appearance of the listing. Listing designer is an interactive utility you can access from the seller's form, but only if you choose to. If you prefer not to use the feature or incur the cost, you can bypass the upgrade and continue creating your auction listing.

What makes Listing designer an interesting utility is its variety of themes. A theme is simply a set of color-coordinated layouts, backgrounds, and borders that gives your listing ad a cohesive feel and a polished look. Ordinarily, to create exciting Web page backgrounds and layouts, you need to know how to use HyperText Markup Language, or HTML. With Listing designer, you can bypass the tediousness of typing HTML and let Listing designer do all the work for you.

You can spend as much time as you need perusing the various theme categories and themes and trying out layouts. You can use the Preview listing link to see how each design looks with your auction text and photos. Listing designer includes a variety of themes ranging from holiday-related backgrounds to eBay category themes.

ENHANCE YOUR AUCTION WITH LISTING DESIGNER

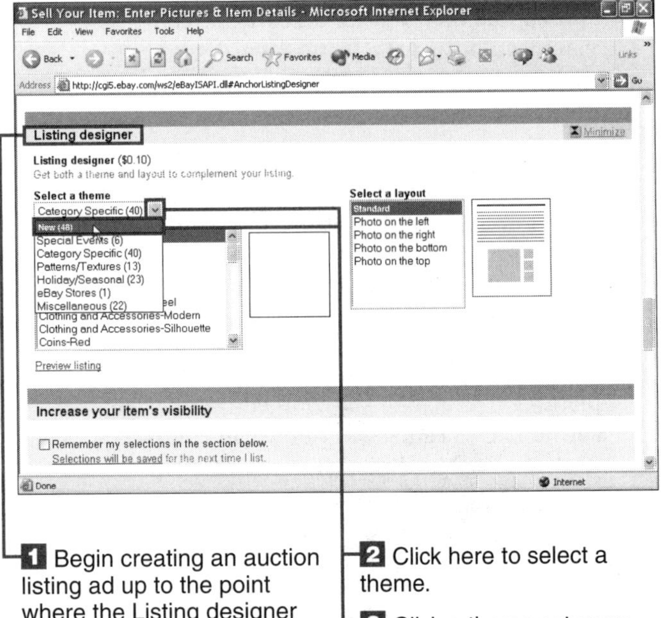

1 Begin creating an auction listing ad up to the point where the Listing designer upgrade appears on the form.

Note: You can find Listing designer on the Enter Pictures & Item Details page of the seller's form.

2 Click here to select a theme.

3 Click a theme category.

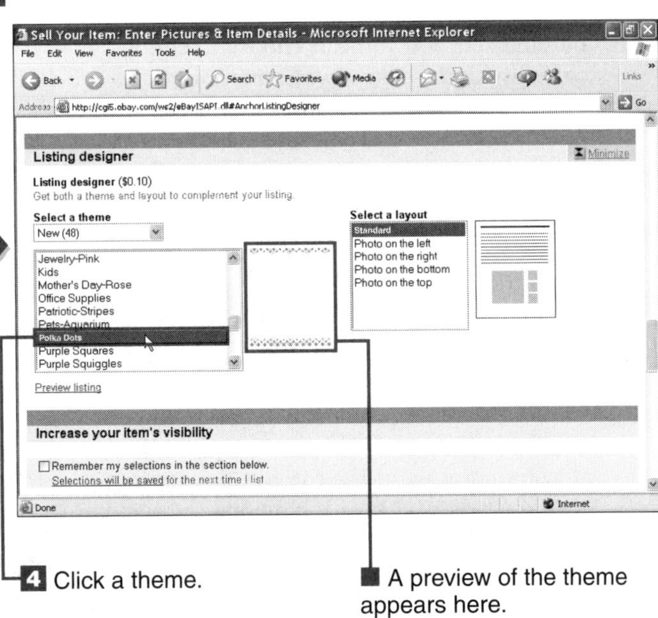

4 Click a theme.

■ A preview of the theme appears here.

How is Listing designer different from Turbo Lister?

✔ Surprisingly, you can find the same themes in Listing designer available in eBay's Turbo Lister program. Turbo Lister, a free download on eBay, is an auction-creation tool you can use to make multiple auction listings offline without using HTML, and then schedule the auctions for posting on eBay. You need 20MB of disk space for Turbo Lister, along with at least 64MB of RAM; however, if these requirements are met, you can easily tap into Turbo Lister's themes for the same cost as using Listing designer on the seller's form. See Chapter 18 to learn more about Turbo Lister.

I decided I do not want to use the theme I selected. How do I undo it before continuing with the ad?

✔ Simply scroll to the top of the list of themes and click the None listing. This removes any theme you previously applied to the ad and resets the Listing designer area of the page back to its default settings. You are not charged for any themes because you chose not to apply a theme to your ad. If you get to the end of the seller's form after assigning a theme, you can change your mind before submitting the ad by returning to the Listing designer section and changing the settings back to the default settings.

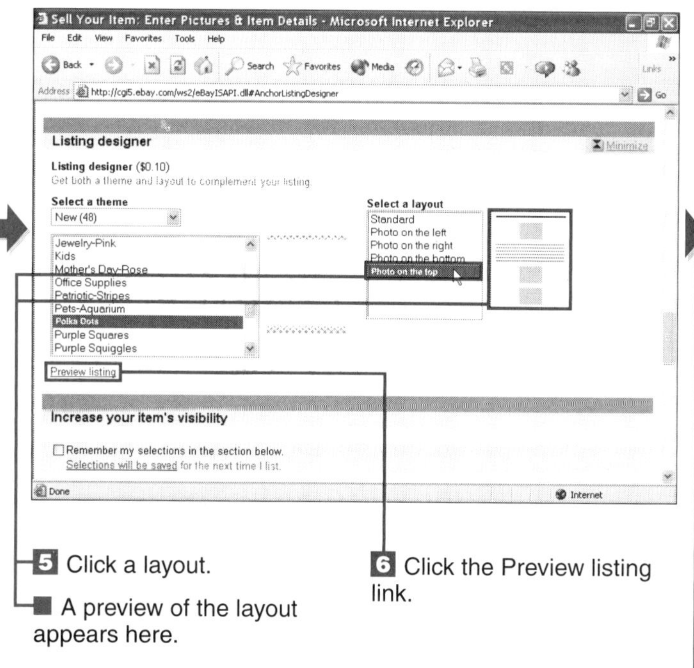

5 Click a layout.

■ A preview of the layout appears here.

6 Click the Preview listing link.

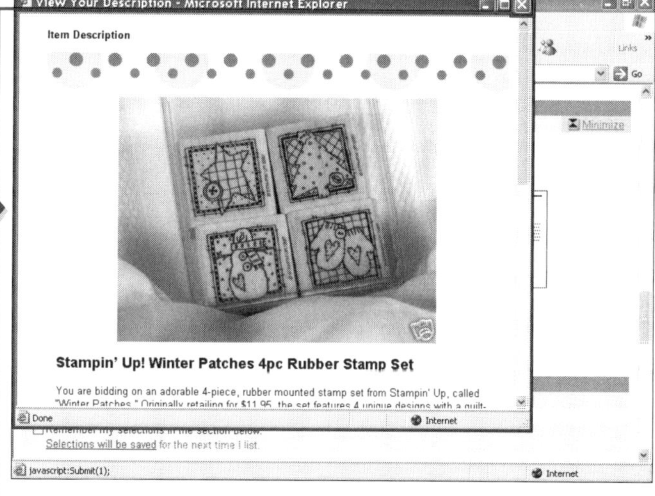

■ eBay opens a new window previewing your ad with the selected theme applied.

7 Click here to close the window.

■ eBay closes the preview window, and the seller's form reappears.

■ You can continue trying out other themes and layouts until you find one you like.

VIEW YOUR LISTING

After you spend time and energy creating an auction listing, it is quite satisfying to view it on eBay as others see it. Depending on how many categories in which you listed your auction, or any upgrade features you assigned, you may see your ad in a variety of places on eBay. Based on keyword searches, your ad may show up on search results pages, too.

eBay assigns every auction a unique item number. You can use the item number to locate your ad. When you complete and post an auction, a congratulatory page appears listing the item number. The number is also available in the confirmation e-mail eBay sends you after you post an auction.

You can also look up your ad based on your User ID. You can use the eBay Search page to search for listing numbers and seller IDs, including your own. See Chapter 2 to learn more about utilizing the eBay search tools.

You may not immediately find your auction on eBay after you post it. It can take up to six hours for eBay to index the listing. You can always find the item by its number, but you may not find it immediately if you conduct a search on the ad's keywords.

VIEW YOUR LISTING

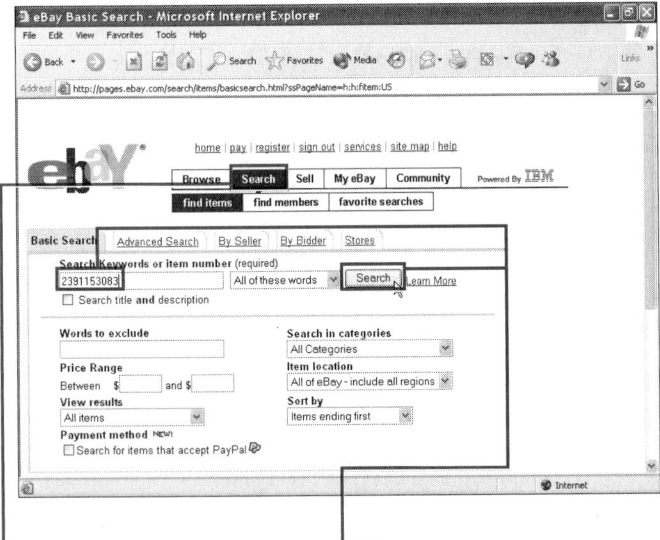

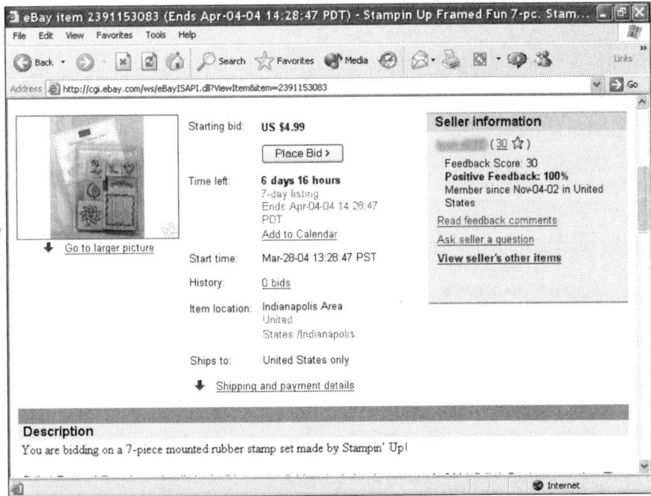

SEARCH BY ITEM NUMBER

1 Click the Search link at the top of any eBay page.

2 Type the item number in the Basic Search text box.

3 Click Search.

■ Your listing appears.

Can I save my listing as an HTML page?

✔ Yes. You may want to save a copy of your ad to file with your eBay business materials and account information. By saving your page as an HTML page, you can view the file in other programs, such as Microsoft Word, as well as offline in your Web browser. To save your ad, first display the listing in your browser window, and then choose File, Save As. A Save As dialog box opens. Navigate to the folder to which you want to store the ad, and then click the Save button. Your browser program saves the file in the Web page format.

How do I send a link to my page to my friends or colleagues?

✔ At the bottom of every auction listing is a link labeled Email this item to a friend. You can click the link to open an e-mail form within eBay. Simply type the user's e-mail address and any additional message you want to convey, and then click the Submit Message button. eBay sends a link to the page along with the message to the e-mail address you specified.

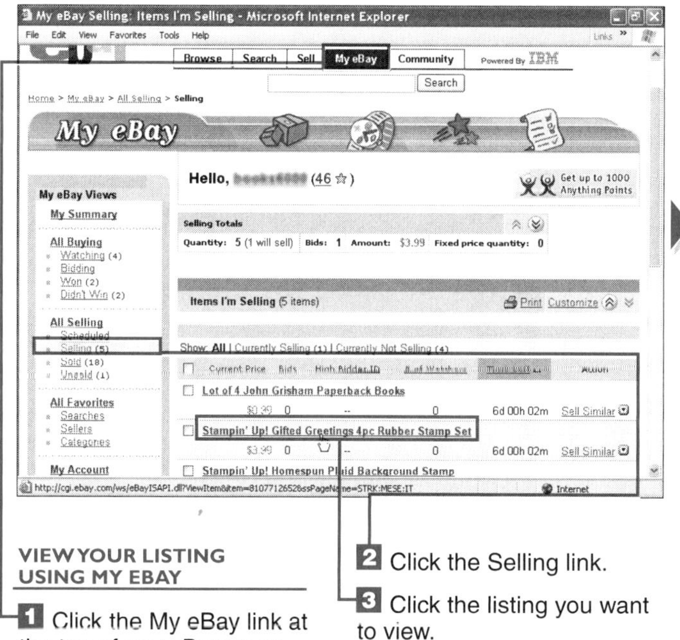

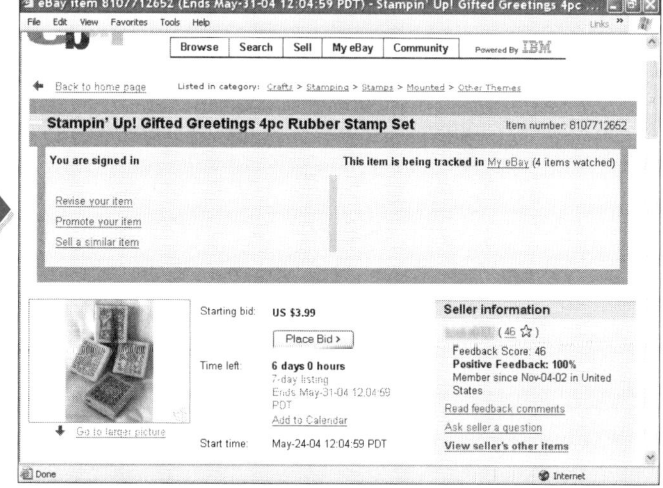

VIEW YOUR LISTING USING MY EBAY

1 Click the My eBay link at the top of any eBay page.

2 Click the Selling link.

3 Click the listing you want to view.

■ Your listing appears.

SECTION III

6) USING MY EBAY

7) MONITORING AND MANAGING YOUR AUCTIONS

8) BRINGING IN THE BIDDERS

MANAGING AND PROMOTING YOUR AUCTION

CUSTOMIZE THE MY EBAY PAGE

You can use the My eBay page as the central operating base for all of your eBay tasks. For example, you can check the current bid on an item you are watching, quickly conduct a favorite search, or check your latest feedback reports. The My eBay page organizes your most common eBay tasks into five different sections, or pages, called *views*. You can quickly access each view using the links in the left pane of the My eBay page, called the *My eBay Views pane*.

Within each main view are subsections, or tables, organizing common eBay activities. For example, the All Buying view lists items you are watching, items on which you are bidding, items you have won, items you did not win, and any buying reminders you set up. You can scroll down the page to view each table, or for faster access, you can click a subsection link in the My eBay Views pane.

By default, eBay displays the Summary view whenever you open the My eBay page. The Summary page is a good place to start because it allows you to quickly ascertain the status of items you are tracking in eBay or items on which you are bidding. If you do more selling than bidding, however, you may prefer to make the All Selling view the opening page on My eBay. You can easily customize which page appears as the first My eBay page by changing your eBay preferences.

CUSTOMIZE THE MY EBAY PAGE

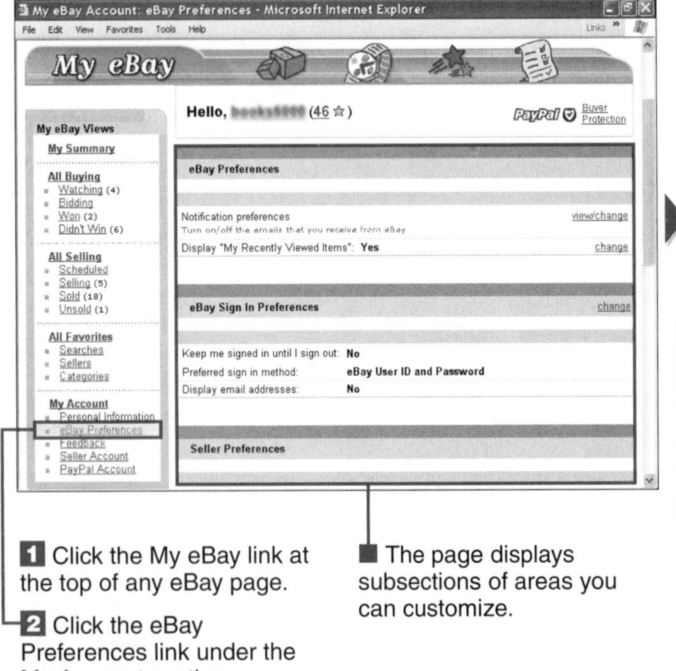

1 Click the My eBay link at the top of any eBay page.

2 Click the eBay Preferences link under the My Account section.

■ The page displays subsections of areas you can customize.

3 Scroll to the My eBay Preferences section of the page.

4 Click here to select the default opening page.

Are there other ways that I can customize the My eBay page?

✔ Yes. At the top of each table section on a view page, you can find control buttons for changing the appearance of the table on the page. For example, to move the section table to another spot on the page, click the Move Table Down or Move Table Up button (<MOVE UP> or <MOVE DOWN>). To further customize the appearance of the section, click the Customize link.

How do I change personal preferences?

✔ Click the Personal Information link under the My Account section in the My eBay Views pane. The top section of the Personal Information page has links for making changes to your personal information, such as your User ID, password, and e-mail address. Any time you need to update your personal information, you can do so from your My eBay page.

What do the Sign In Preferences do?

✔ The eBay Sign In Preferences section allows you to change how you log on to your eBay account. For example, you can tell eBay to keep you logged on for as long as you use the computer, or you can change your preferred logon preference.

What information can I find on the Summary view page?

✔ The Summary view displays a summary of your top tasks on a single screen, such as items you are watching, bidding on, or selling. Rather than access the information by clicking links in the My eBay Views pane, you can display everything and scroll back and forth through the tables and links. The Summary view includes buying and selling reminders and eBay announcements. You can customize which tables appear on the Summary view page; see "Customize a My eBay Table."

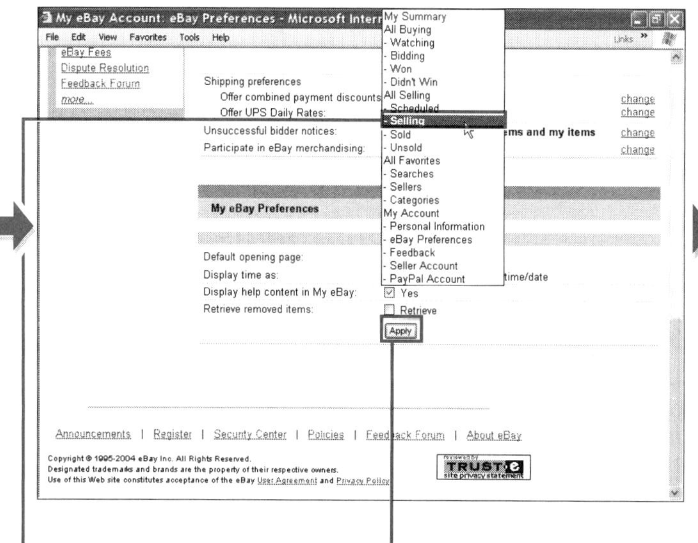

5 Click the page you want to appear each time you display the My eBay page.

6 Click Apply.

■ The next time you click the My eBay link, the designated page appears.

■ In this example, the All Selling view appears first.

Note: To change your default view to another page, you can repeat these steps to select another view.

VIEW ITEMS I'M BIDDING ON OR WATCHING

You can use the All Buying view to keep track of your bids and auction items you are tracking. An important part of the My eBay features, the All Buying view offers several tables to help you keep an eye on listings you want to buy. The page includes four main tables: Items I'm Bidding On, Items I've Won, Items I'm Watching, and Items I Didn't Win.

Each table lets you monitor auctions and presents them as a list based on auction length and dates. eBay automatically adds listings to your page for you as you bid, win, or lose auctions. For example, if you place a bid on an auction for a computer printer, eBay immediately adds the listing to your Buying page and places it in the Items I'm Bidding On table. You can quickly return to the auction listing page by activating the auction link from your Items I'm Buying table.

Several of the tables on the All Buying view are time-sensitive. By default, the page shows active items from the last 31 days. You can choose to view up to the last 60 days of activity. You can add or delete items from the Items I'm Watching table to keep it up-to-date. See the section "Customize a My eBay Table" for more. To add an auction to the watch list, simply activate the Add to Watch List link at the top of any auction listing you view.

VIEW ITEMS I'M BIDDING ON OR WATCHING

1 Click the My eBay link at the top of any eBay page.

2 Under the All Buying section, click the table you want to view.

■ Click the Watching link to view your watch list, or click the Bidding link to view items on which you are bidding.

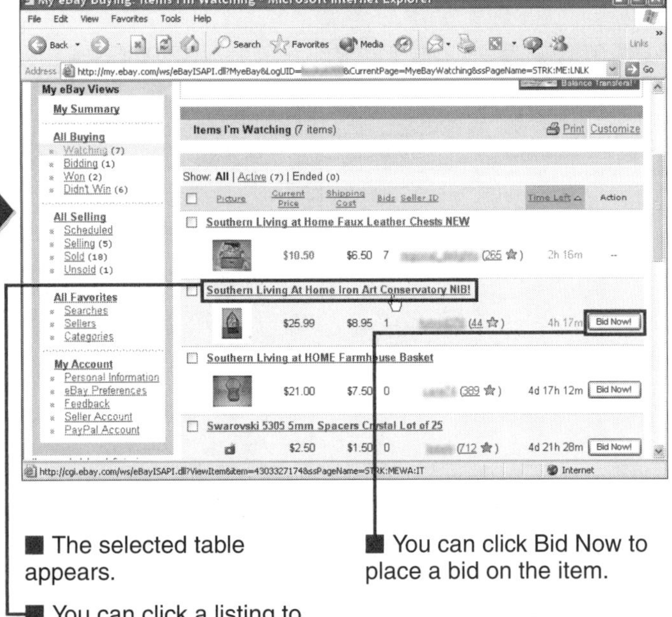

■ The selected table appears.

■ You can click a listing to immediately view the ad page.

■ You can click Bid Now to place a bid on the item.

KEEP TRACK OF FAVORITE SEARCHES

You can use the All Favorites view to access your favorite eBay searches. By saving your searches to one convenient spot, you can quickly conduct a search on your favorite keywords at any time to view a list of current auctions. Located among the sections of the My eBay page, the Favorites page stores up to 100 favorite searches.

You may use the Favorites view to help you watch the progress of bids for items you plan on selling in the future. Checking the items daily can show you their current market value. The tool can also help you check listings from your competitors. You can also use the Favorites view to help you bid on your favorite items each day, or keep an eye out for an item you are looking to add to your inventory.

You can add more searches to the Favorites list whenever you conduct a search on eBay. You can also delete searches you no longer want to track. See Chapter 2 to learn more about searching and saving searches.

KEEP TRACK OF FAVORITE SEARCHES

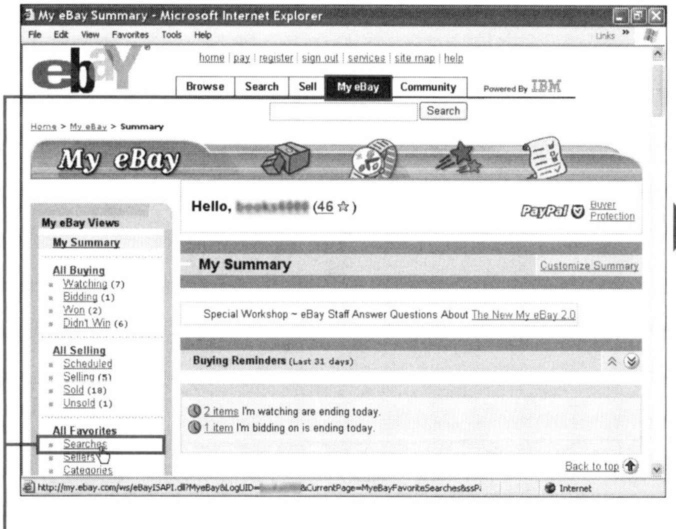

1 Click the My eBay link at the top of any eBay page.

2 Click the Searches link under the All Favorites section.

Note: eBay is constantly fine-tuning the appearance of its Web site, so the appearance of your screen may be different from the screens shown in this task.

■ The My Favorites Searches list appears.

3 Click a search you want to conduct.

Note: See Chapter 2 to learn how to add searches to the list.

■ eBay immediately takes you to a search results page listing the latest matching auctions.

VIEW ITEMS I'M AUCTIONING

The All Selling view of the My eBay page offers you a variety of tools you can use to manage your auctions. The page lists all of your active auctions, as well as items you sold, as tables on the page. Many eBay users prefer using the My eBay page to manage auctions as opposed to using auction services and software.

The Items I'm Selling table of the page keeps a running list of your current auctions. You can quickly check the current bid price, reserve prices, and auction length. eBay color codes the listings to help you determine their status. Auctions in red type indicate no bids yet. Auctions in green type indicate the item has at least one bid.

Beneath the list is a table summarizing your current auctions, so you can quickly see how much you are currently investing in your eBay endeavors. eBay keeps track of the start amount totals and the current bid amount totals.

You can use the Items I've Sold table of the page to view details about the end of the auction. For example, you can check out the name of the winning bidder, payment reminder status, which items are paid for, and which items need feedback. Status icons alert you to which tasks are finished and which await completion.

VIEW ITEMS I'M AUCTIONING

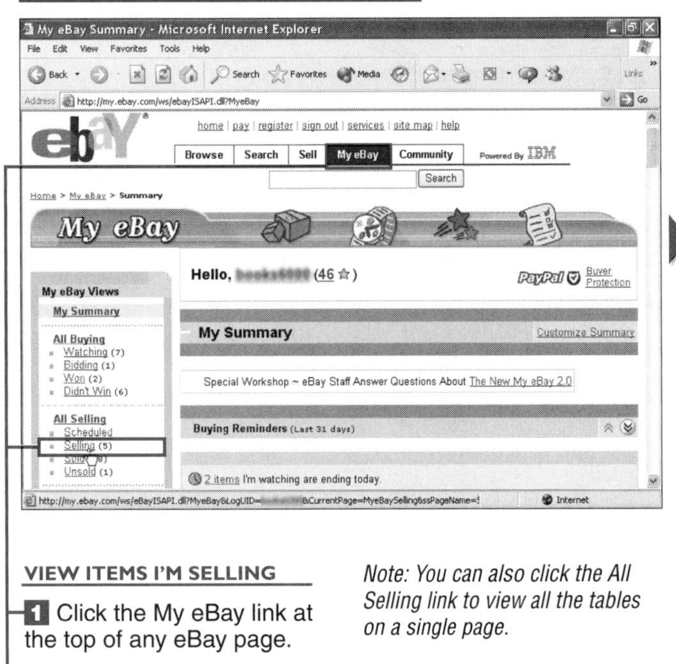

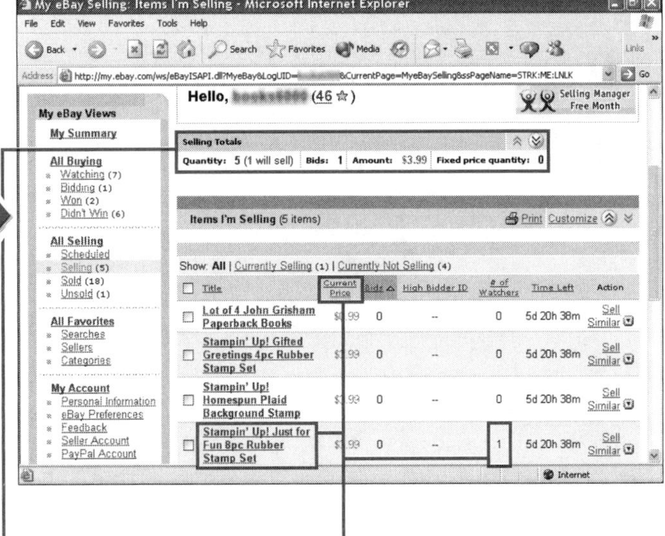

VIEW ITEMS I'M SELLING

1 Click the My eBay link at the top of any eBay page.

2 Click the Selling link.

Note: You can also click the All Selling link to view all the tables on a single page.

- The Items I'm Selling table, which shows your current auctions, appears.
- The Selling Totals area keeps track of your current overall totals.
- You can click any column heading to change how the items are sorted.
- You can click an item link to view the auction page.
- You can view how many people have added your auction to their watch lists.

What can I do with the Selling-Related links?

✔ Below the My eBay Views pane of the All Selling page a list of links related to selling tasks on eBay appears. You can click a link to quickly access the eBay Seller's Guide area, or view more information about eBay's selling policies.

My auction listing has no color. What does that mean?

✔ eBay does not apply color coding to Dutch auctions, eBay store items, or fixed-price auctions. Listings for these types of auctions appear in regular black among your Selling tables.

How do I access my PayPal account from the Selling page?

✔ You can click the PayPal link below the My eBay Views pane of the All Selling page to visit your PayPal account page, make payments for completed auctions, make payments to eBay, or make changes to your payment information. See Chapter 10 to learn more about PayPal.

How can I view a bidder's feedback rating?

✔ To learn more about someone bidding on your auction, you can click the User ID for any bidder listed among your Selling tables to quickly view the person's feedback rating and feedback reports. To learn more about how feedback is used in eBay, see Chapter 11.

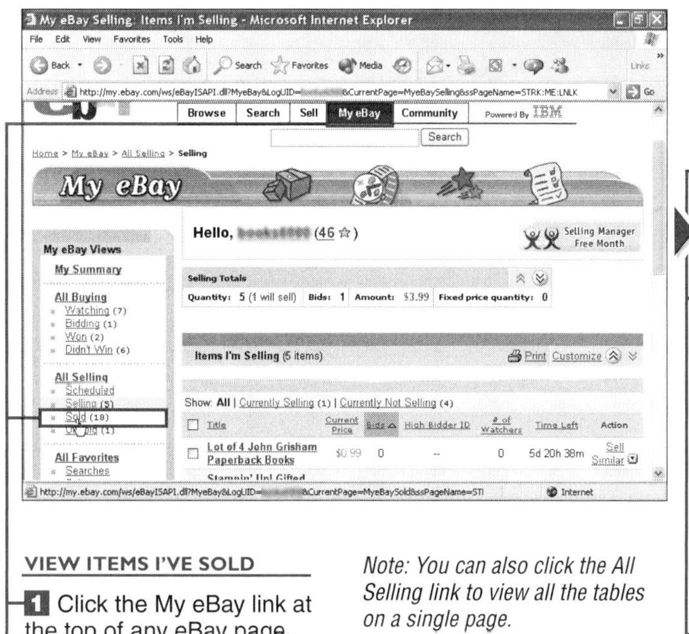

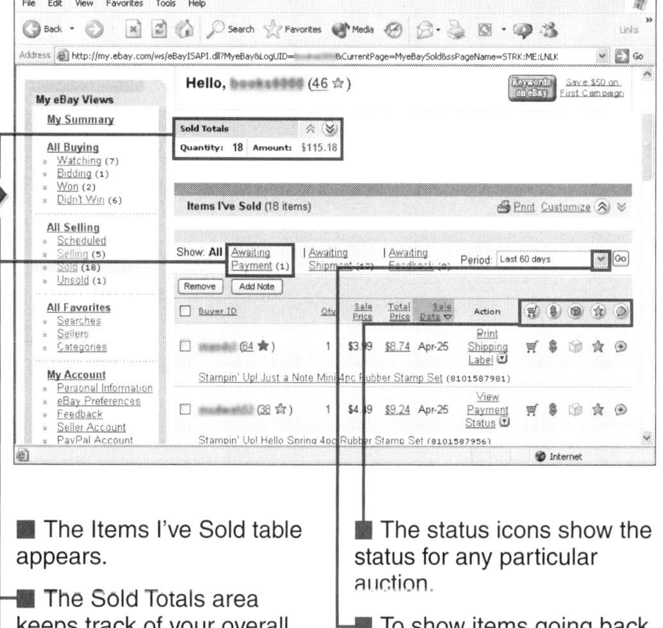

VIEW ITEMS I'VE SOLD

1 Click the My eBay link at the top of any eBay page.

2 Click the Sold link.

Note: You can also click the All Selling link to view all the tables on a single page.

■ The Items I've Sold table appears.

■ The Sold Totals area keeps track of your overall sales.

■ You can click any column heading to change how the items are sorted.

■ The status icons show the status for any particular auction.

■ To show items going back a particular number of days, click here, select a number, and then click Go.

VIEW YOUR EBAY ACCOUNTS

The eBay My Account view is another valuable management tool you can use to help you keep track of the fees and payments you owe to eBay. Although some users prefer to employ an auction management service or program to oversee accounts, you can use the My Account view tools and features for free. As your business grows, you may consider investing in other auction management services, but for just getting started, the My Account view is just what you need.

The My Account view, featured among the various My eBay views, includes several sections to help you view your account information. The My Seller Account Summary section displays your current account balance. This is the amount you owe eBay in current listing fees for posting an ad or final value fees collected at the end of a sale. If your account has not yet incurred any activity, this area of the page shows no data. After your account becomes active, you can see the latest information about your eBay fees.

The My Account Links at the bottom of the My Account view help you to find your way to helpful information about fees and payments you make to eBay.

VIEW YOUR EBAY ACCOUNTS

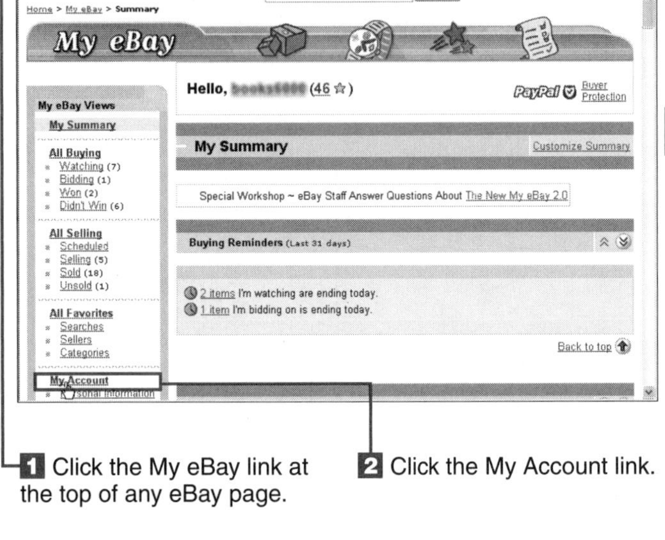

1 Click the My eBay link at the top of any eBay page.

2 Click the My Account link.

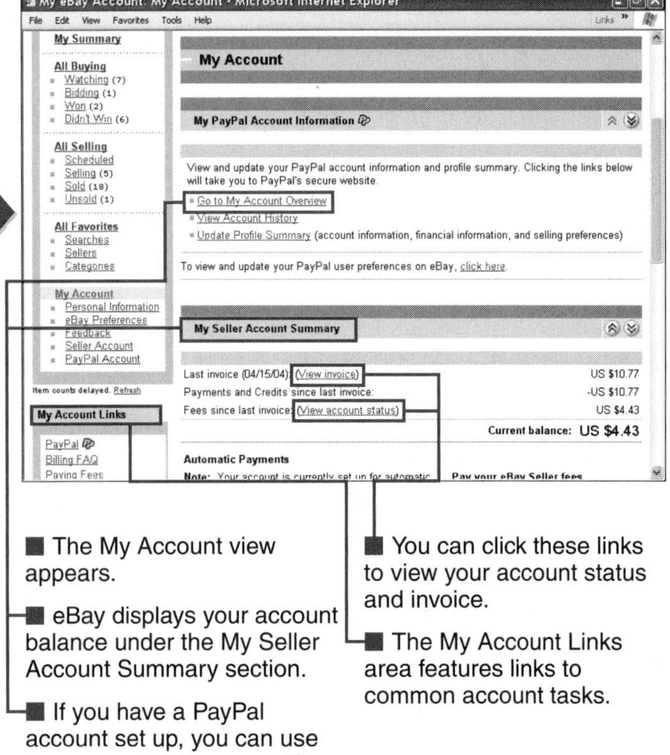

■ The My Account view appears.

■ eBay displays your account balance under the My Seller Account Summary section.

■ If you have a PayPal account set up, you can use the account to pay your eBay seller fees.

■ You can click these links to view your account status and invoice.

■ The My Account Links area features links to common account tasks.

VIEW YOUR FEEDBACK

You can use the Feedback view to check up on your latest feedback reports and overall feedback standing, as well as to view auctions in which you still need to leave feedback. Trust between sellers and buyers is the backbone of trading on eBay, and to help measure each participant's level of trust and security online, eBay's feedback system keeps an ongoing gauge of each user's performance in the transactions they complete. Your eBay feedback rating is a barometer of your online reputation. The more transactions you complete, as a buyer or a seller, the more feedback you accumulate. Each feedback report factors into your overall feedback score.

As a seller, it is your goal to maintain high levels of positive feedback. You can use the Feedback view on your My eBay page to see your latest standing and read individual feedback reports left for you by others. You can also use the page to leave feedback for others, or respond to feedback left to you. The Feedback page gives you a quick way to handle your eBay feedback whenever you log onto your account. To learn more about how feedback works on eBay, see Chapter 11.

VIEW YOUR FEEDBACK

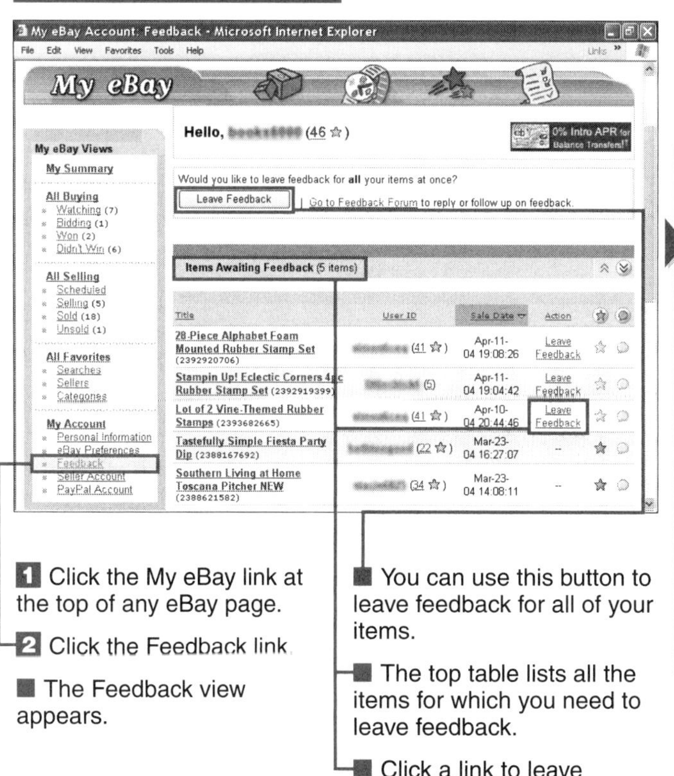

1 Click the My eBay link at the top of any eBay page.

2 Click the Feedback link.

■ The Feedback view appears.

■ You can use this button to leave feedback for all of your items.

■ The top table lists all the items for which you need to leave feedback.

■ Click a link to leave feedback.

■ You can scroll down the page to view your recent feedback reports.

■ You can click this link to view all of your feedback reports.

Note: To learn more about using feedback and viewing feedback reports, see Chapter 11.

CUSTOMIZE A MY EBAY TABLE

You can customize many of the individual tables on the My eBay view pages to suit the way you work with information. For example, you may want to change which columns appear in your Item's I'm Selling table, change their order, or delete columns you no longer want to see in the table. You can also change the number of listed items appearing in a table as well as how the information is displayed.

When you activate the Customize command, eBay opens a page with customizing options pertaining to the current table. When you save the changes, eBay applies them to the current table only. Other customization options include moving the table to another spot on the view page or adding a note to an item. See the next section to learn how to add a note to an item in a table.

How do I return a table to its original settings?

✔ Open the table's Customize page and click the Restore Defaults link. This returns the table to the original default settings.

How do I change the order of my table columns?

✔ Open the table's Customize page and click the column you want to move in the Columns To Display box. Next, click the Move Up or Move Down arrow buttons (⌃ or ⌄) to reposition the column in the table order.

CUSTOMIZE A MY EBAY TABLE

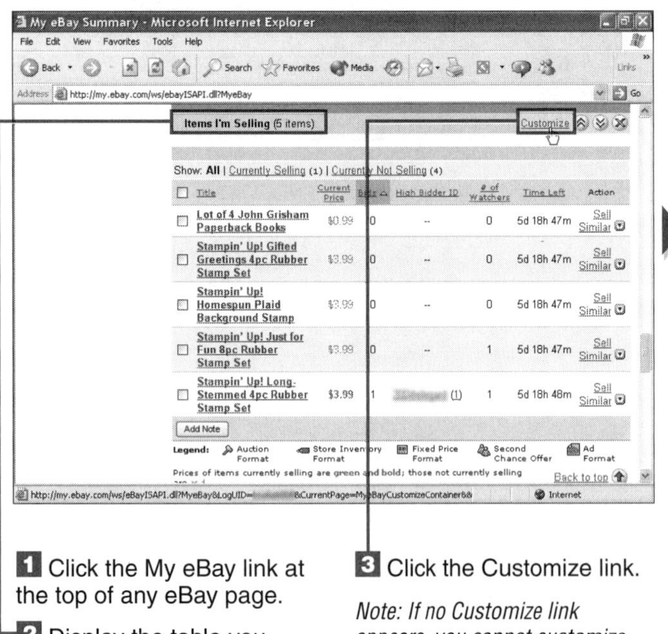

1 Click the My eBay link at the top of any eBay page.

2 Display the table you want to customize.

Note: See the previous sections to learn how to view various tables in the My eBay pages.

3 Click the Customize link.

Note: If no Customize link appears, you cannot customize that particular table.

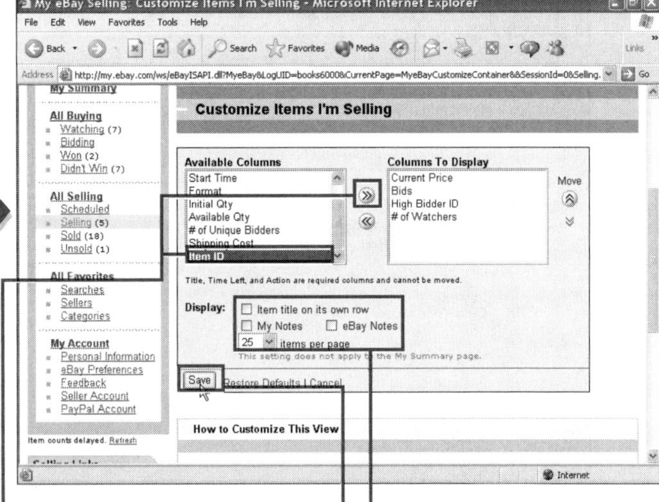

4 On the Customize page, make changes to the table elements.

■ To add a column, select it from the right and click the Add Column button (»).

■ To remove a column, select it from the left and click the Remove Column button («).

■ You can control how items appear with the Display options.

5 Click Save.

■ eBay saves the new settings.

ADD A NOTE TO A TABLE

You can add notes to items in the My eBay page tables to help you remember important tasks, add personalized information about an auction, or help you remember a good or bad experience with a transaction. Notes are simply text notations you can use to help you customize the items you track and manage on the My eBay page. For example, you might want to add a note to an item in your watch list to help you remember to e-mail the seller with a question, or you may add a note detailing transaction information about an item you sold.

Notes appear as text notations with a yellow background in your tables. Only you see the notes; other buyers or sellers cannot see the notes you add to items listed in a table. Notes appear adjacent to the item until you delete the item from the table.

MASTER IT

How do I edit or delete a note?

✔ You can click the Edit link found at the far right side of any note to make changes to the note. When you click the Edit link, the Edit Note page opens and you can change the note text. To delete the note entirely, click the Delete link on the Edit Note page.

ADD A NOTE TO A TABLE

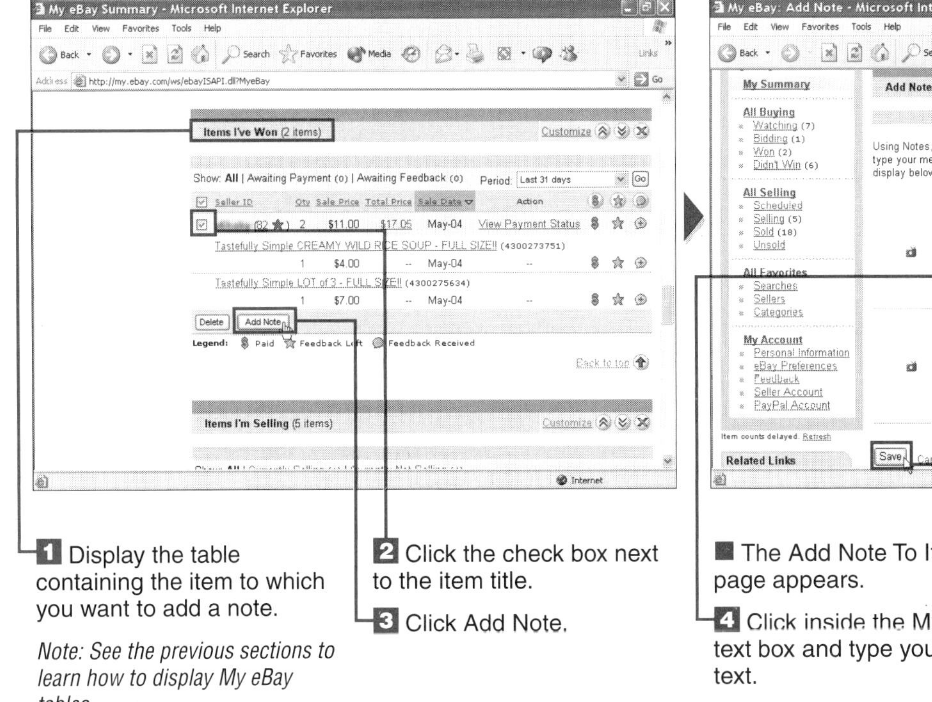

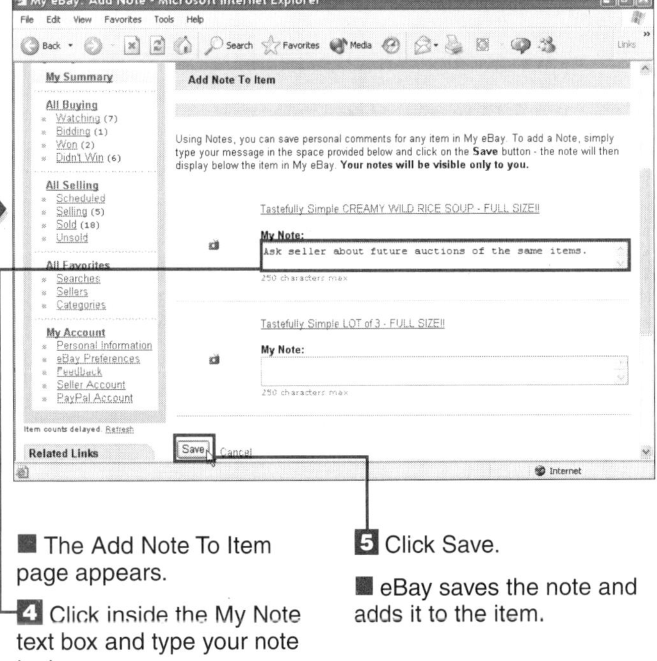

1 Display the table containing the item to which you want to add a note.

Note: See the previous sections to learn how to display My eBay tables.

2 Click the check box next to the item title.

3 Click Add Note.

■ The Add Note To Item page appears.

4 Click inside the My Note text box and type your note text.

5 Click Save.

■ eBay saves the note and adds it to the item.

AUCTION MANAGEMENT OPTIONS

The more items you list, the more winning bids you must track. If you post numerous auctions each week, staying on top of which item is selling, which item is already sold, and which item did not sell can seem like a juggling act. Thankfully, there are numerous tools you can use to help you manage multiple auctions. eBay has quite a few of its own tools available, or you can explore third-party auction management software and services.

My eBay

A simple and free tool you can use to manage your auctions is the My eBay page. The page features several views, or pages, to help you watch other user's listings, track items on which you are bidding, and view your eBay accounts. The page also includes a view that you can use to see any auctions you are currently running, manage the payment and shipping of completed auctions, as well as manage any unsold auctions. You can learn more about using the My eBay page to track listings as you read the rest of this chapter. For information about the other aspects of the page, see Chapter 6.

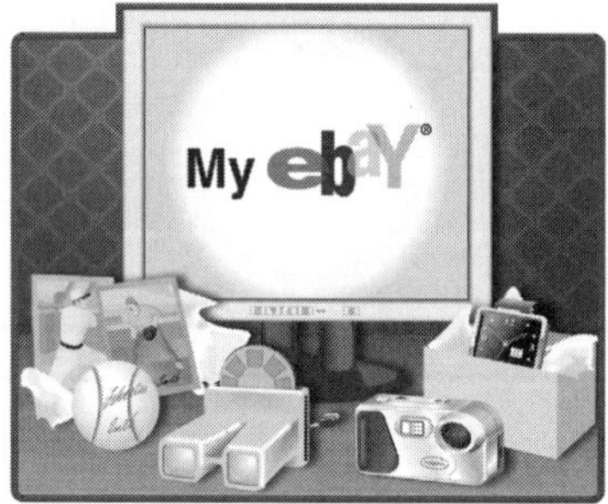

Turbo Lister

You can download eBay's own Turbo Lister program to help you create listings offline. Turbo Lister is a free listing program, and you can use it to create auction ads at your leisure, and then log on to eBay to upload them when you want. You can use Turbo Lister to save listings you use over and over again. You can access a variety of HTML templates or write your own. The program includes features for previewing your ads and scheduling when you want to start your auctions. The program keeps you up-to-date with the latest categories and listing fees by connecting with the eBay Web site.

Until recently, you could use all of the Listing Designer's preformatted themes and layouts for free with Turbo Lister. These themes and layouts are also found on the eBay seller's form, but cost a small fee to use. eBay is now charging additional fees for any ads with Listing Designer themes applied, even if you use Turbo Lister to assign them. For complete control over your listing designs, consider learning how to use HTML. See Chapter 21 to learn more about using HTML with eBay ads. To learn more about using Turbo Lister to create your auctions, see Chapter 18.

Selling Manager

eBay offers another tool, called Selling Manager, specifically to users with higher sales volumes. Selling Manager is an online sales management tool for handling bulk form filing for Non-Paying Bidder Alerts and Final Value Fee Credit requests. Selling Manager also offers a bulk relisting feature, e-mail and feedback templates, as well as management tools to help you track your auctions and stay current on your sales records.

You can use Selling Manager free for a month; after that, the service costs $4.99 per month. You can find Selling Manager among eBay's sellers tools. See Chapter 19 to learn more about this tool.

Selling Manager Pro

A step up from Selling Manager, Selling Manager Pro is another online tool you can use to manage your sales. At a cost of $15.99 per month, Selling Manager Pro adds inventory management features, automated e-mail, monthly sales reports, and listing statistics. Like the regular Selling Manager, you can try the Pro version for a month for free to see if you like it or not. Both Selling Manager and Selling Manager Pro are online programs you can use through eBay. Learn more about these tools in Chapter 19.

Seller's Assistant

You can download and install the Seller's Assistant program to help you manage sales offline. The program features a listing editor to help you design and format your auction ads, automation options for generating e-mails and invoices, and tools for tracking sales information and managing multiple auctions. eBay's Seller's Assistant comes in two versions, Basic and Pro. The basic version of the program is good for low to medium sales volumes, while the pro version is targeted to high-volume sellers and includes more management features. Seller's Assistant costs $9.99 per month, while the pro version is $24. You can try out both versions for free for 30 days. You can learn more about Seller's Assistant in Chapter 19.

Third-Party Programs

You can find a wide variety of auction management software you can use to help you with your eBay sales. Some are free; others charge fees. You can download most of these programs from the Web. Auction management programs are a good choice for users without a broadband Internet connection. The table that follows lists just a few you can explore. You can also do a keyword search on the words *auction management program* to find more on the Web. See Chapter 22 to learn more about programs you can try.

Auction Management Programs	
Auction Wizard 2000	www.auctionwizard2000.com
EZAd	www.etusa.com/auction
Auction Submit	www.auctionsubmit.com
Shooting Star	www.foodogsoftware.com
eLister	www.blackmagik.com/elister.html
Auctiva	www.auctiva.com
AuctionTamer	www.auctiontamer.com/atindex.htm
AuctionSage	www.auctionsagesoftware.com
AuctionFlex	www.auctionflex.com
Auction Messenger	www.auctionmessenger.net
SpoonFeeder	http://spoonfeeder.com

Auction Services

If you have a broadband connection, you may prefer an online auction service to auction software. Auction management services work through your Web browser to help you manage your eBay auctions. Most auction services charge a monthly fee.

Auction Management Services	
Andale	www.andale.com
HammerTap	www.hammertap.com
Zoovy	http://zoovy.com
InkFrog	www.inkfrog.com
AuctionHawk	www.auctionhawk.com
Vendio	www.vendio.com
ChannelAdvisor	http://channeladvisor.com
AuctionHelper	www.auctionhelper.com
DEK Auction Management	http://dekauctionmanager.com
Auction Works	http://auctionworks.com
ManageAuctions	www.manageauctions.com
Meridian	www.noblespirit.com

MONITOR YOUR AUCTIONS

After you post an auction, the next phase of selling on eBay is to sit back and wait. While waiting for your auction to end, you can monitor any bids other users make, answer questions other users e-mail you, and plan ahead for packaging and sending the item.

You can use the My eBay page to monitor your auctions. The All Selling View uses several tables to help you keep track of current auctions, auctions that have ended, and items that have not sold. You can use the Items I'm Selling table to view a complete list of every auction you are currently running. The table keeps track of the number of bids, whether your reserve price is met or not, the current price, the start and end dates, and the amount of time remaining for the auction.

The table also tracks how many users add your listing to their watch lists.

After an auction is over, the Items I've Sold table keeps track of the winning bidders, whether they have made payments or not, payment reminders, and feedback reminders.

The Unsold Items table lists any auctions that fail to collect any bids before closing. If you schedule auctions to appear on eBay, the Pending Items table lists auctions ready and waiting to go.

MONITOR YOUR AUCTIONS

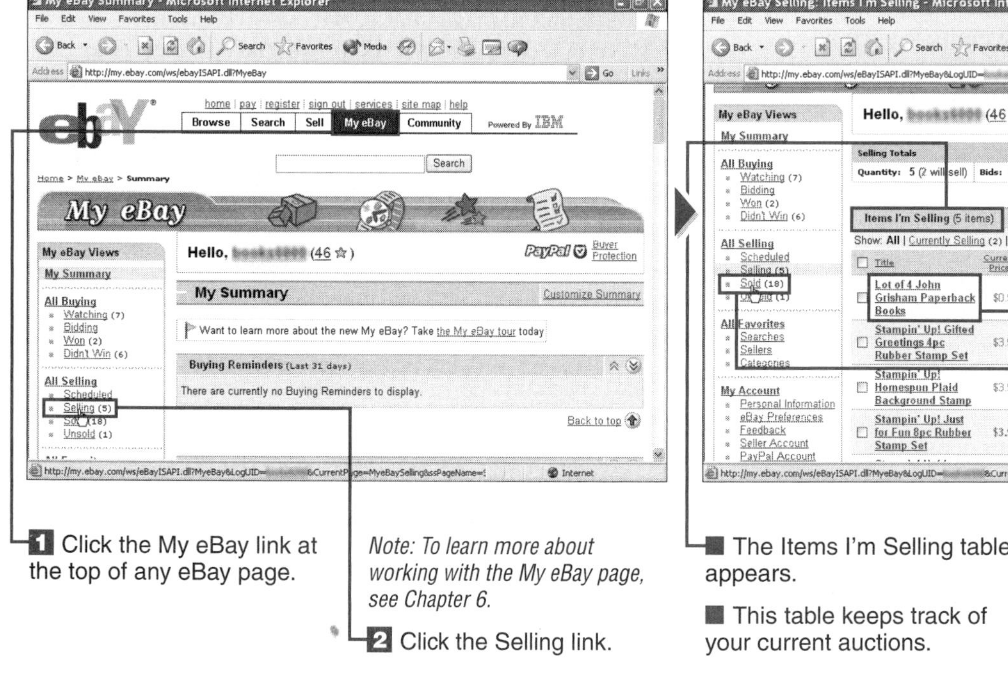

1 Click the My eBay link at the top of any eBay page.

Note: To learn more about working with the My eBay page, see Chapter 6.

2 Click the Selling link.

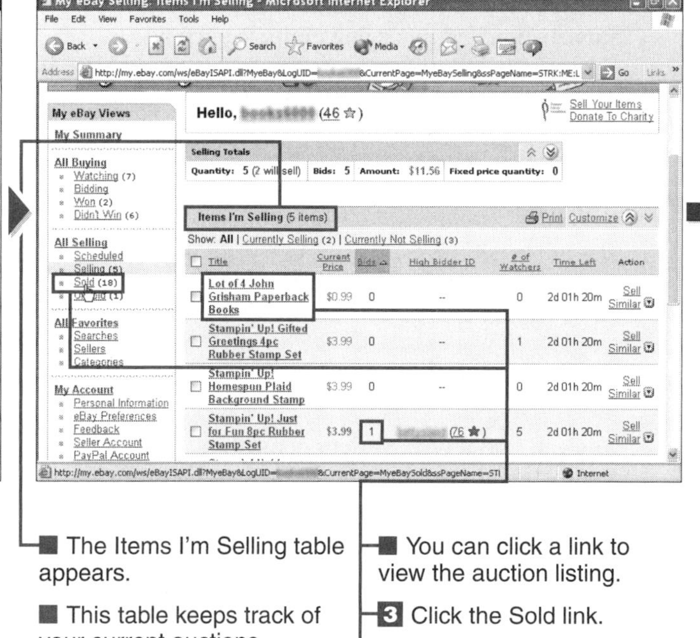

■ The Items I'm Selling table appears.

■ This table keeps track of your current auctions.

■ You can click a link to view the auction listing.

3 Click the Sold link.

■ The number of bids for an item appears in this column.

Am I better off managing my auction with the My eBay page or an auction management service or program?

✔ The more items you sell each week, the more difficult it is to stay on top of your listings, payments, and shipping. While the My eBay All Selling View is good for casual sales or if you are just getting started, you definitely need to compare other programs and services, starting with eBay's own offerings. See the section "Auction Management Options," earlier in this chapter, to learn more about the variety of management tools. See Chapters 18, 19, and 22 to learn more about third-party tools to help you with your eBay sales.

When would I use the Scheduled Items table?

✔ You can consult the Pending Items table on the All Selling View if you schedule auctions to appear on eBay. The table keeps you aprised of pending auctions ready and waiting to be posted. For example, you may prefer to list your auctions on a certain date and time for maximum bidding. You can schedule an auction using the options on the eBay seller's form, as well as in Turbo Lister or other listing programs. Keep in mind, however, that scheduling auctions to appear at a specified time results in additional insertion fees.

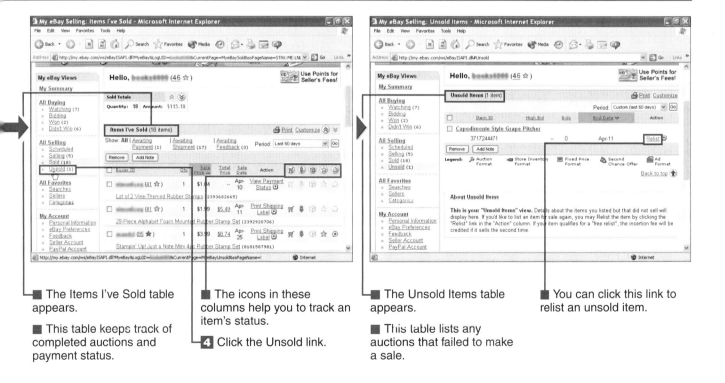

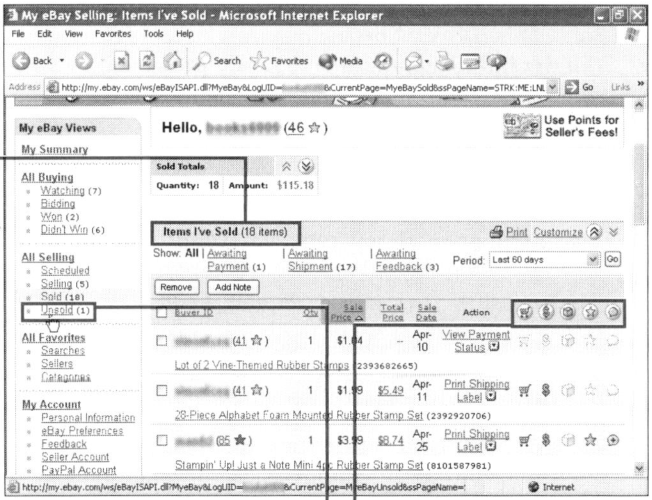

■ The Items I've Sold table appears.

■ This table keeps track of completed auctions and payment status.

■ The icons in these columns help you to track an item's status.

4 Click the Unsold link.

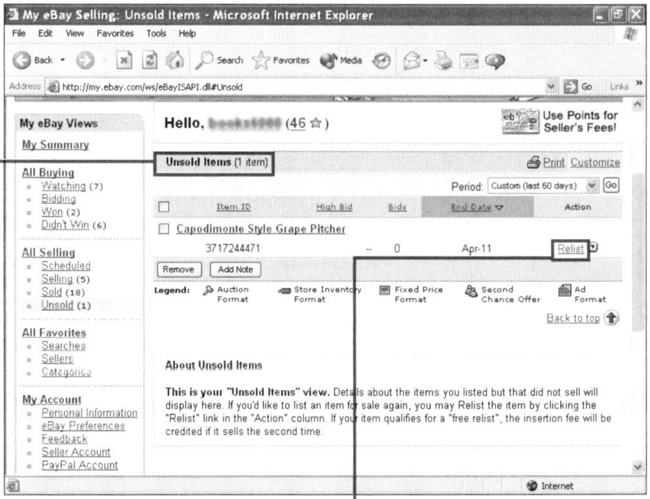

■ The Unsold Items table appears.

■ This table lists any auctions that failed to make a sale.

■ You can click this link to relist an unsold item.

UNDERSTANDING EBAY BIDDING

eBay auctions, particularly traditional and Dutch auctions, stand or fall by the number of bids they receive. When selling an item on eBay, the more bids you receive, the greater the potential to sell the item at a good price.

Proxy Bidding

eBay uses a proxy bidding system to help users bid on auctions. Proxy bidding is a bit confusing at first, but taking time to understand how it works can help you with your auctions. Proxy bidding is designed to make bidding more convenient to the buyer. Normally, a buyer needs to log on to eBay every time he wants to enter a new bid. However, the proxy bidding system lets the bidder enter a maximum price, yet still remain competitive with other bidders. Proxy bidding is built into eBay's auction process, and bidders can choose to take advantage of the system or not.

With the proxy bidding system, eBay bids on your behalf. For example, say you want to bid on a DVD. At the bottom of the auction listing for the DVD, eBay lists the current bid along with a suggestion for the next bid amount, which is slightly more than the current amount. Ordinarily, you just enter the next bid increment and hope to win. Then, you must revisit the page often to see if you are winning, and if you are not, you must enter more bids. However, with proxy bidding, you can enter the maximum amount you are willing to pay for the item, and eBay only bids the amount needed to meet the next bid increment to win the auction, up to the maximum amount you entered.

Say the DVD is currently selling for $5 and you enter the next increment amount to take the winning bid position, which is $5.50. Another user can outbid you later with a bid of $6. If, instead, you enter your maximum bid amount, the highest amount you are willing to pay for the item, eBay can do your bidding for you, so to speak. If you enter $15 as your maximum amount, eBay still only bids $5.50 for you as the bid amount. If another user bids $6, eBay immediately places your proxy bid amount to $6.50 to make you the winning bidder again. This bidding routine continues until your maximum amount is reached. If another bidder bids $15.50, that bidder wins the auction, but at a price beyond what you are willing to pay for the DVD.

Proxy bidding is a bit confusing for new users who do not understand the system is in place within the bidding process. New users look at an auction's bid history and enter what seems like a reasonable amount, only to see the bidding immediately jump to more than their bid. This happens because the previous bidder bid a maximum amount by proxy and eBay keeps upping the bid increments to keep the previous bidder ahead.

Proxy bidding is a huge advantage for buyers because they do not need to return to auctions and rebid every time another user bids more than the winning bid amount. As long as the buyer enters a maximum amount, he or she can simply wait to see if the bid wins or not.

Proxy bidding does not apply to Dutch auctions, however. With Dutch auctions, also called multiple-item auctions, bidders bid on multiples of the same item, and multiple people can win an auction. For example, if there are five of the same DVDs to sell, bidder A might bid for three of the DVDs at $8 each, bidder B bids for one DVD at $10, bidder C bids for one DVD at $12, and bidder D bids for four at $6. At the end of the auction, bidder C is the highest bid, followed by bidder B and bidder A. Bidder D loses the auction. With Dutch auctions, however, the lowest winning bid amount is the final value of the sale. Because bidder A bid the lowest of the winning amount, all the winners pay the lowest winning bid amount, which in this example is $8 for each DVD. To learn more about Dutch auctions, see Chapter 4.

Taking advantage of the proxy bidding system is entirely up to the bidder. Some bidders prefer to forego entering a maximum bid and choose to enter only the minimum bid amount each time. However, doing so requires more time spent monitoring the progress of the auction and entering new bid amounts to maintain the lead in an auction.

Bidding Tips

There are several ways you can increase your chances of winning auctions on eBay. For starters, take advantage of the proxy bidding system by bidding your maximum amount rather than multiple bids of small amounts. This can save you from needing to log on frequently to check your bid price and bid more each time. Plus, it helps to keep you out of bidding wars with other users in which you may end up bidding more than you ever wanted to spend for the item.

Another tip is to always bid a small amount over the recommended bid increment. Going over the bid increment by a few pennies can help you in the case of a tie bid. For example, if the increment amount is $30, bid $30.01 or $30.02. If someone else bids $30, you still win because your bid is slightly more.

If the item you want is available in several auctions, do not bid on more than one auction at a time. Doing so can place you at risk of buying the same item twice. If someone outbids you, and then retracts the bid, leaving you the winning bidder, you still win the auction. Never lose sight of the fact that a bid is a binding contract to purchase the item.

Bidding at the last moment can increase your chances of winning. If you cannot be around to place a bid in the last few moments of an auction, you can use a sniping program to help you. *Sniping* is the act of coming along to win an auction during the last few moments. The bane of many bidders, sniping is a smart and common way to win auctions. Sniping is a legitimate method to win an auction. There are numerous sniping programs you can use, some are free and some charge a monthly fee. Programs like Ezsniper (www.ezsniper.com), Bidnapper (www.bidnapper.com), and AuctionSniper (www.auctionsniper.com) offer free trial versions you can check out and see if you like the program before you buy it. The CD accompanying this book also contains some sniping programs you can try.

Bid Increments

eBay bidding is set up in increments. The increments are determined by ranges. This can also confuse new users. If your auction bidding moves from one range to another in the bidding increments, you can see the bid increment amounts increase. Newer users may wonder, however, why the bidding increments suddenly jump from 50 cents to $1. The table that follows shows the current bid increments eBay uses.

eBay Bid Increments

Current Price	*Bid Increment*
$0.01 – $0.99	$0.05
$1.00 – $4.99	$0.25
$5.00 – $24.99	$0.50
$25.00 – $99.99	$1.00
$100.00 – $249.99	$2.50
$250.00 – $499.99	$5.00
$500.00 – $999.99	$10.00
$1,000.00 – $2,499.99	$25.00
$2,500.00 – $4,999.99	$50.00
$5,000.00 + up	$100.00

HANDLE QUESTIONS FROM EBAY BIDDERS

An important part of managing your auctions is to handle any questions users send you regarding the items you are selling. For example, a potential bidder might want to know more about a flaw you describe in your listing ad, inquire about the origins of the item, or ask about whether you combine shipping for multiple wins.

It is your duty, as the seller, to try to answer any questions as honestly and factually as possible. If you do not know the answer to a question, be honest and state what you do or do not know. Be prompt with your responses, because timeliness can determine whether someone bids on your listing or not. Make a habit of checking your e-mail frequently throughout the day to address any questions that arise.

Answering auction queries is part of the customer service you provide to potential buyers. For that reason, it is essential to use your best communication skills. Always reply to any question with a cordial, friendly tone. You can also use your reply as an opportunity to advertise your other auctions. For example, you might direct the user to another auction for a similar item. A query from another user is a great opportunity to interact with someone viewing your auction.

HANDLE QUESTIONS FROM EBAY BIDDERS

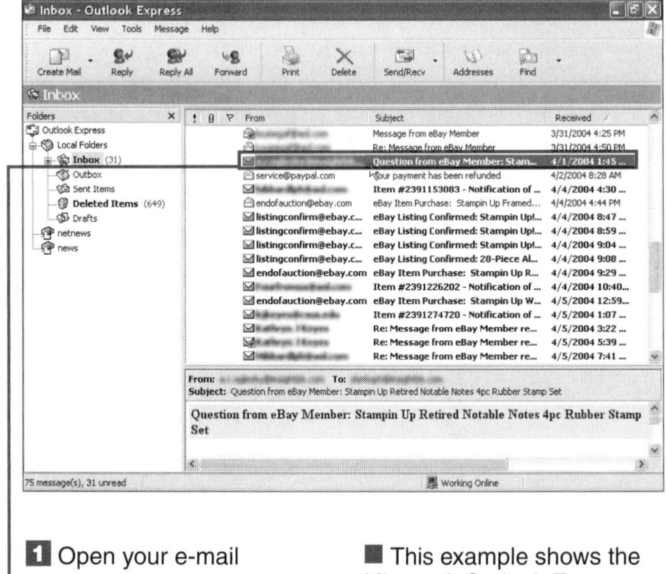

1 Open your e-mail program.

2 Double-click the message you want to view.

■ This example shows the Microsoft Outlook Express program window.

Note: Depending on your e-mail program, you may need to activate different commands to view and respond to e-mail messages.

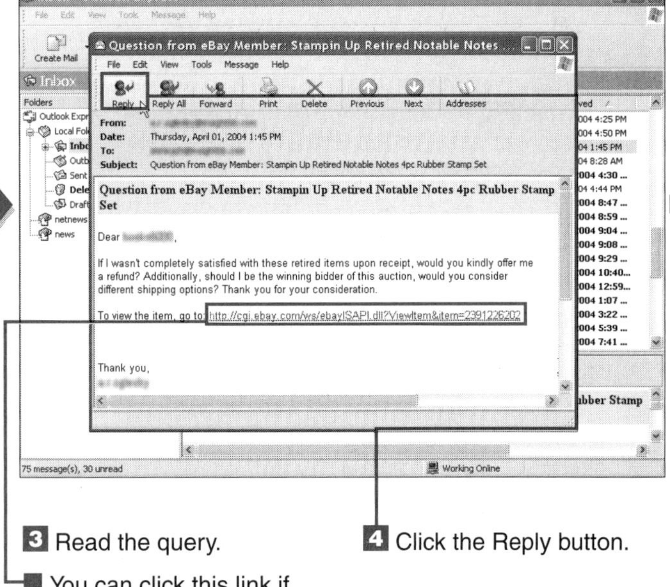

3 Read the query.

■ You can click this link if you need to view the listing.

4 Click the Reply button.

How do I handle an unreasonable request?

✔ Politeness and diplomacy can serve you well with all of your eBay correspondence, but especially with some of the stranger inquiries you may encounter. Start by thanking the bidder for his or her question. State an answer, nicely, to the unreasonable request, and if it is something you decline, say so diplomatically. Encourage the user to continue to bid on your item, and feel free to direct him or her to other items you have for sale. It is never a good idea to ignore a query completely if you want to maintain good customer service.

Someone wants to buy my item outside of the eBay system. How do I respond?

✔ Offers to buy an auction item off of eBay violates eBay policy. Be especially wary of users asking to pay you through a wire transfer service, such as Western Union. Wire transfers are not traceable, and any item sold outside of eBay is not covered by the eBay Purchase Protection Program. You can contact eBay to report the violation, or read the eBay policies to learn more about such violations. See Chapter 12 to learn more about ways to handle auction problems.

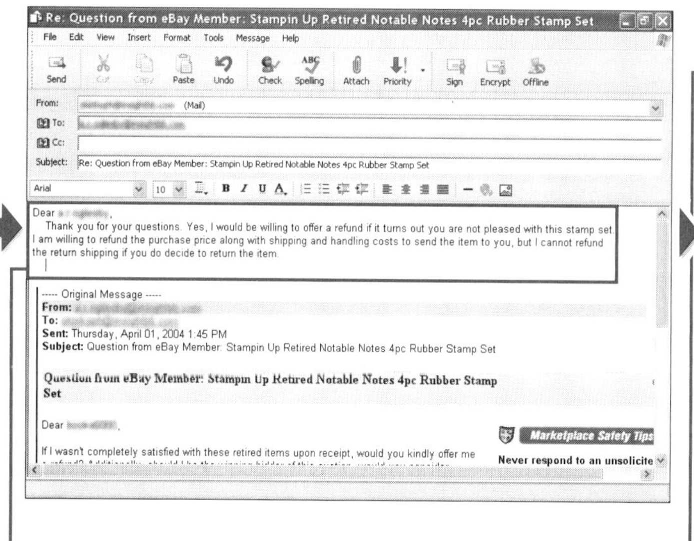

5 Type a response to the query, being sure to answer all of the bidder's questions.

■ You can refer the bidder to other listings currently running, or invite the user to check back for other auctions.

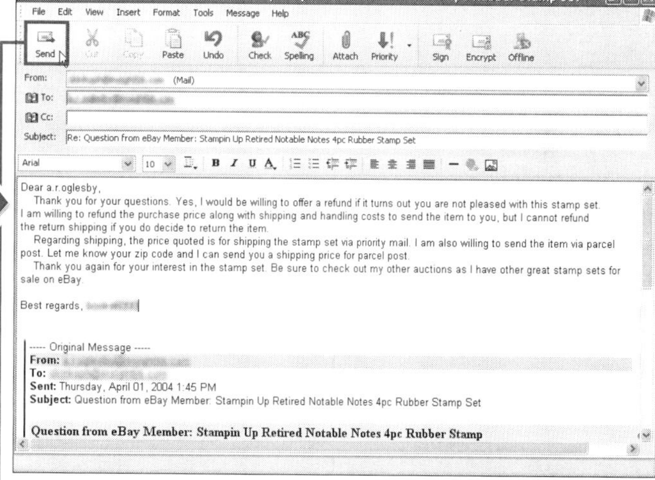

6 Click Send.

■ Your e-mail program sends your reply to the bidder.

CHECK A BIDDER'S FEEDBACK RATING

As you monitor your auctions, you can check on the people who make bids on your items. An eBay user's feedback rating gives you a good idea of the person's online reputation. Although you cannot always take time to check out every bidder, especially if you are away from the computer when the auction ends, it is a good practice. Feedback can warn you of a potential nonpaying buyer or of a difficult-to-please customer.

Along with a feedback rating, you can view a user's feedback report to see what other eBay users say about the transactions they exchanged with the user. Always check for negative feedback, and be sure to read the negative notation. Be on the lookout for trends that might affect your own sale. For example, you might watch out for users who fail to communicate with the seller, or users who have a poor payment history. You should also look out for users who immediately leave negative feedback without contacting the seller to work out any problems with a transaction.

If any potential bidder's poor feedback rating worries you, you can cancel the bid and block the user from bidding again. See the next section, "Cancel a Bid," to learn more.

CHECK A BIDDER'S FEEDBACK RATING

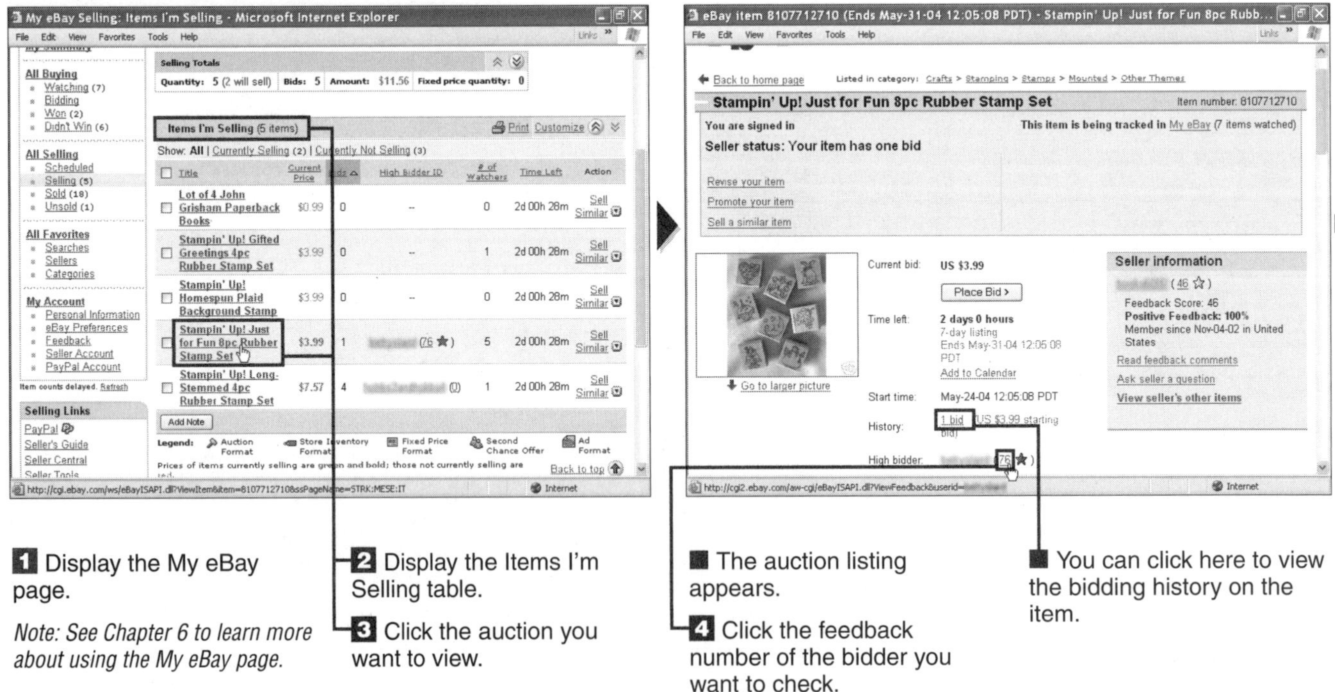

1 Display the My eBay page.

Note: See Chapter 6 to learn more about using the My eBay page.

2 Display the Items I'm Selling table.

3 Click the auction you want to view.

■ The auction listing appears.

4 Click the feedback number of the bidder you want to check.

■ You can click here to view the bidding history on the item.

What constitutes a poor feedback rating?

✔ Experienced users argue over an exact rating number, but generally speaking, anything under 98 percent is cause for a deeper look into the feedback report. Avoid buying or selling from users with poor ratings, or at the very least, take time to read the negative reports that created the lower feedback rating. Are the negatives from inexperienced users who did not know how the feedback system works, or are the complaints more serious in nature, such as failure to pay? Is the feedback recent, or from long ago? Viewing the comments can tell you a lot about the competency and professionalism of a buyer or seller.

Can a user have a negative feedback report removed?

✔ Feedback is permanent. You can add a comment to a feedback comment, and in extreme cases, eBay can remove a negative feedback. Or if two users leave negative feedback for each other and then decide to take it back, they can go through eBay's third-party dispute resolution service, Square Trade (www.squaretrade.com), for help. However, there is a $20 charge for the service. Negative feedback is always a last resort after exhausting every means possible to work out a problem, and should be given out carefully. See Chapter 11 to learn more about how feedback works on eBay.

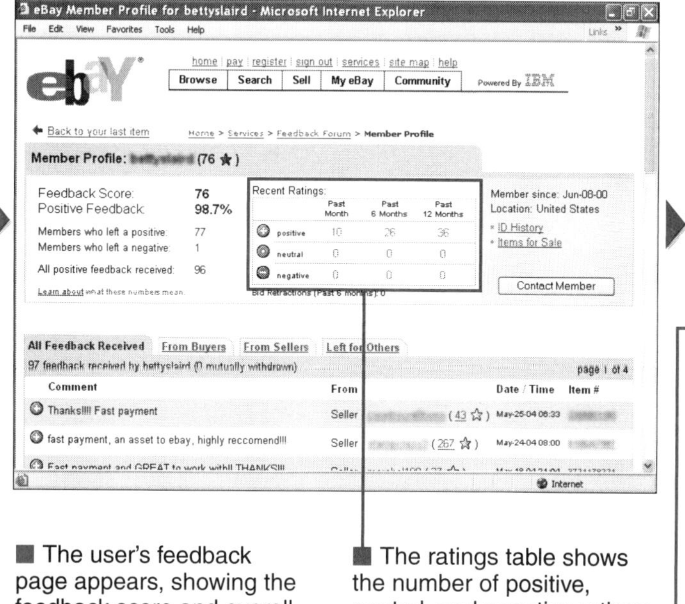

■ The user's feedback page appears, showing the feedback score and overall rating.

■ The ratings table shows the number of positive, neutral, and negative ratings.

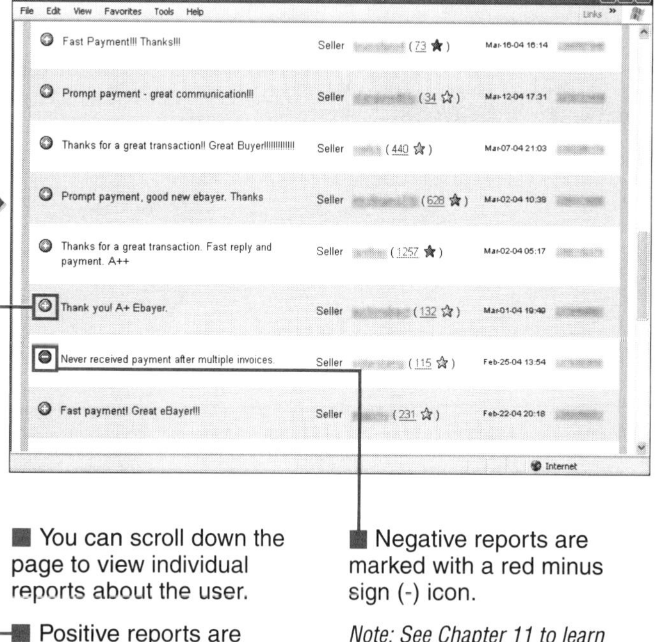

■ You can scroll down the page to view individual reports about the user.

■ Positive reports are marked with a green plus sign (+) icon.

■ Negative reports are marked with a red minus sign (-) icon.

Note: See Chapter 11 to learn more about using feedback in eBay.

CANCEL A BID

You can cancel any bid made on your auction, but you need a valid reason to do so. For example, if you feel a bidder has too many negative feedback reports, you can cancel a bid. Or if a bidder is located overseas and you clearly state in your listing you do not ship internationally, you can cancel the user's bid. From time to time, a bidder may ask you to cancel a bid if he or she wants to back out of the auction. Doing so is up to you, as the seller, however. You may also need to cancel bids to end an auction early.

When a seller ends a bid, it is called canceling, when a buyer ends a bid, it is called retracting. After a bid is cancelled, it cannot be reinstated.

To cancel a bid, you must fill out an eBay form. You need to know the number of the auction and the User ID of the bidder you want to cancel, and you must provide a reason for canceling. The form allows you 80 characters to explain your reason. When you submit the form, eBay sends the user an explanation of the cancellation, and also cancels the bid in your auction.

CANCEL A BID

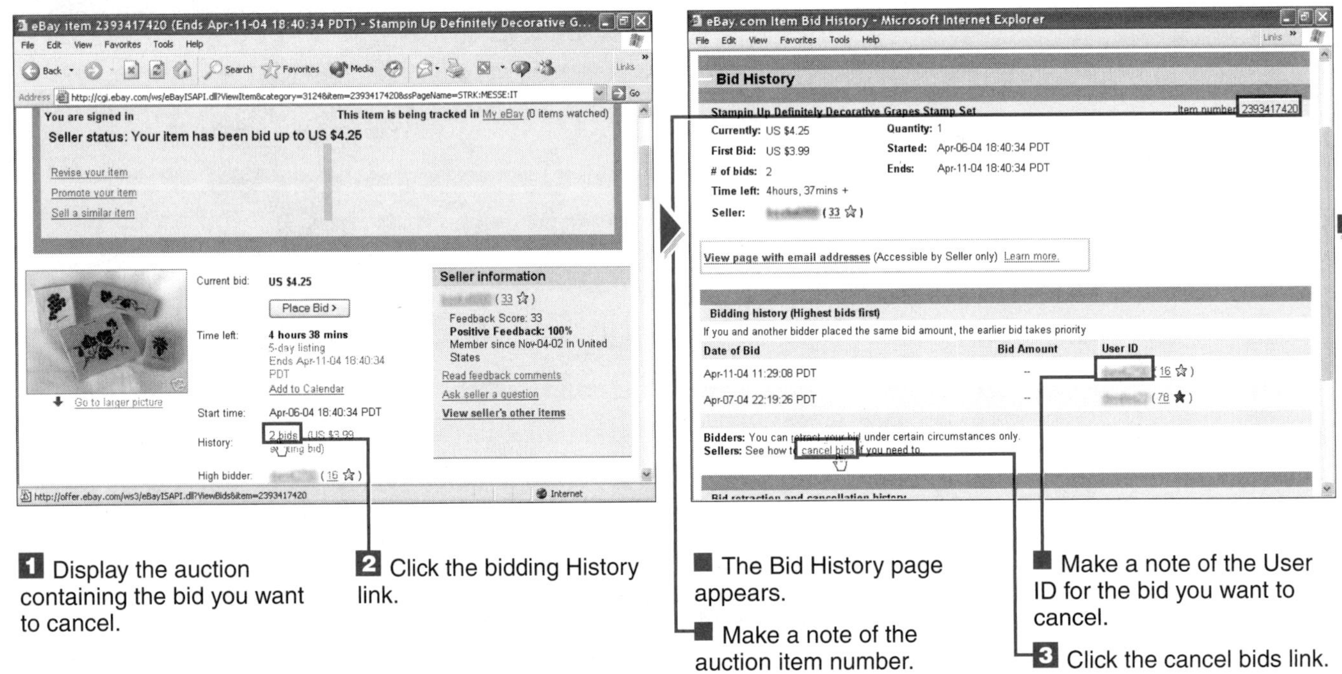

1 Display the auction containing the bid you want to cancel.

2 Click the bidding History link.

■ The Bid History page appears.

■ Make a note of the auction item number.

■ Make a note of the User ID for the bid you want to cancel.

3 Click the cancel bids link.

What rules apply to bid retractions?

✔ eBay allows bid retractions only under certain circumstances. If you entered an incorrect bid amount, you can retract the bid, but then you must immediately correct the mistake with the amount you intended to bid the first time. eBay also allows bid retractions if the seller significantly changes the description, if the seller's contact information is invalid, or if someone has stolen your User ID to make a bid. Retractions also fall under timing rules. You cannot retract a bid during the last 12 hours of an auction. The seller can cancel your bid during that time, if he or she agrees to your request.

As a buyer, how do I retract a bid?

✔ You must fill out the Bid Retraction form to retract a bid. You can find the form at http://offer.ebay.com/ws/eBayISAPI.dll?RetractBidShow.

Does eBay keep track of bid retractions?

✔ Yes. eBay keeps track of bid retractions as part of the feedback rating system, and if you make too many retractions, eBay can suspend your account.

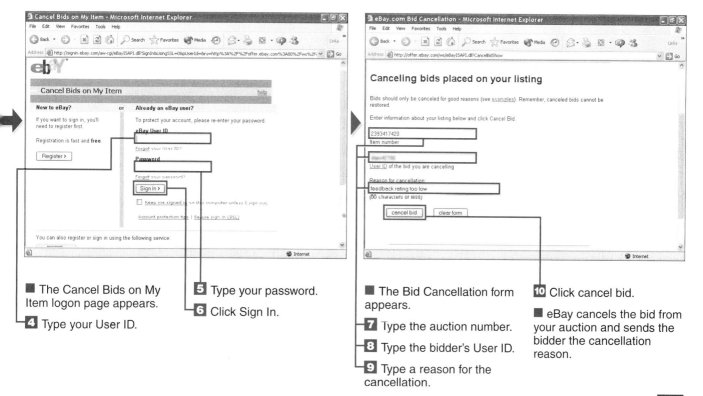

■ The Cancel Bids on My Item logon page appears.

4 Type your User ID.

5 Type your password.

6 Click Sign In.

■ The Bid Cancellation form appears.

7 Type the auction number.

8 Type the bidder's User ID.

9 Type a reason for the cancellation.

10 Click cancel bid.

■ eBay cancels the bid from your auction and sends the bidder the cancellation reason.

CREATE A PRE-APPROVED BIDDERS LIST

You can control the people who participate in your auctions by creating a pre-approved bidders list. This allows you to limit your auction to a specified group of users. This feature is helpful if you want to pre-qualify your bidders, particularly for a high-priced item. Before the bidder can place a bid on your auction, he or she must first contact you for approval. This gives you a chance to verify the identity of the bidder and check his or her feedback rating. You can also use a pre-approved bidders list for Buy It Now auctions.

The pre-approved bidders list is good for the current auction, and you can pre-approve bidders up to the end of the auction. If a bidder tries to place a bid, eBay warns the reader of the restricted bidding and asks the user to contact you via e-mail. To approve bidders, you simply add their name to the list and let them know they can now place a bid.

You need to note the auction number and the User ID of the person you want to add to your list. You can control your pre-approved bidders list by adding and deleting bidders as you see fit. The list is only good for one auction. To use a pre-approved bidders list with another auction, you must create a new list.

CREATE A PRE-APPROVED BIDDERS LIST

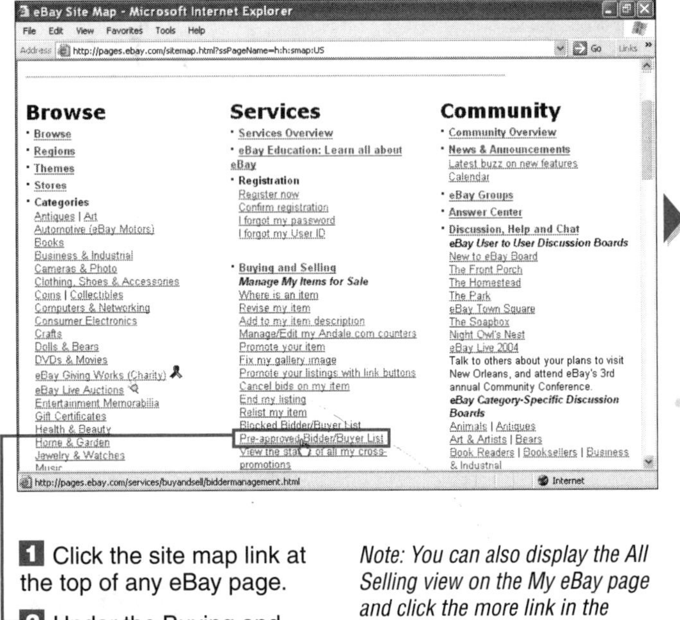

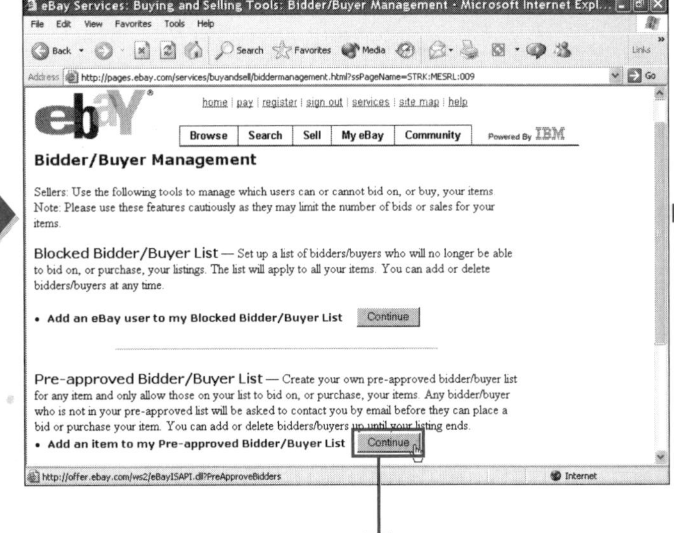

1 Click the site map link at the top of any eBay page.

2 Under the Buying and Selling heading, click the Pre-approved Bidder/Buyer List link.

Note: You can also display the All Selling view on the My eBay page and click the more link in the Selling Links pane to find a list of selling-related links.

■ The Bidder/Buyer Management page appears.

3 Click Continue under the Pre-approved Bidder/Buyer List section.

Are there instances where a pre-approved bidders list is a bad thing?

✔ In recent years, some pre-approval-based auctions have been used in scam auctions in which disreputable users offer an ordinarily high-priced item for a very low price in an effort to lure bidders, and then turn around and offer the item off of eBay with payments made through a wire transfer service. For this reason, pre-approved bidders lists do not always have a good reputation on eBay. To seek advice from other sellers whether the pre-approved bidders list is a good thing or not, be sure to visit eBay's discussion boards. Learn more about eBay discussion boards and chat rooms in Chapters 13 and 14.

Is a pre-approved bidders list the same as blocking someone from bidding on my auction?

✔ No. A blocked bidders list is a list of users you do not want to bid on any of your auctions for as long as you are a registered user on eBay, while the pre-approved bidders list is good only for the current auction. You may want to use a blocked bidders list to block users with whom you have experienced trouble in a past auction. You can learn more about creating a blocked bidders list in Chapter 12.

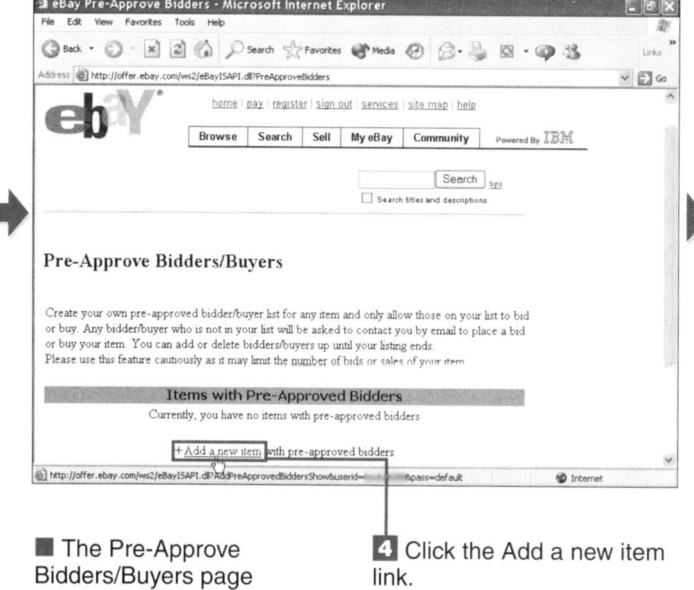

■ The Pre-Approve Bidders/Buyers page appears.

4 Click the Add a new item link.

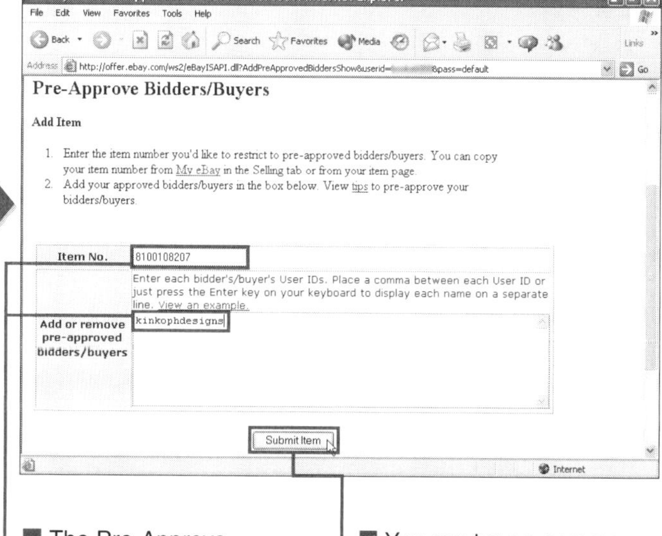

■ The Pre-Approve Bidders/Buyers form appears.

5 Type the number for the auction to which you want to assign the list.

6 Type the User ID you want to add to the list.

■ You can type a comma to separate IDs, or you can press Enter to place each ID on a new line in the list.

7 Click Submit Item.

■ eBay adds the user to the list.

REVISE AN AUCTION

You can revise an auction if you need to make minor changes to the listing. The types of changes you can make, however, are limited based on the amount of time left on the auction. eBay imposes some restrictions on changes based on the 12-hour rule. If the auction has less than 12 hours remaining, you can make changes to increase the listing's visibility, but you are not allowed to make changes to the existing description text. If the auction is newly listed with lots of time remaining, you can make changes to the information, add features such as a Buy It Now option, or change the picture.

eBay also imposes restrictions on changes if an auction has already received bids. With a regular auction that has no bids, you can revise just about everything but the auction format. eBay does not allow you to change the auction format in midstream, so you cannot change a regular auction into a fixed-price auction or vice versa. If your auction already has a bid, you can only add to the description rather than change any existing text, or add features designed to increase the listing's visibility, such as bold the auction listing title or add a color highlight.

If your listing is for a fixed-price auction or an eBay Store, you can change the description and features before the 12-hour rule, but with only 12 hours remaining you are limited to changing the price or quantity and visibility features only.

REVISE AN AUCTION

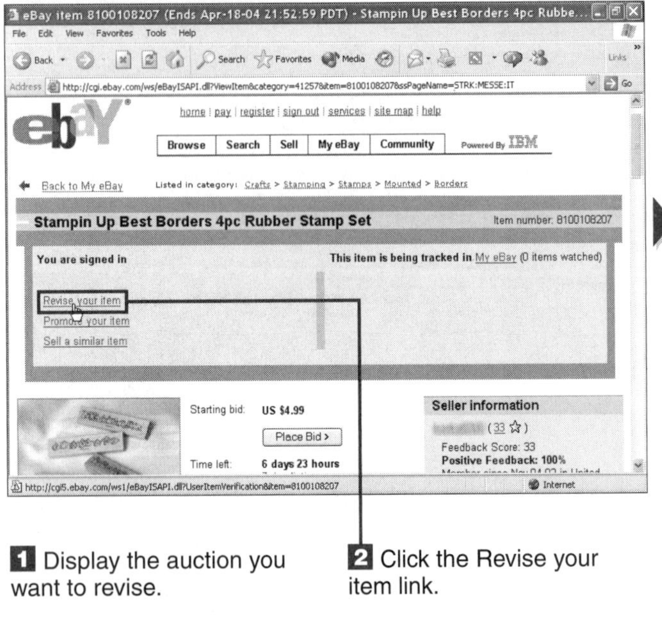

1 Display the auction you want to revise.

2 Click the Revise your item link.

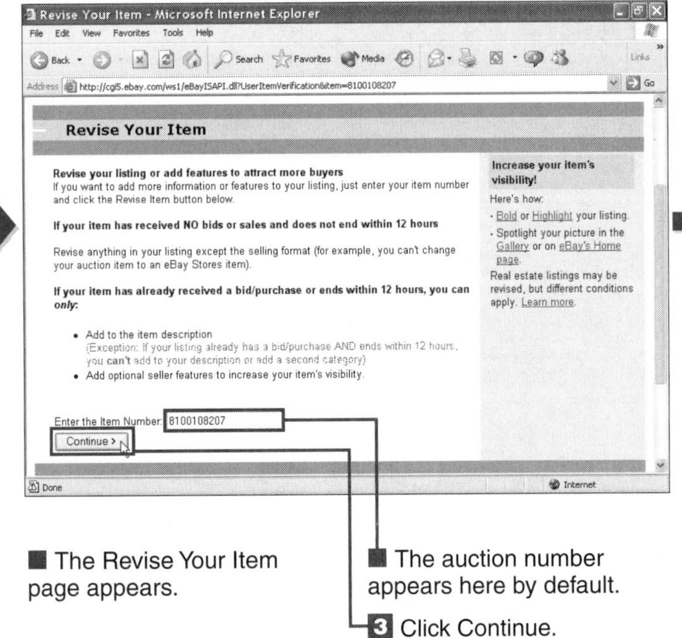

■ The Revise Your Item page appears.

■ The auction number appears here by default.

3 Click Continue.

Is it better to revise an auction, or end it early and relist it?

✔ That depends on how extensive your revisions are. If you are completely revamping the entire description, for example, you should probably end the auction and relist. If the changes are minor, such as adding a sentence or changing the photo, then making a few adjustments to the listing will not cause any problems for you or the bidders. To learn more about ending an auction, see the next section.

Does eBay offer a full list of what revisions are allowed in a posted auction?

✔ Yes. To view a complete list of guidelines for relisting, visit the following link: http://pages.ebay.com/help/sell/questions/revise-item.html. This page spells out what changes can occur before the 12-hour rule, and what changes can occur within the last 12 hours of your auction.

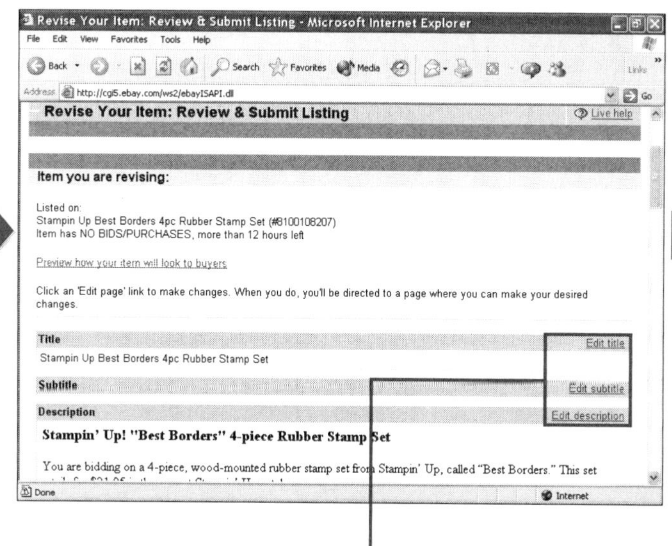

■ Your auction's Revise Your Item: Review & Submit Listing page, a part of the seller's form for creating a listing, appears.

4 Click the Edit link for the section you want to revise and make your revisions.

5 Scroll to the bottom of the page and click the Save Changes button.

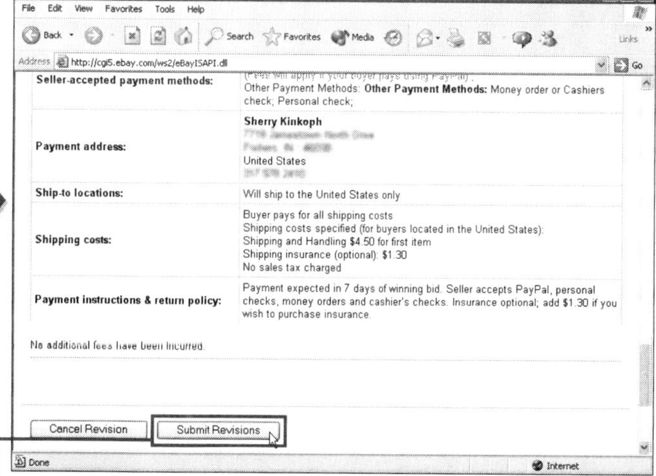

■ The Revise Your Item: Review & Submit Listing page reappears.

6 Scroll to the bottom of the page and click Submit Revisions.

■ eBay adds your revisions to the listing and displays the word Revised next to the Description section of the ad.

END AN AUCTION EARLY

You can end an auction early before the actual expiration time. Although generally frowned upon by eBay, you may need to cancel an auction for a variety of reasons. For example, perhaps the item you were auctioning is suddenly damaged or no longer available, or your listing contained some critical errors regarding the item for sale. You can use the End My Auction Early form to cancel an auction.

Be very careful about choosing to end any auction, even if you have legitimate reasons for doing so. You can be reported as a non-selling seller, for example, so make sure your reason for canceling is a good one. If the auction has already accumulated bids, you must cancel the bids before ending the auction. See the section "Cancel a Bid," earlier in this chapter, to learn more about this action. Make sure you precede the bid cancellations with an e-mail to each bidder explaining why you are canceling, and, if you plan to relist the item with corrected information, mention this in the e-mail. If you fail to contact the bidders, you may end up with some angry customers who may report you to eBay.

END AN AUCTION EARLY

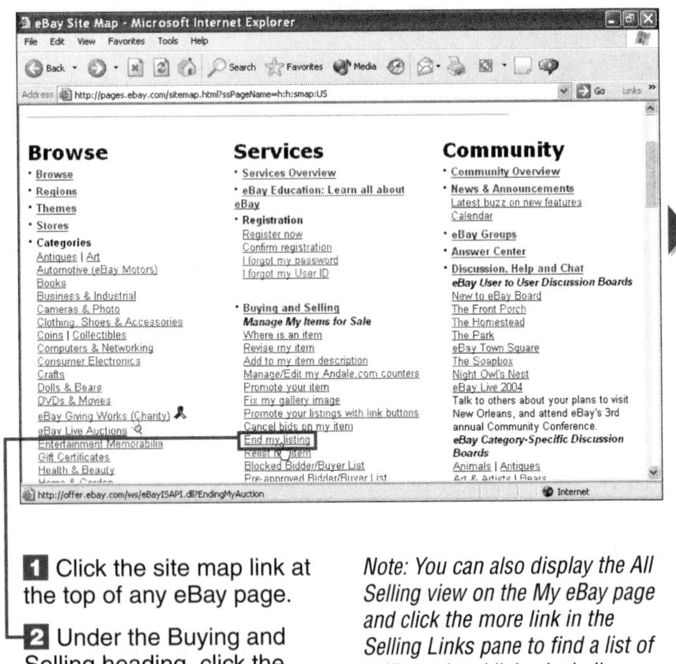

1 Click the site map link at the top of any eBay page.

2 Under the Buying and Selling heading, click the End my listing link.

Note: You can also display the All Selling view on the My eBay page and click the more link in the Selling Links pane to find a list of selling-related links, including a link for ending your listing.

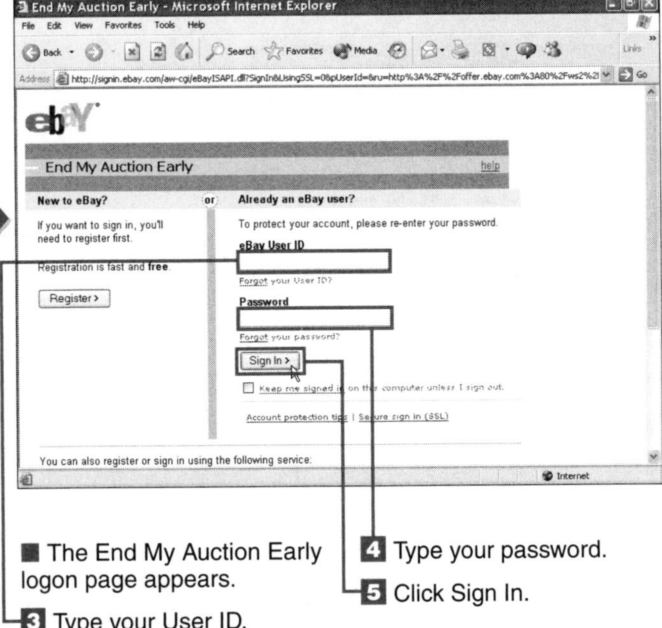

■ The End My Auction Early logon page appears.

3 Type your User ID.

4 Type your password.

5 Click Sign In.

Can I end an auction if it is not selling for the price I hoped for?

✔ No. Ending an auction early in this situation, especially if others already placed bids, is considered fee avoidance. eBay seriously investigates reports of auctions that appear to end early if a desired sale price is not met. This is a violation of eBay policy. To learn more about auction violations, see Chapter 4.

Can I decide not to end the auction in the middle of the process?

✔ Yes. You can close out any eBay activity by clicking another link or clicking the Back browser navigation button to return to the page you want to view. Until you click the designated submission button, the form is not complete.

Am I penalized for ending an auction early?

✔ No. You still incur insertion fees for posting the auction, but no final value fees.

Why does eBay ask me to log on again if I am already signed in?

✔ Repeating the logon procedure for a special task is a safety precaution eBay employs. This keeps other users from ending your auctions for you. If you leave yourself signed in to eBay and walk away from your computer, other users can still use your account; however, when they encounter a repeating logon procedure, they cannot continue without knowing your ID and password.

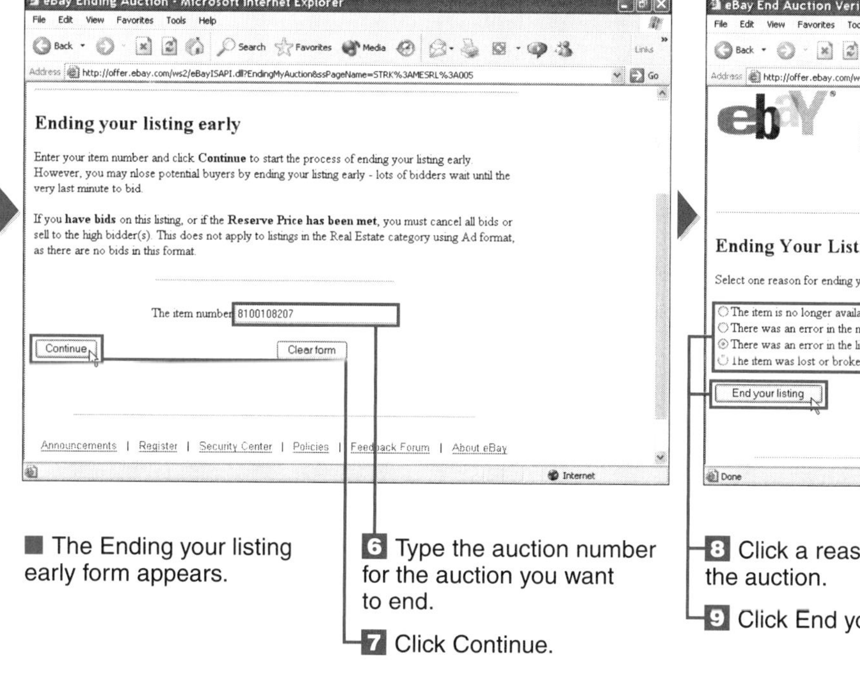

■ The Ending your listing early form appears.

6 Type the auction number for the auction you want to end.

7 Click Continue.

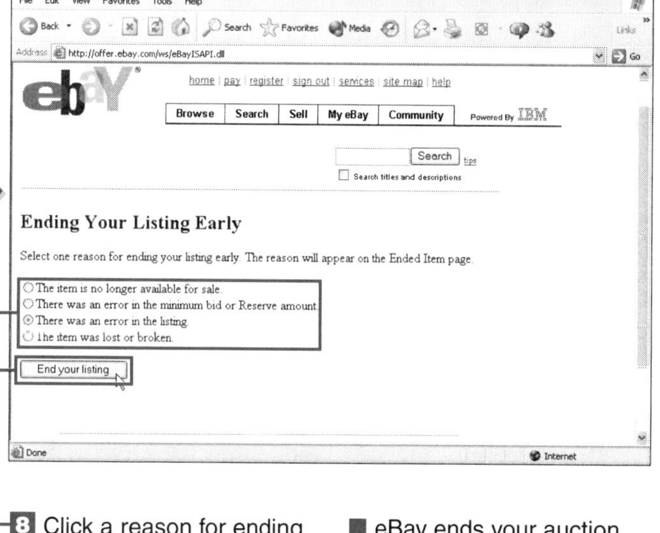

8 Click a reason for ending the auction.

9 Click End your listing.

■ eBay ends your auction listing.

ATTRACT MORE BIDDERS TO YOUR LISTINGS

Unlike a regular marketplace where you can physically display your goods to draw buyers, attracting bidders is a bit more complicated on eBay. In the digital realm, there are fewer ways to have someone look at your item; however, you can employ a few tried and true practices and see if they work.

Basic Tips for Attracting Bidders

To begin to draw the attention of potential bidders, you need to list the auction in the right category for the item. For example, listing a videogame in the Pottery & Glass category may not bring many casual lookers to your listing. Secondly, learn to write good auction titles. eBay searches, typically employed by users looking for certain items, first search through auction title text to find matches, and then look through description text, but only if the option for doing so is selected. Make sure your auction titles contain the most common keywords users would type to look for your item. Research into similar auctions, especially those that receive a lot of bids, can help you discover keywords that attract users. To learn more about writing good auction titles and descriptions, see Chapter 4.

Luck and timing are also other factors in successful auctions. Sometimes the buyers to whom you want to appeal are not visiting eBay while your auction is posted. Keep this in mind as you experiment with what attracts bidders and what does not. Also remember that some items may have more seasonal appeal than others. Selling a pair of ski boots in July, for example, may bring less than top-dollar price, as opposed to selling the boots during ski season.

List in Two Categories

According to eBay, listing an item in two categories can increase the final price by 18 percent. However, eBay's insertion fee doubles when you add a second category to your item, so perhaps eBay has another motivation to suggest a second category. Yet, giving eBay the benefit of the doubt, you can see where a double category listing can increase your auction's potential bidder pool. This is especially true of items that easily span two or more categories. For example, your grandmother's antique vase fits in both the Antiques and the Glass & Pottery categories.

You can easily designate a second category listing in the eBay seller's form. You can also edit an existing listing to appear in a second category. You cannot list real estate or cars in two categories, nor can you list multiple-item auctions, called Dutch auctions, in two categories.

Maximize Auction Length

The length of your auction can play a big part in the volume of bidders you attract. The longer the listing length, the more time for people to find your auction. More people will view a seven-day auction than a three-day auction. The hour you start and end your auction can also affect the number of bidders for your item. Running an auction from a Monday to a Friday may not bring as many bids as ending the same auction on a Sunday. You can learn more about choosing the best auction time in the section "Auction Timing Issues," later in this chapter.

Improve Visibility with Listing Upgrades

Some users strongly believe in eBay's listing upgrades, such as those for increasing a listing's visibility on a search page or in a category browse list. Visibility upgrade features include making the auction title bold, assigning a color bar behind the title, or featuring a photo in the Gallery listing area. Again, eBay's data suggests greater auction success for listings that use visibility upgrades. For example, eBay's data research says making your title appear bold or adding a color band to the title can increase your item's final value price by 25 percent. Placing a thumbnail image of your item photo on the search page results can increase an item's final price by 11 percent. Placing your ad in the Featured area of the search page increases the final value price by 65 percent. Whether your own auctions experience such increases using listing upgrades is really a matter of opinion.

As with other add-on features in eBay, upgrading your listing to include increased visibility can range greatly in price. You can learn more about the individual upgrade features in Chapters 4 and 5. If you do not mind spending the extra fees, you can try out some of the options to find out if they make any difference in your own sales. If you find something that works, and do not mind the additional costs, then take advantage of the edge eBay's visibility upgrades can offer you.

Cross-Promote with eBay Stores

If you create an eBay Store, you can participate in cross-promotional advertising of your wares. An eBay storefront is a one-stop spot to sell your items; your own Web page within eBay. You can list as many items as you want with fixed prices. A plus to using an eBay Store is that you can list your items for sale for longer periods of time, or indefinitely. One the best features of online stores is the ability to promote other items you are selling within an ad. Buyers can quickly link to other listings of interest within your store.

You can try an eBay Store for 30 days for free. To learn more about creating your own eBay Store, see Chapter 23.

Offer Customer-Friendly Features

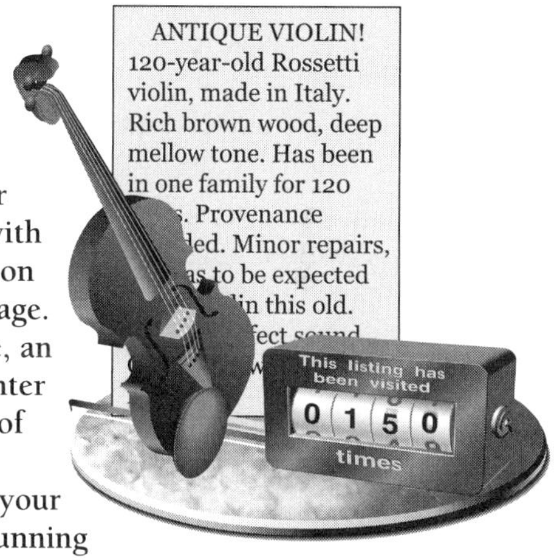

Another way to generate sales is to provide your customers with useful tools on the listing page. For example, an auction counter keeps track of how many people visit your auction. A running count of visitors can make your listing appear to be a hot item among potential bidders. You can learn more about counters in the section "Add a Counter to Your Listing," later in this section.

If you prefer not to list a flat shipping rate, you can include a shipping calculator in your auction. This allows bidders to calculate the shipping and handling costs to send the item to their ZIP code. See the section "Add a Shipping Calculator" to learn more.

On the subject of shipping, consider offering your customers shipping discounts for multiple items they buy. Also, do not overlook the expanded sales potential you can generate by shipping your items overseas. Although international shipping costs are higher, and you must include extra documentation for customs, shipping overseas is not as difficult as you may first imagine. See the section "Offer International Shipping," later in this chapter, to learn more.

AUCTION TIMING ISSUES

The timing of your auction can determine the number of bidders you attract. The key to auction timing is running your auction at a time likely to maximize traffic, yet be a convenience to buyers. When it comes to auction timing, the seller has a great deal of control over the matter. You can choose an auction length when you create your auction listing. The start and end time of an auction is determined by the time of day you post the auction.

Evaluating Auction Lengths

You can select from several auction lengths when creating your listing. eBay auctions can run one, three, five, seven, or 10 days in length. You incur an extra charge when you choose to run a 10-day auction. Your choice of length may depend on the item. For example, if you are selling a ticket to a concert or sporting event, you may need to run a one-day auction. The seven-day auction is the most common auction length used by sellers. It offers the longest exposure for an item, without incurring an extra fee. Many sellers prefer to run a seven-day auction from Sunday to Sunday, gaining a full week of viewing, plus pulling in weekend bidders who log on to shop on eBay while they are at home. Others like to use the five-day or three-day approach, posting their items to fall into the key period of weekend viewing and Sunday auction close.

Pick a Good Start Time

Auction start and end times are often important, too. Many users feel that by ending their auctions in the evening hours, they are more likely to receive a greater number of bids from users home from work. If you are not around to post an auction during key evening hours, you can schedule the auction to go live when you are away. For a fee, eBay posts your auction for you at the designated time, even if you are away from the computer.

Factor In Time Zones

A part of determining start and end times is factoring in time zones. If you sell primarily overseas, you need to consider prime viewing hours for that particular part of the globe. The same holds true in the United States. eBay operates on Pacific time because eBay is located in California. If you end an auction at midnight Pacific time, bidders on the East Coast probably will not see the end of the auction because they are three hours ahead of Pacific time, and probably fast asleep. Some users love to watch the final moments of an auction and place a bid. On the other hand, with proxy bidding — bidding one time with the maximum amount you are willing to pay — auction end times do not really matter as much. Using a sniping program to automatically bid at the last moment for you also takes away the need to see the end of an auction — see Chapter 7 to learn more. As with other aspects of eBay, trial and error may be your best guides to finding the best auction lengths and times for your listings. See Appendix B, "eBay Time Zones," for a handy time zone chart.

OFFER INTERNATIONAL SHIPPING

You can reach an even wider market for your goods and services by selling to users overseas. Many eBay users may feel a bit intimidated selling their items overseas. The process, however, is not much more complicated than selling items domestically. American goods are in high demand outside of the United States, and purchasing them through eBay can often be a huge cost savings for the foreign buyer. Language is not really a barrier, either, because many people speak and write English around the world. Payment is not a problem because PayPal is now the leading international online currency for global users.

Shipping Costs

Shipping costs are significantly more expensive, of course, and you need to include an invoice of the item for customs. Customs charges can be expensive for higher-priced items. eBay offers you a variety of tools to help you calculate costs for overseas buyers. All of the major shipping carriers can help you complete the appropriate documentation needed to help the item pass through customs. For example, the Postal Service and UPS can help you fill out documentation online for overseas shipments. Different regulations can come into play based on the value of the item. For example, items valued at more than $500 require a shipper's export declaration to pass through U.S. Customs.

Choosing Countries

You can specify which countries you are willing to ship to when you complete the eBay seller's form. You may want to start with some easier destinations, such as Canada, because the Postal Service can assist you. Canadian buyers are responsible for paying duty fees, a goods and services tax, and in the case of higher-priced goods, customs fees. In most instances, buyers pay these fees upon receiving a shipment from the United States.

Choosing a Currency

You can also pick which currency you want to accept, which is typically your own. Do not worry about converting currency. eBay's international sites offer currency conversion programs that overseas users can utilize to help them make payments. You can also find a Universal Currency Converter on the U.S. eBay site at http://pages.ebay.com/services/buyandsell/currencyconverter.html.

For more information about international selling, see eBay's help pages. You can also read about U.S. government export restrictions at www.bis.doc.gov/ComplianceAndEnforcement/index.htm#LTC. These regulations may apply to the item you want to sell, particularly if it is a foodstuff, software, or an agricultural product. You can also talk to other eBay sellers who sell successfully overseas by visiting the eBay discussion boards. See Chapter 14 to learn more about communicating with other eBay users.

PROMOTE YOUR AUCTIONS WITH LISTING UPGRADES

You can enhance your listing after you post an auction by adding listing upgrades. eBay's listing upgrades are designed to help users promote their auctions. Listing upgrades primarily focus on ways to increase an auction's visibility. Users typically find their way to your auction listings through a casual browsing of the eBay categories, or by conducting a keyword search. As users browse the list of auctions in a category or a list of search results, listing upgrades can help a listing stand out in the crowd.

For example, you can choose to make your auction title bold, or add a band of color to the title. Either upgrade can help draw the attention of potential bidders. You can also choose to include a thumbnail photo of the item in the Gallery area of a list of auctions.

eBay charges additional fees for listing upgrades; however, you may find the cost worthwhile if you end up attracting more bidders. If you do not mind the extra expense, you can try a few upgrade options and test their effectiveness. You can also test listing upgrades by looking out for them when browsing or searching for auctions yourself.

PROMOTE YOUR AUCTIONS WITH LISTING UPGRADES

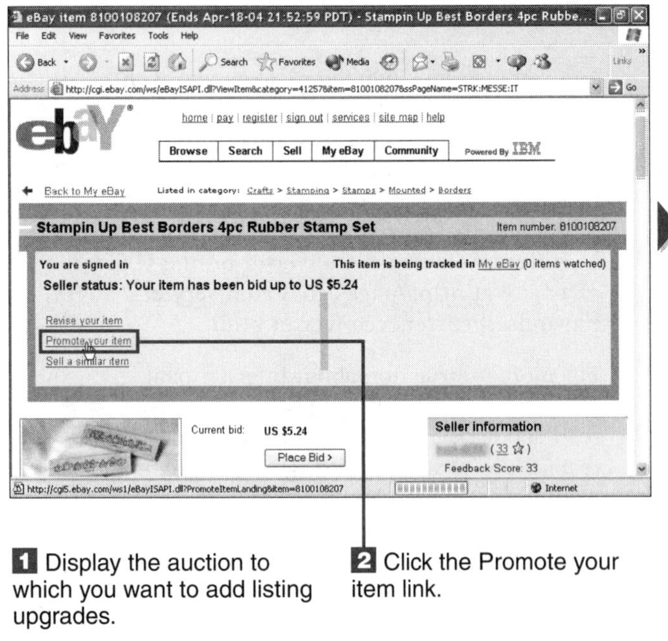

1 Display the auction to which you want to add listing upgrades.

2 Click the Promote your item link.

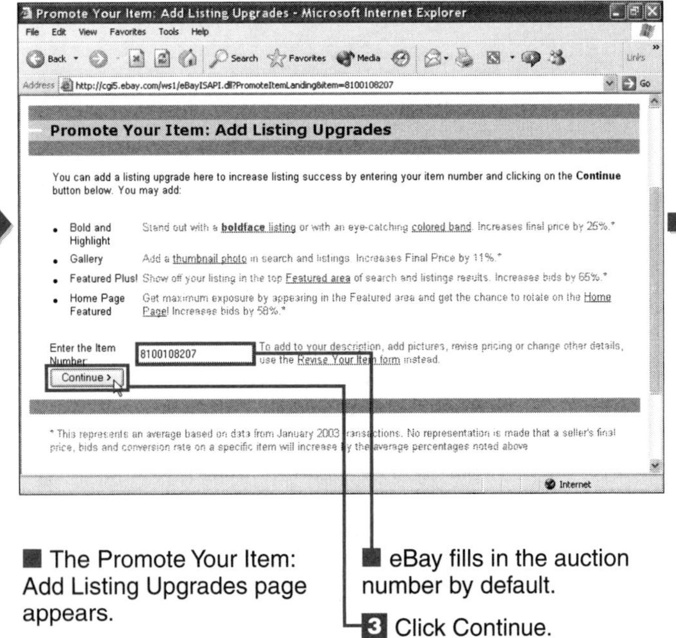

■ The Promote Your Item: Add Listing Upgrades page appears.

■ eBay fills in the auction number by default.

3 Click Continue.

Are listing upgrades the same as revising an auction?

✔ No. When you revise an auction, you can make changes to the auction title, description text, terms of sale, and photos. eBay limits the amount of changes you can make depending on when the auction ends. If the auction has less than 12 hours to go, you cannot make too many changes to the auction. If the auction still has plenty of time remaining, eBay allows you to change a few more listing items. You can, however, add listing upgrades when you edit a listing. To learn more about revising an auction to make changes to the text, see Chapter 7.

Where can I learn more about eBay's study regarding the success of listing upgrades?

✔ For more information about the research, visit the following URL: http://pages.ebay.com/sellercentral/tools.html#programs.

Does eBay offer any advertising tools I can use?

✔ You can sign up for the eBay Keywords, eBay's keyword advertising program, to help you advertise your listings through banners and text ad links. To learn more about this service and its costs, visit the following eBay page at https://ebay.admarketplace.net/ebay/servlet/ebay.

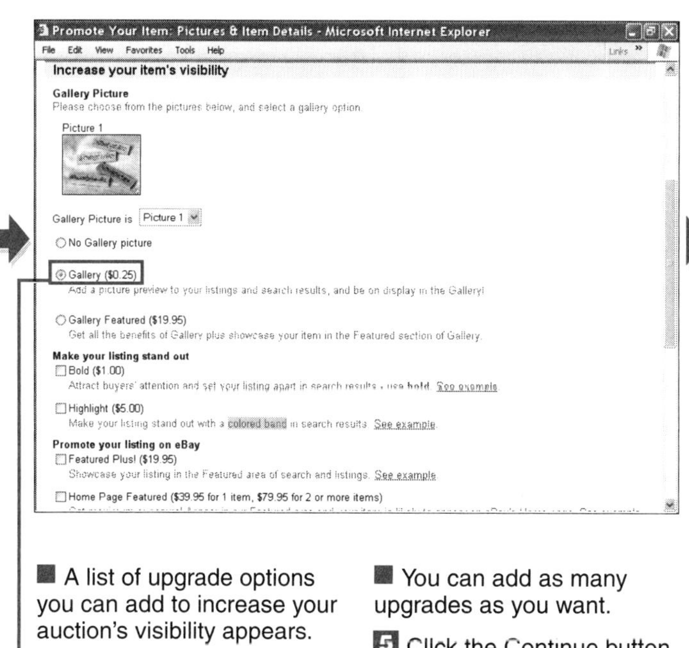

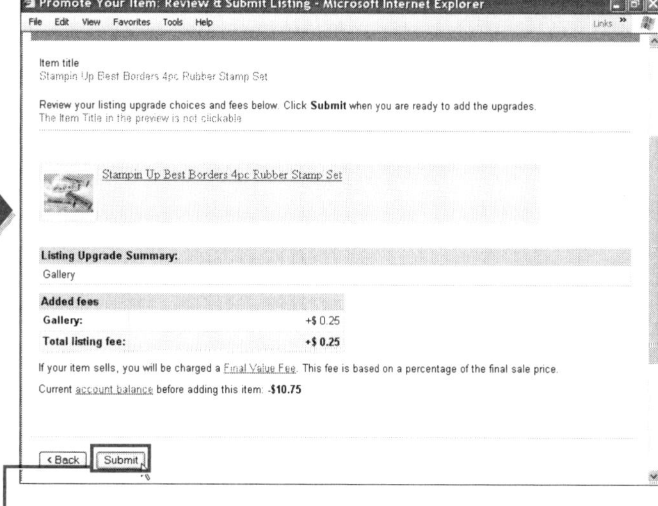

■ A list of upgrade options you can add to increase your auction's visibility appears.

4 Scroll through the list of options and click the ones you want to add.

■ You can add as many upgrades as you want.

5 Click the Continue button at the bottom of the page.

■ A summary of your selections and the resulting additional fees appears.

6 Click Submit.

■ eBay applies the upgrades to your auction.

ADD A COUNTER TO YOUR LISTING

You can use a counter in your listing auction to keep track of how many users stop to visit your auction. Not only does it count each time someone views a page, it can also help generate excitement over your item. The more people who view your auction and see how many other people are viewing it, the more the item seems like a hot deal.

You can add a counter to your listing for free. eBay offers two styles of counters — Andale and LED — and one hidden counter. The Andale-style counter displays a regular-looking number as the counter. The green LED-style counter resembles a digital display, much like your digital clock. If you choose to add a hidden counter to your auction, only you can see the number of hits, or views, your page accrues.

You can designate a specific counter when you fill out the Pictures & Details page, the third page on the eBay seller's form. The very first time you create an auction, the counter display is set to No counter unless you choose to add a counter to your listing.

ADD A COUNTER TO YOUR LISTING

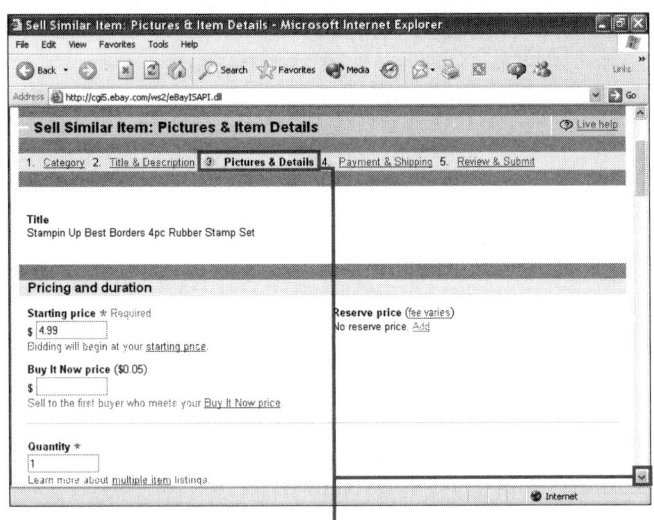

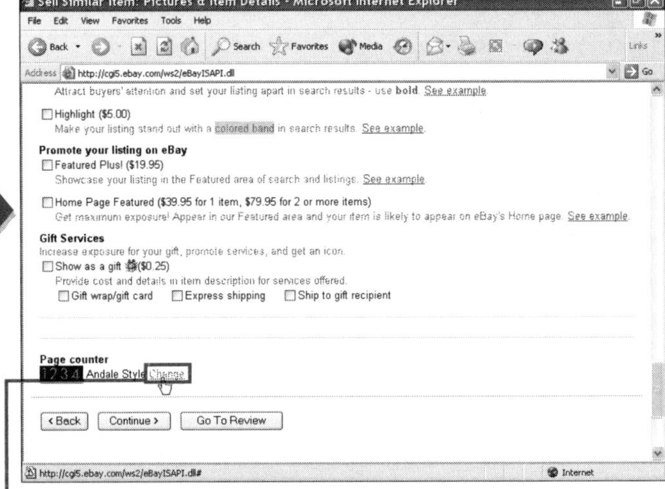

1 Use the seller's form to create a listing, or revise an existing listing.

2 Navigate to the Pictures & Item Details page, which is page 3 on the form.

3 Click here to scroll to the bottom of the form page.

4 Under the Page counter options, click the Change link.

Why should I use a private counter?

✔ If you prefer to keep the number of visits shielded, you can use the hidden counter. In order to view the count, you must log into a password-protected page.

Can I add other types of counters to my auctions?

✔ Yes. There are numerous sites around the Web that offer free counters. In addition, some auction management software and services offer counters that go so far as to tally hourly visits to your page. To use such counters, you must sign up with the auction service and use its features to create your auction listings along with any counter you want to add.

People are viewing my listing, but not making any bids. Should I be worried?

✔ Not at all. You should be more worried if no one has viewed your auction at all. Savvy bidders know to wait and bid near the close of an auction, often bidding at the last minute. Many auctions typically see the majority of bids in the last few remaining minutes of the auction. Many users also employ sniping programs to help them place their highest maximum bids at the last minute, so wait until the auction is completely over before worrying about lack of bids.

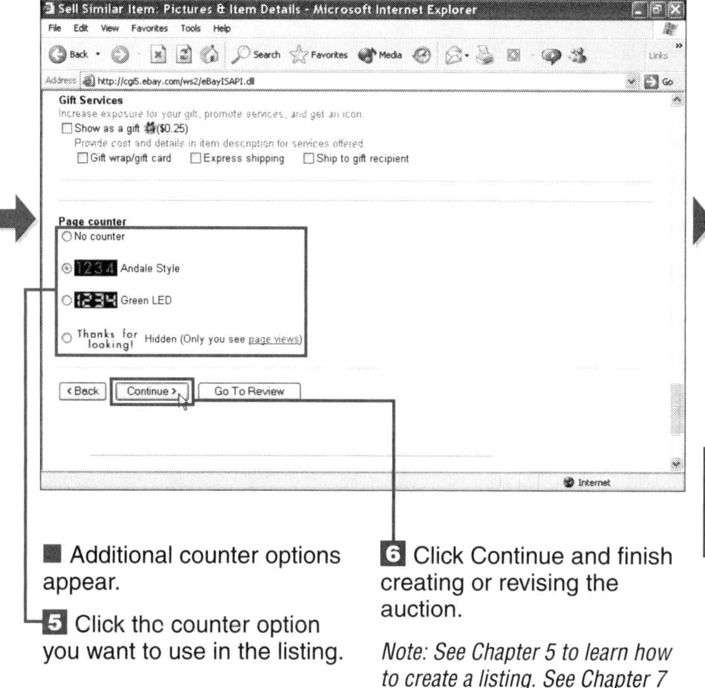

■ Additional counter options appear.

5 Click the counter option you want to use in the listing.

6 Click Continue and finish creating or revising the auction.

Note: See Chapter 5 to learn how to create a listing. See Chapter 7 to learn how to revise a listing.

■ When you view the auction, the counter appears at the bottom of the description area.

ADD A SHIPPING CALCULATOR

You can add a free shipping calculator to your auction that lets bidders find out what it costs to ship the item to their area. When you fill out the seller's form for creating an auction listing, you can choose whether to list a flat shipping rate or offer calculated shipping rates. If you choose the calculated shipping rates option, eBay adds a shipping calculator to the auction that allows bidders to type their ZIP codes and calculate shipping costs. Calculated shipping rates appeal to buyers who want to pay shipping costs based on their location in the country.

You can set up a shipping calculator to calculate costs for sending a package by USPS or UPS. You simply enter the package weight, size, and seller ZIP code, plus add any handling fee for packaging, and the shipping calculator is ready to go. After you post the auction, the shipping calculator appears in the shipping and payment details area of the listing. Users can type their ZIP codes and generate an accurate shipping cost for the item.

You can set up a shipping calculator to appear in your auction when you complete the Payment & Shipping page, the fourth page of the eBay seller's form.

ADD A SHIPPING CALCULATOR

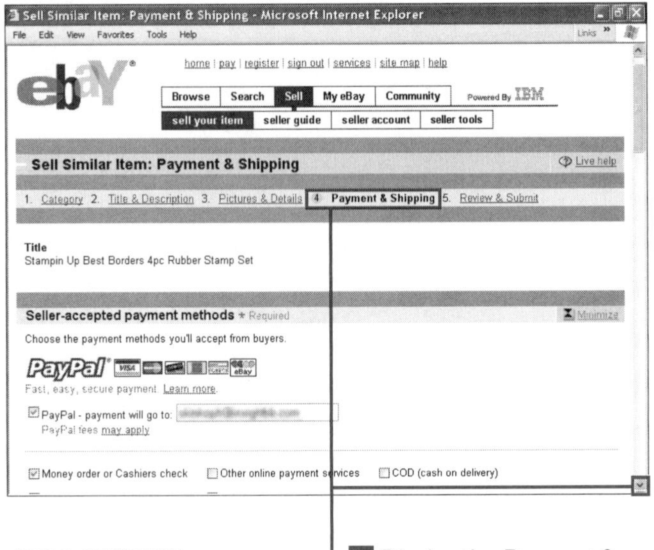

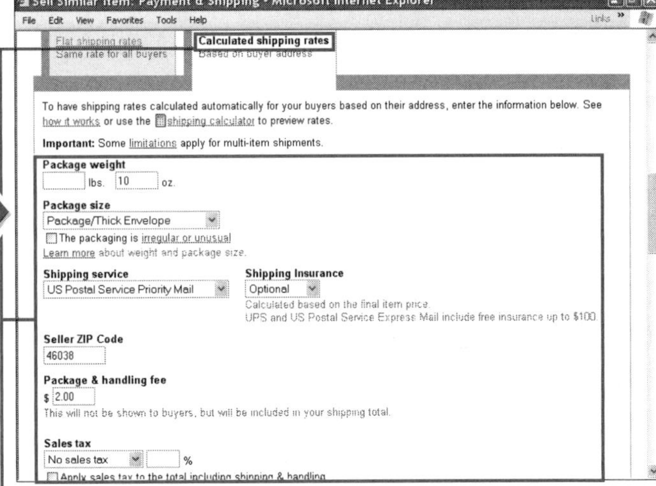

ADD A SHIPPING CALCULATOR

1 Use the seller's form to create a listing, or revise an existing listing.

2 Display the Payment & Shipping page, page 4 on the form.

3 Click here to scroll to the middle of the form page.

4 Under the Shipping Costs section, click the Calculated shipping rates tab.

■ A form for setting up the shipping calculator appears.

5 Fill in the shipping rates details for the item you want to sell.

6 Click the Continue button at the bottom of the page and finish creating or revising the auction.

Note: See Chapter 5 to create a listing. See Chapter 7 to revise a listing.

How does the shipping calculator figure insurance costs?

✔ If insurance is included in the shipping costs, the amount is not calculated until the auction is over because it is based on the final price of the item. If you offer insurance to your buyers, be sure to make a note of the additional cost and let them know it is calculated based on the final value.

Does the bidder see my handling charge?

✔ No. You designate a packaging and handling charge when you set up the shipping calculator. Remember to be reasonable in your handling charges. eBay frowns on users who try to make a profit by charging excessive handling fees.

Can I override the shipping charges after the auction ends?

✔ Yes. You can change the shipping information in the eBay invoice you send to the user, but make sure you and the buyer are in agreement about the new shipping rates you enter. The buyer cannot make changes to the shipping amounts when paying by PayPal.

How do I know if I am entering the right shipping rate information?

✔ Do your homework; know how much the item will weigh when it is packaged properly. You can use the links on the Calculated shipping rates tab in the seller's form to help you determine the rate information.

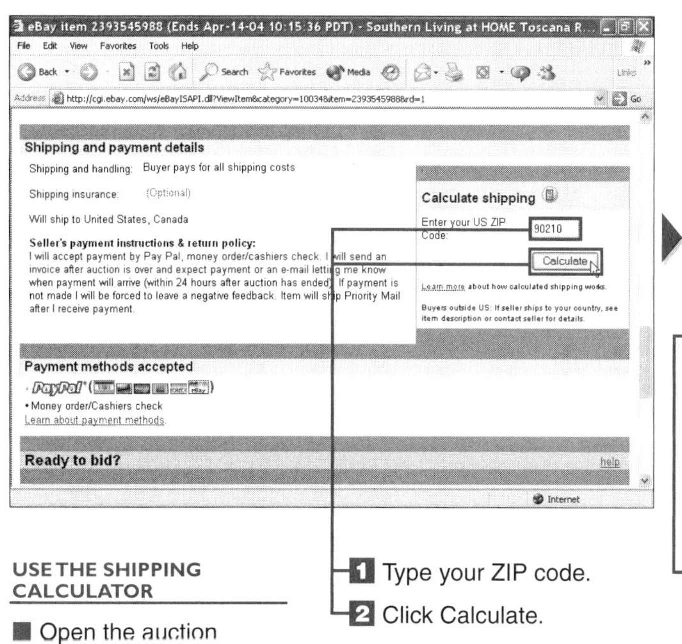

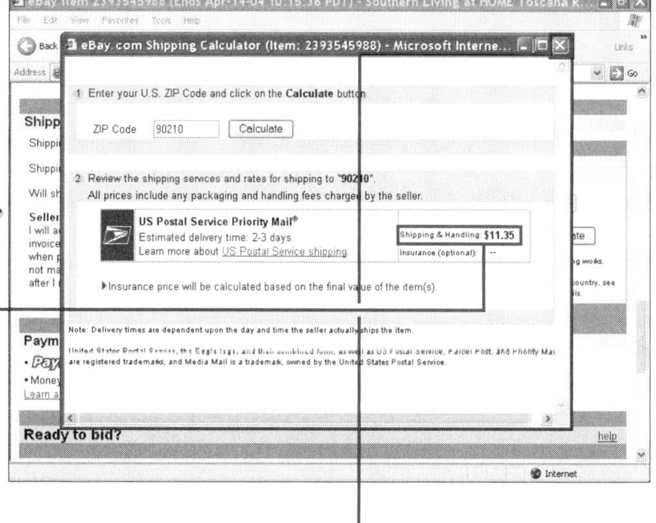

USE THE SHIPPING CALCULATOR

■ Open the auction containing the shipping calculator you want to use.

1 Type your ZIP code.

2 Click Calculate.

■ The shipping calculator displays your shipping costs in a separate window.

■ Click here to close the calculator window.

LINK TO YOUR AUCTIONS

If you have a Web site, you can link to your eBay auctions to attract more bidders or advertise your wares. Although eBay has quite a few restrictions for linking to your auctions or other Web sites from within eBay, you can certainly add a link to eBay on your own Web page. You may want to link to a list of your current auctions, or to a specific auction that you are running. Keep in mind that linking to a current auction means the link is only valid for a short time.

In order to link to your auctions, you must know the URL of each item you are currently running. To learn the URL of any auction, simply display the auction page and look at your browser window's address bar. You can use the Copy and Paste commands to copy and paste the URLs of your auction pages into your own Web pages to use as links.

To make your links more professional, consider adding an official eBay button to your Web page. As long as you agree to the Link License Agreement, you can use the eBay logo button on your Web pages to help promote your auctions.

LINK TO YOUR AUCTIONS

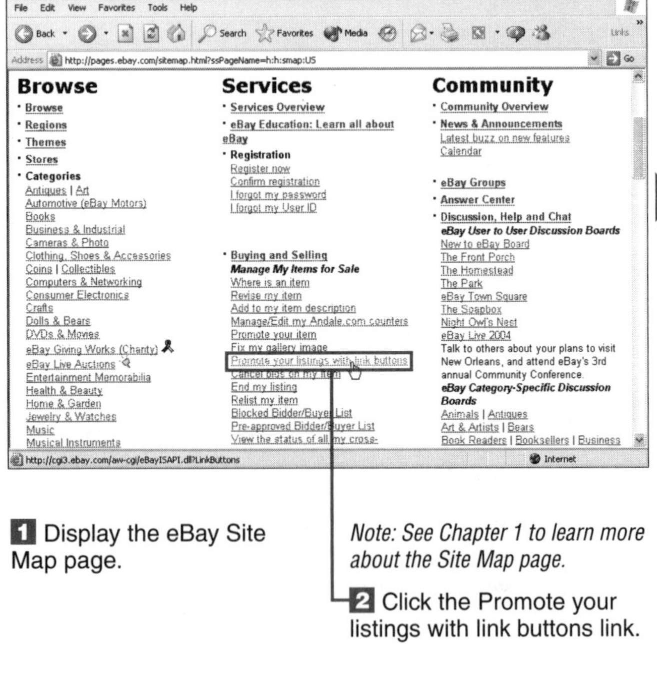

1 Display the eBay Site Map page.

Note: See Chapter 1 to learn more about the Site Map page.

2 Click the Promote your listings with link buttons link.

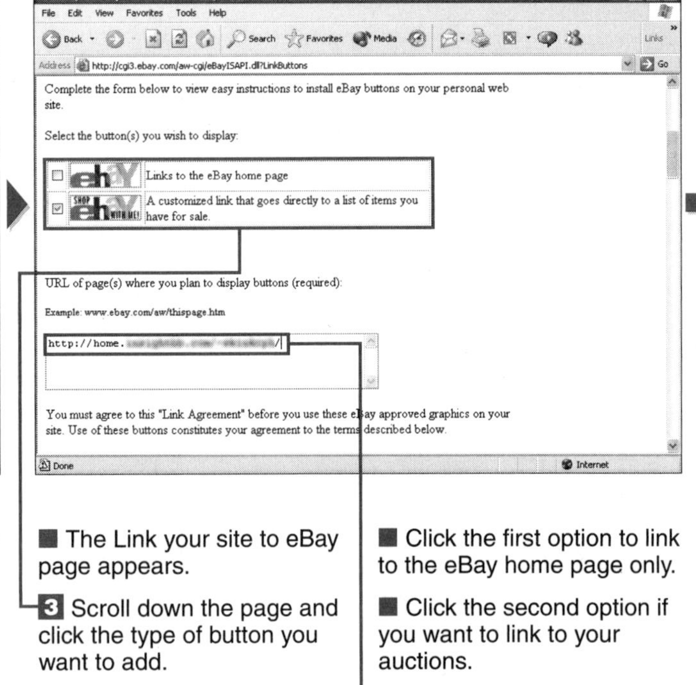

■ The Link your site to eBay page appears.

3 Scroll down the page and click the type of button you want to add.

■ Click the first option to link to the eBay home page only.

■ Click the second option if you want to link to your auctions.

4 Type the URL for your Web page.

Can I link from an auction to my Web page?

✔ No. eBay does not allow you to link to any off-site Web pages. There are some exceptions to the link rule. For example, you can link to a manufacturer's Web site to allow bidders to view specs for an item, but you cannot link to a page in which the item is also sold by the manufacturer. eBay views this as direct competition to the sale on eBay.

Where can I view more guidelines regarding links on eBay?

✔ You can visit the following URL to view eBay's link policy page: http://pages.ebay.com/help/policies/listing-links.html.

Can I add a link in my auction to my About Me page?

✔ Yes. eBay does allow you to link to your About Me page from your auction listing. You can use the About Me page to promote yourself and your sales interests, or anything else you want to share with eBay users. You can also add a link on your About Me page to your own Web site, even it it is an e-commerce site, a place where you sell items. To learn more about using the About Me page to promote yourself and your auctions, see Chapter 3.

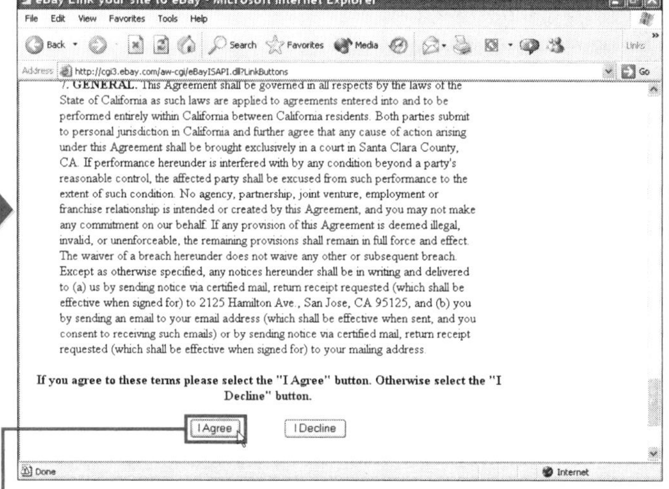

5 Scroll down the page to read the Link License Agreement and click I Agree.

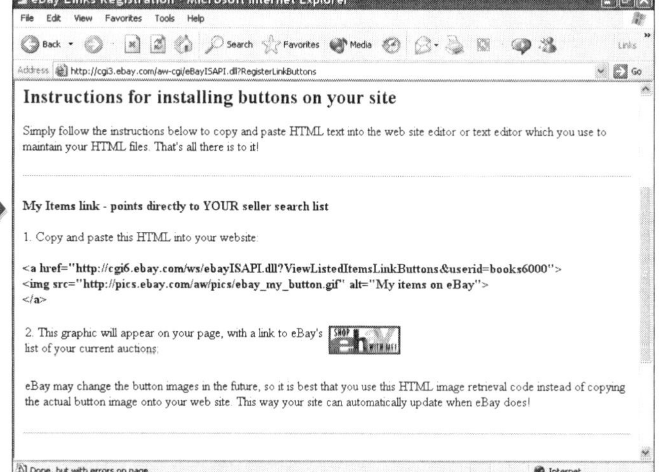

■ A page of instructions for installing the eBay link buttons to your Web page appears.

■ You can copy and paste the HTML code into your Web page.

SECTION IV

9) FINALIZING THE SALE

10) USE PAYPAL WITH AUCTIONS

AFTER THE AUCTION ENDS

11) KEEPING TRACK OF FEEDBACK

12) WHEN GOOD AUCTIONS GO BAD

Dear eBay Buyer,
Congratulations on winning my auction!
With shipping and handling, the total comes to $19.95. I will ship the item on receipt of a check or money order in that amount. Thank you for bidding.
Sincerely,
eBay Seller

CONFIRMATION NOTICE
09285051304
Date Sept. 19, 2004
To Scott C. Warner
2211 Fairway Dr.
Chicago, IL 60611

END-OF-AUCTION COMMUNICATION

Waiting for an auction to end is often a lesson in patience, but when the sale is over, you typically find yourself in a flurry of activity. Much of your end-of-auction activity involves communication. You can expect to encounter or engage in several types of communication after a sale. eBay communicates with you by alerting you to the end of your auction, and, as the seller, you communicate with the buyer to establish payment and shipping. In turn, the buyer may also communicate with you regarding questions about shipping and payment. If the buyer pays through PayPal, PayPal also communicates with you regarding a completed transaction. All of this communication involves your e-mail account. For that reason, it is important to check your messages frequently throughout the day to stay on top of your sales.

E-mailing within eBay

eBay's Web site offers a variety of built-in features to help you communicate with your buyers. The built-in e-mail form is the easiest way to communicate with the buyer. eBay's e-mail form is simply a text box appearing on the Web page where you can type your message text. By default, the form already references the buyer's name and e-mail address, along with the auction number. The form also includes an option for sending yourself a copy of your correspondence to help you keep a record of your messages. This is a good practice to follow in case something goes wrong later. For example, if the buyer does not like the item, or suddenly disagrees with the terms of sale, you have a copy of your previous exchanges to back up your position.

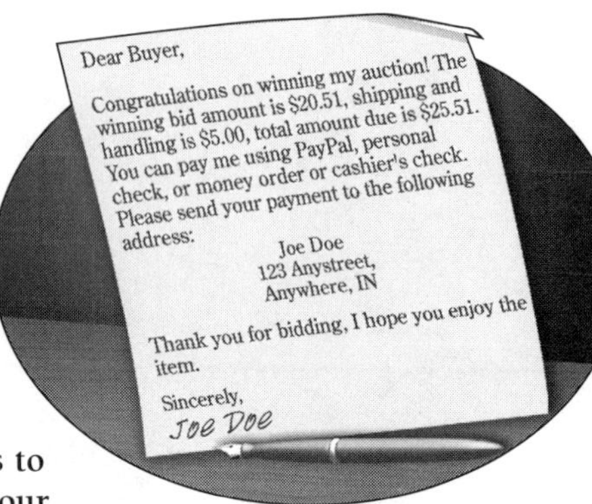
Dear Buyer,

Congratulations on winning my auction! The winning bid amount is $20.51, shipping and handling is $5.00, total amount due is $25.51. You can pay me using PayPal, personal check, or money order or cashier's check. Please send your payment to the following address:

Joe Doe
123 Anystreet,
Anywhere, IN

Thank you for bidding, I hope you enjoy the item.

Sincerely,
Joe Doe

Notify the Winner

Communication is essential to offering your buyers good customer service. Your first step is to send the winning bidder a notification congratulating him or her on the win and detailing the payment and shipping costs. If the buyer does not pay after a couple of days, you can send a payment reminder through eBay, kindly prompting the buyer to follow through with the sale.

Communicate with the Buyer

As a courtesy, you can also send the buyer messages during key points of the transaction, such as a note saying you received payment, or another note telling the buyer when you shipped the item. For example, your shipping notice might give the buyer tracking information or let them know when to expect the item to arrive. Your shipping notice might also prompt the buyer to let you know, in return, when the item arrives safely and whether he or she is satisfied with the purchase. Keeping good communication lines open throughout the end of auction activity can help create positive feedback.

UNDERSTANDING EBAY'S CHECKOUT PROCEDURE

After your auction is over, the buyer can pay for the item through eBay's checkout feature. eBay offers an integrated checkout feature that helps you generate the correct totals for your auction payments and expedite the communication and payment between you and the buyer. eBay's checkout feature also lists the buyer's shipping address automatically.

Find Checkout Options

Checkout options are part of the eBay seller's form, the online form you complete to create and list an auction. You can use the checkout options with traditional auctions, Buy It Now auctions, and fixed-price listings, including those found in an eBay Store. The feature is free for both sellers and buyers. The feature is also available if you use Turbo Lister or eBay's Seller's Assistant to create and manage your auctions.

Define Payment and Shipping Costs

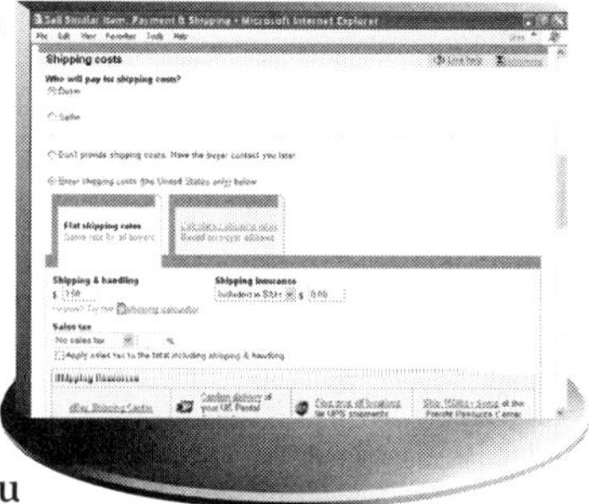

You can activate the checkout feature by filling in the payment methods and shipping costs areas of the seller's form. You can choose to define a flat shipping and handling rate, or you can calculate costs based on the buyer's shipping ZIP code. As part of defining shipping costs, you can also define any insurance costs for shipping and any sales tax, if it applies. If the buyer pays through check or money order, the checkout feature lists your payment address where the buyer can send the payment.

The shipping costs you specify on the seller's form apply to U.S. buyers. If your auctions include international buyers, they need to contact you for the correct payment amount before proceeding with the checkout process.

If you leave the shipping costs undefined in your listing, the eBay checkout feature cannot help your buyers complete the transaction quickly and smoothly when they win an auction. Instead, winning buyers have to contact you for all the pertinent information, which means more work for you, more communication back and forth, and more hassles for the buyer, who must wait to find out the total payment amount you want. To save yourself and your customer some time and effort, take advantage of the eBay checkout feature. To learn more about creating an auction listing with the seller's form and filling in the payment and shipping costs, see Chapters 4 and 5.

Track Checkout Features

eBay can also help you keep track of payments made and which sales are still pending in the Items I've Sold table on the Selling tab of the My eBay page. The Next Steps/Status column can tell you whether a user has paid through PayPal. If the buyer is using another payment method, it is up to you to keep track of who has paid and who has not. You may prefer to use an auction management or database program to help you track auction payments.

VIEW END OF AUCTION NOTIFICATIONS

One of the most satisfying aspects of selling items on eBay is receiving an End of Auction notification for a successful sale. In terms of auction management, the notification lets you know one of your auctions is over. eBay notifies sellers at every auction close with an e-mail message containing details about the sale, including the auction number, so you can keep track of which item sold. The notification lets you know the name of the winning bidder and the winning amount, along with any predetermined shipping and handling amounts to be paid.

The End of Auction notification also includes links for viewing the listing, contacting the winner, and creating and sending an invoice. The bottom of the message includes more links to other related areas on eBay.

MASTER IT

Can I control which auction notifications eBay sends me?

✔ Yes. If you prefer not to receive a new e-mail notification every time an auction ends, you can turn off the option in your eBay preference settings. From the My eBay page, click the eBay Preferences link, and then click the view/change link for your notification preferences. You must log on to your account again, but you can then view a page to select which types of e-mail messages you want to receive from eBay.

VIEW END OF AUCTION NOTIFICATIONS

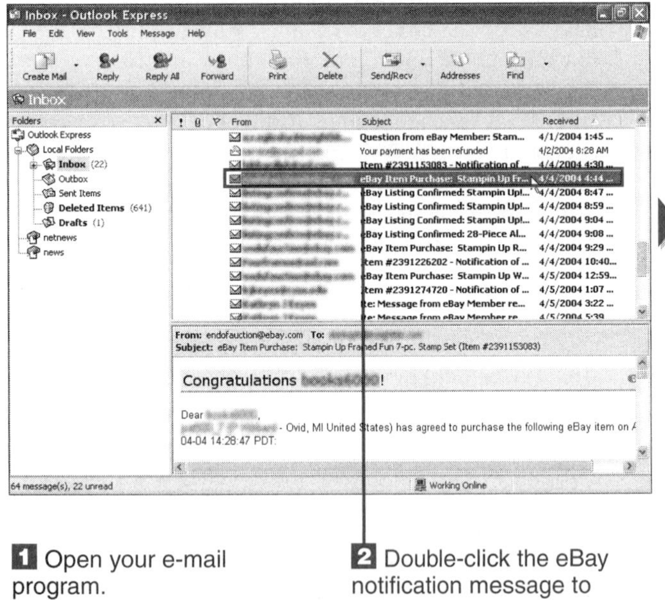

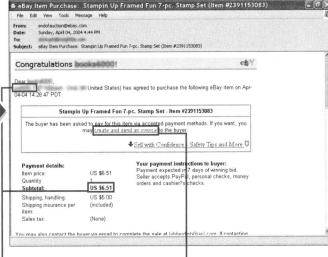

1 Open your e-mail program.

2 Double-click the eBay notification message to open it.

■ The notification message tells you the name of the winning bidder.

■ The amount of the winning bid appears here.

■ You can click this link to create an invoice if the buyer has not yet paid for the item.

NOTIFY A WINNER

After an auction ends, you can contact the winning bidder. It is good practice to contact the winning buyer as soon as the auction is over, or at least within the first few hours after the auction ends. Being the first to make contact shows the buyer you are a competent seller and gives the buyer more confidence in your attention to customer service. eBay recommends contacting the buyer within three days; however, if good customer service and repeat sales are your goal, it is better to contact the buyer much sooner than three days after the auction is over.

The easiest way to contact the buyer is through the All Sellers view on the My eBay page. You can also use this method to let a buyer know when you ship an item or when you receive payment. When contacting the buyer, be sure to reference the correct auction, congratulate him or her on the win, and provide the appropriate shipping and payment information. Be sure to use a cordial, friendly tone in your correspondence. You do not need to send a lengthy message, just a brief congratulatory note with details about how to pay for the auction.

If you intend to automate your winner notifications, take time to personalize your response. Boilerplate, bulk-generated notifications only irritate buyers and show a lack of attention to detail.

NOTIFY A WINNER

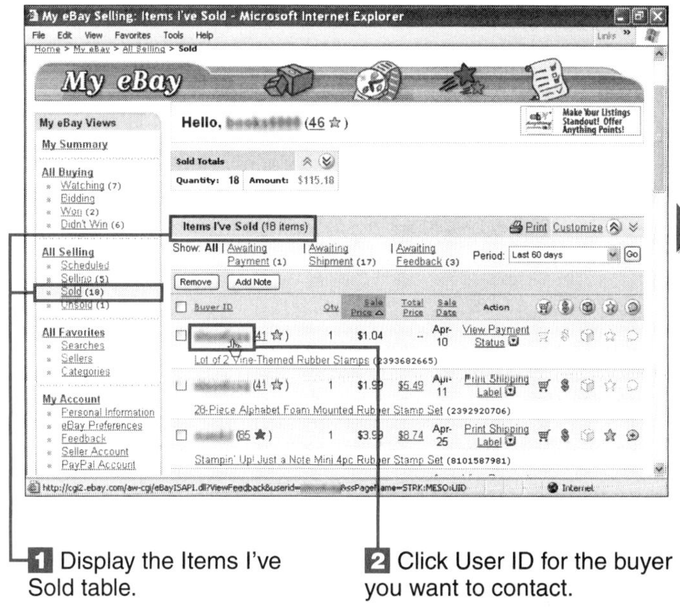

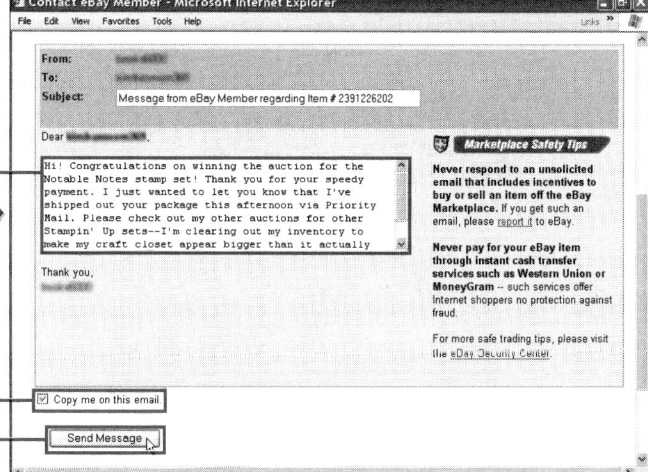

1 Display the Items I've Sold table.

Note: See Chapter 7 to learn how to view the Selling tables.

2 Click User ID for the buyer you want to contact.

■ The Contact eBay Member page appears.

3 Type your message text.

■ Click this option to send a copy of the message to yourself.

4 Click Send Message.

■ eBay e-mails your message.

Note: You can also use your own e-mail program to notify a winner. You can find the buyer's e-mail address by clicking the Contact the buyer link on the auction listing page.

SEND AN INVOICE

You can send an invoice to winning bidders if they have not yet paid for an item. For example, you might send an invoice as soon as the auction ends. An invoice is simply a prewritten summary of an auction win and includes details about the amount of the winning bid along with shipping and handling charges, or taxes. To help you figure out any shipping charges if you have not done so prior to the auction end, the invoice also includes the winning bidder's ZIP code and a shipping calculator.

The eBay All Selling view on the My eBay page includes a feature for generating an invoice and sending it to the winning bidder. The invoice form also includes a text box where you can type your payment instructions for the winning bidder. You can also use the text box to generate a personal note that congratulates the buyer for winning the auction, or thanks him or her for bidding on your item.

After you complete the form, eBay e-mails the invoice to the winning bidder. You can also choose to e-mail yourself a copy of the invoice. This is handy if you are trying to keep records of every successful sale you make on eBay.

SEND AN INVOICE

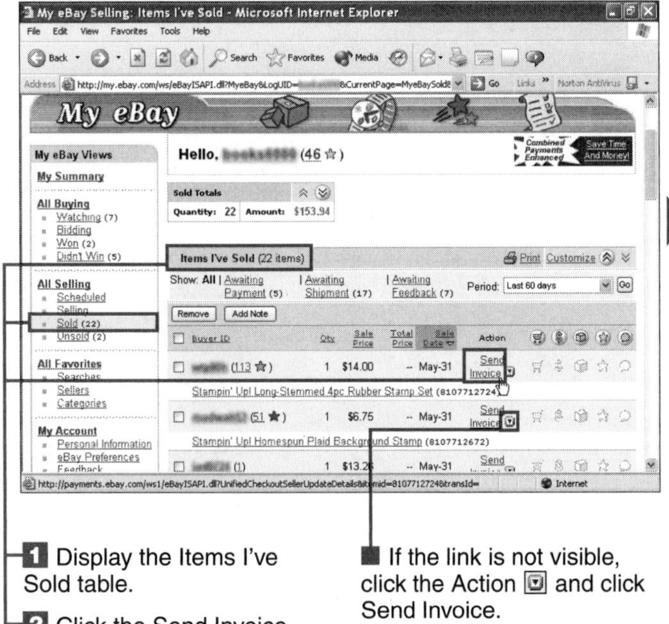

1 Display the Items I've Sold table.

2 Click the Send Invoice.

■ If the link is not visible, click the Action ▣ and click Send Invoice.

Note: If you have already sent an invoice or the buyer has already paid it, the Send Invoice action is not available.

■ The Send Invoice to Buyer page appears.

■ The form includes prewritten invoice information, including options for setting shipping and handling charges.

■ You can make changes to the shipping and handling information, if needed.

I tried to send an invoice, but eBay will not let me. Why not?

✔ The Send Invoice option only appears on your All Selling page if the buyer has not yet paid for the auction. If the buyer pays immediately after winning an auction with PayPal, for example, the link is not available. The same is true if you try to send an invoice from your End of Auction notification e-mail, which also includes a link for creating and sending an invoice. If you want to send an invoice with the item later, you can print out the PayPal details page.

Why does eBay fill in my payment instructions for me on the invoice?

✔ The invoice automatically includes any text you entered in the Seller's Payment Instructions & Return Policy area of your auction listing. You enter this data when you fill out the seller's form to create an auction listing. If you leave this area blank, it appears blank on the eBay-generated invoice. It is a good idea to always give details in this area of the listing and in the invoice. This information is important for the buyer to understand your terms of sale, including payments, shipping and handling costs, and your policy regarding refunds.

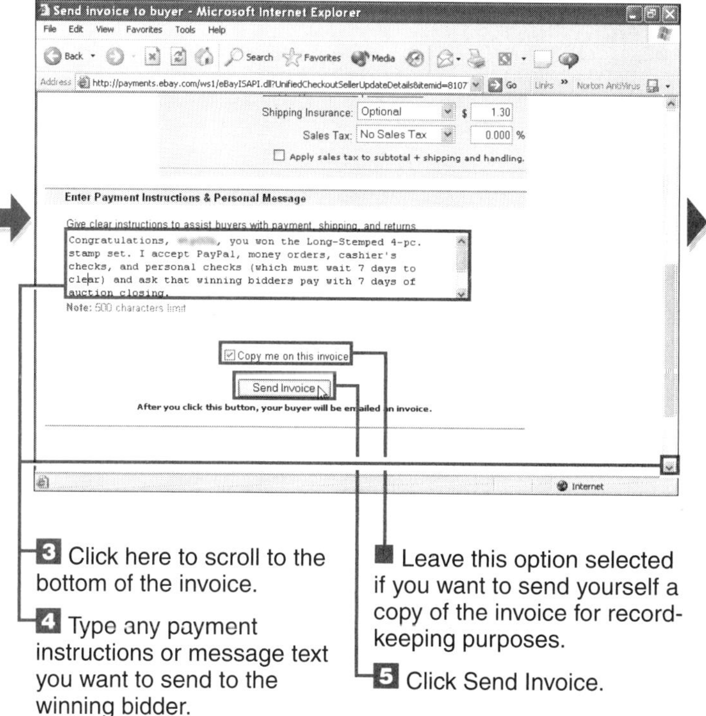

3 Click here to scroll to the bottom of the invoice.

4 Type any payment instructions or message text you want to send to the winning bidder.

■ Leave this option selected if you want to send yourself a copy of the invoice for record-keeping purposes.

5 Click Send Invoice.

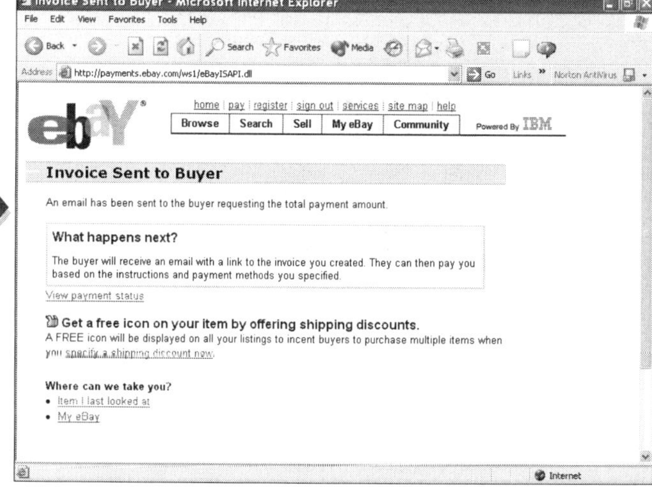

■ eBay sends the invoice and displays a page confirming the action.

SEND A PAYMENT REMINDER

Most buyers on eBay are very responsible and promptly send payment for the auctions they win. However, situations can arise in which you need to remind a buyer of his or her commitment to pay for the item. You do not want to pester the buyer, but you want to know whether the buyer plans on paying, because you may want to relist the item or offer it to another bidder.

You must also keep in mind that personal situations can arise, such as an impromptu out-of-town trip or an illness, that can keep the buyer from promptly paying for an auction. Technical problems are another type of situation that can cause a buyer not to notice an auction win right away. For example, the computer is not functioning properly, or the Internet connection is not operable.

If you do not hear from the winner after three days, you can use eBay's payment reminder feature to remind the buyer of the win. eBay's payment reminder is a form letter containing details about the auction, the amount due, payment instructions, and your contact information.

SEND A PAYMENT REMINDER

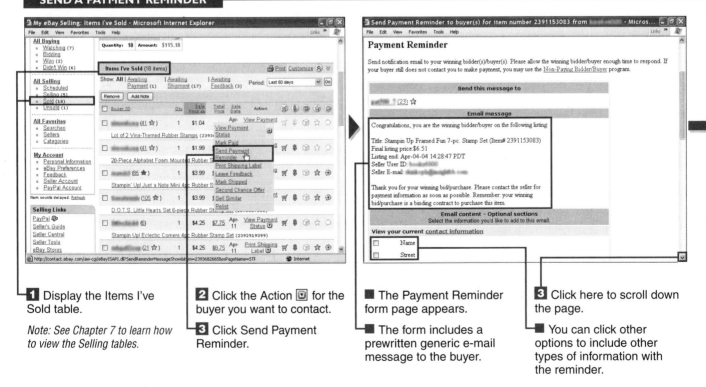

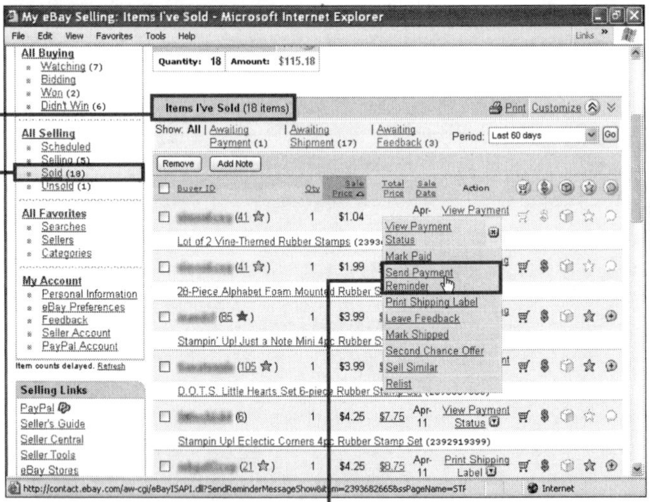

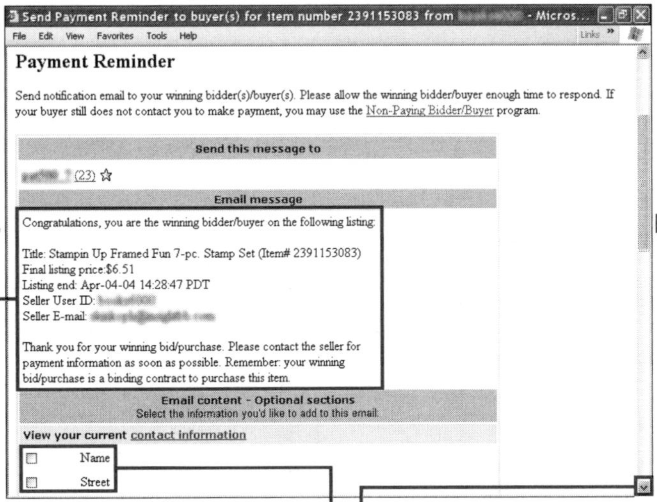

1 Display the Items I've Sold table.

Note: See Chapter 7 to learn how to view the Selling tables.

2 Click the Action ▾ for the buyer you want to contact.

3 Click Send Payment Reminder.

■ The Payment Reminder form page appears.

■ The form includes a prewritten generic e-mail message to the buyer.

3 Click here to scroll down the page.

■ You can click other options to include other types of information with the reminder.

Can I send a payment reminder through my own e-mail program instead?

✔ Yes. Be sure to reference the auction number and provide a link to the listing to help the buyer procede through the eBay checkout feature. As with any other correspondence among eBay users, it is in your best interest to remain professional at all times. Diplomacy takes a bit of practice, but be friendly yet clear in your communication. Simply remind the buyer of the auction he or she won, the payment amout due, ways to make the payment, and a deadline for doing so. Refrain from any subtle or overt threats of leaving negative feedback or reporting the buyer for nonpayment.

I do not see an active link for a payment reminder. Why not?

✔ eBay does not allow you to access the payment reminder form for at least three days following an auction. This control helps to ensure that sellers give buyers enough time to respond to the win.

What if the buyer still does not pay me?

✔ If you do not hear from the buyer after the payment reminder, you may want to request the buyer's contact information and give him or her a call, or send a personal e-mail. Perhaps their computer or Internet connection is down and they have been unable to complete the auction process. If a reasonable amount of time passes and you still do not receive payment, you may need to file a nonpaying buyer report. See Chapter 12 to learn more.

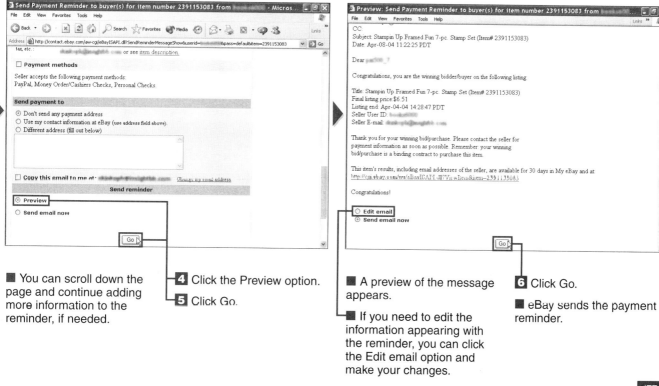

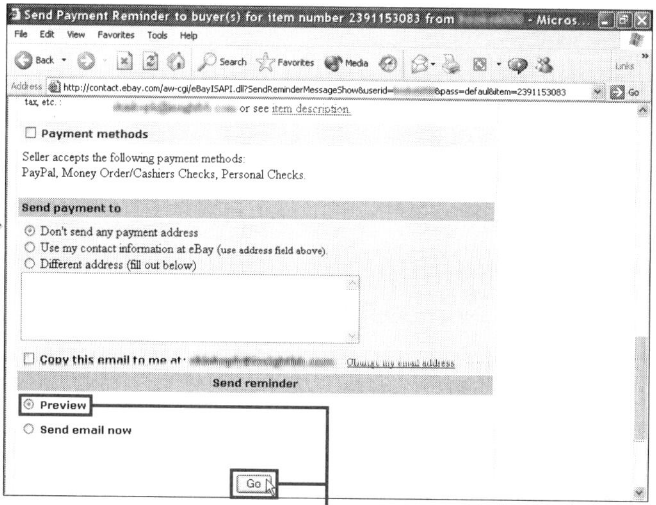

■ You can scroll down the page and continue adding more information to the reminder, if needed.

4 Click the Preview option.

5 Click Go.

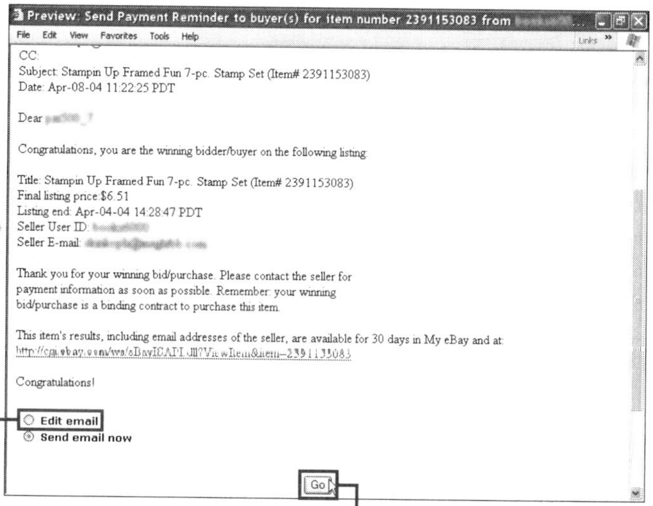

■ A preview of the message appears.

■ If you need to edit the information appearing with the reminder, you can click the Edit email option and make your changes.

6 Click Go.

■ eBay sends the payment reminder.

REQUEST CONTACT INFORMATION

At the end of the auction, you can request the buyer's contact information. Basic contact information includes the name, city, and phone number the users provide to create their eBay accounts. For example, you may need to request contact information in order to phone the buyer. You may also request contact information if you need to verify the person's name, city, and phone number. The buyer can do the same for you. eBay then sends the contact information to your e-mail address. Even if only one-half of the transaction party requests the information, both users receive the contact information for the other user via e-mail.

When requesting contact information, you can only use the information within the framework of the eBay Privacy Policy. Contact information is considered private, and is exchanged between the parties involved in a transaction, such as a bidder, a buyer, or a seller. The exchange of information can only occur to facilitate a sale or purchase.

eBay allows bidders to request contact information about a seller while an auction is going on, and sellers can request contact information from anyone bidding on their auctions. You need to know the other user's ID in order to request contact information.

REQUEST CONTACT INFORMATION

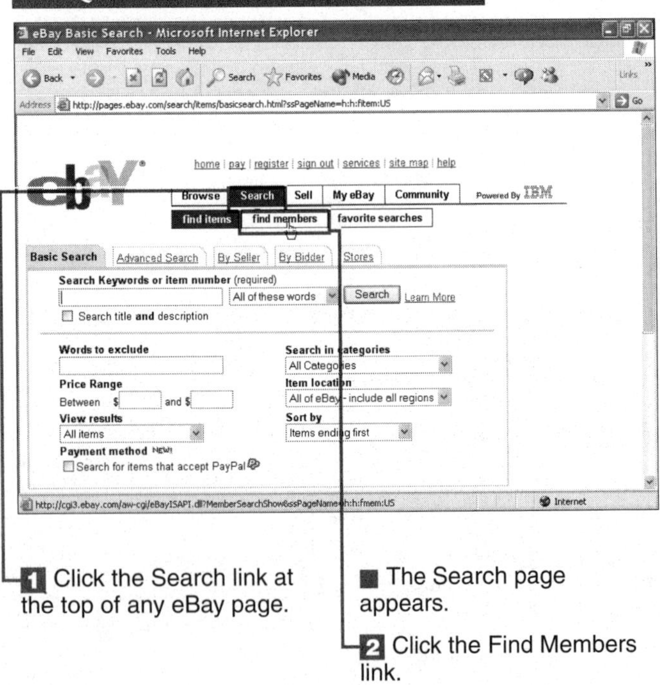

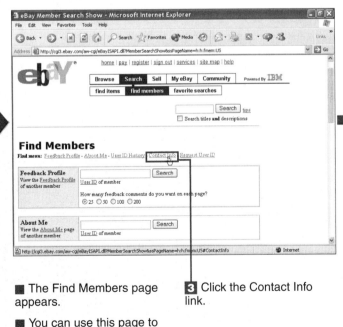

■1 Click the Search link at the top of any eBay page.

■ The Search page appears.

■2 Click the Find Members link.

■ The Find Members page appears.

■ You can use this page to look up information about other users.

■3 Click the Contact Info link.

What if someone's contact information is invalid?

✔ It is very important to keep your contact information up to date on eBay. Failure to provide accurate contact information can result in a suspension of your eBay account. If you do encounter invalid contact information for another user, you can report the violation to eBay. You need the User ID in order to report the violation. To file a report, click the Help link at the top of any eBay page, and then click the Contact Us link. This opens the Contact Us form that you can fill out to report the User ID to eBay.

How do I update my own contact information if something changes?

✔ If you change your address, phone number, or e-mail address, be sure to update the information in your eBay account. You can update your information using the My eBay page. Click the Personal Information link and then click the corresponding link from the Personal Information section of the page. For example, to change your e-mail address, click the change link next to Email address information. To change your address, click the change link under the Address Information section of the Personal Information page.

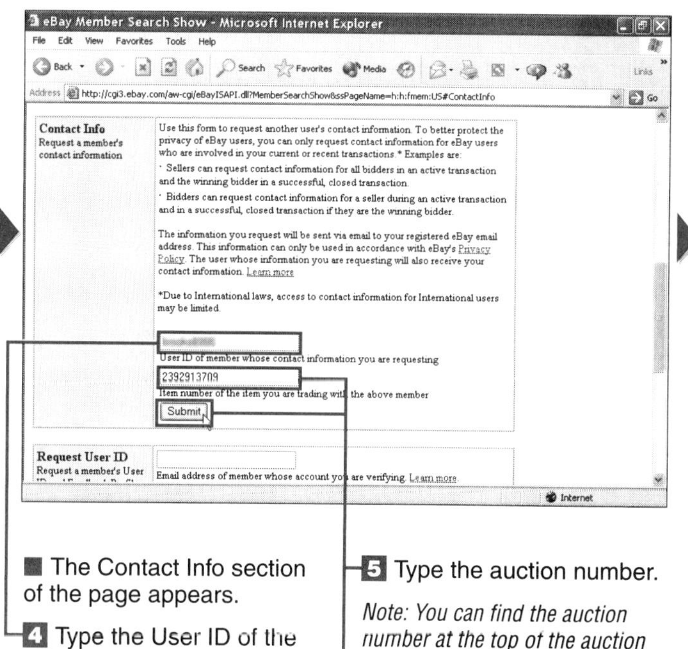

■ The Contact Info section of the page appears.

4 Type the User ID of the buyer or seller.

5 Type the auction number.

Note: You can find the auction number at the top of the auction listing page.

6 Click Submit.

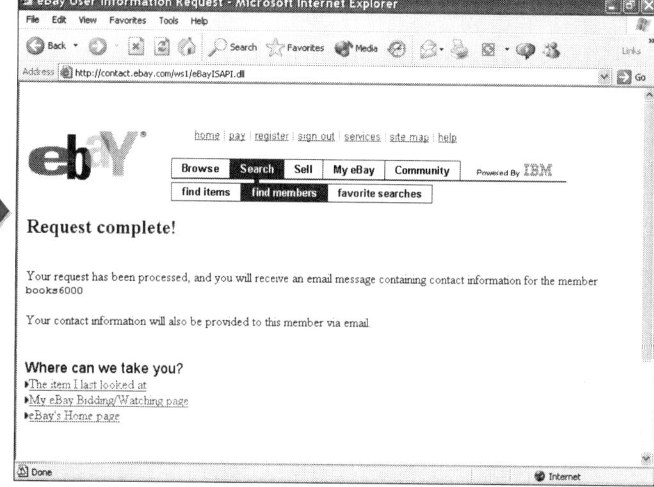

■ A Request complete page appears.

■ eBay sends a User Information Request e-mail to both users containing the basic contact information.

PAY YOUR EBAY FEES

As you list auctions and make sales on eBay, you accumulate fees. Insertion fees, also called listing fees, accrue for every auction you post. Insertion fees are nonrefundable, and vary based on the starting price of your item and the type of listing you post. For example, in a regular auction with a starting price of $5, the insertion fee is 35 cents. Insertion fees are added to your account as soon as you post an auction.

Final value fees accrue after your auction ends, and are based on the final sale price of the item, not including shipping and handling, also called the final value. For example, if your item sells from $0–$25, the final value fee is 5.25 percent of the closing value.

The Accounts tab on the My eBay page keeps track of the fees you owe eBay. You can choose to pay your eBay fees by credit card, through your checking account, or with your PayPal account. You can also mail a check or money order to eBay. For example, you can charge your fees to your credit card on a monthly basis, or you can instruct eBay to deduct the fees directly from your checking account each month.

PAY YOUR EBAY FEES

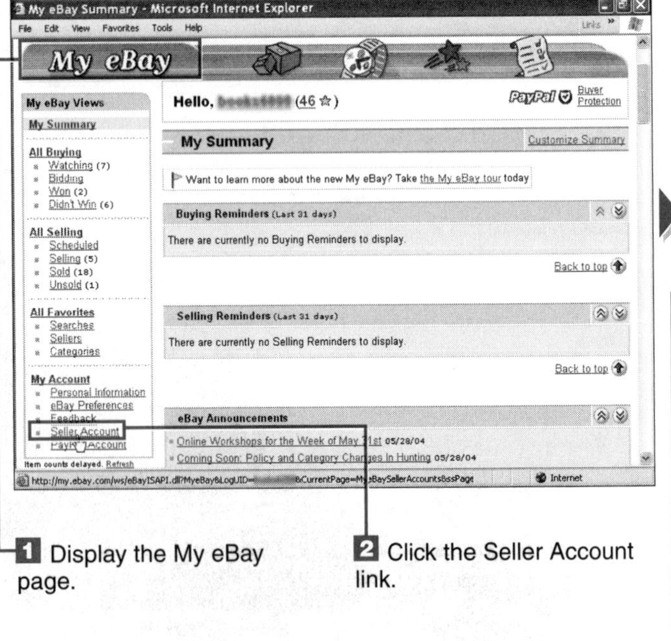

1 Display the My eBay page.

2 Click the Seller Account link.

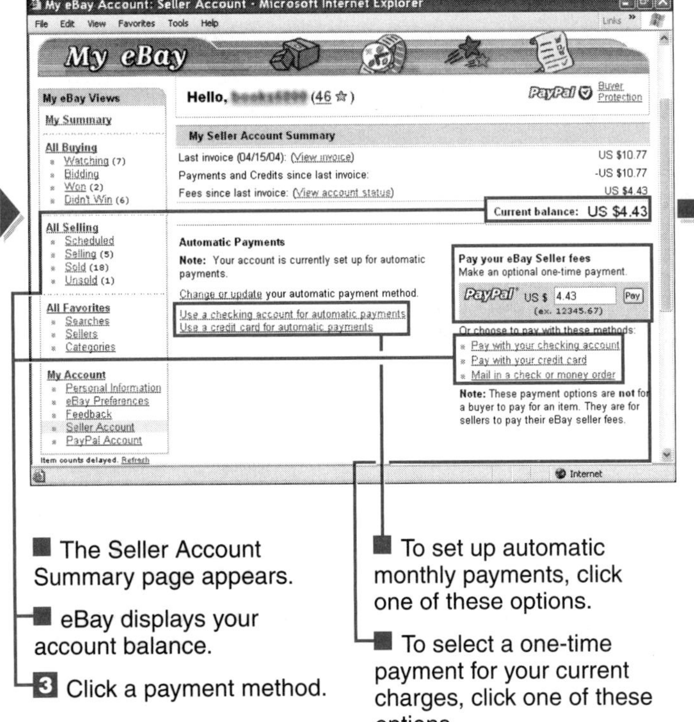

■ The Seller Account Summary page appears.

■ eBay displays your account balance.

3 Click a payment method.

■ To set up automatic monthly payments, click one of these options.

■ To select a one-time payment for your current charges, click one of these options.

Where can I find a list of the current fees?

✔ For a complete list of current eBay fees, click the Fees & credits link at the bottom of the My Account page. This opens a page detailing both insertion and final value fees.

What if my auction does not sell or the sale falls through. Do I still pay final value fees?

✔ You can relist an unsold item without paying a final value fee. You incur another insertion fee, however. If the buyer fails to purchase the item, you can file for a final value fee credit seven days after the auction. See Chapter 12 to learn more about both scenarios.

What is the difference between a one-time pay and monthly payments?

✔ If you are a casual eBay seller, you may only sell items sporadically, so making a one-time payment may work best for you. You can pay your fees after you conduct your auctions, and your slate is clean until you list more auctions again. If you sell consistently, you may prefer to set up your fees for monthly deduction from your credit card or checking account. This allows eBay to deduct your fees at the end of each month automatically.

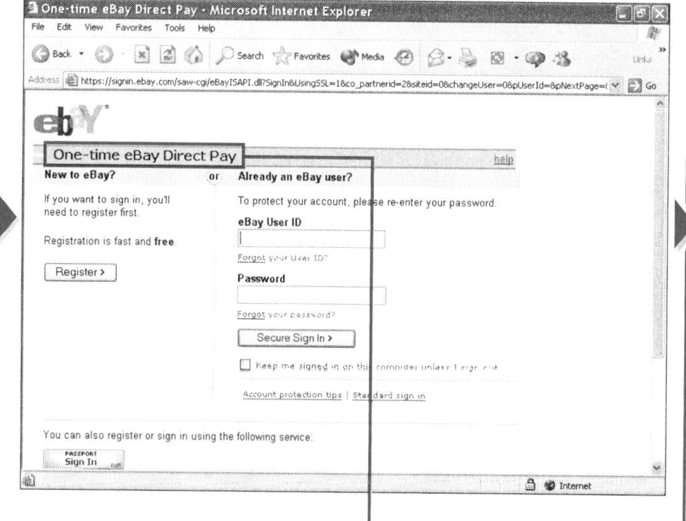

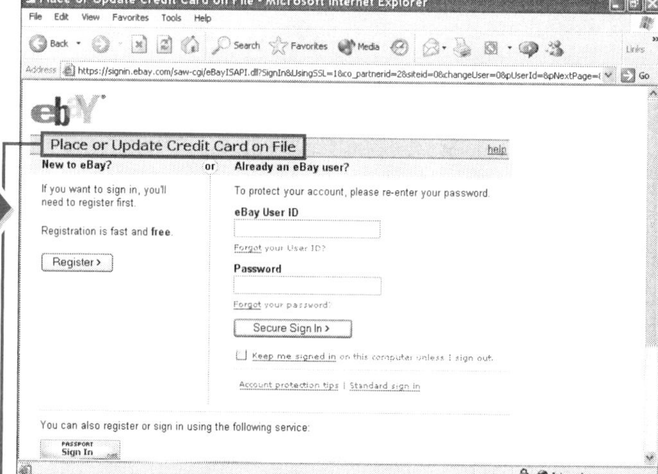

■ Depending on the payment method you select, follow the on-screen prompts to log on and pay your fees.

■ In this example, you can log on and make a one-time payment through Direct Pay and deduct the fees from your checking account.

■ In this example, you can log on and make a monthly payment with your credit card.

PACK AND SHIP AN ITEM

An important part of finalizing any sale on eBay is sending the auctioned item to the winning bidder. Although it is tempting to view the shipment of items as a last-minute task, serious sellers know to treat shipping as a critical part of closing the sale. Your overall success on eBay relies on your shipping practices. If you package an item poorly and it breaks in transit, you can jeopardize a sale and potentially accumulate a negative feedback report. Continue packaging items badly and you can really damage your online reputation.

Packing Tips

The more items you sell, the more items you pack and ship. Take time to pack items carefully and securely. If you have ever been on the receiving end of a poorly packaged item, you know the displeasure and frustration that comes from opening a box only to find the contents broken and damaged. Granted, some of the blame goes to the people handling the package in transit, but most of the blame goes to the person who did not properly prepare the item for shipping.

The packages you send are the only real form of physical contact you make with your buyers. Attention to detail speaks highly about your quality of customer service, and results in positive feedback from your buyers, which is read in turn by potential bidders and garners trust with others who want to bid on your auctions. Good packaging equals positive feedback.

For starters, use the appropriate package, whether it is a bubble envelope or a strong box. Consider the weather of the item's destination, and package for rain or snow accordingly. Boxes and other packages often sit on front porches and are subject to inclement weather. If dampness or wetness can easily damage your item, be sure to ship it in a watertight box or package. Also make your outside labels easy to read and waterproof as well.

As for the inside of the package, do not skimp on the packing material. Wrap items to survive extremely rough handling, using layers of your favorite packing materials, such as bubble wrap, foam peanuts, and crumpled newspaper. You might also include a note in the shipment with any additional information about the item, or a copy of the original invoice.

You can find all types of packing materials and boxes for sale on eBay, as well as other sites on the Internet. Some shipping services also offer packing materials, such as USPS Priority Mail.

Find a Shipping Carrier

The final phase of shipping is to take your packages to a shipping carrier or make arrangements for pickup. Major carriers include the United States Post Office (USPS), United Parcel Service (UPS), and Federal Express (FedEx). As advised in earlier chapters, take time to compare the shipping prices among the major carriers in your area. Be sure to factor in drive time and the time you spend standing in line to ship your packages when determining which service to use. You may find one service preferable for larger packages and another for smaller ones.

You should also factor in the costs of extra shipping features, such as insurance and delivery confirmation. Some services include these extra features as part of their shipping, while others do not. A good way to investigate any shipping questions and rates is to log on to the company's Web site to learn the latest rates and options. Each of the major shipping carriers offers an interactive Web site, and some include features for purchasing and printing out shipping labels and postage.

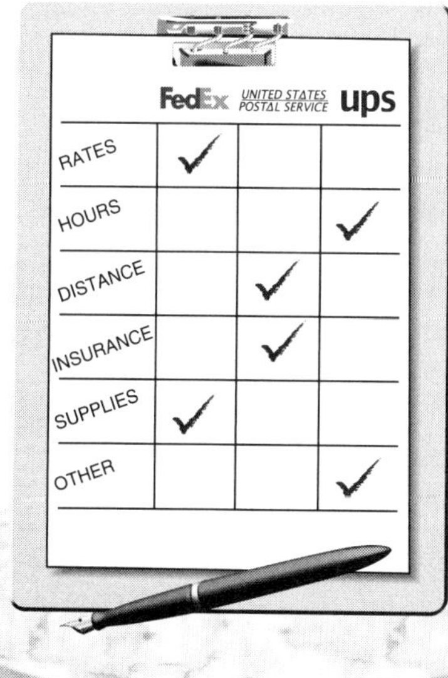

Handle Shipping Problems

Regardless of what extra shipping options you add on, until the package arrives in the hands of the winning bidder, it is still in your realm of responsibility. For your own protection, invest in delivery confirmation for all of your items. This helps you to know the package is received. You can track the shipment and rest assured it arrived in the right spot. If the buyer says the item never arrived, your confirmation number proves otherwise. In the same manner, tracking numbers can also help you determine the success of a shipment. Spending a few extra cents for confirmation or tracking numbers is worth it for your peace of mind.

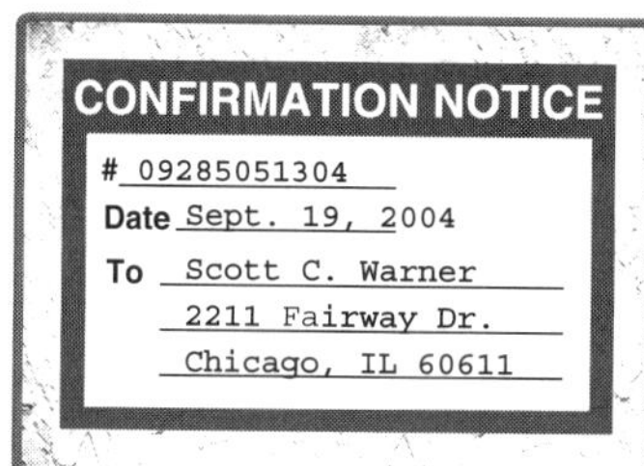

If problems do arrive with a shipment, it really is your responsibility, as the seller, to file for any insurance claims, no matter if the insurance was purchased by you or the buyer. It is also good policy to offer refunds for items lost or damaged in shipping. If you have doubts about whether a buyer is being truthful or not about a lost or damaged item, consult the buyer's feedback report to spot any trends. If other sellers report similar claims, it may be a chronic problem for the buyer.

Although defining a good return policy in your auction listing might seem like a good way to dissuade disreputable buyers out to scam you with false shipping claims, a restrictive return policy might also repel honest bidders. As a seller, you must tackle each shipping problem individually as it arrives, and offering good customers a refund for a lost or damaged item is a good business practice. Be flexible in your stance, but be careful about buyers with lots of negative feedback. Most shipping problems can be avoided by packing items to withstand the transit process.

SIGN UP FOR A PAYPAL ACCOUNT

PayPal is an eBay-owned service that enables you to pay for auctions and other eBay transactions online using credit cards and bank account transfers. In a nutshell, PayPal helps make completing an eBay sale easy. The service saves sellers from having to set up merchant accounts with their banks to accept credit cards. The service also saves buyers and sellers the time and risk involved in sending and receiving personal checks and money orders.

Because PayPal is owned by eBay, it is tightly integrated into the eBay selling process. When you create your auctions, you can easily advertise to buyers that they can pay for your auction using PayPal. When a buyer wins an auction from a seller that accepts PayPal, he or she can go to PayPal to pay for the transaction by clicking a link in the confirmation e-mail or on the auction page itself.

When someone purchases an eBay item from you using PayPal, PayPal sends you an e-mail notification that you have new funds in your PayPal account. You can withdraw the funds from your PayPal account by requesting that a check be sent to you by U.S. mail or by requesting an electronic funds transfer to your bank account.

SIGN UP FOR A PAYPAL ACCOUNT

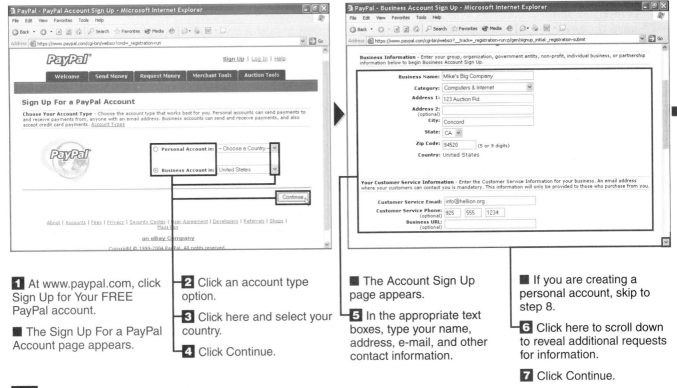

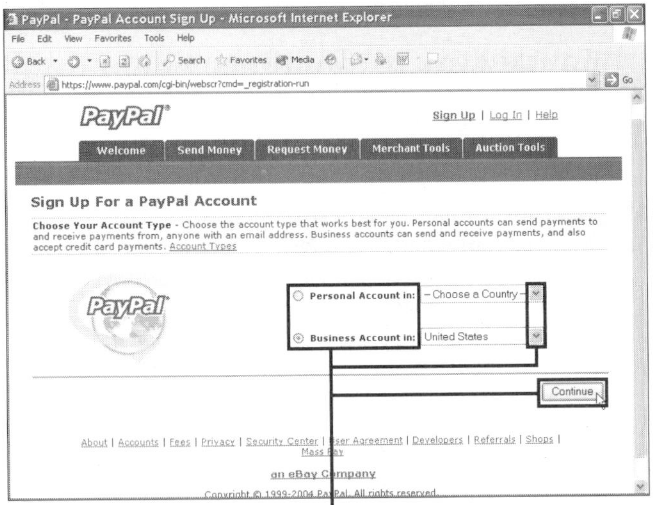

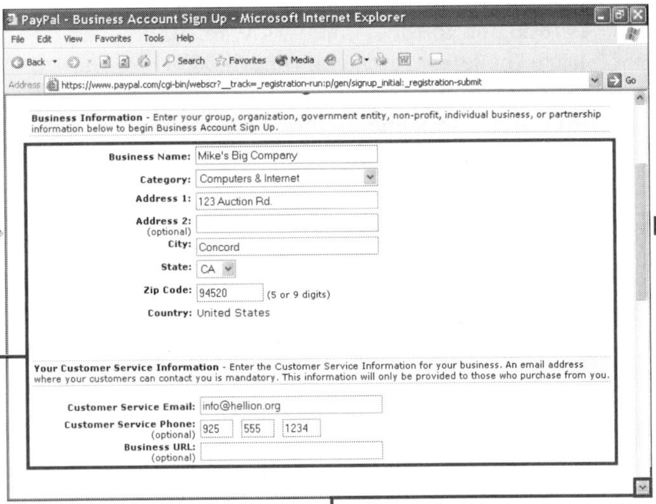

1 At www.paypal.com, click Sign Up for Your FREE PayPal account.

■ The Sign Up For a PayPal Account page appears.

2 Click an account type option.

3 Click here and select your country.

4 Click Continue.

■ The Account Sign Up page appears.

5 In the appropriate text boxes, type your name, address, e-mail, and other contact information.

■ If you are creating a personal account, skip to step 8.

6 Click here to scroll down to reveal additional requests for information.

7 Click Continue.

Why is selecting a hard-to-guess password important?

✔ You probably use your e-mail address, which is also your PayPal logon, for a variety of different functions on the Internet. This address is most likely stored on many different online servers and may even be on some publicly viewable Web pages. For this reason, you should assume lots of people have access to your e-mail address. This makes selecting a hard-to-guess password very important. You should not use a password that you use on another site, because someone with access to the other site's account information could potentially find out your e-mail address and password and access your PayPal account.

Why do I have to type the letters and numbers in the security measure box?

✔ PayPal requires that a person signing up for an account do this to prove that he or she is a real person and not an automated piece of software. The letters and numbers in the box appear in such a way that it is practically impossible for automated Web-browsing software to recognize the symbols.

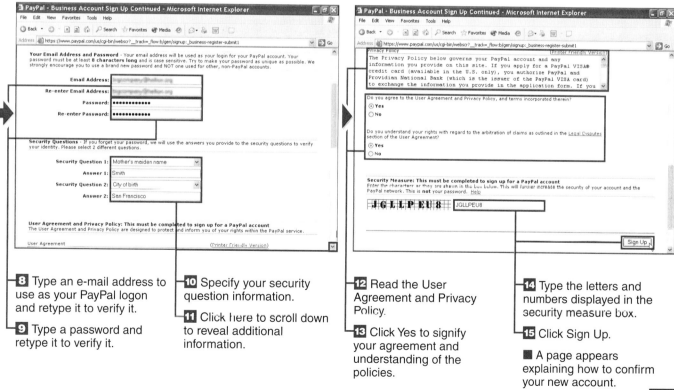

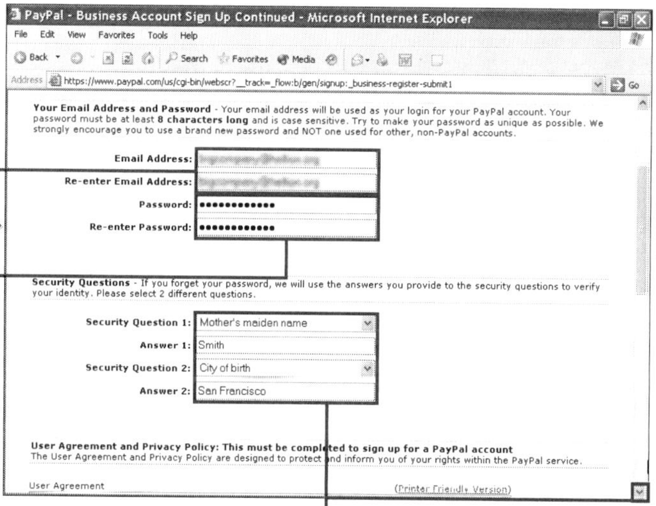

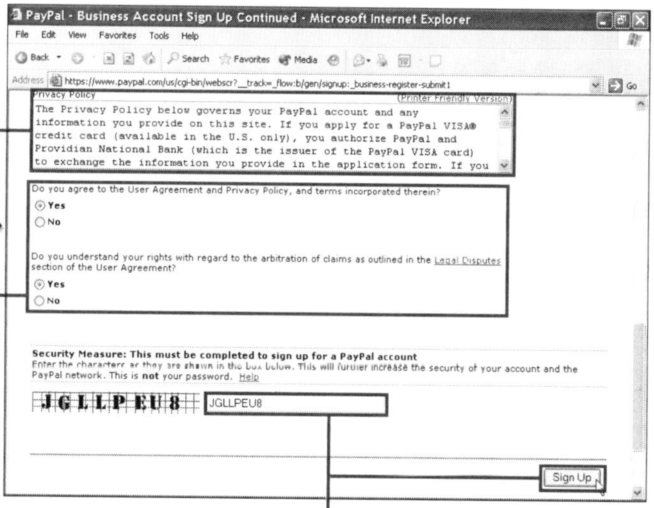

8 Type an e-mail address to use as your PayPal logon and retype it to verify it.

9 Type a password and retype it to verify it.

10 Specify your security question information.

11 Click here to scroll down to reveal additional information.

12 Read the User Agreement and Privacy Policy.

13 Click Yes to signify your agreement and understanding of the policies.

14 Type the letters and numbers displayed in the security measure box.

15 Click Sign Up.

■ A page appears explaining how to confirm your new account.

CONFIRM YOUR ACCOUNT VIA E-MAIL

Your e-mail address is the ID that you use to log in to your PayPal account. It is also the way PayPal communicates with you about payments sent, payments received, and other critical information. Consequently, PayPal needs to verify that an e-mail address is legitimate and that it belongs to the actual account owner before an account can be activated.

After you register, PayPal sends a message to your e-mail account. The e-mail message contains a link that returns you to PayPal. Here you are asked to enter your password. If you enter the correct password, your account is confirmed.

PayPal allows you to associate up to seven secondary e-mail addresses with your account. To make one of these secondary addresses your primary address, which is the e-mail address that you must log on with, you must verify the secondary address. You cannot associate an e-mail address with your account if it is currently associated with another PayPal account.

CONFIRM YOUR ACCOUNT VIA E-MAIL

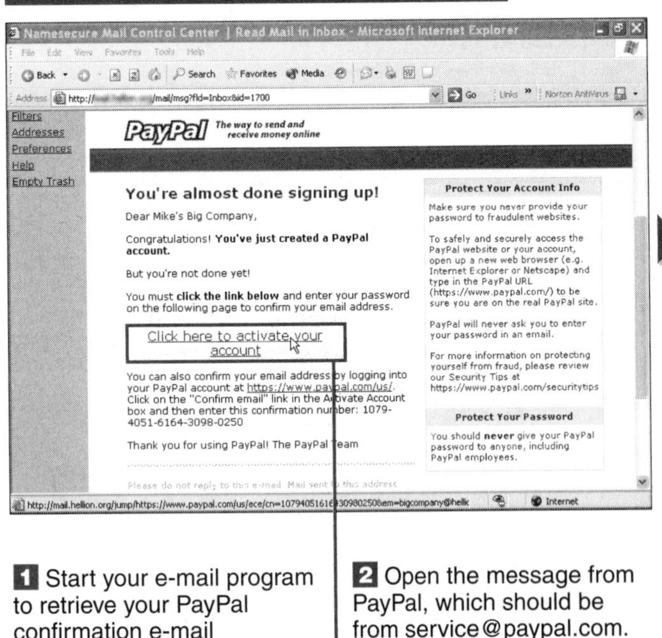

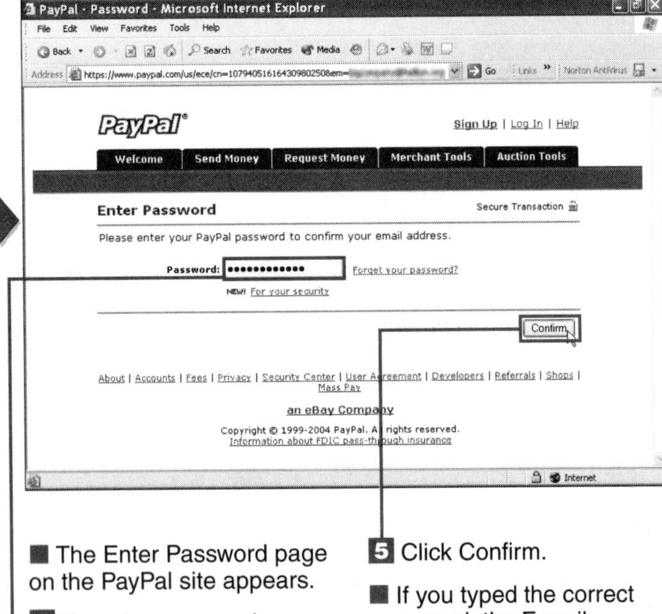

1 Start your e-mail program to retrieve your PayPal confirmation e-mail message, which is sent to the address you specified when you signed up for a new account.

2 Open the message from PayPal, which should be from service@paypal.com.

3 Click the Click here to activate your account link.

■ The Enter Password page on the PayPal site appears.

4 Type the password you specified when you signed up for a new account.

5 Click Confirm.

■ If you typed the correct password, the E-mail Confirmed page appears, confirming your account activation.

LOG ON TO PAYPAL

You can access your PayPal account by typing your e-mail address and password in the fields on the Member Log In page and clicking the Log In button. The e-mail address must match the e-mail address that you submitted when you signed up or, if you have associated multiple addresses with your account, your primary PayPal e-mail address.

If you forget your password, you can retrieve it by clicking the Forget your password? link on the PayPal login page. From the page that appears, you can enter any e-mail address that is associated with your PayPal account. You password will be sent to the address you specify.

You can update the e-mail address or password that you log on with in the Profile area of your PayPal account. Click the My Account tab and then the Profile tab. Then click the Email or Password link.

I am repeatedly being asked to log on when I navigate PayPal. What can I do?

✔ To avoid being repeatedly asked to log on, make sure that cookies are enabled on your Web browser. See the user documentation for your browser for details.

LOG ON TO PAYPAL

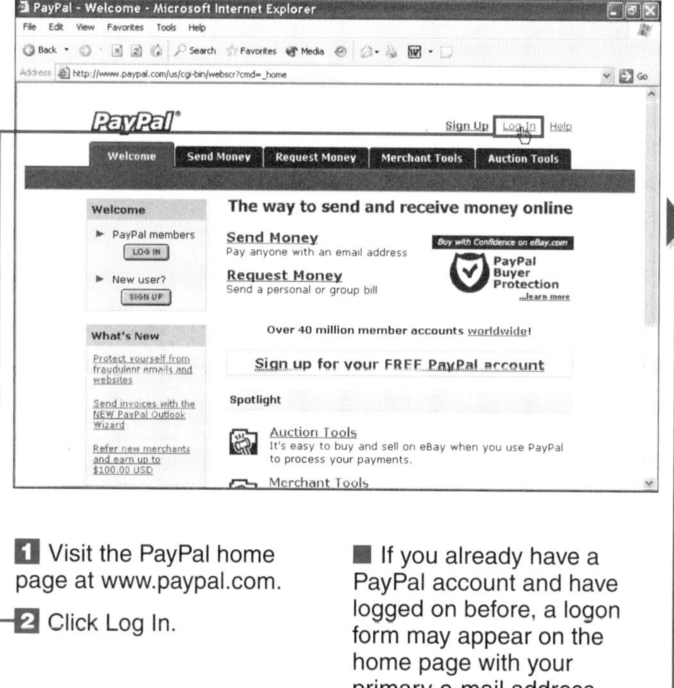

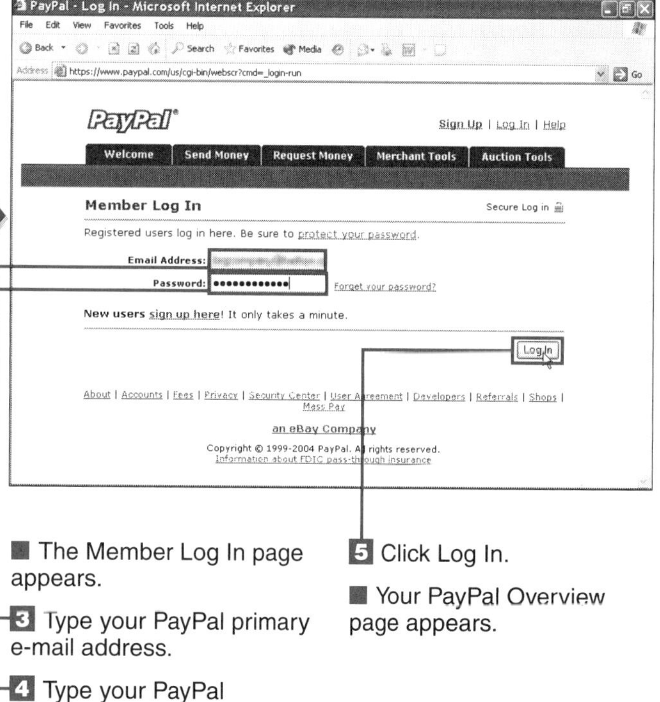

1 Visit the PayPal home page at www.paypal.com.

2 Click Log In.

■ If you already have a PayPal account and have logged on before, a logon form may appear on the home page with your primary e-mail address automatically filled in.

■ The Member Log In page appears.

3 Type your PayPal primary e-mail address.

4 Type your PayPal password.

5 Click Log In.

■ Your PayPal Overview page appears.

CREATE AND MANAGE AUCTION ACCOUNTS

To begin using many of the auction-specific features at PayPal, you must create an auction account inside your PayPal account. You create an auction account by specifying your eBay User ID and password in the Auction Accounts section of your PayPal account profile. Specifying this information allows PayPal to communicate with eBay and integrate the auction process at eBay with the payment process at PayPal.

After you have created an auction account, PayPal gives you access to several auction-related features. You can turn on the Winning Buyer Notification to automatically send an e-mail from PayPal to your winning bidder when your eBay auction listings close. Winning Buyer Notification saves you from having to create a customized invoice for each buyer and makes it easy for buyers to use PayPal as a payment method.

You can also turn on Automatic Logos to add PayPal and associated credit card images to all of your eBay listings. The images appear in the Payment Methods Accepted section, and tell buyers that PayPal is among your accepted payment methods. To inform buyers that you *prefer* PayPal as a payment option, you can also turn on the PayPal Preferred option in your PayPal account.

CREATE AND MANAGE AUCTION ACCOUNTS

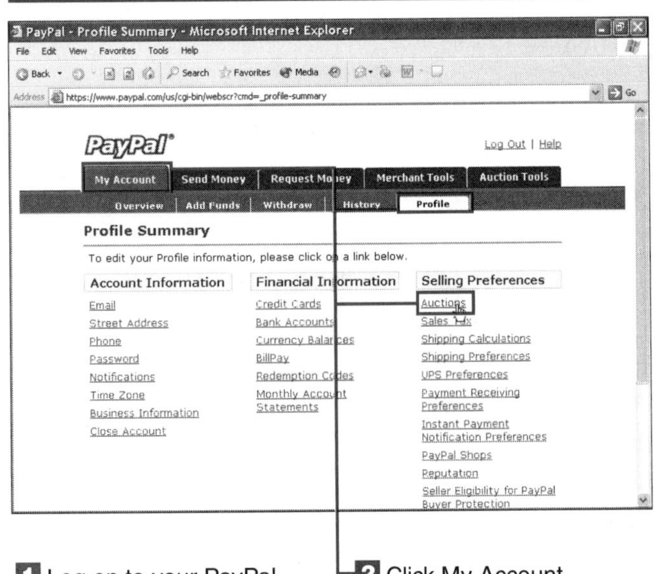

1 Log on to your PayPal account.

Note: See the section "Log On to PayPal" for details.

2 Click My Account.

3 Click Profile.

4 Click Auctions.

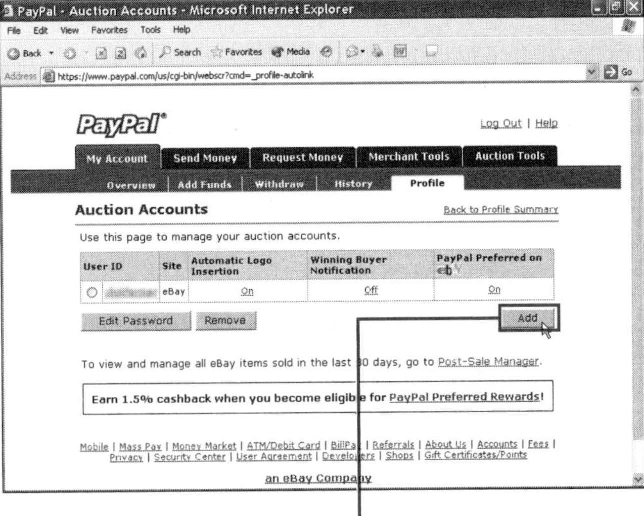

■ The Auction Accounts page appears.

■ PayPal displays any existing auction accounts.

5 Click Add.

How do I turn on Winning Buyer Notification or Automatic Logos?

✔ Log on to your PayPal account and go to the Auction Accounts page. You can turn on Winning Buyer Notification or Automatic Logos by clicking the Off link in the column for that feature. After you activate the feature, an On link appears in the column.

If I turn the Automatic Logos option on or off while an auction is underway, will the information listed in the auction change?

✔ No. Changing the Automatic Logos option will only affect what appears on future auctions, not on auctions that are currently underway. Current auction information does not change.

How can a buyer access PayPal to pay for my auction items?

✔ If you have specified PayPal as one of the payment options in your eBay auction information, the winning bidder can click the PayPal link on the auction page itself, in the confirmation e-mail from eBay, or from a Winning Buyer Notification e-mail from PayPal. Clicking any of these links takes buyers to a PayPal page where they can pay for the auction item. Buyers need to sign up for a PayPal account to pay with the service.

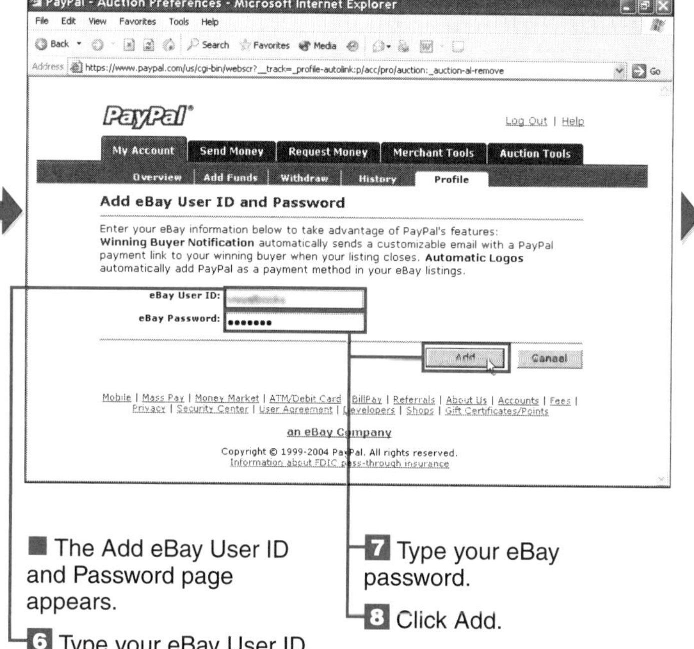

■ The Add eBay User ID and Password page appears.

6 Type your eBay User ID.

7 Type your eBay password.

8 Click Add.

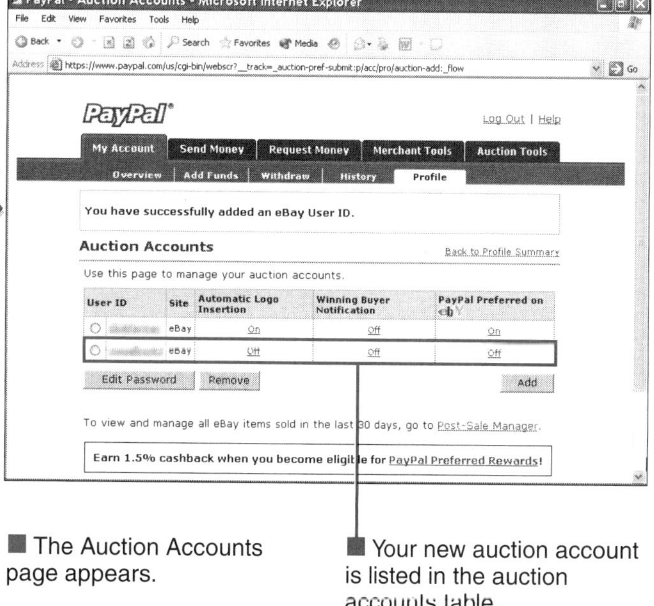

■ The Auction Accounts page appears.

■ Your new auction account is listed in the auction accounts table.

MAKE AN AUCTION PAYMENT USING PAYPAL

If an eBay seller offers PayPal as a payment method for a listing, buyers can use PayPal to pay for the item online using their credit card or bank account. PayPal makes completing an auction convenient for both the buyer and seller. The buyer can often pay for the item within minutes of the end of an auction. When the auction has been paid for, the seller can put the package in the mail.

eBay and PayPal are tightly integrated: The final selling price and shipping fees from an auction are carried over to the PayPal payment forms when you use PayPal to make a payment. The transaction details in the My eBay section also show which listings have been successfully paid for using PayPal.

PayPal accepts payments from buyers in the United States as well as more than 30 countries. For a complete list of these countries and the specific services offered, click the Help link in the upper right corner of the PayPal pages. PayPal currently accepts the following currencies: U.S. dollar, Canadian dollar, euro, pound sterling, and yen.

MAKE AN AUCTION PAYMENT USING PAYPAL

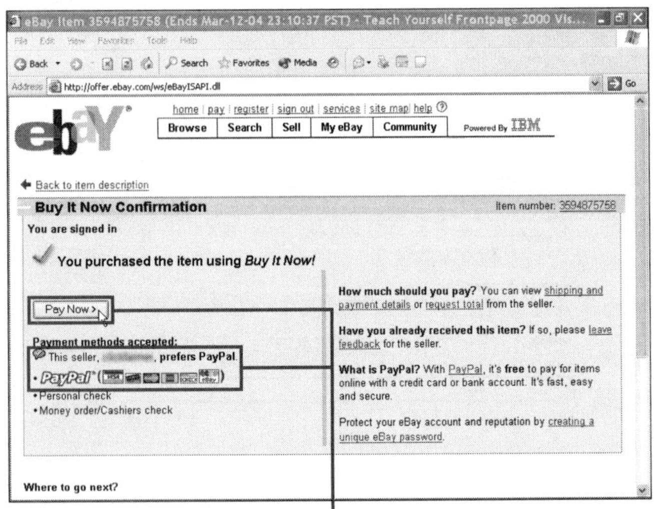

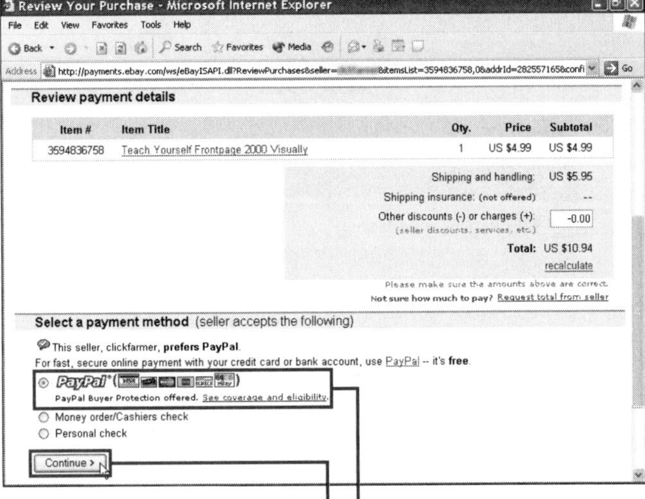

1 Log on to your eBay account.

2 Open the eBay auction page for the item you won.

■ You can find links to recent items you have won in the My eBay section.

■ If the buyer accepts PayPal, it will say so under the Payment methods accepted.

3 Click Pay Now.

■ The Review Your Purchase page appears.

4 Review your shipping and payment details.

5 Click the PayPal payment option you want to use.

6 Click Continue.

How can I adjust the payment amount I send to a seller?

✔ In some cases, a buyer may need to adjust the payment amount that is sent to a seller so that it is different than the amount stated on the eBay listing. This may happen when the seller offers a discount to buyers purchasing more than one item, or when the shipping fees need to be changed because of the location of the buyer. You can adjust the payment by typing a number in the Other discounts or charges text box on the Review Your Purchase page. Type a minus sign (-) before the number to decrease the payment, or a plus sign (+) to increase the payment. Click the recalculate link for the new total.

Will a seller see the credit card information of a buyer who pays for an auction through PayPal?

✔ No. A buyer's credit card information is encrypted and hidden from view through the PayPal servers to protect buyers from unauthorized use of their cards.

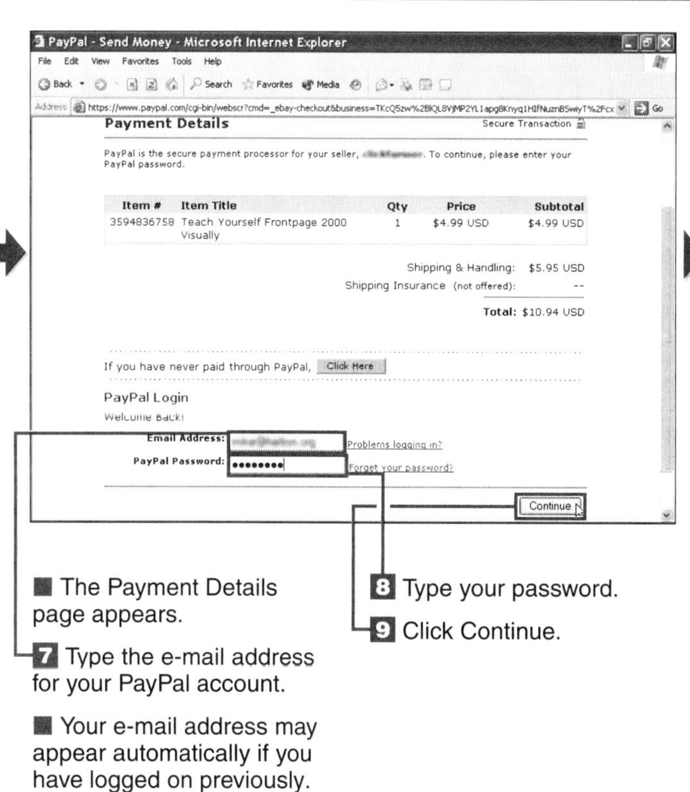

■ The Payment Details page appears.

7 Type the e-mail address for your PayPal account.

■ Your e-mail address may appear automatically if you have logged on previously.

8 Type your password.

9 Click Continue.

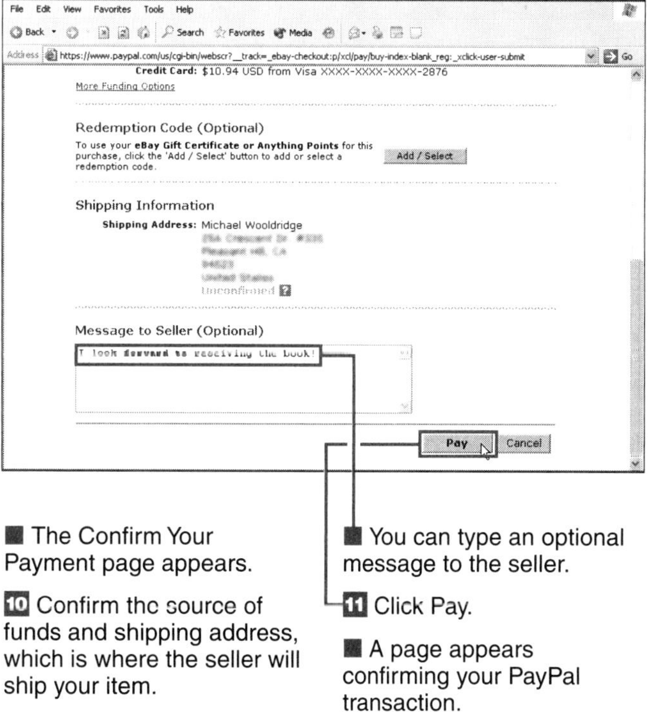

■ The Confirm Your Payment page appears.

10 Confirm the source of funds and shipping address, which is where the seller will ship your item.

■ You can type an optional message to the seller.

11 Click Pay.

■ A page appears confirming your PayPal transaction.

USE PAYPAL POST-SALE MANAGER

The Post-Sale Manager at PayPal lets you view your recent eBay sales and manage their invoicing, payments, shipping, and feedback. Post-Sale Manager works with any eBay listing through which you successfully sell an item. Items are displayed in the Post-Sale Manager for up to 30 days after the close of the listing.

The Invoice column in the Post-Sale Manager allows you to send a customized invoice to the buyer after an auction has ended. The invoice contains instructions for using PayPal and a link to the PayPal page where the buyer can make a payment. If you have Winning Buyer Notification turned on, invoices are sent out automatically and Auto is displayed in the Invoice column.

After a buyer has paid for an item through PayPal, the Invoice column displays nothing. The Invoice column also displays nothing if you have specified that the buyer made a non-PayPal payment for the item. You can specify this by clicking the Edit button in the Payment Status column of the manager.

You can remove an item from the Post-Sale Manager by clicking the Select option and then the Remove button. Note, however, that after items have been removed, they cannot be reimported into the Post-Sale Manager.

USE PAYPAL POST-SALE MANAGER

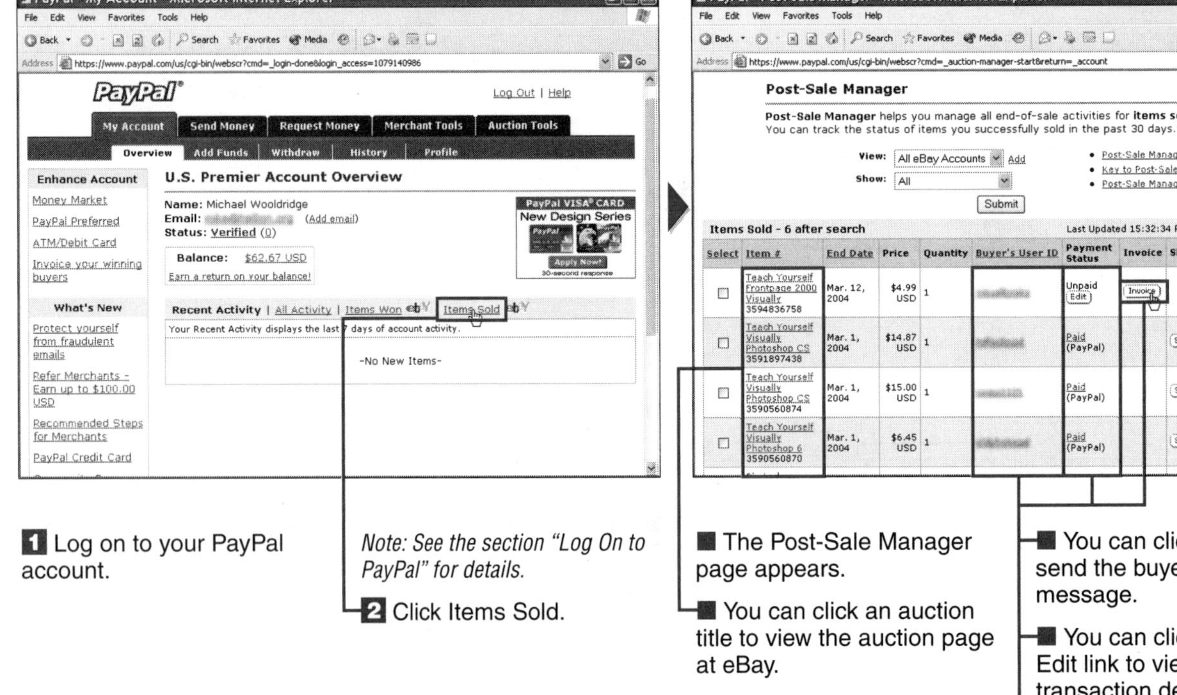

1 Log on to your PayPal account.

Note: See the section "Log On to PayPal" for details.

2 Click Items Sold.

■ The Post-Sale Manager page appears.

■ You can click an auction title to view the auction page at eBay.

■ You can click a User ID to send the buyer an e-mail message.

■ You can click a Paid or Edit link to view the transaction details.

3 Click Invoice for an item.

What do the Post-Sale Manager table headings mean?

✔ **Select**: Clicking an option in this column allows you to invoice or delete a transaction using the buttons at the bottom of the page.

Item: The eBay auction title and item number.

End Date: The date that the eBay listing ended.

Price: The selling price of the auction, not including shipping fees.

Quantity: How many items were purchased.

Buyer's User ID: The user ID of the winning buyer.

Payment Status: Whether the transaction has been paid for, through PayPal or some other method.

Invoice: The invoice status of the item. This will be blank if the buyer has paid already through PayPal.

Shipping: The shipping status of the item. You can click the Ship button to purchase and print a shipping label.

Feedback: The feedback status of the transaction. It will show Done for feedback sent through the Post-Sale Manager.

Memo: Lets you to leave a memo about the transaction.

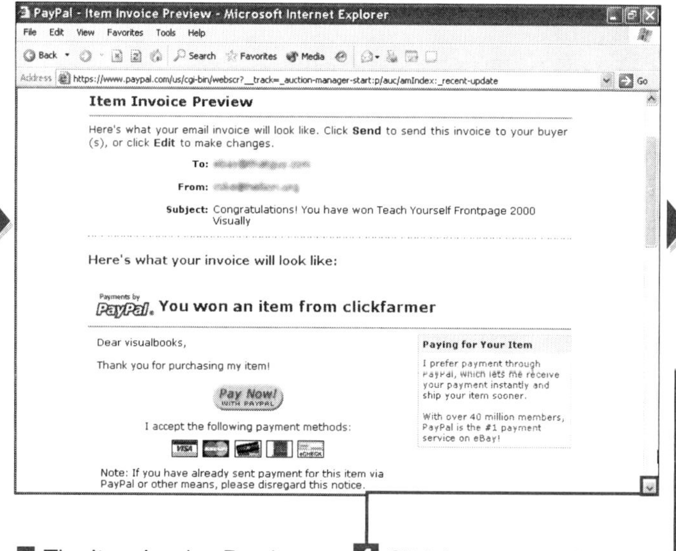

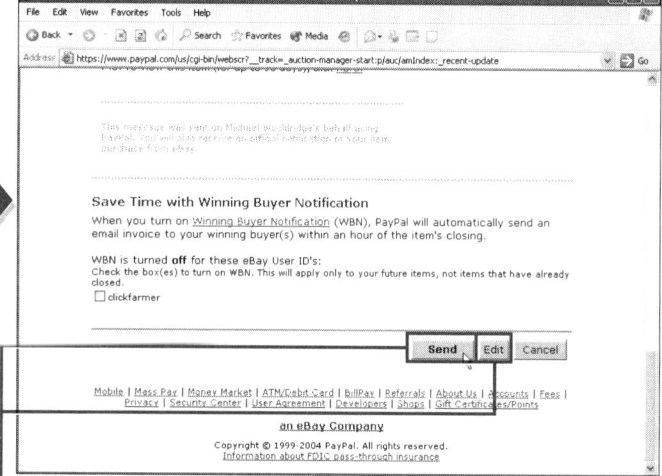

■ The Item Invoice Preview page appears.

■ The page shows a preview of the invoice information to be sent to the buyer.

4 Click here to scroll to the bottom of the page.

5 Click Send.

■ You can click Edit to make changes in invoice information before sending.

■ PayPal sends the buyer the invoice by e-mail.

■ The Invoice button in the Post-Sale Manager changes to Sent.

SHIP A PACKAGE VIA PAYPAL

PayPal Shipping lets you purchase U.S. Postal Service and UPS shipping labels for your packages through the PayPal Web site. After you purchase the label, you can print it from your Web browser, affix it to your package, and drop the package off with the shipping service for delivery to your buyer.

To ship a package from the PayPal site, click the Ship button for the transaction in the Post-Sale Manager or on the History page. You can also ship a package by clicking the Print Shipping Label button for sold items in the My eBay section on the eBay site.

To ship a package, you need to know the type of packaging to be used, such as a USPS Priority Mail envelope or a UPS shipping tube. You also need to know the weight of the entire package, including the container and any packing materials.

When shipping through the U.S. Postal Service, you can pay for shipping labels with your PayPal account balance, with an instant transfer from your bank account, or with your credit card. With UPS shipping, you can pay with your PayPal account balance or you can charge it to your UPS Account, if you have one.

SHIP A PACKAGE VIA PAYPAL

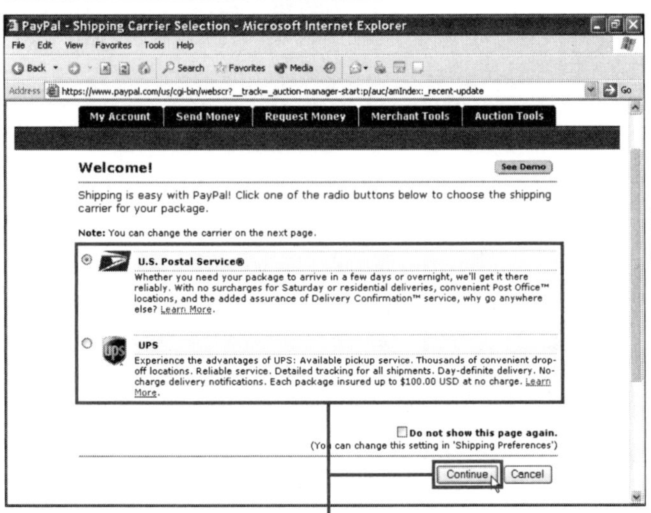

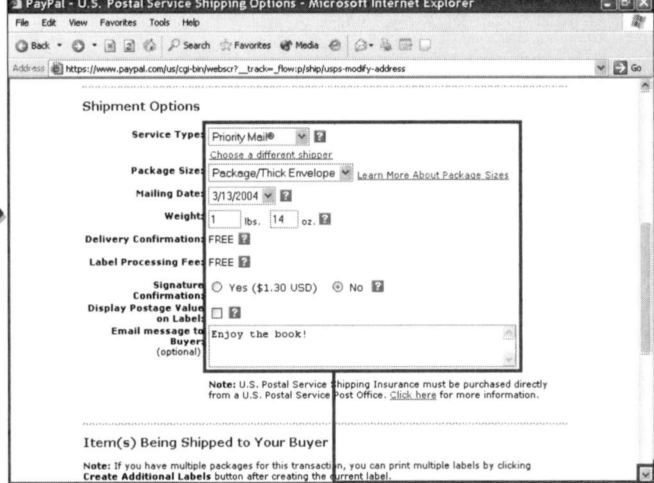

1 Log on to PayPal and open the Post-Sale Manager page.

Note: See the section "Use PayPal Post-Sale Manager" for details.

2 In the Shipping column, click Ship for an item.

■ The Shipping Carrier Selection page appears.

3 Click a shipping carrier option.

4 Click Continue.

■ The Shipment Options page appears.

5 Confirm the shipping address information at the top of the page.

6 Specify your shipping options, such as service type, package size, and package weight.

7 Click here to scroll down to the bottom of the page for additional options.

8 Click Continue.

The shipping label does not appear after I pay for it. What can I do?

✔ The completed label appears in a separate browser popup window after you pay for it. If you have a utility installed on your browser that stops popup windows, you should disable it before you create your shipping label.

How do I attach the shipping label to my package?

✔ You can use glue or tape to attach the shipping label to your package. However, if you use tape, do not tape over the barcode information. Place the label on your package so that it does not wrap around any edges.

What type of printer setup should I use for creating my shipping labels?

✔ To print your label, you should use a laser printer or a high-quality inkjet printer set to at least 600 dots per inch. Low-quality printers, or printers set to print at low dpi, may not create the crisp barcode lines that shipping scanners can read.

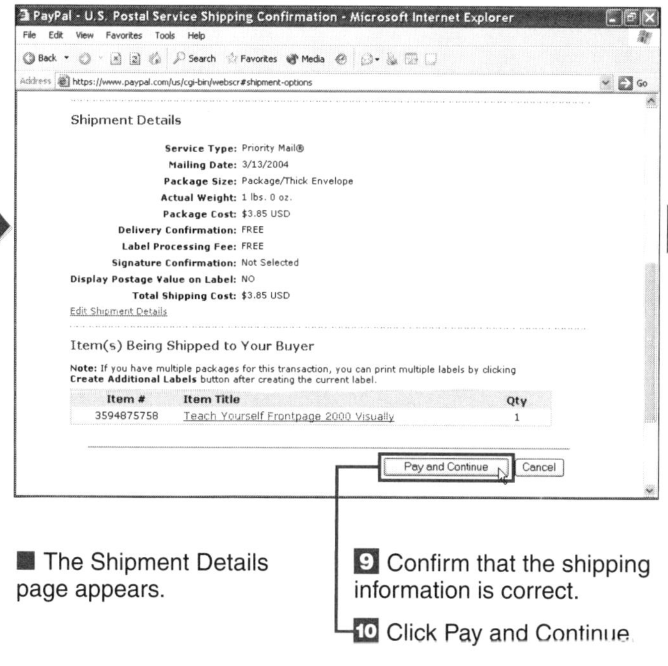

■ The Shipment Details page appears.

9 Confirm that the shipping information is correct.

10 Click Pay and Continue.

■ A Print Postage page appears in a new window.

■ A sample shipping label appears at the bottom of the page.

■ Directions explain how to use the label.

11 Click Print Label.

■ Your browser sends the label to your printer for printing.

TRACK A SHIPPED PACKAGE

After you create a shipping label for a package at PayPal and ship it via the U.S. Postal Service or UPS, you can track the package as it travels to the buyer's address. The tracking page at the U.S. Postal Service or UPS displays an electronic trail of the facilities the package has stopped at as it moves to its destination. It also tells you the time and date when the package reaches the buyer.

Tracking your packages helps you keep tabs on which of your transactions is complete. You can also see how long a package takes to reach its destination and determine whether different shipping options live up to your expectations.

You can view tracking information at the PayPal site through the History section or the Post-Sale Manager. In both places, transactions for which shipping labels have been created display a tracking button. Clicking the button takes you to a tracking page on the U.S. Postal Service or UPS site.

You can also track packages that have been shipped through PayPal from the My eBay page for your eBay account.

TRACK A SHIPPED PACKAGE

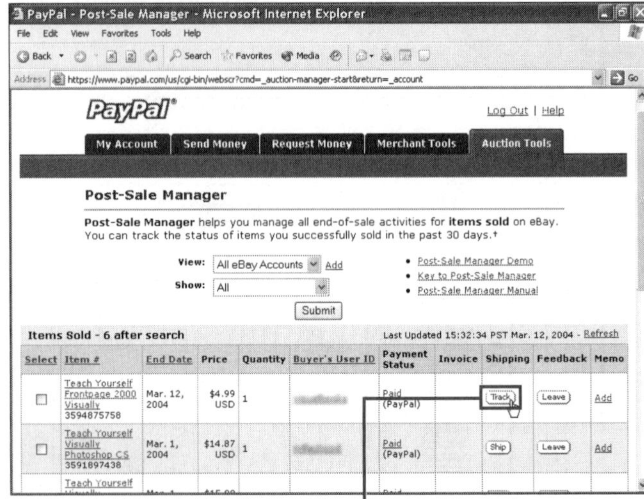

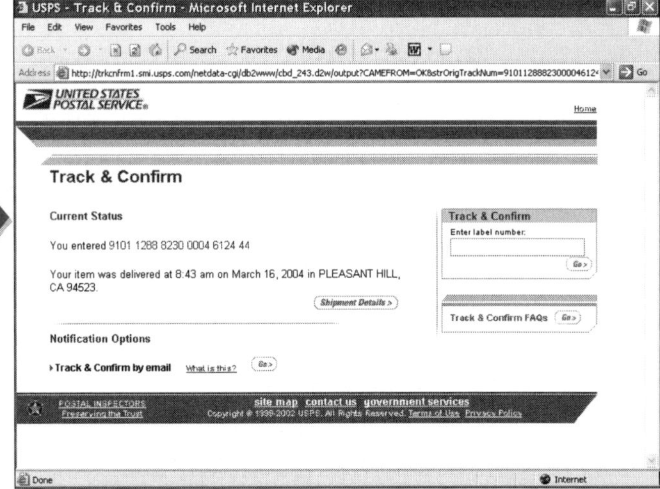

FROM POST-SALE MANAGER

1 Log on to PayPal and open the Post-Sale Manager page.

Note: See the section "Use PayPal Post-Sale Manager" for details.

2 In the Shipping column for an item, click Track.

Note: The Track button appears after you create and purchase a shipping label through PayPal Shipping. See the section "Ship a Package via PayPal" for details.

■ A tracking page appears in a new browser window with any tracking information for the package.

■ If the package has yet to be sent, no tracking information is displayed.

How can I get confirmation that a package I ship reaches the right person?

✔ For packages sent via the U.S. Postal Service, you can request a signature confirmation. This will require that the addressee signs for the package when it is delivered. After the package reaches the destination and a signature is gathered, you can visit the tracking page at the USPS Web site (www.usps.com/shipping/trackandconfirm.htm) and request that the signature be faxed or mailed to you.

Signature confirmation can be added to USPS Priority Mail packages for an extra fee. The service is free if you send a package by USPS Express Mail.

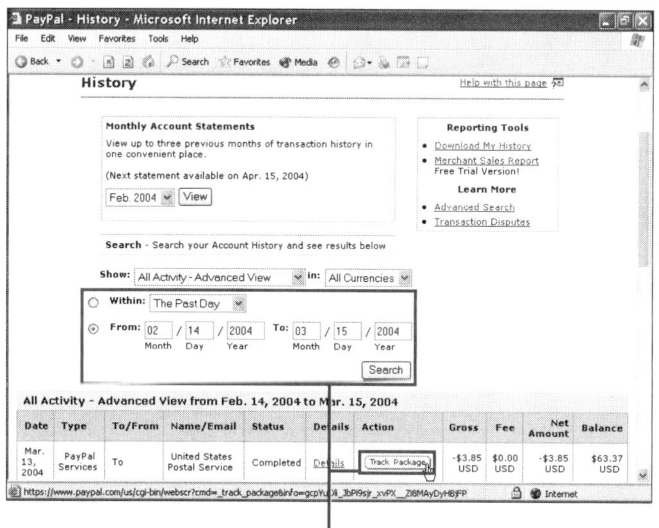

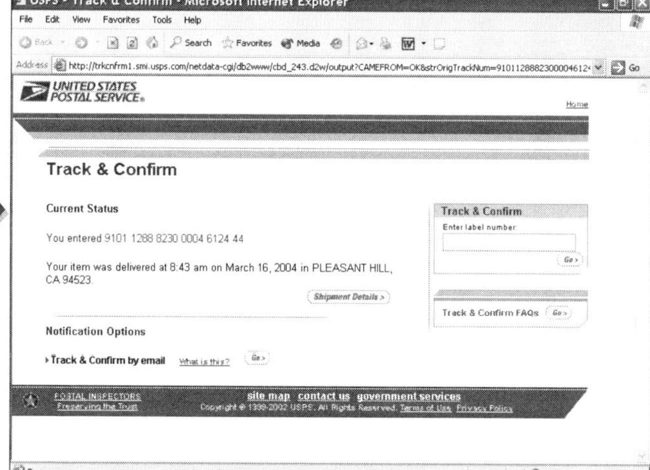

FROM HISTORY

1 Log on to PayPal.

2 Click the My Account tab.

3 Click History.

■ You can change the search settings on the History page to view a specific date range.

4 In the Action column for an item, click Track Package.

■ A tracking page appears in a new browser window with any tracking information for the package.

■ If the package has yet to be sent, no tracking information is displayed.

VIEW YOUR PAYPAL HISTORY

Your PayPal History contains a log of all your PayPal transactions whether they are payments you have made or payments you have received. Through History, you can view PayPal activity that occurred during a specific time period, find out which buyers have paid for their auctions through PayPal, and look at the details of a particular transaction. A table on the PayPal History page displays when and with whom each transaction occurred, and the monies and PayPal fees involved.

To view details of an auction transaction made through PayPal, you can click a Details link for that transaction in the History table. This shows you the eBay auction number, the auction title, and other details. Clicking the auction title takes you to the auction page on the eBay site.

You can download your History to save an offline record of your PayPal transactions on your computer. You have the choice of downloading your History as a comma- or tab-delimited file. Both types of files can be opened with most spreadsheet programs. You can also download your history as a Quicken or QuickBooks file.

VIEW YOUR PAYPAL HISTORY

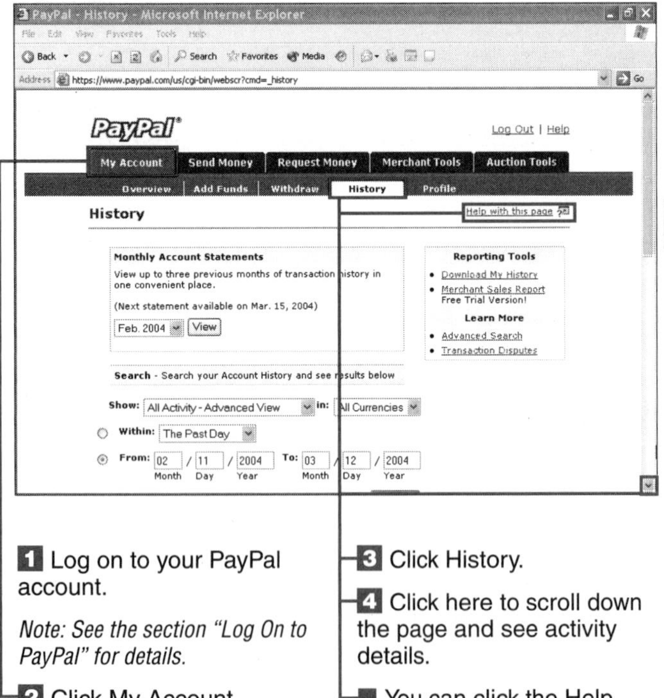

1 Log on to your PayPal account.

Note: See the section "Log On to PayPal" for details.

2 Click My Account.

3 Click History.

4 Click here to scroll down the page and see activity details.

■ You can click the Help with this page link to find out more about PayPal History.

All Activity - Advanced View from Feb. 11, 2004 to Mar. 12, 2004

Date	Type	To/From	Name/Email	Status	Details	Action	Gross	Fee	Net Amount	Balance
Mar. 3, 2004	Payment	From		Completed	Details	Ship	$19.95 USD	-$0.88 USD	$19.07 USD	$62.67 USD
Mar. 1, 2004	Payment	From		Completed	Details	Ship	$19.82 USD	-$0.87 USD	$18.95 USD	$43.60 USD
Mar. 1, 2004	Update	From		Completed	Details		$13.95 USD	-$0.70 USD	$13.25 USD	$24.65 USD
Mar. 1, 2004	Payment	From		Completed	Details	Ship	$13.95 USD	-$0.70 USD	$13.25 USD	$11.40 USD
Mar. 1, 2004	Payment	From		Completed	Details	Ship	$11.40 USD	$0.00 USD	$11.40 USD	$11.40 USD
Feb. 27, 2004	Payment	To		Completed	Details		-$19.99 USD	$0.00 USD	-$19.99 USD	$0.00 USD
Feb. 27, 2004	Transfer	From		Completed	Details		$3.05 USD	$0.00 USD	$3.05 USD	$19.99 USD
Feb. 25, 2004	Payment	From		Completed	Details	Ship	$16.94 USD	$0.00 USD	$16.94 USD	$16.94 USD
Feb. 23, 2004	Payment	To		Completed	Details		-$49.95 USD	$0.00 USD	-$49.95 USD	$0.00 USD
Feb. 23,	Transfer	From		Completed	Details		$49.95 USD	$0.00 USD	$49.95 USD	$49.95 USD

■ A table displays your PayPal History.

5 Click a Details link for an auction transaction.

What are Monthly Account Statements?

✔ Accessible from the History page, Monthly Account Statements let you view and print a monthly summary of the activity in your PayPal account. You can view and print a statement for any of the previous three months.

What happens if I click the Ship button in the History table?

✔ Clicking the Ship button takes you through a series of pages that enable you to create and print a shipping label and pay shipping fees for a PayPal transaction. For more details about this process, see the section "Ship a Package via PayPal."

What are Merchant Sales Reports?

✔ Similar to your account History, Merchant Sales Reports provide weekly analyses of your PayPal revenue. This information can help you measure and manage your PayPal-based business. You can view them by clicking the Merchant Sales Report link in the Reporting Tools box of your History page.

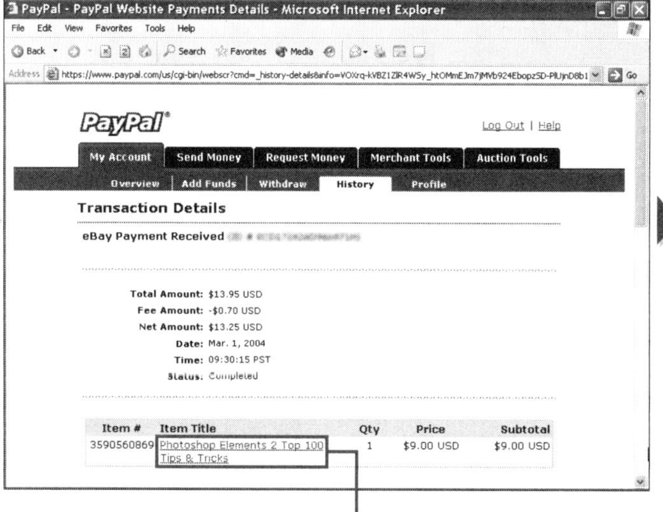

■ Details of the auction transaction appear.

6 Click the item title.

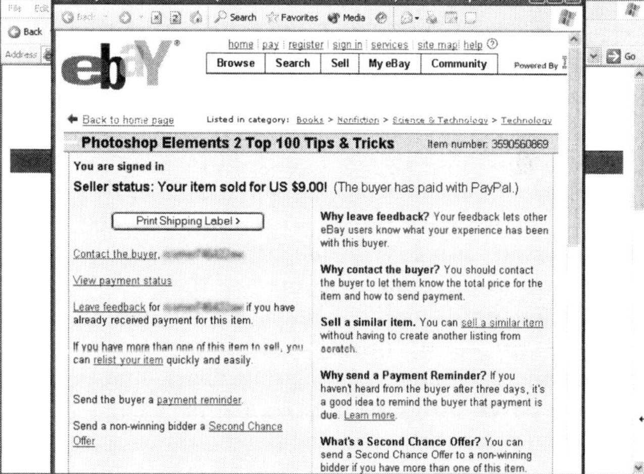

■ A new window appears, showing the eBay auction page for that transaction.

UNDERSTANDING FEEDBACK

eBay's buying and selling structure is built on a unique foundation of feedback. Feedback is a voluntary process of reporting your auction experience for a particular item. As a buyer, your feedback tells others about your experience with a particular seller. As a seller, your feedback tells other sellers what your experience was like with a particular buyer. Over the course of time, your accumulation of feedback tells everyone about your buying and selling reputation on eBay, and basically describes your success rate as an eBay business.

The exchange of feedback is what makes eBay a distinct community, allowing users to interact with each other. Because eBay's auction transactions require a lot of trust on both the buying and selling ends, feedback becomes an essential part of determining whether others want to interact with you. What makes feedback so important to you as a user is its permanency. Like a record of school grades, your feedback record is permanent for as long as you are a registered eBay user, even if you change e-mail addresses. Because feedback is permanent, it is up to you to maintain a good reputation.

Leaving feedback for others is strictly voluntary. Some users never leave feedback, regardless of whether the transaction was good or not. However, to really be a part of eBay's community, it is in your best interest to participate fully in the feedback process, especially if you want others to view your eBay business as a serious endeavor. Without your feedback, others do not gain any knowledge about the level of trust or competency of a particular buyer or seller.

How Feedback Works

You can only leave feedback for another eBay user if you win an auction or if you sell an item to a winning bidder or Buy It Now purchaser. Feedback reports always pertain to a particular auction listing. Buyers can report feedback about the seller, essentially summing up the transaction experience. For example, as a buyer, your feedback report might mention the speediness of the shipping, the level of communication with the seller, or the quality of the item you purchased. Sellers can leave feedback about the buyer, including whether the payment was prompt or noting the quality of communication.

Buyers and sellers both use a feedback form to evaluate a transaction. The form allows you to note the experience as positive, neutral, or negative. In addition, the form includes a text box you can use to further describe the transaction. After filling out the form, the feedback is posted to the user's feedback report, viewable by anyone else on eBay.

Feedback Scores

Next to every user's ID is a feedback number, also called a *score*. The feedback score pertains to the user's overall feedback standing. The number represents the total of completed transactions with unique users. The higher the number, the more feedback accumulated by the user.

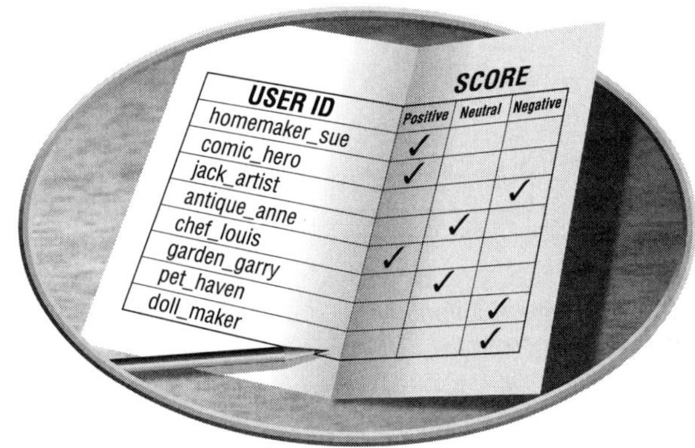

You accumulate positive points for every positive transaction, zero points for neutral transactions, and negative points for negative transactions. In addition, if you attain certain feedback number levels, colored star icons appear alongside your feedback score. For example, when you reach a feedback score of 10, you can see a yellow star next to your score.

However, just looking at a feedback number does not tell you about the person's reputation. Rather, the feedback number indicates a level of eBay experience. To really determine reputation, you need to look at the actual feedback report — the notations reported by others.

Feedback Notations

Feedback notations tell others about your experience, your history, your level of professionalism, and your ability to communicate and work well with others. Gaining positive feedback is a goal for anyone starting an eBay business. The more successful your transactions, the more others are willing to buy from you and make repeat purchases.

If you start accumulating negative reports, your eBay business is likely to suffer. Negative reports immediately send up red flags to other users that you may not be a good businessperson to deal with, and if you accumulate a negative feedback of –4, eBay can close your account.

Before you ever bid on an auction, take a moment to check out the seller's feedback report. If a person has a large number of negative comments, you may reconsider making a bid. If you see a high number of negative reports, take into consideration the total number of sales as well as the total number of negative reports. For example, if a user has a feedback score of 80, and two negatives, chances are that the seller simply encountered two buyers he could not please. If the same rating included 12 negatives, the rating serves as a caution to you about the user's abilities and service. Be sure to read the negative comments to spot any trends you want to avoid, such as failure to pay or deliver in a timely fashion.

Determining Feedback

eBay allows users up to 90 days to leave feedback. This lengthy amount of time gives sellers and buyers time to work out any issues that may arise with a transaction. As a general rule, if the seller receives payment and the buyer receives the item, the transaction is considered a positive experience and both parties leave appropriate feedback. For example, as a seller, if the buyer follows your terms of sale and pays you in a timely manner, you can certainly rate the experience as positive.

Not every transaction runs smoothly, however, and payments can arrive late or communication channels may not always operate properly. If the end result still works out in favor of both parties, positive feedback is in order. Negative reports should only be reserved for extreme situations and grievous problems, such as failure to pay or failure to ship. Negative feedback should never be used as a threat or personal attack against another user. You should always try to work out problems before leaving feedback.

VIEW FEEDBACK

As you complete buys or sales on eBay, you begin to accumulate a feedback rating. A feedback rating, or score, alerts other eBay users to your online reputation. You can view your own feedback in several ways. An initial glance at your eBay User ID shows a number following your ID in parentheses. This number indicates your total number of unique feedback reports. For example, a feedback of (17) indicates you have completed 17 transactions with unique users. If you buy more than one item from the same seller, that feedback report only counts as one point in your feedback rating.

In addition to a feedback point system, you can also view actual feedback reports. Reports are simply the written evaluations about your customer service or buying reputation. Your feedback report lists all the notations you receive about the auction items you win or sell. The report also lists the feedback you give to others. As you complete more auctions, your feedback report grows in length.

You can view your own feedback through the My eBay page or by interacting directly with the feedback number next to your ID. You can also use this method to view the feedback about others, such as users bidding on your auctions.

VIEW FEEDBACK

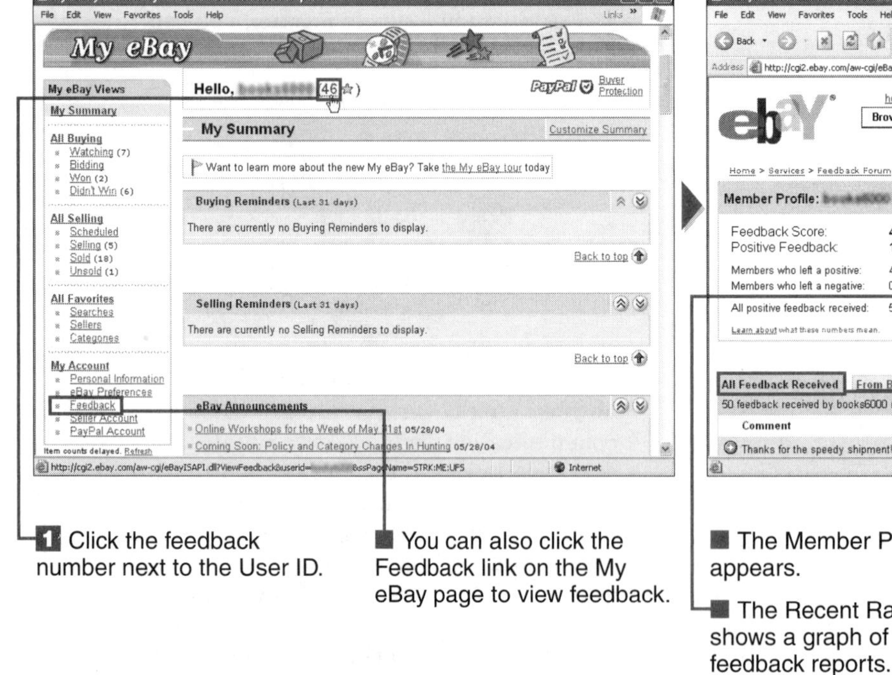

1 Click the feedback number next to the User ID.

■ You can also click the Feedback link on the My eBay page to view feedback.

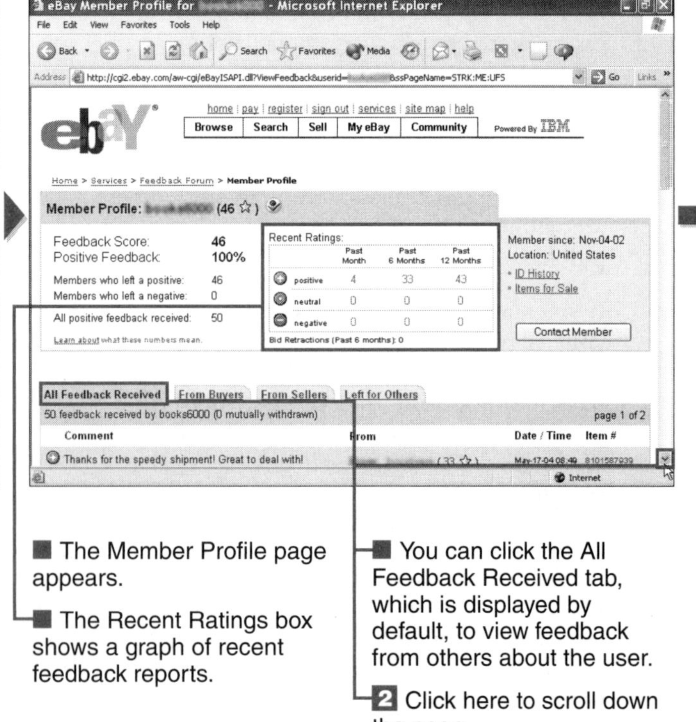

■ The Member Profile page appears.

■ The Recent Ratings box shows a graph of recent feedback reports.

■ You can click the All Feedback Received tab, which is displayed by default, to view feedback from others about the user.

2 Click here to scroll down the page.

The seller's feedback is hidden. Why?

✔ eBay allows users to keep their feedback comments hidden as a privacy feature. Although the comments are hidden, the ratings are not, and other users can still see how many positive, neutral, and negative feedback points the person has accumulated. Hiding comments can bring immediate suspicion to your feedback profile, because other users assume you are trying to hide negative reports. In some cases, you may need to hide your feedback comments temporarily until eBay fixes a problem if someone has violated the Feedback Abuse policy and entered contact information or profanity into his or her comments about you. If you are uncomfortable with anyone's hidden feedback, block that user's bidding or do not bid on the user's auction.

How do I view feedback from the My eBay page?

✔ You can click the Feedback tab to quickly view your eBay feedback. To view all your feedback, including feedback from sellers, buyers, and feedback you left for others, click the See All Feedback link.

What are bid retractions?

✔ Your feedback profile also keeps track of any bid retractions you make. Bid retractions occur when you accidentally bid the wrong amount, but you must immediately bid the right amount after placing a retraction. Bid retractions are also allowed if the auction listing changes significantly or the seller has invalid contact information. Be mindful that eBay investigates bid retractions.

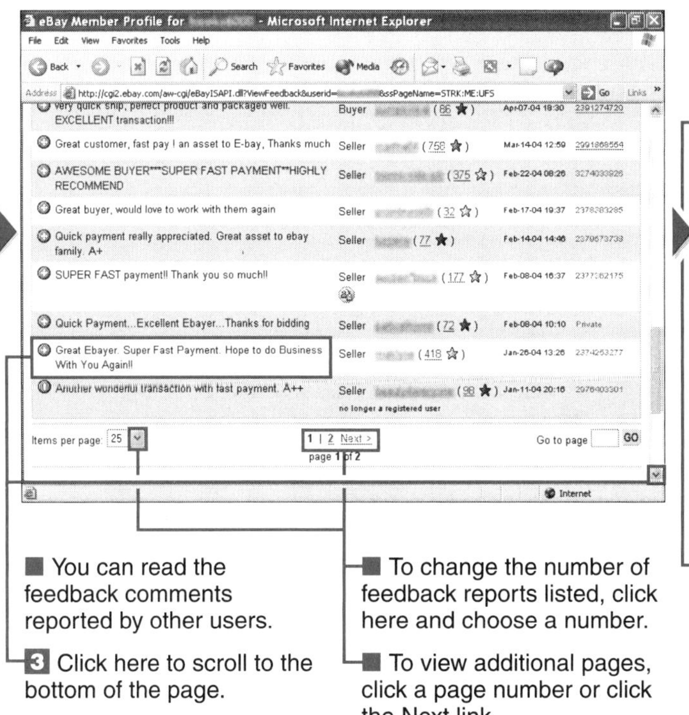

■ You can read the feedback comments reported by other users.

3 Click here to scroll to the bottom of the page.

■ To change the number of feedback reports listed, click here and choose a number.

■ To view additional pages, click a page number or click the Next link.

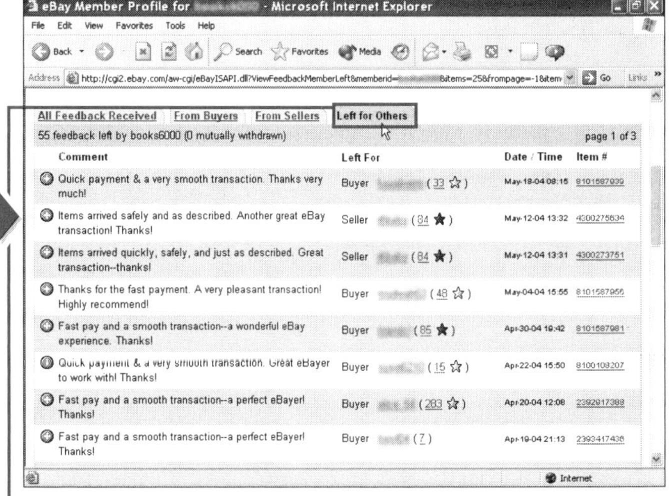

4 Scroll to the top of the page and click the Left for Others tab.

■ eBay displays all the feedback the current user left for others.

LEAVE FEEDBACK

After you complete an auction transaction, whether as a buyer or as a seller, you can leave feedback about the process. The Feedback Forum page includes a form you can fill out about the transaction, including three ways to rate the experience: positive, neutral, or negative. You can also add a text comment to further describe the experience. The Comment text box only allows up to 80 characters, including punctuation.

eBay users employ a variety of phrases to summarize a transaction. Comments can range from high praise to factual notes. For example, positive comments can include phrases like "quick payment, excellent eBayer" to "easy transaction, great product, A+." It is in your best interest to remain professional in your report notations at all times. When leaving feedback for others, being friendly, concise, factual, and grammatically correct can go a long way in building a good business reputation.

You have up to 90 days to leave feedback for a transaction. The feedback you leave for others is permanent, so use good judgment when filling out the feedback form. Your comments carry more weight when they avoid emotion, speculation, or accusations. Negative feedback should always be a last resort after attempting to correct any problems.

LEAVE FEEDBACK

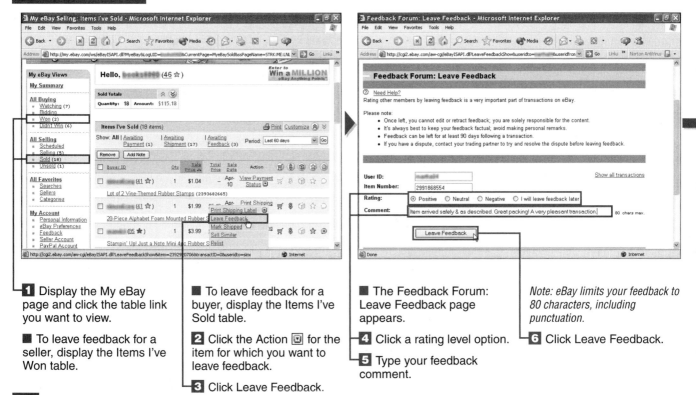

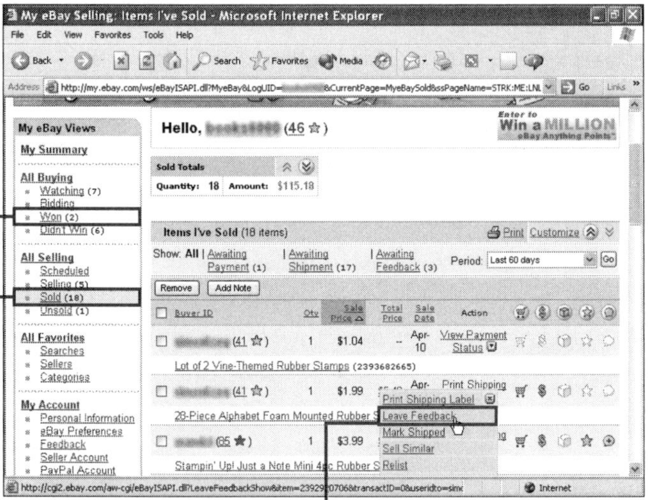

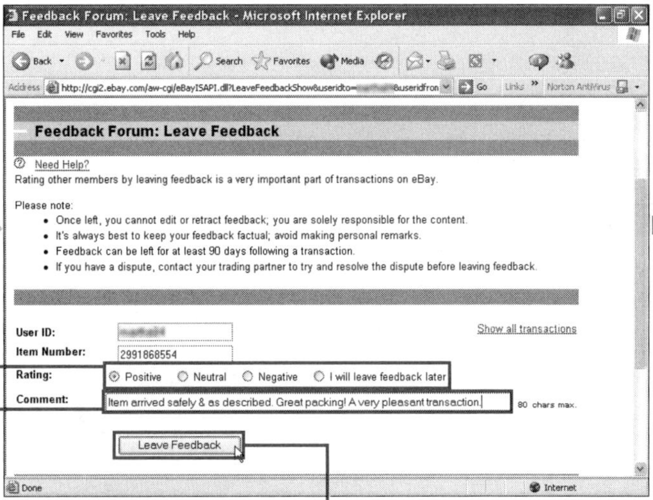

1 Display the My eBay page and click the table link you want to view.

■ To leave feedback for a seller, display the Items I've Won table.

■ To leave feedback for a buyer, display the Items I've Sold table.

2 Click the Action for the item for which you want to leave feedback.

3 Click Leave Feedback.

■ The Feedback Forum: Leave Feedback page appears.

4 Click a rating level option.

5 Type your feedback comment.

Note: eBay limits your feedback to 80 characters, including punctuation.

6 Click Leave Feedback.

A buyer has not left me feedback. What can I do?

✔ You cannot force anyone to leave feedback. Feedback is a voluntary action. You can consider sending the buyer an e-mail asking if the item has been received and if the buyer is happy with the purchase, and then gently remind the buyer to leave feedback. Just remember, some users never leave feedback, positive or otherwise.

Can I edit the feedback I just left for someone?

✔ No. You cannot edit any feedback comment you leave. As soon as you submit the comment, the notation is permanent. For that reason alone, you should be very careful about leaving feedback, especially negative feedback.

What types of situations warrant negative feedback?

✔ Leaving negative feedback is always a last resort when you cannot work out your differences with the other user. You should only leave negative feedback if the buyer or seller has seriously transgressed regarding a transaction, such as refusing to pay or ship.

Where do I report feedback violations?

✔ You can report a violation to eBay by clicking the Help link at the top of any eBay page, and then clicking the Contact Us link on the Help page. A form appears that you can use to specify the type of problem you want to report.

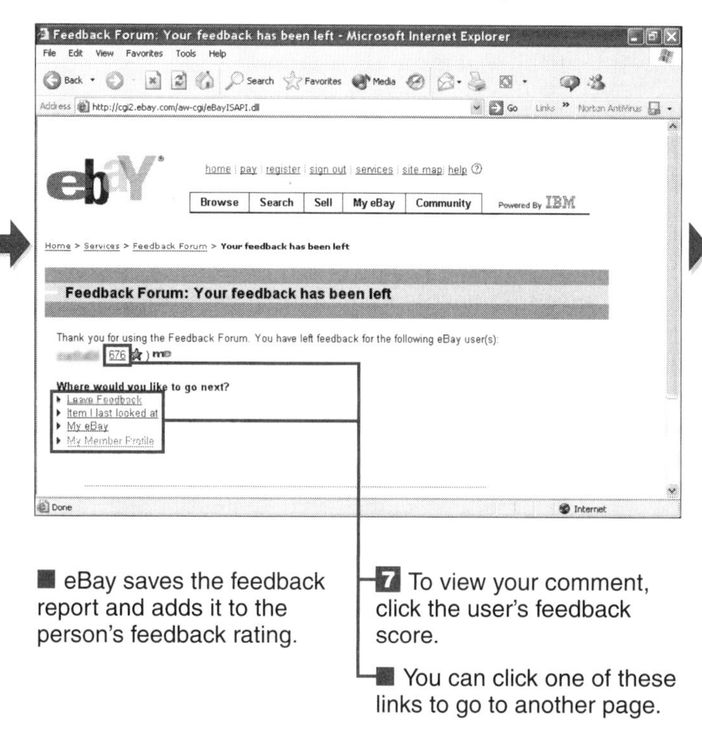

■ eBay saves the feedback report and adds it to the person's feedback rating.

7 To view your comment, click the user's feedback score.

■ You can click one of these links to go to another page.

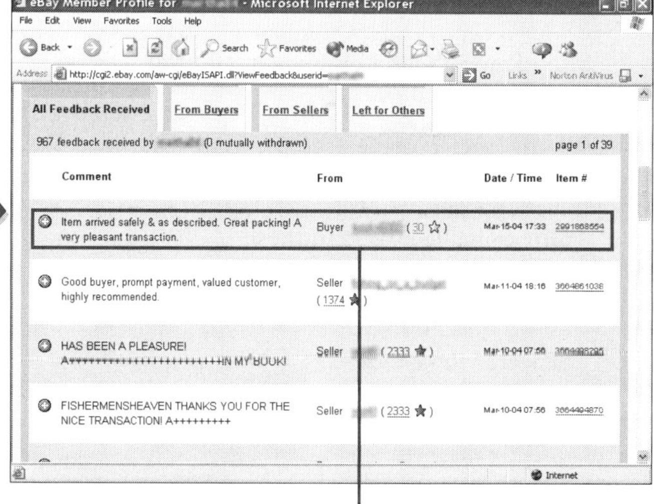

■ The user's feedback profile page appears.

■ You can view your comment in the list.

RECOURSES FOR NEGATIVE FEEDBACK

Negative feedback can greatly affect how others perceive you and your eBay business. The more you buy and sell, the more likely you are to encounter a negative feedback situation at some point in time. This is especially true as eBay continues to grow and inexperienced users interact with the system without fully understanding the feedback process and its intent. Because feedback is permanent, recipients of negative feedback do not have much recourse to reverse the damage. However, depending on the severity of the situation, you can respond to negative feedback in several ways.

The Reality of Negative Feedback

Acquiring negative feedback can be quite frustrating, especially when you know the rating is not justified. Most eBay sellers are honest and want to make sure each sale is a complete success, ending with a satisfied buyer. Unfortunately, you simply cannot please every buyer on eBay. Some buyers make outlandish requests or fail to read your auction listing properly and comply with your terms of sale. Other buyers may not let you know about a problem at all until they post their feedback.

Sadly, after posting negative feedback, there is no way to reverse the situation. You can chalk up negative feedback from unreasonable buyers in these situations as just a part of the ongoing eBay experience. Serious eBayers who check your feedback comments can quickly discern situations in which hard-to-please buyers are involved. Feedback comments are viewed as opinions, and disagreements are bound to happen between users. As you make more sales, you can rest assured the comment will work its way to the back of your growing list of feedback.

Responding to Feedback

If you do receive negative feedback, you can add a response to explain the situation. Always limit your response to stating the facts, such as "No payment; auction ended 3/12; NPB filed 3/26." The more professional your response, the more trustworthy you appear to other users. For example, if a buyer does not pay, state the fact along with the date you filed a nonpaying buyer report. An emotional response may indicate to others that the negative feedback is warranted.

If, on the other hand, the mistake is yours, admit your error in your response. For example, "mistakenly offered an out-of-stock item; made reasonable offer to substitute," "buyer did not alert me to problem; would have addressed immediately," or "item lost in shipping; offered complete refund." Being upfront about your mistake says a lot about your level of honesty and responsibility.

Before you ever respond to negative feedback, allow yourself a cooling-off period. Do not respond in anger or with name-calling. Do not respond with sarcasm or blame. Instead, be accurate and calm. It might help to write your response on paper and view it at a later time to ensure you are fair in your statements.

Feedback Abuse

Sadly, feedback is easily abused on eBay. It is not uncommon to encounter retaliatory, negative feedback, in which one user leaves negative feedback about a transaction, and the receiving user retaliates with his or her own negative feedback. Another common situation is to threaten another user with negative feedback if demands are not met.

eBay offers a Feedback Abuse policy in these situations. The policy prohibits the use of inappropriate language in feedback statements, including profanity, obscenities, and racist text. The Feedback Abuse policy also prohibits harassment, publishing contact information, and references to eBay investigations. To view the policy, visit the eBay help pages or click the Policies link at the bottom of any eBay page. If you feel a negative feedback comment falls under the prohibited policy guidelines, you can report the situation to eBay by clicking the Feedback Forum link at the bottom of any eBay page and following the disputes links. If eBay finds the feedback violates the policy, eBay will remove both the rating and the comment entirely.

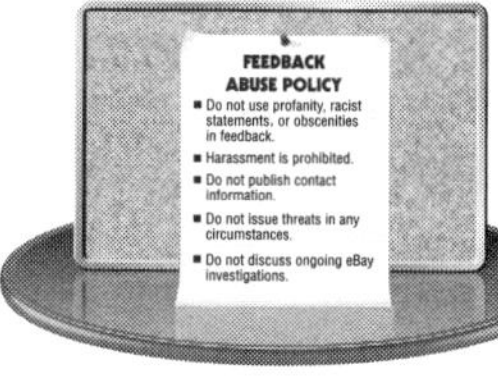

Mutual Feedback Withdrawal

If both users agree to a resolution and desire to withdraw negative feedback, eBay's Mutual Feedback Withdrawal form comes into play. Both members complete the form and submit it to eBay. If approved, the users' feedback scores are adjusted. The negative comments remain in the feedback notation area, but eBay adds a notation indicating the feedback is mutually withdrawn. This feature can only be activated one time for a single transaction, and only within 90 days of the transaction end date. You can request up to five withdrawals per 30 days.

If either party does not agree to the feedback withdrawal, the action is null and void and the feedback remains as is.

SquareTrade

Another option for resolving negative feedback disputes is to file a case with SquareTrade. SquareTrade is eBay's preferred mediation service. You can link to the SquareTrade site through eBay's help pages. The service also works with partnerships such as PayPal and Verisign. There is no charge to file a case with SquareTrade. If the user with whom you have a problem responds to the SquareTrade invitation to resolve the dispute, a professional mediator may be hired for a nominal fee. The mediator steps in to help both parties reach a resolution by corresponding with both sides and drawing a settlement agreeement. If both parties accept the agreement, the negative feedback may be eligible for withdrawal. If the other user refuses the mediation, SquareTrade may still assist in withdrawing the negative feedback comment(s) if the case meets the guidelines for feedback withdrawal set by eBay.

Steps to Avoid Negative Feedback

To help prevent negative feedback in the future, take time to evaluate your auction listings and terms of sale, your correspondence tone, and your online demeanor. Maintaining a professional, friendly attitude is a major factor in many online disputes. If people perceive you as rude, inflexible, and difficult to deal with, chances are good that you will encounter more negative feedback in the future. It is also crucial to keep up timely correspondence with the people from whom you buy and to whom you sell on eBay. If you have a problem with a transaction, be sure to communicate with the person on the other end. Lastly, politeness and diplomacy go a long way in creating a positive atmosphere for all of your auction transactions, and reflect well on your eBay business.

RESPOND TO FEEDBACK

You can add a response comment to feedback others leave you on eBay. For example, you may want to add a response to remind you about details of the transaction. For example, you may respond to a positive comment by adding sizing, color, or quantity details about the item. You can also use the response feature to respond to negative or neutral feedback. eBay's response feature allows you to tell your side of the comment in 80 characters or less. For every feedback comment you receive, you can respond once in return.

You can use a standard form to type your feedback response. After you submit your comment, the response appears directly beneath the feedback comment on your feedback profile page.

By addressing negative feedback comments, you can alert other eBayers to your side of a dispute. It is good practice to use the same guidelines for posting feedback to any responses you make; stick to the facts, and be professional and careful in your statements.

If you previously left a negative feedback for another user and wish to correct it, you can use the response feature to try to remedy the situation.

RESPOND TO FEEDBACK

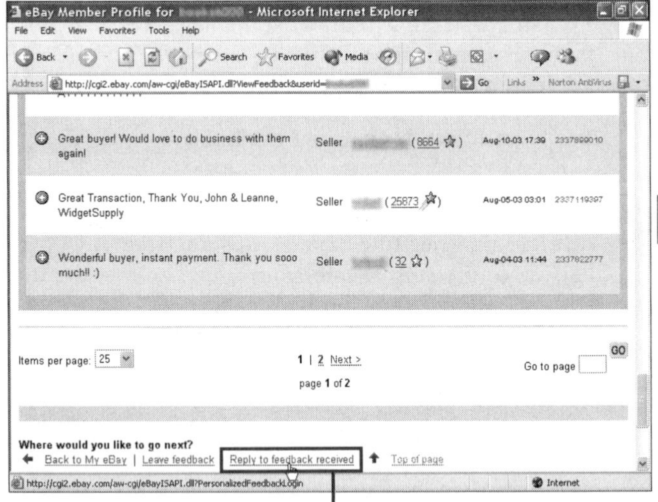

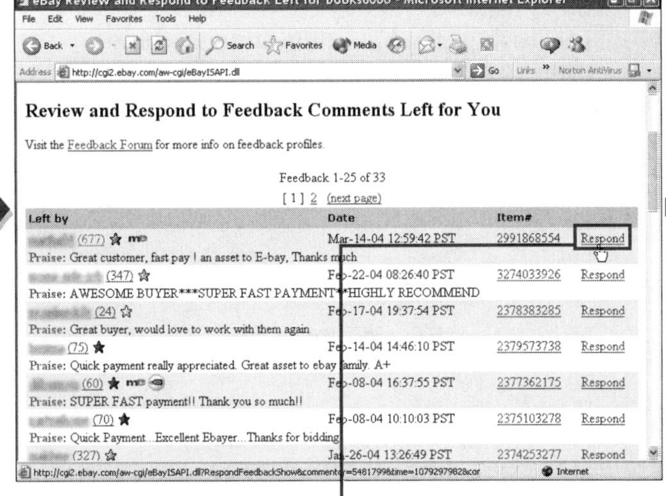

1 Display your feedback profile page.

Note: See the section "View Feedback," earlier in this chapter, to learn how to view feedback comments.

2 Click the Review and Respond link at the top of the page, or the Reply to feedback received link at the bottom of the page.

Note: Depending on your screen resolution setting, your links may vary in placement on the page.

■ eBay may ask you to choose the number of comments you want to view; make a selection and click View Feedback.

■ The feedback listing with a Respond link activated appears.

3 Click the Respond link for the comment to which you want to respond.

If I exit the feedback page before clicking the Submit button, are my comments still saved?

✔ No. Your comments are not saved unless you click the Leave Feedback or Leave Response button on the feedback reporting pages.

How do I evaluate other users' feedback when determining whether to bid?

✔ Check the seller's feedback comments to determine how he or she conducts business. Feedback can tell you how the seller resolves conflicts, whether he or she responds in retaliation, or whether the negative feedback happened recently or a long time ago. If the feedback you see raises any doubts, pass up the auction and wait for another.

I accidentally left feedback for the wrong person. How do I correct this?

✔ You cannot edit existing feedback. All feedback comments you make are permanent. For that reason, eBay posts warnings on all the feedback reporting pages telling users to be careful about leaving feedback. However, people still make mistakes, leaving feedback for the wrong person, or leaving negative feedback out of anger. Although you cannot edit existing feedback, you can add a feedback response. You can also seek help for feedback problems through eBay or eBay's mediation service, SquareTrade. See the section "Recourses for Negative Feedback" to learn more.

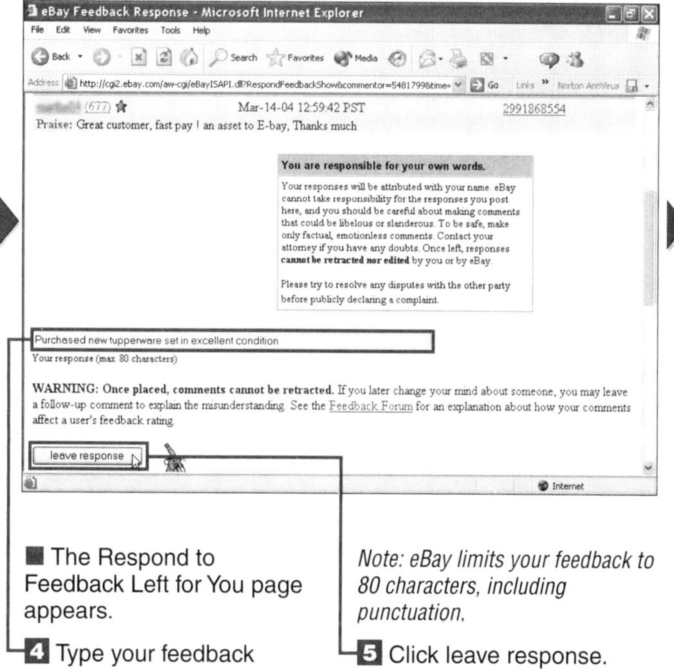

■ The Respond to Feedback Left for You page appears.

4 Type your feedback response.

Note: eBay limits your feedback to 80 characters, including punctuation.

5 Click leave response.

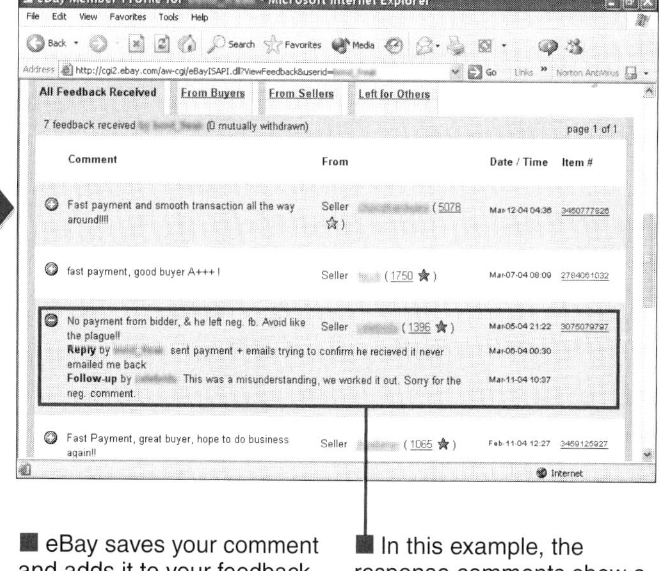

■ eBay saves your comment and adds it to your feedback profile page.

■ In this example, the response comments show a mutual resolution to an original negative comment.

WHAT TO DO IF AN AUCTION FALLS THROUGH

There are times when an auction may not go as planned. An item may not sell, a bidder may ask to cancel a bid, or a buyer may renege on a commitment to purchase an item. An auction can also fall through after you ship an item if the recipient suffers from buyer's remorse. While the vast majority of online auctions are a success, you may encounter problems from time to time with nonpaying buyers, nonselling sellers, and auctions that simply fail to find a market. Thankfully, there are several paths you can take to remedy a failed transaction.

No Bidders

If an item does not attract any bidders at all by the end of the auction, you can try listing the item again. For example, you might try listing the item under another category, changing the auction title, or lowering the starting price. Sometimes the timing may be off in attracting bids for your item, and listing the item in another week or another month solves the problem. With some items, trial and error is a necessity to find just the right niche.

eBay lets you relist an unsold item a second time; if the item sells the second time around, eBay refunds the insertion fee for the second listing. If the item still does not sell again, no insertion fee refund is offered. Please note that the original listing fee is never refunded. You can learn more about relisting an auction in the section "Relist an Unsold Item," later in this chapter.

If you frequently find your items not selling, you may need to take a hard look at your auction listings to figure out why. Do your ads properly describe the item? Are you listing your auctions in the right categories, and are you writing good auction titles? Take time to study the eBay marketplace for similar items. Make note of the categories used for successful auctions, and study the listing descriptions to find ways to improve your own auctions.

You may also need to do a little self-examination regarding your selling practices. Are you practicing diplomacy in your eBay communications with others? Is your feedback rating keeping others from bidding? Are you placing too many restrictions in your terms of sale? These issues can also thwart your sales on eBay.

You can also seek selling advice among eBay's many discussion boards. See Chapter 14 to learn more about accessing the eBay message boards.

Bad Bidders

Another way in which an auction can fail is to encounter an inexperienced bidder or a bidder who thinks eBay is a game rather than a marketplace. Sadly, not everyone who uses eBay understands how the auction process works. This is especially true with some new users. Newer users sometimes bid on an item and then change their minds in midstream, suddenly retracting their bid for no reason.

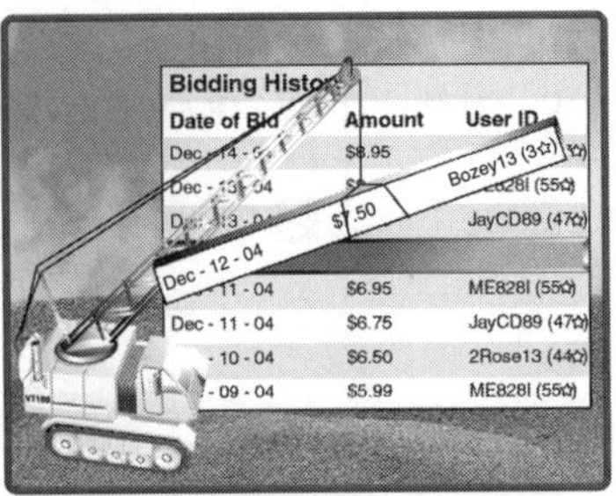

Amount
User ID
Bozey13
$7.50
JayCD89 (47)
Dec - 12 - 04
$6.95
ME828I (55)
Dec - 11 - 04
$6.75
JayCD89 (47)
$6.50
2Rose13 (44)
$5.99
ME828I (55)

Technically, the only time users are allowed to retract a bid is if they accidentally type a wrong bid amount the first time, and follow up with a correct bid amount. eBay considers this a typographical error, but the user must correct the mistake immediately with the intended bid amount.

eBay policy also allows bid retractions if the auction item changes significantly after the bid is placed or if the seller cannot be reached for questions because of an invalid phone number or e-mail message. Bid retractions are not allowed during the last 12 hours of an auction unless the seller agrees to the retraction. eBay keeps track of bid retractions; if a buyer makes them a habit, eBay can suspend the account. As a seller, you can report violations to eBay for investigation.

In eBay terminology, buyers *retract* bids and sellers *cancel* bids. As a seller, you can cancel any bid on your auction. For example, you may look at a bidder's feedback rating and find an ongoing pattern of nonpayment. If you do not want to risk the same problem happening to your auction, you can cancel the bid. As a seller, you have the right to cancel any bid as you see fit. You may want to engage this right when you encounter bidders of questionable background.

Bad Buyers

Nothing is more frustrating to a seller than encountering an uncooperative buyer. Some of the more disreputable users on eBay bid and win auctions, and then refuse to pay for the item. Known as deadbeat bidders/buyers, this type of customer never responds to the winning bid notifications or payment reminders, or worse yet, promises to pay, but never sends you the payment.

Classified as nonpaying bidders, the only recourse for the seller is to file a Non-Paying Bidder (NPB) Alert form with eBay. This serves as a wake-up call to the nonpaying bidder, who also receives a copy of the form encouraging the buyer to complete the transaction. Sometimes this works, but if it does not, you can proceed with filing a form requesting your final value fee, called the Final Value Fee Credit (FVFC). Some buyers do not realize the fees charged by eBay and PayPal for listing and selling items online. Refusing to pay costs the seller money in fees.

You are eligible to file the NPB report seven days after the end of the auction. If the buyer still does not respond, you can file the FVFC report ten days after the NPB. You can also employ eBay's second-chance option and offer the item to another bidder.

On the other hand, do not immediately classify someone as a nonpaying bidder if you do not receive a response to your e-mails. The person may be experiencing legitimate computer or Internet connection problems. Be reasonable in your deadlines, and continue to contact the buyer by phone, if possible. If you do not hear from someone after three days, send a payment reminder. See Chapter 9 to learn more about the payment reminder feature. Always make sure you have exhausted all means of contacting the buyer before giving him or her up as a nonpaying bidder.

In addition to nonpaying bidders, you may also encounter nonselling sellers. If a seller refuses to accept payment or send an item you paid for, you can report him or her to eBay. As a buyer, you are covered by eBay's Buyer Protection Program. See the eBay Help pages to learn more.

CONTINUED

WHAT TO DO IF AN AUCTION FALLS THROUGH (CONTINUED)

Unhappy Customers

Because the eBay marketplace is made up of all kinds of people, you can expect to run across some hard-to-please customers occasionally. When they receive the item, they may claim it does not live up to its description or it is damaged in some way, and demand a refund. Buyer's remorse can happen on eBay as well. A buyer receives the item, and then decides he or she paid too much or does not like the color or size of the item.

When you encounter unhappy customers, you can instruct them to send the item back for a refund, or you can refuse to take back the item. By law, you do not have to refund an auction sale. Taking the refusal approach typically results in negative feedback from the buyer, while taking the refund approach can smoothly put a close to the transaction. If you are serious about selling on eBay, it is in your best interest to refund the money paid for the item and create a happy customer. Why leave yourself open to negative feedback? You can always list the item for sale again. It is important, however, that you instruct the buyer to send back the item before issuing a refund.

Refunding the costs for shipping in either direction is up to you. Shipping is always an extra cost outside of the winning bid amount. Some sellers refund the original shipping amount only. It is up to you and the buyer to reach an agreement regarding shipping costs.

In some cases, both you and the buyer may agree to end the transaction amicably. If the buyer made a legitimate mistake in purchasing the item, he or she can offer to refund your fees to close the transaction on a positive note. In this scenario, you can file a nonpaying bidder report but mark the transaction dissolution as mutually agreed upon. Doing so does not put a black mark on the buyer's record, yet still allows you to file the Final Value Fee Credit report.

Disreputable Users

As a seller, you must also watch out for eBay scams and disreputable users. eBay accounts can be hijacked by illegal users who then turn around and use the account to place a false auction and steal an unsuspecting bidder's money. To keep yourself safe, never give out your eBay password, and always take precautions to safeguard your computer's connection to the Internet.

Some auction practices practically scream scam, such as listings that only accept payment through Western Union or MoneyGram. eBay never recommends paying through instant cash wire transfer services because the transfer is not traceable, is fraught with criminal misuse, and is not covered by the eBay Purchase Protection Program. Other scams include listings for electronic items for too-good-to-be-true prices. If an auction does sound too good to be true, it generally is.

Also be on the lookout for illegal bidding practices. Shill bidding, for example, is a practice in which two or more bidders working together bid up the price of an item to generate a higher sale. Shill bidding can also happen with one user using several accounts. Shill bidding is illegal on eBay. If you suspect shill bidding occurring in an auction, report it to eBay. See Chapter 4 to learn more about auction violations.

Watch out for e-mail scams and messages purporting to be from eBay. eBay never asks for account information, such as passwords, in an e-mail message. If you receive a suspicious eBay e-mail message, report it to eBay.

Ways to Resolve an Auction Dispute

When you do encounter problems with a transaction, it is extremely important to negotiate a good ending for both parties. Arguing, accusing, and blaming are not good tactics to practice, especially in the form of e-mail communications. Instead, always state your case clearly and factually, without letting emotion enter into the dialog. If a buyer fails to meet your terms of sale, gently remind him or her of the agreement to do so when the bid was placed and the auction won. In some instances, you may need to cut your losses and simply make the best of a bad situation.

If you and the buyer are unable to reach a resolution, you can seek mediation. eBay's discussion boards, such as the SafeHarbor board, are a great place to look for advice, or you can consult eBay's Help pages or live help for answers. For $20, you can also enlist eBay's third-party dispute resolution provider, SquareTrade, to help you resolve your differences. SquareTrade hears both sides of the disagreement and tries to mediate a solution between the two parties.

Negative Feedback

The eBay system is based on the feedback reports users generate for transactions to rate their satisfaction with the experience. Sadly, many users abuse the feedback system when it comes to resolving problems with a transaction. Negative feedback is always the last thing to worry about as a seller or as a buyer. If, after doing what you can to resolve a situation, it still ends unsatisfactorily, you can leave the other user a negative feedback report.

For example, in an auction in which the buyer refuses to pay, even after you followed all the eBay guidelines and procedures to prompt a close to the transaction, you can leave negative feedback briefly detailing the experience. Stick to the facts, simply stating the end-of-auction date, no payment received, and the date you filed the NPB. Never indulge in emotional responses or name calling of any kind; doing so makes you appear immature and unprofessional.

It is not uncommon for either party of a failed transaction to threaten negative feedback. Do not use feedback as a weapon, but only as a last recourse to warn others users about the buyer or seller. To learn more about using feedback in eBay, see Chapter 11.

RELIST AN UNSOLD ITEM

You can relist an auction if it fails to generate any bids. Relisting an auction results in another insertion fee, but if the item sells the second time, the fee is refunded. You can also relist an auction if you encounter a *nonpaying bidder*, a situation in which the winning bidder fails to pay.

eBay allows you to relist an item within 90 days of the original listing. The relisting option applies only to traditional auctions and fixed-price auctions.

Before you relist an auction, you might consider making some changes to the auction listing. Treat the relist option as a second chance for attracting bidders, taking time to examine what might have failed to garner a bid the first time. For example, you may need to change the category in which the item was listed, or write a better auction title. Perhaps you need to replace the photo, or adjust your shipping and handling rates or other terms of sale.

You can also lower the starting price for the item. You cannot raise the starting price more than the original starting price, nor can you add a reserve price unless the original listing also had a reserve price.

RELIST AN UNSOLD ITEM

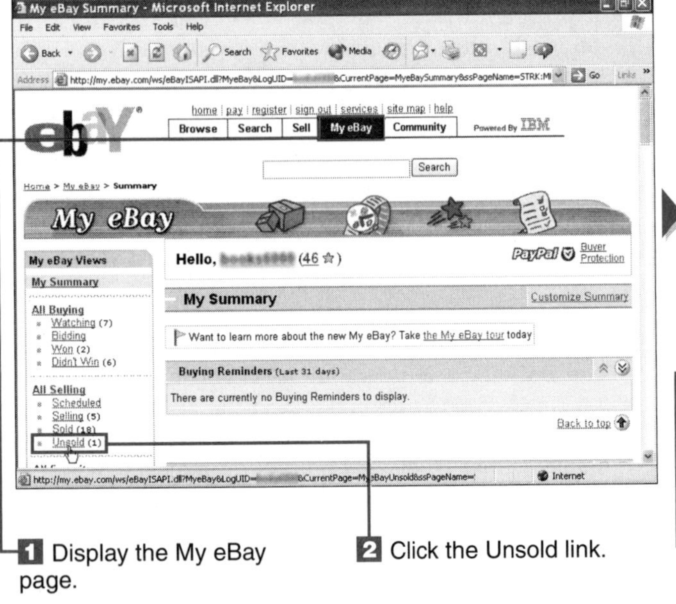

1 Display the My eBay page.

2 Click the Unsold link.

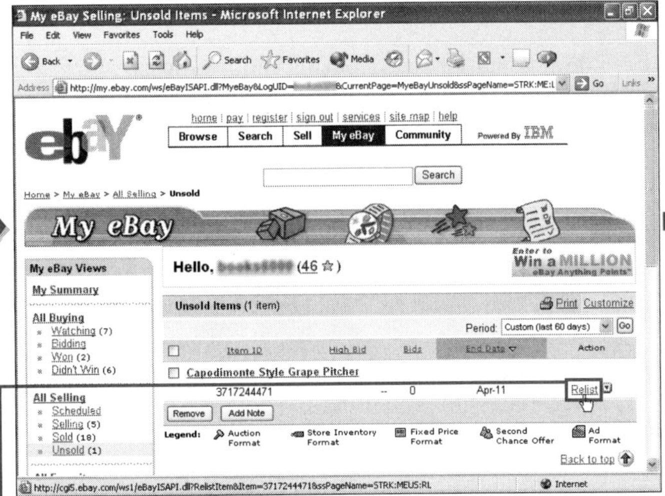

3 Click the Relist link for the auction you want to relist.

Note: You can also relist an item from the auction page; click the Relist your item link at the top of the page.

Can I use the relist command to post a similar auction?

✔ Yes. If you want to auction another item identical to the one you just sold, you can use the relist feature to help you duplicate your listing without having to retype everything. This is a great timesaver. Just remember, however, the new listing you create based on a previous listing is treated as a new auction.

If my item does not sell, do I have to pay final value fees?

✔ No. eBay does not charge any final value fees for unsold items. eBay does charge insertion fees, however.

Can I relist an item I relisted already and receive the insertion fee refund?

✔ No. You cannot relist the same item a third time and qualify for eBay's relisting credit. The relist insertion fee credit only works for an item you did not sell the first time and want to try selling a second time. If the item still does not sell with the second listing, you can certainly continue listing the item, but you incur insertion fees each time you relist.

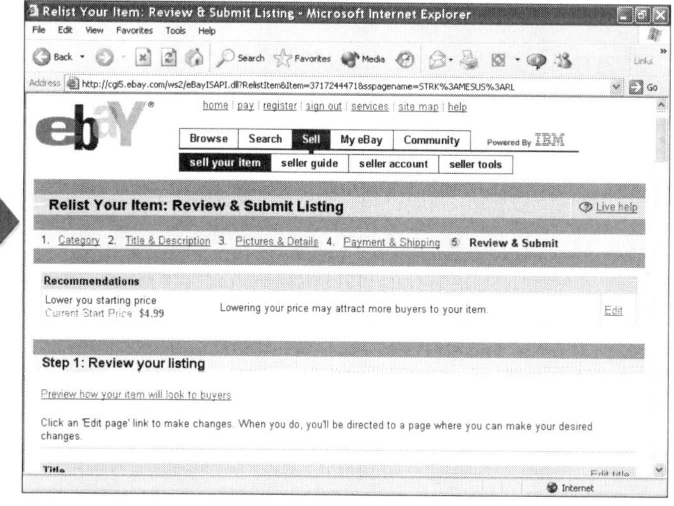

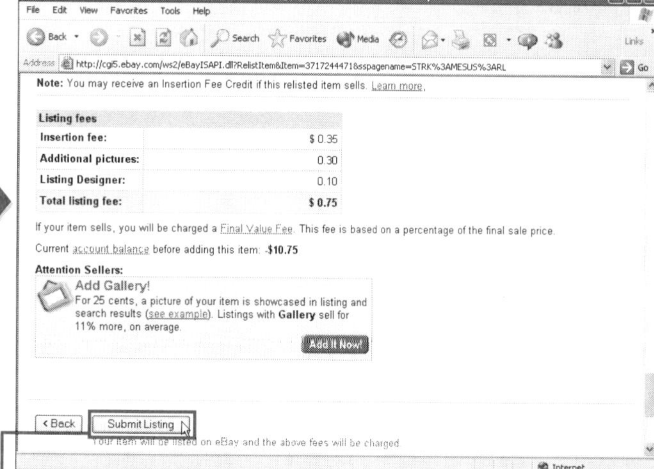

■ The Relist Your Item: Review & Submit Listing page appears.

■ This page is the same as the Review & Submit page of the seller's form.

4 Review the listing and make any changes you want.

5 Click Submit Listing at the bottom of the Review & Submit Listing page.

■ eBay relists your item.

SEND A SECOND-CHANCE OFFER

If the first buyer for your auction falls through, you can offer the item to another bidder. However, you must offer the item at the other bidder's price, not the winning bid price. You can send a second-chance offer to any bidder from your auction. The second-chance offer is only available from closed auction listings, and only if the auctions include nonwinning bidders, which simply means auctions with more than one bid.

You can also use the second-chance offer to sell another of the same item to bidders on the original auction listing. This allows you to sell to both the winning bidder as well as others who bid on the auction. The second-chance offer can also be used to offer the item to the highest bidder of a reserve auction in which the reserve is not met.

Offering a second-chance option is free, until someone accepts the offer. If a bidder accepts the offer, he or she can proceed through the regular eBay checkout procedure. You incur a final value fee after the second-chance bidder completes the transaction.

SEND A SECOND-CHANCE OFFER

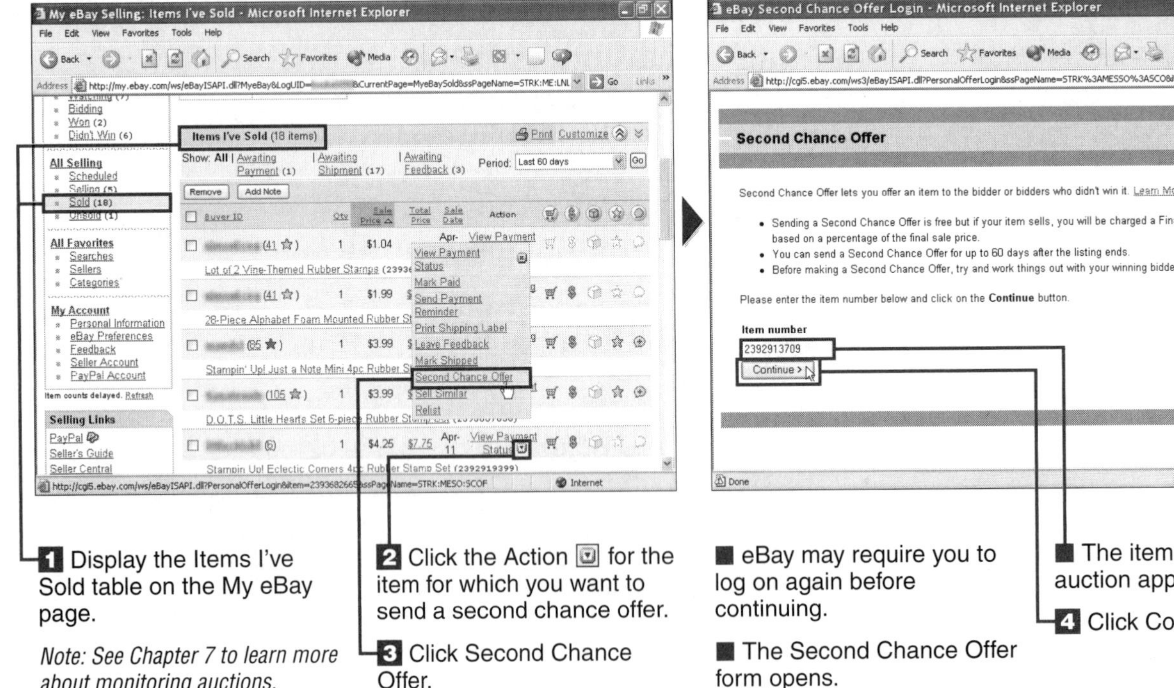

1 Display the Items I've Sold table on the My eBay page.

Note: See Chapter 7 to learn more about monitoring auctions.

2 Click the Action ▾ for the item for which you want to send a second chance offer.

3 Click Second Chance Offer.

■ eBay may require you to log on again before continuing.

■ The Second Chance Offer form opens.

■ The item number for the auction appears by default.

4 Click Continue.

How many users can I send a second-chance offer to?

✔ If you only have one item to sell, you can send a second-chance offer to one user at a time. If the first person chooses not to take you up on the offer, you can send the second-chance offer to another bidder on the item's bid history list. If you have multiples of the same item to sell, you can send out multiple second-chance offers.

Can buyers still leave feedback on a second-chance offer purchase?

✔ Yes. eBay treats the second-chance offer like any other auction. You and the buyer can leave feedback, and you pay a final value fee for the item sold.

As a buyer, is there a way to never receive second-chance offers?

✔ Yes. You can set up your eBay preferences to tell eBay never to send you second-chance offers. You can quickly set and reset your preferences through the My eBay page. Click the eBay Preferences link on the My eBay page, and then click the view/change link next to Notification preferences. You must log on to your eBay account again; then, you can deselect the Second Chance Offer Notice option (☑ changes to ☐) to turn off this feature. This prevents eBay from sending you any second-chance offers via e-mail.

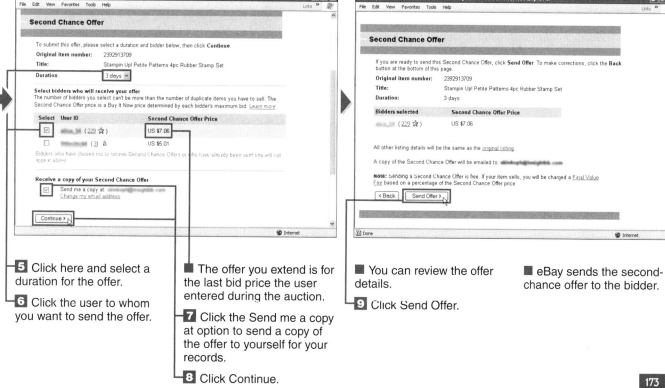

5 Click here and select a duration for the offer.

6 Click the user to whom you want to send the offer.

■ The offer you extend is for the last bid price the user entered during the auction.

7 Click the Send me a copy at option to send a copy of the offer to yourself for your records.

8 Click Continue.

■ You can review the offer details.

9 Click Send Offer.

■ eBay sends the second-chance offer to the bidder.

FILE A NON-PAYING BIDDER ALERT

If a winning bidder fails to pay you after the auction, you can file a Non-Paying Bidder Alert with eBay, also called an *NPB*. Although most users honor their winning bids, you may encounter nonpaying bidders from time to time. Although eBay posts warnings about the seriousness of bidding throughout the site, especially on the pages in which bids are entered, some people treat bidding as a frivolous game. Although the winning bidder enters a legally binding contract with the seller, some users simply refuse to comply.

The NPB is actually a generic, yet official, eBay e-mail message prompting the user to pay for the auction. eBay also sends you a copy of the report. If the buyer does not respond to the NPB, it goes on his or her permanent record. You must file an NPB as a prerequisite to collecting your final value fee credit.

Before you ever take steps to file an NPB, make a concerted effort to contact the buyer. If, after three days, the bidder does not respond to your winner's notification message, send a payment reminder. If you still receive no response after a reasonable amount of time, file the nonpaying bidder report. You can file the report seven days after the end of the auction, but no later than 45 days after the auction.

FILE A NON-PAYING BIDDER ALERT

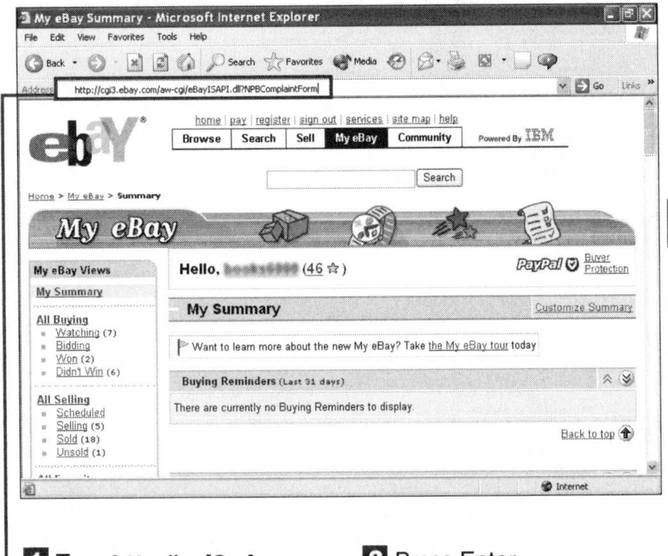

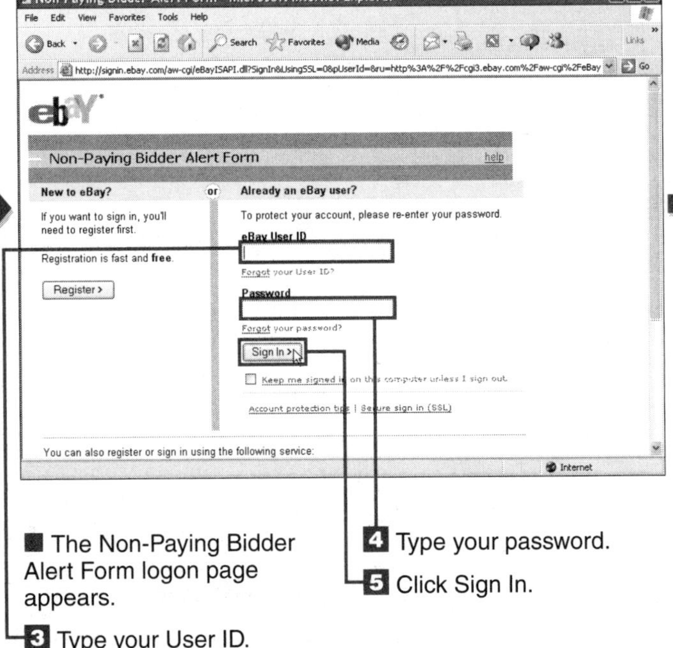

1 Type **http://cgi3.ebay.com/aw-cgi/eBayISAPI.dll?NPBComplaintForm** into your browser's address bar.

2 Press Enter.

Note: You can also access the form by clicking the Site Map link. Then, click the Request final value fee credit link in the middle column to access pages that help you with the forms.

■ The Non-Paying Bidder Alert Form logon page appears.

3 Type your User ID.

4 Type your password.

5 Click Sign In.

What happens if a user receives several NPBs?

✔ If a user receives three Non-Paying Bidder Alerts, eBay suspends the account indefinitely. As you can imagine, not paying for auctions is a serious eBay offense, and to discourage users from pursuing a pattern of nonpayment, the repercussions are harsh.

What if I receive an unwarranted NPB?

✔ If you, as the buyer, receive an NPB you feel is not warranted, you can appeal the notice. To make an appeal, you must have proof of payment or proof of an agreement with the seller to excuse you from paying. To appeal an NPB, consult the eBay Help pages, or visit http://pages.ebay.com/help/policies/appeal-npb.html. You can make your appeal by e-mail, regular mail, or by fax.

How do I remove an NPB after it is filed?

✔ If your buyer comes through with a payment, you can use the Remove Non-Paying Buyer Warning form to remove the alert. Type **http://pages.ebay.com/help/policies/appeal-npb.html** in your Web browser's address window, and then click the nonpaying bidder/buyer warning removal link found near the bottom of the help page. Log on to your eBay account again and follow the directions on the form for removing an NPB.

Who sees an NPB?

✔ Only the seller, the buyer, and eBay know about the NPB, unless the buyer accumulates three NPBs, in which case the account is suspended.

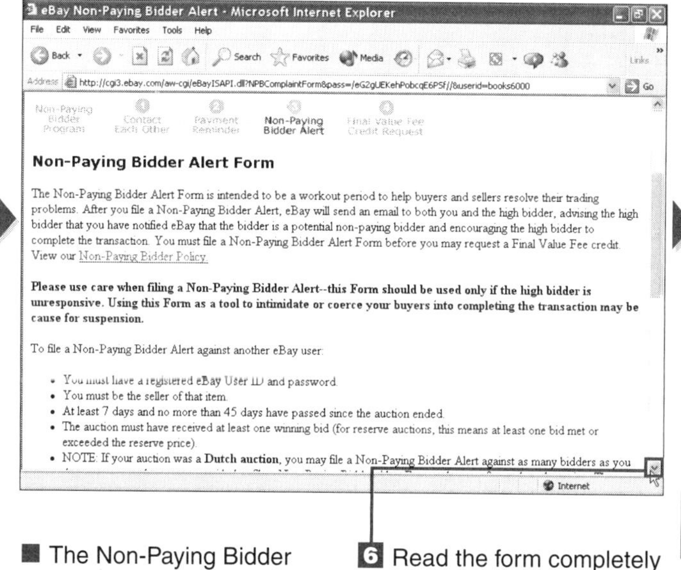

■ The Non-Paying Bidder Alert Form page appears.

6 Read the form completely and click here to scroll down the page.

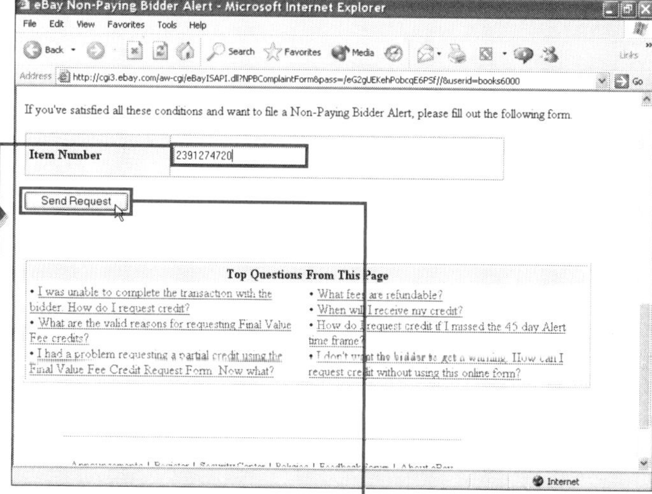

7 Type the item number for the auction in which you have a nonpaying bidder.

8 Click Send Request.

■ eBay files the report and sends a copy to the nonpaying bidder.

REQUEST A FINAL VALUE FEE CREDIT

If the sale does not go through as planned, whether from a mutual dissolution with the buyer or because the buyer fails to complete the transaction, you must notify eBay in order to receive credit for the final value fee. The final value fee is the amount you owe eBay after you sell an item. Until you file for the credit, eBay treats the auction as a successful transaction and tries to collect its fees.

You can use the Final Value Fee Credit form, also called the FVFC, to request a credit. Before you can file an FVFC, you must first file a Non-Paying Bidder Alert, or NPB. Even if you and the buyer agree to a legitimate reason for dissolving a transaction, you must still file an NPB. The NPB form includes an option for mutually canceling a transaction. In the case of a nonpaying bidder, the NPB goes on the user's record.

You can file an FVFC at any time up to 60 days after the close of the auction, but you must wait at least 10 days to file an FVFC after you file an NPB. After you file the report, eBay credits your account.

REQUEST A FINAL VALUE FEE CREDIT

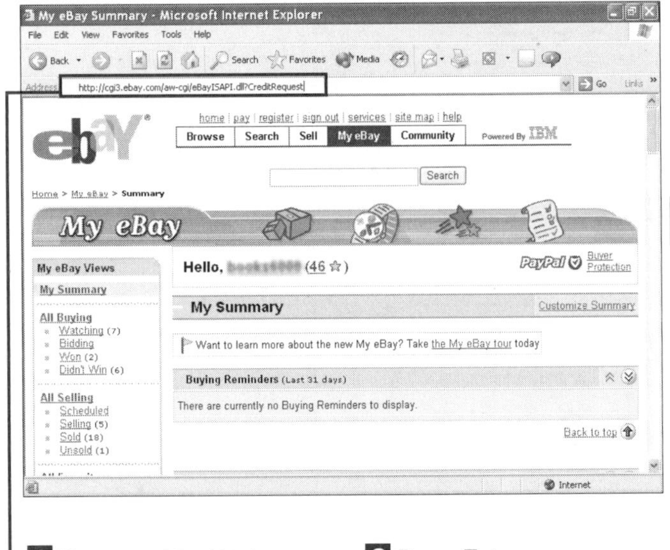

1 Type **http://cgi3.ebay.com/aw-cgi/eBayISAPI.dll?CreditRequest** into your browser's address bar.

2 Press Enter.

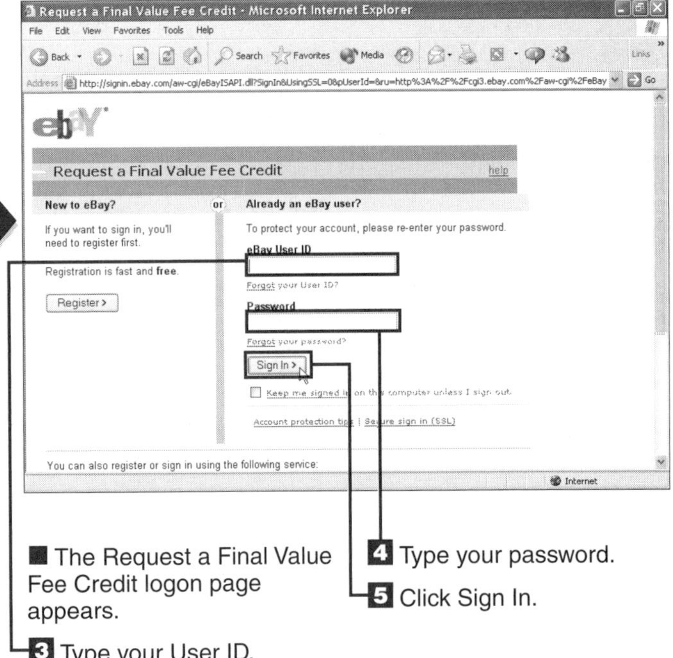

■ The Request a Final Value Fee Credit logon page appears.

3 Type your User ID.

4 Type your password.

5 Click Sign In.

What if I file my FVFC, but then the buyer pays me?

✔ If you work things out with a buyer after you file an FVFC, you must fill out the Non-Paying Buyer Warning Removal form. This removes the black mark from the buyer's record. eBay then charges the credit back to your account again. Type **http://pages.ebay.com/help/policies/appeal-npb.html** in your browser's address bar, and then click the nonpaying bidder/buyer warning removal link found near the bottom of the help page. Log on to your eBay account and fill out the form for removing an NPB.

Where can I find a list of the fees eBay charges?

✔ To view a current list of all the fees eBay charges to sellers, click the Sellers Guide link below the views pane on the All Selling view page. This opens the Seller's Guide help pages. You can then click the fees link under the Listing Your Item topic to view a page of current eBay charges. eBay frequently makes changes to fees throughout the year, so remember to check the fees page from time to time to stay up-to-date about your eBay charges.

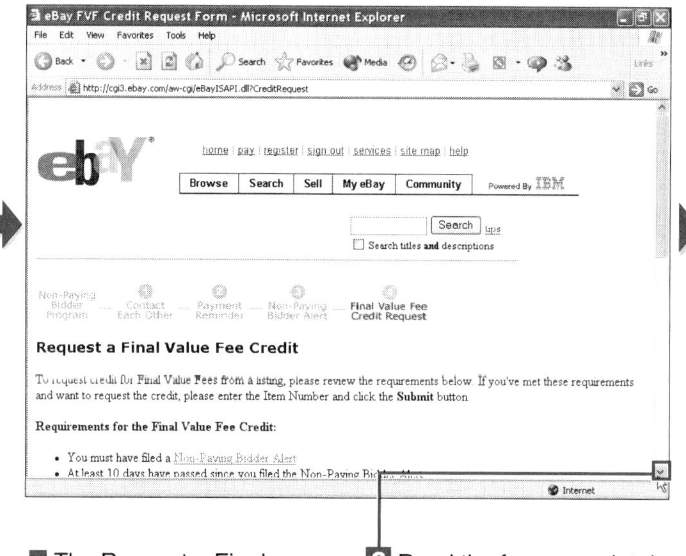

■ The Request a Final Value Fee Credit form appears.

6 Read the form completely and click here to scroll down the page.

Note: You must file an NPB report before completing the FVFC. See the previous task to learn how to file an NPB.

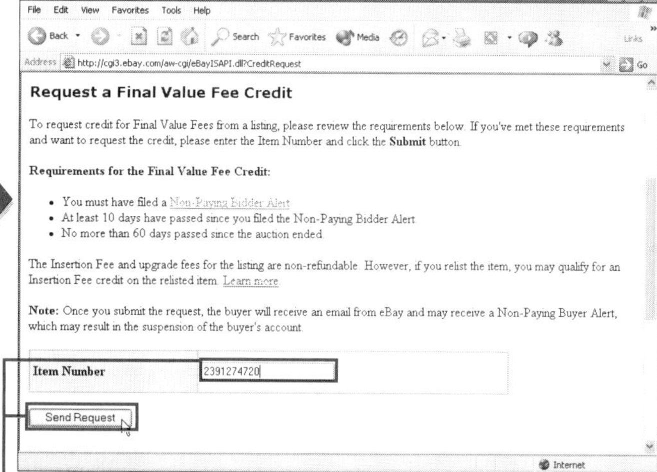

7 Type the item number for the auction in which you are requesting a credit.

8 Click Send Request.

■ eBay processes the form.

Note: It may take 24 hours for the credit to appear on your account.

STOP UNWELCOME BIDDERS

When you encounter questionable bidders in your auctions, you can block them from bidding. You can keep a running list of users to whom you do not want to sell, and you can add to and subtract from the list as needed. Called the blocked bidder/buyer list, the list applies to all the auctions you post on eBay. If any person from the list tries to bid on one of your auctions, eBay blocks the bid automatically.

For example, if you encountered a nonpaying buyer in the past, you can add that name to the list. Or if a bidder has a poor feedback rating, you can block him or her from bidding. eBay allows you to block up to 1,000 users. Hopefully, you will never run into 1,000 bad bidders, but knowing you have a tool to avoid them can help you run your auctions more efficiently.

In order to block a bidder, you must know the bidder's User ID. You can note the ID from the Bid History list on your auction listing page, or you can locate the ID from previous auctions or e-mail correspondence.

STOP UNWELCOME BIDDERS

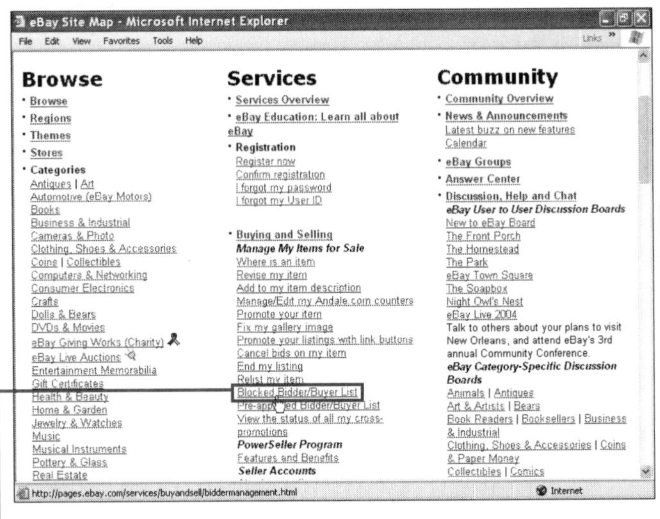

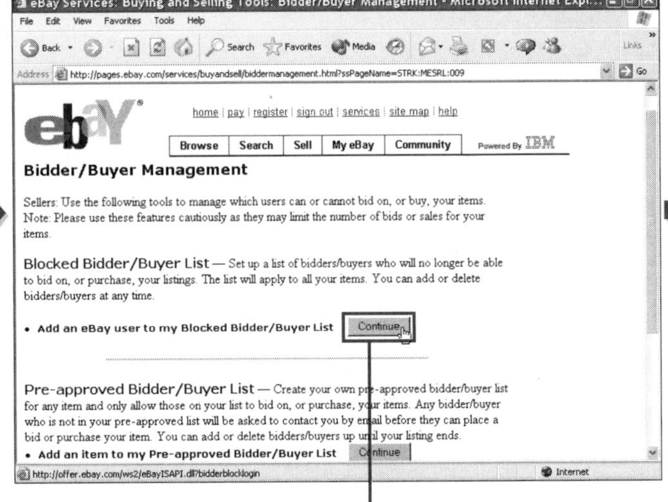

1 Click the site map link at the top of any eBay page.

2 Under the Buying and Selling heading, click the Blocked Bidder/Buyer List link.

Note: You can also display the All Selling view on the My eBay page and click the more link in the Selling Links pane to find a list of selling-related links.

■ The Bidder/Buyer Management page appears.

3 Click Continue under the Blocked Bidder/Buyer List section.

How do I remove a user from my blocked bidders list?

✔ Follow the steps in the steps below to open the blocked bidders list, and then delete the ID you want to remove from the list. Click the Submit button to save your changes, and eBay updates the list.

How do I find a person's User ID if I only know the user's e-mail address?

✔ You can use eBay's Search page to help you find a User ID. The By Bidder tab features a link for looking up different types of information about a user, including his or her About Me page, ID history, and User ID. To learn more about searching for a bidder, see Chapter 2.

How do I cancel a single bid?

✔ You need a valid reason for canceling any user's bid, particularly because the cancelation notice is sent to the bidder. It is only polite to tell them why you are cancelling the bid. You can cancel a bid in your auction if you feel the bidder has too many negative feedbacks and is a potential nonpaying bidder. You can also cancel a bid if the bidder is ignoring your terms of sale, such as no overseas bids. You can cancel a bid from your auction's Bid History page. See Chapter 7 to learn how to perform a bid cancellation.

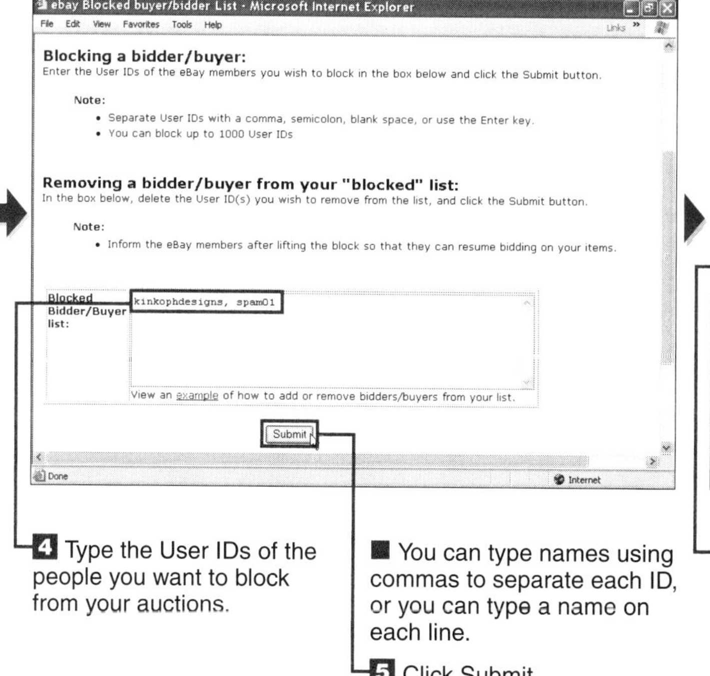

4 Type the User IDs of the people you want to block from your auctions.

■ You can type names using commas to separate each ID, or you can type a name on each line.

5 Click Submit.

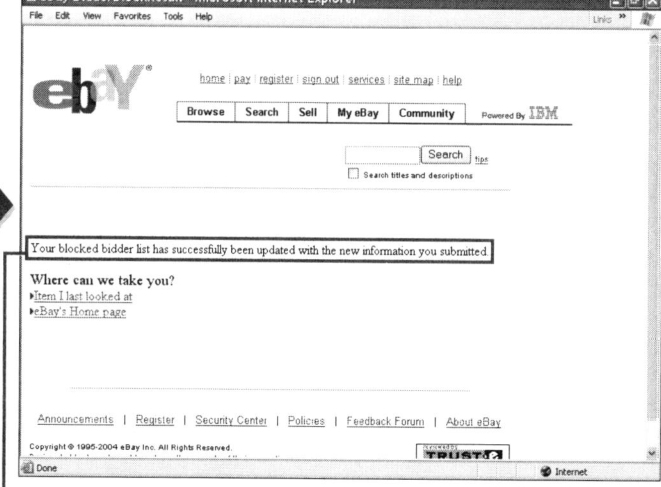

■ eBay adds the name or names to your list and a message confirming the action appears.

BLOCK EBAY USERS FROM E-MAILING YOU

If your communication with a fellow eBayer goes totally awry, you can block the user from e-mailing you. You can use your e-mail editor program to block incoming messages from certain users. Depending on your e-mail program, you may need to use different steps for blocking unwanted e-mail. The steps below show how to block senders using Microsoft Outlook Express, a popular e-mail program.

Generally speaking, the only times you may ever need to block eBay users from e-mailing you is if they do so incessantly, above and beyond the confines of an auction transaction, or if they harass you over a transaction that did not have a happy outcome. It is not unheard of for some eBay users to indulge in vitriolic arguments over an auction with e-mail correspondence filled with threats and offensive language. For your own safety, never exchange abusive e-mails, no matter how tempting it is to set the other person straight. Continuing the argument is not likely to dissuade an angry user. If the harassment escalates, you can contact eBay for help.

Although rare, cyber-stalking can also occur when a person might continue to contact you in a manner that makes you uncomfortable long after an auction is complete. For your own safety, it is advisable to block the bidder's e-mail.

Use your blocking feature wisely. Do not block ordinary e-mail inquiries from reaching you or eBay can suspend your account. Invalid contact information, such as an inaccessible e-mail address, is an eBay violation.

BLOCK EBAY USERS FROM E-MAILING YOU

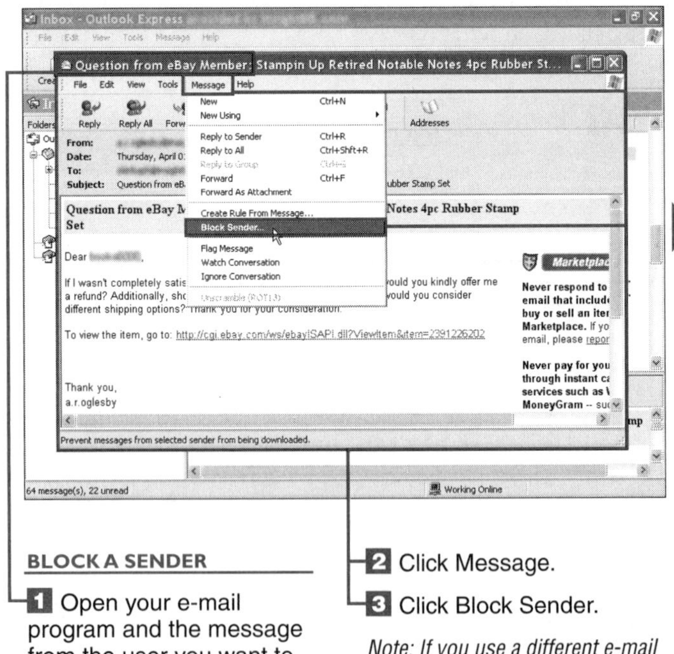

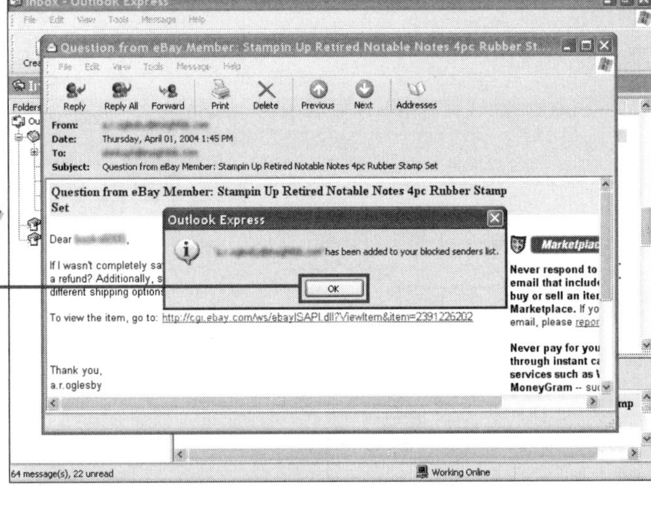

BLOCK A SENDER

1 Open your e-mail program and the message from the user you want to block.

■ This example shows Outlook Express.

2 Click Message.

3 Click Block Sender.

Note: If you use a different e-mail program, your commands for blocking senders may differ than those shown in these steps.

■ A dialog box appears, confirming the new setting.

4 Click OK.

■ The program blocks the receipt of future e-mails from the sender you selected.

Can a user switch IDs and e-mail addresses and still interfere with my auctions and e-mail?

✔ Yes. It is not unheard of for irrational users to take their unhappiness with a transaction to extremes and continue to plague you by using new IDs and e-mail addresses. Contact eBay for help in dealing with the situation.

I am having trouble receiving e-mail notifications from eBay. Why?

✔ If your e-mail program has a spam filtering feature, you may need to adjust the message settings in order to receive correspondence from eBay and eBay users. Check your program's Help files for more information about fine-tuning the spam filtering feature.

What do I do if a disgruntled buyer starts harassing me via e-mail?

✔ You can report the user to eBay. Make sure you save all of the e-mails you receive from the buyer and include them in your violation report. See the next section, "Report a Violation to eBay," to learn more about contacting eBay for help with abusive users. You can also contact eBay's Live Help area for immediate assistance and advice. See Chapter 13 to learn how to use Live Chat. If the harassment extends into threats of violence, you may need to contact your local authorities for additional help.

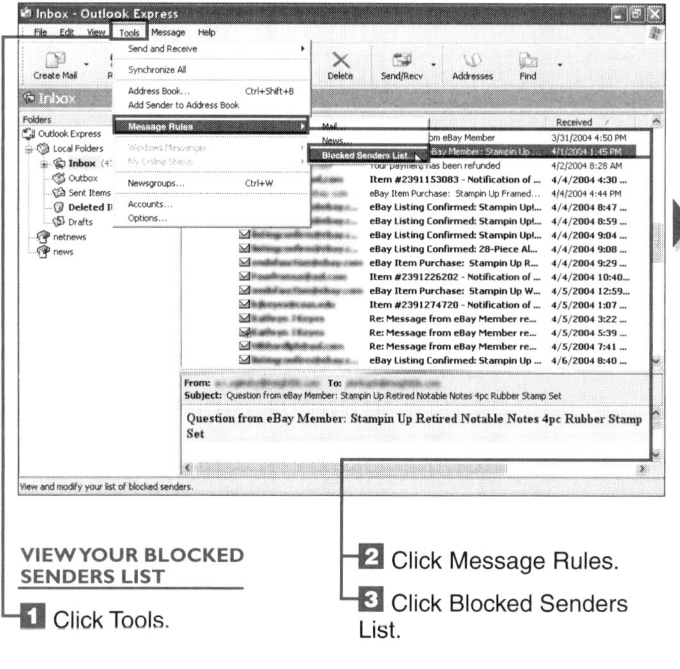

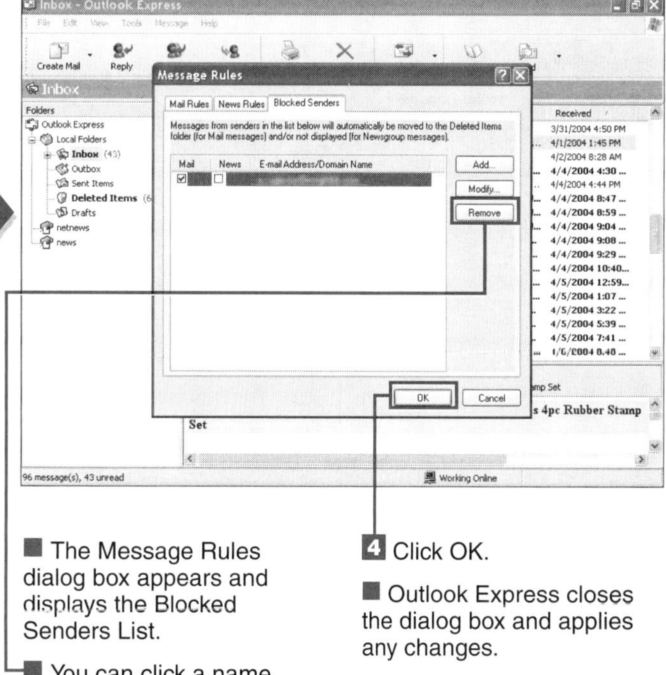

VIEW YOUR BLOCKED SENDERS LIST

1 Click Tools.

2 Click Message Rules.

3 Click Blocked Senders List.

■ The Message Rules dialog box appears and displays the Blocked Senders List.

■ You can click a name on the list and then click Remove to remove the selected user from the list.

4 Click OK.

■ Outlook Express closes the dialog box and applies any changes.

REPORT A VIOLATION TO EBAY

If you suspect or know that another user is violating an eBay policy, you can report the abuse to eBay. You can report blatant violations of auction listing rules and bidding guidelines. For example, if someone tries to offer you a sale outside of eBay, deliberately interferes with the bidding going on in your auction, or retracts a bid without placing a corrected bid amount, you can contact eBay.

The contact form includes a number of categories you can use to help define the nature of your problem. You can also contact eBay to report e-mail threats, online harassment, and other problems that arise from transaction disputes. Make sure your information regarding the problem is clear, factual, and thorough. Include the auction number, User ID, and any e-mails you receive relating to the problem.

After you contact eBay, eBay looks into the problem. eBay investigates the circumstances surrounding the issue and the user's previous trading record. You may not hear back from eBay regarding the offense, due to privacy issues; however, eBay can take action if the complaint is valid. eBay can take action in the form of a formal warning, a temporary sanction, or an indefinite suspension of the user's account.

REPORT A VIOLATION TO EBAY

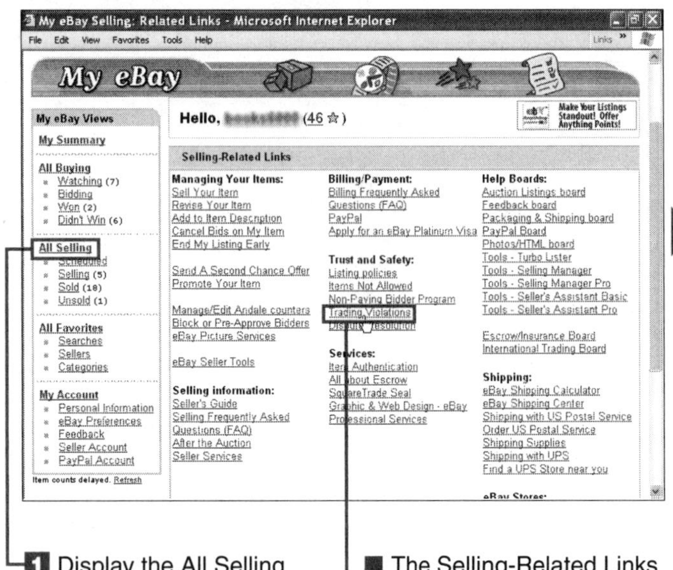

1 Display the All Selling view on the My eBay page.

2 In the Selling Links pane, below the My eBay Views pane, click the more link.

■ The Selling-Related Links page appears.

3 Click the Trading Violations link.

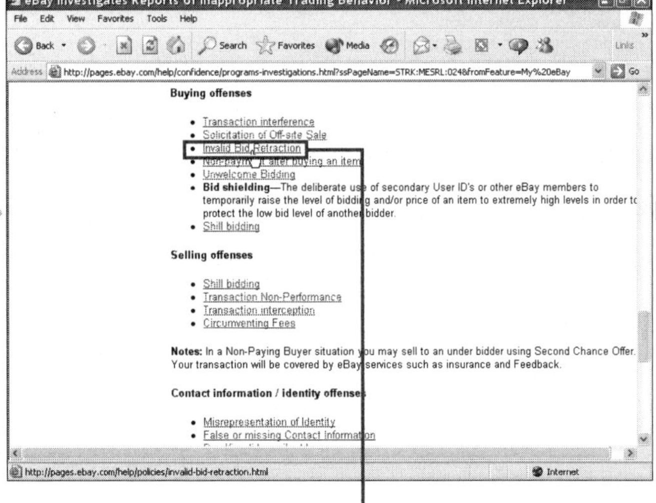

■ The help page listing types of trading violations appears.

4 Click the link for the type of violation you want to report.

Where can I find more information about eBay's policies?

✔ You can click the Policies link at the bottom of any eBay page to find a help page detailing different policy guidelines. To learn more about auction violations, see Chapter 4. To learn more about viewing eBay rules, see Chapter 1.

Can I speak to a live eBay representitive to ask more about a problem?

✔ eBay does not offer a phone number for live help, but you can seek advice through the live online help service. eBay's Live Help is a staffed area on the Web site that allows users to chat live with customer service people. To learn more about eBay chat, see Chapter 13.

How do I know if eBay has looked into the problem?

✔ eBay cannot divulge the results of any online investigation. However, you can keep track of a user's status to find out if an account is suspended. Simply conduct a search of the person's User ID, or visit an auction page in which the person's ID is posted.

I submitted three NPBs against the same buyer for three different auctions. Why does the User ID still appear as a registered user?

✔ Non-Paying Bidder Alerts must be filed from three unique eBay users before an account can be suspended.

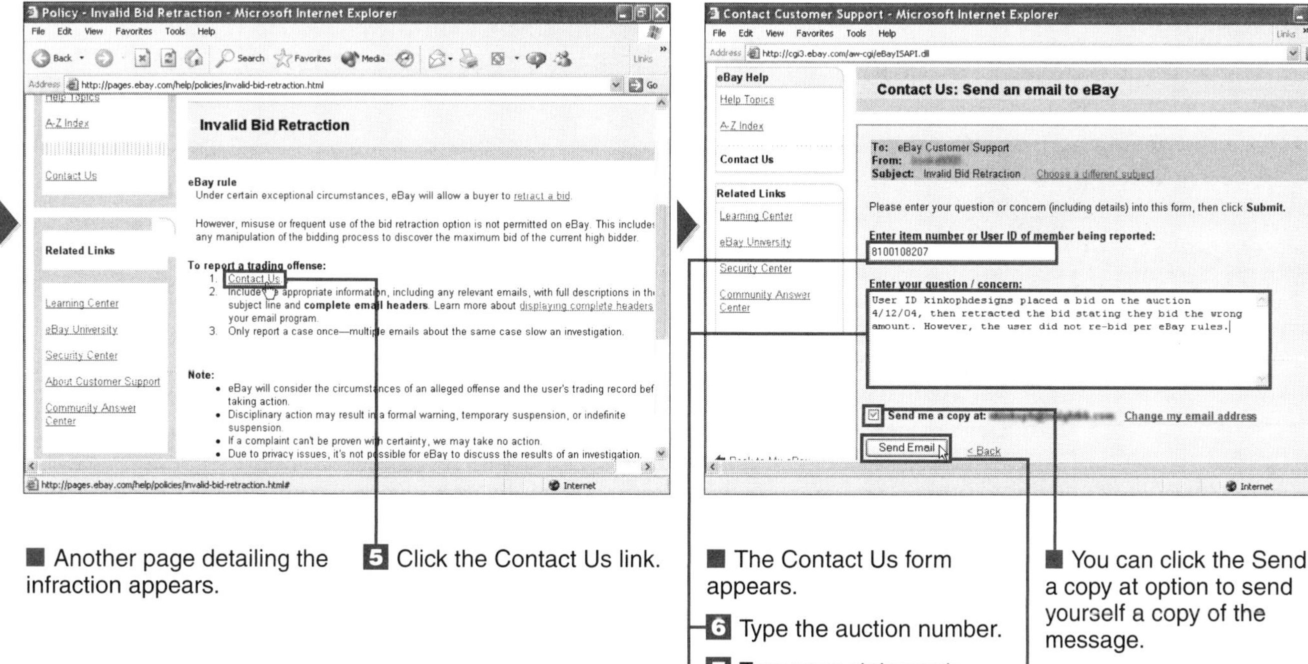

■ Another page detailing the infraction appears.

5 Click the Contact Us link.

■ The Contact Us form appears.

6 Type the auction number.

7 Type your statements regarding the violation.

■ You can click the Send me a copy at option to send yourself a copy of the message.

8 Click Send Email.

■ The report is submitted.

SECTION V

13) FINDING HELP WITH EBAY

14) USING EBAY COMMUNITY RESOURCES

15) SELLING HIGH-PRICED ITEMS ON EBAY

TAKING ADVANTAGE OF EBAY SERVICES AND RESOURCES

16) GETTING SELLING HELP

17) USING EBAY GROUPS

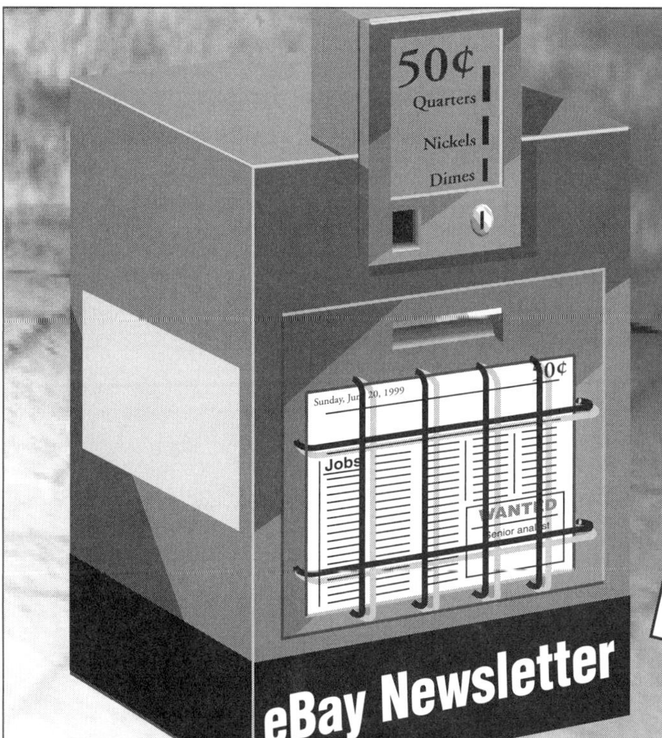

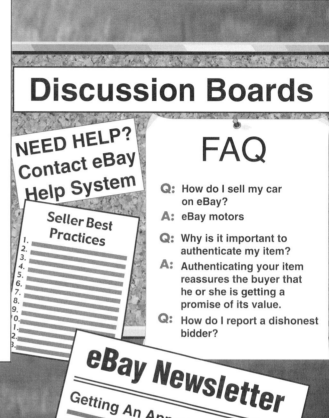

FIND HELP THROUGH THE EBAY HELP PAGES

You can locate help with eBay tasks by consulting the Help links and pages of the Web site. Knowing where to look for answers is an important part of identifying resources to help you succeed in your eBay business. The eBay Help pages offer a plethora of topics ranging from how to buy or sell an item to how to contact the eBay support team.

The eBay Help pages are the first area to consult when you run across any problem with buying or selling an auction item. Before you try contacting eBay directly or posting a question on the discussion boards, look for information in the Help pages. This can save you time, and more often than not, you can find the information for which you are looking.

Help topics are grouped by subject. For example, if you are looking for help with a seller-related topic, you can start with the Selling subject group. Each group lists subgroups of help topics, further detailing areas of help. When you find the topic you want to view, you can open a page detailing information about the topic. The help text may include additional links you can follow to learn more about a topic.

FIND HELP THROUGH THE EBAY HELP PAGES

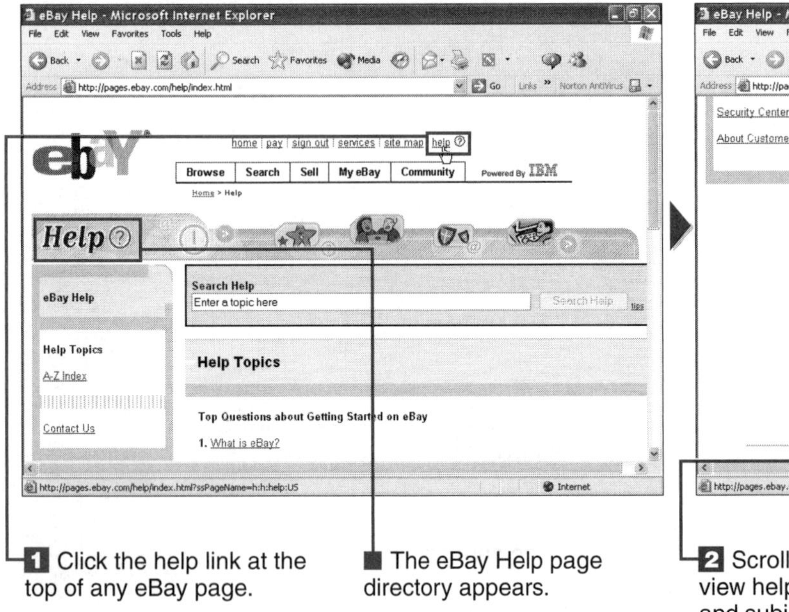

1 Click the help link at the top of any eBay page.

■ The eBay Help page directory appears.

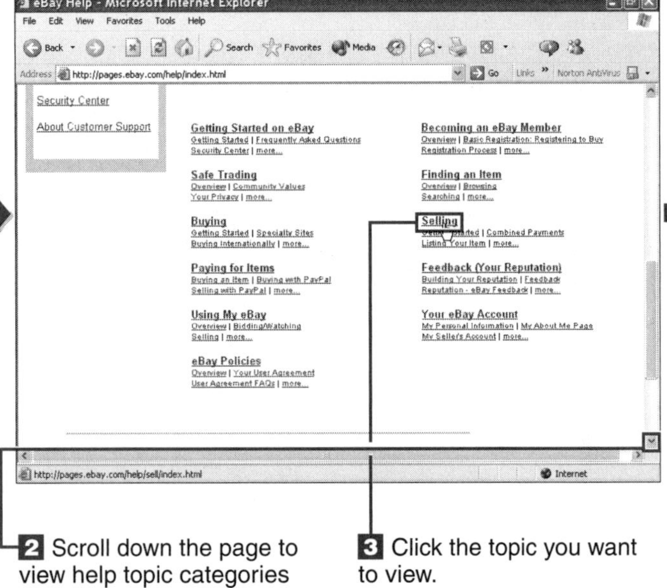

2 Scroll down the page to view help topic categories and subjects.

3 Click the topic you want to view.

How do I print an eBay help topic?

✔ The quickest way to print an eBay help topic is to right-click a blank area of the topic page and click Print from the popup menu that appears. This immediately opens the Print dialog box, and you can set any print options before activating the Print command. When you print in this manner, the entire Web page prints, including all the artwork and extraneous links and information surrounding the help topic. For better results, you can choose to print only a portion of a Web page instead. First select the text you want to print, and then click Selection (○ changes to ◉) in the Print dialog box.

What are the questions links at the top of the Help pages?

✔ Each major Help subject lists five of the most popular subject-related questions at the top of the page. These are questions eBay staff are commonly asked by users visiting the Help area of eBay. Be sure to check the top five questions to see if they relate to your own question. To view a question's answer, simply click on the question link. If you cannot find a topic covering your question, you can conduct a search of the eBay Help pages. See the next section, "Search the eBay Help System," to learn more.

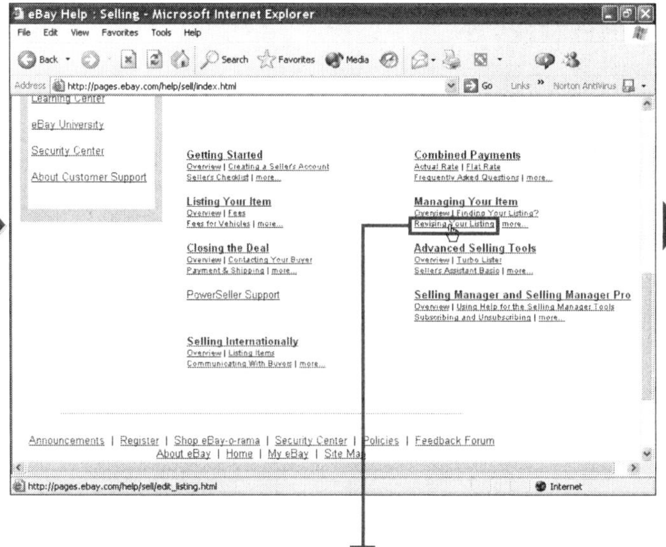

■ Another Web page appears, displaying additional topic categories.

4 Click the topic you want to view.

■ You can also click other links to view more topics.

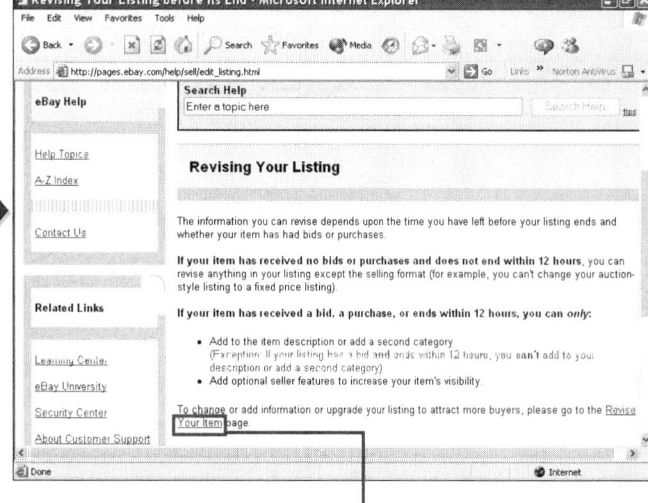

■ A Web page appears, displaying information about the topic.

■ You can click links to view related information.

SEARCH THE EBAY HELP SYSTEM

You can search the eBay Help pages for a particular word or phrase. If a glance through the Help topics does not reveal the information you need, you can type a keyword and search the Help pages for the information you are seeking. For example, you can type the keyword *listings* to view all the related information about auction listings in eBay.

Typing your own search keywords can save you time when looking for specific information. Rather than wade through all the available Help topics, you can narrow your search to just the ones featuring your keyword or words.

When eBay displays a list of possible matches, you can search through the topics that most closely match the one about which you want to find more information.

If your search fails to produce any results, try another keyword or a different version of the same word. For example, try a plural version of the keyword or a different keyword that means the same thing.

SEARCH THE EBAY HELP SYSTEM

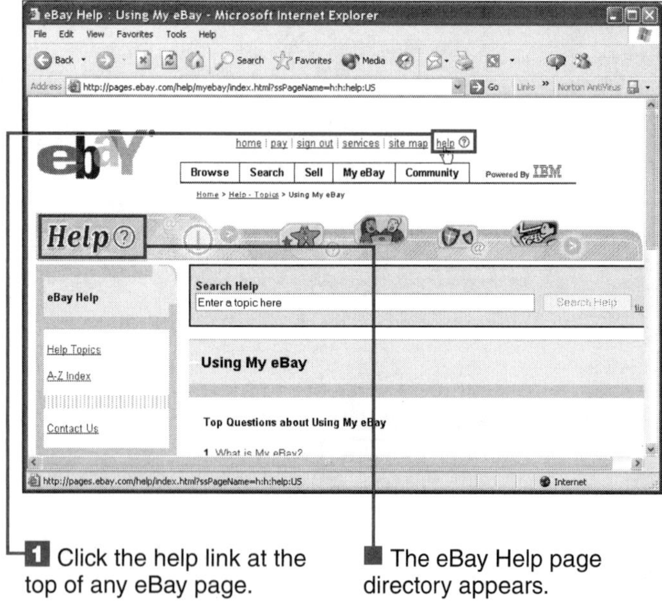

1 Click the help link at the top of any eBay page.

■ The eBay Help page directory appears.

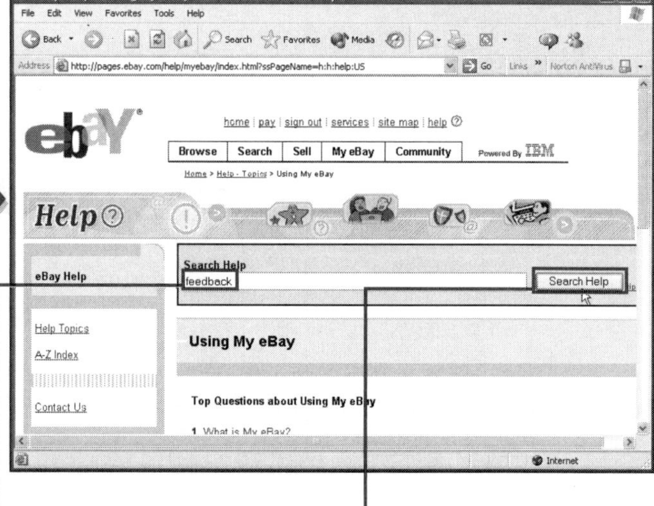

2 Type a keyword or keywords for which you want to search.

3 Click the Search Help button.

Can I view an alphabetical list of Help topics?

✔ Yes. You can use eBay's A-Z Index to quickly view all of the Help topics listed alphabetically. For example, if you want to view all of eBay's topics related to the word *auction*, you can open the A-Z Index and display all the topics that start with the letter A. To view the index page, click the A-Z Index link in the left pane of any Help page window. The A-Z list appears, and you can click a letter to view topics alphabetically. When you see a topic you want to read more about, simply click the topic link to open a page of information about the topic.

Does the Search feature search auction listings?

✔ No. The Search feature only searches through the eBay Help pages. To search for auction listing titles, use the Browse or Search features outside of the eBay Help area pages.

Can I search for a phrase or sentence?

✔ Yes. A better approach, however, is to simplify your search terms. eBay's Help system search results show only the pages that include all the search terms you type, so be sure to include only the words for which you want information. Complete sentences and case-sensitive keywords are not necessary for a search through the eBay Help pages.

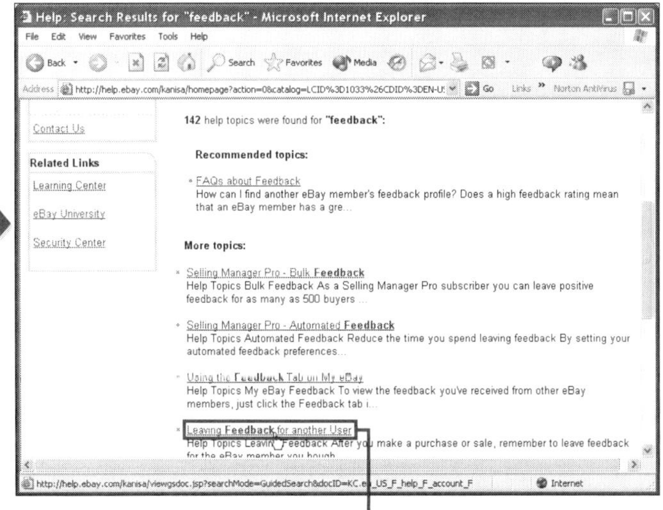

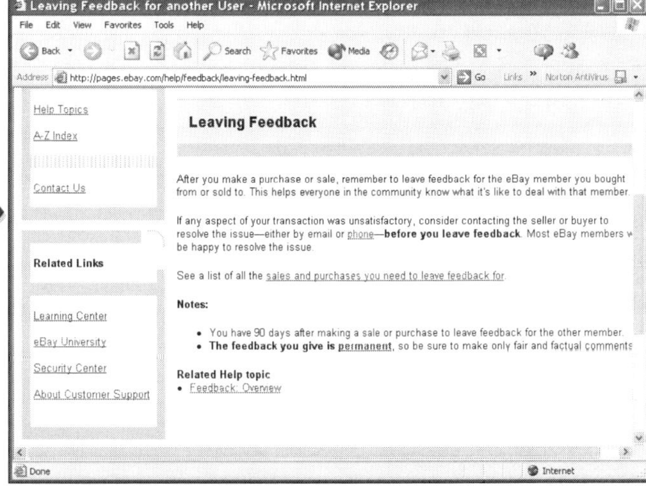

■ Another Web page appears, displaying subjects related to your keyword.

4 Click the topic you want to view.

■ You can also click other subject links to view more topics.

■ A Web page appears, displaying information about the topic.

CONTACT EBAY FOR HELP

Another method of finding help with eBay tasks and topics is to contact eBay itself. You can contact eBay's customer support team through e-mail and receive a response to your question within 24 to 72 hours. For example, if you have a particular issue or question that is not addressed in any of the Help system topics, you can e-mail the information to the customer support team for extra assistance with your problem.

To help you receive the fastest response to your issue or question, you can narrow your question by selecting categories in the eBay e-mail form. In narrowing your question, be sure to select a category topic that most closely relates to your question or issue. You can use the eBay e-mail form to ask a question or report something wrong with an auction, a buyer or seller, or the eBay Web pages. If you report a listing violation, however, you may not hear back from eBay directly.

In some instances, you may be directed to eBay's live help chat area to address the issue or question category you select. In this case, you can type your question and receive an instant reply rather than an e-mail reply.

CONTACT EBAY FOR HELP

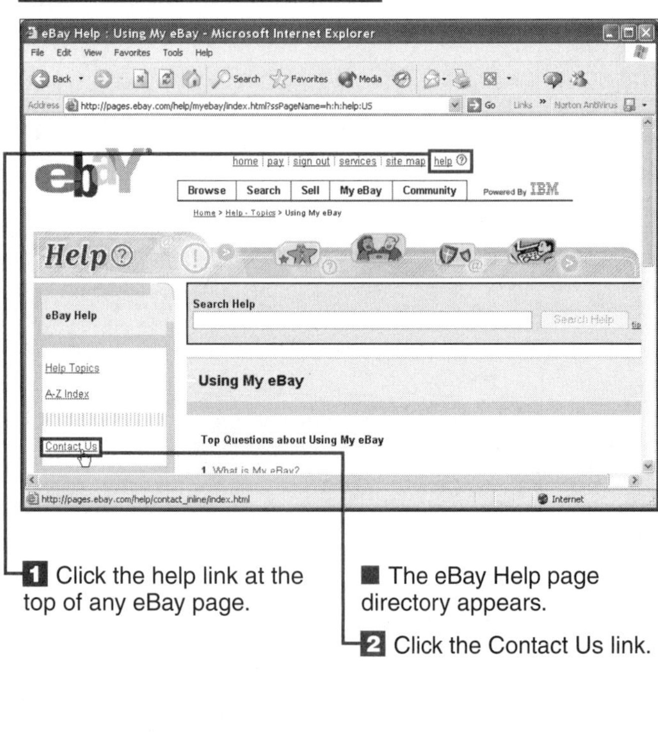

1 Click the help link at the top of any eBay page.

■ The eBay Help page directory appears.

2 Click the Contact Us link.

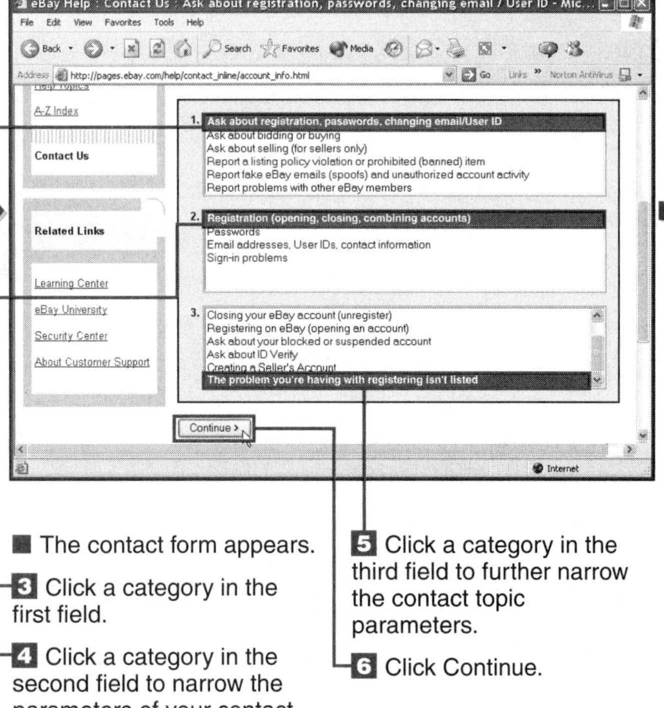

■ The contact form appears.

3 Click a category in the first field.

4 Click a category in the second field to narrow the parameters of your contact topic.

5 Click a category in the third field to further narrow the contact topic parameters.

6 Click Continue.

Can I find live help from eBay's customer support team?

✔ Yes. Click the eBay home link at the top of any eBay page, and then click the Live Help link located in the upper-right corner of the home page. This opens a live chat window that you can use to contact eBay immediately and ask a question. Note, however, that this feature is often very busy and unavailable during peak hours, or the wait time is very long. Be sure to consult the online Help system before using the Live Help feature. Most basic questions and answers are covered in the Help pages or in eBay's Answer Center.

How do I contact eBay through a phone number?

✔ eBay does not offer a telephone number on its Web site. However, you can write to the corporate headquarters. Display the eBay home page, scroll to the bottom of the page, and click the About eBay link. Click the Contact Information link to view a page with the corporate address.

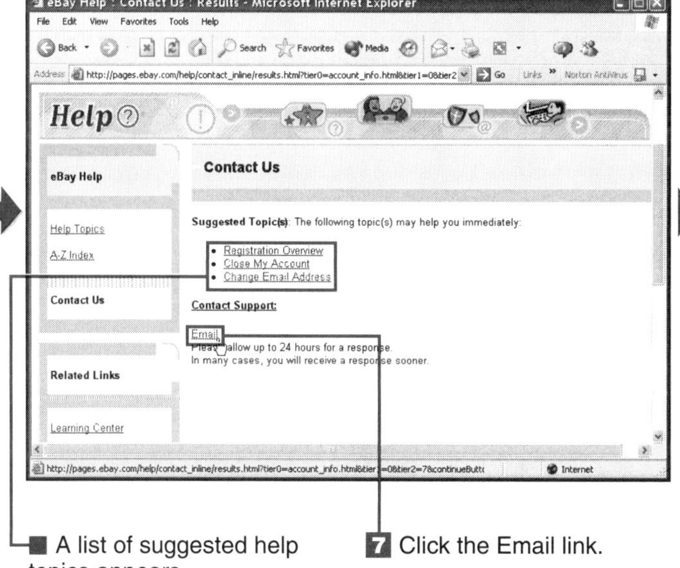

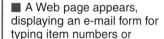

■ A list of suggested help topics appears.

Note: See the section "Find Help Through the eBay Help Pages," earlier in this chapter, to learn more about viewing eBay's Help pages.

7 Click the Email link.

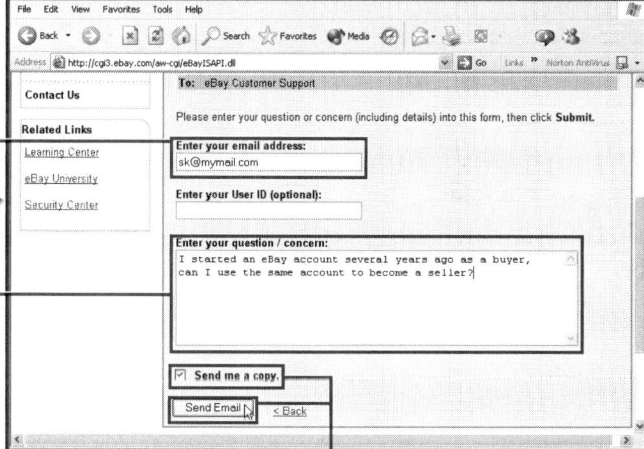

■ A Web page appears, displaying an e-mail form for typing item numbers or questions.

8 Use the required fields to ask your question or report an issue.

Note: Depending on the categories you select, the form may offer different fields.

■ Leave this option selected if you want to send a copy of the e-mail to yourself.

9 Click Send Email.

■ eBay sends your query to the customer support team.

FIND HELP THROUGH THE ANSWER CENTER

You can use eBay's discussion boards to find help with problems or concerns about auction listings, payment methods, feedback issues, and more. eBay's many discussion boards offer a wealth of knowledge posted by other eBay users. When looking for immediate help, the Answer Center discussion board is a great resource for questions you may have about buying or selling items on eBay.

The Answer Center includes discussion areas for all the major aspects of eBay, including dealing with eBay stores, international trading, and packaging and shipping issues. The eBay discussion boards offer dynamic communication between all levels of eBay users, from the novice buyer to the experienced seller. The boards work by allowing users to exchange information, opinions, and ideas. Users can post a question on a board and receive answers from other users or from eBay's own customer service staff. For example, you can post a question about an auction listing description and get responses from five other eBay users offering their own advice.

Before posting a question, however, scroll through the current postings to see if another user has already asked a similar question.

FIND HELP THROUGH THE ANSWER CENTER

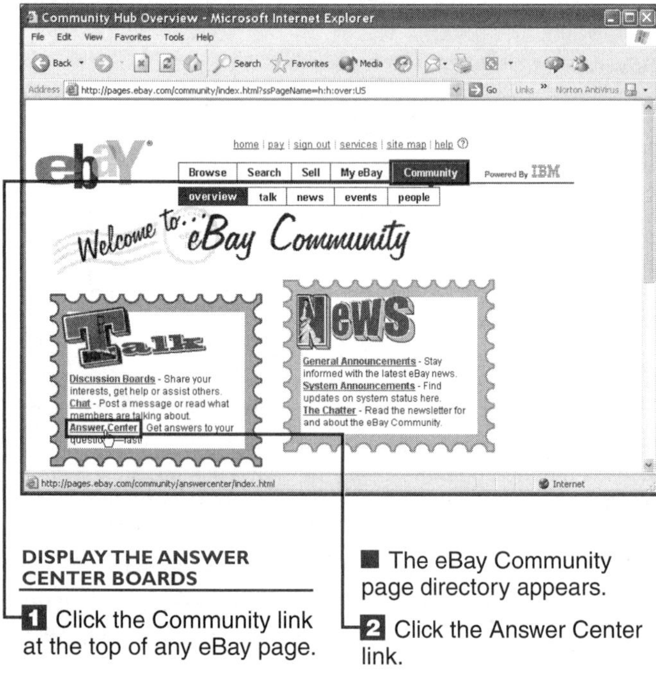

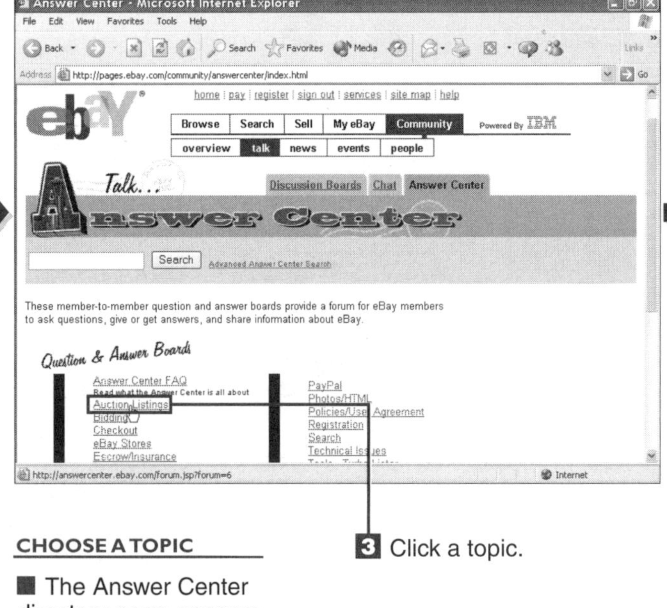

DISPLAY THE ANSWER CENTER BOARDS

1 Click the Community link at the top of any eBay page.

■ The eBay Community page directory appears.

2 Click the Answer Center link.

CHOOSE A TOPIC

■ The Answer Center directory page appears.

3 Click a topic.

How do I view more pages of message postings?

✔ You can click page numbers at the bottom of any discussion board page to view more message postings. Depending on the discussion board topic, thousands of messages may be available to view. You can conduct a discussion board search to find messages and replies related to your own situation. See the next page to learn how to search the discussion boards.

Is there any information I can access to learn more about using the Answer Center?

✔ Yes. You can click the general Answer Center discussion board, called the Answer Center FAQ, at the top of the directory page to view a page of frequently asked questions. Here you can read more information about how the feature works.

How do I post a new message on a discussion board?

✔ See the section "Post a Question in the Answer Center," later in this chapter, to learn how to log on and add your own question to a discussion board.

How do the Answer Center question-and-answer boards differ from the other community boards?

✔ The primary purpose of the Answer Center discussion boards is to help other users with eBay problems and issues. The other eBay boards are more community-driven and focused on other interests that are often unrelated to eBay. You can use the other discussion boards to meet other eBay users, talk about marketing and product ideas, and discuss myriad other subjects. The Answer Center boards focus strictly on answering help-related questions and problems.

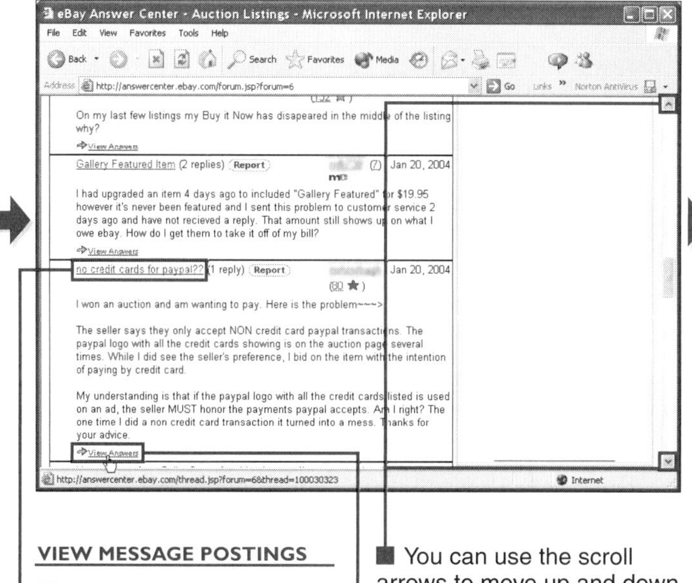

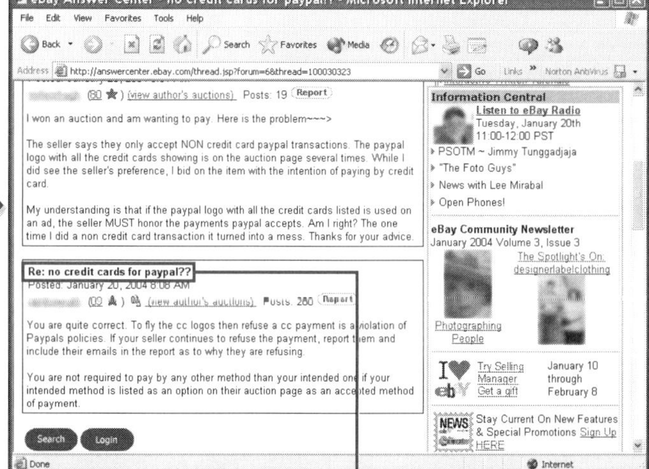

VIEW MESSAGE POSTINGS

■ The discussion board appears, displaying discussion posts.

4 Scroll through the list and click on a post that you want to read.

■ You can use the scroll arrows to move up and down the message posts.

5 Click the View Answers link to view the replies posted by other users.

VIEW MESSAGE REPLIES

■ A page appears, displaying the original question and any answers to the posted question.

■ Answers to the original message appear with Re: in front of the original question.

CONTINUED

FIND HELP THROUGH THE ANSWER CENTER (CONTINUED)

If a casual viewing of the first several pages of message posts does not reveal any topics related to the area in which you need help, you can conduct a search of the message postings with the search feature found at the bottom of the discussion board pages. You can do a keyword search of messages throughout the current Answer Center discussion board topic.

When searching a discussion board, you can search for a particular word or phrase. The discussion board search form allows you to narrow your search, if needed. For example, you can search for message postings from a particular eBay user if you know the user's ID, or you can search for postings from a certain period of time, such as messages posted in the last seven days.

You can also set the number of message postings you want to appear on a page. By default, eBay's Answer Center displays ten messages at a time, but you can choose to view 15 or 30 messages per page.

After filling out the search form, you can conduct a search. The Answer Center displays message postings that match the criteria you set as a list of search results. You can then view each result to read the original message posting along with any replies.

FIND HELP THROUGH THE ANSWER CENTER (CONTINUED)

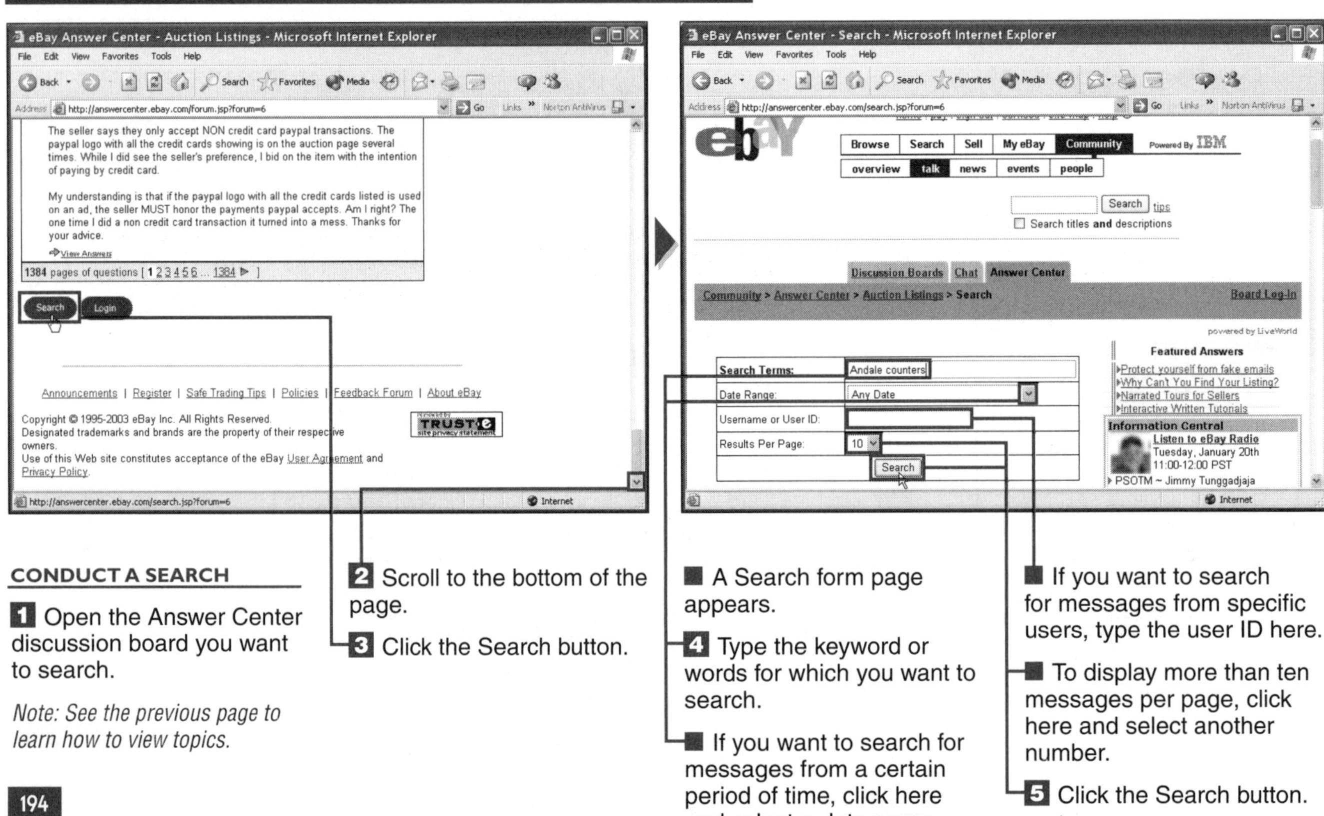

CONDUCT A SEARCH

1 Open the Answer Center discussion board you want to search.

Note: See the previous page to learn how to view topics.

2 Scroll to the bottom of the page.

3 Click the Search button.

■ A Search form page appears.

4 Type the keyword or words for which you want to search.

■ If you want to search for messages from a certain period of time, click here and select a date range.

■ If you want to search for messages from specific users, type the user ID here.

■ To display more than ten messages per page, click here and select another number.

5 Click the Search button.

I tried to conduct a search, but ended up viewing auction listings instead. What happened?

✔ If you click the Search icon at the top of any discussion board page, including the Answer Center, eBay searches through the auction listings instead of the message board postings. You must click the Search button at the bottom of the discussion board page to search only through message postings.

My search did not produce any results. What do I do now?

✔ Try generalizing your search by using fewer and more general keywords. Before conducting a search, scan other message board postings to see what questions other users are posting and how they are worded. This can help you define your own message board search terms.

How often should I check the Answer Center for new questions or answers to posted questions?

✔ Because eBay users reply to questions throughout the day, it is a good idea to check the Answer Center often. For example, if you find a message posted that matches your own situation, check the board at the beginning and end of the day to see what new replies are posted. If you log on to the board, you can set up a watch to keep track of updates. The watch list feature is only available when you log on to the discussion board area. See the next section to learn about logging on; see the next section's tip area to learn more about setting up a watch list.

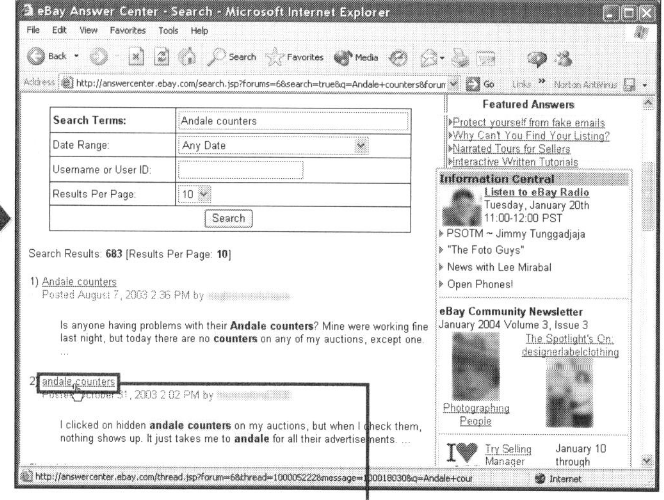

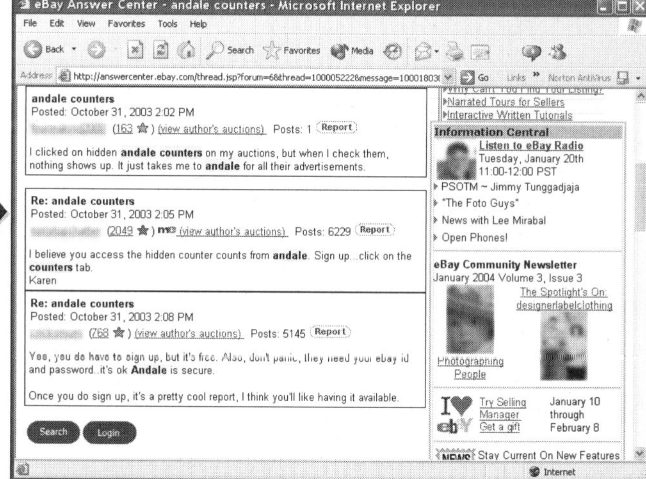

VIEW SEARCH RESULTS

■ eBay displays the search results.

6 Click the message you want to view.

VIEW A MESSAGE POSTING

■ The original message and its replies appear.

POST A QUESTION IN THE ANSWER CENTER

If browsing and searching the Answer Center discussion boards does not reveal the information you need, you can post your own question. Posting a question allows other eBay users to view your message and offer any replies.

In order to post a question or answer another user's question, you must log on to the discussion board using your eBay User ID and password. Even if you already logged on to eBay to make a bid or view auction listings, you must log on again in order to use the discussion board area of the site.

When you post a new question, a message form appears. You can specify a subject as well as type in your question in detail. Keep your subject line brief and to the point. When other users search the message boards, eBay conducts a search of the messages' subject lines.

Check spelling and grammar before posting your message. The message form includes a spell-check feature for proofing your message. Clear communication can greatly benefit anyone reading and answering your question.

Before posting a question, scroll through the current postings to see if another user has already asked a similar question.

POST A QUESTION IN THE ANSWER CENTER

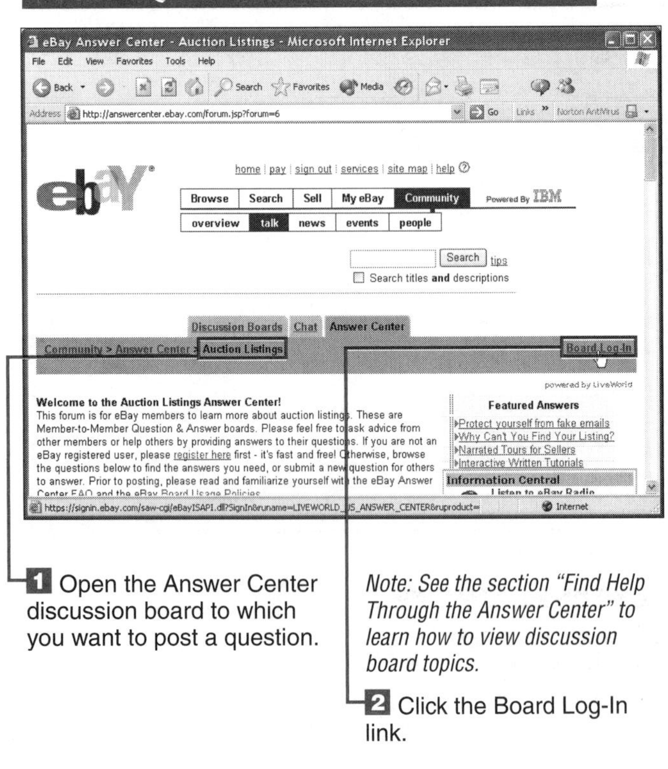

1 Open the Answer Center discussion board to which you want to post a question.

Note: See the section "Find Help Through the Answer Center" to learn how to view discussion board topics.

2 Click the Board Log-In link.

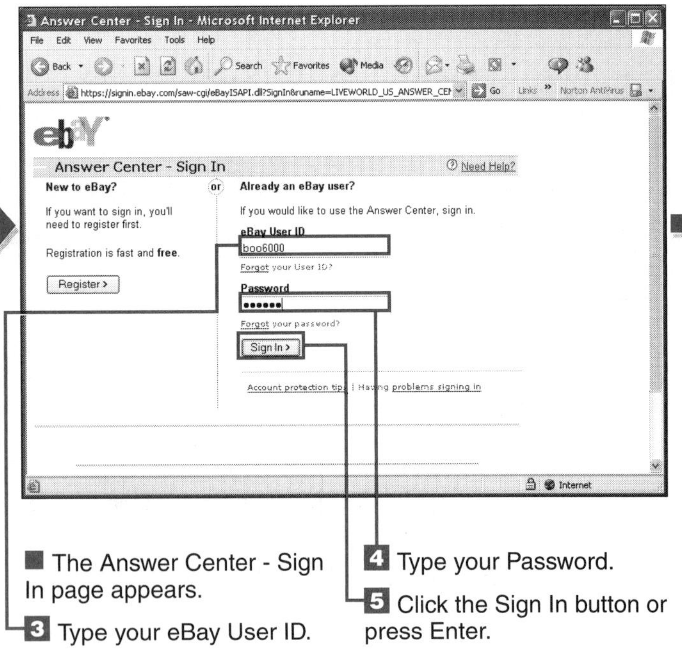

■ The Answer Center - Sign In page appears.

3 Type your eBay User ID.

4 Type your Password.

5 Click the Sign In button or press Enter.

The Answer Center will not let me answer another user's question. Why not?

✔ You cannot answer other users' questions unless you have a feedback rating of 10 or more. This stipulation helps keep new users from possibly giving out incorrect information. eBay figures that the more feedback you have, the more experienced you are. See Chapter 11 to learn more about feedback ratings.

Is there a limit to how many message replies can appear with a question?

✔ Yes. eBay only allows 10 replies to a question on the discussion boards. If you are the 11th person to respond to a question, eBay will not let you post your reply.

Can I tell eBay to contact me if I get any replies to my message post?

✔ Yes. You can set up a watch feature to watch the question and send an e-mail when the question receives an updated reply. To set up the watch feature for a message, display the question and its current replies. Click the Watch this Question link at the top of the question area. This opens a Watch List where you can keep track of and manage the message questions you are tracking. You can tell eBay to e-mail you immediately, daily, or weekly when anyone replies.

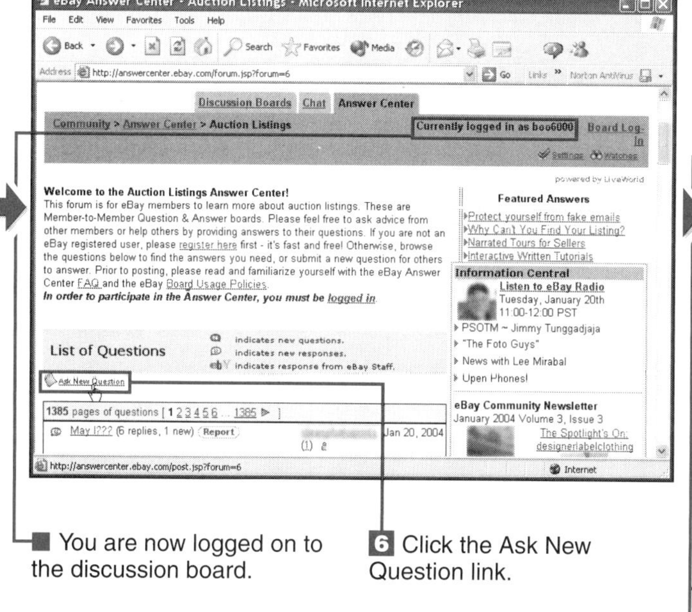

■ You are now logged on to the discussion board.

6 Click the Ask New Question link.

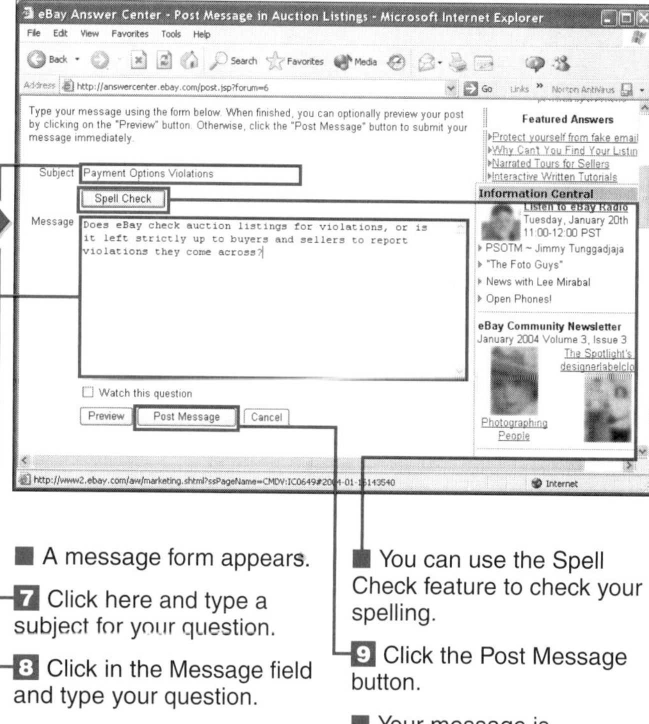

■ A message form appears.

7 Click here and type a subject for your question.

8 Click in the Message field and type your question.

■ You can use the Spell Check feature to check your spelling.

9 Click the Post Message button.

■ Your message is immediately added to the discussion board posts.

FIND IMMEDIATE HELP WITH EBAY CHAT

You can use eBay's live chat rooms to find immediate help with your eBay problems. Live chat rooms offer dynamic conversations between eBay users who are logged on at the same time as you. For example, if you are having a problem with an auction that ends in less than an hour, cannot find the information you want from eBay's online Help system, and do not have time to wait for an e-mail answer, try posting your question in the eBay Q&A chat room.

The eBay Q&A chat room is specifically for users experiencing problems and wanting to ask a quick question. The chat room is typically populated at all hours of the day with users willing to lend a helping hand to others having problems.

Be aware that not all the chat is professional in nature. In most instances, however, you can find someone to help you if you ask your question politely.

To use the eBay chat rooms, you must first log on to the boards using your eBay User ID and password. You must log on even if you previously logged on to bid on an item or perform another eBay task.

FIND IMMEDIATE HELP WITH EBAY CHAT

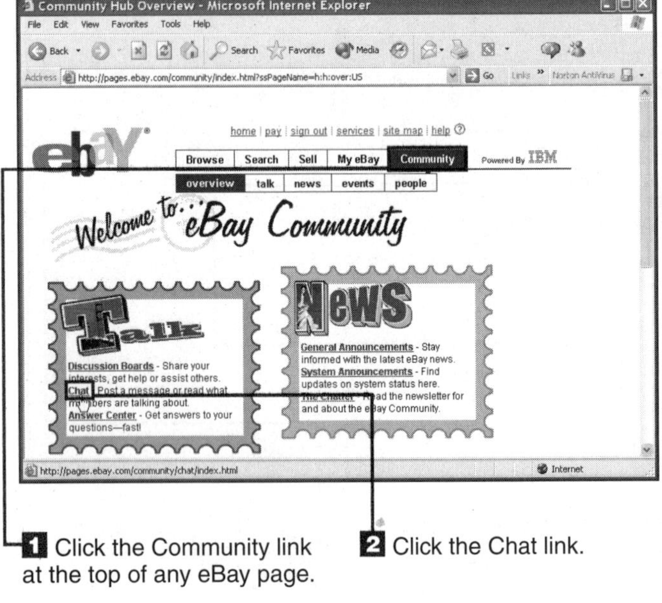

1 Click the Community link at the top of any eBay page.

2 Click the Chat link.

■ The Chat directory page appears.

3 Click a chat room that you want to join.

■ You can select the eBay Q&A chat room for immediate help with any eBay questions.

What other types of chat rooms are available?

✔ eBay features several general topic chat rooms as well as more than 20 category-related chat rooms. For example, if you are an avid collector of Elvis memorabilia, you may want to visit the Elvis chat room from time to time to learn about Elvis-related items and share new information with other Elvis collectors. Although you cannot buy or sell items in a chat room, you can certainly talk about your hobby with other enthusiasts. To find a listing of all available chat rooms on eBay, return to the Chat directory page, click the Community link, and then click the Chat link under the Talk area.

Are there rules or guidelines I should follow when participating in an eBay chat room?

✔ Yes. You can click the eBay Board Usage Policies link at the top of any chat room page and view a list of rules and guidelines for posting messages both in chat rooms and eBay discussion boards. For example, you cannot use profanity in your message text or post contact information about another user. You cannot sell or buy items through chat rooms or discussion boards, or conduct any type of product trading outside of the auction listing format. If you violate the rules, eBay can suspend you from the chat rooms or message boards.

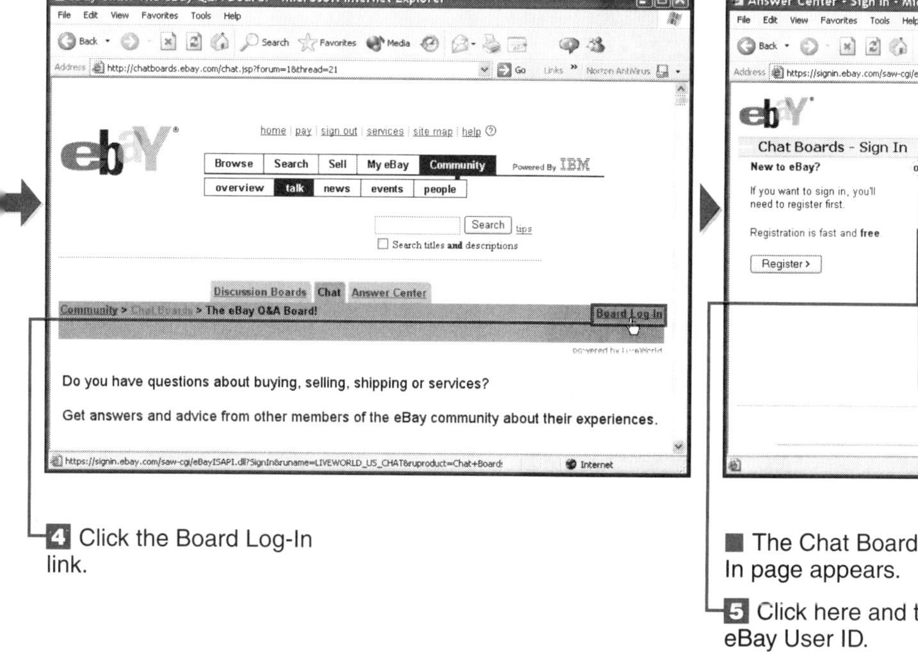

4 Click the Board Log-In link.

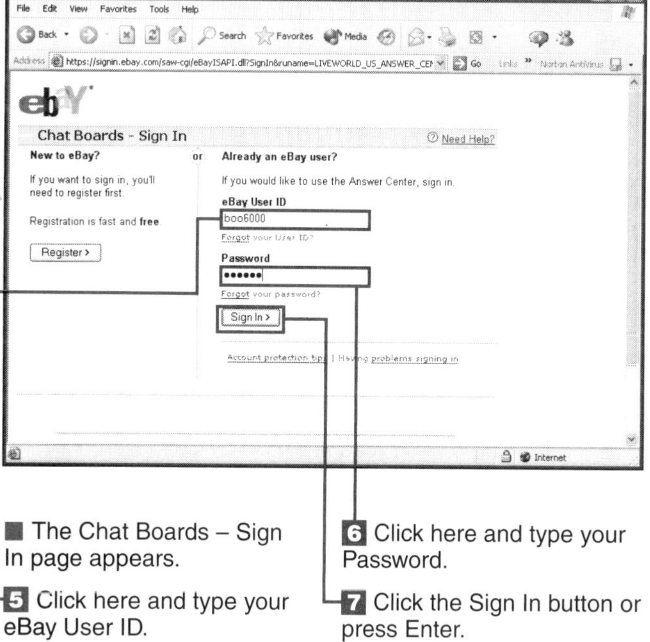

■ The Chat Boards – Sign In page appears.

5 Click here and type your eBay User ID.

6 Click here and type your Password.

7 Click the Sign In button or press Enter.

CONTINUED

FIND IMMEDIATE HELP WITH EBAY CHAT (CONTINUED)

The eBay Q&A chat room posts questions and answers in the form of scrolling messages. The newest messages appear at the top of the page. To continue seeing new messages, you must refresh the page from time to time.

Messages posted in a chat room continue to generate more messages as well as new ones added to the conversation. As such, it is often difficult to follow the conversation because someone may be posting an answer to a question farther down the page. Learning to read live messages takes a bit of practice.

To post a question, you can use the message form that appears near the top of the chat room page. The form consists of a text box for typing your question or conversational text, and a submission button that actually posts your message to the ever-scrolling list of conversations.

After you post your message, click the Refresh button in your browser window to refresh the ongoing conversations and view any responses to your message. You can continue conversing with other users by returning to the message form and posting new messages to add to the scrolling conversation.

FIND IMMEDIATE HELP WITH EBAY CHAT (CONTINUED)

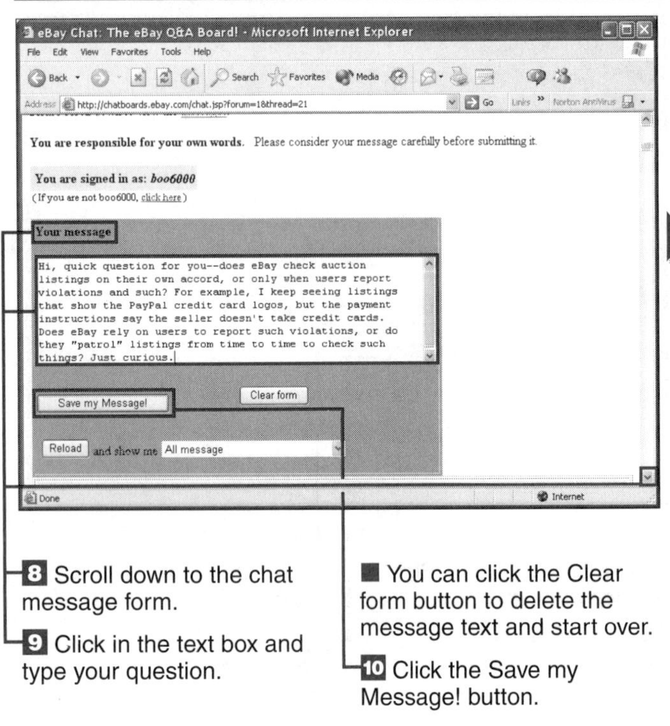

8 Scroll down to the chat message form.

9 Click in the text box and type your question.

■ You can click the Clear form button to delete the message text and start over.

10 Click the Save my Message! button.

■ eBay adds your message to the live chat room postings.

11 Scroll down the page to see your message.

I can no longer see my question in the scrolling conversations. Is there any way I can see my original question again?

✔ No. There is a limit as to how many message boxes appear in an eBay chat room. Because live chat is always changing, your original question is only onscreen for a short amount of time as others answer or add more questions. Unfortunately, you cannot scroll back beyond the bottom-most message on the page. If you did not see an answer to your question, you can type it again and see if anyone answers.

If I have an eBay emergency, where do I go for help?

✔ From the Chat directory page, you can click the Emergency Contact chat room link to talk to other eBay users about immediate problems. Experienced users can direct you to important eBay Help pages or offer advice with a problem. You can also try asking a question of eBay's live help feature. From the eBay home page, click the Live Help link to post a question to an eBay customer assistant. Be aware that live help is often delayed, so be prepared to wait for several minutes before you can communicate with a live person regarding your question.

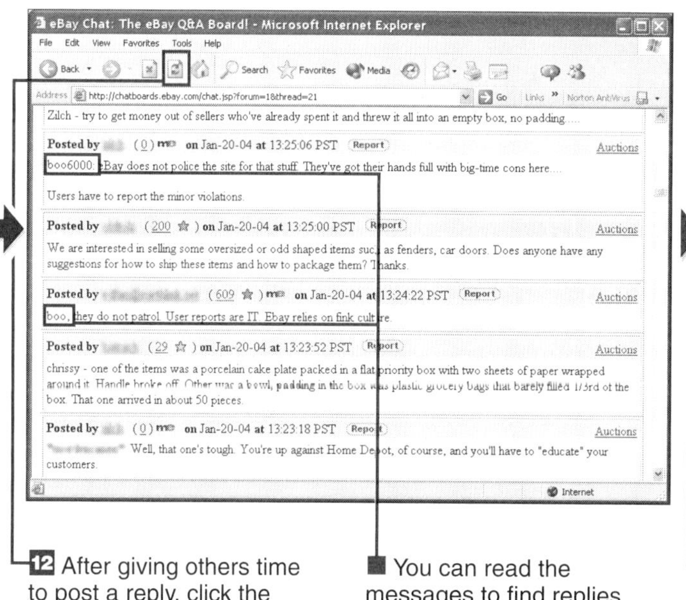

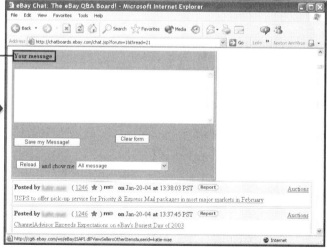

12 After giving others time to post a reply, click the Refresh button.

■ You can read the messages to find replies to your question.

■ To post additional questions or replies, you can return to the message form and repeat steps 9 and 10.

VIEW EBAY ANNOUNCEMENTS

For the latest eBay information, you can visit the News pages to read eBay announcements and system news. eBay news can include anything from eBay scams users should watch out for to information about new services to changes to existing eBay services.

The General Announcements page displays information about category listing changes, new eBay features, policy changes, and more. You can use the General Announcements page to learn about upcoming changes to the eBay system, changes in fees and policies, upcoming online seminars, and other important news. To keep on top of upcoming events and happenings, be sure to check the General Announcements page with some degree of frequency. This is especially important when you are maintaining an eBay business online.

The System Announcements page posts information about system status issues, such as scheduled maintenance times when the eBay site may not work as smoothly as it should, category listing problems, and other technical announcements. You can visit this page if you experience a problem accessing the eBay site or an auction listing to find out if your problem was isolated or experienced by everyone else using eBay.

VIEW EBAY ANNOUNCEMENTS

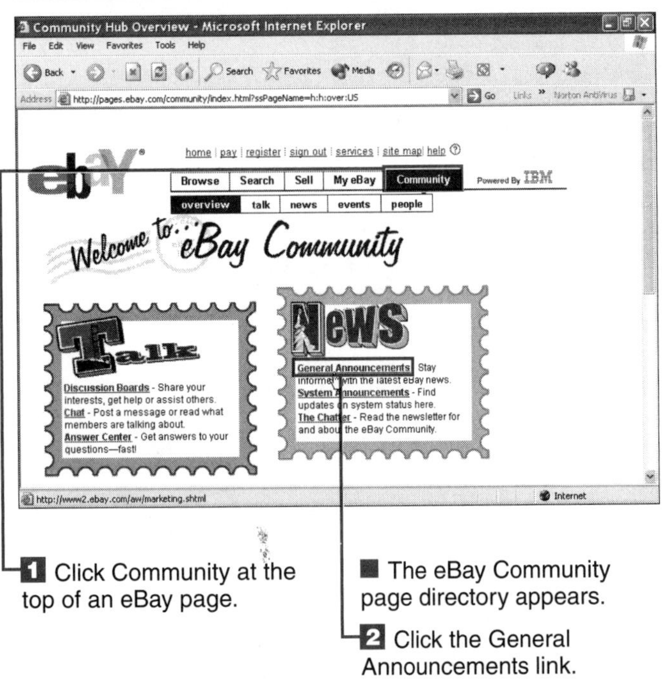

1 Click Community at the top of an eBay page.

■ The eBay Community page directory appears.

2 Click the General Announcements link.

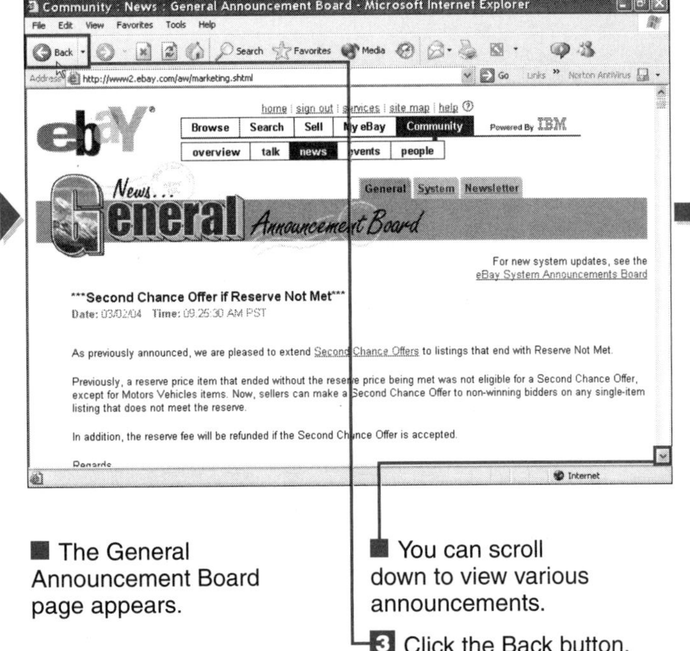

■ The General Announcement Board page appears.

■ You can scroll down to view various announcements.

3 Click the Back button.

Where else can I find eBay news?

✔ Throughout different categories and among the eBay community, you can find newsletters to help keep members up-to-date about important issues, policies, and news. For example, eBay's own newsletter, *The Chatter*, keeps you informed about eBay success stories and upcoming events. In addition to the general newsletter, some individual categories also put out newsletters for people who share similar interests. See the section "Sign Up for eBay Newsletters" to learn more about tapping into newsletters as a way to learn more about the eBay community.

Are there any other eBay publications I can consult?

✔ eBay used to publish its own magazine a couple of years ago, but the venture did not last long. You can, however, find plenty of information about eBay on other Internet Web sites. For example, sites like Auction Bytes (www.auctionbytes.com), Auction Guide (www.auctionguide.com), and Auction Insights (www.auctioninsights.com), are good places to find a wealth of online auction information. You can do a Web search on the keywords *auction tips* to find more sites to check out.

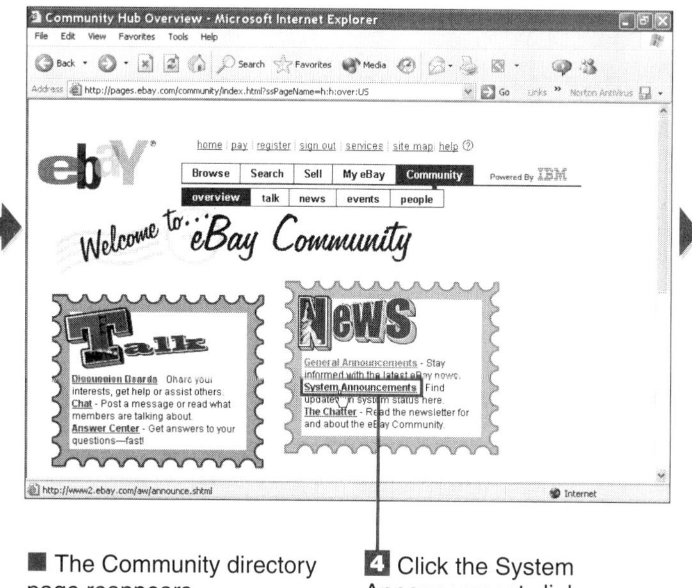

■ The Community directory page reappears.

4 Click the System Announcements link.

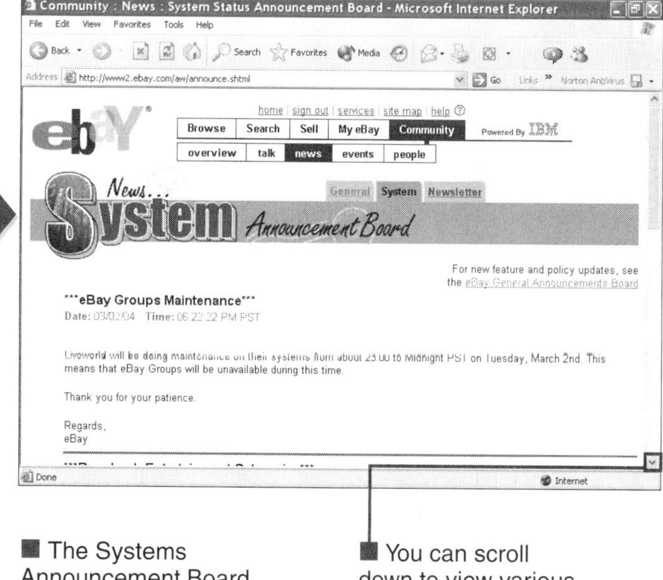

■ The Systems Announcement Board page appears.

■ You can scroll down to view various announcements.

READ EBAY DISCUSSION BOARDS

Some of the best places to learn about eBay tips and techniques are the many eBay online message boards. Message boards, also called *discussion boards* on eBay, are electronic bulletin boards that allow members to communicate questions and ideas, and engage in general conversation about eBay and its many facets. Discussion boards also allow eBay users with similar interests to participate in online discussions about problems and concerns. Users post messages on a particular board, and other users come along and reply. To participate in any of eBay's discussion boards, you must be a registered user. You do not need to be a registered user to read the boards.

You can find discussion boards through eBay's Community page. As you build your eBay business, be sure to visit the Seller Central discussion board from time to time to learn about the latest selling tools and resources.

The Workshops Board is another good source for learning about specific aspects of eBay, such as how to sell clothing or find cost-effective shipping methods. eBay workshops are run by eBay's community development team and often sponsor special guests and eBay experts. Workshop discussions are archived on the Workshops Board, so you can still learn about a topic without needing to attend the online workshop.

READ EBAY DISCUSSION BOARDS

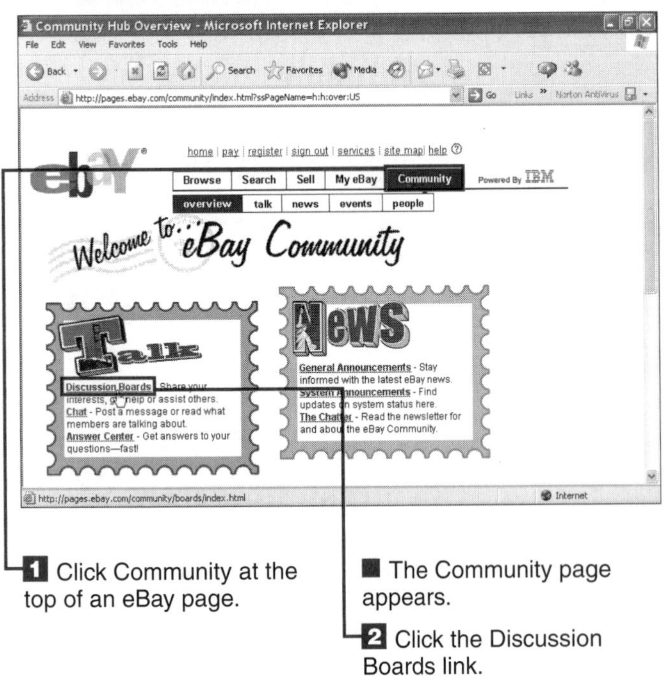

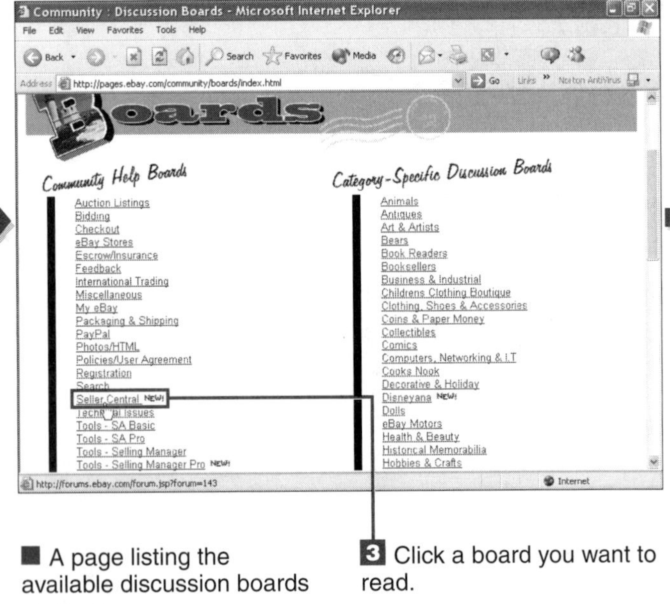

1 Click Community at the top of an eBay page.

■ The Community page appears.

2 Click the Discussion Boards link.

■ A page listing the available discussion boards appears.

3 Click a board you want to read.

How do I post a new message topic?

✔ To add a new message to the board, you must first log on to the discussion board using your eBay User ID and password. After logging on, you can scroll to the bottom of the page and click the Add Discussion button. This button does not appear unless you log on to the discussion board. When you activate the Add Discussion button, a new message form page opens. Fill in the subject title and the message text, and then click the Post Message button. eBay adds your message to the board. There may be a delay between the time you post and when you see the message appear on the board.

Are there any rules for posting messages?

✔ Yes. Obvious rules include using appropriate language. The boards also restrict you from posting contact information about another user, posting private e-mails, and posting obscene material. Make sure you fully understand what is and is not allowed on the board before posting a single message or posting a reply to an existing message. To learn about board policies, click the Board Usage Policies link at the top of the discussion board.

How many messages stay on a board?

✔ eBay keeps a little over 1,000 messages posted, with newer posts appearing on the first page of the discussion board. To find a message or topic, use the Search button at the bottom of the discussion board page.

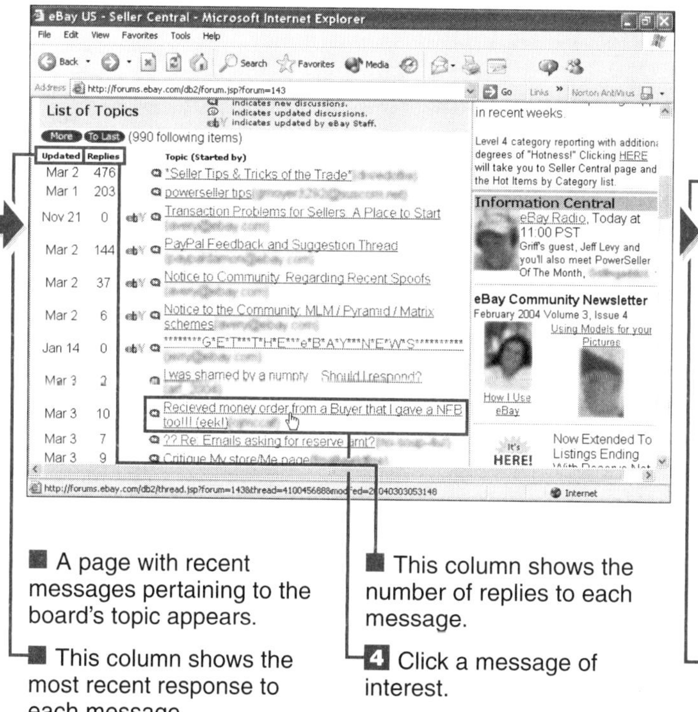

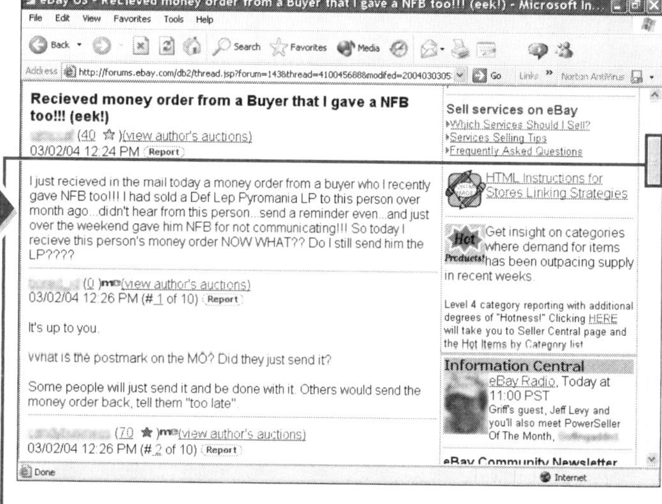

■ A page with recent messages pertaining to the board's topic appears.

■ This column shows the most recent response to each message.

■ This column shows the number of replies to each message.

4 Click a message of interest.

■ The original message and any replies it has received appear.

■ You can scroll through the replies to read responses by other users to the original message post.

■ You can add your own reply by filling out the message form at the bottom of the page.

Note: You must log on to the discussion board before you can post a message or a reply.

SIGN UP FOR EBAY NEWSLETTERS

You can use eBay newsletters as another way to stay on top of the latest news and information about any particular eBay auction category. Category newsletters, called *newsflashes*, are electronic newsletters offering information about upcoming events, seller tips, and special offers.

Published monthly, eBay newsletters are tailored to a variety of unique categories. For example, the *Antiques Seller Newsflash* is tailor-made for online antique sellers, while the *Coins Seller Newsflash* is geared toward collectible coins. Each newsflash lists the hottest-selling items for a particular category, as well as links to useful eBay tools and information. Be sure to check out the newsflash each month to find the latest news about your category of interest. Not all categories offer a newsletter, but check your favorite category often to see if a newsletter is available.

eBay also has a general eBay community newsletter called *The Chatter* that you can use to learn more about the eBay community at large. One of the most useful newsletters for an eBay business is the *Seller Newsflash*. You can sign up to have the newsletter delivered to your e-mail address.

SIGN UP FOR EBAY NEWSLETTERS

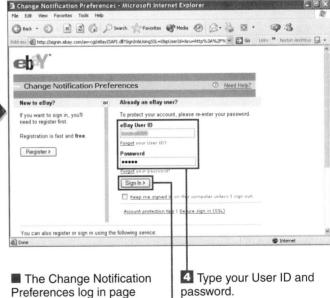

Don't miss out-sign up for eBay email today and get advance notice of upcoming events, promotions, and your monthly Seller Newsflash!

1 Type **http://pages.ebay.com/sellercentral/newsflash.html** in your browser window.

2 Click the Go button or press Enter.

■ The Seller Central page appears.

3 Click the sign up link.

■ The Change Notification Preferences log in page appears.

4 Type your User ID and password.

5 Click Sign In.

How do I sign up for other category newsletters?

✔ You can use the same technique of changing your notification preferences to sign up for other eBay newsletters. To find other newsletters, start by browsing the category to which you want to subscribe. Click the Browse link and choose the category. Scroll to the bottom of the category page and look for a newsletter option among the category's Category Community Links area. If the category does offer a newsletter, click the link and follow the signup prompts. Not all categories offer newsletters. Among those that do are the Antiques, Toys & Hobbies, and Clothing, Shoes & Accessories categories.

How do I unsubscribe to the Seller Newsflash?

✔ Repeat the steps shown below, but click the eBay Email option in step 7 to deselect it (☑ changes to ☐). After you save your changes, eBay no longer e-mails you the newsletter.

Can I read a current newsletter without having to subscribe?

✔ Many of the category newsletters permit you to read the latest edition without signing up to receive the newsletter by e-mail. For example, if you display the Toys & Hobbies category and click the Read the Latest Seller Newsletter link, eBay opens the newsletter page for you to peruse online.

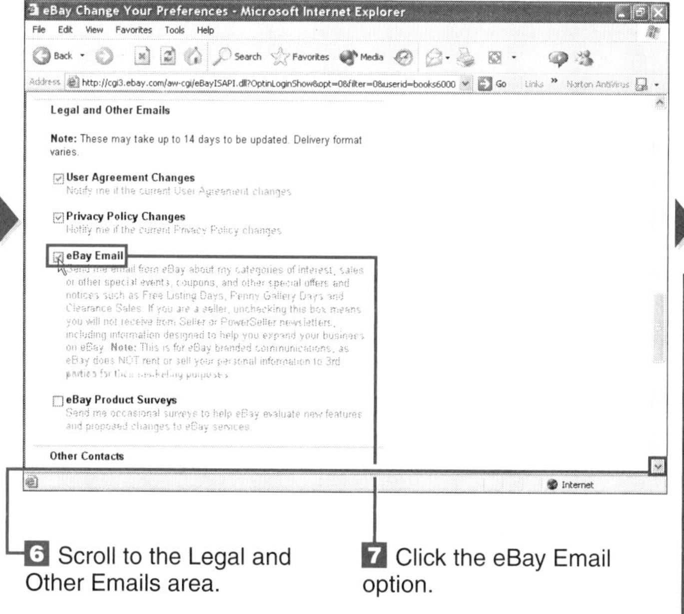

6 Scroll to the Legal and Other Emails area.

7 Click the eBay Email option.

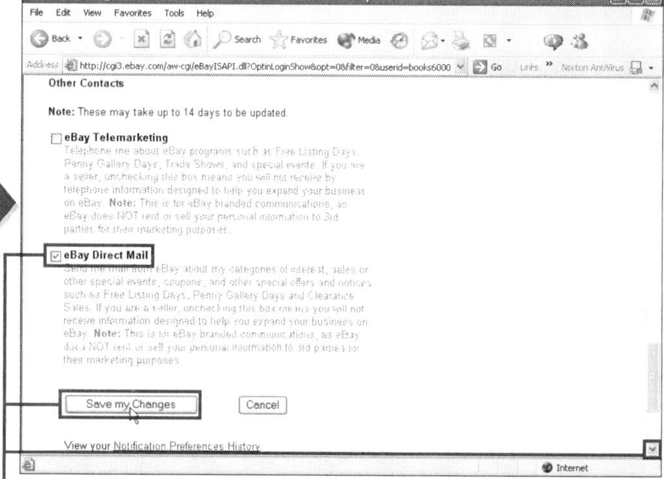

8 Scroll to the bottom of the page.

9 Click the eBay Direct Mail option.

10 Click Save my Changes.

■ eBay saves your notification settings, and you are now signed up to receive eBay Email and the Seller Newsflash.

FIND SELLER TUTORIALS

Among eBay's many resources, you can find online tutorials to help you learn more about certain aspects of eBay. For example, you can view seller tutorials to learn more about creating auction listings and selling items on eBay.

A tutorial is simply an online guide that explains a concept or procedure step by step. Tutorials are often comprised of several pages of information in which you can stop and read each page before progressing to the next. eBay offers both written tutorials, which include illustrations of what you can expect to see on your computer screen, and several audio tutorials, called *audio tours*. To fully utilize an audio tour, your computer needs a speaker and a volume control. Tutorials often appear when eBay introduces a new feature, so check the Help area from time to time for the availability of new tutorials.

eBay's seller tutorials show you how to create a seller account on eBay, create an auction listing, work with auction payments, and track your listings and sales. eBay lists several seller tutorials in the Help area of the Web site. You can also find additional tutorials and help in the Seller Central area of eBay.

FIND SELLER TUTORIALS

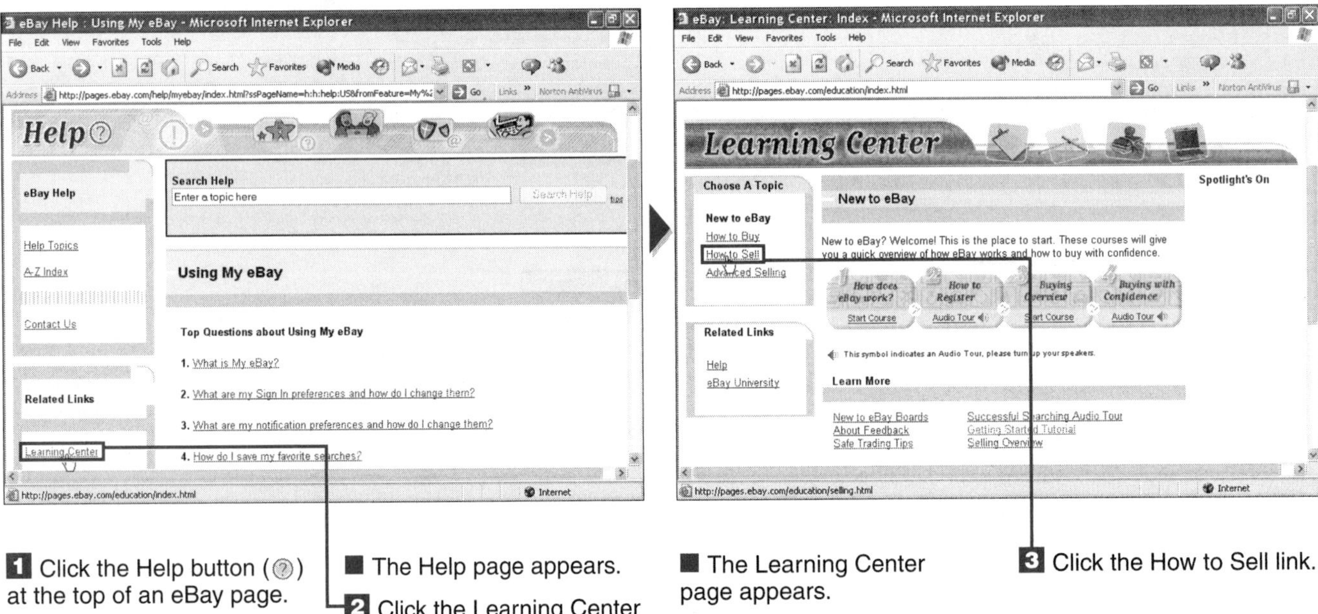

■1 Click the Help button (?) at the top of an eBay page.

■ The Help page appears.

■2 Click the Learning Center link.

■ The Learning Center page appears.

■3 Click the How to Sell link.

What is eBay University?

✔ If you prefer to learn in an actual classroom environment, eBay offers classes in large cities across the United States. For example, you can take a course on selling basics, which covers everything you need to know to start selling on eBay. The Beyond the Basics course teaches you how to utilize helpful eBay listing tools, PayPal, and more. You can sign up for the courses online and pay a registration fee. You can also look for free 90-minute courses in your area. To learn more about eBay University, display the Help page and click the eBay University link.

Does eBay offer online seminars?

✔ Yes. The site offers ongoing seminars, called *workshops*, that you can attend, as well as online classes through the eBay University area. For a fee, you can take an online course that teaches about a specific topic, such as improving your listings. The course includes reading, a live chat with the instructor, and a certificate of completion. Online workshops are often given by eBay experts and eBay personnel. The workshops are structured as live chat rooms in which participants can log in, listen to the speaker, and interact with chat questions. You can find workshops through the Community page.

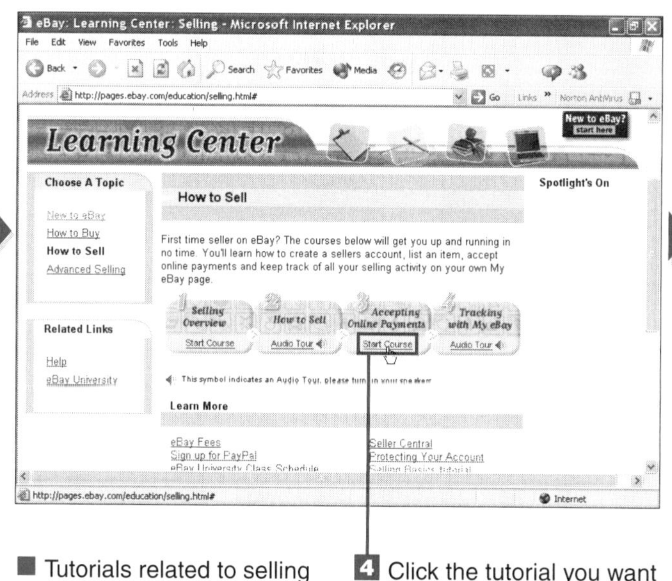

■ Tutorials related to selling items on eBay appear.

4 Click the tutorial you want to hear or view.

■ eBay opens the tutorial as a new window.

■ You can click the Next Step and Previous Step links to navigate the tutorial pages.

5 When finished, click here to close the tutorial window.

SELL REAL ESTATE

eBay features a real estate section where sellers can list homes, commercial buildings, land, timeshares, and other properties. Selling your property on eBay can be a cost-effective way to get regional, national, and international exposure. Because of the high price of many real estate transactions and the complexities of real estate sales, such listings have guidelines that differ from those for other eBay listings.

Real Estate Auction Format

The *auction* format for real estate is similar to the non-real estate format on eBay in that it involves a set time limit and a single winning bidder. In eBay real estate auctions, however, the winning buyer and seller are not legally bound to buy and sell the posted property. As eBay describes it, "A bid on a property is an indication of willingness in good faith to proceed to contract discussions." At the end of the auction, the seller contacts the high bidder to discuss entering into a contract for the property.

Real Estate Ad Format

eBay users also have the option of posting details about their property in an *ad* format rather than an auction format. When a seller uses the ad format, no bidding takes place. The ad format allows you to receive leads from multiple interested buyers over a set period of time — 30 or 90 days — rather than from a single high bidder. Instead of bidding a dollar amount, interested buyers fill out a contact form on eBay, and the information is sent to the seller

Real Estate Fees

There are special insertion fees for real estate listings. There are no final value fees associated with real estate on eBay.

Listing Type	*Insertion Fee*
3-, 5-, 7-, and 10-day auctions	$100
30-day auction	$150
30-day ad	$150
90-day ad	$300

A Better Real Estate Listing

The more detailed information you provide about your property in your description, the more likely you are to be matched with one or more interested buyers. Qualities such as location, numbers of bedrooms and baths, square footage, acreage, and architectural style are all important to buyers, and many conduct searches using these criteria. Multiple photos of a home or building are almost always a must to attract serious attention from buyers. Adding photos to your real estate listing costs the same as adding them to a non-real estate listing. If you provide an address for your property, eBay has free tools that allow potential buyers to view area maps and information about the property's neighborhood.

Sell a Timeshare

eBay's timeshare category connects eBay buyers with sellers offering part ownership in vacation properties. Timeshare auctions have a different fee structure — a $35 listing fee and a $35 final value fee. On the Timeshare Seller Help page, eBay offers a link to a timeshare valuation estimator that helps sellers set a fair selling price for timeshare listings. Note that many locales include special rules for timeshare transactions, including "cooling off" periods where a buyer can cancel the deal for any reason.

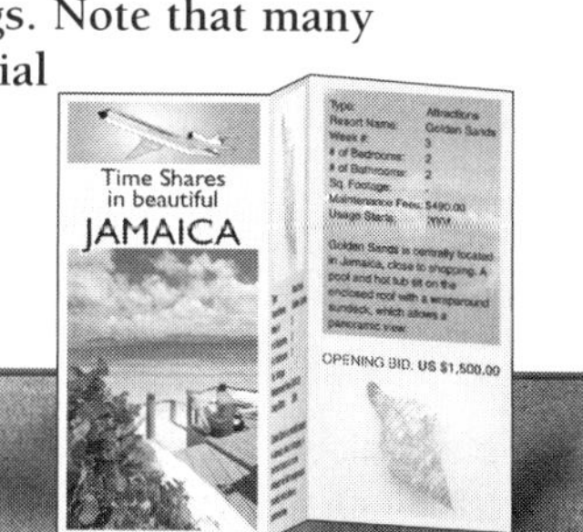

Sell Land

The eBay real estate section features a land category, where you can sell residential, commercial, and industrial properties. Putting land up for sale involves special considerations. Zoning, which determines how a piece of property can be used, plays a strong role in land sales. You will want to understand any zoning restrictions on your property and include those in your description. For example, can the land be subdivided? What types of structures are allowed? Photos can be a valuable asset for a land listing, especially if the land has a view or is near water. You may consider working with an appraiser or real estate agent to set a smart selling price for your land.

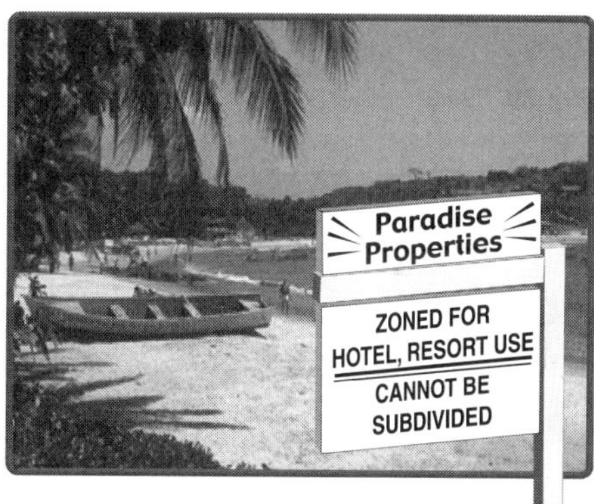

Get Help

Real estate buyers and sellers can trade tips with one another through the Real Estate & Timeshares Discussion Board. See Chapter 14 for more information on reading and posting to eBay discussions. Trading assistants — experienced sellers who will sell your items for a fee — can also be of help in completing a successful real estate transaction. eBay offers a searchable directory of trading assistants, some of whom specialize in real estate auctions. For more information, see the section "Find a Trading Assistant" in Chapter 16.

SEARCH REAL ESTATE AUCTIONS

You can search for residential homes, commercial buildings, land, timeshares, and other properties through the real estate section of eBay. The real estate search forms enable you to conduct a basic search of real estate titles and descriptions, or perform more advanced searches that specify the number of bedrooms and bathrooms, city and state, price range, and other information.

Listings that appear in the search results can be in two formats. Real estate *auctions* last for 30 days or less, and require you to bid against other interested buyers, just like non-real estate auctions. Real estate *ads* are like classified ads in the newspaper. A property description is listed with a price, and there is no limit as to the number of people who can contact the seller professing an interest. Both types of listings appear in the search results.

Unlike regular auctions, real estate auctions on eBay can last for as long as 30 days while real estate ads can appear for as long as 90 days. This gives you time to research the properties and locations before you make a bid.

SEARCH REAL ESTATE AUCTIONS

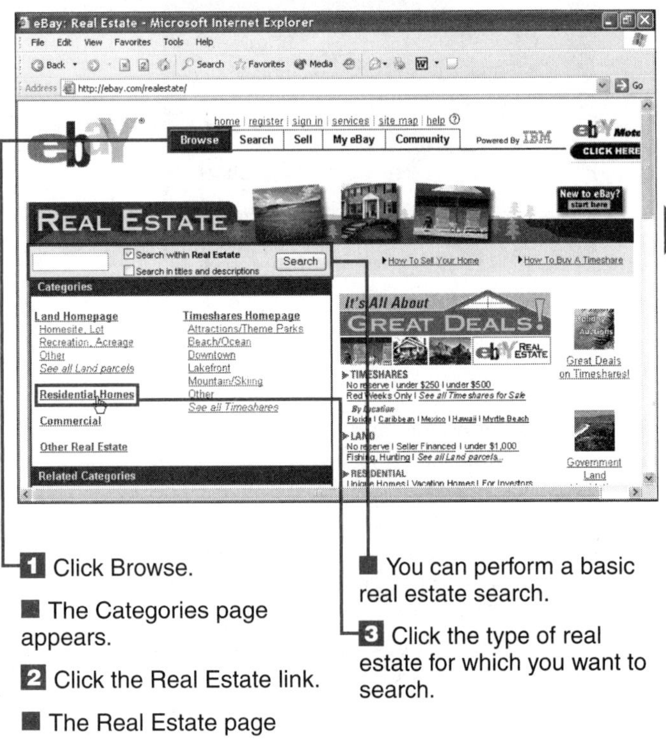

1 Click Browse.

■ The Categories page appears.

2 Click the Real Estate link.

■ The Real Estate page appears.

■ You can perform a basic real estate search.

3 Click the type of real estate for which you want to search.

■ A Real Estate Category appears.

4 Select a state or province and city.

5 Select a sale type.

■ You can limit your search to new, existing, or foreclosed homes.

6 Specify the number of bedrooms and bathrooms.

7 Type an optional keyword.

8 Click Show Items.

Where can I get more information on timeshares?

✔ eBay has a separate timeshare page where you can search for timeshares or browse for timeshare properties in different locations such as near the beach or in the mountains. To view it, click the Timeshares for Sale link on the main real estate page. eBay also has a category for Vacation Rentals, where you can bid on rentals of timeshares and other property rather than ownership.

How can I require that bidders make a deposit before bidding on my real estate?

✔ To encourage serious bidding only, sellers of real estate may want to require that bidders put down a deposit toward the purchase of a property before bidding. Companies such as eDeposit (www.edeposit.com) offer this service to sellers. With eDeposit, a seller can include a form in a listing description that allows bidders to place funds from their eDeposit account toward the purchase. Bidders must first sign up for and make a deposit to their eDeposit accounts.

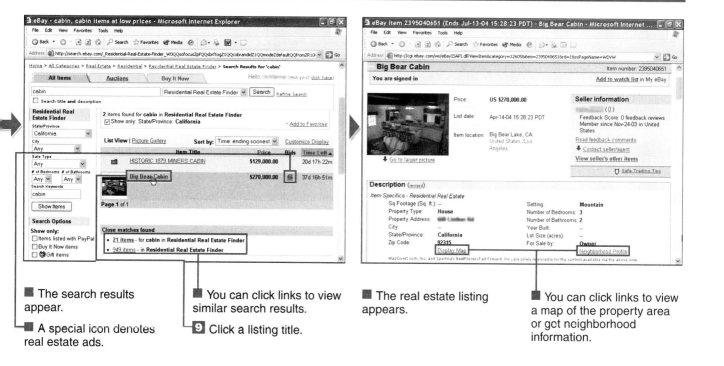

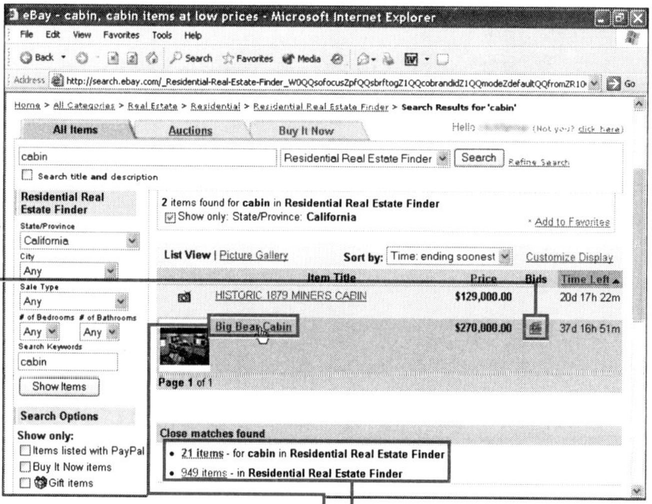

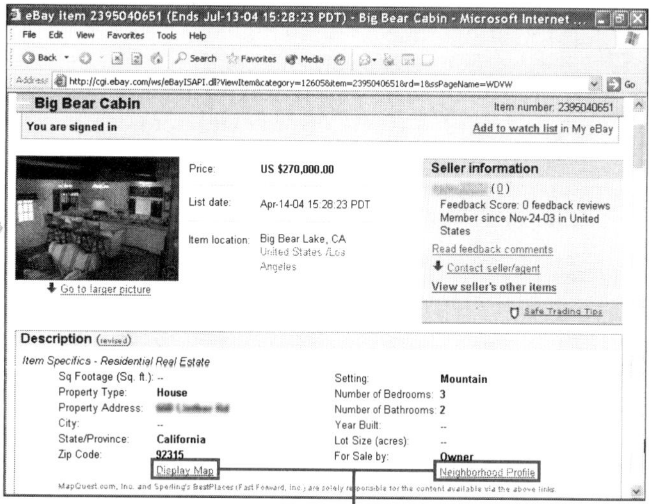

■ The search results appear.

■ A special icon denotes real estate ads.

■ You can click links to view similar search results.

9 Click a listing title.

■ The real estate listing appears.

■ You can click links to view a map of the property area or get neighborhood information.

SELL AN AUTOMOBILE OR OTHER VEHICLE

eBay Motors is a site within eBay devoted to auctions for cars, trucks, boats, aircraft, and other vehicles. The site features thousands of vehicle listings from both private parties and dealers. It also includes resources — some at eBay, some at third-party Web sites — that can help ensure your buying or selling experience is a success. These resources include used-car pricing guides, vehicle inspection services, auto-shipping companies, and others.

Vehicle Listing Fees

There is a $40 nonrefundable insertion fee for listing most vehicles at eBay Motors. Insertion fees for motorcycles are $30.00. Unlike regular auctions, eBay does not charge a final value fee at the close of a vehicle auction. Instead, eBay charges a transaction services fee when your auction receives its first bid or, if you set a reserve price, at the time of the first bid over that reserve. For passenger vehicles, the transaction services fee is $40.00; for motorcycles, it is $30.00. You will not be charged a transaction services fee if there are no bids on your item, or if there are no bids that meet your reserve price.

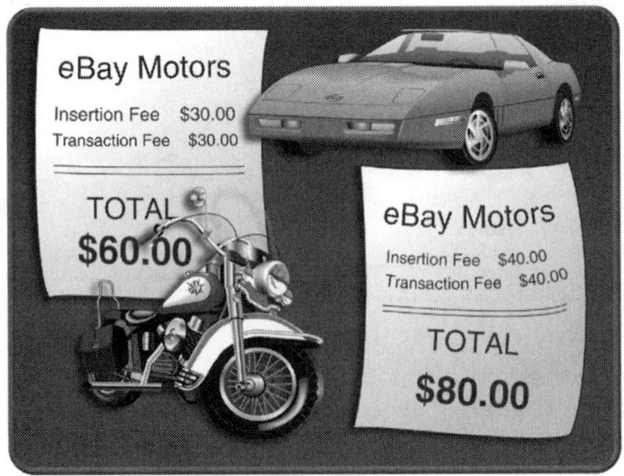

Set a Fair Price

Setting a fair price for your vehicle is key to attracting bidder attention and completing the sale. To determine a decent selling price, check out vehicle pricing guidelines at sites such as www.kbb.com, www.nadaguides.com, or www.edmunds.com. You can also look at final prices achieved on other eBay listings for similar cars by clicking the Completed Items link in the search results. In general, it can be a good idea to set the starting price low to attract bidder attention. If you're using a reserve price, consider setting it at a level at which you are willing to let the car go rather than the price you expect. For more on setting a reserve price in an auction, see Chapter 4.

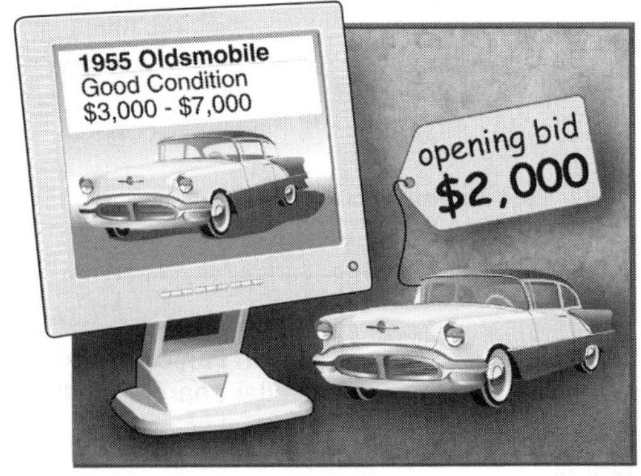

Photograph Your Vehicle

Your buyers will probably not have a chance to see your vehicle in person before making a bid, so it is critical that you give them a comprehensive look at what you're selling through photos. Try to take pictures of all sides of the vehicle, as well as of the front and back seats, dashboard, trunk, and engine. You might also consider photographing the odometer, plus any special customization or damage that the vehicle has. For more information about optimizing your photos for posting on

Vehicle Listing Tools

There are a variety of services that can help you create detailed, professional-looking vehicle listings and post them to eBay Motors. At CARad (www.carad.com), eBay's specialized vehicle listing service, you provide basic information about your car, such as its make, model, and year or vehicle identification number, and the CARad Web site automatically generates an auction listing with detailed information about the car. You can customize your listing by selecting from different auction templates and uploading photos of the vehicle. The service also offers preformatted e-mail messages to send interested buyers and tools for managing multiple vehicle auctions. Using CARad costs $9.95 per auction, in addition to the regular eBay auction

Provide a Vehicle History

Buyers will have more confidence about placing bids on your auctions if you include a complete history of the vehicle in question. You should also provide the vehicle identification number (VIN), so that buyers can look up information on the vehicle themselves using a vehicle history service such as CARFAX (www.carfax.com). eBay requires vehicle identification numbers when listing 1992 or newer vehicles. eBay features its own vehicle history service where buyers and sellers can perform searches. A search can reveal details such as the odometer history, salvage or flood records, accident and theft reports, and other information about a car that can affect its value.

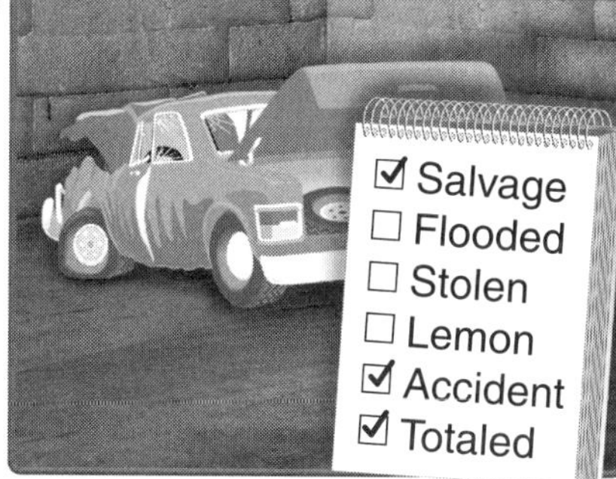

Lowering Your Price

One difference between eBay Motors auctions and other auctions is that a seller may lower the reserve or Buy It Now price at any time before the auction has met the reserve price or the auction has ended. When a reserve or Buy It Now price has been lowered, eBay notifies all bidders by e-mail. If a seller lowers the reserve or Buy It Now price below the maximum bid of the high bidder, the maximum bid of the high bidder is then lowered to $1 below the new price. The new price is then revealed to the high bidder by e-mail. This allows the high bidder to confirm that he or she is still interested in the vehicle. For more information about setting reserve and Buy It Now prices, see Chapters 1 and 4.

SEARCH VEHICLE AUCTIONS

The eBay Motors search page enables you to find exactly the types of cars, motorcycles, or other vehicles you are interested in. For passenger cars, the search lets you specify the make, model, year, and price of the car, as well as keywords in the title and description to include or exclude. You can also limit your search to major metropolitan regions of the United States.

The search form lets you find auctions held by a particular seller, which is useful if you want to examine the inventory of a dealer that lists on eBay Motors. You can also search by bidder, which will list the vehicle auctions that an eBay user is currently bidding on. This lets sellers find out what their potential buyers are interested in, or lets buyers view their current auction bids.

On the search results page, you can filter the information to include only those vehicles for sale that include a warranty. You can also filter auctions to show only those that offer Secure Pay, which is an escrow service that verifies the funds from a buyer and enables the buyer to inspect the auto before completing payment.

SEARCH VEHICLE AUCTIONS

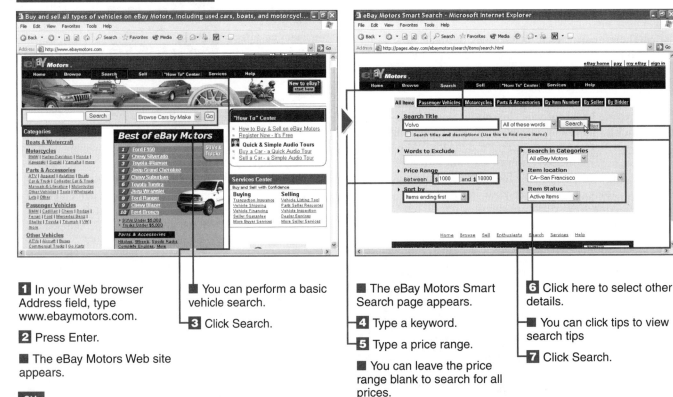

1 In your Web browser Address field, type www.ebaymotors.com.

2 Press Enter.

■ The eBay Motors Web site appears.

■ You can perform a basic vehicle search.

3 Click Search.

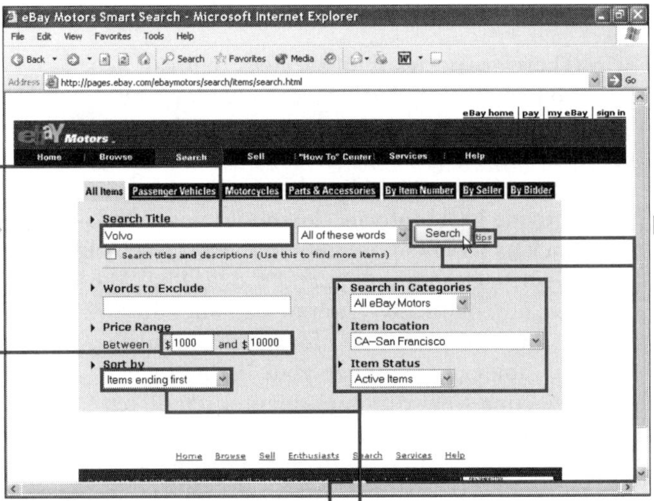

■ The eBay Motors Smart Search page appears.

4 Type a keyword.

5 Type a price range.

■ You can leave the price range blank to search for all prices.

6 Click here to select other details.

■ You can click tips to view search tips

7 Click Search.

Does eBay offer purchase insurance for vehicles obtained through eBay Motors?

✔ Yes. eBay offers purchase Insurance that protects buyers against cases of fraud and material misrepresentation. The coverage maximum is the vehicle purchase price, up to $20,000, with a $500 buyer co-pay. This program is provided free on all eligible eBay Motors passenger vehicle transactions. Some examples where insurance applies include buying a car and never receiving it, receiving a stolen car, receiving a make or model that was different than that described in the listing, and never receiving a title with the vehicle. For more details, click Vehicle Purchase Protection on the eBay Motors home page.

How can I have my auction vehicle inspected?

✔ eBay partners with two companies, SRS and Pep Boys, to offer buyers and sellers vehicle inspection services. Sellers can include inspection information in their auctions to make them more attractive to buyers, while buyers can have independent inspections performed after auctions close at the seller's location to verify the condition of the car is as it was described. Click Vehicle Inspection, which is located in the Selling column of the Services Center section on the eBay Motors home page, for more information.

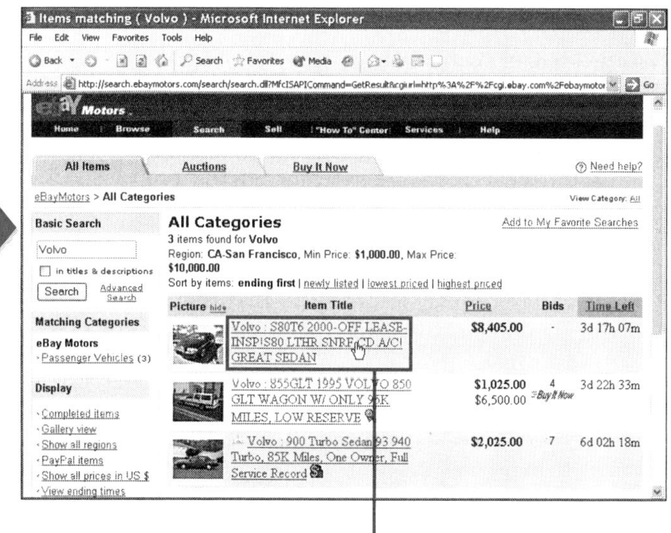

■ The search results appear.

8 Click a listing title.

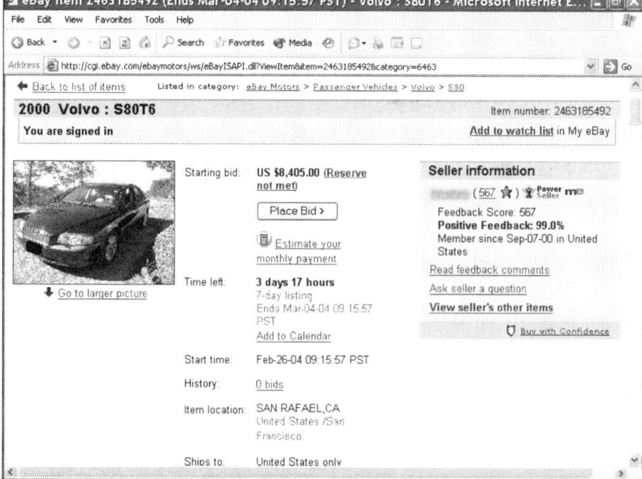

■ The vehicle listing appears.

SELL JEWELRY

More than 30,000 pieces of jewelry and watches sell every day on eBay. Jewelry sellers can maximize their auction success by writing detailed descriptions, including clear photos, and certifying their products through established organizations in the industry.

Top-Selling Jewelry

According to eBay, jewelry that is new, authentic, and certified, and that is listed with a low starting price and low reserve price tends to sell best. Buyers visit eBay daily looking for good deals, so many jewelers use eBay as a liquidation channel, rather than trying to sell items at auction for full price. Including good photos with your jewelry auctions and having positive feedback from past transactions can also help ensure your jewelry items sell well.

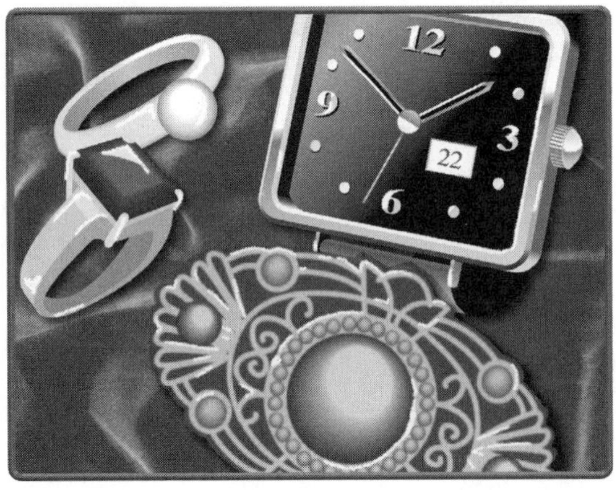

Describe Your Jewelry

The more details you include in your jewelry description, the greater the chance that buyers will be encouraged to bid. For gems, you should include the stone type, stone size and weight, stone shape, and stone descriptions such as clarity and color. For rings, be sure to include the ring size; for necklaces and bracelets, include the length. Condition is a selling point, so mention whether it is new or used. Certification is also something buyers look for, so if your product is certified by organizations such as the International Gemological Institute or the Gemological Institute of America, be sure to state that.

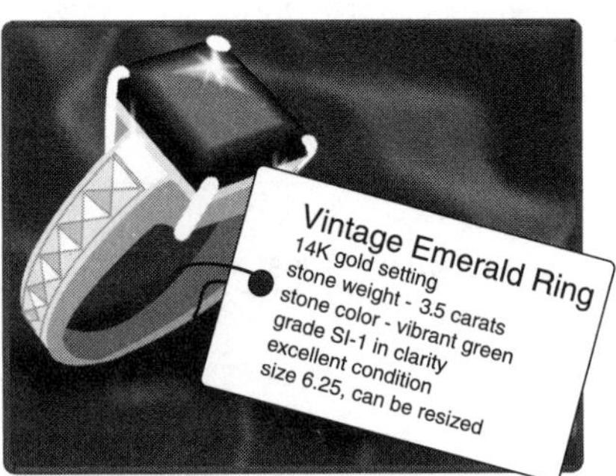

Vintage Emerald Ring
14K gold setting
stone weight - 3.5 carats
stone color - vibrant green
grade SI-1 in clarity
excellent condition
size 6.25, can be resized

Include Photos

Shooting photos of your items with a digital camera is a great way to attract attention to your jewelry auctions. Try to include several digital photos taken from multiple angles with every item that you list. You can also include photographs of any gemstone certifications. It is important to take your photos in good light and shoot on a contrasting background. You should also be careful that the photos you post are not blurry. Most photo-editing software can help improve photos that have slight blurring. See Chapter 20 for more information.

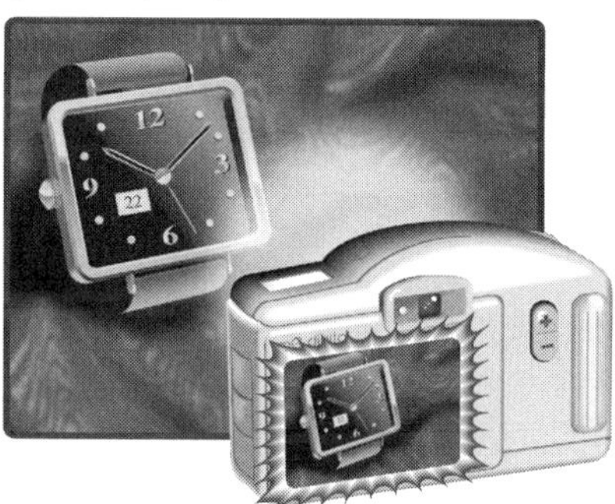

Offer a Return Policy

Offering a return policy can provide a sense of security to prospective customers, especially new customers. eBay does not require that jewelry sellers have a return policy. However, the majority of eBay jewelry sellers offer some sort of return privilege to their customers. You should determine what yours is and include it clearly on the listings that you post.

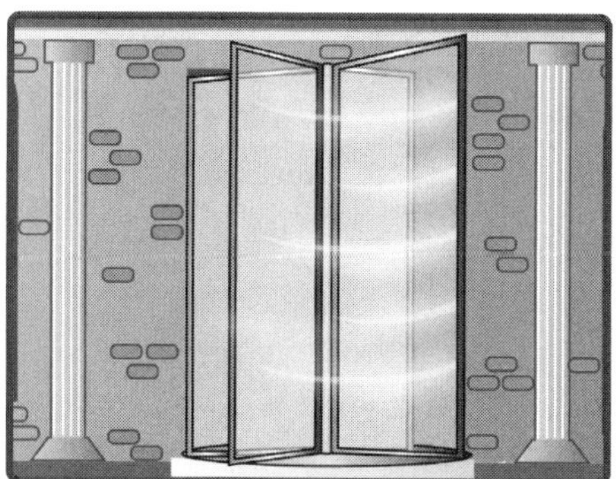

Certify Jewelry

To help jewelry sellers guarantee the authenticity of the items they sell at auction, eBay has established an Authenticator Pre-Certified Jewelry (APJ) Program through which sellers can have their wares certified by the International Gemological Institute (IGI). Jewelry in the program is graded by three gemologists, and gemstones are laser-inscribed with an identifiable marking that can assist law enforcement in case of theft or loss. Buyers who purchase the jewelry receive IGI grading certificates. SalesLink, a third-party logistics company, provides assistance with storage and fulfillment of orders. Click the Authenticator Pre-Certified Jewelry link on the Jewelry and Watches category page for more details.

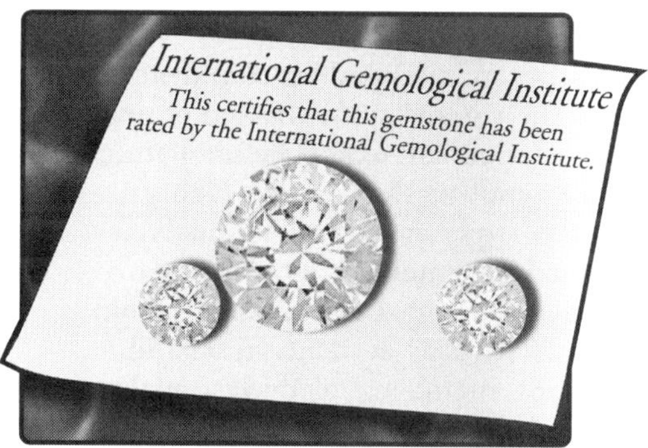
International Gemological Institute
This certifies that this gemstone has been rated by the International Gemological Institute.

Get Help

eBay has a discussion board devoted to jewelry, where buyers and sellers can discuss the ins and outs of auctioning gemstones, rings, necklaces, watches, and similar goods. The board is an excellent way to hear from seasoned eBay jewelers about the ways to market your items effectively, complete transactions successfully, and guard against fraud. To view the discussion boards, click the Community link at the top of the eBay pages, and then click Discussion Boards. For more information about reading and posting to the boards, see Chapter 14.

AUTHENTICATE OR GRADE YOUR ITEMS

eBay partners with services that offer professional opinions on the authenticity or condition of various types of items. Authentication means determining whether an item is genuine and described appropriately. Because of their training and experience, expert authenticators can often detect counterfeits. Grading is a way of specifying the physical condition of an item, such as "near-mint condition" or "fair quality." The details of the grading system depend on the type of item being graded. For more information, click the services link on the main eBay naviation page and then, on the page that appears, click the Opinions, Authentication & Grading link under Selling Services.

Why Grade or Authenticate?

Sellers can increase bidder confidence by having their items authenticated or graded by an independent expert before listing them. Promoting the fact that highly qualified, experienced professionals have examined their items is a good way to increase the number of bids and the bid amount. The eBay authentication and grading partners have pledged to make independent experts available to sellers at reasonable prices.

Grade Stamps

eBay partners with several philatelic organizations for the grading of postage stamps. Buyers or sellers can mail stamps to the organizations, where they are inspected and graded by one or more experts and returned. When grading stamps, graders take into account any tears, creases, perforations, or cancellations, the condition of the adhesive gum, and other characteristics.

Grade Coins

eBay partners with the Numismatic Guaranty Corporation and PCGS for the grading of collectible coins. Coins are graded on a 70-point scale that takes into account their metal color, wear on their faces and edge, and other characteristics. Graded coins are given a serial number and are encapsulated in a protective holder.

Authenticate Books

eBay partners with PKBooks for authenticating books for buyers. After a buyer purchases the service, the company forwards the auction information to a panel of experts that verifies the book based on the description and photos included in the auction. The opinion includes whether the item is authentic, whether its authenticity cannot be determined, or whether it is not authentic.

Grade Sports Cards

eBay partners with PSA Sports and SGC for authenticating baseball and other sports trading cards. Grading takes into account the condition of card corners, fading, stains, pinholes, and other characteristics. PSA Sports uses a 10-point scale in its grading; SGC uses a 100-point scale. After a card is examined and graded, it is placed in a plastic container that protects it from further wear and tear, and returned to its owner.

Authenticate Beanie Babies

eBay partners with Peggy Gallagher Enterprises for the authentication of collectible Beanie Baby plush toys, some of which can fetch thousands of dollars at auction. Buyers or sellers ship their Beanie Babies to Gallagher, who inspects them and their attached tags, issues a certificate of authenticity, and seals the Beanie Baby with the certificate in a tamper-proof case.

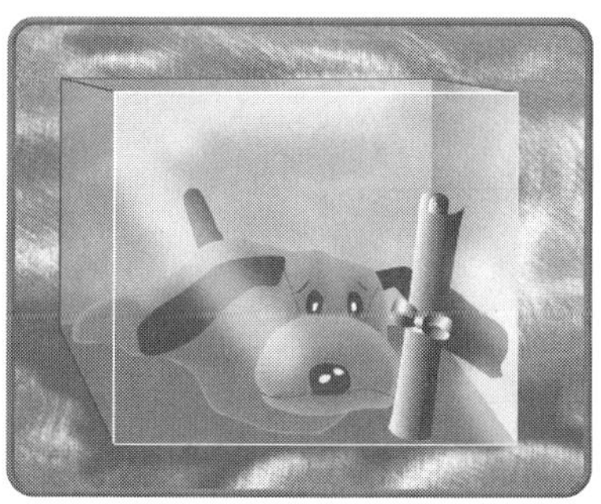

USE AN ESCROW SERVICE

An escrow service is a company that collects a buyer's payment and holds it while the seller sends a purchased item to the buyer. Typically, when the buyer receives and approves the item from the seller within an agreed time frame, the escrow service then sends the payment to the seller. Sellers can specify whether or not they are willing to use an escrow service when they create an auction.

When to Use Escrow

Typically, escrow services are used for high-value purchases of $500 or more. Escrow is well suited for auction items such as automobiles, motorcycles, domain names, jewelry, specialized computer equipment, and other expensive items. eBay's partner for escrow services is Escrow.com, a licensed and reputable escrow provider. eBay recommends that buyers and sellers do not use other escrow services due to the chance of fraud. The following steps outline how the escrow process works through Escrow.com.

Step 1: Buyer and Seller Agree to Terms

Both parties need to first agree to terms, which include a description of the merchandise, sale price, number of days for the buyer's inspection, and shipping information. Either the buyer or seller signs in to the Escrow.com Web site and creates a transaction. The initiating party defines the terms of the transaction, including the e-mail address of the other party, length of inspection period, party responsible for paying the escrow fee, and shipping costs. The other party is notified by e-mail and agrees to the terms of the transaction provided by the initiating party.

Step 2: Buyer Pays the Escrow Service

As soon as the parties agree to terms, the buyer submits payment to the escrow service. The payment includes the cost of the item purchased, shipping fees if the buyer is responsible for them, plus escrow service fees. The escrow service verifies the payment and secures it in a non-interest-bearing trust account. After payment is secured, the escrow service notifies the seller to ship the merchandise to the buyer.

Step 3: Seller Ships the Merchandise

Next, the seller ships the merchandise to the buyer using an approved delivery service. The seller must initially pay for shipping fees. If the buyer is responsible for paying the shipping costs, the seller is reimbursed when the transaction is complete. After the seller has shipped the merchandise, he or she signs in to Escrow.com and provides the tracking information, which allows both parties to track the shipment. The inspection period begins after Escrow.com confirms delivery of the merchandise.

Step 4: Buyer Accepts the Merchandise and Escrow Service Pays Seller

The buyer gets to examine the merchandise during the agreed-upon inspection period. When the buyer notifies Escrow.com that he or she accepts the merchandise, or when the inspection period expires, Escrow.com disburses payment. Escrow.com sends the funds to the seller with escrow fees and any relevant shipping costs deducted.

When a Buyer Rejects the Merchandise

The buyer can reject the merchandise during the inspection period by notifying Escrow.com. A buyer who rejects merchandise has ten days to ship the merchandise back to the seller's address. Upon delivery of the shipment, the seller must accept or reject the returned merchandise within ten days. If the seller accepts the returned merchandise, Escrow.com reimburses the buyer the purchase amount, less escrow and applicable shipping fees. If the seller rejects the returned merchandise, Escrow.com holds the funds until the dispute is resolved.

ACCESS SELLER CENTRAL

You can access seller tips, information about auction management tools, and other selling resources from the eBay Seller Central page.

The Getting Started section features profiles from which users just beginning to sell on eBay can learn. You can read profiles of individual sellers who have had success auctioning niche products, small companies who have turned to eBay to complement their bricks-and-mortar businesses, and enterprise firms who have built thriving sales channels on eBay.

The Advanced Selling section introduces the variety of tools that you can use to streamline your responsibilities before, during, and after your auctions. It also gives you a look at what lies in store after you have hit it big, and the opportunities that come with being a PowerSeller on eBay.

If you prefer to learn about selling by listening, there is an audio tour that leads you step-by-step through the process of setting up a seller's account and listing your first auction.

You can also access the Merchandising Calendar in Seller Central. This calendar shows what product categories will be featured in the upcoming weeks on the eBay home page. Coordinating your listings with the calendar can help you gain maximum exposure for your auction items.

ACCESS SELLER CENTRAL

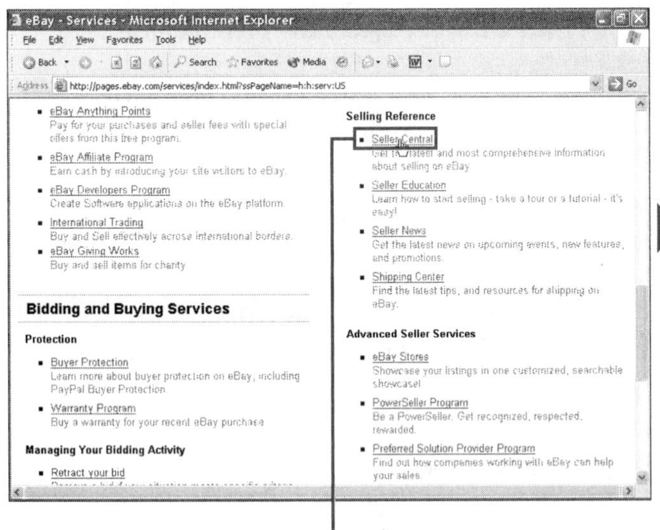

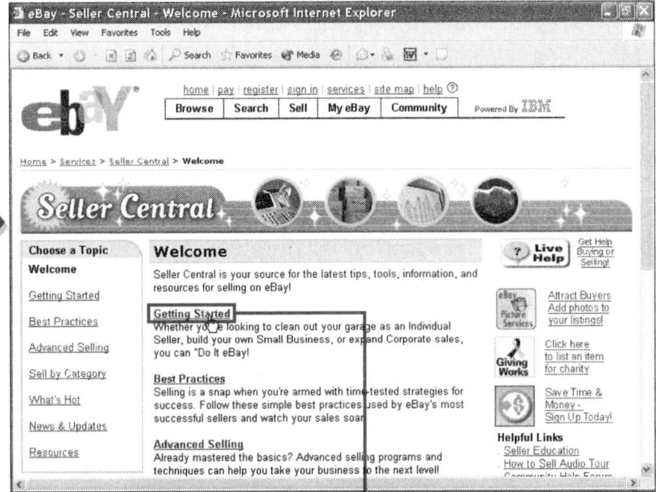

1 Click the services link from the navigation area at the top of an eBay page.

■ The Services page appears.

2 Under Selling Reference, click Seller Central.

■ The Seller Central page appears.

3 Click a link to view seller resources.

VIEW SELLER BEST PRACTICES

In the Seller Central area of eBay, you can access a set of Best Practices pages where you can find time-tested strategies that help ensure that you get the highest selling prices possible for your auctions. Hints in the Best Practices section include common-sense guidelines that beginning sellers should keep in mind as well as tips about some of the newer features of eBay about which even experienced sellers might not be aware. The following are some highlights. For more information, click the Best Practices link in the Seller Central area.

Pricing

Setting a price for your auction item can be a tricky balancing act. You want to place your price high enough to ensure you cover your costs and make a profit, but you also want to attract buyers to start bidding by offering what seems to be a bargain. Researching completed items that are the same or similar to yours tells you what kind of bidding you can expect. Pricing your auction at least as low as previous sales prices can increase the chances of seeing some bids.

Choosing a Format

There are several formats with which to sell items on eBay. *Classic auctions* work well for items that are hard to find because they do not put a limit on the price that such items can fetch. The price can climb as more bidders join the fray. However, if you have many commodity-type items to sell, and the items also have a steady track record in terms of what they have sold for previously, you can offer your items in a *fixed-price auction*. This way, buyers know what they are going to pay for the items at the outset. A compromise between the auction and fixed-price formats is offering a *Buy It Now* option with your auctions. This allows you to offer a price above your initial opening price that buyers can pay if they want to end the auction immediately and win the item. For more information about formats, see Chapter 4.

Merchandising Your Goods

Price is not the only element you have at your disposal to lure customers. You can include a lengthy description with your item so that buyers know exactly on what they are bidding. The description can include not only the condition of the item but also any shipping options available to the winner. Photos can be invaluable tools for closing a sale if your item is one of a kind. The first photo is free when you use the photo hosting service at eBay. See Chapter 20 for more details about photos. Additionally, building an attractive About Me page in the My eBay section can give the buyers confidence that they are dealing with an experienced, trustworthy seller.

Promotional Upgrades

All listings are not created equal. For a little extra money, you can make your auction stand out in the crowd. For an extra 25 cents, you can have a smaller *thumbnail* version of your item photo appear next to the listing title in the search results. An extra 75 cents highlights your listing in a colored box in the search results. An additional $1 can get you a bold-text listing. For higher-ticket items, you can spend $19.95 to ensure that your auction gets "featured" status at the very top of the search results pages.

ACCESS SELL BY CATEGORY HELP

In the Sell by Category section, eBay offers a number of selling resources specific to each of its top-level item categories. The section currently features resources for 24 different item categories, including Antiques, Books, Coins, Home, Jewelry, Sports, Stamps, and others.

The Seller's Edge articles in the Sell by Category section feature general tips about increasing sales in your auctions and eBay storefronts, such as updating your seller templates to include color, business logos, and product photos. Other Seller's Edge articles are specific to a category, such as a recent jewelry-oriented feature on laser inscription for diamonds that helps ensure the identity and authenticity of for-sale gems.

The In the Field pages profile sellers who have had success marketing particular types of goods on eBay. Recent articles have included seller tips about sourcing specialty items from wholesalers as well as how to maximize your feedback rating as you complete your auctions.

The In Demand areas list the current top-selling items as well as popular keyword searches for different categories. For example, the In Demand page for Entertainment lists recent best-selling movies and music CDs on eBay. On the page for Clothing, you can view the most popular searches for shoes, handbags, accessories, and other subcategories.

ACCESS SELL BY CATEGORY HELP

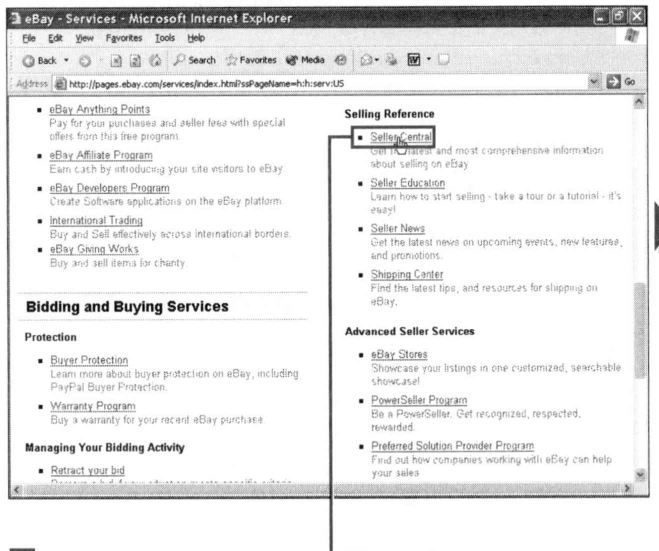

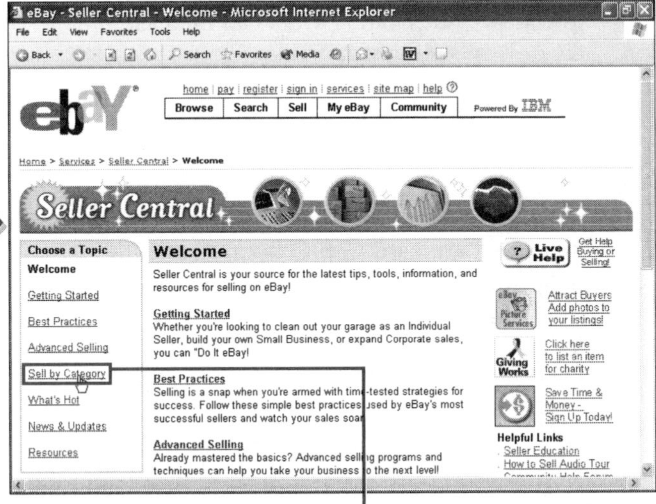

1 Click the services link from the navigation area at the top of an eBay page.

■ The Services page appears.

2 Under Selling Reference, click Seller Central.

■ The Seller Central page appears.

3 Click Sell by Category.

How can I interact with other eBay users that sell the same types of products that I do?

✔ There are links to category-specific discussion boards in the Sell by Category section. This is a place for sellers to view, post, and reply to information about specific types of products. For more information about discussion boards, see Chapter 14. You can also search for eBay Groups that focus on your favorite products. For more information about groups, see Chapter 17.

How can I view all the categories and subcategories that eBay uses to organize its auctions?

✔ The category structure at eBay runs many levels deep and includes thousands of different subcategories. Click the Browse button in the top navigation area of the eBay site, and the main categories and subcategories under which you can list your auctions briefly appear. Clicking the Category Overview link on this page takes you to an exhaustive listing of all the categories.

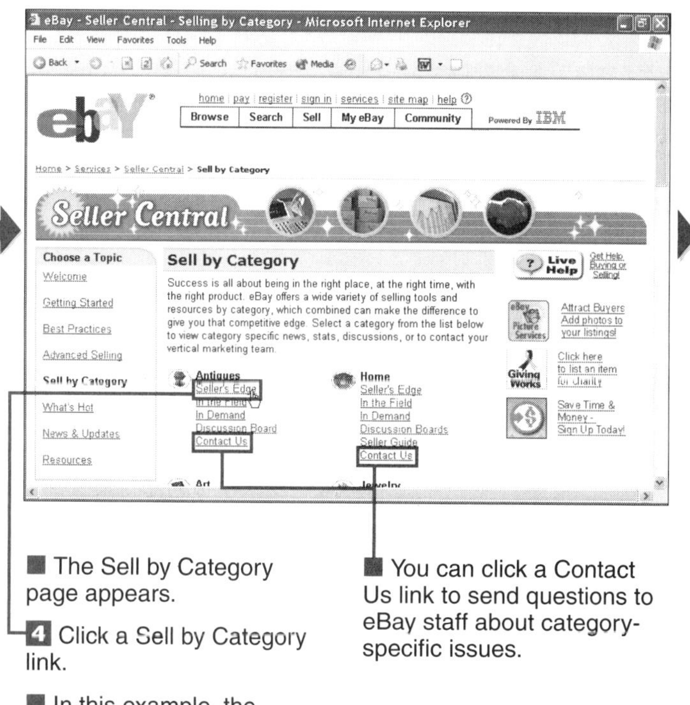

■ The Sell by Category page appears.

4 Click a Sell by Category link.

■ In this example, the Seller's Edge link under the Antiques category is clicked.

■ You can click a Contact Us link to send questions to eBay staff about category-specific issues.

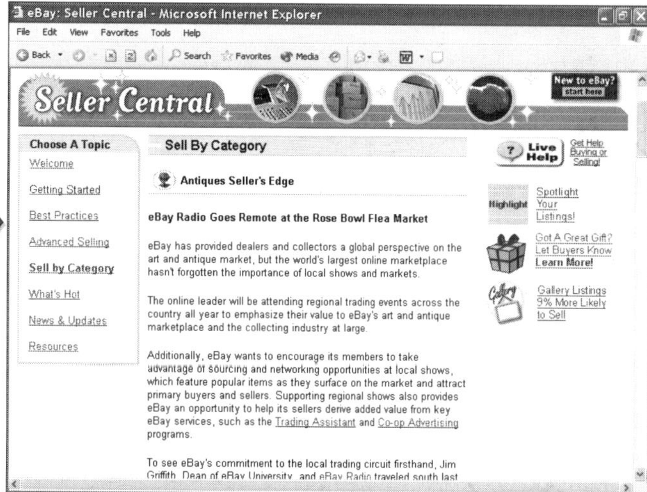

■ Information specific to a particular item category appears.

VIEW TOP-SELLING CATEGORIES

Every month, eBay publishes a list of the auction categories that had the most selling activity during the previous month. Checking this list can be a useful way to discover selling trends on the site and choose classes of products that will sell well for your own business.

The criteria eBay uses to determine what categories are "hot" is complicated. First, the numbers of bids on items in a category must have grown by at least 1 percent over the previous month. Second, the bid growth must have been at least 1.5 times the listings growth for that category. Third, the bids per item for the category must be greater than the average for other categories under the parent category. Fourth, the category must receive at least 100 bids a month.

Popular categories are further described using a degree of hotness — super hot, very hot, or hot. The degree of hotness is determined by comparing the rise in the number of bids in a category compared to the rise in the number of listings. More information about ranking criteria can be found in the Hot Categories Report.

VIEW TOP-SELLING CATEGORIES

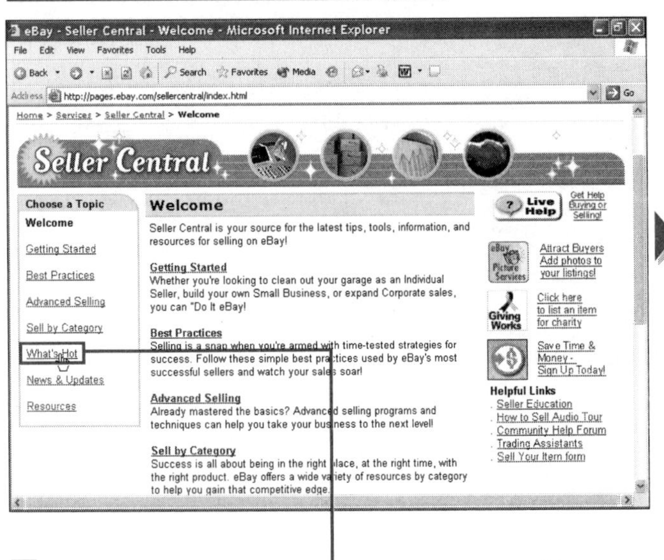

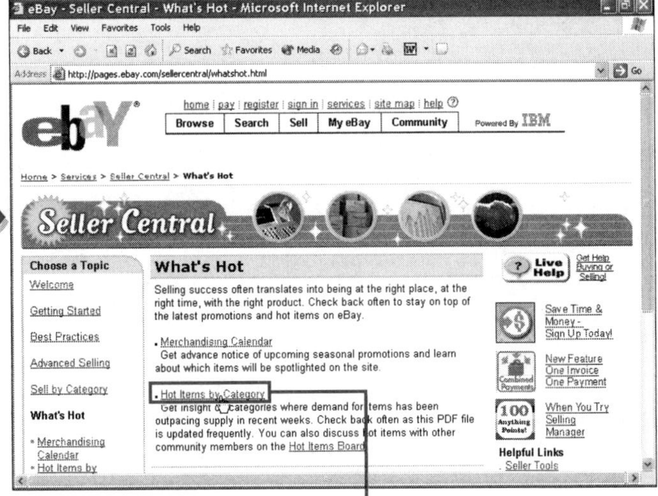

1 Access the Seller Central page.

Note: See the section "Access Seller Central" for details.

2 Click What's Hot.

■ The What's Hot page appears.

3 Click Hot Items by Category.

What do the different levels mean in the Hot Categories Report?

✔ The hierarchy of categories can span many levels at eBay. For example, Books, Children, Young Adult Fiction, and Science Fiction is a sequence of four descending categories. In this sequence, "Children" is at level 2. The report looks at the auctions at and below the fourth level — in this case, at and below Science Fiction — to determine the categories that go in its list. So, if there were a significant number of sales of science-fiction-related collectibles in the past month, Science Fiction could show up as a hot category.

What do I need to read the Hot Categories Report?

✔ eBay publishes its Hot Categories Report as a PDF file, which means you will have to have a PDF reader such as Adobe Reader to view it. A copy of Adobe Reader is included on the CD-ROM that comes with this book.

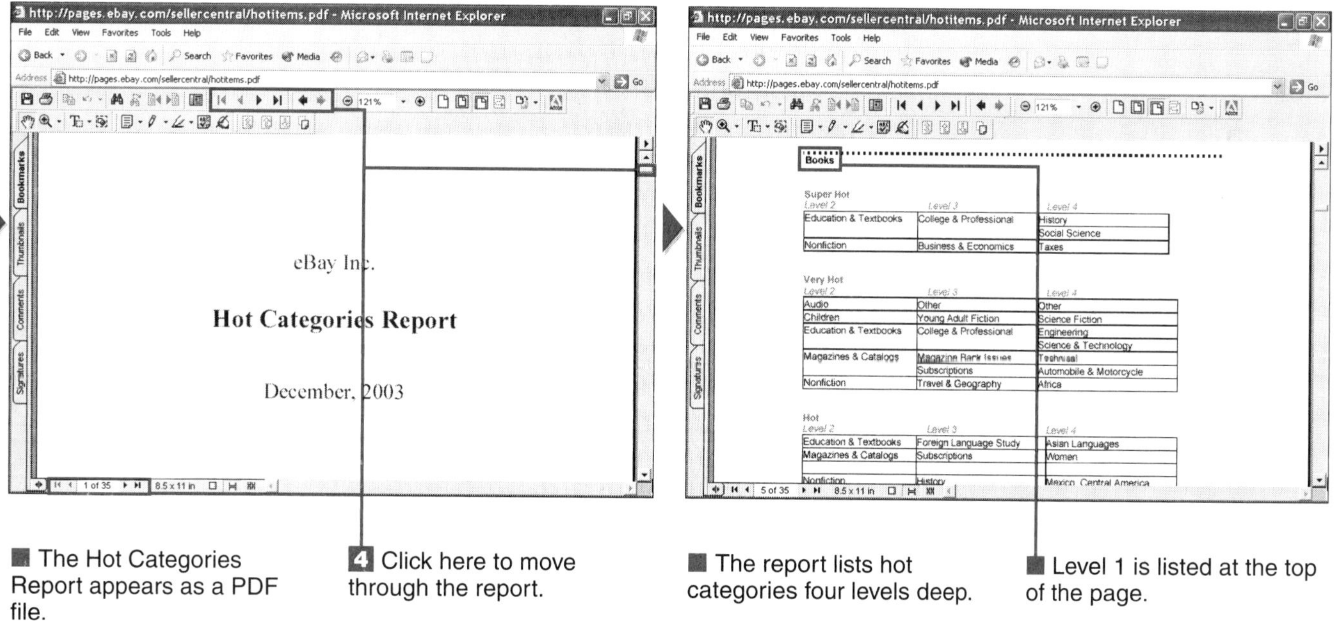

■ The Hot Categories Report appears as a PDF file.

4 Click here to move through the report.

■ The report lists hot categories four levels deep.

■ Level 1 is listed at the top of the page.

SIGN UP FOR THE SELLER NEWSLETTER

Every month, eBay puts out a newsletter devoted to useful selling information called Seller Newsflash. Subscribing to the newsletter is an easy way to keep up to date on eBay news and special eBay promotions that can help you save money on your auction fees. eBay delivers the newsletter via e-mail to users who sign up for it under their account preferences.

eBay often announces special price breaks in the newsletter, such as "free listing days" during which auction listing fees are waived. It also highlights upcoming seller sweepstakes. In the past, eBay has held sweepstakes to celebrate the half-billionth auction listing and sweepstakes that awarded winners all-expenses-paid trips to eBay headquarters in San Jose, California.

Some of the content features in the newsletter are archived on pages in the Seller Central area of the eBay site. For example, you can find old Seller's Edge and In the Field articles in the Sell by Category area of Seller Central. See the section "Access Seller Central," earlier in this chapter, for more information.

SIGN UP FOR THE SELLER NEWSLETTER

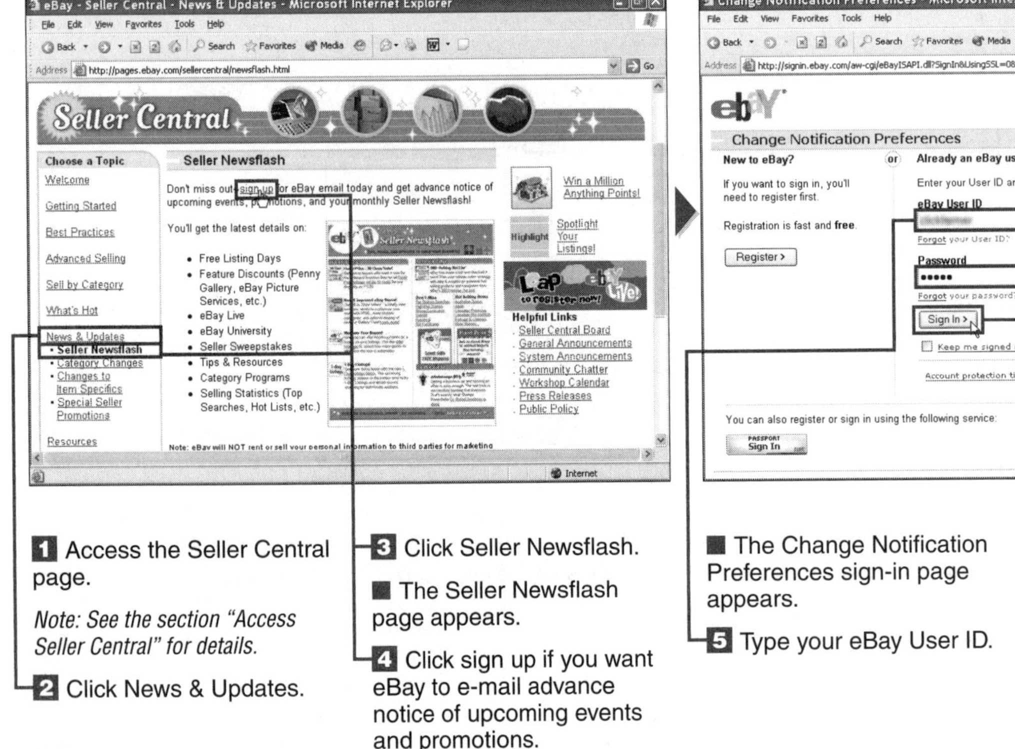

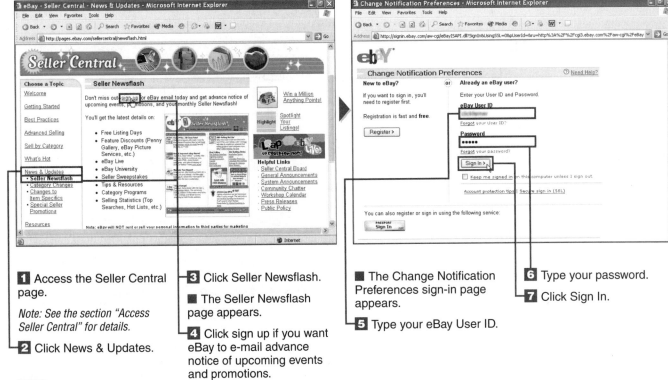

1 Access the Seller Central page.

Note: See the section "Access Seller Central" for details.

2 Click News & Updates.

3 Click Seller Newsflash.

■ The Seller Newsflash page appears.

4 Click sign up if you want eBay to e-mail advance notice of upcoming events and promotions.

■ The Change Notification Preferences sign-in page appears.

5 Type your eBay User ID.

6 Type your password.

7 Click Sign In.

Is there a newsletter for buyers?

✔ Yes. There is a general eBay newsletter called The Chatter, which includes articles and links of interest to both sellers and buyers. You can access current and past issues by clicking the Community link at the top of any eBay page. On the Community page that appears, click The Chatter link in the News section. Signing up for the seller newsletter also signs you up for The Chatter newsletter.

Can I access past issues of Seller Newsflash?

✔ You can, but it takes a little work. eBay does not provide links to past Seller Newsflash issues in the sellers area of the site, or on the site map. But you can perform a search on a search engine such as Google for Seller Newsflash and usually find links to a few past issues. You get the best results if you restrict your search to results from the eBay.com site.

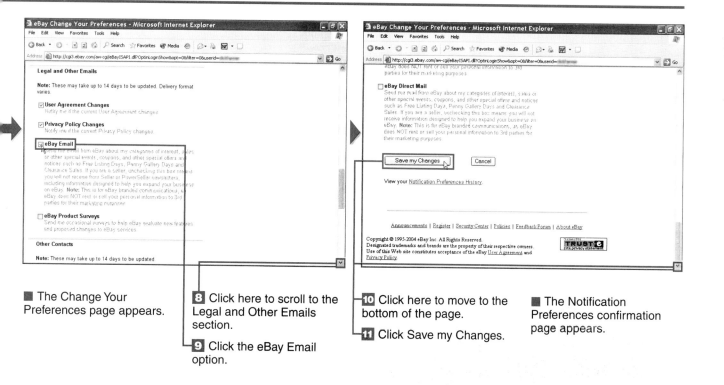

■ The Change Your Preferences page appears.

8 Click here to scroll to the Legal and Other Emails section.

9 Click the eBay Email option.

10 Click here to move to the bottom of the page.

11 Click Save my Changes.

■ The Notification Preferences confirmation page appears.

FIND A TRADING ASSISTANT

Some sellers may not feel they have the time or expertise to sell their products on eBay. eBay has created a valuable resource for such sellers — the trading assistant.

Trading assistants are experienced eBay sellers who sell products for others, usually for a fee. The trading assistants set the fees themselves, not eBay. Trading assistants usually charge per item sold or for a percentage of the selling price; they may also charge a fee for picking up items or returning unsold items.

Typically, you may want to use a trading assistant that is in your local area because the assistant needs to obtain the items in order to list them properly and to ship them to winning bidders. You can search for a trading assistant in the trading assistant directory on eBay by postal code, telephone area code, or country. At the time of this writing, there were more than 18,000 trading assistants listed in the United States.

Note that trading assistants are not employees of eBay, or licensed by eBay in any way. You should read their contact information, contact them with questions, and ask for client references to make sure they are a good fit for you and for the products you want to sell.

FIND A TRADING ASSISTANT

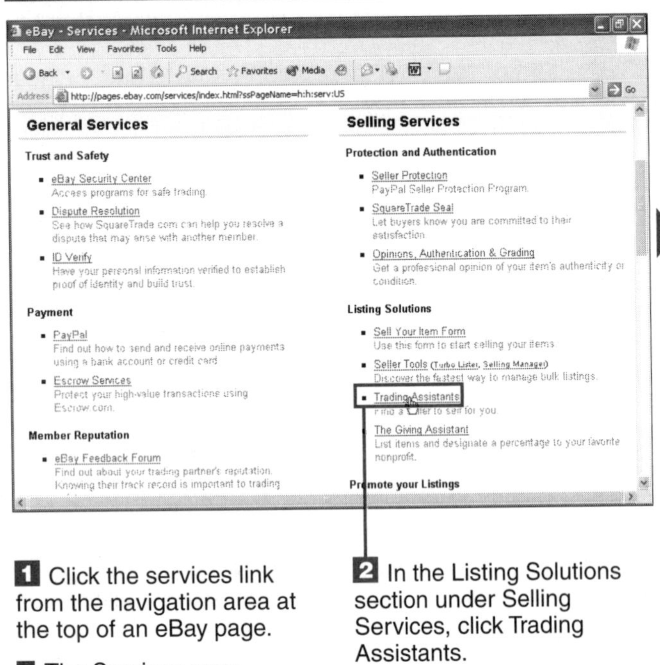

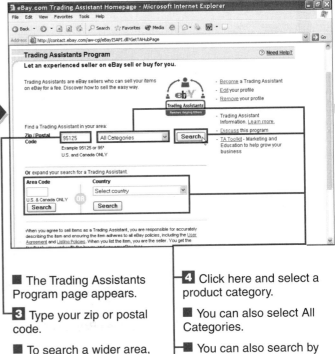

1 Click the services link from the navigation area at the top of an eBay page.

■ The Services page appears.

2 In the Listing Solutions section under Selling Services, click Trading Assistants.

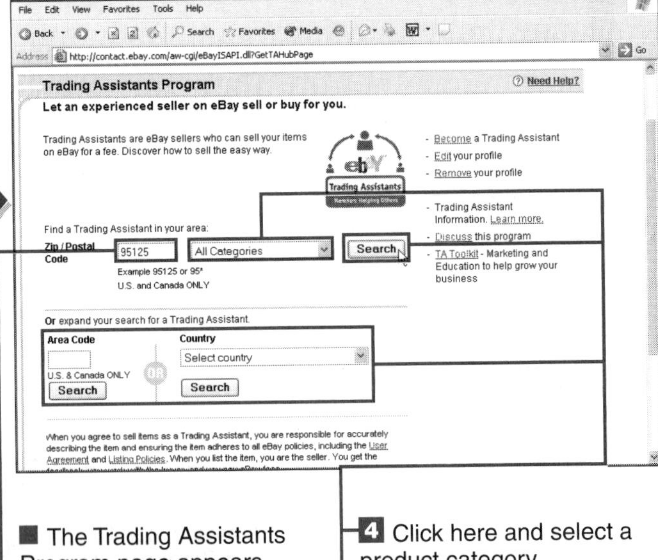

■ The Trading Assistants Program page appears.

3 Type your zip or postal code.

■ To search a wider area, you can type * as a wildcard in your postal code.

4 Click here and select a product category.

■ You can also select All Categories.

■ You can also search by area code or country.

5 Click Search.

Who will receive feedback from a sale when I use a trading assistant?

✔ The trading assistant will be the one listing your auction items, and will be the one who receives any feedback — positive, negative, or neutral — that the buyers choose to leave.

What happens if the trading assistant is unsuccessful in selling my items?

✔ What happens is up to you and the trading assistant to decide. If you want the items back, you can discuss whether you will pick them up or the trading assistant will return them. As is sometimes the case, the trading assistant may also be willing to donate unsold items to charity.

How do I contact a trading assistant?

✔ The contact information in the trading assistant directory lists the user ID of each assistant. You can click user ID to visit the assistant's profile page, which enables you to e-mail the assistant. The contact information in the directory may also include a primary and secondary phone number.

Who is charged the auction fees when I use a trading assistant?

✔ The user who lists an auction item for sale is charged the listing fee and any selling fee. Because the trading assistant lists your items, he or she also incurs the auction fees.

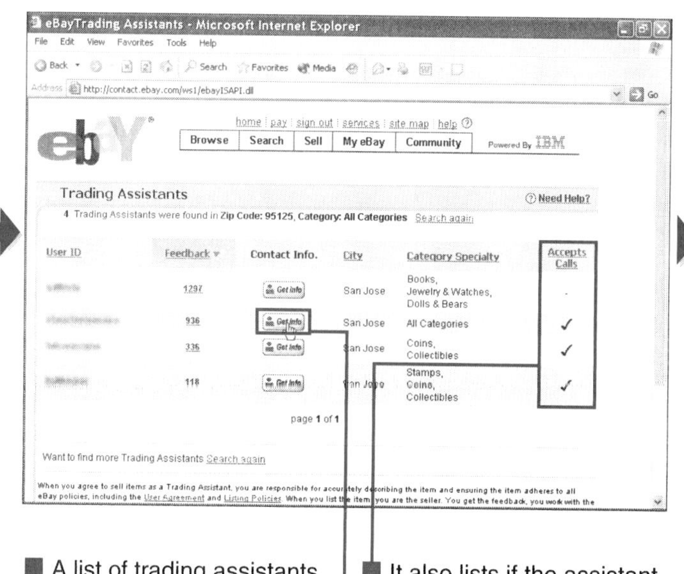

■ A list of trading assistants in your region appears.

■ The list includes the feedback rating, location, and specialties for each assistant.

■ It also lists if the assistant accepts telephone calls.

6 Click Get Info for an assistant.

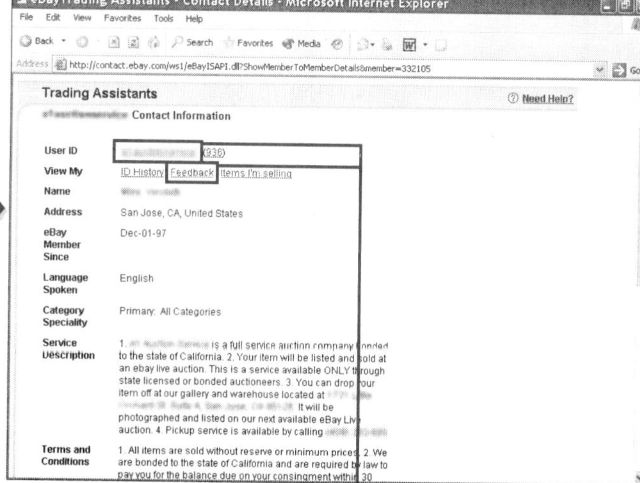

■ The Contact Information page appears.

■ The page lists details about services, terms and conditions, and fees.

■ You can click links to view the user profile or feedback for the assistant.

■ If the assistant has listed a phone number, it appears at the bottom of the page.

BECOME A TRADING ASSISTANT

Sellers who find they have a knack for creating winning auctions on eBay can put their talents to profitable use through the Trading Assistant program. This program connects buyers looking for help selling their items with experienced eBay sellers who are willing to sell for others, usually for a fee.

As a trading assistant, you set your own terms and conditions for working with your clients, including what you charge for selling their products. Most trading assistants charge clients a flat fee per item listed plus a percentage of the final selling price. These fees help cover the listing and selling fees for the auctions, which are charged to the trading assistant.

To become a trading assistant, you must have sold at least four items on eBay in the past 30 days. You must also have a feedback rating of at least 50, with no more than 2 percent of your feedback being negative.

If you become a trading assistant, you are responsible for checking what local laws apply to your selling on eBay for others. You should be particularly careful with sales of real estate and cars, which often require special licenses.

BECOME A TRADING ASSISTANT

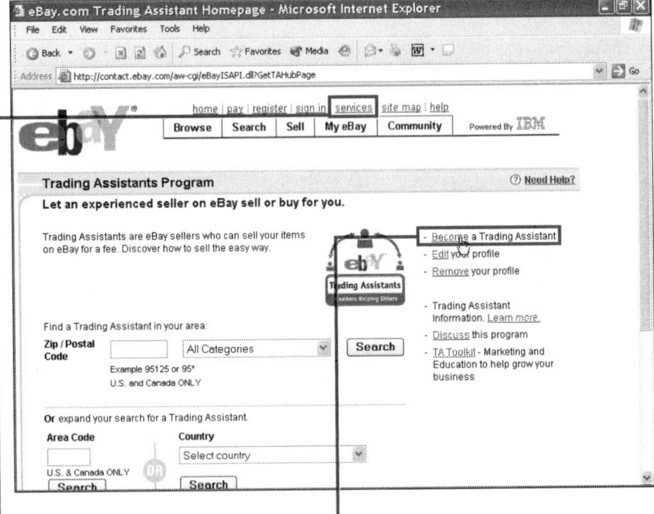

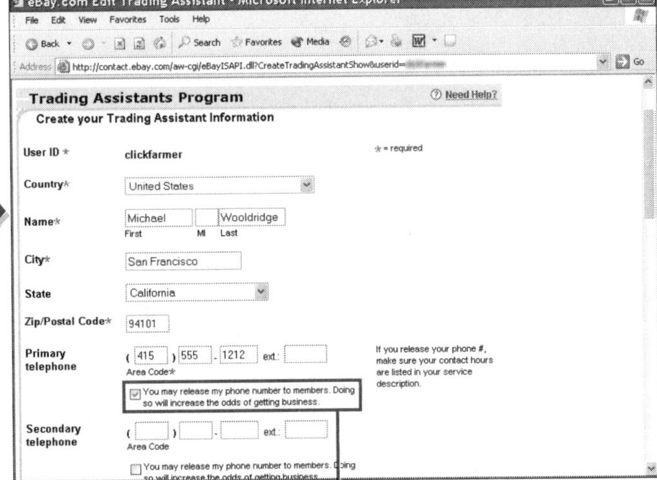

1 Click the services link from the navigation area at the top of an eBay page.

■ The Services page appears.

2 In the Listing Solutions section under Selling Services, click Trading Assistants.

■ The Trading Assistants Program page appears.

3 Click Become a Trading Assistant.

4 If you are not signed in, the Sign In page appears. Sign in to your eBay account.

■ The Create your Trading Assistant Information page appears.

5 Specify your contact information.

■ You can click a checkbox to display your phone number to eBay users searching for trading assistants.

What does it cost to register as a trading assistant?

✔ It currently costs nothing to register as a trading assistant, although eBay reserves the right to charge for this in the future.

Where can I get tips about selling for others from other trading assistants?

✔ There is a discussion board where trading assistants can discuss issues related to selling for others on eBay. Click the Trading Assistant link listed in the Community Help Boards section on the main Discussion Boards page. For more details on discussion boards, see Chapter 14.

Where can I find help promoting myself as a trading assistant?

✔ eBay provides collateral material to registered trading assistants to help them promote their services. The collateral material includes posters that you can print to advertise your services and images that you can display on your Web site. eBay also offers a co-op marketing program where trading assistants can be reimbursed for 25 percent of their marketing costs when they advertise their services locally.

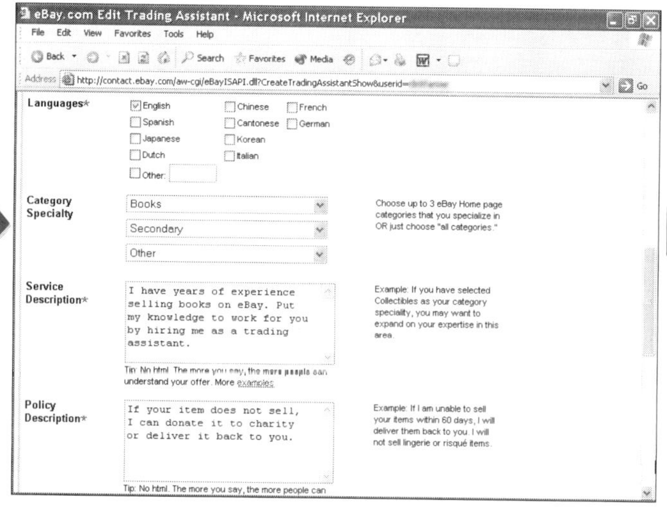

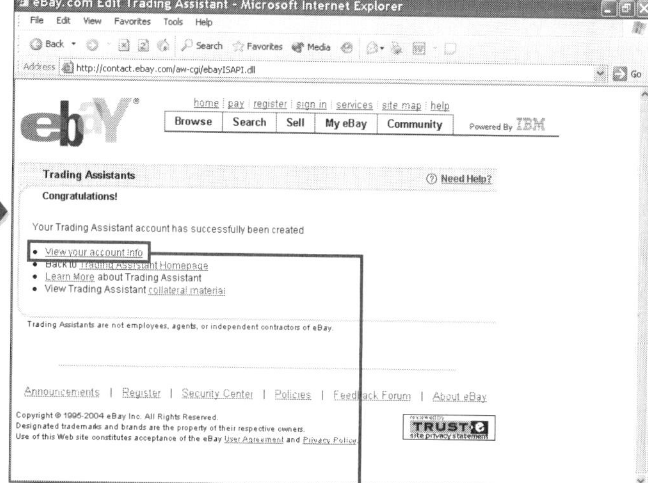

6 Scroll down and specify your languages, category specialties, and descriptions of your services, policies, and fees.

7 Click the Continue button at the bottom of the page.

■ A confirmation page appears.

■ You can click the View your account info link to view your new trading assistant listing.

BROWSE EBAY GROUPS

eBay Groups are online communities within the eBay site, where users with common interests can trade tips and help one another buy and sell. Through the group pages, group members can participate in discussions and polls, view group calendars, and post pictures to online photo albums.

eBay Groups are similar to some of the groups found on Yahoo! and other community Web sites. eBay Groups can be an invaluable resource for getting answers to questions about eBay, in addition to the Help pages, discussion boards, and tutorials on the site.

There are more than 1,000 groups on eBay. Some are oriented toward collectibles, such as antiques, coins, jewelry, pottery, and trading cards; Others are regional. There are groups for eBay users from every state, for example, as well as groups for users in Australia, Great Britain, Singapore, and other countries. There are also seller groups that focus on seller tools, strategies, and stores, as well as how to become a successful trading assistant.

You can view limited information about the groups as you browse them. To view more information, including messages posted to a group by members, you need to join.

BROWSE EBAY GROUPS

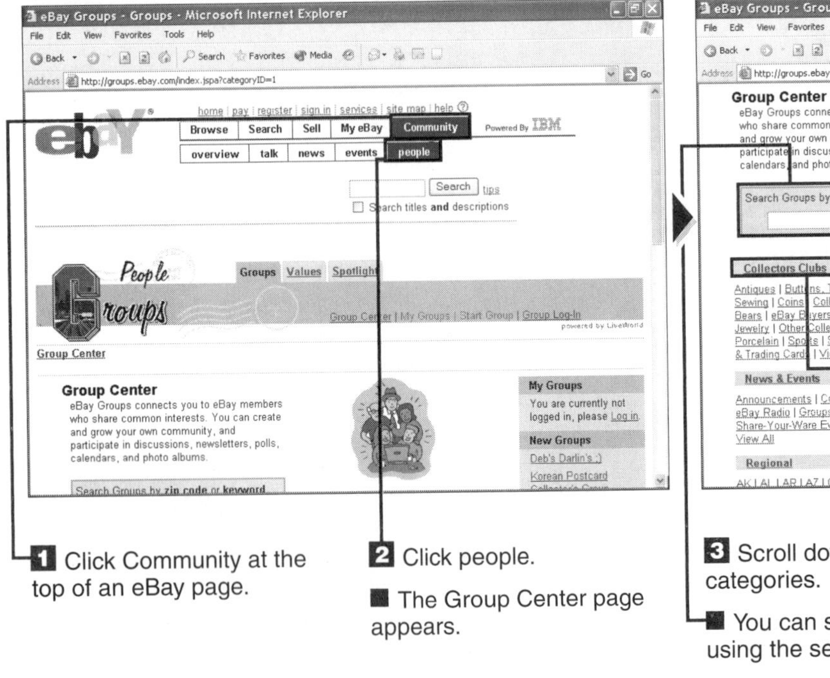

■1 Click Community at the top of an eBay page.

■2 Click people.

■ The Group Center page appears.

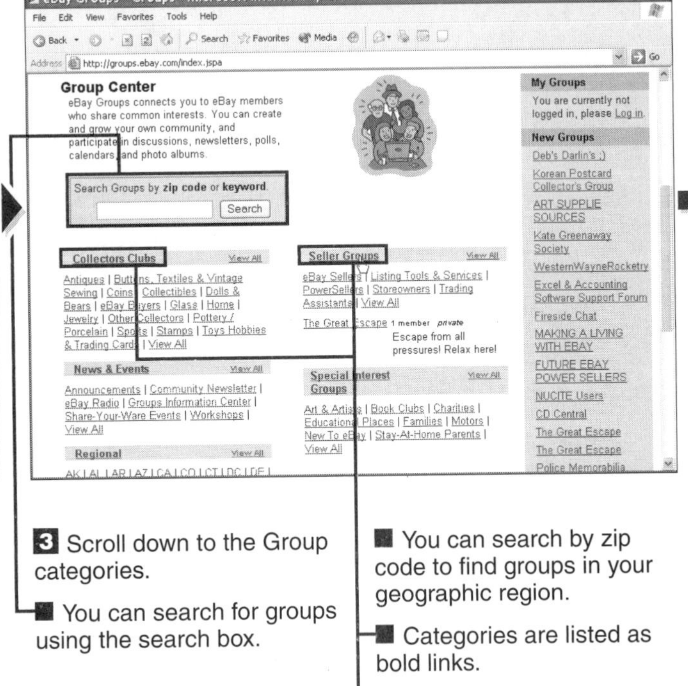

■3 Scroll down to the Group categories.

■ You can search for groups using the search box.

■ You can search by zip code to find groups in your geographic region.

■ Categories are listed as bold links.

■4 Click a Group category.

Is eBay the company responsible for running the groups?

✔ For the most part, the operation of the groups on the eBay site is the responsibility of the eBay users who are members of the group, not eBay company employees. As it explains on the Group Usage Policy page, eBay does not "manage, moderate, or direct the operations of Groups or the content related to those Groups, including materials posted by Group members."

What is not allowed on eBay Groups?

✔ Just because groups are run by eBay users, not eBay the company, does not mean they are a complete free-for-all. Group members can be sanctioned for activities such as posting the private information of other members, posting hateful or obscene material, or impersonating eBay staff or other group members. You can learn more about group rules and restricted activities on the Groups Usage Policy page.

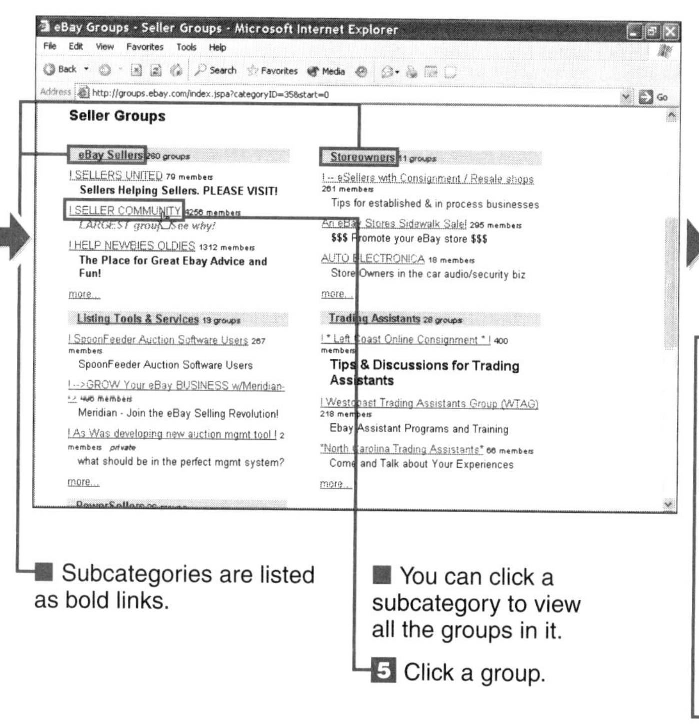

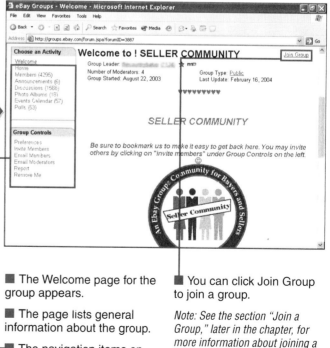

■ Subcategories are listed as bold links.

■ You can click a subcategory to view all the groups in it.

5 Click a group.

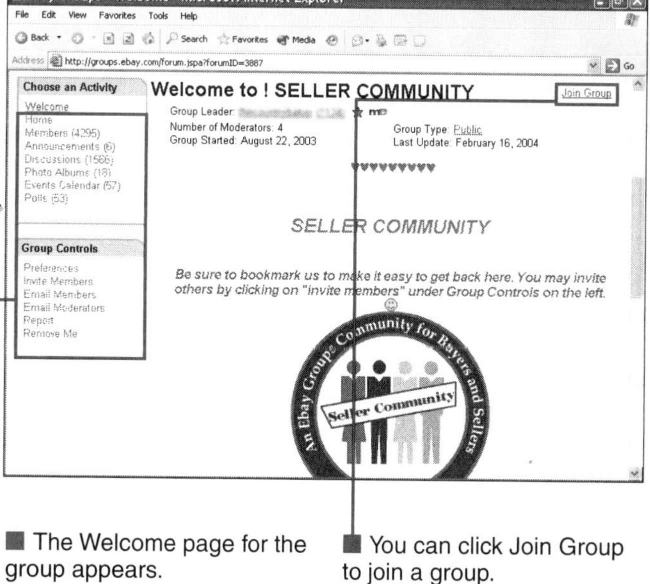

■ The Welcome page for the group appears.

■ The page lists general information about the group.

■ The navigation items on the left side are not clickable until you join the group.

■ You can click Join Group to join a group.

Note: See the section "Join a Group," later in the chapter, for more information about joining a group.

JOIN A GROUP

To participate in an eBay Group, you first have to join. Some groups are public, which means approval is automatic after you click the link to join the group. Other groups are private, meaning you have to be approved by the leader or one of the moderators of the group to become a member. For example, private groups can be restricted to eBay users that are of a certain regional area or that have specific buying or selling interests. You receive an e-mail message from the group moderators telling you if you have been approved for a private group.

After your membership has been approved, you can read and post messages, communicate with other members, upload photos, vote on poll topics, and participate in other features of the group.

After you join a group, you are listed in the membership roster of the group. The membership page lists information about each member, including User IDs, links to current auctions, personal profiles, and the last time each member visited the group pages.

Listed at the top of the member page are the group leader and moderators, who are responsible for approving group members and maintaining the discussions, polls, and other features of the group. Moderators are selected by the group leader to help maintain the group.

JOIN A GROUP

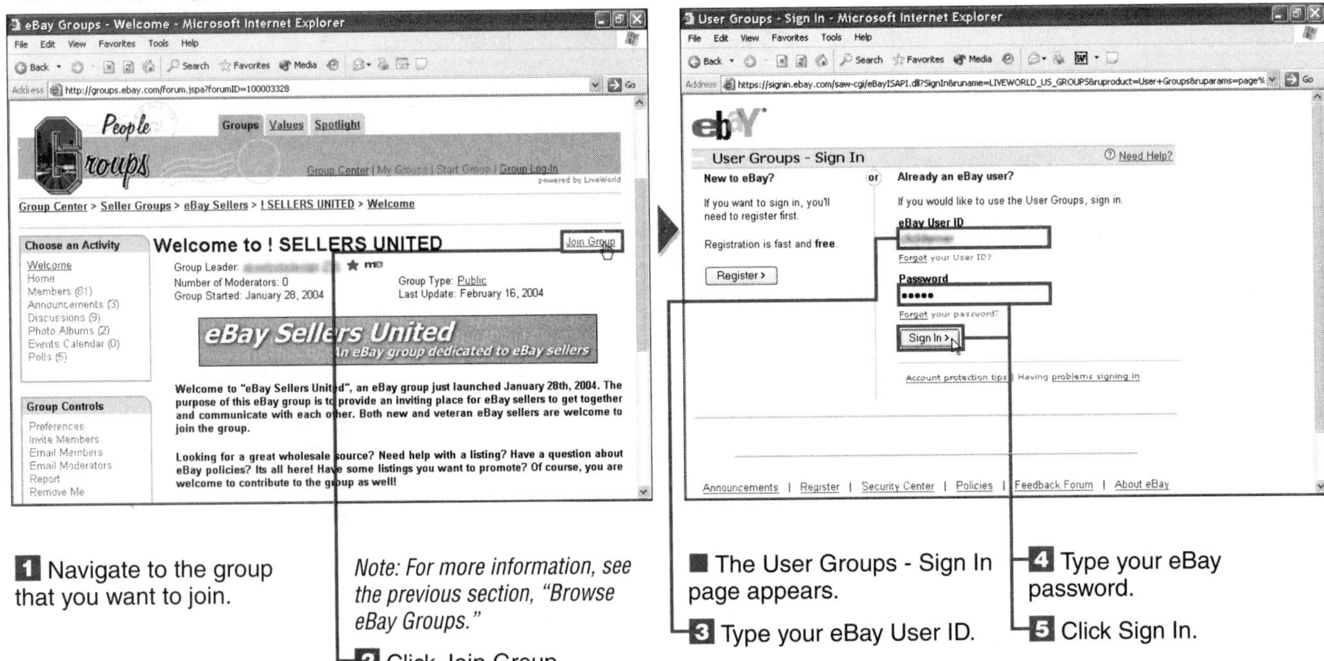

1 Navigate to the group that you want to join.

Note: For more information, see the previous section, "Browse eBay Groups."

2 Click Join Group.

■ The User Groups - Sign In page appears.

3 Type your eBay User ID.

4 Type your eBay password.

5 Click Sign In.

Will my private information be viewable by group members after I join?

✔ Other members will not be able to see your real name, address, or other private information. The only information viewable is your eBay User ID, your current auctions, and whatever you have posted on your profile page. There is also a link to your About Me page, if you have created one, on your profile page. Basically, other members can only see the information that all eBay members can see.

How do I create a member profile for a group?

✔ Click the Preferences link under the Group Controls section on a groups page, which opens the Preferences page. Under Edit Your Settings, click the Your Profile tab. Here, you can enter profile information for other members to see. You might want to include the types of auction items that you are interested in or details about any eBay-related hobbies.

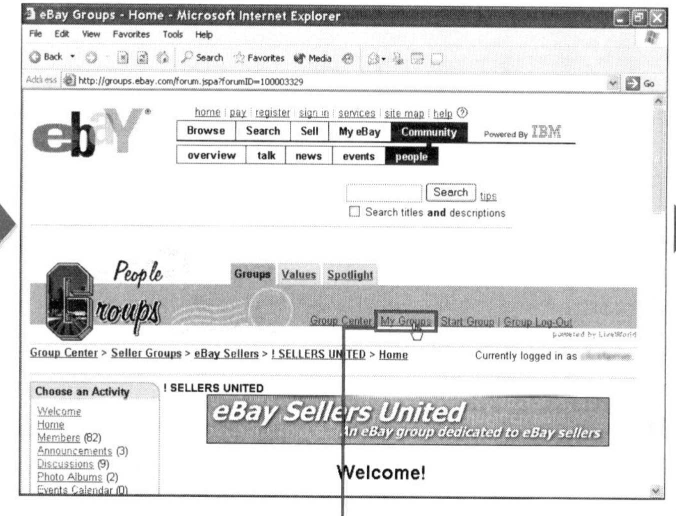

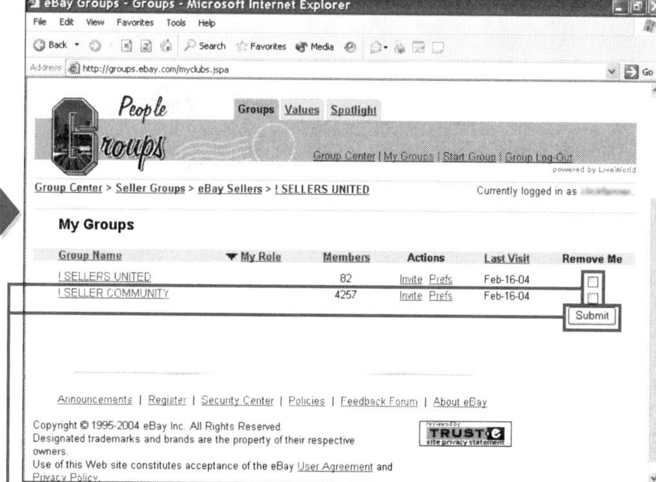

■ If the group you are joining is a public group, the Welcome page appears, as shown here.

■ If the group you are joining is a private group, a request form appears allowing you to send a message to the group requesting membership.

6 Click My Groups.

■ A page appears that displays information about the groups you have joined.

LEAVE A GROUP

1 Click the Remove Me option next to the group you want to leave.

2 Click Submit.

3 On the confirmation page, click Submit to leave the group.

■ You can click Cancel to remain a member.

SEARCH WITHIN A GROUP

You can access a search page inside each eBay Group to find information about a specific topic. The search function can be handy in large groups whose discussion pages include thousands of messages.

The Group or Component menu on the search page allows you to limit your search to a certain area of the group. For example, you can use keywords to search the photo albums in a group to find photo album descriptions that include those keywords. You can also use keywords to search the polls of a group to look for those keywords in the instructions that accompany the different polls.

The date range option on the search page lets you limit your search to recent or not-so-recent information. Including a date range in a search is useful if you are not interested in older discussion postings or if you want to limit your results to postings made during a particular time frame.

The search page also enables you to search for information submitted by a specific group member. This can be useful if there are experts in the group who post discussion messages that are particularly interesting or informative.

SEARCH WITHIN A GROUP

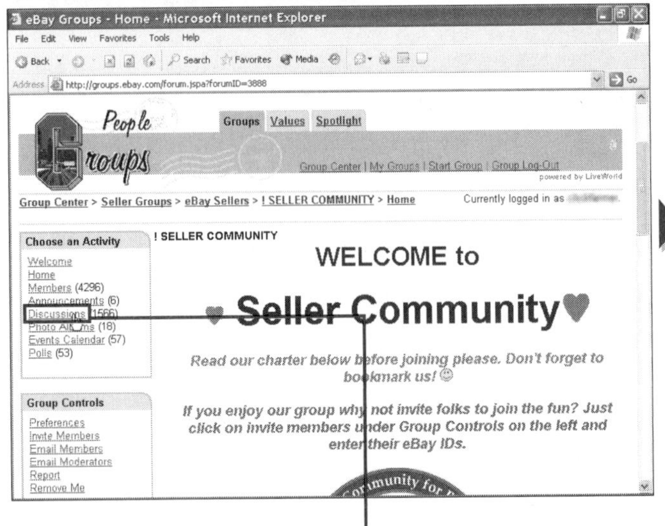

1 Navigate to the group within which you want to search.

2 In the Choose an Activity section, click Discussions.

■ The Discussions page appears.

3 Click Search Discussions.

Can I search for more than one keyword in my searches?

✔ Yes. You can include multiple keywords in the search terms field. For example, if you type "stamps philately," the search returns messages that include stamps, philately, or both words.

How do I specify that keywords in my search are required?

✔ You can add a plus sign (+) before a keyword to specify that the keyword must be in the search results. For example, if you type "+stamps +philately" and perform a search, only messages that include both stamps and philately will be returned.

How can I search for all keywords that begin with a certain string of letters?

✔ You can add an asterisk (*) to the end of a keyword to search for words that begin with a certain string of letters. For example, a search for the keyword "auto*" will return results that include the words such as auto, automobile, or automatic. Note that adding * to the beginning of a string of letters does not work similarly. For example, you cannot search for messages that include hardware or software by typing "*ware" as a keyword.

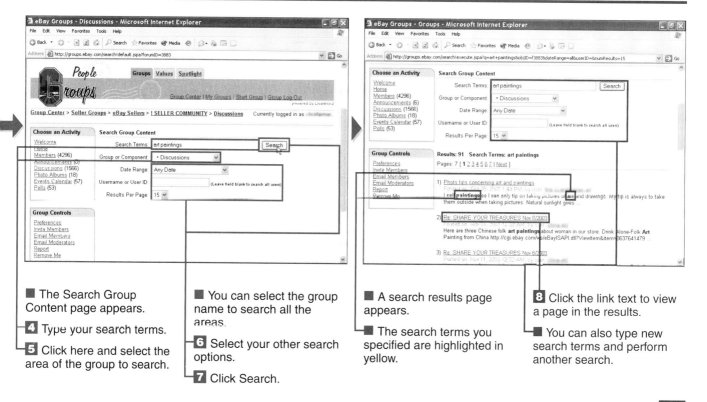

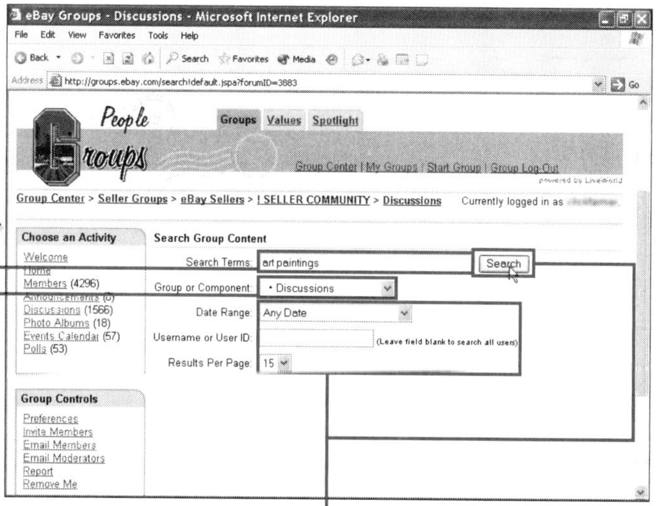

■ The Search Group Content page appears.

4 Type your search terms.

5 Click here and select the area of the group to search.

■ You can select the group name to search all the areas.

6 Select your other search options.

7 Click Search.

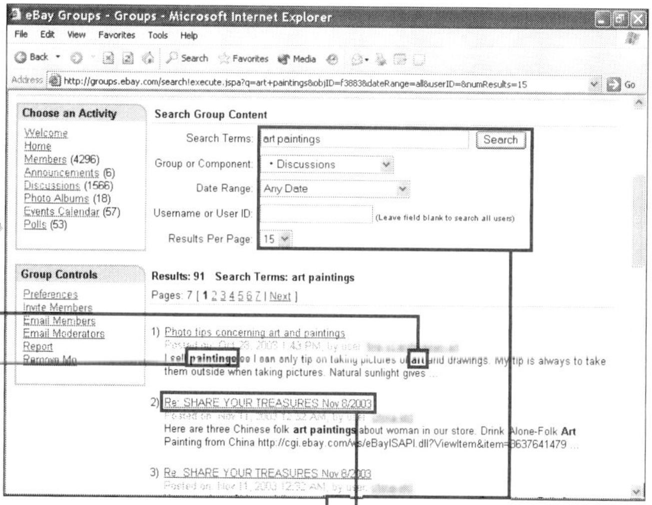

■ A search results page appears.

■ The search terms you specified are highlighted in yellow.

8 Click the link text to view a page in the results.

■ You can also type new search terms and perform another search.

READ A DISCUSSION MESSAGE

The most useful information in eBay Groups is usually found in the messages posted to the group discussion areas. The discussion areas are where members can chat with one another about their successes and failures buying and selling on eBay. Because many of the groups serve a social as well as a business function, discussions can also focus on non-eBay subjects such as current events and even the weather.

In the sellers-oriented groups, discussion topics can range from tips on making your auctions more compelling to the best ways to deal with uncooperative buyers. Browsing the selling discussion groups is a good way to pick up tried-and-true strategies from seasoned veterans that can help make your eBay-based business more efficient and profitable.

You can control how much information displays in the discussion areas by clicking the Preferences link in the Group Controls section on the left side of the group pages. The Preferences page enables you to specify how many discussion topics display per page, as well as how many messages display when you click into a discussion.

READ A DISCUSSION MESSAGE

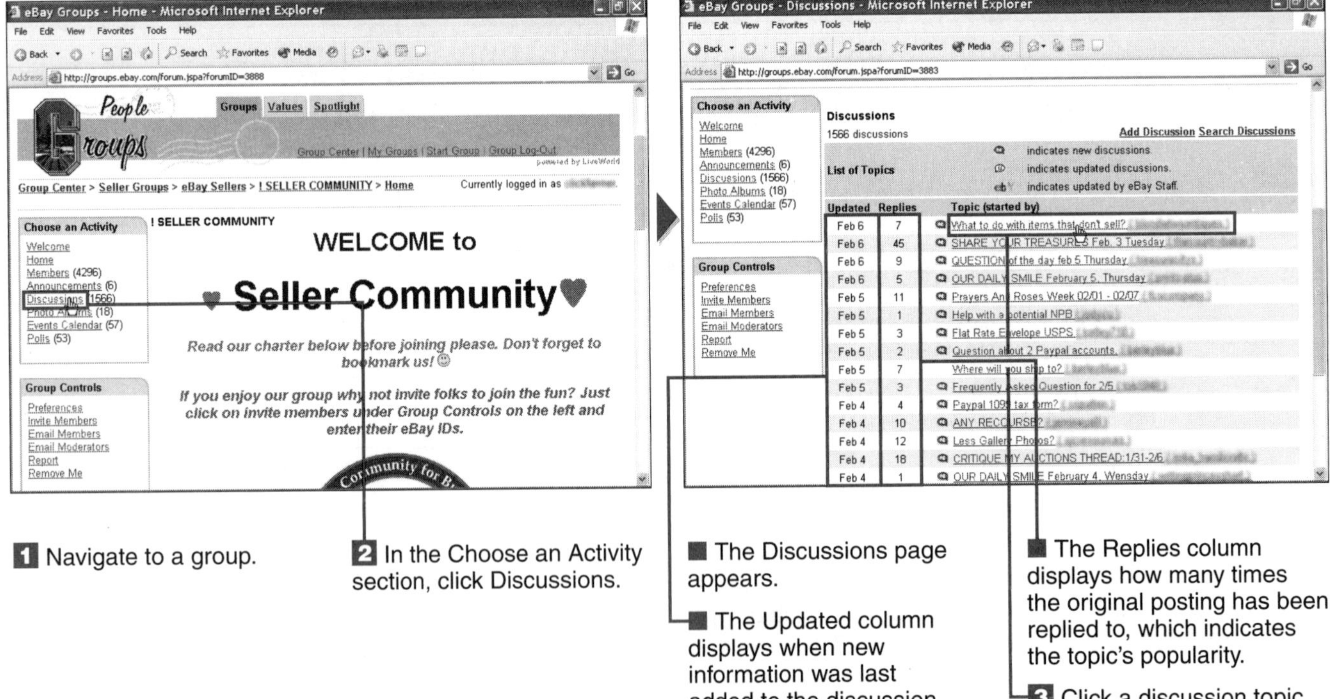

1 Navigate to a group.

2 In the Choose an Activity section, click Discussions.

■ The Discussions page appears.

■ The Updated column displays when new information was last added to the discussion.

■ The Replies column displays how many times the original posting has been replied to, which indicates the topic's popularity.

3 Click a discussion topic.

Can I read the discussions of a group if I am not a member?

✔ No. To read the messages posted to the discussion area of a group, you have to be a member of the group.

How do I search through the discussions in a group?

✔ Access the group search page by clicking the Search Discussions link at the top right of the discussions pages. For more information, see the previous section, "Search Within a Group."

How can I stay abreast of discussions that I am interested in?

✔ You can set up a "watch" on a specific group discussion that you find interesting. Watched topics show up under the Watches tab in your eBay Groups preferences. You can click the General Settings tab in your preferences and select the Notify me by email option (◯ changes to ◉) under Watch Preferences to have new postings sent to the e-mail address associated with your account.

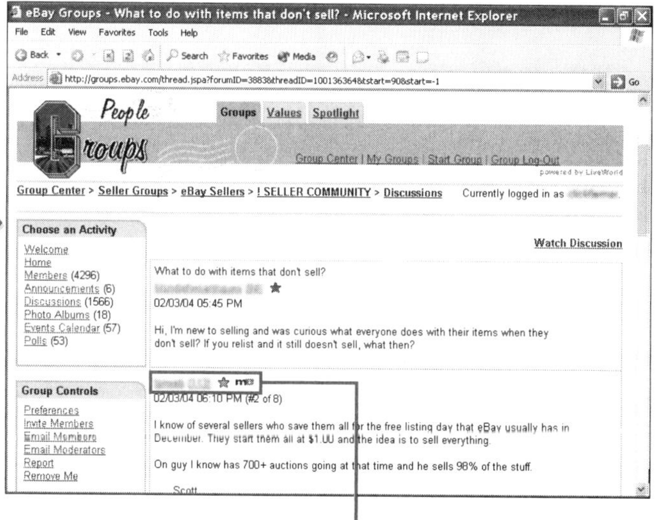

■ A page listing the messages in the discussion appears.

■ Messages are displayed in descending order with the most recent appearing on top.

■ You can click the name of the member who posted the message to see more information about the member.

■ You can scroll to the bottom of the page to reply to current messages.

Note: For more information, see the next section, "Post a Discussion Message."

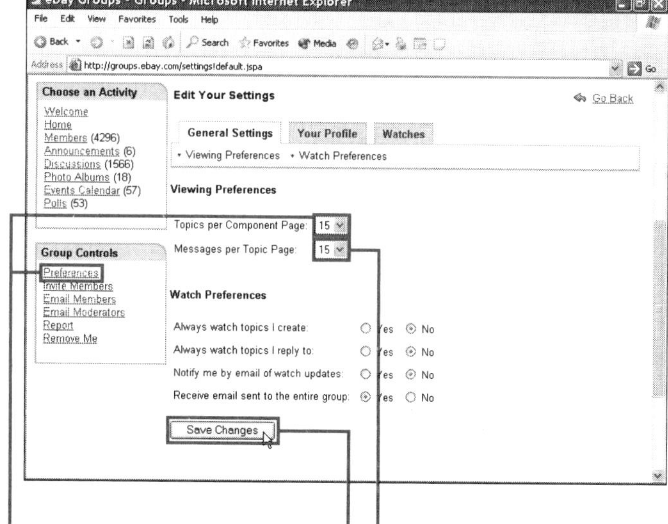

CHANGE VIEWING PREFERENCES

1 In the Group Controls section, click Preferences.

2 Click here and select the number of topics to view on the Discussions page.

3 Click here and select the number of messages to view on a topic page.

4 Click Save Changes.

■ The changes are saved.

POST A DISCUSSION MESSAGE

You can interact with eBay users who share your interests by posting a message to a group discussion. Posting a new message creates a new discussion in the Discussions area of the group. The discussion appears on the top of the discussions list, and other members of the group can read and reply to your posting. Replies to a message appear under the original message in the discussion area pages.

To post a message to a group, you must first become a member of the group. See the section "Join a Group," earlier in the chapter, for more information.

Some groups, especially large ones and ones that are devoted to a niche interest, may have rules that govern what types of discussions are appropriate for the group. Check the Welcome page or the Group Charter page, which is linked from the bottom of the Welcome page, to see if there are such rules before posting.

POST A DISCUSSION MESSAGE

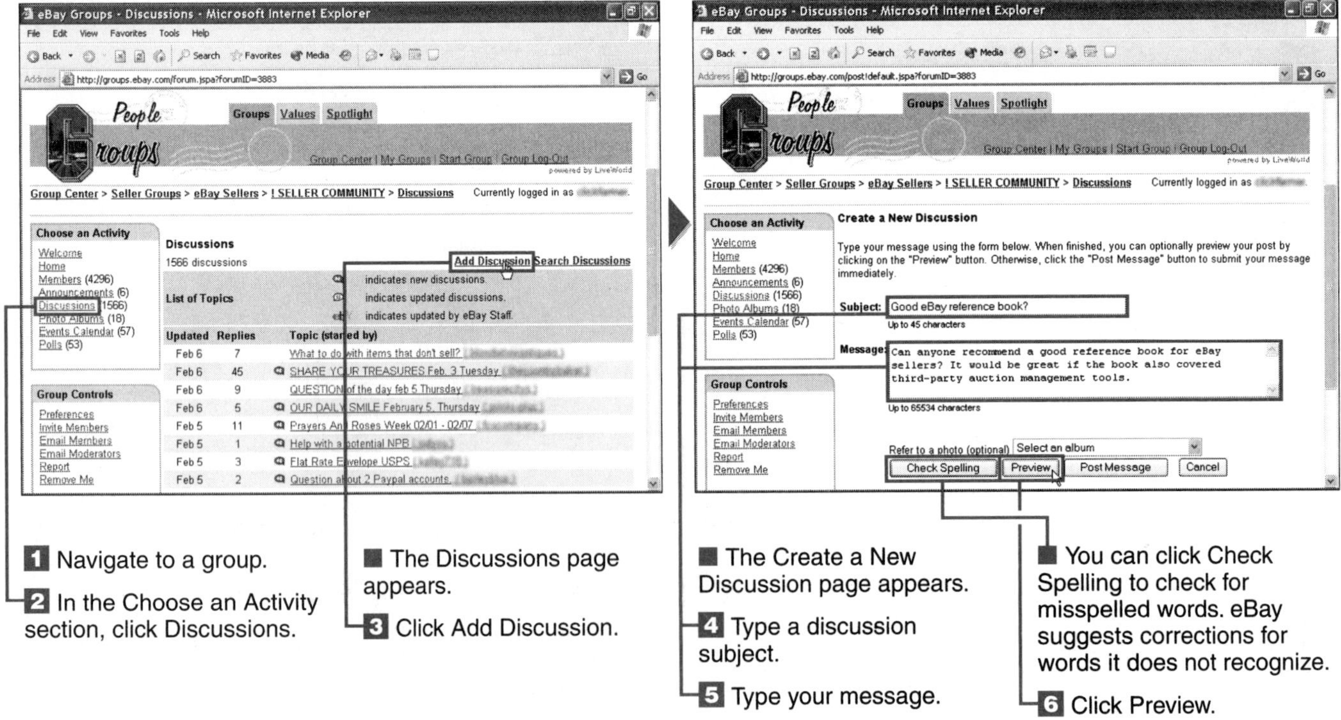

1 Navigate to a group.

2 In the Choose an Activity section, click Discussions.

■ The Discussions page appears.

3 Click Add Discussion.

■ The Create a New Discussion page appears.

4 Type a discussion subject.

5 Type your message.

■ You can click Check Spelling to check for misspelled words. eBay suggests corrections for words it does not recognize.

6 Click Preview.

Can I add HTML to my group discussion messages?

✔ Yes. You can add HTML tags to your group discussion messages to format your message text or to add images or hyperlinks to your messages. This can be useful if your message references a particular product and you want to include a picture of that product. It is also handy if you want to include links to relevant auctions in your message. For details about HTML, see Chapter 21.

How do I respond to an existing discussion message?

✔ An alternative to posting a new discussion message is posting a reply to an existing discussion message. There is a reply form located at the bottom of each discussion message page. You can reply to the messages that are on the current page by submitting the form. The number of replies submitted to each message is listed on the main Discussions page.

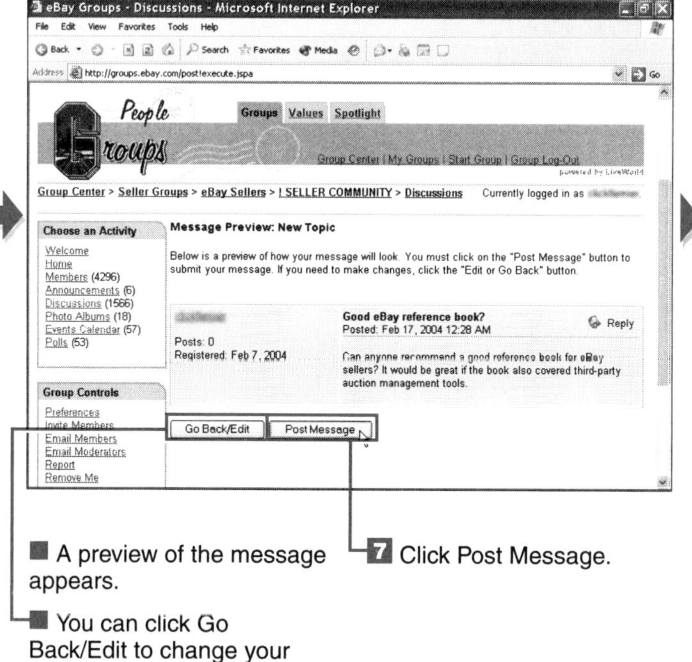

■ A preview of the message appears.

■ You can click Go Back/Edit to change your message before posting.

7 Click Post Message.

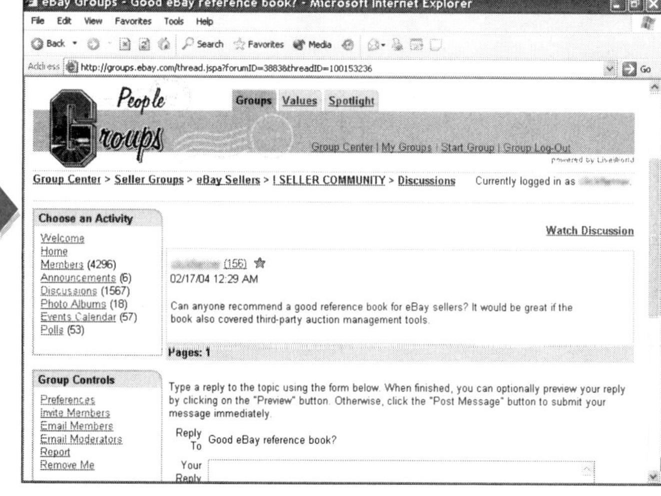

■ The page displaying your newly posted message appears.

START A GROUP

If want to create a forum for eBay users with a common interest, you can start your own eBay Group. Starting a group can be a useful way to meet other motivated eBay users and establish yourself as a leader in the eBay community.

It is a good idea to browse the lists of existing eBay Groups before you start your own group. That way, you can see if any groups already exist that cover your topic of interest. Joining and participating in similar groups can give you an idea of the level of interest that exists for your topic and the types of discussions in which eBay users are interested in participating.

Starting a group makes you the group leader and requires you to assume certain responsibilities. For example, you will need to approve any photo album submissions that are made to the group before those photos can be viewed online. If you start a private group, you are required to approve members who request to join the group. You are also required to write the group descriptions and charter to tell other eBay users what the group is all about.

eBay Groups policy requires you to have a certain amount of experience using eBay before you start a group. You must be an eBay member for at least 90 days and have accumulated a minimum feedback level of 50.

START A GROUP

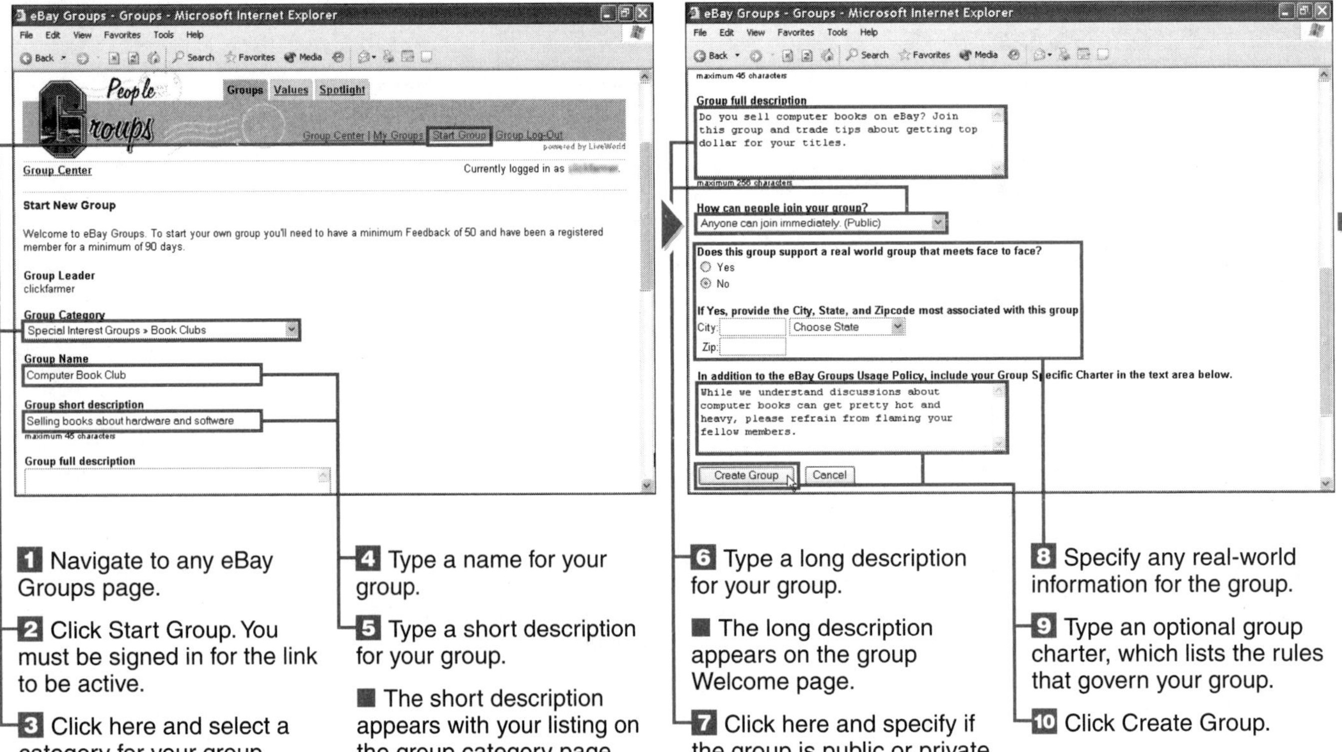

1 Navigate to any eBay Groups page.

2 Click Start Group. You must be signed in for the link to be active.

3 Click here and select a category for your group.

4 Type a name for your group.

5 Type a short description for your group.

■ The short description appears with your listing on the group category page.

6 Type a long description for your group.

■ The long description appears on the group Welcome page.

7 Click here and specify if the group is public or private.

8 Specify any real-world information for the group.

9 Type an optional group charter, which lists the rules that govern your group.

10 Click Create Group.

How can I let people know about my new eBay Group?

✔ After your new eBay Group has been approved, it will be linked from the main eBay Group Center page under the category and subcategory that you chose when you created the group. You can also invite eBay users to join your group directly. You may want to invite eBay users with whom you have previously done business and who might be interested in your group topic. To invite users, click the Invite Members link on the left side of your group pages. You will need to know the eBay User ID of the members whom you want to invite.

As a group leader, can I have people help me manage my group?

✔ A group leader can deputize members of the group to be moderators, who can then help with the tasks involved in running the group. Group leaders can add moderators by clicking Group Management under Group Controls for their group.

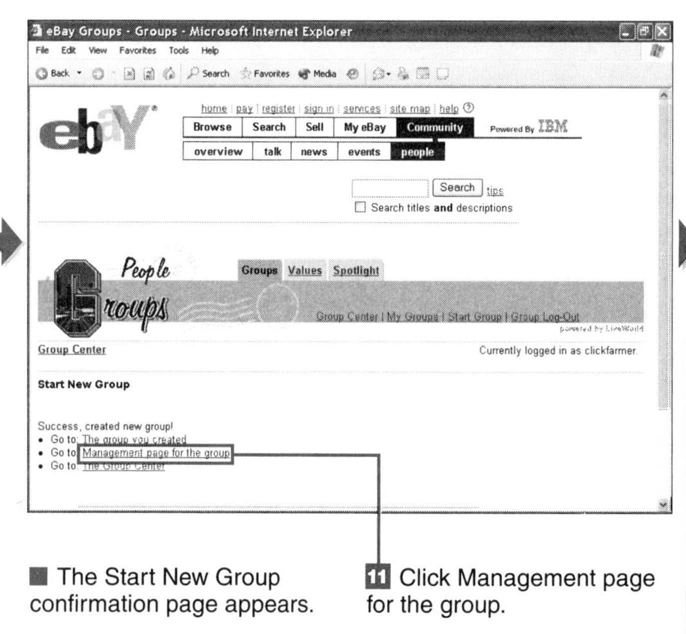

■ The Start New Group confirmation page appears.

11 Click Management page for the group.

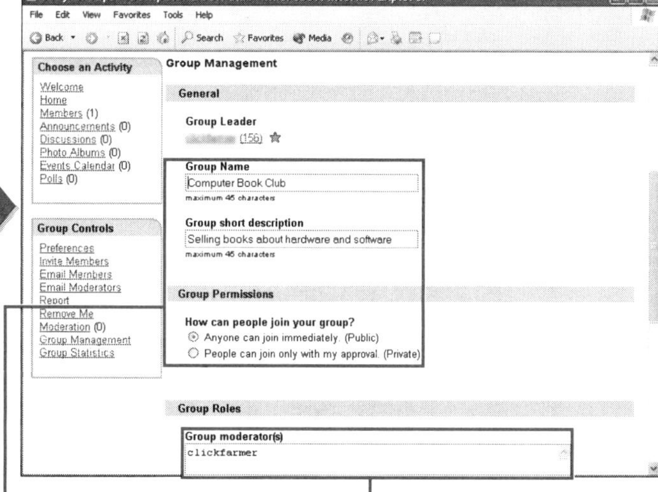

■ The Group Management page for the group appears.

■ You can update information about the group by typing information and clicking different options.

■ You can type the User IDs of moderators who you have authorized to help manage the group.

SECTION VI

ADVANCED TECHNIQUES:

18) LIST ITEMS AUTOMATICALLY WITH TURBO LISTER

19) USING SELLER'S ASSISTANT AND SELLING MANAGER

AUCTION TOOLS, PHOTO EDITING, AND HTML

20) MAKE BEST USE OF PHOTOS

21) USING HTML IN EBAY LISTINGS

22) THIRD-PARTY AUCTION SOFTWARE

<P>This antique cabinet was built in <B>1872</B>.
I purchased it in <I>1982</I>.</P>

CREATE A NEW LISTING ITEM

eBay Turbo Lister is a program that enables you to create and manage for-sale items on your computer and, when you're ready to sell, upload them to eBay. Even if you are an individual with just a few items to sell online, Turbo Lister can save you time by letting you create and edit your listings offline, upload them in batches, and reuse the stored listings later if the items do not sell or if you have multiple items. With the program, you can create listings for regular auctions, fixed-price auctions, real estate ads, and items for your eBay Store. You can download Turbo Lister here: http://www.ebay.com/turbo_lister.

Creating a new listing is similar to creating a new listing online at eBay. First, the program asks for your eBay user ID and password so it can upload your listings to your eBay account later on.

Next, you choose one or two categories for the listing. The categories displayed in the program come from the eBay site, and the program updates any category changes when it periodically checks for software updates online. If you choose two categories for your item, buyers can find your listing in two places when they browse the listings on the eBay site. Note that your insertion fees and some upgrade fees double if you choose two categories.

CREATE A NEW LISTING ITEM

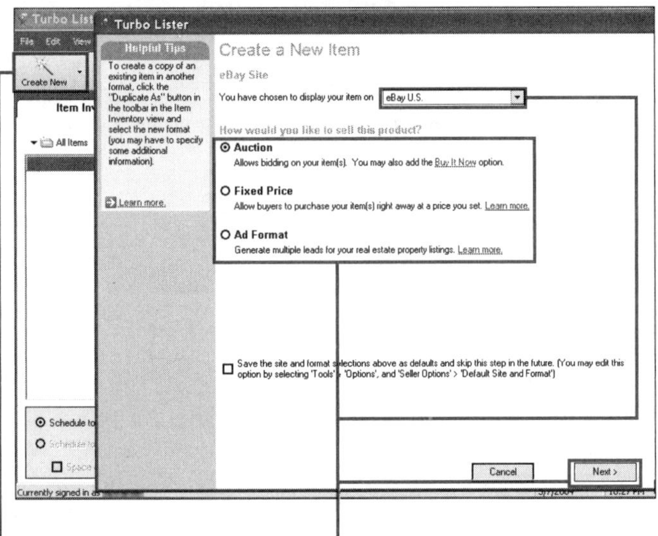

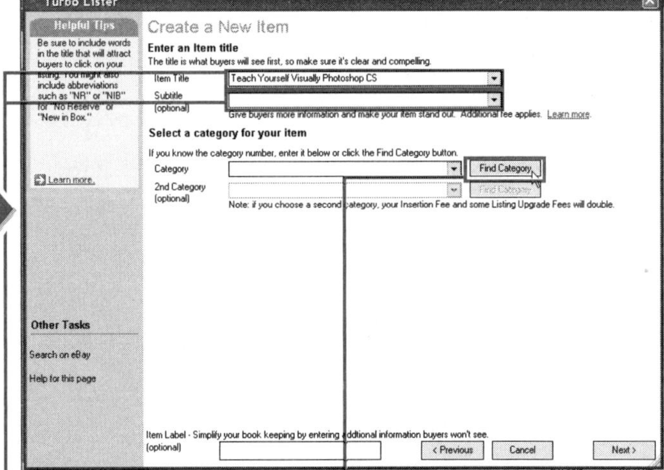

1 Start Turbo Lister and click Create New.

■ You can download the program by typing **http://www.ebay.com/turbo_lister/** into your browser's address bar.

■ The Create a New Item Turbo Lister window appears.

2 Click here and select the eBay site where you want to display your listing.

3 Click a listing type option.

4 Click Next.

5 Type a title for your listing.

■ You can type an optional subtitle.

Note: Posting a listing with a subtitle requires additional fees.

6 Click Find Category.

How can I change the personal options that I specified when I installed Turbo Lister?

✔ You can choose Tools and then Options. This allows you to change the address to which buyers should send payment and the default information for the auctions that you set up through Turbo Lister. You can save time by setting your default information such as shipping costs and payment types accepted before you start creating your listings. See the section "Define Default Listing Information," later in this chapter, for more details.

What version of Turbo Lister should I download?

✔ When you download the program, you have the choice of downloading a small version, which connects to eBay to retrieve the information that you specifically need to create and manage your listings, or a large version, which includes everything. To save download time and space on your hard drive, you should choose the small version, unless you plan to use Turbo Lister on a computer that is not connected to the Internet.

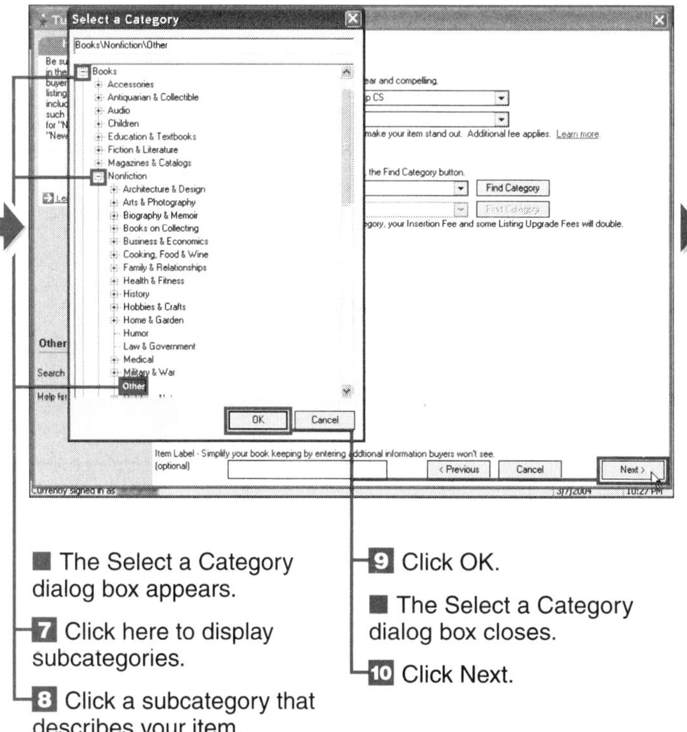

■ The Select a Category dialog box appears.

7 Click here to display subcategories.

8 Click a subcategory that describes your item.

9 Click OK.

■ The Select a Category dialog box closes.

10 Click Next.

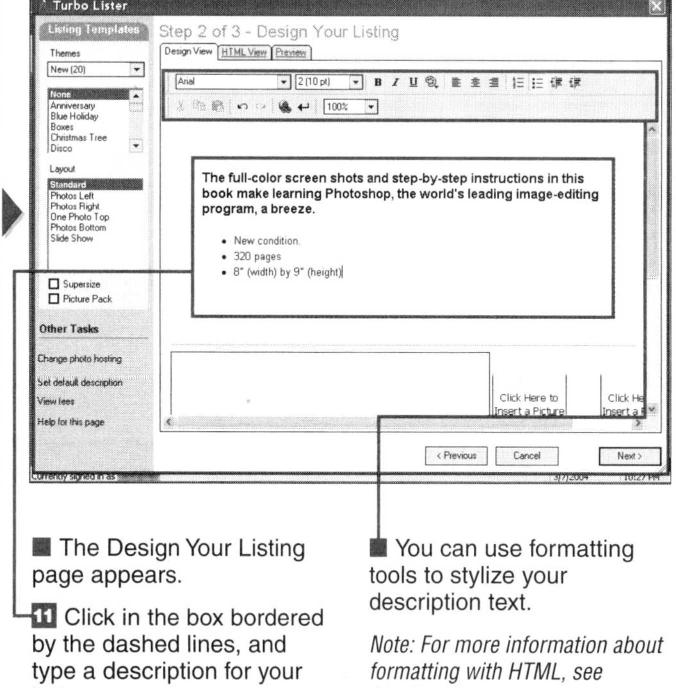

■ The Design Your Listing page appears.

11 Click in the box bordered by the dashed lines, and type a description for your listing.

■ You can use formatting tools to stylize your description text.

Note: For more information about formatting with HTML, see Chapter 21.

CONTINUED

CREATE A NEW LISTING ITEM (CONTINUED)

The Design Your Listing interface in Turbo Lister allows you to use HTML formatting to create a professional-looking description of your item. You do not need to know HTML to use the interface. Type your description in the text box, and then use buttons and menus to add the HTML formatting.

If you want to write your HTML by hand, you can click the HTML View tab, which displays the raw HTML code. For more information about using HTML, see Chapter 21.

You can also customize your listing by choosing from a variety of ready-made themes. Choosing a theme adds a colorful background to the description area of the auction, with imagery appropriate for the given theme. You can choose themes that go with an item category such as baby or computer, a holiday such as Christmas or Hanukkah, or an event such as a wedding. The layouts let you organize the text and photos of your listing in different ways, such as with photos above or to one side of the text.

After you specify the price and payment information in the final dialog box, you save your listing. Then it is ready for uploading to eBay.

CREATE A NEW LISTING ITEM (CONTINUED)

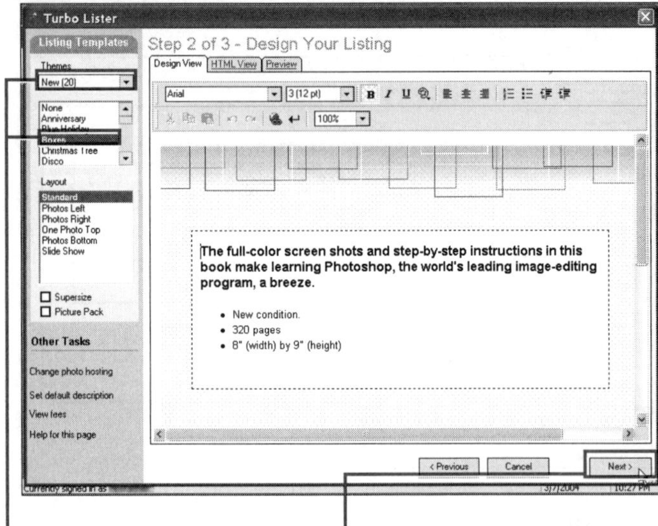

12 Click here and select a theme category.

13 Click a theme.

■ Turbo Lister adds a colorful background to your listing.

■ You can click a layout to arrange your description and photos.

Note: For more information, see the section "Add Photos to a Listing."

14 Click Next.

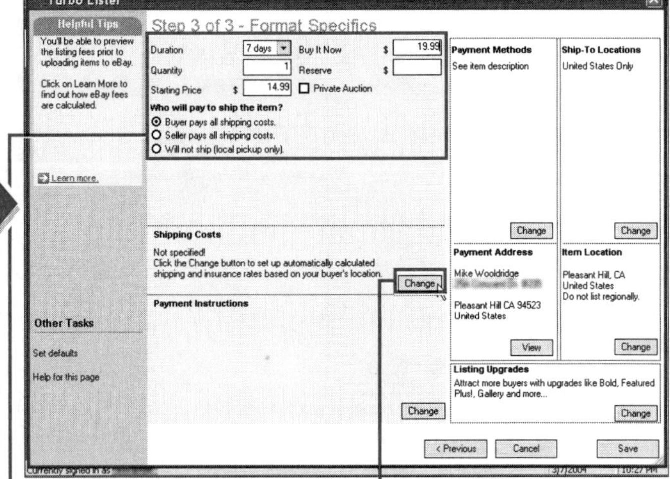

■ The Format Specifics page appears.

15 Specify duration, quantity, pricing, and shipping payment information.

16 Click Change to enter more listing information.

■ In this example, the Shipping Costs category has been selected.

How do I insert a clickable hyperlink into my description?

✔ You can click [icon] in the Design Your Listing page to insert a hyperlink. Turbo Lister asks for the text to be hyperlinked and the hyperlink URL. The URL is the Web address that users are taken to when they click the link. You can get the URL by opening the destination page in a Web browser and copying the information that appears in the address bar.

What if I do not want a special theme or layout for my listing?

✔ On the Design Your Listing page, you can select None from the Themes list, and Standard from the Layout list. This gives your listing a plain appearance without any extra color or imagery.

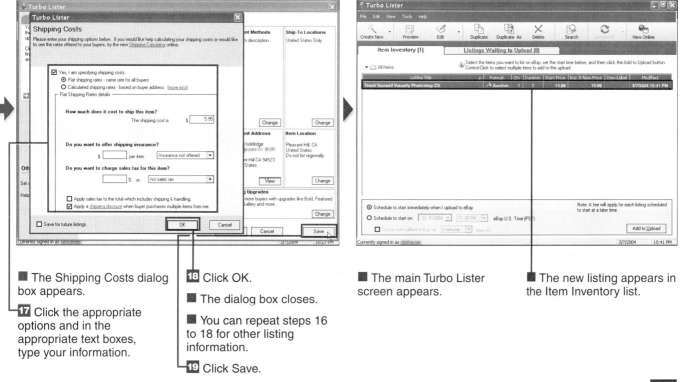

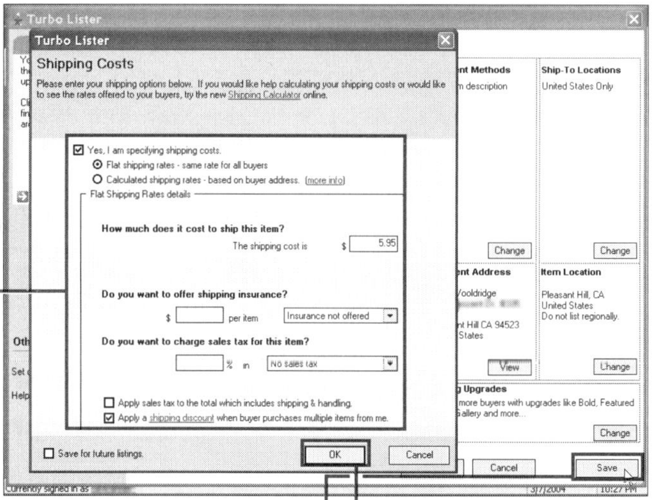

■ The Shipping Costs dialog box appears.

17 Click the appropriate options and in the appropriate text boxes, type your information.

18 Click OK.

■ The dialog box closes.

■ You can repeat steps 16 to 18 for other listing information.

19 Click Save.

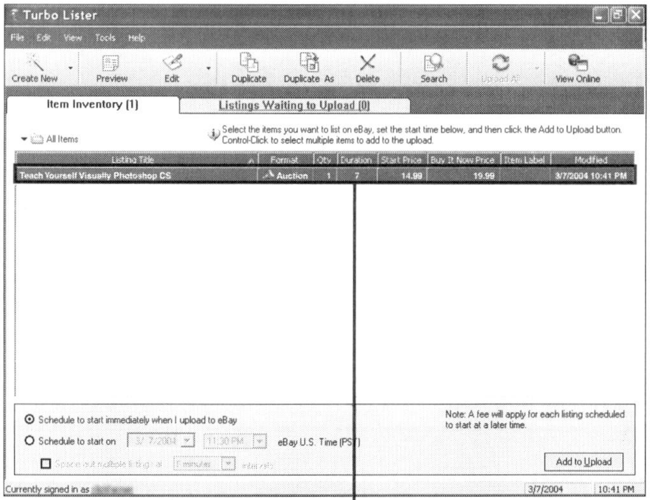

■ The main Turbo Lister screen appears.

■ The new listing appears in the Item Inventory list.

ADD PHOTOS TO A LISTING

eBay allows sellers to include up to six photos with their listings. The first photo is free, while additional photos cost 15 cents each. Any photo fees are charged after you upload your listings to the eBay site, along with your other fees. No fees are charged when you initially add photos in Turbo Lister.

You add your photos on the Design Your Listing page, below the description area. Clicking one of the picture boxes opens a dialog box from which you can choose any image file that is stored on your computer hard drive and add it to your listing. You should use images that are saved in the JPEG (.jpg) or GIF (.gif) formats, the two most common Web formats. eBay recommends that you use photos that are no larger than 400 pixels in width by 300 pixels in height. For more information about preparing photos for eBay auctions, see Chapter 20.

Turbo Lister also gives you the option to supersize your photos, which lets you insert images up to 800 pixels in width by 600 pixels in height. This costs an extra 75 cents per photo. For another 75 cents, you can also choose the Slide Show layout and have your added photos appear as a slide show.

ADD PHOTOS TO A LISTING

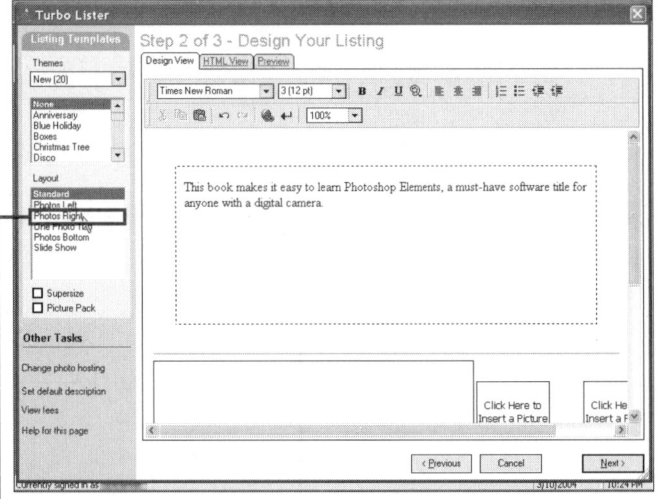

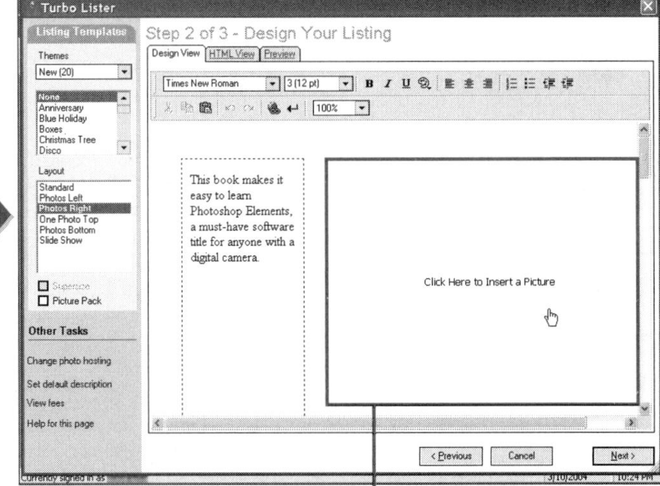

1 Start a new Turbo Lister listing.

Note: See "Create a New Listing Item" for details.

2 On the Design Your Listing page, click a layout to determine how your photos are arranged.

■ If you want to add photos to an existing listing, click the Add/Manage Photos button from the Edit Item page.

Note: See "Edit a Listing" for more information.

■ If you click a new layout, the arrangement of the text and photos changes.

3 Click a picture box.

What if I want to host my photos on my own Web server and include them in my listings?

✔ You can click Change photo hosting under Other Tasks on the Design Your Listing page. This allows you to specify that you want to host your own photos. After you select this option, Turbo Lister includes an Insert Picture button (📷) in the toolbar area. Clicking the button allows you to type a URL where the photo is stored on your Web server. Hosting your own images lets you avoid eBay's photo fees when you include more than one photo in your listing.

If I include a stock photo through the pre-filled information feature, does that count as my first free photo?

✔ The pre-filled information feature lets you automatically add descriptive information to certain types of items, such as author, page count, and publisher information for books. The feature can also include stock photos, such as cover art for music CDs. If you include a stock photo, it does not count as your free photo. You can still include another photo with your listing and not be charged any extra fees. See "Use Pre-filled Information" for more information.

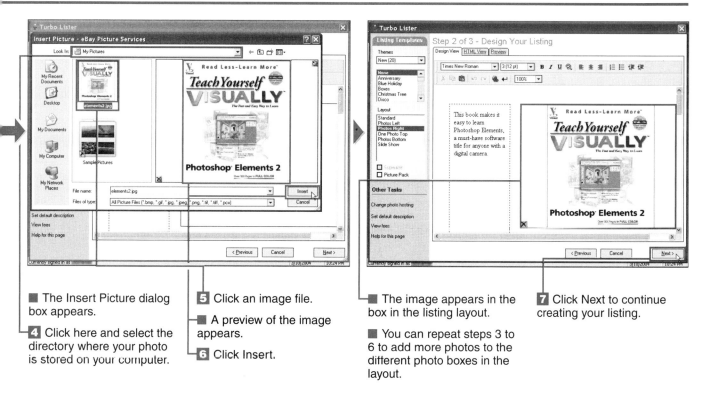

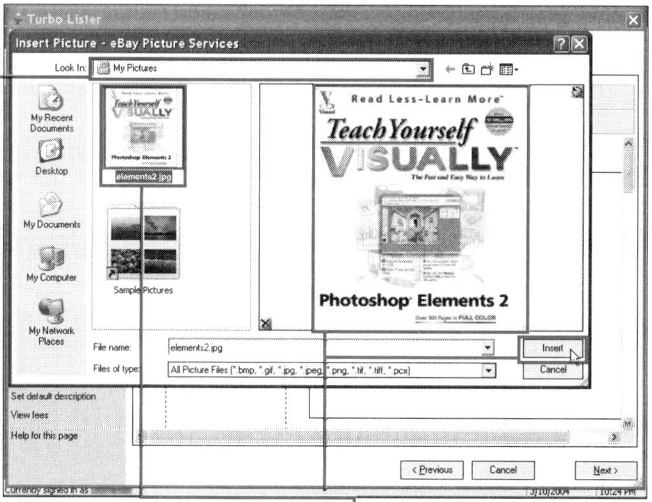

■ The Insert Picture dialog box appears.

4 Click here and select the directory where your photo is stored on your computer.

5 Click an image file.

■ A preview of the image appears.

6 Click Insert.

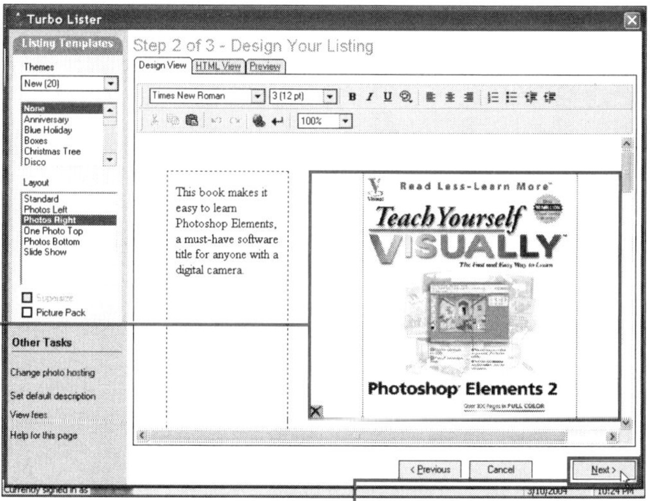

■ The image appears in the box in the listing layout.

■ You can repeat steps 3 to 6 to add more photos to the different photo boxes in the layout.

7 Click Next to continue creating your listing.

ADD A COUNTER TO A LISTING

You can add a graphic to the bottom of your listing page that counts the number of times eBay users visit your page. Andale, an eBay partner, provides the counters available in Turbo Lister. You can add a counter to your listing for free.

Turbo Lister gives you two numeric styles, and a style that hides the number of visits from visitors to the page. To view the visits measured by a hidden counter, you need to set up and log on to your account at the Andale Web site (www.andale.com). To change the style of your counter, you can click the counter graphic at the bottom of the Design Your Listing dialog box. You can select None in the style menu if you do not want to place a counter on your listing.

Besides giving you a feel for how popular your listing is, it can also help you measure the effectiveness of some of eBay's upgrade features. For example, you can add a bold, highlight, or gallery feature to some of your listings and not others, and track whether the added emphasis to the upgraded listings brings in more traffic.

ADD A COUNTER TO A LISTING

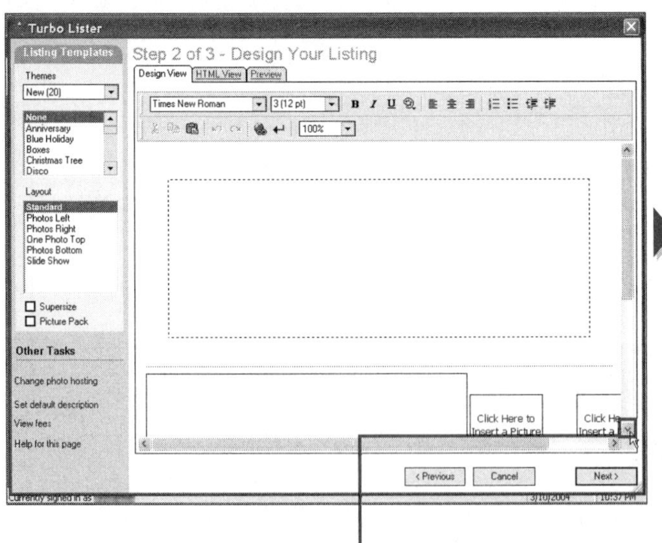

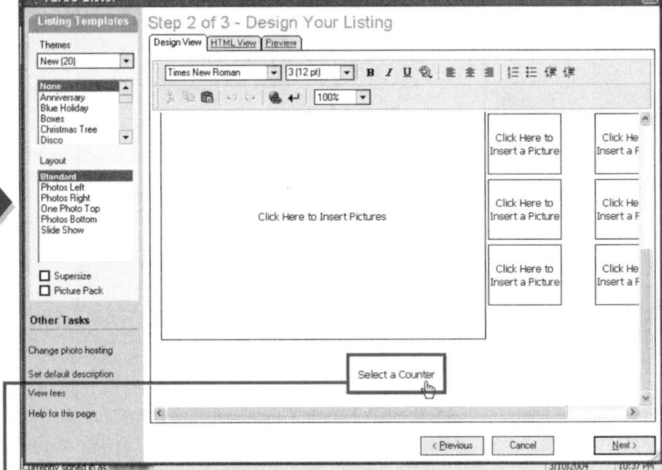

1 Start a new Turbo Lister listing.

Note: See "Create a New Listing Item" for details.

2 On the Design Your Listing page, click here to scroll to the bottom of your listing.

3 Click Select a Counter.

Do I need to add a new counter if I relist an item?

✔ No. When you relist an auction, you do not need to add a new counter. The counter will stay on the page and be reset to zero. If you want to remove the counter before relisting, you can turn the counter feature off in Turbo Lister. Click the Add/Manage Photos button on the Edit Item page. Then click the counter graphic, and select None from the menu. For more about editing your listings, see the next section, "Edit a Listing."

Will a counter add to its count if I reload a page?

✔ Counters keep track of visitors, and will not increment the count if a visitor reloads a page in the browser. The count that is displayed represents the number of unique visitors to a given auction.

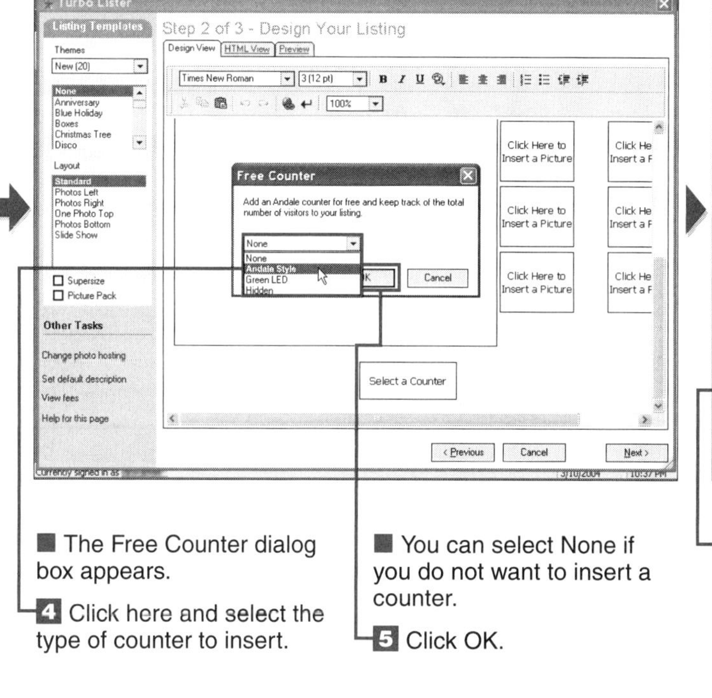

■ The Free Counter dialog box appears.

4 Click here and select the type of counter to insert.

■ You can select None if you do not want to insert a counter.

5 Click OK.

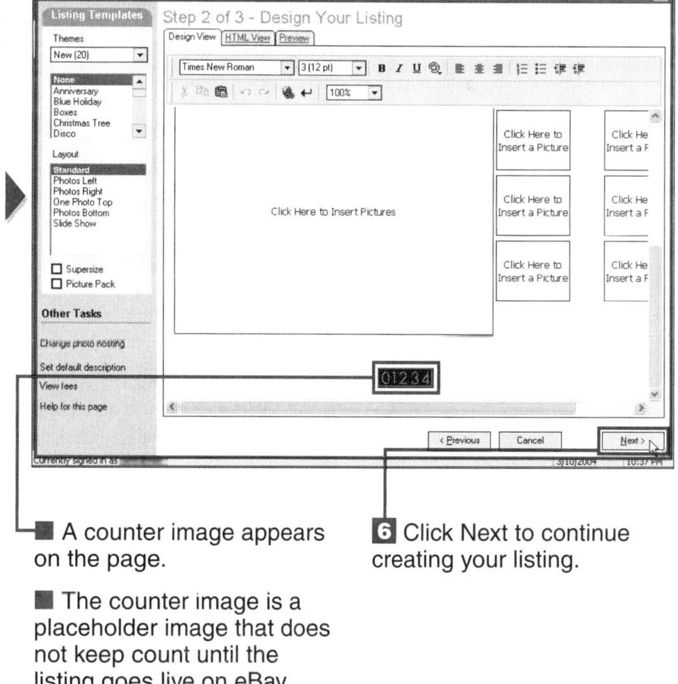

■ A counter image appears on the page.

■ The counter image is a placeholder image that does not keep count until the listing goes live on eBay.

6 Click Next to continue creating your listing.

EDIT A LISTING

You can edit any listing that you create and save in Turbo Lister. You can update the title and description, swap photos, adjust pricing, and change shipping options. Being able to easily edit your listings offline is one of the advantages of Turbo Lister. You can continue to tweak the details of what you are selling up to the time you upload them for sale online.

You can also edit listings for items that do not sell on eBay before you upload those listings again. You may want to lower the starting or reserve prices of such listings, make the descriptions more comprehensive, or add more photos.

When editing a listing, the Auction Details dialog box enables you to edit the raw information about the auction such as pricing and shipping details. Clicking the Design View button opens the Design Your Listing interface, which lets you change the theme and layout, as well as the photos. After you are finished editing and have clicked the Save button, the old information for the listing is overwritten with the new information. If you want to keep the old information, you can duplicate a listing using the Duplicate button on the main Turbo Lister page, and then edit the duplicate.

EDIT A LISTING

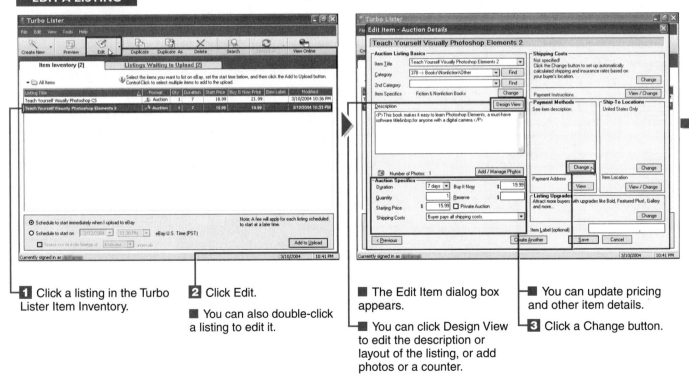

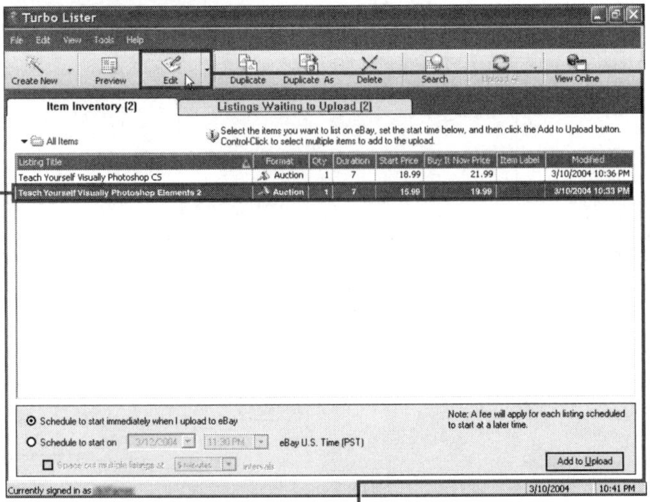

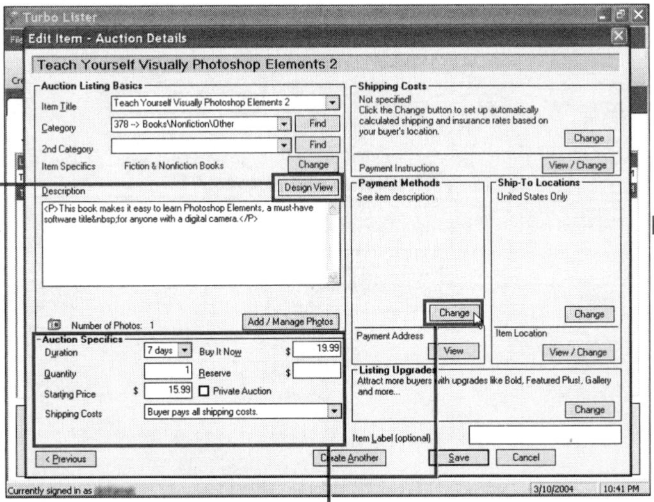

1 Click a listing in the Turbo Lister Item Inventory.

2 Click Edit.

■ You can also double-click a listing to edit it.

■ The Edit Item dialog box appears.

■ You can click Design View to edit the description or layout of the listing, or add photos or a counter.

■ You can update pricing and other item details.

3 Click a Change button.

How do I edit any pre-filled information that I have included with my listing?

✔ If you have included any pre-filled information with a book, CD, movie, or other item for which this is available, you can view it by clicking the Change button next to Item Specifics in the Auction Details dialog box. You can then change certain editable information such as condition of the item. You cannot change information such as the pre-filled title, author, and date published. You can delete the listing and re-create it without the pre-filled information added or with different information. See "Use Pre-filled Information" for more information.

Can I edit a listing after I have moved it to the Listings Waiting to Upload list?

✔ No. You cannot edit the listings in the Listings Waiting to Upload list. The Edit button is disabled when that list is viewed. The only way to update a listing that has been moved there is to delete it from the Listings Waiting to Upload list, and then edit the listing copy that is in the Item Inventory. After you have edited the copy there, you can move the listing back to the Listings Waiting to Upload list. For more information about uploading, see the section "Upload a Listing," later in this chapter.

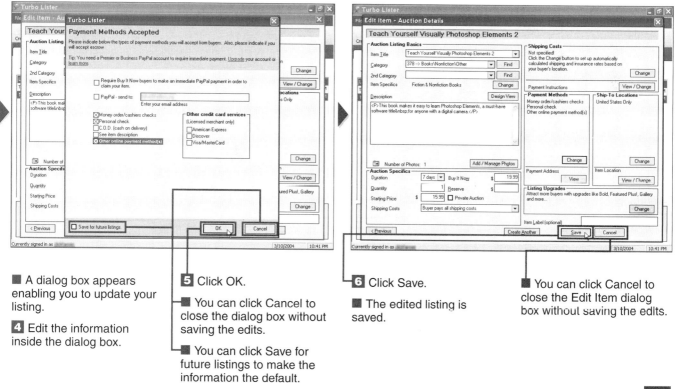

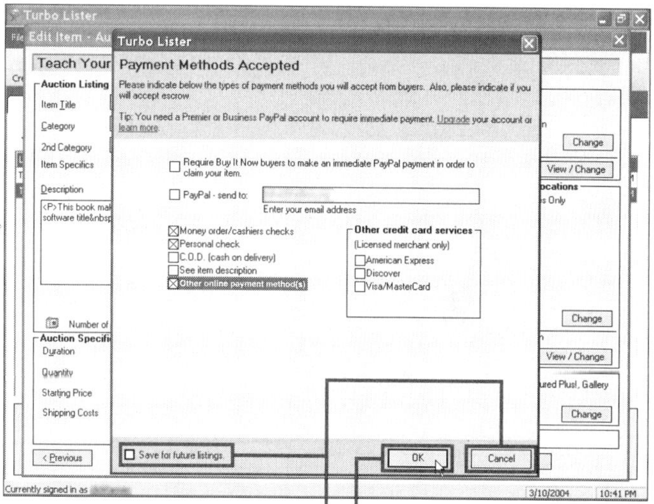

■ A dialog box appears enabling you to update your listing.

4 Edit the information inside the dialog box.

5 Click OK.

■ You can click Cancel to close the dialog box without saving the edits.

■ You can click Save for future listings to make the information the default.

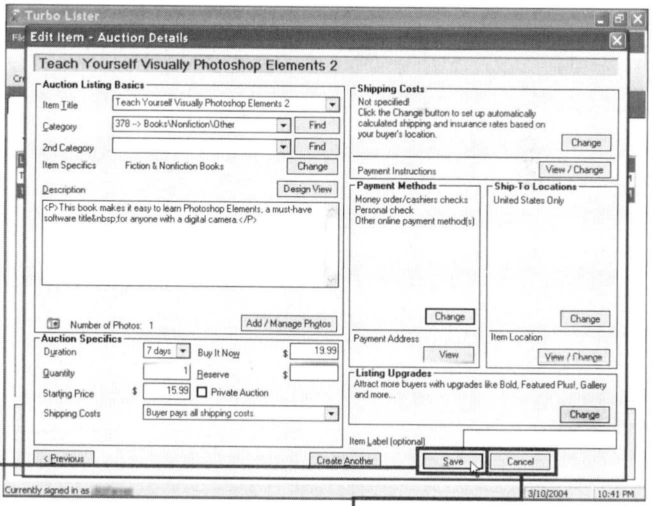

6 Click Save.

■ The edited listing is saved.

■ You can click Cancel to close the Edit Item dialog box without saving the edits.

USE PRE-FILLED INFORMATION

You can create more comprehensive listings for books, movies, music, video games, and other products using the pre-filled information feature. The feature saves you time by automatically filling in such details as author, artist, page count, publisher, and other standard information. Some types of pre-filled information even come with stock photos — for example, pictures of book covers or CD cover art — that you can include with your listings for free. After adding pre-filled information to your listing, you can add your own description and photos to personalize it.

Turbo Lister attempts to find pre-filled information for your items by using their unique product identifiers, such as the ISBNs or UPCs. You can also have Turbo Lister search by words in the title, or product-specific keywords such as the director for movies or author for books. You can add one set of pre-filled information to each listing.

Muze, Inc., not eBay, provides the pre-filled information and stock photos. eBay recommends that you confirm the accuracy of the information before you include it in your listing.

USE PRE-FILLED INFORMATION

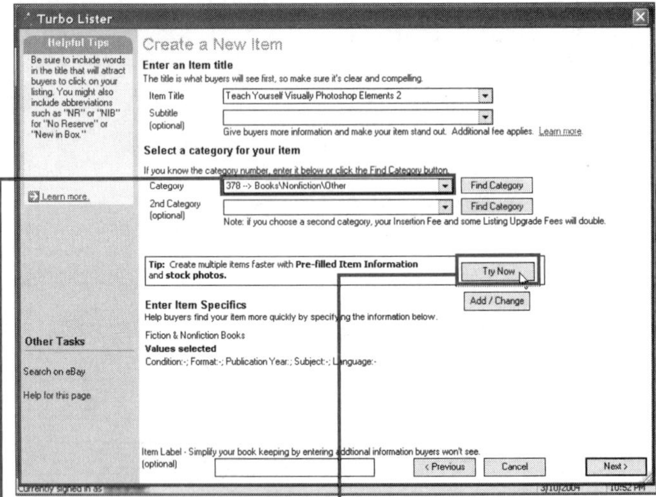

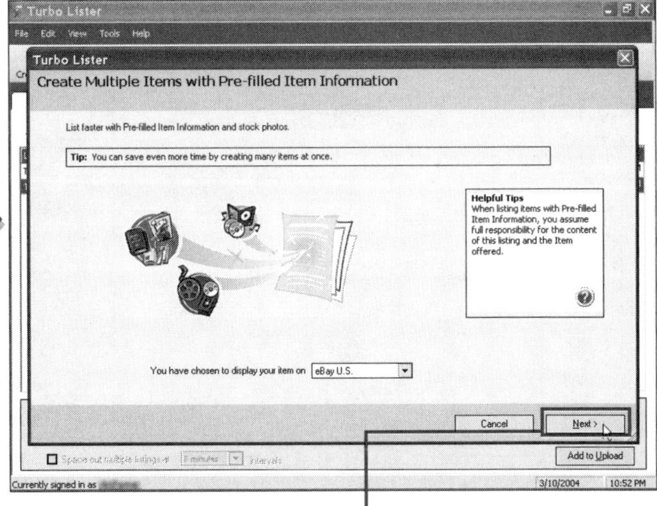

1 Start a new Turbo Lister listing.

Note: See "Create a New Listing Item" for details.

2 Select a category under Books or Entertainment.

■ Most of the subcategories under Books and Entertainment offer the pre-filled information feature.

3 Click Try Now.

■ The pre-filled information form appears.

■ The Create Multiple Items with Pre-filled Item Information dialog box appears.

4 Click Next.

What is a UPC?

✔ UPC stands for Universal Product Code, a 12-digit code for identifying a wide range of products. UPCs are associated with the bar codes on packaging, and enable prices to be scanned electronically and products to be inventoried.

What is an ISBN?

✔ ISBN stands for International Standard Book Number, a 10-digit code for identifying books and book-like products such as audio books. Similar to UPCs, ISBNs are also associated with bar codes for pricing and inventory purposes.

Can I use a stock image as the gallery image for my listing?

✔ You can specify that the stock image in the pre-filled information be the gallery image for your listing on the Listing Upgrades page. To open this page, click the Change button in the Listing Upgrades section when you edit your listing. The gallery image is the small image that appears next to the listing title when you browse or search for items on eBay. A gallery image is an upgrade that costs 25 cents to add to each listing.

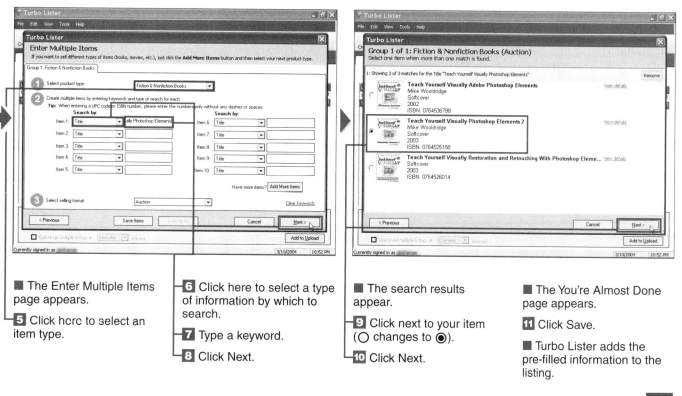

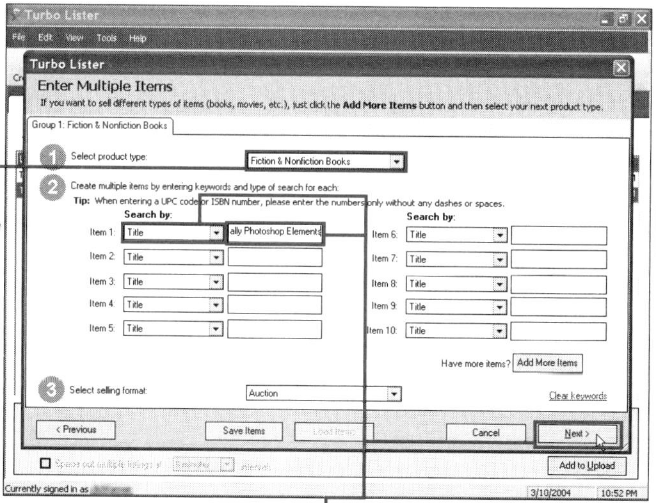

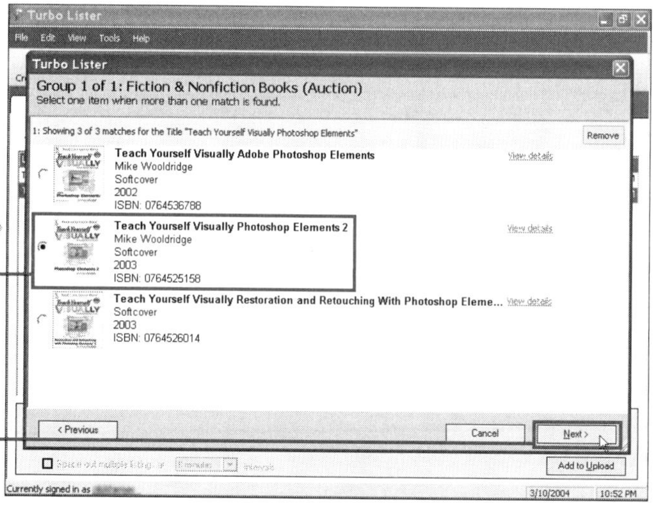

■ The Enter Multiple Items page appears.

5 Click here to select an item type.

6 Click here to select a type of information by which to search.

7 Type a keyword.

8 Click Next.

■ The search results appear.

9 Click next to your item (○ changes to ◉).

10 Click Next.

■ The You're Almost Done page appears.

11 Click Save.

■ Turbo Lister adds the pre-filled information to the listing.

SCHEDULE A LISTING

You can schedule your listings to determine when they go live on the eBay site. Listings can be scheduled to start immediately and to start at a later time.

Listings that are scheduled to start immediately are live the instant you upload them to eBay. You can avoid paying additional listing fees when you start your listings immediately.

You can also schedule a listing to start later than the current date and time. The advantage to a listing that starts at a later date is that you can coordinate the ending time to fall at a particular date and time when you think buyers will be most likely to see the listings. The disadvantage to starting a listing at a later date is that it costs an additional 10 cents per item in fees.

If you are scheduling multiple items to start in advance of the current date, you can spread out their start times by a given interval, for example, five or ten minutes. This can be optimal for items that are similar and will conceivably attract the same buyers. If you schedule all the items to end at the same time, buyers that want to make their bids right before the ending time may only be able to bid on a single item. Spreading out the start times allow potential buyers to bid on more than one.

SCHEDULE A LISTING

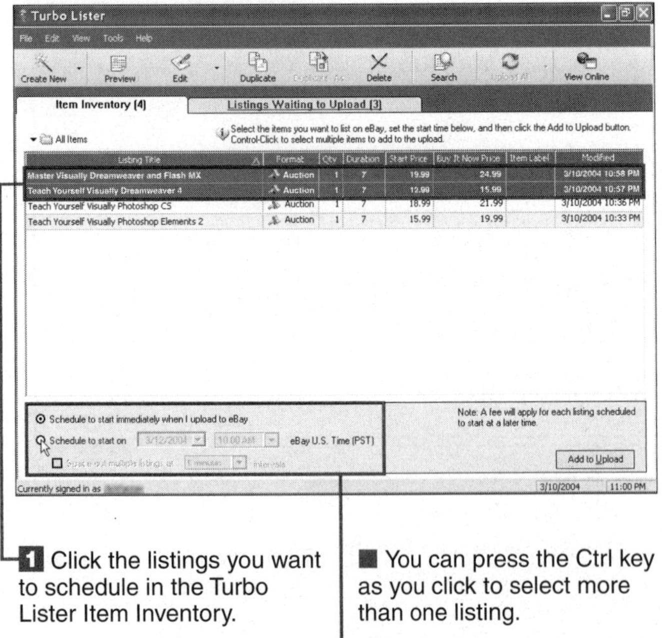

1 Click the listings you want to schedule in the Turbo Lister Item Inventory.

■ You can press the Ctrl key as you click to select more than one listing.

2 Click a scheduling option.

■ If you click the Schedule to start immediately when I upload to eBay option, you are finished.

Note: See "Upload a Listing" for details about the next steps.

3 If you click the Schedule to start on option, click here to select the date.

4 In the calendar that appears, click a date to start the listings.

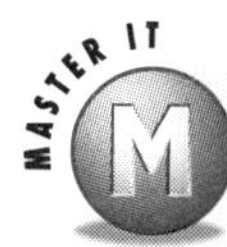

How much in advance can I schedule a listing to start?

✔ You can schedule a listing to start up to three weeks in advance of the current date and time.

When is the best time to schedule items to start?

✔ One strategy is to pick a start time that results in an ending time during which a lot of users visit the eBay sites. Items that are ending soon get better exposure in the eBay search results, so having listings end at times when a lot of people will be searching the eBay site — for example, during the day in the U.S. for listings posted to the U.S. eBay site — can increase the chances of getting a bid.

Is there a maximum number of items I can schedule?

✔ Yes. You can schedule a maximum of 3,000 items, using Turbo Lister, at a given time.

Can I change the start time for a listing after I have moved it to the Listings Waiting to Upload list?

✔ Yes. Click the listing to highlight it and then click the Change Start Time button. A dialog box appears allowing you to change the start time.

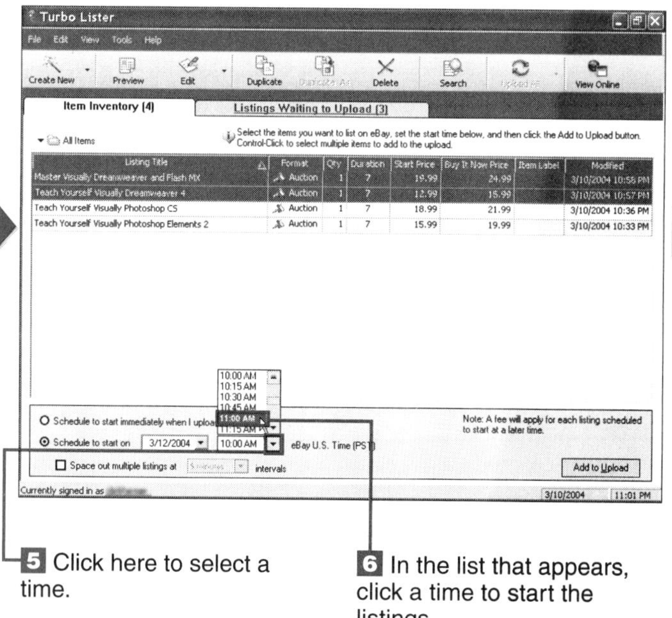

5 Click here to select a time.

6 In the list that appears, click a time to start the listings.

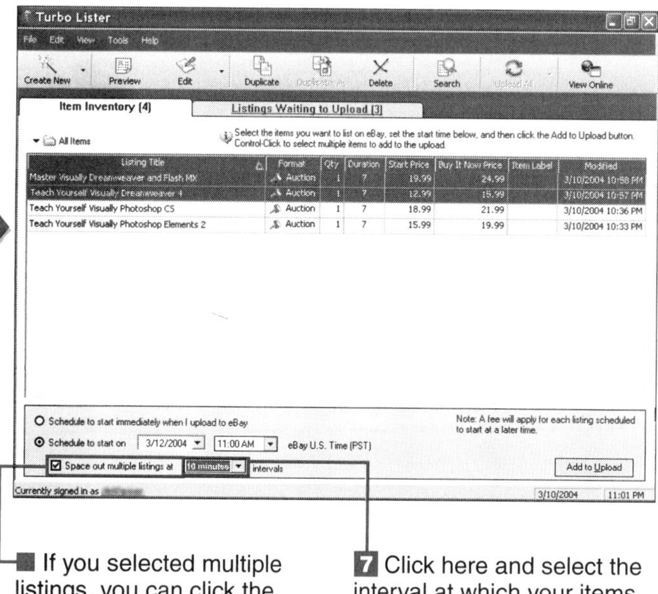

■ If you selected multiple listings, you can click the Space out multiple listings option to space out their start times.

7 Click here and select the interval at which your items should appear.

■ Your listings are scheduled and ready for upload.

UPLOAD A LISTING

You can upload your listings in Turbo Lister to move them from your local computer to the eBay Web site. Before you upload your listings from Turbo Lister, check to see that your descriptions, photos, and prices are correct, and your theme and layout settings are what you expect. You can view the theme and layout for a listing by previewing it. See the section "Preview a Listing," later in this chapter, for details.

If you scheduled a listing to start immediately, it will go live when you upload it. If you scheduled a listing to start at a time in the future, it will have a pending status until its start time. You can view your pending listings in the My eBay area.

Listings upload in the order that they appear in the Listings Waiting to Upload window, with the top listing uploading first. This is important to remember in cases where you have specified that the start times of your listings be spaced out by a certain interval. The interval and upload order determines when each listing goes live. You can change the order by selecting a listing and clicking the up or down arrows at the bottom left of the Listings Waiting to Upload screen.

UPLOAD A LISTING

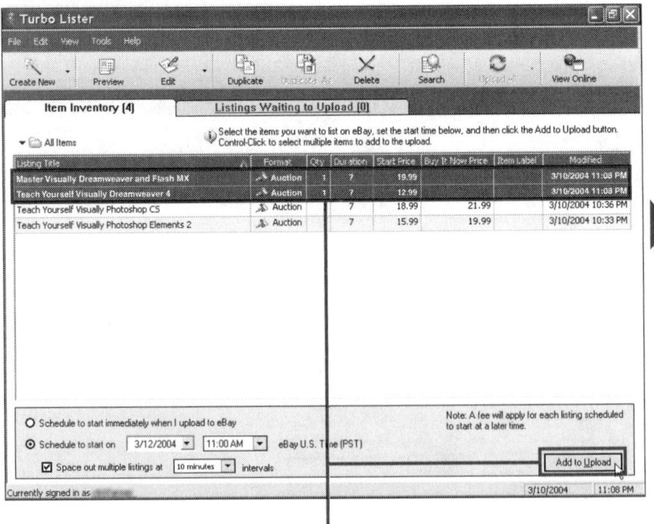

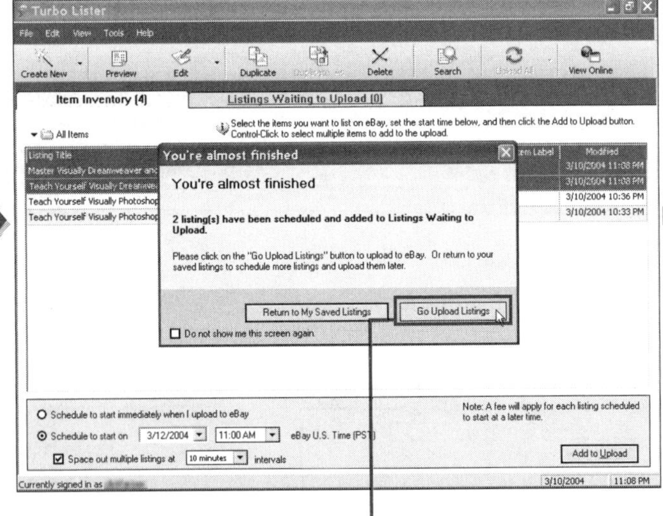

1 Schedule the listings that you want to upload.

Note: See the previous section, "Schedule a Listing," for details.

2 Click the listings you want to upload in the Turbo Lister Item Inventory.

■ You can press the Ctrl key as you click to select more than one listing.

3 Click Add to Upload.

■ A You're almost finished dialog box appears.

4 Click Go Upload Listings.

How do I update the Turbo Lister software?

✔ The software automatically updates itself with the latest information available each time you upload your listings to eBay. You can update the software manually by choosing Check for Program Updates from the Tools menu. You can also have the program automatically download updates when you launch it by clicking Tools, Options, and then the Advanced Options item in the dialog box that appears.

Can I delete a listing that I have already uploaded?

✔ Yes, as long as it is at least one hour before its scheduled start time. To delete a listing, click the View Online button in Turbo Lister, which takes you to the My eBay area. Under Pending Listings, click the Delete button next to the listing that you want to delete.

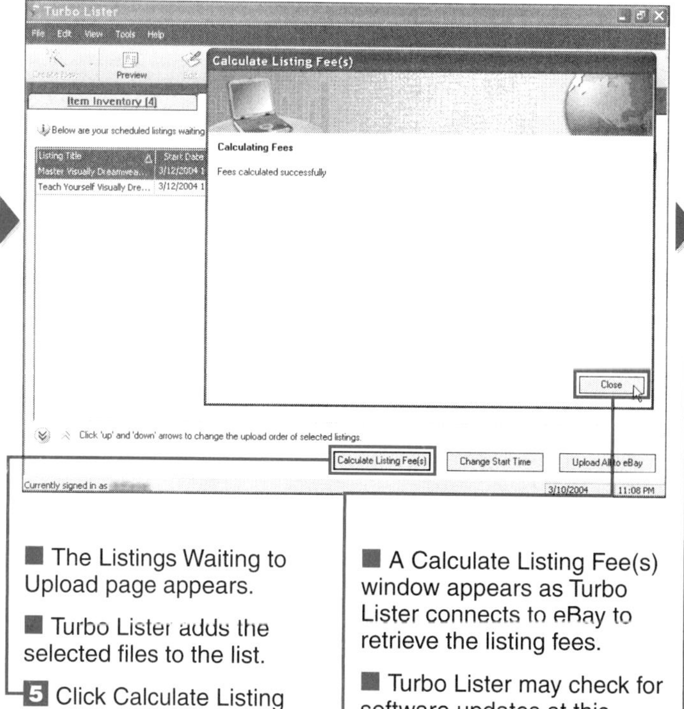

■ The Listings Waiting to Upload page appears.

■ Turbo Lister adds the selected files to the list.

5 Click Calculate Listing Fee(s).

■ A Calculate Listing Fee(s) window appears as Turbo Lister connects to eBay to retrieve the listing fees.

■ Turbo Lister may check for software updates at this time.

6 Click Close.

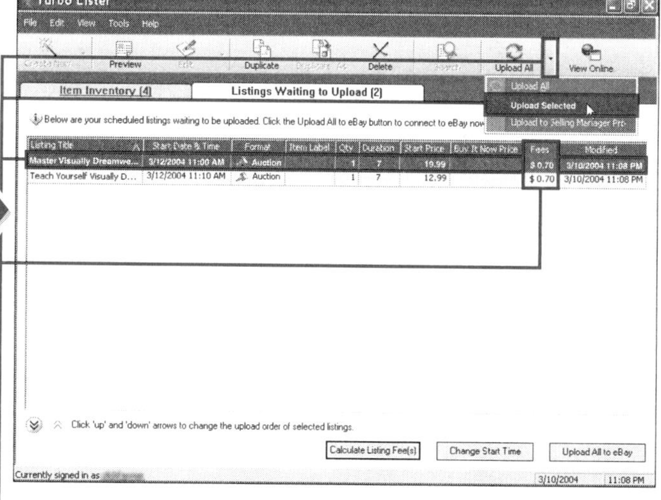

■ The fees for the listings appear.

7 Click a listing to select it.

8 Click here to select an upload option.

9 Click Upload Selected.

■ You can click Upload All to upload all the items on the list.

10 On the Upload Listings confirmation page that appears, click Continue to complete the upload.

DEFINE DEFAULT LISTING INFORMATION

You can set default settings in Turbo Lister for your regular auctions, real estate ads, fixed-price auctions, and eBay Store items. Creating defaults can save you time as you input the information for each listing in Turbo Lister. Often, your information is the same across different listings for such details as shipping terms, payment options, ship-to addresses, and return policies. It's a good idea to input these default settings options before starting to input your listings.

The most basic default settings for Turbo Listing are the eBay site selection and listing type selection. You can specify these under the Seller Options menu on the Options & Preferences page. Selecting a default eBay site lets you specify from where you usually sell your products, be it at the U.S. eBay site or a site in a foreign country.

Turbo Lister also lets you specify default settings for listing upgrades. This includes the Bold or Highlight options for emphasizing listings in search results, and the Subtitle option for adding an extra line of text below the listing title. Note that listing upgrades involve extra fees in addition to the regular eBay insertion fees.

DEFINE DEFAULT LISTING INFORMATION

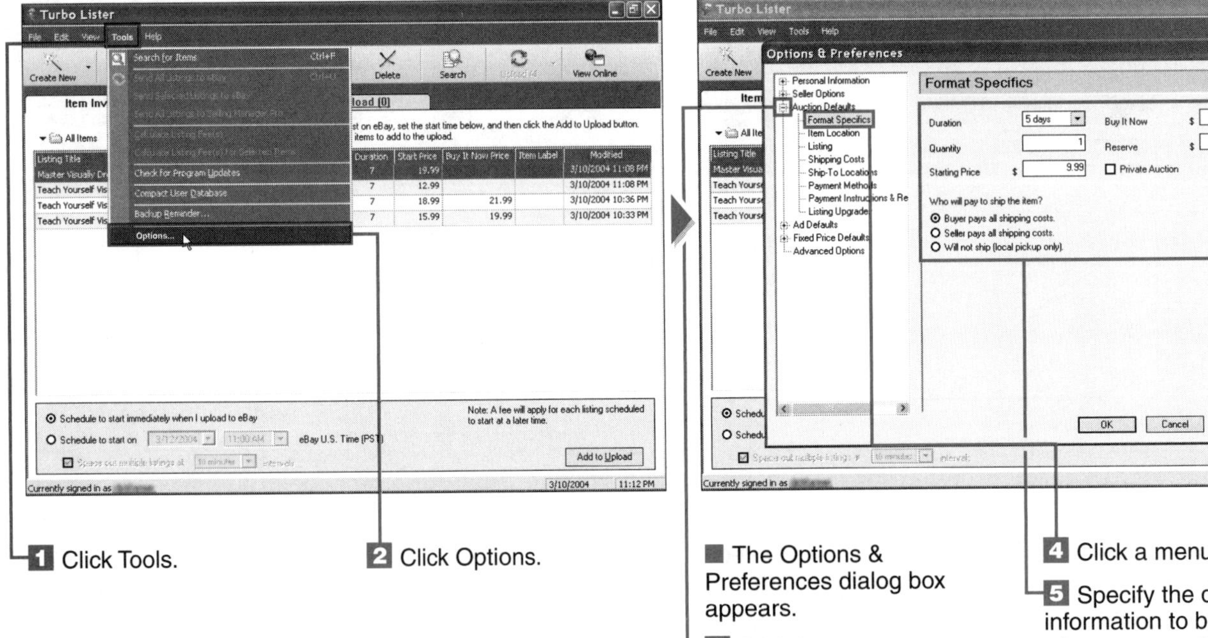

1 Click Tools.

2 Click Options.

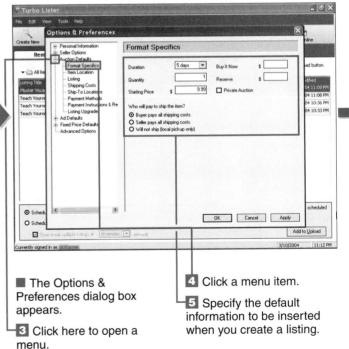

■ The Options & Preferences dialog box appears.

3 Click here to open a menu.

4 Click a menu item.

5 Specify the default information to be inserted when you create a listing.

How do I specify that I only accept PayPal payments for all my listings?

✔ In the Options & Preferences dialog box, click the Payment Methods menu item. Click the PayPal option (☐ changes to ☑) and type your e-mail address in the accompanying text box. Your e-mail address may already be in the box if Turbo Lister has downloaded your eBay user information. Deselect all other payment methods (☑ changes to ☐). Note that there are separate Payment Methods sections for both Auction Defaults and Fixed Price Defaults. You need to adjust your settings in both places.

How do I specify a return policy for all my listings?

✔ You can specify a return policy in the Payment Instructions & Return Policy section of the Auction Defaults and Fixed Price Defaults section in the Options & Preferences dialog box. A return policy can include under what circumstances a buyer may return an item and how it should be returned.

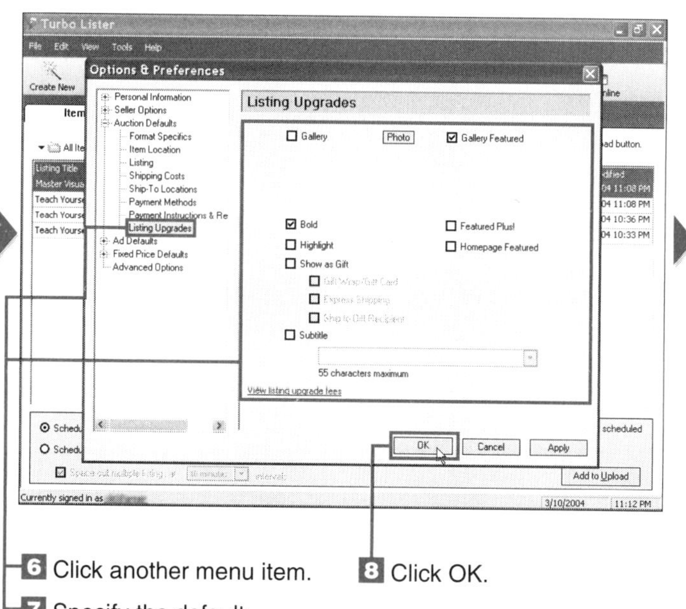

6 Click another menu item.

7 Specify the default information.

8 Click OK.

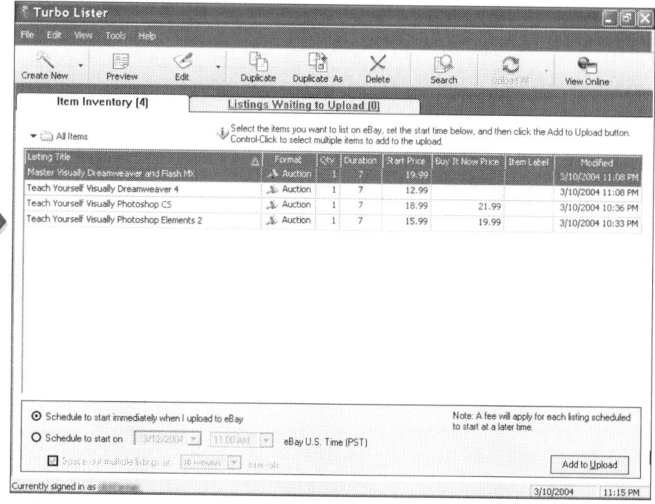

■ The default information updates and the main Turbo Lister page appears.

PREVIEW A LISTING

You can preview your listings to get an idea about how they will appear on the eBay Web site. Turbo Lister offers a preview function on the main Turbo Lister toolbar as well as from the Design Your Listings page.

You can select a listing in the Item Inventory or Listings Waiting to Upload lists and click the Preview button on the toolbar. This opens a window that shows a summary of your listing information, including duration, quantity, and pricing. It also shows a preview of your description and photos as they will look online. This preview includes any HTML formatting.

You can also preview the description and photos when you create or edit a listing. Click the Preview tab on the Design Your Listing page to see how the description and photos will be arranged and formatted.

Note that the preview functions do not show you everything that you will see when the listing is posted online. As soon as the auction has started, the listing will include seller and bidder information, the time left in the auction, and other information that cannot be accurately previewed offline.

PREVIEW A LISTING

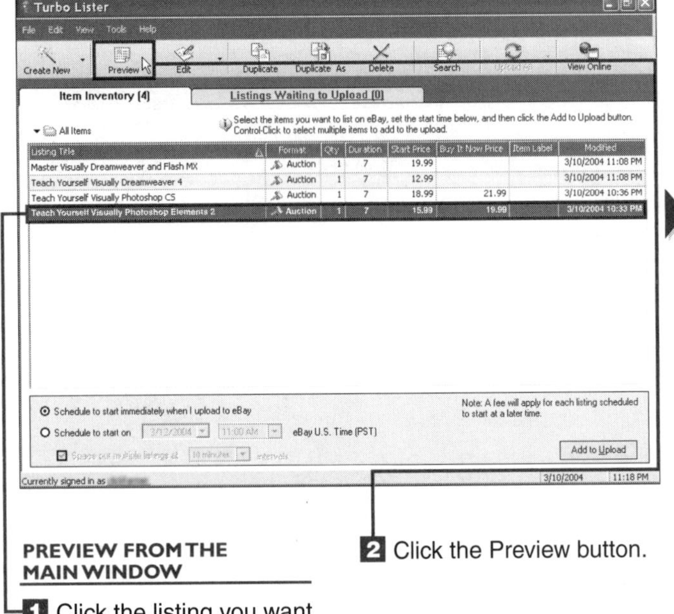

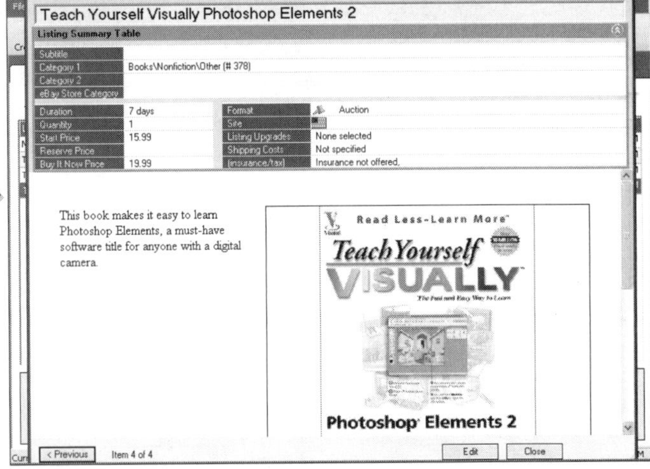

PREVIEW FROM THE MAIN WINDOW

1 Click the listing you want to preview.

2 Click the Preview button.

■ A Preview Item window appears with a summary of the listing on top and the description and any photos on the bottom.

Will my images display during a preview?

✔ There are two ways to add images to your listings. You can have eBay add them using either their photo service or the pre-filled information feature in Turbo Lister. You can also add them by writing HTML that references an image that is already online. Regardless of how you add them, the images should display during a preview. Reasons they might not display include your Internet connection being down or your making a mistake in your HTML. For more about HTML, see Chapter 21.

What does the View Online button do?

✔ Clicking the View Online button on the Turbo Lister toolbar takes you to the My eBay area for your account. There you can view your listings that are pending, currently selling, or have ended. You will have to log on before you can view your My eBay page. If you have not uploaded your listings to eBay yet, they will not appear in your My eBay area.

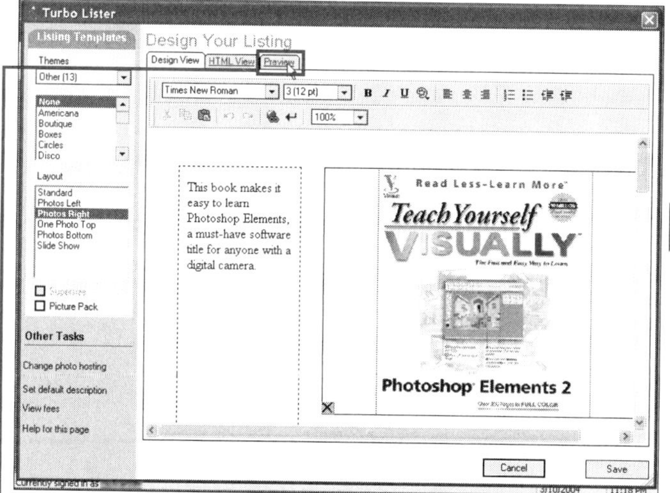

PREVIEW FROM DESIGN YOUR LISTING

1 Click the Preview tab.

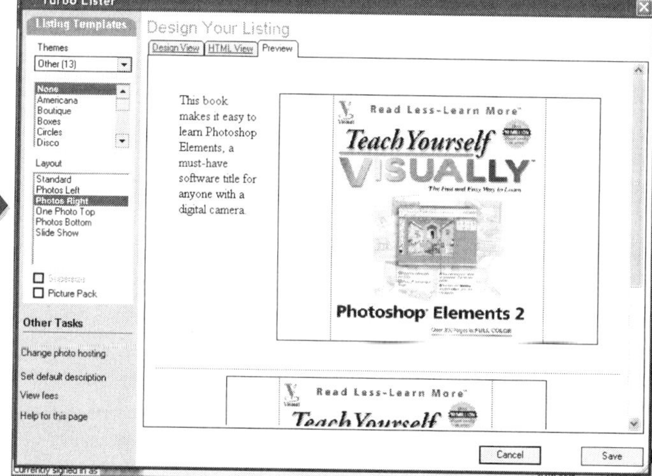

■ Turbo Lister displays how the listing description and any photos will appear online.

CREATE A LISTING WITH SELLER'S ASSISTANT

Seller's Assistant is software that you can run on your local computer that helps you manage and monitor your auctions on eBay. Seller's Assistant offers a quicker way to create your listings, compared to creating them online, by automatically filling in much of the data that appears on all of your listings.

The Seller's Assistant listing creation features are similar to those found in the Turbo Lister software, which is described in Chapter 18. Unlike Turbo Lister, however, Seller's Assistant allows you to monitor the bidding on your listings while they are live on the eBay site. It also helps you communicate with your buyers via e-mail when your auctions end.

If you have created eBay auctions before, the information in the Seller's Assistant New Listing dialog box will look familiar. An advantage that you have with Seller's Assistant is that you can view and enter most of the information on a single screen. This saves you time because you do not have to click through a sequence of pages online at the eBay site to type your title, description, price, and other information for your listing.

Seller's Assistant comes in both Basic and Pro versions, both of which require a paid monthly subscription. Currently eBay offers the first 30 days free.

CREATE A LISTING WITH SELLER'S ASSISTANT

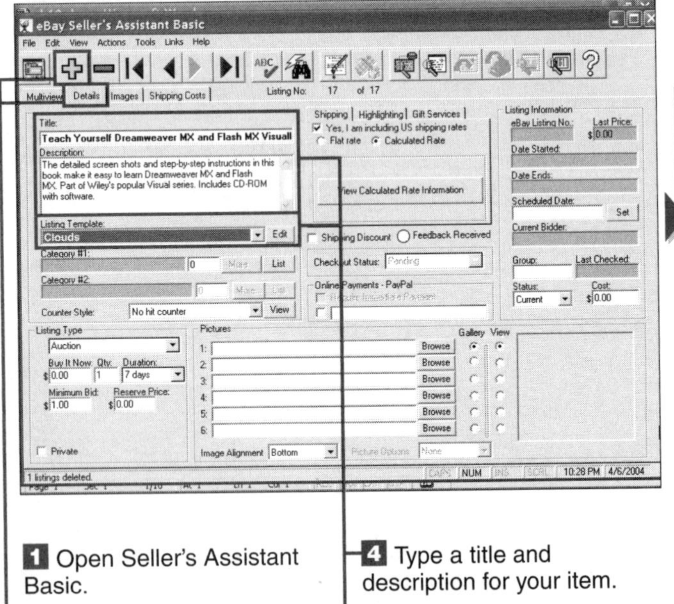

1 Open Seller's Assistant Basic.

2 Click the New Listing button (⊕).

3 Click the Details tab.

4 Type a title and description for your item.

5 Click ▾ and select a template. You can click Edit to preview and change the template styles and colors.

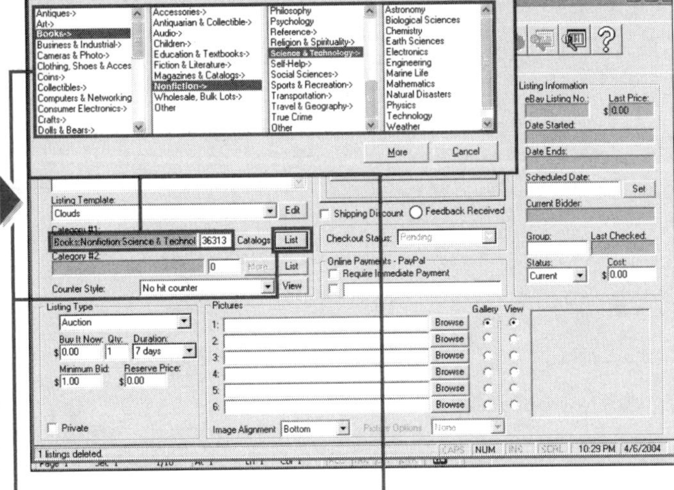

6 Click List.

■ The Select Category window appears.

7 Click the category and subcategories for your item.

■ The window closes automatically, and the category information appears in the Category #1 field.

Where do I download Seller's Assistant?

✔ You can download the Seller's Assistant software at http://pages.ebay.com/sellers_assistant. You can also get to the Seller's Assistant download page through the eBay Site Map.

How can I update the default information that appears in each new listing that I create?

✔ You can click File and then Options, or click the Options button (). This lets you change the default format, pricing, and payment information, as well as your mailing address. You can also update the mail server settings that Seller's Assistant uses to send e-mail to your buyers. Changing these options does not affect the information for the listings that you have already created in Seller's Assistant.

Can I create a new listing by duplicating an existing one?

✔ Yes. Click the Multiview tab to view all of your listings in Seller's Assistant. Select the listing that you want to duplicate. Click File and then Duplicate Listing. As soon as you have duplicated a listing, you can click the Details tab for that listing and edit the title, description, pricing, and other information.

How do I import my existing listings into Seller's Assistant?

✔ Click File, Import, and then Import from eBay Listings. A window opens that enables you to specify a date range. You can retrieve listings that are up to 29 days old.

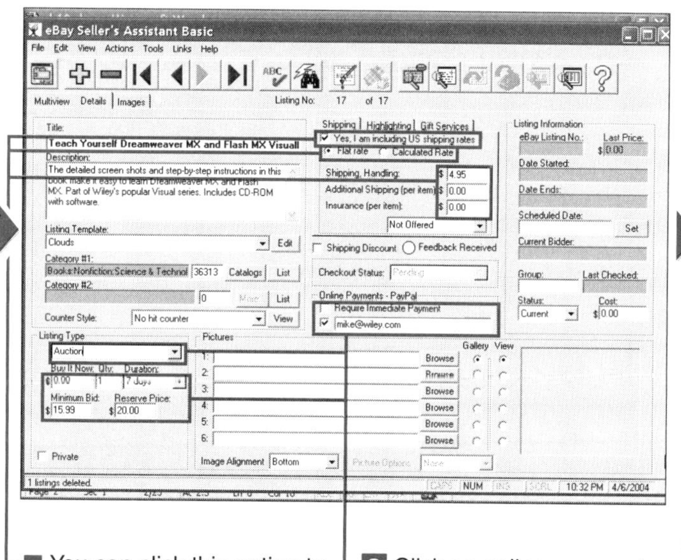

■ You can click this option to include U.S. shipping rates.

■ You can click this option to specify a flat rate or a calculated rate.

8 Type your shipping fees.

9 Click an online payment option.

10 Specify your listing type.

11 Specify your price, quantity, and duration information.

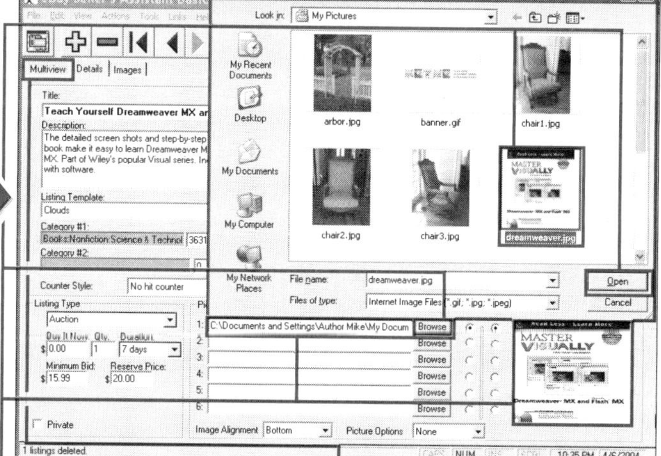

12 Click Browse to add a photo to your listing.

13 Click a photo file on your computer, and click Open to add the photo.

■ The file path appears, and a preview image appears.

■ You can repeat steps 12 and 13 for additional photos.

14 Click the Multiview tab to return to the overview screen displaying your listings.

PREVIEW AND UPLOAD A LISTING WITH SELLER'S ASSISTANT

After you create a listing in Seller's Assistant, you can preview it and then upload it to the eBay Web site.

Previewing your listing enables you to see how the description will appear online through a Web browser. If you have selected one of the Seller's Assistant templates, previewing will display the font styles and background colors as they are defined by the template.

If you have included images in your description using HTML code, those images will appear in the preview. For more information about this, see Chapter 21. If you are adding photos using eBay Picture Services, there will be placeholder text showing where the photos will appear.

Above the preview area, Seller's Assistant lists the information associated with the listing, including the format, price, shipping costs (if you have specified them), and any listing upgrades you have selected. Below the preview area are listed the fees associated with the listing. After you have double-checked the listing information, you can submit the listing to the eBay site. You can edit your listing information by closing the preview window and making changes in the Details panel.

PREVIEW AND UPLOAD A LISTING WITH SELLER'S ASSISTANT

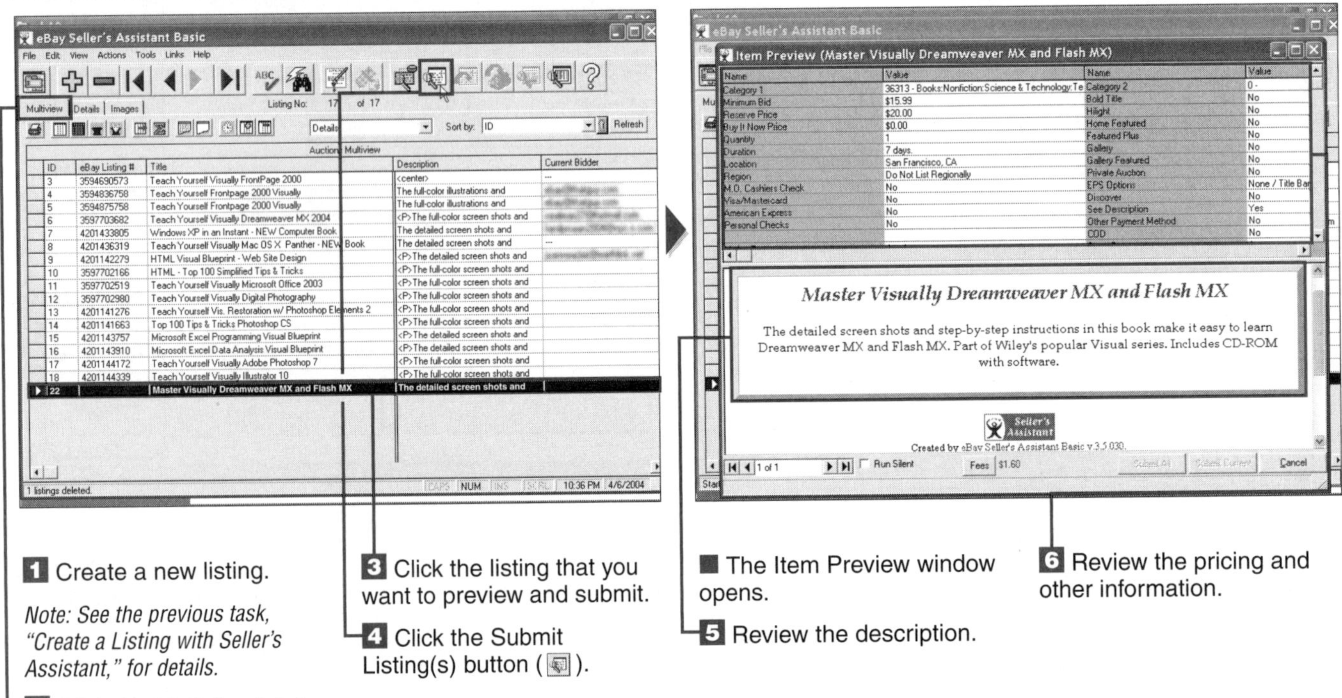

1 Create a new listing.

Note: See the previous task, "Create a Listing with Seller's Assistant," for details.

2 Click the Multiview tab to view all of your listings.

3 Click the listing that you want to preview and submit.

4 Click the Submit Listing(s) button ( ).

■ The Item Preview window opens.

5 Review the description.

6 Review the pricing and other information.

How do I submit multiple listings at the same time?

✔ You can select multiple listings in the Multiview window by pressing Ctrl while clicking each listing you want to submit. Clicking the Submit Listings button ( ) opens the preview window and allows you to cycle through the previews for the different listings by clicking the controls at the bottom-left corner of the window (, , , and). You can click Submit All to submit all of the listings at the same time, or click Submit Current to submit them one at a time.

How do I preview a listing without submitting it?

✔ Select the listing in Multiview and click the Preview from Local Drive button ( ).

How do I view the listing that I have submitted on eBay?

✔ You can select a listing in the Multiview window, click View, and then click Current Listing at eBay to open a browser window with the listing displayed. You can also right-click the listing in the Multiview window.

How do I schedule a listing to start sometime in the future?

✔ On the right side of the Details window for the listing, click the Set button under Scheduled Date to open a window that allows you to specify a start date and time. Note that starting a listing in the future instead of immediately after submission is an upgrade feature, and costs 10 cents.

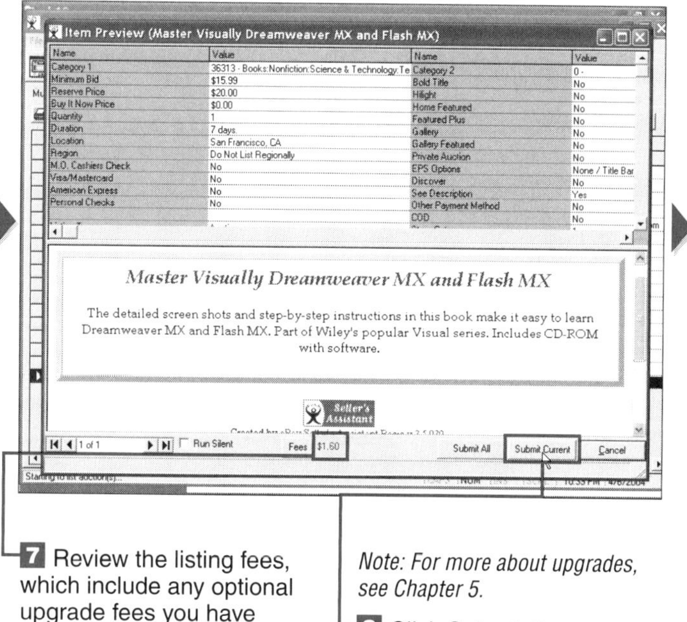

7 Review the listing fees, which include any optional upgrade fees you have selected.

Note: For more about upgrades, see Chapter 5.

8 Click Submit Current.

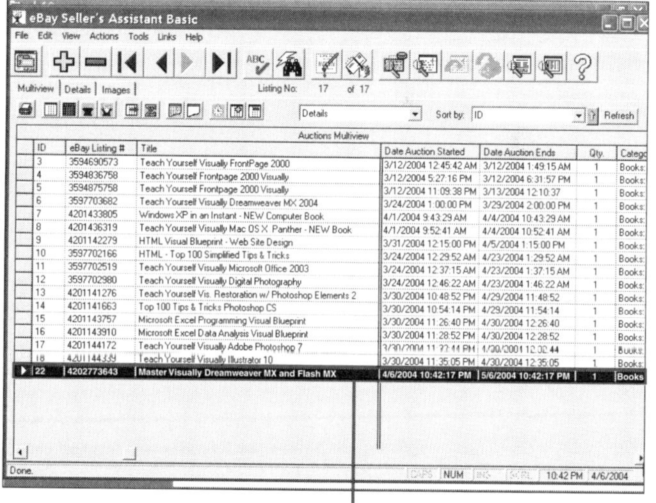

■ Seller's Assistant submits the listing to eBay.

■ An eBay listing number appears for the submitted listing.

PROCESS A COMPLETED LISTING WITH SELLER'S ASSISTANT

Seller's Assistant offers a number of features that can help you manage the tasks that are necessary after a listing has ended successfully. This includes keeping track of when you inform buyers of their status, when you receive payment, when a payment has cleared, and whether you have left feedback for a transaction.

One handy feature of Seller's Assistant is that it includes e-mail functionality that enables you to send e-mail messages to the winning bidder from within the program. This includes sending e-mail to notify buyers that they are the winning bidders, that their payments have been received, or that their listing items have been shipped.

The Seller's Assistant can either send e-mail messages directly through your ISP's mail server, or it can work in conjunction with stand-alone e-mail programs such as Microsoft Outlook. You specify how the e-mail messages should be handled in the Seller's Assistant Options window. You can also specify the text for your generic notification e-mail messages through the Options window.

Information entered about a listing in the Post-Listing Processing window — such as when you have notified a buyer about payment received or an item shipped — also appears in fields in the Multiview window, allowing you to check on the status of completed listings at a glance.

PROCESS A COMPLETED LISTING WITH SELLER'S ASSISTANT

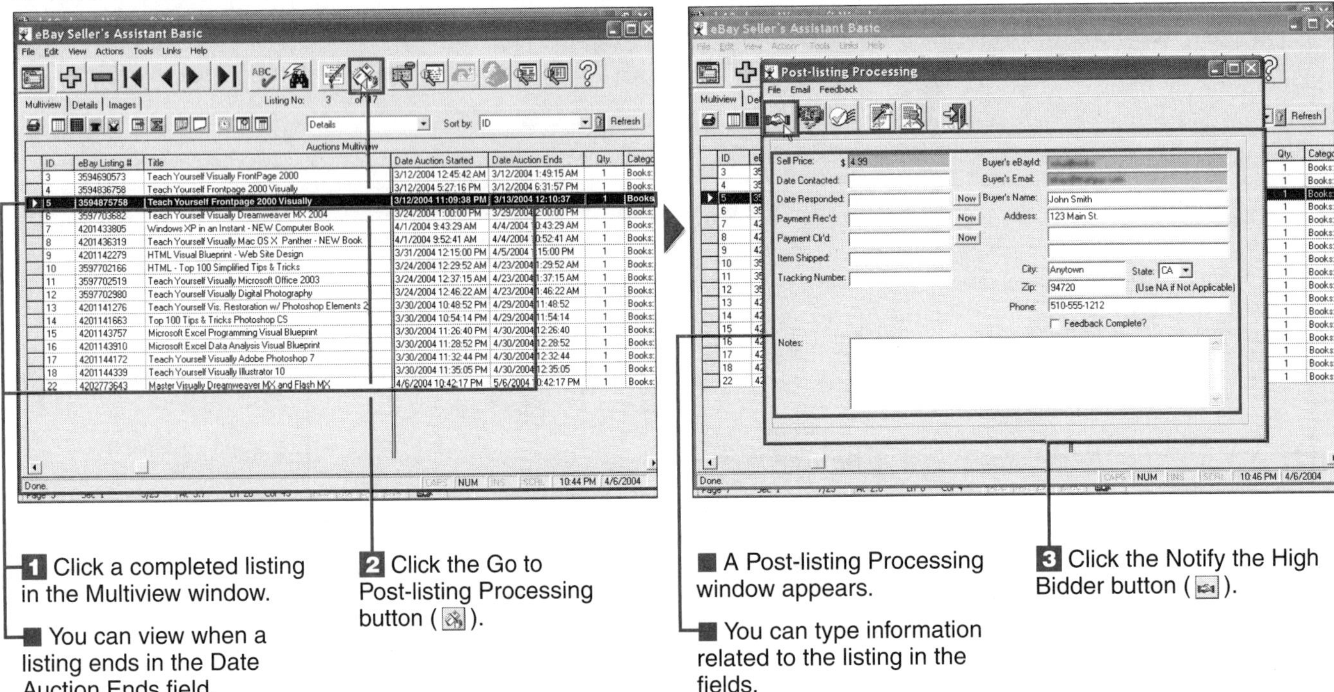

1 Click a completed listing in the Multiview window.

■ You can view when a listing ends in the Date Auction Ends field.

2 Click the Go to Post-listing Processing button ( ).

■ A Post-listing Processing window appears.

■ You can type information related to the listing in the fields.

3 Click the Notify the High Bidder button ( ).

How can I notify buyers that they did not meet the reserve price?

✔ If the reserve price is not met, an extra Reserve Not Met button ( ) appears at the top of the Post-Listing Notification window. You can click it to send a customized message to the high bidder saying that he or she did not meet the reserve price for the auction. If you decide to sell the item to the high bidder anyway, you can click the Notify High Bidder button ( ), just as you would for an auction where the reserve price is met.

What happens after I send a shipment notification?

✔ After you send a shipment notice for a listing in Seller's Assistant, the program offers to perform cleanup tasks for the listing. This includes deleting photos for the listing off of your local hard drive, leaving feedback for the customer, and archiving the listing. After you archive a listing, it will not be shown in the regular Multiview window. You can view archived listings by selecting the Archived Listings command under the View menu.

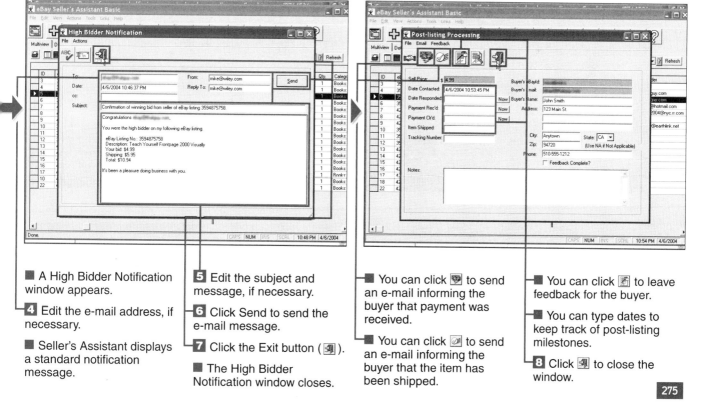

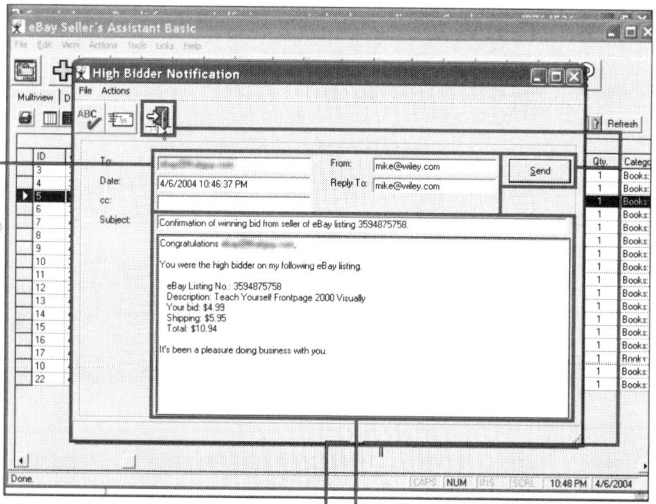

■ A High Bidder Notification window appears.

4 Edit the e-mail address, if necessary.

■ Seller's Assistant displays a standard notification message.

5 Edit the subject and message, if necessary.

6 Click Send to send the e-mail message.

7 Click the Exit button ( ).

■ The High Bidder Notification window closes.

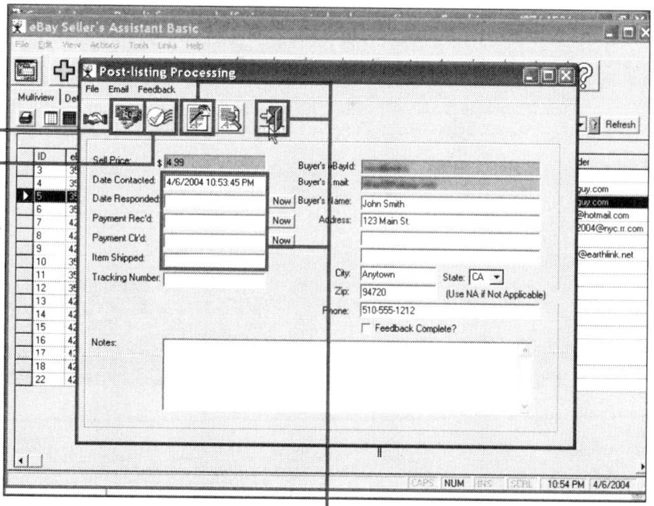

■ You can click to send an e-mail informing the buyer that payment was received.

■ You can click to send an e-mail informing the buyer that the item has been shipped.

■ You can click to leave feedback for the buyer.

■ You can type dates to keep track of post-listing milestones.

8 Click to close the window.

MAKE A BATCH UPDATE WITH SELLER'S ASSISTANT PRO

Often, you may want to change the same listing information for a number of listings in Seller's Assistant. Because doing this one listing at a time can be tedious, the Pro version of the program offers a batch change feature.

The batch change feature can be useful if you make changes to the categories of your eBay Store and need to revise the categorization for all of your listings. You can do this by changing the Store Category field during a batch change.

Another reason you may want to update several listings at a time is when postage costs change. The batch change feature allows you to update the shipping fees for several listings at the same time to reflect the new postage prices.

You can also make batch changes to listings that have already been sold. You can make these changes by clicking the Batch Change button from the Sales window. This can be useful if you are sorting through recent checks and money orders and want to specify the payment-received date for a number of items. It can also be useful if you have just made a trip to the post office, and want to specify which listings have had their items shipped.

MAKE A BATCH UPDATE WITH SELLER'S ASSISTANT PRO

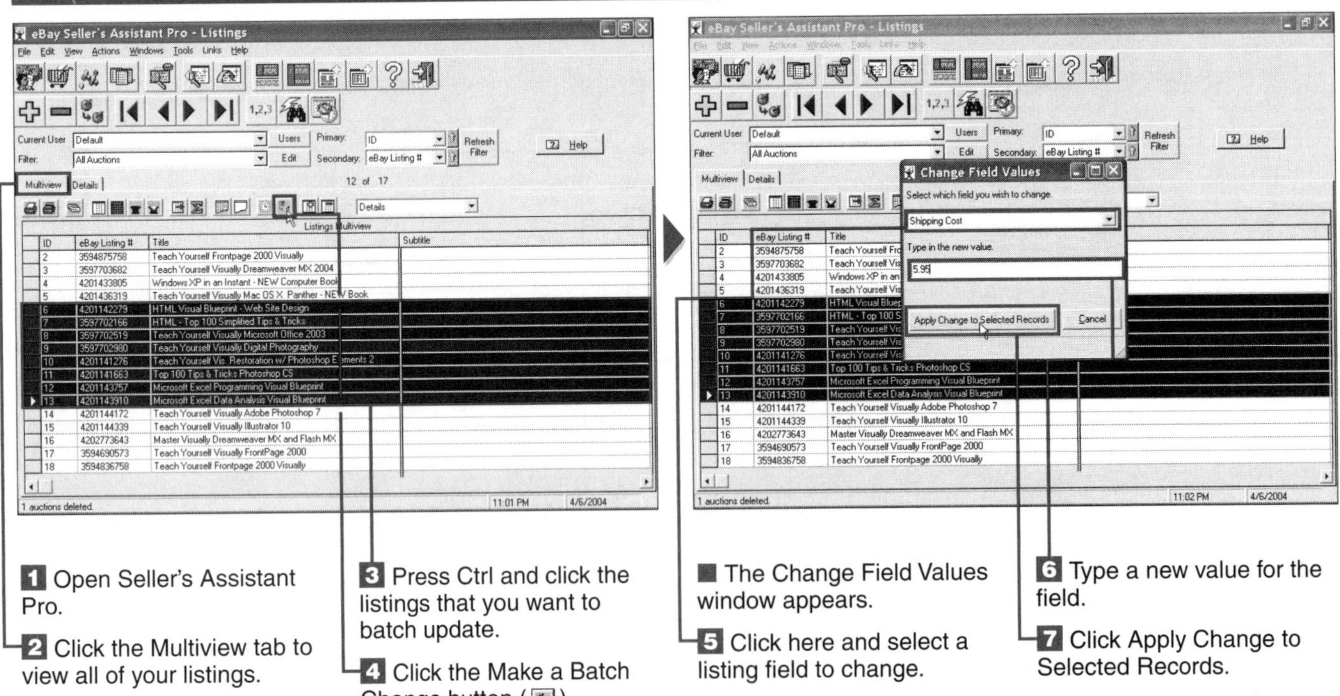

1 Open Seller's Assistant Pro.

2 Click the Multiview tab to view all of your listings.

3 Press Ctrl and click the listings that you want to batch update.

4 Click the Make a Batch Change button ( ).

■ The Change Field Values window appears.

5 Click here and select a listing field to change.

6 Type a new value for the field.

7 Click Apply Change to Selected Records.

How can I combine several batch processing operations?

✔ You can group several batch operations together in Seller's Assistant Pro using the *automaton* feature. For example, when you ship your items, you can start an automaton that can send an e-mail to notify your buyers that the item was shipped, set the status of each item shipped, and delete associated images. You can set up an automaton from the Sales window. Click the View the Sale Information button (), and then click the Edit button next to the Automaton menu at the top of the Sales window that opens.

How can I manage feedback for my listings?

✔ Seller's Assistant Pro's Feedback Studio enables you to manage the eBay feedback for your listings. Click to access it. You can create and save generic messages for positive, neutral, and negative feedback that you can send to buyers after a listing has been completed. The studio also lets you send batches of positive feedback to multiple buyers. Seller's Assistant does not allow you to send neutral and negative feedback in batches. You must send that feedback one listing at a time.

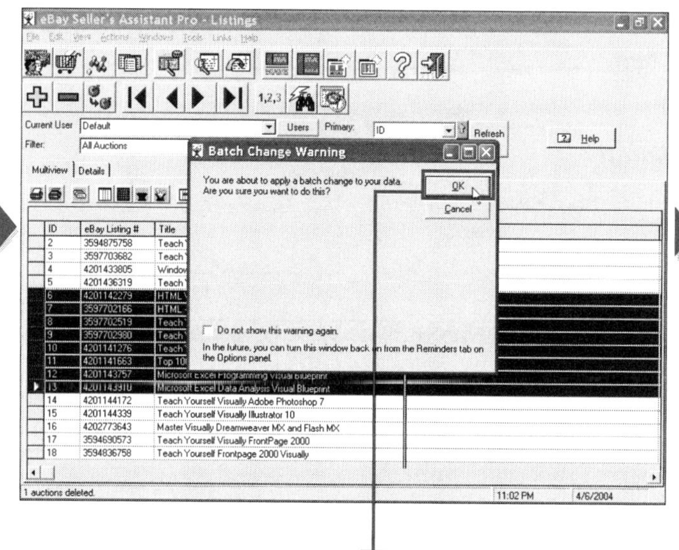

■ A Batch Change Warning dialog box appears.

8 Click OK to confirm the batch change.

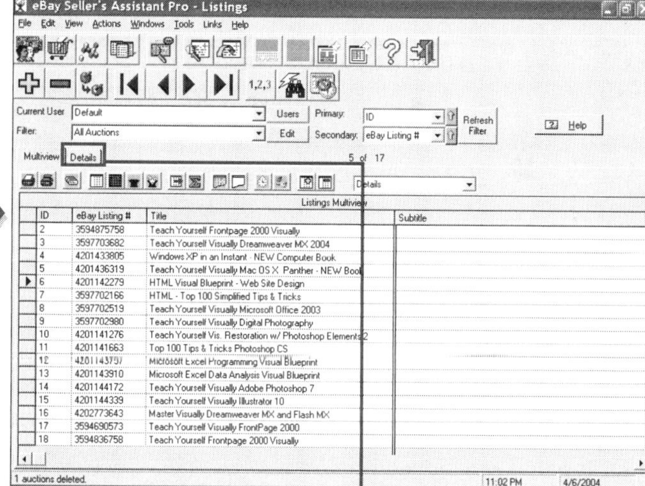

■ Seller's Assistant Pro makes the batch change in all the selected listings.

■ You can select a listing and click the Details tab to view the updated information for a listing.

CREATE A SALES REPORT WITH SELLER'S ASSISTANT PRO

One of the added features that Seller's Assistant Pro offers over the Basic version is a set of full-featured reports that can be run on your eBay listings. You can run reports on all of your listings — including pending, in-progress, and completed listings — or just a subset.

The standard set of reports that Seller's Assistant includes can help you understand which types of auctions are generating the most profits; keep track of your sales dollars from month to month and year to year; and perform housekeeping tasks such as totaling the amount of sales tax you have collected over a given period.

If the standard set of reports does not include what you are looking for, you can create your own customized reports in the Reports Studio. By clicking the Design tab, you can create a new report from scratch or make edits to an existing report. You can add fields to your reports by clicking and dragging items from the available database fields. Creating a custom report can be useful if you want to send a special order summary to customers along with each item shipped.

CREATE A SALES REPORT WITH SELLER'S ASSISTANT PRO

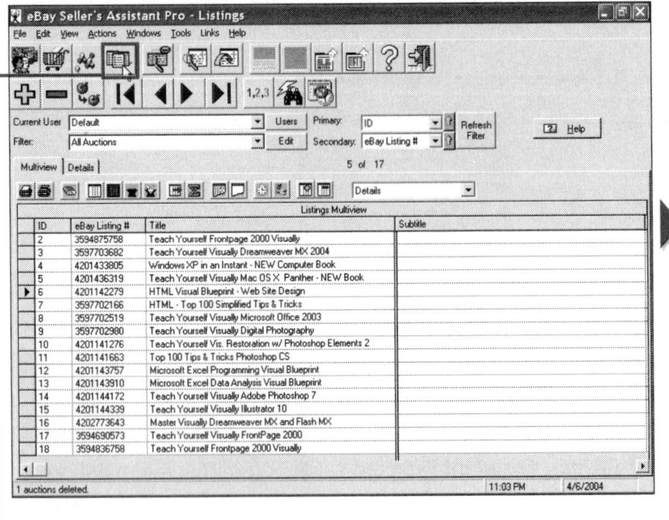

1 Click the View the Listing Reports button ( ).

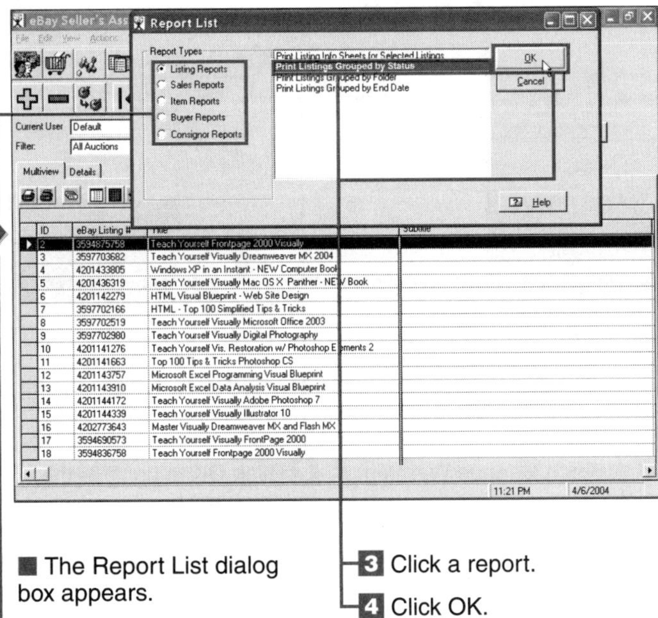

■ The Report List dialog box appears.

2 Click a report type option.

3 Click a report.

4 Click OK.

What listing reports are available?

✔ You can create the following listing reports in Seller's Assistant Pro.

Listing Report Name	Description
Print Single Listing Info Sheet	Displays all information for the currently selected listing
Print Listings Grouped by Status	Displays all listings within selected statuses sorted by status
Print Listings Grouped by Folder	Displays all listings within selected folders sorted by folder
Print Listings Grouped by End Date	Displays all listings within a date range sorted by end date

What sales reports are available?

✔ You can create the following sales reports in Seller's Assistant Pro.

Sales Report Name	Description
Print Single Sale Info Sheet	Displays all information for the currently selected sale
Print List of Sales	Displays information for sales within a date range sorted by end date
Print Sales for a Buyer	Displays all sales for the buyer of the currently selected sale
Print Profit and Loss Report	Displays an earning report for your sales based on the information from the Profit/Loss window
Print Tax Collected Report	Displays the sales tax you have collected

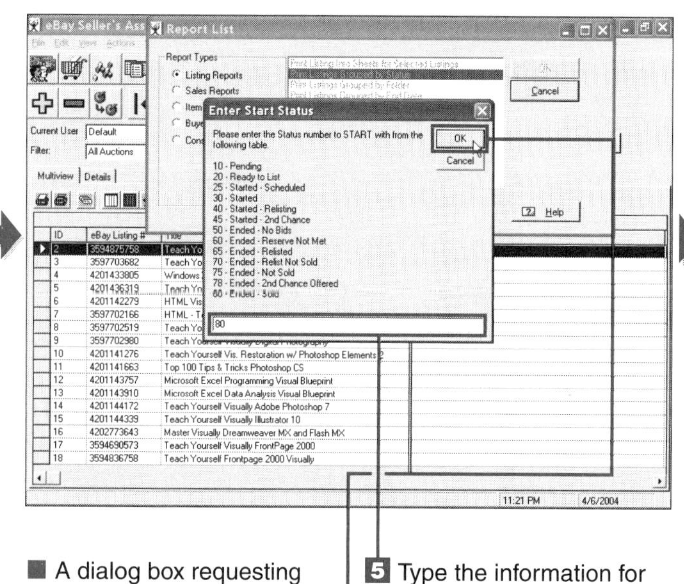

■ A dialog box requesting additional information may appear, depending on the report chosen.

5 Type the information for the report.

6 Click OK.

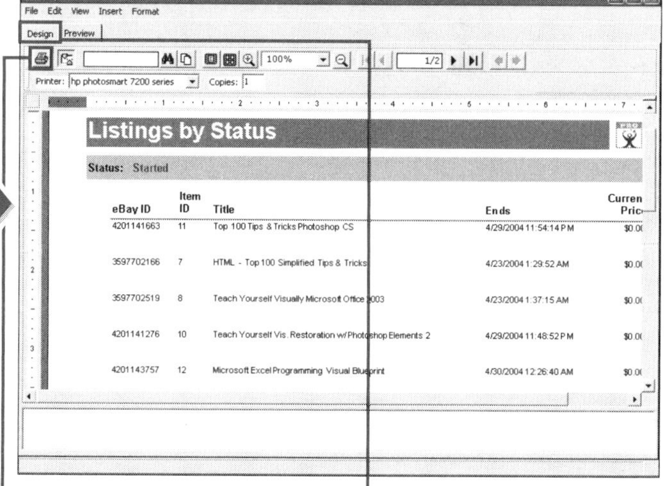

■ A Report Studio window appears, displaying the report.

■ You can click 🖨 to print the report.

■ You can click the Design tab to make edits to the current report template.

VIEW A SOLD LISTING IN SELLING MANAGER

If you sell more than ten items per month on eBay and prefer to manage your listings online, you should consider subscribing to Selling Manager, eBay's online tool that tracks and manages your sales after they have been listed.

Selling Manager shows you which activities you have completed for each of your listings and what you still have left to do. E-mail and feedback templates enable you to manage communication with your buyers more efficiently. You can also print labels and invoices directly from sales records.

When you subscribe to the service, which costs $4.99 per month, the Selling Manager interface is automatically available through your My eBay page. You can click the Selling Manager tab in My eBay to view it.

As an eBay listing progresses, it moves through the different pages in Selling Manager. The Pending Listings page displays items that have yet to go live. Active Listings displays items currently on sale. When a listing ends, it moves to either the Sold Listings page or Unsold Listings page. When you have finished processing a listing, you can move it to Archived Listings.

Selling Manager is a sales management tool, not a listing tool. You cannot create listings with it. You can use the free Turbo Lister software to create listings in bulk, or you can upgrade to Selling Manager Pro. See Chapter 18 for details about how to use Turbo Lister. See "List Multiple Items with Selling Manager Pro" for more about the Pro version.

VIEW A SOLD LISTING IN SELLING MANAGER

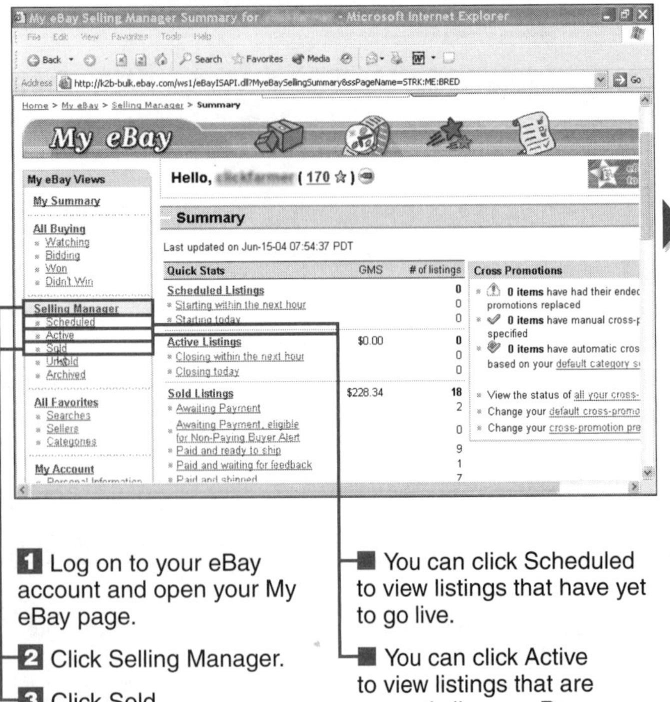

1 Log on to your eBay account and open your My eBay page.

2 Click Selling Manager.

3 Click Sold.

■ You can click Scheduled to view listings that have yet to go live.

■ You can click Active to view listings that are currently live on eBay.

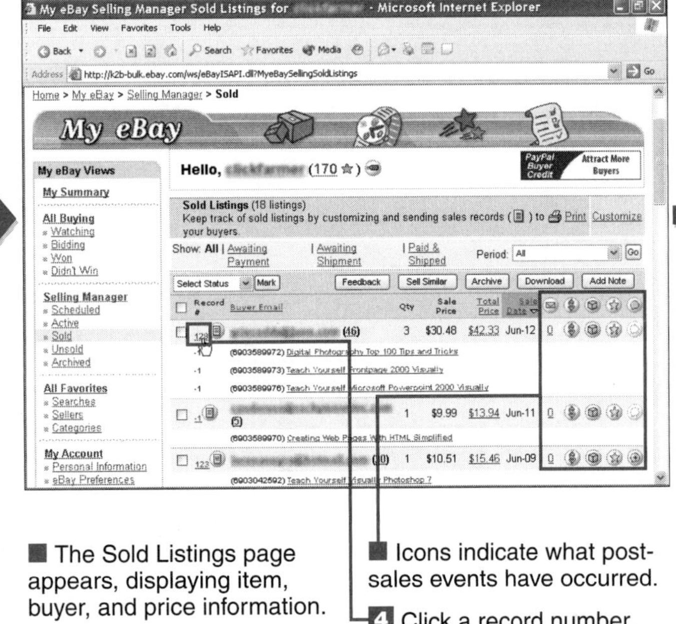

■ The Sold Listings page appears, displaying item, buyer, and price information.

■ Icons indicate what post-sales events have occurred.

4 Click a record number.

How do I subscribe to Selling Manager?

✔ Click the services link at the top of any eBay page. Click the Selling Manager link in the Listing Solutions section of the Services page. On the Selling Manager page that appears, click the Subscribe Now link. You can unsubscribe by clicking the Subscribe/Unsubscribe link on the Selling Manager page. eBay currently offers a 30-day free trial for Selling Manager.

How is eBay Selling Manager different from Seller's Assistant Basic?

✔ Seller's Assistant Basic is a desktop software program that creates and uploads eBay listings, and helps with sales management tasks such as tracking items, sending feedback, and e-mailing buyers. See the tasks earlier in this chapter for more information about Seller's Assistant. Selling Manager is an online tool that appears on a seller's My eBay page. Unlike Seller's Assistant, Selling Manager does not allow you to create new listings. Selling Manager is a newer tool than Seller's Assistant, and eBay is promoting it as a preferred alternative to Seller's Assistant. Both tools require paid subscriptions to use.

What do icons on the Sold Listings page mean?

✔ The icons represent different information about a sale.

Icon	Description
🛒	Checkout is complete.
$	Payment has been received.
📦	Item has been shipped.
☆	You have left feedback.
💬	You have received feedback.

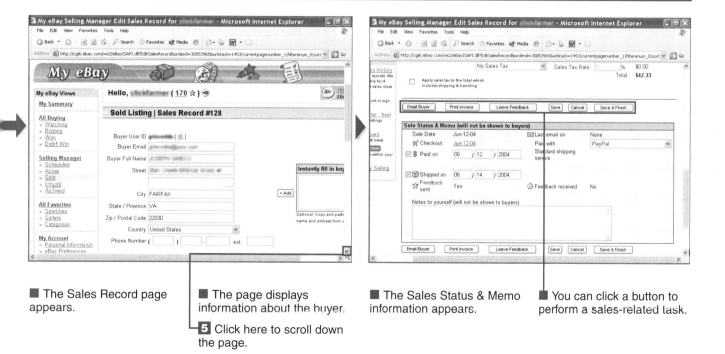

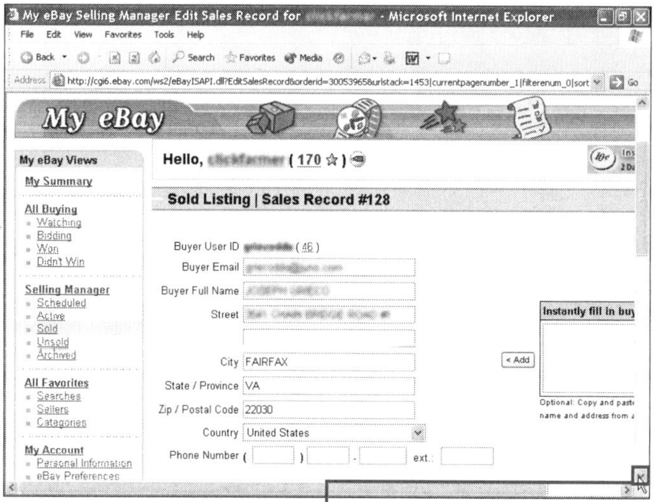

■ The Sales Record page appears.

■ The page displays information about the buyer.

5 Click here to scroll down the page.

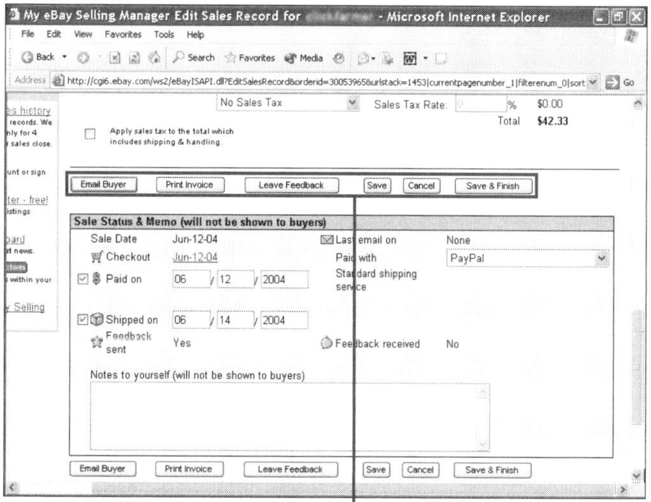

■ The Sales Status & Memo information appears.

■ You can click a button to perform a sales-related task.

E-MAIL A BUYER WITH SELLING MANAGER

Selling Manager allows you to e-mail your buyers from the sales record of a listing. The e-mail tool enables you to use message templates so that you don't have to type the same messages again and again.

Selling Manager comes with seven templates that correspond to common post-sales questions and tasks. These templates include Winning Buyer Notification, Payment Reminder, Payment Received Notification, Request for Shipping Address, Feedback Reminder, Shipping Notification, and Personalized E-mail. You can edit the templates to suit your preferences.

The Winning Buyer Notification informs buyers that they have won your item and can purchase it using the payment methods specified in your listing. The e-mail includes the URL for your listing, final price, and the mailing address where buyers can send payment, if applicable.

The Feedback Reminder encourages a buyer to leave feedback for you after the transaction is complete. Sending such messages can help you maximize your feedback rating and present an appearance of trustworthiness to future buyers.

For times when you want to start from scratch, the Personalized E-mail template includes empty subject and message fields in which you can type your personalized text.

E-MAIL A BUYER WITH SELLING MANAGER

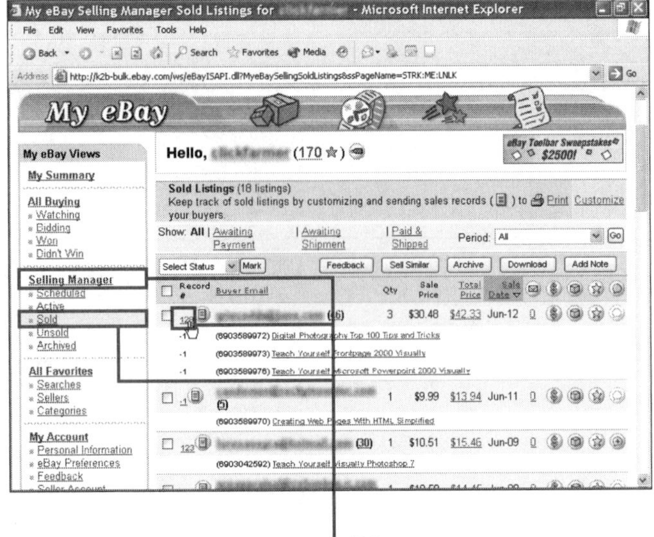

Note: To use this feature, you must already be a Selling Manager subscriber. See "View a Sold Listing in Selling Manager" for details.

1 Log on to your eBay account and open your My eBay page.

2 Click Selling Manager.

3 Click Sold.

■ Your sold listings appear.

4 Click a record number.

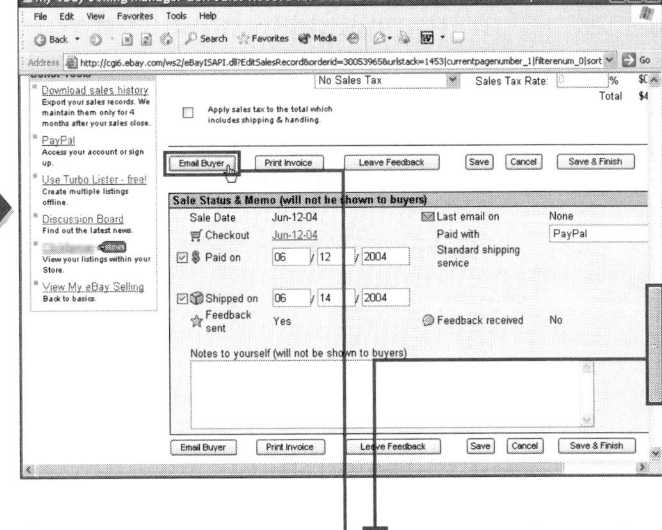

■ The sales record for the listing appears.

5 Click here to scroll down the page.

6 Click Email Buyer.

How do I automatically transfer information from my listings into my e-mail templates?

✔ You can use the AutoText feature in your e-mail templates to automatically insert the buyer's name, closing price, item URL, or other listing-specific text into the e-mail subject or message. You can reference such information using special variables inside curly brackets, for example, {BUYERUSERNAME}. You can easily insert this code by selecting from the AutoText menu, and clicking the Insert button. Click Edit Templates on the Email Buyer page to use AutoText.

Can I restore an e-mail template that I have edited to its default state?

✔ You can restore an e-mail template to its default state by clicking the Reset to Default button at the bottom of the Edit E-mail Templates page.

Can I send e-mail in bulk using the e-mail templates feature?

✔ If you are using Selling Manager Pro, you can send e-mail to as many as 500 buyers at one time from the Sold Listings page. To upgrade to the Pro version, click the Subscribe/Unsubscribe link on the Selling Manager information page at http://pages.ebaycom/ selling_manager.

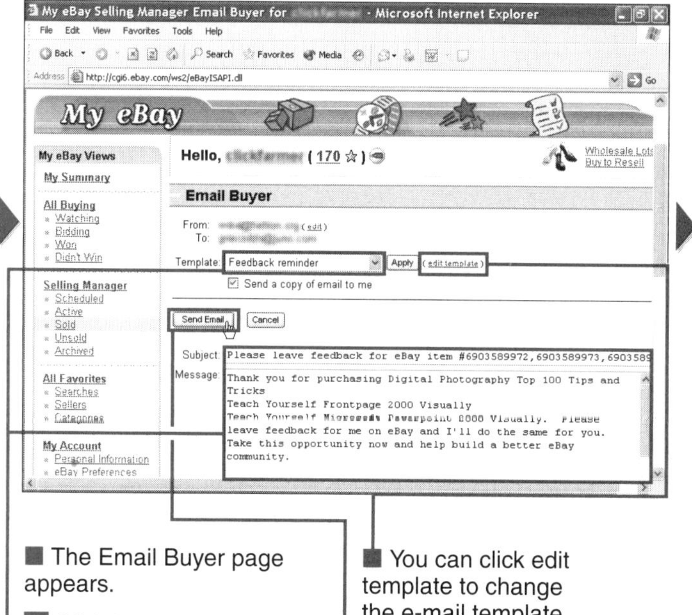

■ The Email Buyer page appears.

7 Click here and select a message template.

■ The subject and message text for that template appears. You can edit the text to change the e-mail message content.

■ You can click edit template to change the e-mail template.

8 Click Send Email.

■ Selling Manager sends the e-mail to the buyer's e-mail address.

■ The sales record appears with a confirmation of the sent e-mail.

■ In the Sale Status & Memo section, the Last email on date changes to the current date.

PRINT AN INVOICE WITH SELLING MANAGER

As a Selling Manager subscriber, you can print invoices to include with your shipped items or to keep yourself as a paper-based record of your transactions. You can also print shipping labels to affix to your packages.

Selling Manager allows you to customize an invoice by editing the template used to create the invoice. This enables you to insert the URL of your company Web site or eBay Store, if you have one. You can add a company logo or the graphic that appears on your eBay Store pages. You can also add a personalized message, such as thanking your customers and inviting them to buy again in the future.

The buyer name and address that appears on the invoice and shipping label is the same information that appears on the Sales Record page for the listing in Sales Manager. If you want to update this information, you can change it in the fields on the Sales Record page.

If you choose to print an invoice for your own records from the Print page, the invoice will include payment, shipping, and feedback dates at the bottom of the invoice, in addition to any seller notes you have added to the listing in Selling Manager.

PRINT AN INVOICE WITH SELLING MANAGER

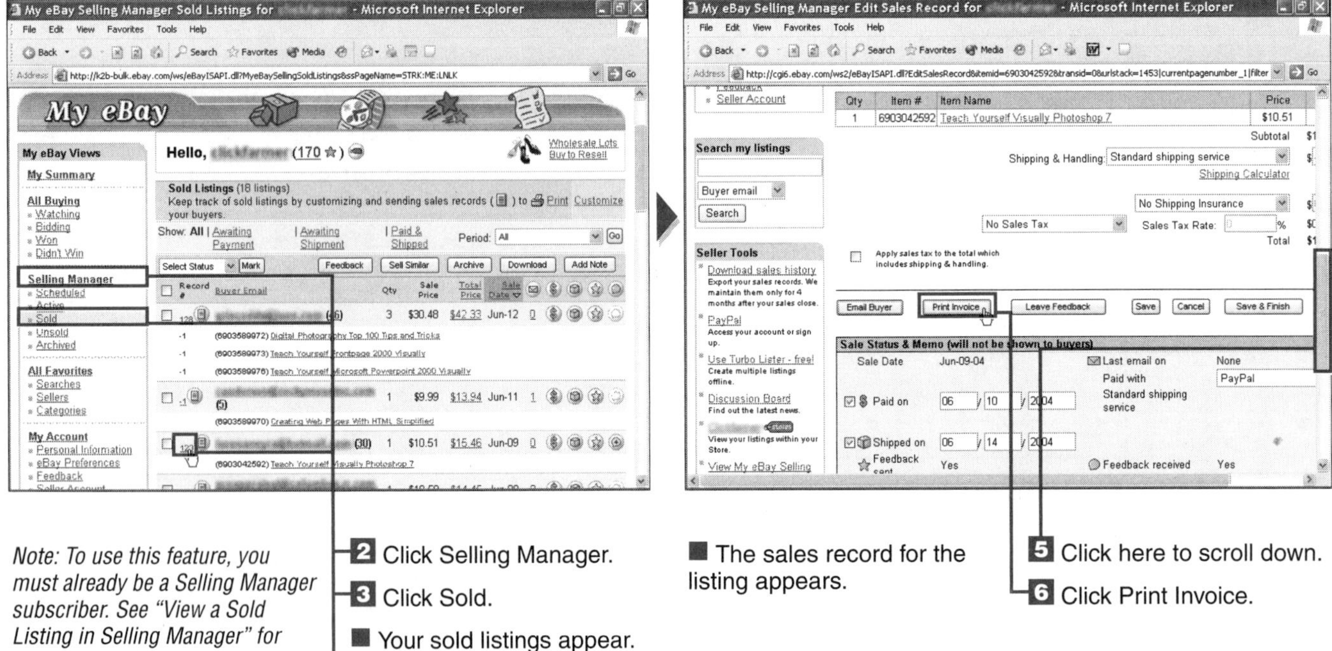

Note: To use this feature, you must already be a Selling Manager subscriber. See "View a Sold Listing in Selling Manager" for details.

1 Log on to your eBay account and open your My eBay page.

2 Click Selling Manager.

3 Click Sold.

■ Your sold listings appear.

4 Click a record number.

■ The sales record for the listing appears.

5 Click here to scroll down.

6 Click Print Invoice.

How can I pay for postage and create a shipping label with Selling Manager?

✔ If you click the US Postal Service postage or UPS shipping Label option (○ changes to ◉) on the Print page and then click the Continue button, Selling Manager transfers you to the PayPal site, where you can pay for postage and print a label for shipping through the U.S. Postal Service or UPS. You will need to know the weight of your package to be able to do this. For more information, see Chapter 10.

How can I make sure my invoices print properly?

✔ To print invoices properly, your browser should be configured to print background colors and images. In Microsoft Internet Explorer, you can do this by clicking Tools, Internet Options, and then the Advanced tab. Under the Printing settings, make sure the Print background colors and images option is checked (☐ changes to ☑).

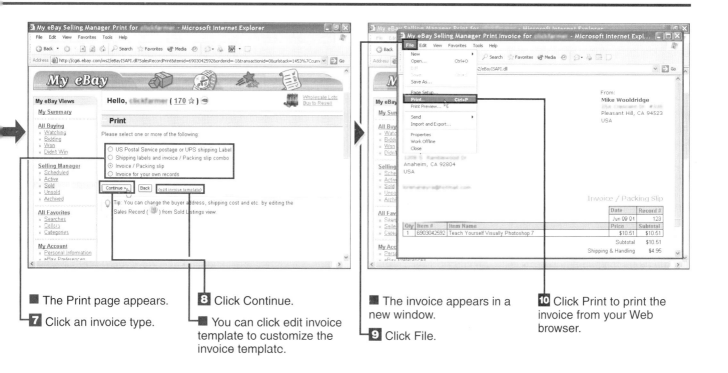

■ The Print page appears.

7 Click an invoice type.

8 Click Continue.

■ You can click edit invoice template to customize the invoice template.

■ The invoice appears in a new window.

9 Click File.

10 Click Print to print the invoice from your Web browser.

LEAVE FEEDBACK WITH SELLING MANAGER

Selling Manager enables you to leave feedback for your buyers from the sales record for a listing. Leaving prompt feedback for your buyers helps ensure that they leave feedback for you. Building your feedback rating on eBay is an important way to establish yourself as an experienced and trustworthy seller.

The feedback feature in Selling Manager allows you to store standard comments that you can leave for your buyers. This lets you avoid typing the same comments again and again. The feedback feature in Selling Manager comes with five standard positive comments already filled in when you subscribe. All of the comments in the feature are editable, and you can store up to ten comments at one time.

If you subscribe to Selling Manager Pro, you can leave positive feedback for as many as 500 buyers at one time from the Sold Listings View. Listings that have feedback successfully posted during a bulk submission have their feedback icon updated on the Summary page. Feedback messages that error during submission have an alert displayed on the Summary page. You can then try to send feedback for such transactions manually.

LEAVE FEEDBACK WITH SELLING MANAGER

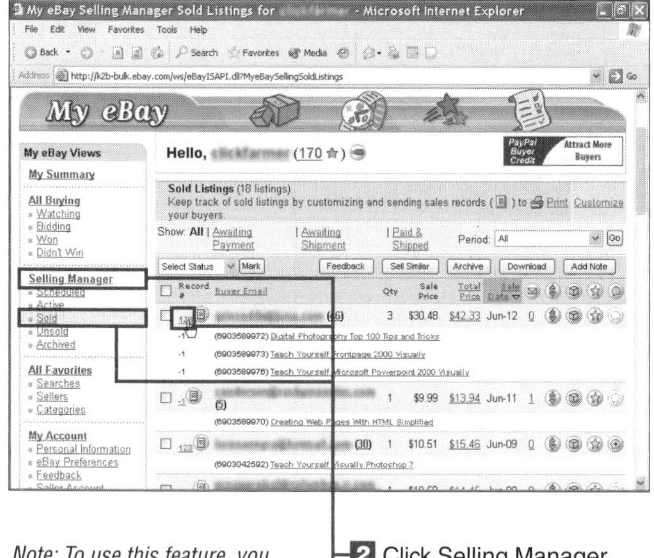

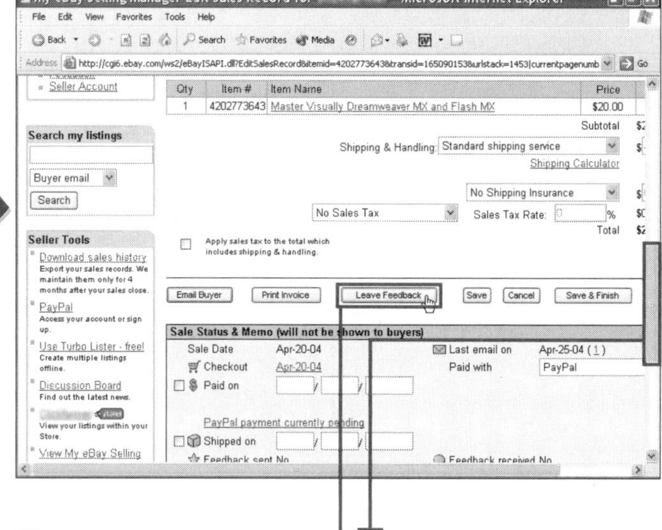

Note: To use this feature, you must already be a Selling Manager subscriber. See "View a Sold Listing in Selling Manager" for details.

1 Log on to your eBay account and open your My eBay page.

2 Click Selling Manager.

3 Click Sold.

■ Your sold listings appear.

4 Click a record number.

■ The sales record for the listing appears.

5 Click here to scroll down.

6 Click Leave Feedback.

Can I store neutral or negative feedback comments?

✔ No. You can only store positive feedback comments. If you choose to leave neutral or negative feedback through the Selling Manager, the stored comment option is grayed out and you must type a custom comment.

How can I tell if a buyer has left feedback for me?

✔ An icon (☐) appears in the Feedback Received column on the Summary page of the Selling Manager.

Can I leave feedback for a listing that I have archived?

✔ You can leave feedback for archived listings for up to three months after the listing has ended. From your My eBay page, click the Selling Manager tab and then the Archived Listings link. Click the record number for the listing, and then click the Leave Feedback button.

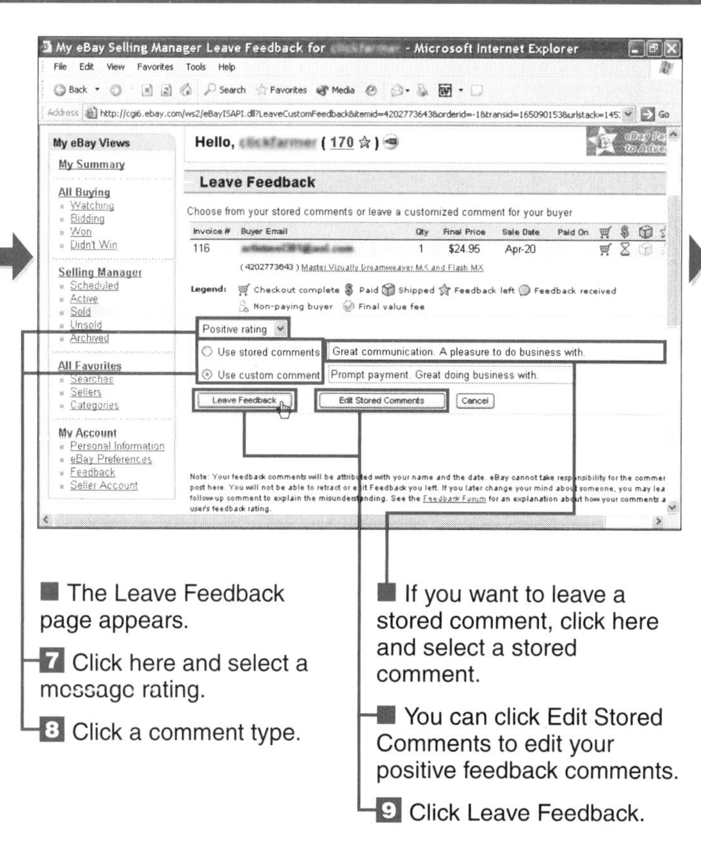

■ The Leave Feedback page appears.

7 Click here and select a message rating.

8 Click a comment type.

■ If you want to leave a stored comment, click here and select a stored comment.

■ You can click Edit Stored Comments to edit your positive feedback comments.

9 Click Leave Feedback.

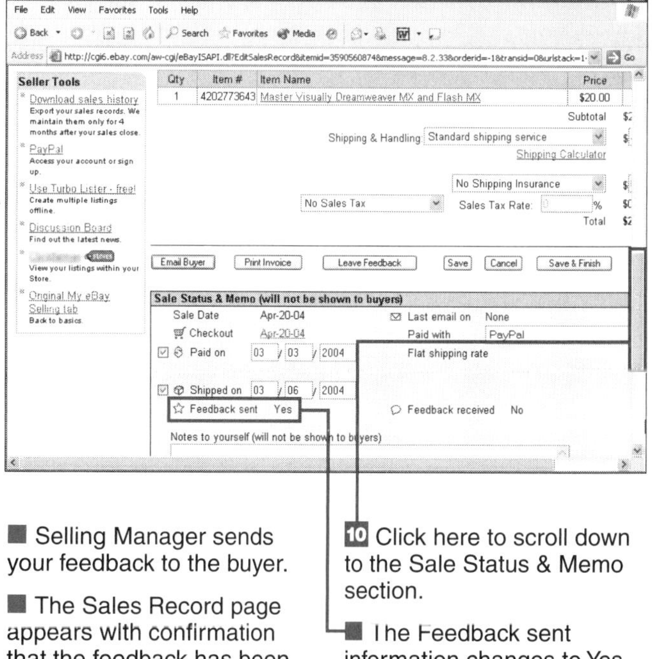

■ Selling Manager sends your feedback to the buyer.

■ The Sales Record page appears with confirmation that the feedback has been sent.

10 Click here to scroll down to the Sale Status & Memo section.

■ The Feedback sent information changes to Yes.

LIST MULTIPLE ITEMS WITH SELLING MANAGER PRO

Selling Manager Pro allows you to create multiple new eBay listings at the same time, saving you from entering the same information again and again each time you list. Bulk listing can be a real timesaver if you use eBay to sell large quantities of the same or very similar items. It is less useful when your listings are one-of-a-kind items.

Before you can bulk-list items, you must add those items to your inventory in Selling Manager Pro.

Adding items to you inventory is very similar to creating regular listings on the eBay site. After you create a product name for your new listing, you continue through the same pages where you describe your item, add pictures, specify pricing, and so on. At the end of the listing creation process, you save your item to your inventory rather than listing it live on the eBay Web site.

To use the bulk-listing feature, you must upgrade from regular Selling Manager to Selling Manager Pro. To upgrade, click the services link at the top of an eBay page, and then click Selling Manager under the Listing Solutions section of the Services page. You can also go to http://pages.ebay.com/selling_manager.

On the Selling Manager page, click the Subscribe/Unsubscribe link under the Selling Manager Pro heading on the right side.

LIST MULTIPLE ITEMS WITH SELLING MANAGER PRO

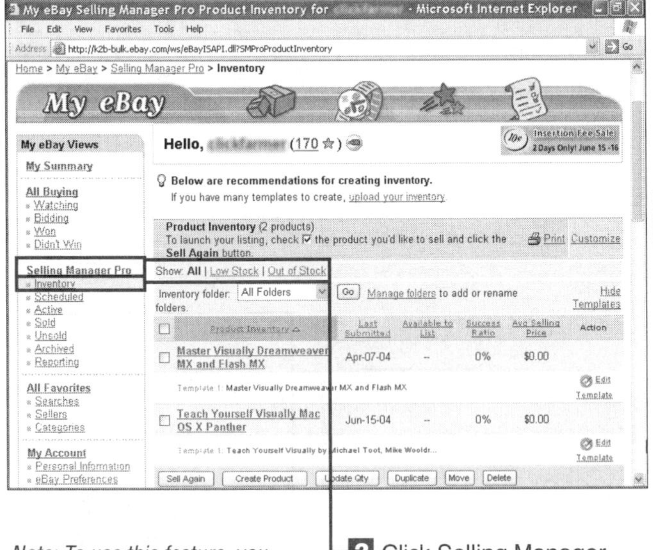

Note: To use this feature, you must already be a Selling Manager Pro subscriber.

1 Log on to your eBay account and open your My eBay page.

2 Click Selling Manager Pro.

3 Click Inventory.

■ Your inventory appears.

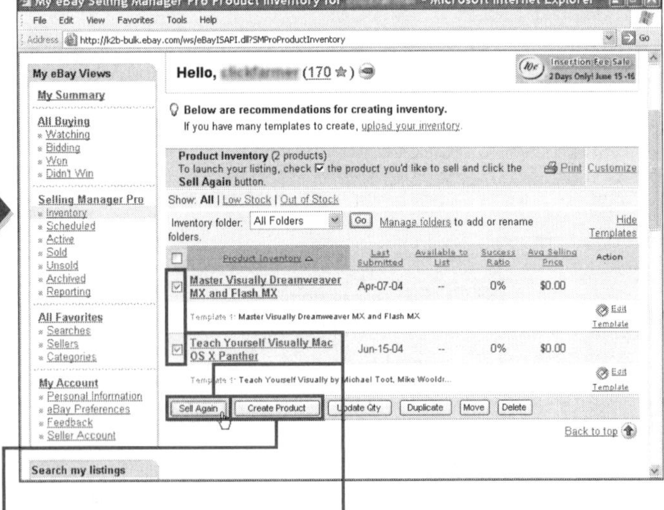

■ You can create a new listing by clicking Create Product, which is similar to creating a regular eBay listing.

4 Click to select the products that you want to list.

5 Click Sell Again.

How can I organize different types of products within Selling Manager Pro?

✔ You can create product folders in Selling Manager Pro, and organize the different types of products within your inventory inside those folders. When you start out with Selling Manager Pro, you are given a single folder named My Products. If needed, you can add additional folders as well as delete the original My Products folder. Click the Manager Folders link on the Product Inventory page to add, delete, or rename folders.

I've just created a new folder. How do I move an item into it?

✔ On the Product Inventory page, select the item you want to move (☐ changes to ☑) and then click the Move button. A Move Products page appears, where you can specify a destination folder.

How does the quantity value of a product work?

✔ When you create a new inventory item in Selling Manager Pro, you have the opportunity to assign a quantity value to it. This quantity value is decremented each time your product sells on eBay. You can manage the quantity value for an inventory item by selecting the item on the Product Inventory page (☐ changes to ☑) and clicking the Update Qty button.

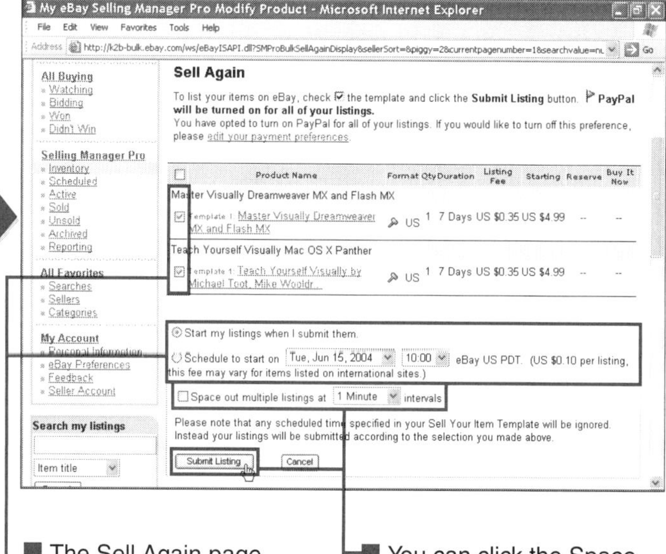

■ The Sell Again page appears.

6 Make sure the products that you want to list are selected.

7 Click an option to specify when the listings appear.

■ You can click the Space out multiple listings at option (☐ changes to ☑), and then click the intervals ▾ to set the intervals.

8 Click Submit Listing.

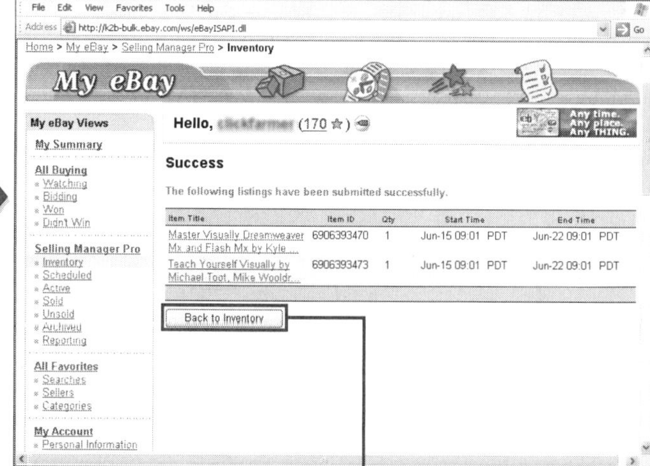

■ A Success page appears confirming that your listings have been submitted.

■ You can click Back to Inventory to list more products.

DISPLAYING PHOTOS IN YOUR AUCTIONS

Photos can appear in several places in your eBay listing. You can add one or more photos of your item to the description area of your listing, along with the descriptive text. The number of photos that appear depends on how many you submit to eBay, or on how many you reference in the HTML of your description. If you add photos to your description using eBay's Picture Services, the first photo added also appears at the top-right of your auction page in the preview box. This gives viewers a better idea of what you are selling when the auction page first appears. You can also have a miniature version your first photo appear in eBay search results by adding a Gallery upgrade to your listing.

Photo Hosting Options

For a photo to appear in your auction listing, it must be hosted on a Web server somewhere. eBay can host your photos on its servers if you use eBay Picture Services when you create your auction. With eBay Picture Services, the first photo for each auction is hosted for free. eBay charges 15 cents for each additional photo.

If you have space available on your own Web server, you can host your photos there and reference them using HTML in your auction description. See the section "Add a Photo Using HTML" in Chapter 21 for details on using this option. There are also third-party services that can host your auction photos for a fee. See the section "Upload a Photo to an Online Host," later in this chapter, for more information.

eBay Picture Services

eBay's Picture Services allow you to display up to six different photos with each listing. After you have added a photo to your listing, you can crop it and rotate it using eBay's online editing tools. To do more complex editing, you need to use photo-editing software on your computer.

eBay offers several upgrade options with its Picture Services. You can turn multiple photos into a rotating slide show; you can also supersize your photos, which allows a viewer to click a link to view a larger version of each photo. See the sections "Add a Supersize Photo to an Auction" and "Add a Slide Show to an Auction," later in this chapter, for more information about these upgrades.

Auction Photo Formats

When you display images on the Web, you should save your images as either JPEG or GIF files. Both file formats are supported almost universally by Web browsers. However, for photos of auction items, you should usually choose the JPEG format, because it can display millions of colors in a single image and is thus better suited for photographic images. GIF images can only handle a maximum of 256 colors.

If you are using eBay's Picture Services to display your photos, you have the added option of uploading images saved as BMP, TIF, or PNG files to eBay when you create a new listing. eBay reformats such files to JPEG before adding them to your auction.

Image Editor Options

The photo correction tasks in this chapter feature step-by-step examples using Adobe Photoshop Elements, a popular image editor. Photoshop Elements enables you to adjust lighting levels, shift colors, overlay type, combine several images into one, and more. Photoshop Elements is available for both PCs and Macintosh.

Some third-party auction management utilities also include tools that you can use to improve auction photos before you upload them to eBay. Auction Wizard 2000, for example, allows you sharpen blurry images, adjust brightness and contrast, and make rudimentary color tweaks. You can find a trial version of this program on the CD-ROM for this book.

Improving Photos Prior to Upload

Many times, having a clear, high-quality photo of your item in your listing can make the difference between getting top dollar for your auction and not getting any bids at all. If you're serious about selling on eBay, it's worth the expense and effort to acquire a decent image-editing program and learn how to use it to improve the photos you post to eBay.

By allowing you to adjust the lighting and colors in digital photos, image-editing programs help you bring out the subtle details of photographed objects and ensure your photos accurately represent the real thing. Image editors can also optimize the file sizes of photos to ensure that they download quickly for all of your potential bidders, no matter what type of Internet connection they have.

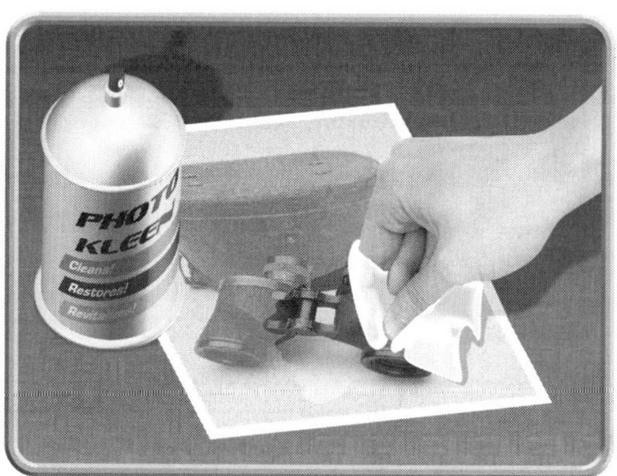

CROP OR ROTATE YOUR AUCTION PHOTOS

If you use eBay Picture Services to host your auction photos, you have the opportunity to crop or rotate your photos before they go live.

Cropping allows you to remove extraneous elements from your image so that the focus is on the item that you want to sell. You can crop by clicking and dragging the corners or sides of the small version of the photo that appears on the Enter Pictures & Item Details page.

Rotating allows you to switch your photos between portrait and landscape orientation. Portrait orientation is when a photo is taller than it is wide. Landscape orientation is when a photo is wider than it is tall.

If you want to make more advanced edits to your photos, such as lighting or color correction, you have to make them before you add them to your auction. Adobe Photoshop Elements is a popular program for editing photos taken with a digital camera or captured with a scanner. See other tasks in this chapter for details about using the program.

CROP OR ROTATE YOUR AUCTION PHOTOS

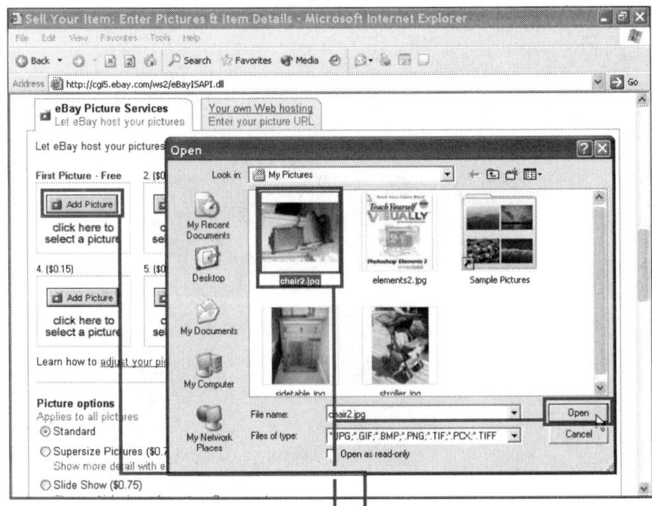

1 Create a new eBay auction listing.

Note: For more information on creating a new eBay listing, see Chapter 5.

2 If you have yet to upgrade to the full-featured version of eBay Picture Services, click the Upgrade link in the eBay Picture Services box to do so.

3 Click Add Picture.

■ The Open dialog box appears.

4 Click a photo to add to the listing.

5 Click Open.

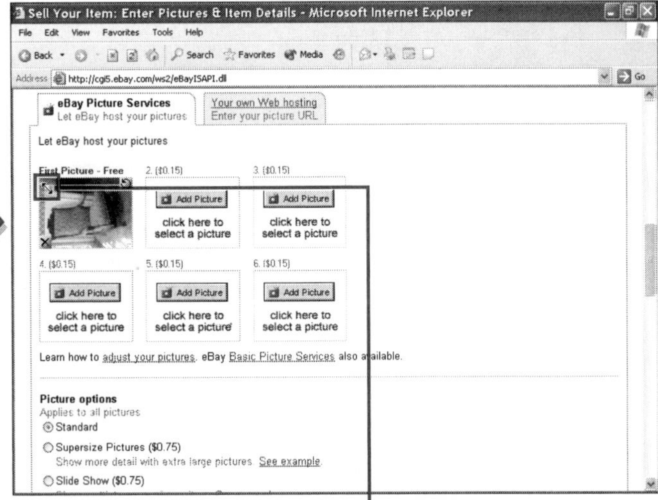

■ eBay adds the photo to your listing.

6 Click and drag the corner or edge of the photo to crop it.

My browser isn't showing the crop and rotate features. Why?

✔ The crop and rotate features are available with the full-featured version of eBay Picture Services. To use the full-featured version, you must have a PC with at least Windows 95 and Microsoft Internet Explorer 4. Macintosh users or users of the Netscape browser can use the basic version of Picture Services, which does not include the crop and rotate features.

Will my photo appear smaller on my auction listing if I crop it?

✔ eBay's hosting services will not display images larger than 400 by 300 pixels, and shrinks images that are larger to this maximum size. If your cropped photo is smaller than 400 by 300 pixels, the cropped version will be smaller than the original. If it is equal to or larger than 400 by 300 pixels, then it will be the same size as it would be if you hadn't cropped it.

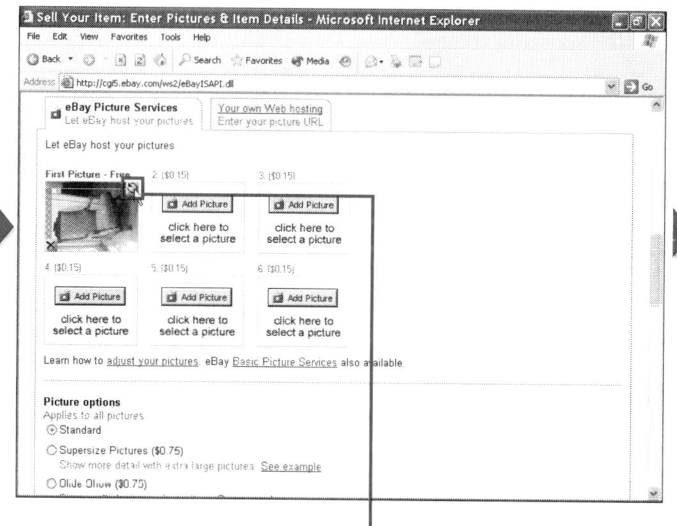

■ The part of the photo within the white box will appear in your auction description.

7 Click the Rotate button ( ).

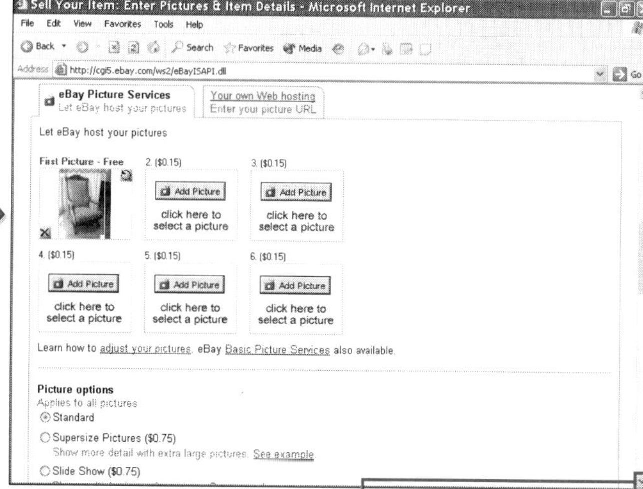

■ eBay rotates the photo 90 degrees.

■ You can click the Rotate button more to continue to rotate the photo.

8 Scroll down and click Continue to continue creating your auction.

■ eBay adds the edited photo to your listing.

RESIZE A PHOTO

You can resize an image to make it fit within the confines of your eBay auction listing. Scaling a photo down in size can also reduce the file size of the photo, and result in faster downloads for viewers. This can be important for people viewing your auction via slower dial-up Internet connections.

When you use the photo hosting service at eBay, eBay automatically reduces the size of large photos to 300 by 400 pixels. This is done to make sure auction content displays quickly. If you host your own photos, you can put photos that are larger than this limit in your auctions. However, it is a good idea not to use photos that are larger than 600 pixels in width to ensure that buyers can see the entire picture without scrolling.

Resizing involves changing the pixel dimensions of an image. Pixels are the tiny, solid-color squares that make up every digital image. Decreasing the number of pixels in an image decreases its size and scales it down on a Web page. Increasing the number of pixels makes an image larger.

RESIZE A PHOTO

1 Open Photoshop Elements, and then open the photo that you want to resize.

2 Click Image.

3 Click Resize.

4 Click Image Size.

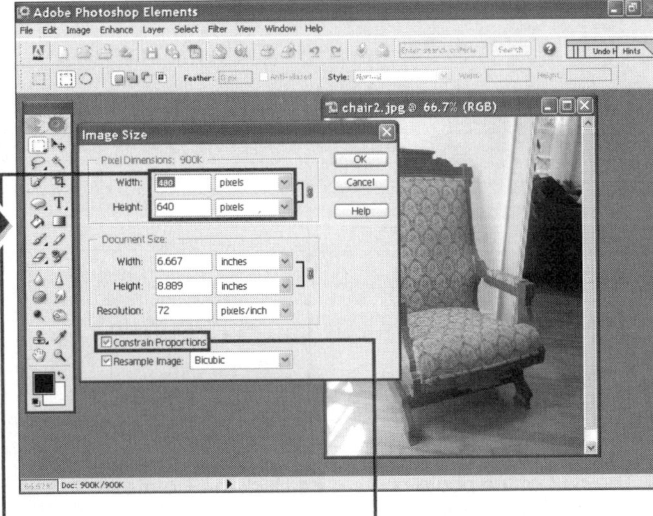

■ The Image Size dialog box appears listing the width and height of the image in pixels as well as other document size information.

5 Click the Constrain Proportions option to cause both dimensions to change proportionally as you resize.

What can I do to improve the quality of a resized photo?

✔ Resizing changes the number of pixels in a photo, which can add blur. You can offset this blurring in Photoshop Elements by applying one of the program's sharpen filters. Click Filter and then Sharpen to access them. You can also help ensure that your photos look good by not enlarging them. Enlarging a photo decreases its quality much more noticeably than shrinking it does.

What is the difference between the on-screen size and print size of a photo?

✔ On-screen size, which is the size at which a photo appears on the eBay Web site, depends only on the number of pixels that make up a photo. Print size depends on the number of pixels as well as the print resolution, which is the density of the pixels on the printed page. Higher pixel resolutions print smaller images while lower resolutions print larger images, given the same on-screen size.

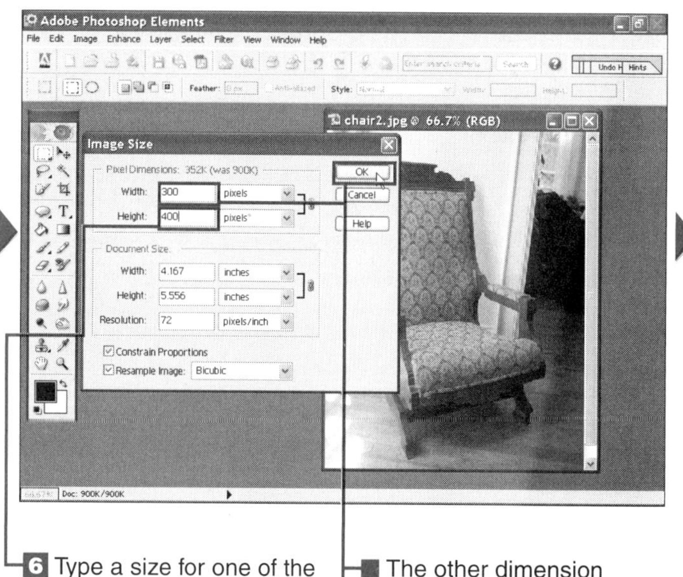

6 Type a size for one of the dimensions.

■ The other dimension changes proportionally.

7 Click OK.

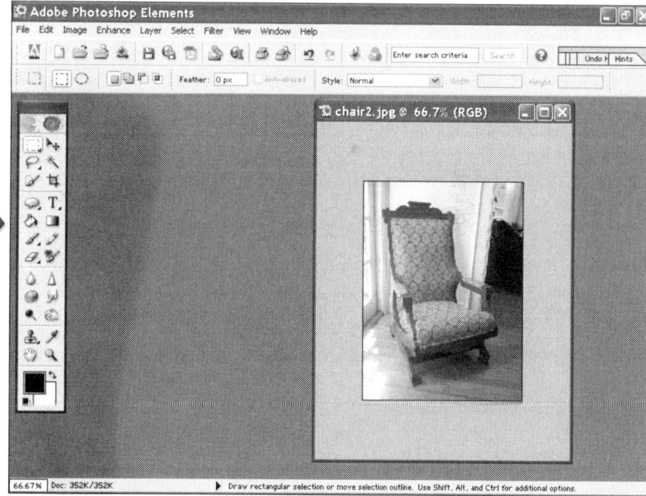

■ The image resizes.

Note: To save the resized image for use with your eBay listing, see the section "Optimize the File Size of a Photo," later in this chapter.

CORRECT LIGHTING IN A PHOTO

You can easily improve brightness, contrast, and other lighting characteristics of your photo by using the Levels command in Photoshop Elements. This can be helpful if you shot your photo in poor lighting conditions or you used a low-quality digital camera or scanner. The Levels command enables you to convert a dull, low-contrast photograph into a clearer, more colorful image, drawing out details that may otherwise be missed with less-than-perfect lighting.

The Levels command allows you to make individual adjustments to the highlights, midtones, and shadows of an image. When you open the Levels command, you see a graph that represents the density of the pixels in the shadow, midtone, and highlight regions of the image. Underneath the graph are three sliders that you can use to redistribute the lighting in the image and boost the contrast. Below these sliders is another set of sliders called the Output Levels sliders that allow you to reduce the range of shadow and highlight details, decreasing the contrast.

Clicking the Preview option in the Levels dialog box allows you to watch the lighting in your image change as you make adjustments.

CORRECT LIGHTING IN A PHOTO

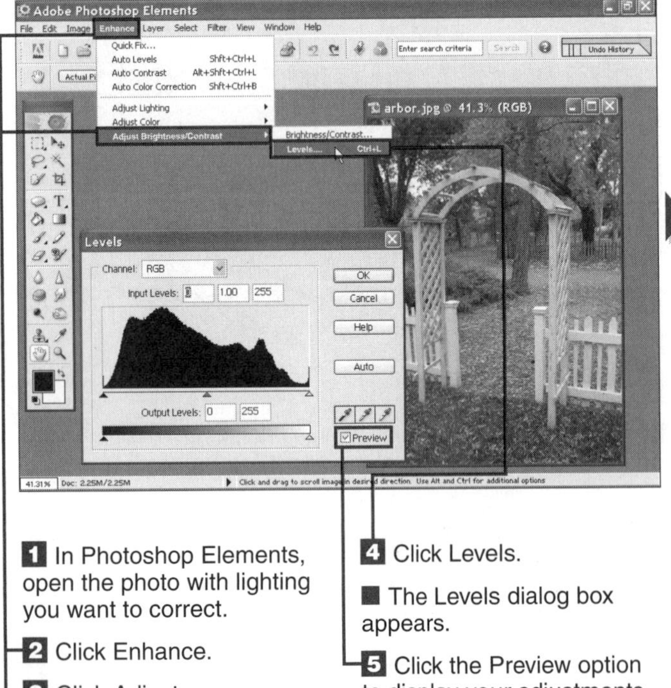

1 In Photoshop Elements, open the photo with lighting you want to correct.

2 Click Enhance.

3 Click Adjust Brightness/Contrast.

4 Click Levels.

■ The Levels dialog box appears.

5 Click the Preview option to display your adjustments to the photo as you make them.

■ You can click and drag the Input sliders to adjust the shadows, midtones, and highlights.

6 Click and drag ▲ to the right to darken shadows and increase contrast.

7 Click and drag △ to the left to lighten the bright areas of the image and increase contrast.

8 Click and drag ▲ to adjust the midtones in the image.

How can I adjust the brightness levels automatically?

✔ You can click Enhance and then Auto Levels in Photoshop Elements. The program converts the very lightest pixels in the image to white and the very darkest pixels in the image to black. This command is similar to the Auto Contrast command in the same menu and can quickly improve the contrast of an overly gray photograph.

What is the Brightness/Contrast command?

✔ The Brightness/Contrast command, which is located under the Enhance and Adjust Brightness/Contrast menu commands in Photoshop Elements, provides a less powerful way to adjust the lighting in your photograph. With this command, you have two sliders rather than the five in the Levels dialog box. It can be adequate if your photo has minor lighting problems and you want to make improvements quickly.

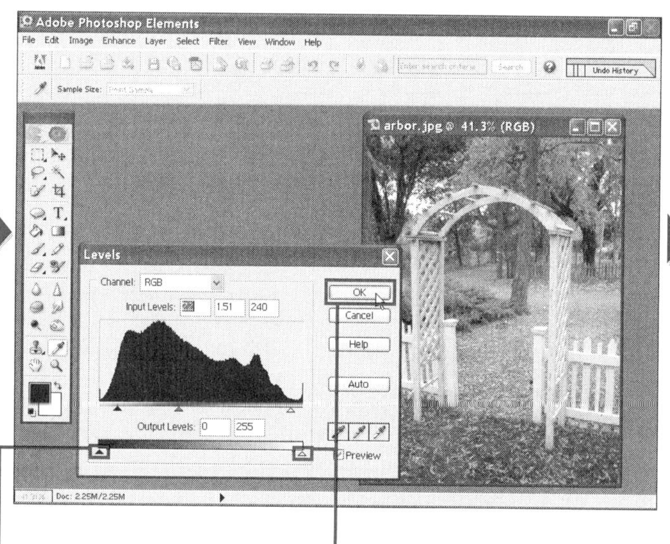

■ Use the Output sliders to decrease contrast, and to make the image either lighter or darker.

9 Click and drag ▲ to the right to lighten the image.

10 Click and drag △ to the left to darken the image.

11 Click OK.

■ Photoshop Elements makes the light adjustments.

CORRECT COLOR IN A PHOTO

You can quickly and easily adjust the color of a photo in Photoshop Elements by using the program's Hue/Saturation dialog box. This offers an effective way to intensify the colors in a washed-out photograph, or tone down parts of an image that is overly bright.

Changing the *hue* enables you to shift the colors in your photo to different colors in the spectrum. This can be useful if your photo has an abnormal colorcast due to poor lighting. Adjusting the *saturation* allows you to increase or decrease the color intensity of the selected object. You may want to boost the intensity of colors in your auction photos if color is one of the selling points for your items.

Adjusting color using the hue and saturation settings keeps the lighting and contrast of the object intact. There is no loss in detail, which means the objects in your photos remain crisp and clear.

CORRECT COLOR IN A PHOTO

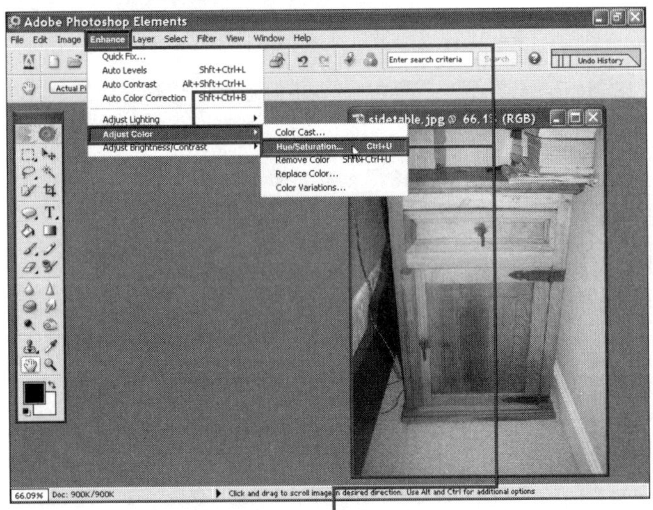

1 In Photoshop Elements, open the photo in which you want to correct the color.

2 Click Enhance.

3 Click Adjust Color.

4 Click Hue/Saturation.

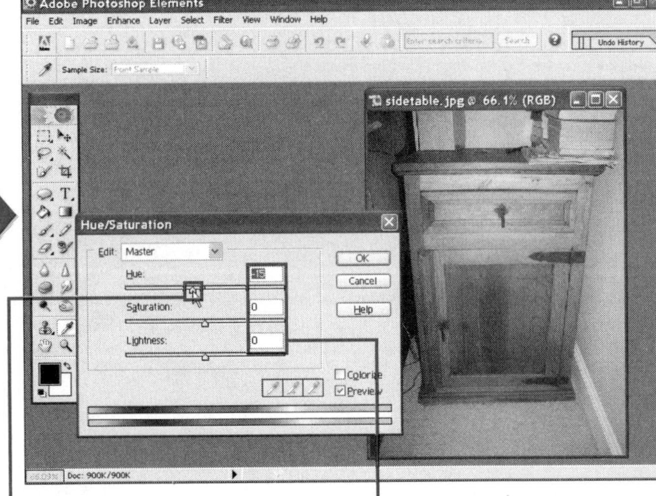

■ The Hue/Saturation dialog box appears.

5 Click and drag the Hue △.

■ You can also type a positive or negative number in the fields.

■ The colors in the photo change.

In what order do the colors change when I adjust the hue of a photo?

✔ As you click and drag the Hue slider (△) in Photoshop Elements, colors in your photo change according to their position in the color spectrum, which is also their order in a rainbow. This means that as you move the slider to the right, red colors in your image turn orange, yellow, green, blue, and then purple.

Is there another way to remove a colorcast in Photoshop Elements?

✔ Yes, you can use the Color Cast tool. Click Enhance, Adjust Color, and then Color Cast. You can then click the eyedropper that appears (↖ changes to ✒) on an area of the photo that should be devoid of color — namely, an area that should be white, gray, or black. Elements adjusts the overall color based on the tint of the clicked pixel.

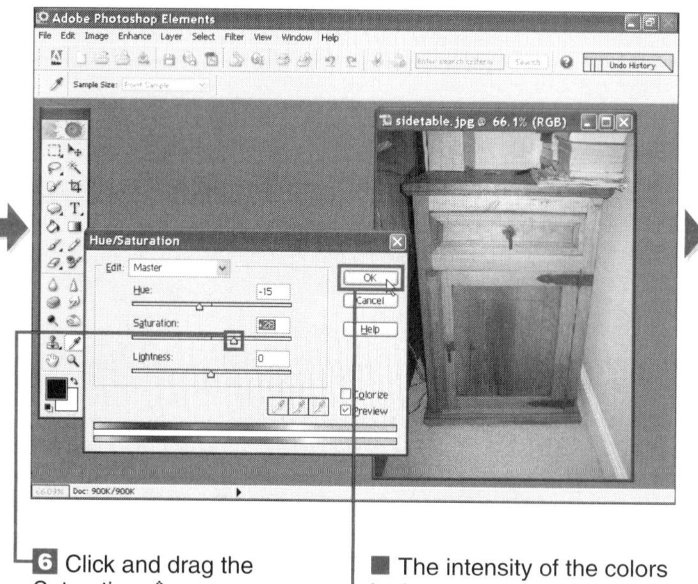

6 Click and drag the Saturation △.

■ The intensity of the colors in the photo changes.

7 Click OK.

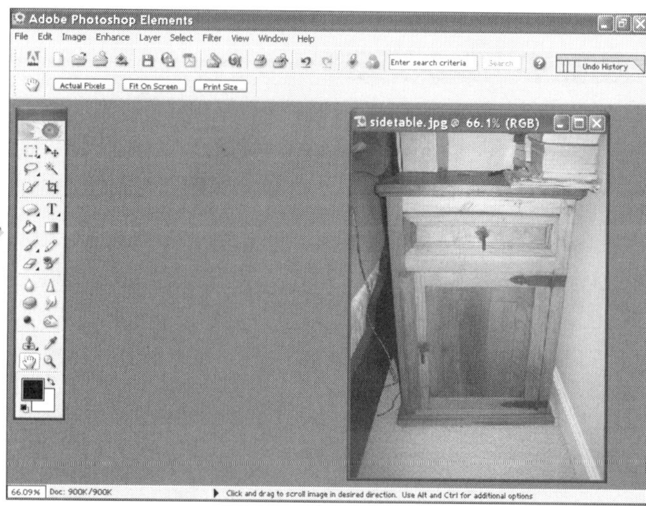

■ The color adjustment is applied.

ADD TYPE TO A PHOTO

You can add type to a photo in order to give it a title or to label objects inside it. The type tools in Photoshop Elements allow you to easily specify the color, font style, size, and other characteristics of type.

Adding type to an eBay auction photo can enable you to add your item description right on the photo instead of with accompanying HTML-based text. If you decide to add lots of descriptive text to your image, make sure it is large enough — at least 12 points in size — to be easily viewed on monitors of different resolutions.

Adding type can also be useful for distinguishing the pictures as your own, such as when you add a copyright symbol (©), for example. Adding such information can dissuade other eBay sellers from using your images for auctions of the same item.

When you add type to your photo in Photoshop Elements, the type is created on a separate image layer. This keeps it separate from the photographic content in your image, and allows you to easily reposition the type or change its color, font style, or size. You can also delete the type by deleting the layer.

ADD TYPE TO A PHOTO

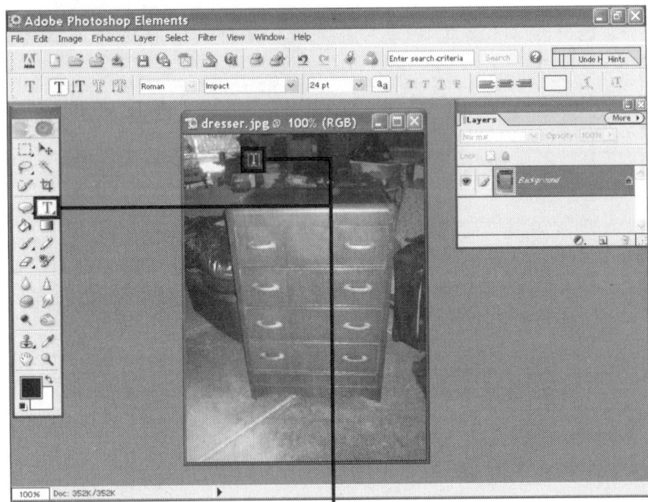

1 In Photoshop Elements, open the photo to which you want to add type.

2 Click the Type tool (T).

3 Click in the photo where you want the new type to begin.

4 Click ▾ and select a style, font, and size for your type.

5 Click the Color box to select a color for your type.

How can I edit the type in my Photoshop Elements photo?

✔ You can edit your type to change letters, words, or sentences by clicking the Type tool (T) and then clicking the type layer that you wish to edit. Then you can click inside the text in your photo and type new content or press the Backspace key to delete letters. You can also press the arrow keys to navigate within your text as you edit.

Can I reposition the type in my photo?

✔ Yes. Click the type layer that you want to move, and then click the Move tool (Move tool icon). With the tool, you can click and drag to move the type to a different part of the photo. You can press the Shift key as you move your type to constrain it in the horizontal or vertical direction. With the Move tool activated, you can also use the arrow keys on your keyboard to move your type layer in small increments.

6 Type your text.

■ You can press Enter to create a line break.

7 When you finish typing your text, click ✔ or press Enter on your keyboard's number pad.

■ You can click ⊘ or press Esc to cancel.

■ Photoshop Elements places the type on its own layer.

OPTIMIZE THE FILE SIZE OF A PHOTO

By optimizing your auction photos in Photoshop Elements, you can ensure that they download quickly and look good when potential buyers view them online. For most eBay photos, you want to save your image file in the JPEG — or Joint Photographic Experts Group — format. Because it supports millions of colors in a single image, the JPEG format is especially suitable for photographs and other images with continuous tones.

When you save a photo as a JPEG file, you specify a quality setting for the resulting image. The higher the quality you specify, the greater the file size of the image. This tradeoff allows you to balance the need for high-quality images against the need for smaller images that download fast.

The JPEG format is especially good at compressing photographic image information to create files that are compact. When saved in a JPEG format, a typical 1MB uncompressed TIFF image can be reduced to less than 100K. eBay recommends that you try to keep your auction photos at sizes less than 50K. You can reduce photo file sizes by shrinking the dimensions of your photo before optimizing. See the section "Resize a Photo," earlier in this chapter, for more information.

OPTIMIZE THE FILE SIZE OF A PHOTO

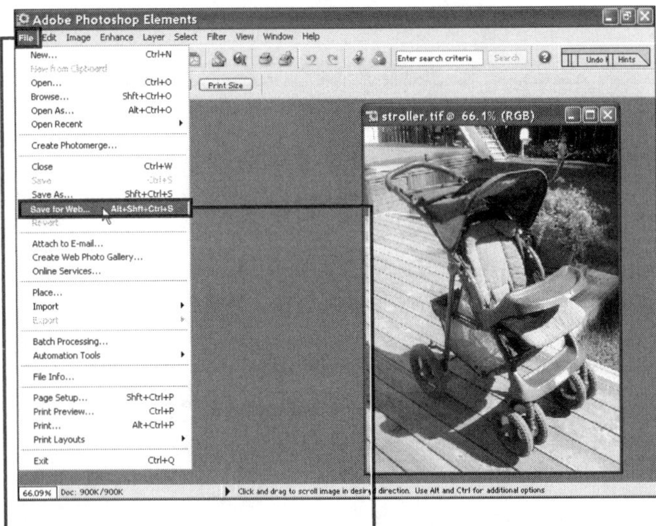

1 In Photoshop Elements, open the photo you want to optimize.

2 Click File.

3 Click Save for Web.

■ The Save For Web dialog box appears.

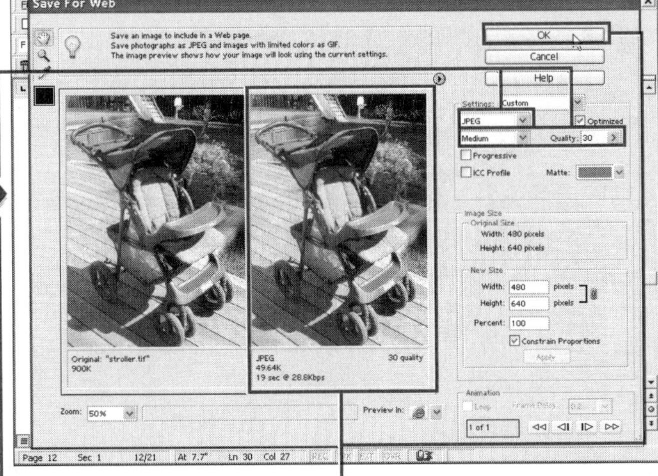

4 Click here and select JPEG.

5 Select a JPEG quality setting.

■ You can select a descriptive setting or a numeric value from 0, the lowest quality, to 100, the highest quality.

Note: The higher the quality, the larger the resulting file.

■ You can use the preview window to check that file quality and size are acceptable.

6 Click OK.

What is a GIF file?

✔ Along with JPEG, GIF is the other most common Web image format. GIF stands for Graphics Interchange Format. Because the format supports only up to 256 colors in a single image, the GIF format is more suitable for solid-color illustrations rather than photographs. You can optimize your images as GIFs by selecting GIF instead of JPEG in the Save For Web dialog box.

How does the JPEG image format compress my photo so that it has a small file size?

✔ JPEG is known as a *lossy* file format, because there is a loss of some image information when an image is saved in the JPEG format. How much information depends on the quality setting you choose — the lower the quality, the greater the information loss. This information loss can show up as blurriness in the final JPEG image. The blurriness, which is usually only slight, is the price you pay for having a small file size.

■ The Save Optimized As dialog box appears.

7 Click here and select a folder in which to save the file.

8 Type a filename with a .jpg extension.

9 Click Save.

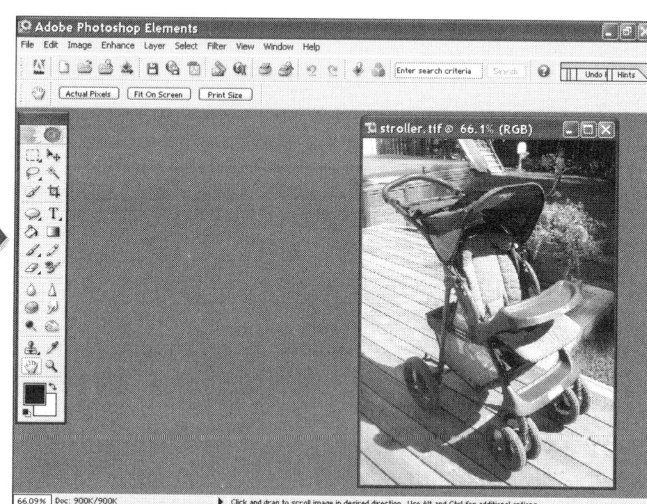

■ Photoshop Elements saves the JPEG file in the specified folder.

■ You can open the folder to access the file.

■ The original image file remains open.

CREATE A PHOTOMONTAGE

You can arrange several photos onto a single canvas to create a *photomontage*. This can be useful if you have several photos of an auction item that you want to merge into a single image file. Creating a single image file can help you save on listing fees because eBay charges extra fees after the first photo when you use its photo hosting service.

Photoshop Elements makes it easy to create a montage by enabling you to copy and paste images into a central image window, organize the pasted images into separate image layers, and move them relative to one another with the Layers palette and Move tool.

The first step to making a montage is to create the canvas on which to combine the different photos. The canvas should be large enough to accommodate all the content you plan to add to the montage.

As you copy and paste each of the montage photos into the central canvas in Photoshop Elements, each is automatically placed onto its own layer. This is convenient, because you can then move the photos independently of one another by selecting a layer and then moving the photo with the Move tool.

CREATE A PHOTOMONTAGE

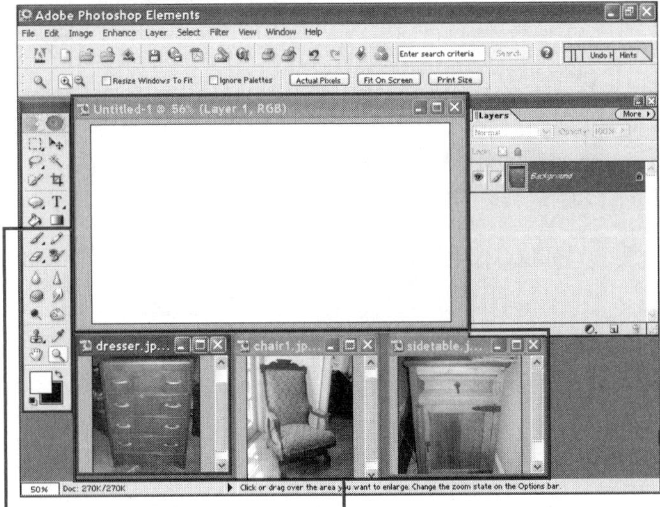

1 In Photoshop Elements, create a canvas on which to create the montage.

■ You can create a blank canvas in Photoshop Elements by clicking File and then New. In the dialog box that appears, you can name the canvas and specify the dimensions.

2 Open the photos you want to use in the montage.

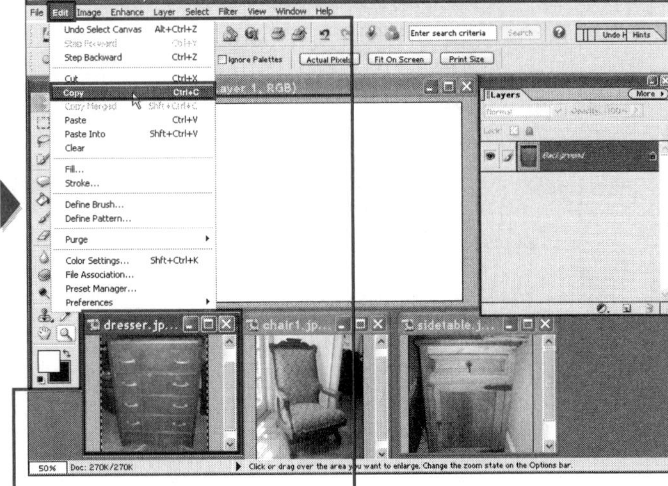

3 Click a photo.

4 Press Ctrl+A to select all the pixels in the photo.

5 Click Edit.

6 Click Copy.

How do I overlap photos in a montage?

✔ In the example, the photos that make up the montage are in separate image layers, which allows you to move them over and under one another. Overlapping the different layers slightly can give your composition a sophisticated, artsy look. Changing how overlapping photos are stacked relative to one another is as easy as clicking and dragging the different layers in the Layers palette. Click and drag a layer up to place it above other layers in the montage; drag it down to place it below other layers in the montage.

Can I add text to my montage?

✔ You can title or add text effects to your montage in Photoshop Elements by mixing type layers among the image layers. Type layers can be moved and shuffled just like image layers can. For more information about type, see the section "Add Type to a Photo," earlier in this chapter.

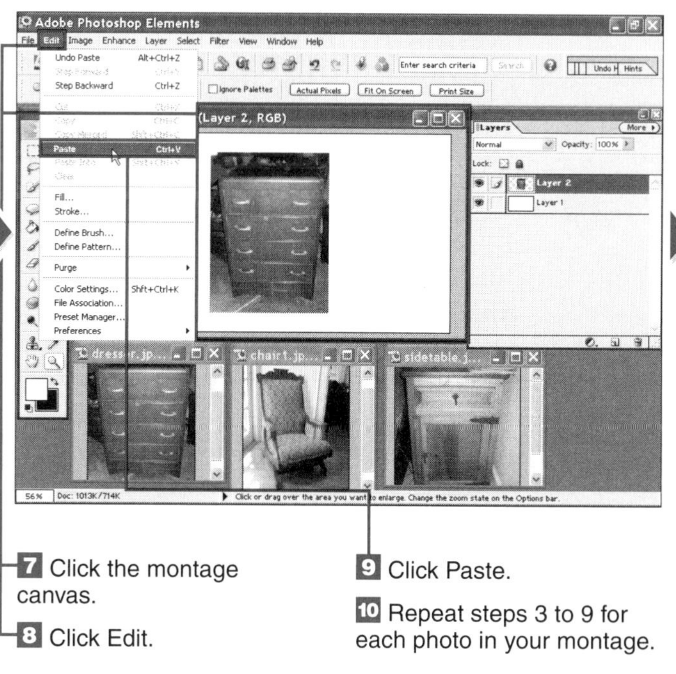

7 Click the montage canvas.

8 Click Edit.

9 Click Paste.

10 Repeat steps 3 to 9 for each photo in your montage.

11 Click a photo layer in the montage.

12 Click the Move tool (▶+).

13 Click and drag the photo to arrange it in the montage.

14 Repeat steps 11 to 13 for each photo in the montage.

■ Photoshop Elements creates the montage.

ADD A SUPERSIZE PHOTO TO AN AUCTION

Sellers who want to give potential buyers a closer look at their items can use eBay's Supersize upgrade option for photos. This displays them at a size twice that of regular auction photos. Available to sellers who use the eBay hosting service, the Supersize feature costs 75 cents in addition to the regular photo fees.

Regular photos hosted by eBay are displayed at up to 400 pixels wide by 300 pixels high in size. Supersize photos are displayed at up to 600 by 800 pixels. When you supersize a photo in a listing, eBay provides a link next to the photo that viewers can click to see the larger version.

eBay recommends that your photo be at least 440 pixels in width by 330 pixels in height if you are going to use the Supersize feature. This size should be the original size of the photo. Increasing a smaller photo to this size or larger is not recommended because enlarging can decrease the quality of a photo and add blurring.

MASTER IT

Does eBay offer a discount for listings that include multiple Supersized photos?

✔ eBay offers a Picture Pack feature that allows you to post up to six photos in a listing, with the Supersize feature included for all the photos. Listings that have the Picture Pack feature also automatically get the Gallery upgrade, which means a small photo is displayed when the listing appears in eBay search results. Picture Pack costs $1. If purchased individually, the Picture Pack options cost $1.75.

ADD A SUPERSIZE PHOTO TO AN AUCTION

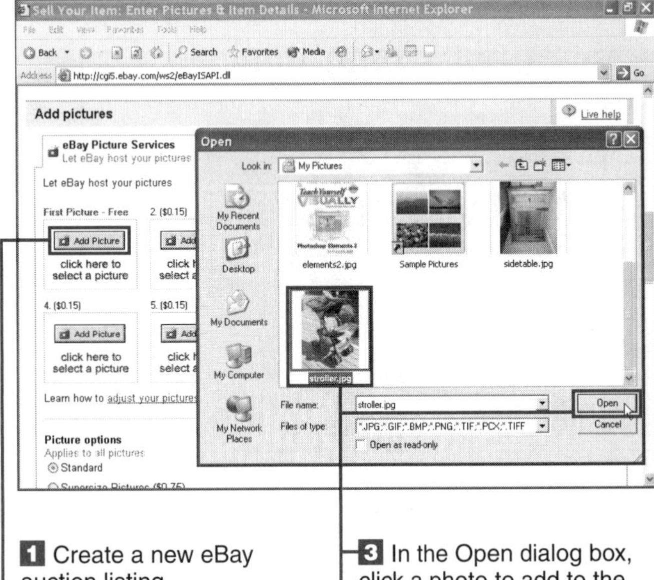

1 Create a new eBay auction listing.

Note: To create a new eBay listing, see Chapter 5.

2 On the Enter Pictures & Item Details page, click Add Picture.

3 In the Open dialog box, click a photo to add to the listing.

4 Click Open.

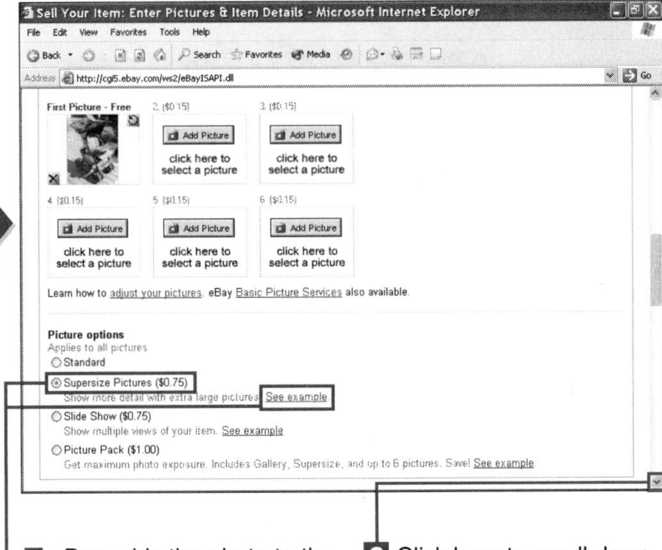

■ eBay adds the photo to the listing.

5 Click the Supersize Pictures option.

■ You can click See example for more information about the Supersize feature.

6 Click here to scroll down the page; click Continue to continue creating your listing.

■ eBay supersizes the photos in your listing.

ADD A SLIDE SHOW TO AN AUCTION

You can add a set of pictures to your auction that can automatically cycle in a single window with the eBay Slide Show feature. Slide Show is available if you are using eBay's picture hosting service for your auction. It costs 75 cents in addition to the 15 cents per picture fee for each image after the first one.

Slide Show is a useful feature if you want to display what an item looks like from various angles, but want to keep your item description relatively compact. You can also use the Slide Show feature for an animated effect. You can present a sequence of photos in succession to show how an item moves or changes over time.

The Slide Show interface includes a play button and stop button, plus buttons to cycle forward and backward through the photos individually.

Can I add a slide show to my auction if I host my auction photos myself?

✔ While you cannot use the eBay Slide Show feature if you host your photos yourself, you can create something similar using an animated GIF file. This type of image file can display several photos consecutively. Many image editors, including Photoshop Elements, can save animated GIF files.

You can also create a slide show using multiple photo files and JavaScript code.

ADD A SLIDE SHOW TO AN AUCTION

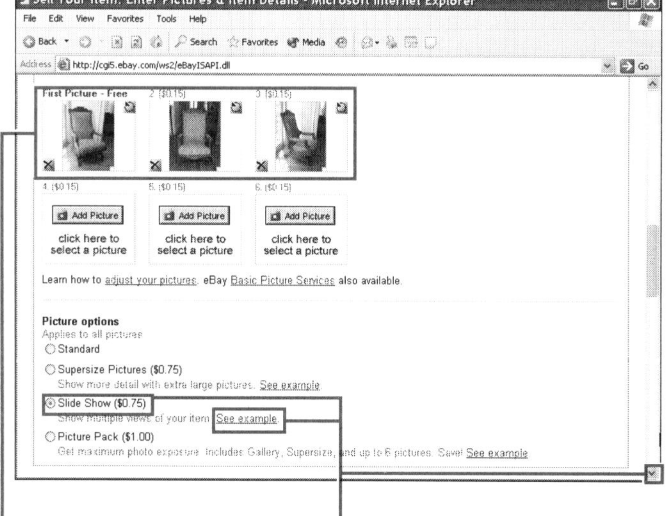

1 Create a new eBay auction listing.

Note: To create a new auction listing, see Chapter 5.

2 On the Enter Pictures & Item Details page, add more than one photo to your auction listing.

3 Click the Slide Show option.

■ You can click See example to view more information about the Slide Show feature.

4 Click here to scroll down and click Continue.

■ The Enter Payment & Shipping page appears.

5 Scroll down and click Continue.

■ The Review & Submit Listing page appears.

■ Your slide show is displayed.

■ You can click the control buttons to test it.

UPLOAD A PHOTO TO AN ONLINE HOST

Photos that appear on your eBay auction pages do not have to be stored on the eBay Web servers — they can be stored on a server anywhere on the Web. Online photo-hosting services take advantage of this fact by offering space on their Web servers where people can store their photos while their auctions are underway. Some photo hosts include www.pixhost.com and www.pongo.com.

Third-party photo hosting services used to be more popular before eBay offered its own photo-hosting service. Now that eBay offers such a service — and even hosts the first photo for each listing for free — third-party hosting services really make the most sense for people who include many photos in their auctions, or who find the limits of eBay's Picture Services too restrictive.

After you have uploaded the photo to a hosting service, you can access the photo via its Web address or URL (Uniform Resource Locator). Most services give you the URL for the photo right after you have uploaded it. To have the photo appear in your eBay auction, you need to add the URL to your listing either on the Pictures & Item Details page or in the HTML of your item description.

UPLOAD A PHOTO TO AN ONLINE HOST

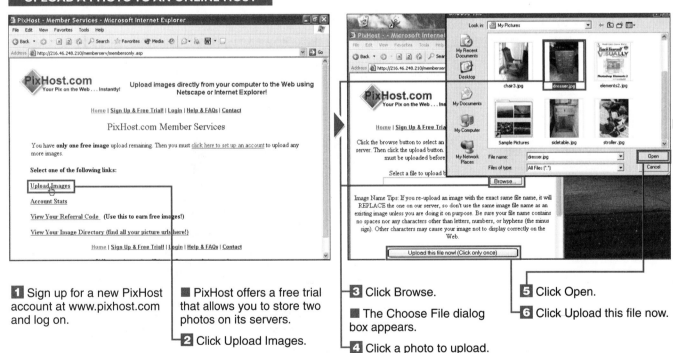

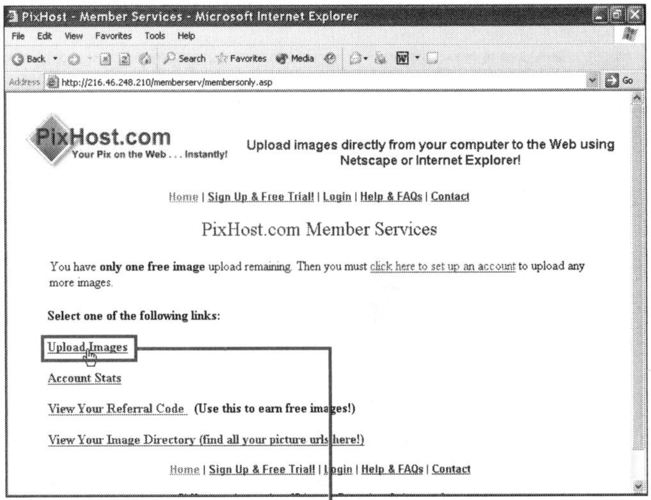

1 Sign up for a new PixHost account at www.pixhost.com and log on.

■ PixHost offers a free trial that allows you to store two photos on its servers.

2 Click Upload Images.

3 Click Browse.

■ The Choose File dialog box appears.

4 Click a photo to upload.

5 Click Open.

6 Click Upload this file now.

How much does it cost to host a photo at a hosting service?

✔ Most photo-hosting services recommended by eBay charge 50 cents per average-size photo for a month's storage. The services sometimes charge more to host photos that are over a certain file size.

In contrast, eBay charges 15 cents per photo after the first free photo. However, eBay hosts photos only for the duration of a listing. Using a non-eBay photo host can be economical if you use more than one photo per listing and use the same photos in multiple listings.

I want to include more than one photo from a photo-hosting service. How do I do it?

✔ On the Enter Pictures & Item Details page, eBay allows you to type the URL for one externally hosted photo. If you want to display more than one photo from a photo-hosting service, you need to insert the additional photos using HTML in your description. See Chapter 21 for more about HTML.

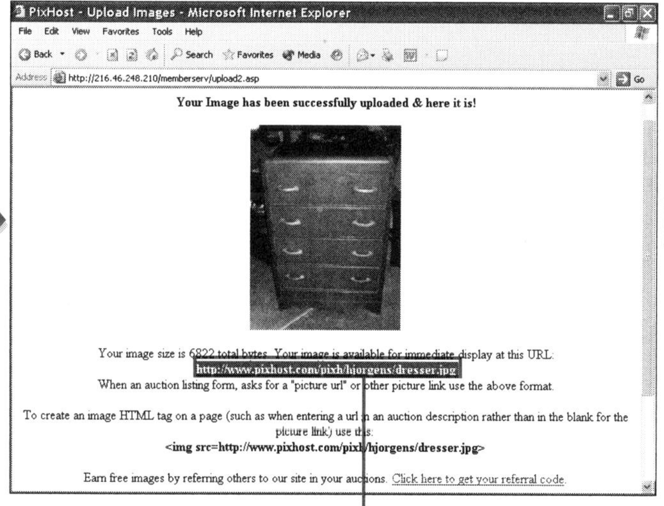

■ PixHost uploads the file from your computer to its servers.

■ The uploaded photo appears.

7 Click and drag to select the photo URL.

8 Press Ctrl+C to copy the URL.

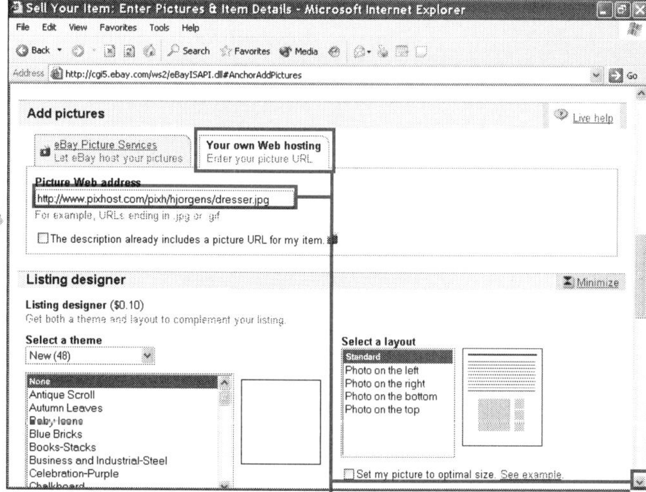

ADD THE PHOTO TO A LISTING

9 Create a new eBay auction listing.

Note: For more information on creating a new listing, see Chapter 5.

10 On the Enter Pictures & Item Details page, click Your own Web hosting.

11 Press Ctrl+V to paste the URL into the Picture Web address field.

12 Click here to scroll down, and click Continue to finish creating your auction.

UNDERSTANDING HTML

Hypertext Markup Language, or HTML, is the formatting language that you use to create Web pages. When you open a Web page in a browser, HTML code tells the browser how to display the text, images, and other content on the page. Every page on the eBay Web site has HTML code associated with it. That code tells Web browsers how to format the auction information, arrange the photos, and build the forms that enable buyers to make their bids.

The Official Standard

The World Wide Web Consortium (W3C), an international body made up of members from industry, academia, and government, maintains the official HTML standard. The consortium makes recommendations as to what new HTML features should be adopted. Developers of browsers, servers, and HTML editors can then follow these guidelines when building their products. As of this writing, the current HTML standard is version 4.01, which you can view at www.w3c.org.

HTML Tags

The basic unit of HTML is a *tag*. You can recognize HTML tags by their angle brackets:

```
<P>This antique dresser was built
in <B>1780</B>.<BR>I purchased it
in <I>1980</I>.</P>
```

Some HTML tags work in twos. Opening and closing tags surround content in a document and control the formatting of the content. For example, <B> tags cause text to be bold. Closing tags are distinguished by a forward slash, /. Other tags can stand alone. For example, the <BR> tag adds a line break. HTML tags are not case sensitive — they can be uppercase, lowercase, or mixed case. Uppercase tag names are used in the examples in this book to make the HTML code stand out.

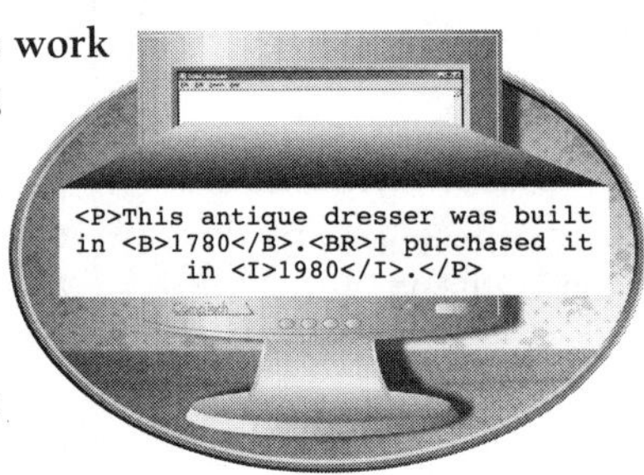
<P>This antique dresser was built
in <B>1780</B>.
I purchased it
in <I>1980</I>.</P>

HTML Attributes

You can modify the effect of an HTML tag by adding extra information known as attributes. Attributes are name/value pairs — such as `ALIGN="Right"` — that live inside the HTML angle brackets to the right of the tag name. As an example, you can add the align attribute to a <P> (paragraph) tag to align a paragraph in various ways:

```
<P ALIGN="Right">I accept PayPal
as a payment method. I also
accept personal checks.</P>
```

This HTML aligns the two-sentence paragraph to the right side of the Web browser window.

Editing HTML Documents

Because HTML documents are plain text files, you can open and edit them with any text editor. In fact, in the early days of the Web, most people created their pages with simple editors such as Windows Notepad and Macintosh SimpleText. But writing HTML by hand can be a slow, tedious process. Web editors such as Macromedia Dreamweaver and Microsoft FrontPage can save you time by automating the writing of tags and giving you a visual WYSIWYG — What You See Is What You Get — interface in which to work.

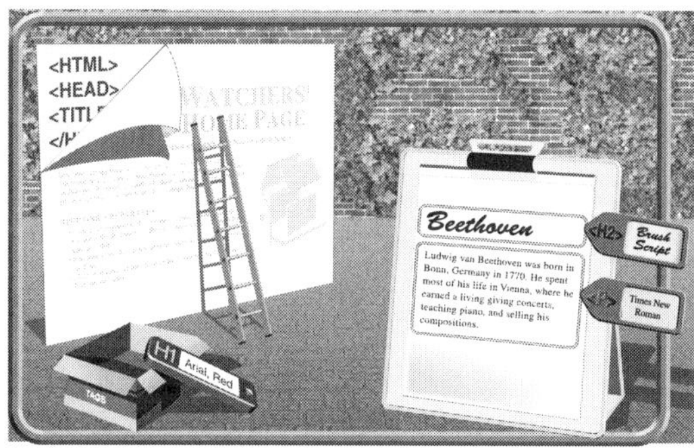

Anatomy of an Auction Listing

Sellers have only partial control over the HTML that makes up an eBay auction page. The HTML at the top of an auction page, which contains site navigation links, the auction title, and seller and bidder information, is controlled by eBay. So is the HTML at the bottom of an auction page, which includes payment methods accepted, a bidding form, and more navigation. The seller controls the auction description, which is in the middle of the page. This part of the page can include both text and images.

What You Can Do with HTML

HTML gives you a variety of capabilities when it comes to creating an eBay listing. You can change the size, color, and emphasis of text, or create bulleted or numbered lists of text items. You can add photos of your auction items or insert decorative graphics to give your listing description a theme. You can also include hyperlinks to other Web pages to give potential buyers access to additional information about your products.

Reasons to Use HTML

One reason to use HTML is it can help make your listings look more professional. By aligning photos and adjusting text size, you can also fit more auction information into a smaller space. Inserting photos using HTML can help you save money by avoiding the extra fees that eBay charges when you include multiple photos through its photo hosting service. While creating listings with HTML can take some time, you can streamline the process by saving ready-made templates that you can quickly fill in when you need to create new auctions.

CREATE PARAGRAPHS

The most basic HTML tag for formatting your auction listings is the <P>, or paragraph, tag. Surrounding text with paragraph tags adds extra spacing before and after the text.

To add paragraph formatting with HTML in your eBay listing descriptions, you can click the Enter your own HTML tab in the Item description text box. To preview how your HTML formatting is coming along, you can click the Standard tab in the Item description text box. In Standard view, HTML tags are interpreted and you can see how your description will appear in a Web browser.

Web browsers generally ignore extra white space in HTML. That is why adding hard returns before and after text in your HTML does not generate a paragraph. You need to surround the sentences with an opening <P> tag and a closing </P> tag.

You can customize the look of your paragraphs with the ALIGN attribute, which enables you to align paragraph text to the *left*, *right*, or *center* of the page. You can also *justify* a paragraph, which spaces the text so that margins are equal on both sides.

CREATE PARAGRAPHS

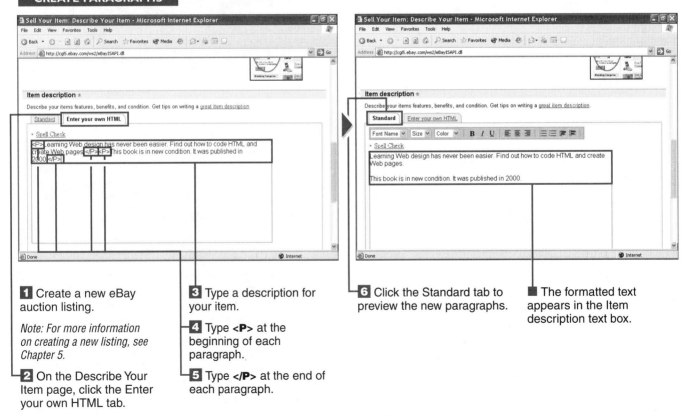

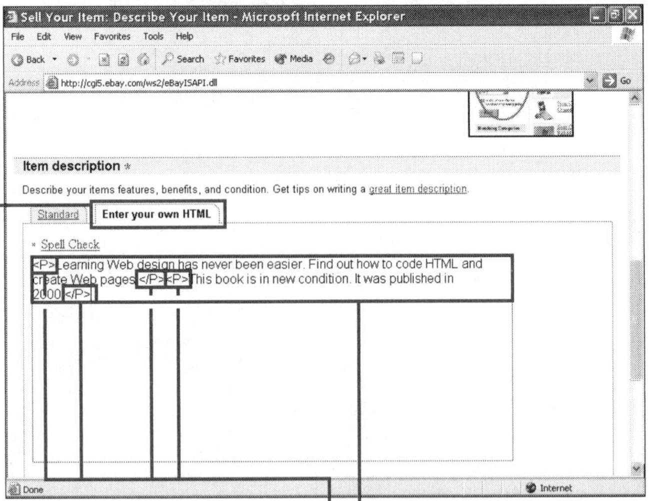

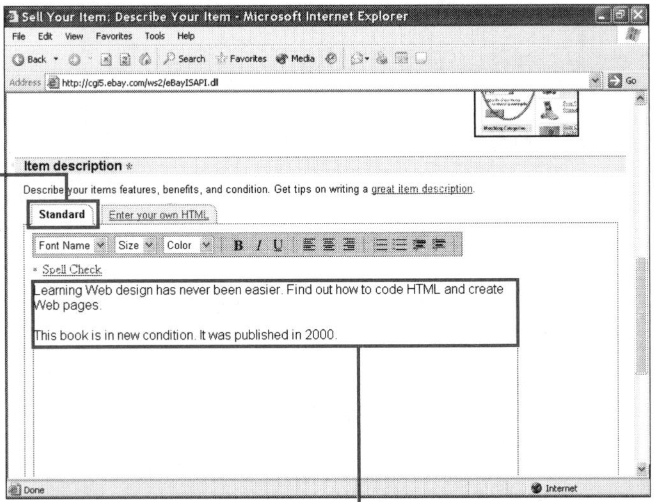

1 Create a new eBay auction listing.

Note: For more information on creating a new listing, see Chapter 5.

2 On the Describe Your Item page, click the Enter your own HTML tab.

3 Type a description for your item.

4 Type **<P>** at the beginning of each paragraph.

5 Type **</P>** at the end of each paragraph.

6 Click the Standard tab to preview the new paragraphs.

■ The formatted text appears in the Item description text box.

How can I make a browser recognize the white space in my HTML?

✔ You can add the <PRE> tag to your HTML to keep a browser from ignoring the white space, which is its usual behavior. A browser keeps spaces and line breaks intact between any opening <PRE> and closing </PRE> tags in your HTML code. The drawback to using the <PRE> tag is that browsers won't automatically wrap text inside <PRE> tags when a sentence reaches the right side of the window. You have to know when to add the line breaks yourself, which can be tricky because you do not necessarily know the size of the browser window.

How can I indent the first line of a paragraph?

✔ You can indent the first line of a paragraph by adding nonbreaking spaces to your HTML code. Type ** ** for each space:

```
<P>   My
indented one-sentence
paragraph.</P>
```

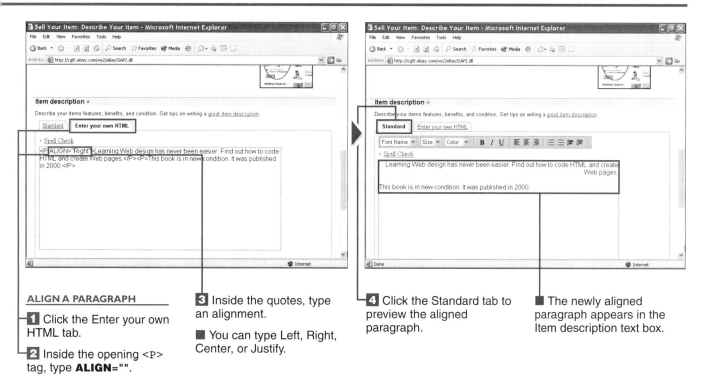

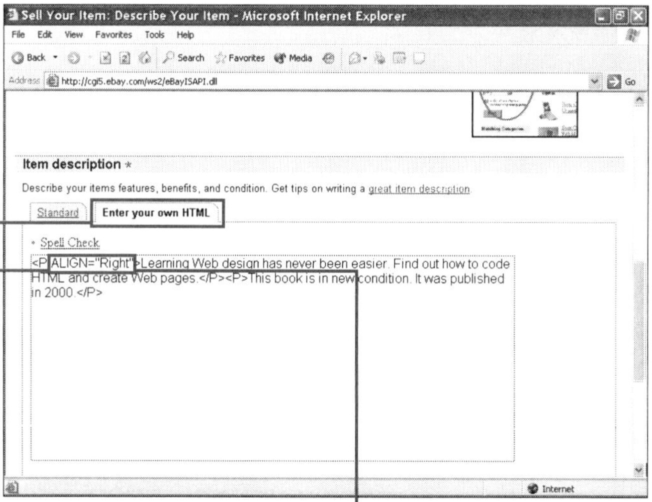

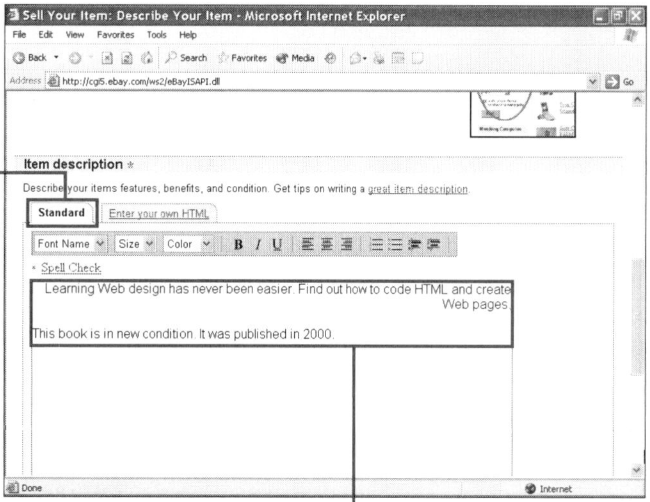

ALIGN A PARAGRAPH

1 Click the Enter your own HTML tab.

2 Inside the opening <P> tag, type **ALIGN=""**.

3 Inside the quotes, type an alignment.

■ You can type Left, Right, Center, or Justify.

4 Click the Standard tab to preview the aligned paragraph.

■ The newly aligned paragraph appears in the Item description text box.

SET FONT STYLE AND SIZE

Using the FACE attribute with the <FONT> tag allows you to change the font style to make the words in your eBay descriptions look more interesting. You can specify a specific font style such as Verdana or Courier, or a font category such as sans-serif or monospace. If you do not specify a particular font, most browsers display Web page text in Times New Roman (Windows) or Times (Macintosh).

You can specify any style of font that you want in the FACE attribute; however, Web browsers can display only fonts that are installed on the computer on which they are running. Because of this, you will most likely want to limit your font choices to the more popular ones, such as Arial, Verdana, Georgia, Comic Sans, and Courier.

Additionally, you can specify the size of the font using the SIZE attribute to emphasize or de-emphasize sections of text. You can specify an absolute size from 1 to 7 for your font; 3 is equivalent to the default text size. You can also specify a relative size, such as +1 or –2, and the font increases or decreases relative to its current size.

If you do not want to use HTML, you can change the font name and size of the text using the Font Name and Size menus in the Standard view of the Item description text box.

SET FONT STYLE AND SIZE

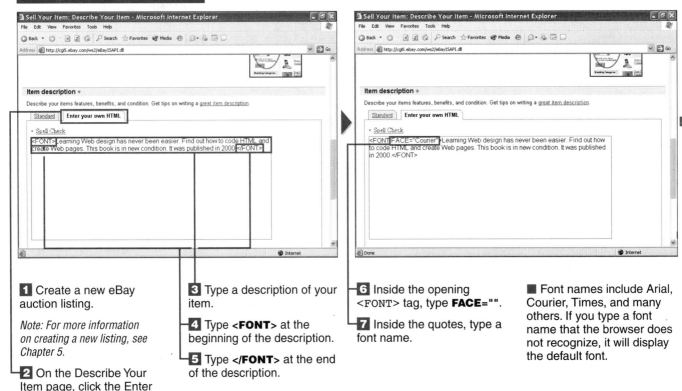

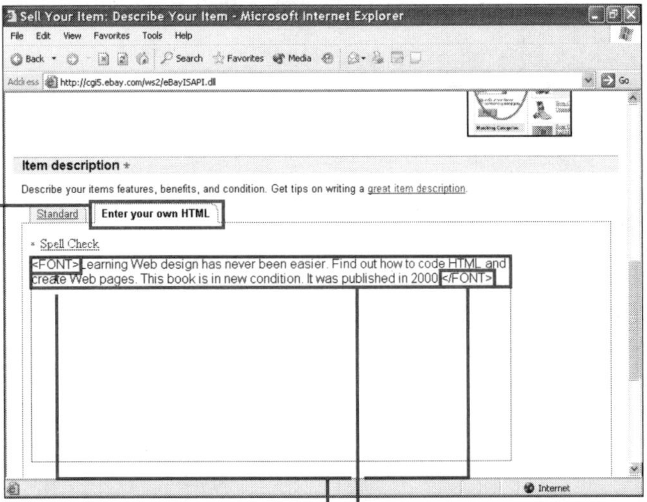

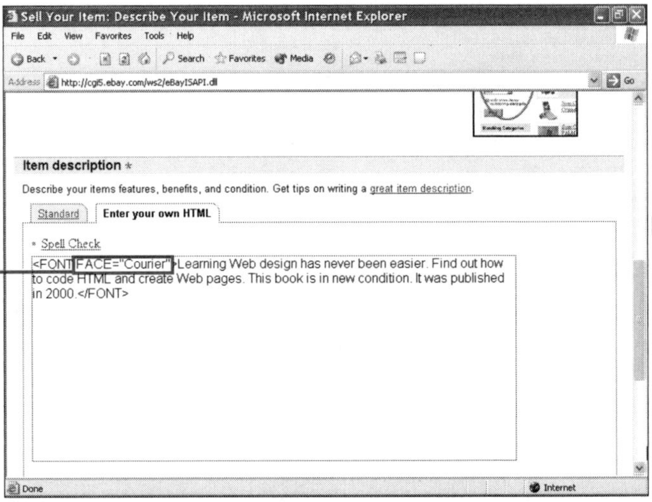

1 Create a new eBay auction listing.

Note: For more information on creating a new listing, see Chapter 5.

2 On the Describe Your Item page, click the Enter your own HTML tab.

3 Type a description of your item.

4 Type **<FONT>** at the beginning of the description.

5 Type **</FONT>** at the end of the description.

6 Inside the opening <FONT> tag, type **FACE=""**.

7 Inside the quotes, type a font name.

■ Font names include Arial, Courier, Times, and many others. If you type a font name that the browser does not recognize, it will display the default font.

What is the actual size of FONT-formatted text?

✔ In most browsers, size 3, the default size, is 12 points. Size 1, the smallest, is 8 points. Size 7, the largest, is 36 points. Note that users can change their default browser settings so that fonts are displayed at larger or smaller sizes, so actual sizes can vary among browsers.

What are serifs?

✔ Serifs are the tiny, curved decorations on the ends of the vertical and horizontal strokes of some letters. Serif fonts include Times and Palatino. Sans-serif fonts — fonts without serifs — include Arial and Verdana.

Do I have to use the FACE and SIZE attributes together?

✔ You can use the FACE and SIZE attributes in the same <FONT> tag, as is done in the steps below. Or you can use them separately. For example, `<FONT FACE="Arial">eBay </FONT>` or `<FONT SIZE="6"> Auctions</FONT>`.

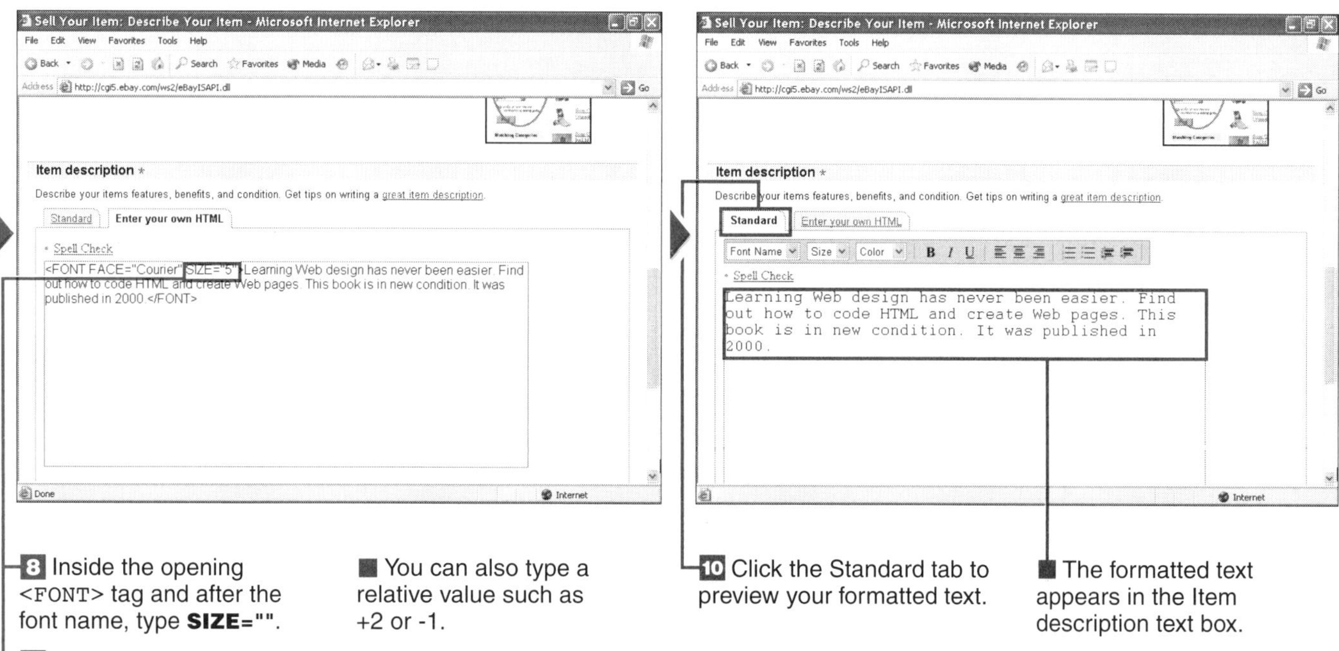

8 Inside the opening <FONT> tag and after the font name, type **SIZE=""**.

9 Inside the quotes, type a number from 1 to 7.

■ You can also type a relative value such as +2 or -1.

10 Click the Standard tab to preview your formatted text.

■ The formatted text appears in the Item description text box.

EMPHASIZE TEXT

You can emphasize text on your Web page with several different HTML tags, including the bold, italic, and underline tags. Emphasizing text in your eBay auction descriptions can draw the viewer's eye to important words or sentences.

To make text in your description bold, you can use the <B> tag. This gives your text a heavier weight than the surrounding text. An alternative to the <B> tag is the <STRONG> tag, which produces the same effect in most Web browsers.

You can italicize, or slant, text in your description with the <I> tag. You should preview your italicized text before posting it live, because some italicized text can be difficult to read at small sizes or with certain font styles. An alternative to the <I> tag is the <EM> tag, which produces the same effect in most Web browsers.

The <U> tag can be used to underline text. Underlining should be used sparingly because it is usually used to designate hyperlink text in Web pages. For more information about hyperlinks, see the section "Create a Hyperlink," later in this chapter.

If you do not want to use HTML, you can change the emphasis of the text by highlighting it and clicking the **B**, *I*, and U buttons in the Standard view of the Item description text box.

EMPHASIZE TEXT

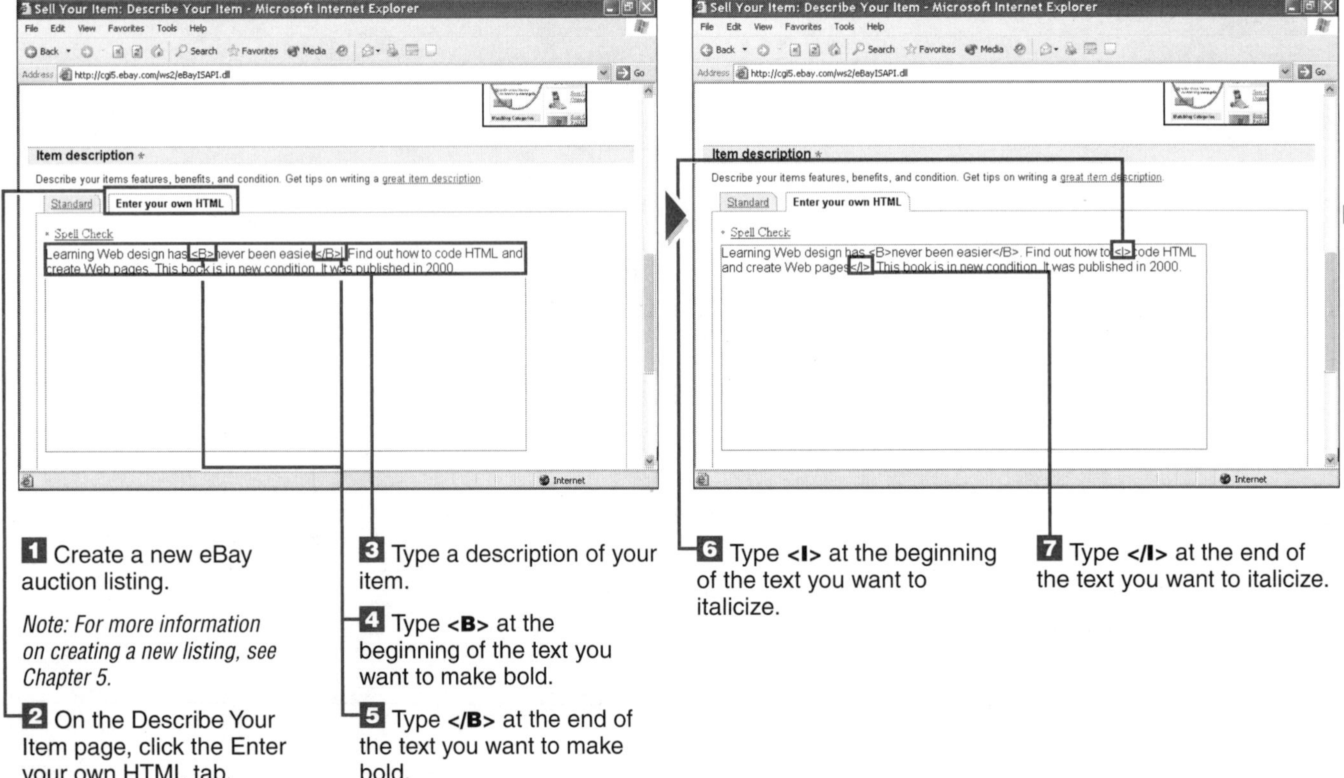

1 Create a new eBay auction listing.

Note: For more information on creating a new listing, see Chapter 5.

2 On the Describe Your Item page, click the Enter your own HTML tab.

3 Type a description of your item.

4 Type **<B>** at the beginning of the text you want to make bold.

5 Type **</B>** at the end of the text you want to make bold.

6 Type **<I>** at the beginning of the text you want to italicize.

7 Type **</I>** at the end of the text you want to italicize.

How do I make text that is both bold and italicized?

✔ To apply both bold and italic formatting to the same text, you can nest HTML tags. For example, `<B><I>Very emphasized</I></B>`. Note that the inner HTML tag should be closed before the outer HTML tag to ensure that the code works correctly in all browsers.

I want to add text to my listing in a style or format that is not supported by HTML. Can I do it?

✔ If you want text that is especially fancy — for example, with a drop shadow behind it or with a rainbow-colored gradient — you can create the text as an image file in an image editor and then insert the image using HTML. For more information about image editors, see Chapter 20. For more about inserting images, see the section "Add a Photo Using HTML," later in this chapter.

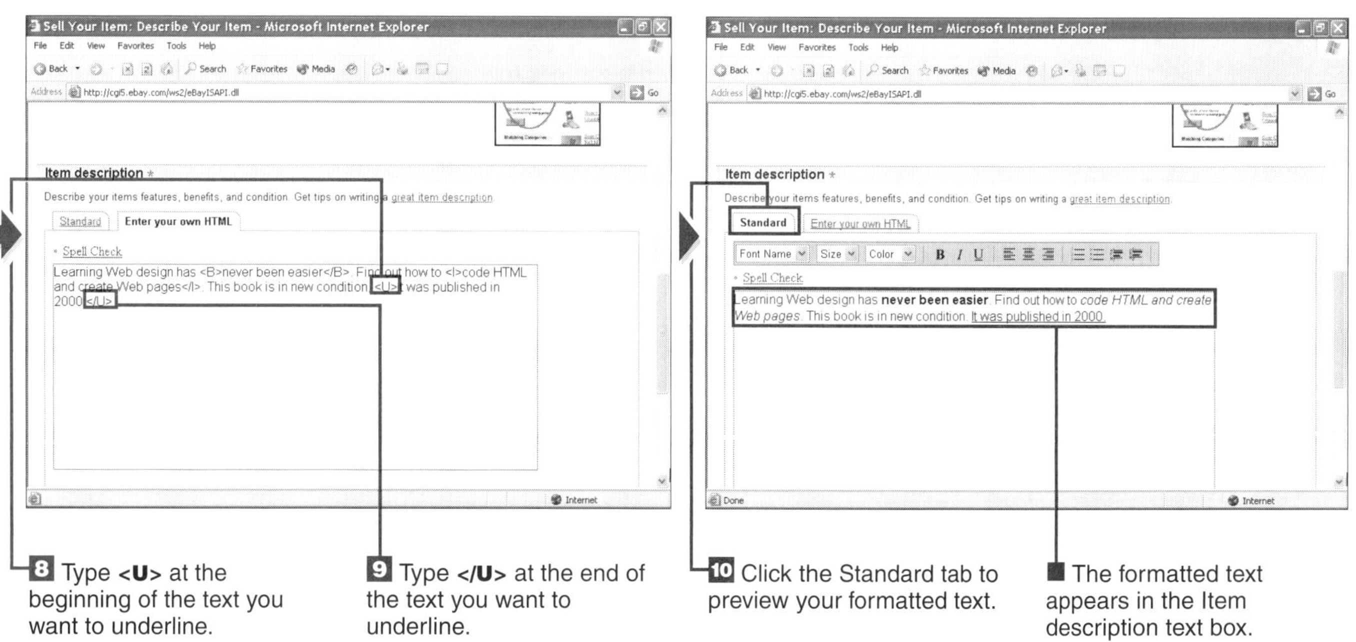

8 Type **<U>** at the beginning of the text you want to underline.

9 Type **</U>** at the end of the text you want to underline.

10 Click the Standard tab to preview your formatted text.

■ The formatted text appears in the Item description text box.

CHANGE TEXT COLOR

You can change the color of text on all or part of your auction description to make it more visually interesting. The default color for text on a Web page is black. When changing the color of text, you use the <FONT> tag and the COLOR attribute. You set the COLOR attribute to either the name or the hexadecimal value for the color.

A hexadecimal value is composed of a number sign, #, followed by three pairs of letters or numbers. The three pairs of letters or numbers specify the amount of red, green, and blue in the resulting color, respectively. There are 16 colors defined by the HTML standard that you can specify by name; see the table on the next page. To ensure that your text is readable, make sure its color contrasts with the white background color of the eBay auction page.

If you do not want to use HTML, you can change the color of the text in your description using the Color menu in the Standard view of the Item description text box.

CHANGE TEXT COLOR

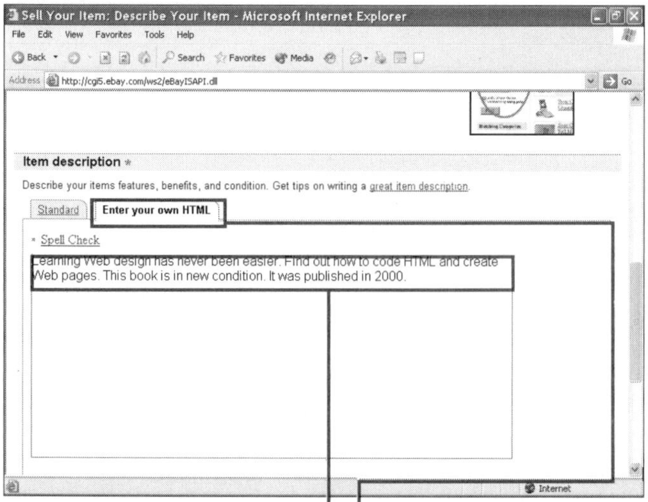

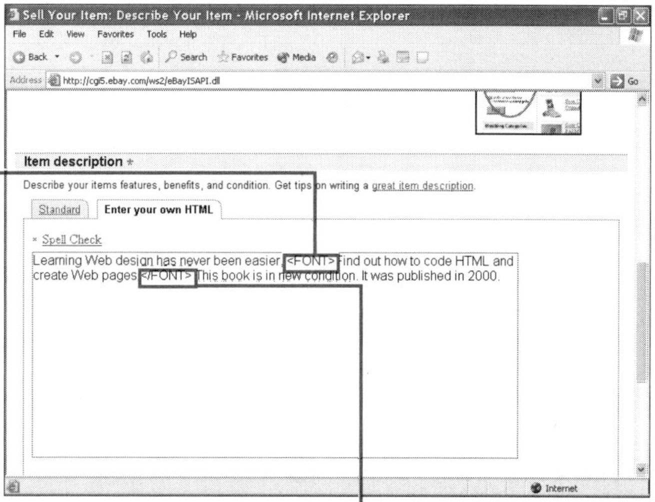

1 Create a new eBay auction listing.

Note: For more information on creating a new listing, see Chapter 5.

2 On the Describe Your Item page, click the Enter your own HTML tab.

3 Type a description of your item.

4 Type **<FONT>** at the beginning of the text you want to color.

5 Type **</FONT>** at the end of the text you want to color.

What are the standard color names that I can use with the COLOR attribute?

✔ The following table shows the 16 standard colors names and their corresponding hexadecimal values:

Color Name	Color Code	Color Name	Color Code
Aqua	#00FFFF	Navy	#000080
Black	#000000	Olive	#808000
Blue	#0000FF	Purple	#800080
Fuchsia	#FF00FF	Red	#FF0000
Gray	#808080	Silver	#C0C0C0
Green	#008000	Teal	#008080
Lime	#00FF00	White	#FFFFFF
Maroon	#800000	Yellow	#FFFF00

What if I use a color name that is not on the official list of 16?

✔ Many modern Web browsers display many colors in addition to the 16 defined in the HTML standard. For example, crimson, goldenrod, and plum are all color names that Microsoft Internet Explorer will understand and display. You can see a list of more than 100 nonstandard color names here: www.htmlgoodies.com/tutors/colors.html. If a Web browser does not recognize a name in the COLOR attribute, it ignores the attribute and keeps the text the default color.

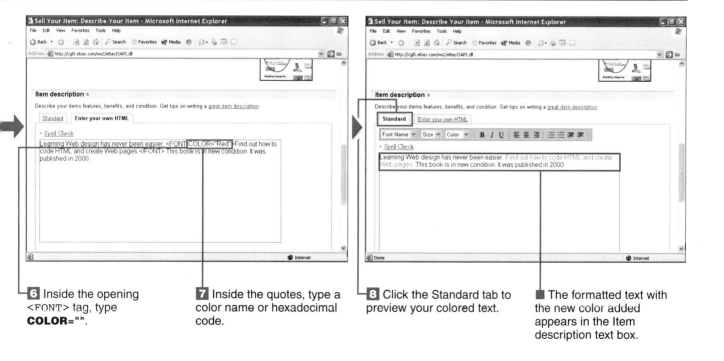

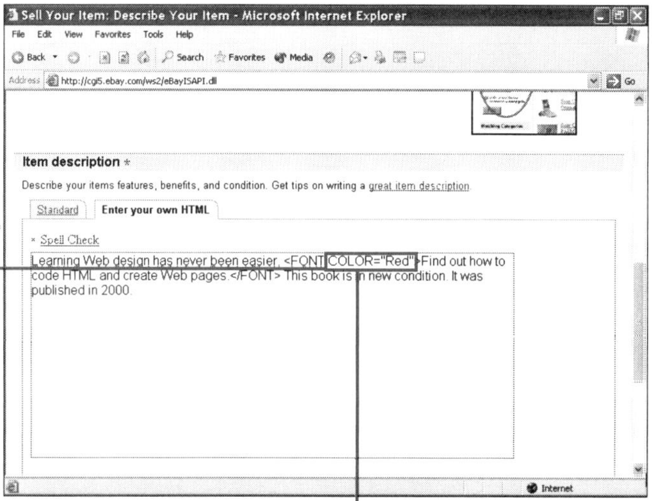

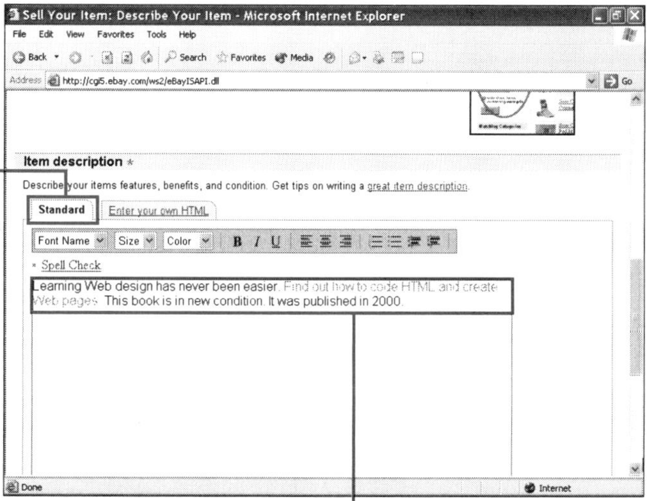

6 Inside the opening <FONT> tag, type **COLOR=""**.

7 Inside the quotes, type a color name or hexadecimal code.

8 Click the Standard tab to preview your colored text.

■ The formatted text with the new color added appears in the Item description text box.

CREATE A HYPERLINK

You can create clickable hyperlinks in your auction descriptions that lead to related information on other pages on the Web. You create links using the <A> tag with an HREF attribute that specifies the Web address, also known as a URL (Uniform Resource Locator), of the destination page.

You can link to any other page on the Web as long as you know its address. You can get a Web page's address by opening the page in your Web browser and copying the text that appears in the browser's address field.

You may want to add hyperlinks to your eBay auctions if you have an online Web site that sells similar items. You can also link to your eBay Store, if you have one. For more information about setting up an eBay Store, see Chapter 23.

When viewed in a browser, hyperlink text is usually underlined and in a color different from other text. Viewers can change this default characteristic in their browser settings. Designers can change it in Web pages by using more advanced HTML as well as style sheets.

CREATE A HYPERLINK

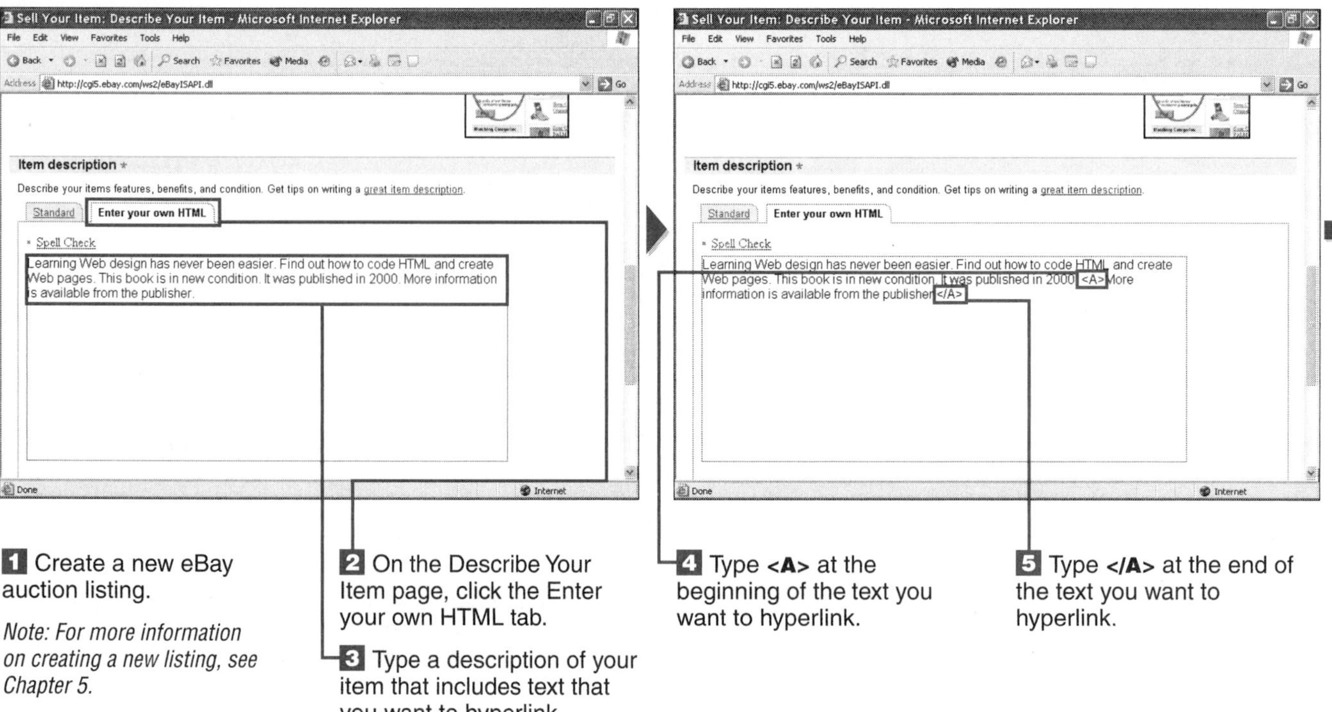

1 Create a new eBay auction listing.

Note: For more information on creating a new listing, see Chapter 5.

2 On the Describe Your Item page, click the Enter your own HTML tab.

3 Type a description of your item that includes text that you want to hyperlink.

4 Type **<A>** at the beginning of the text you want to hyperlink.

5 Type **</A>** at the end of the text you want to hyperlink.

How can I test the hyperlinks in my description?

✔ You have a chance to review your completed listing at the end of the auction creation process. At that point, you can test your hyperlinks to make sure that all of them direct you to the correct pages. You can also test your hyperlink URL by copying it, pasting it into the address bar of a Web browser, and pressing Enter.

How do I create a hyperlink that opens a destination page in a new browser window?

✔ You can specify that a hyperlink opens a new browser window by adding a `TARGET` attribute with a `_blank` value. For example:

```
<A HREF="http://www.ebay.com
"TARGET="_blank">eBay Link</A>
```

Can I create an image hyperlink?

✔ Yes. You turn an image into a clickable link by surrounding the `<IMG>` tag with `<A>` tags. For example:

```
<A HREF="http://wiley.com>
<IMG SRC="http://wiley.com/
book.gif"></A>
```

For more information about images, see the section "Add a Photo Using HTML," later in this chapter.

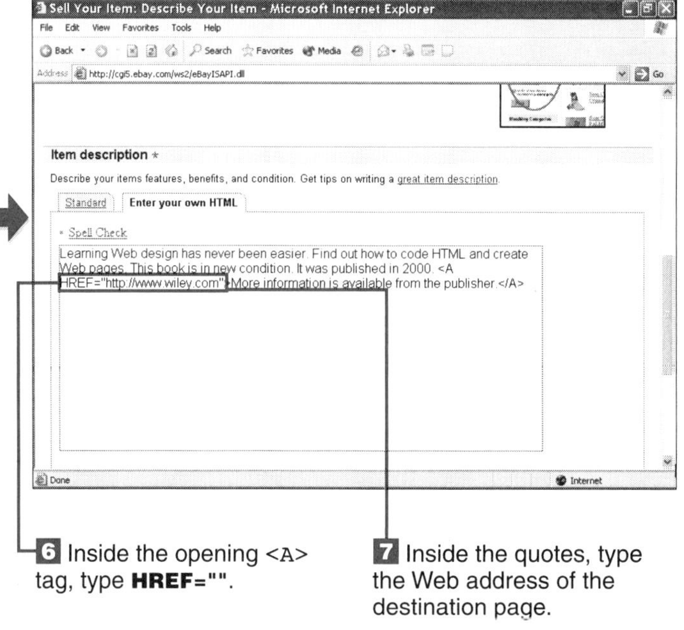

6 Inside the opening `<A>` tag, type **HREF=""**.

7 Inside the quotes, type the Web address of the destination page.

Note: Make sure you include the http:// at the beginning of the Web address.

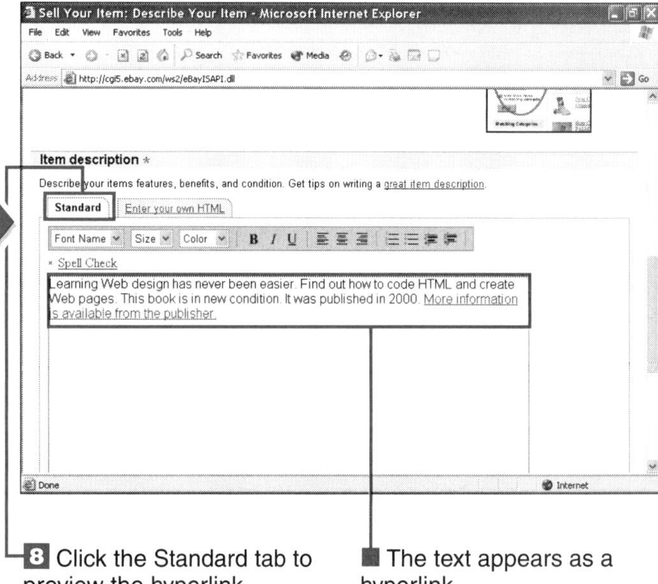

8 Click the Standard tab to preview the hyperlink.

■ The text appears as a hyperlink.

ADD A LINE BREAK

Adding line breaks to your auction descriptions enables you to keep adjacent lines of related text close together. Line breaks are an alternative to paragraph breaks, which add more space between lines of text. See the section "Create Paragraphs," earlier in this chapter. Line breaks can be useful when displaying content such as addresses.

You can use line breaks with nontext elements as well. Putting a line break between images, for example, can ensure that they stay close together.

You can create line breaks inside HTML paragraphs. Inserting line breaks inside a paragraph does not affect the alignment of the text inside the paragraph. For example, if you right-align paragraph text and add a new line break, the text before and after the break stays right-aligned.

You can easily add lots of vertical space on your page by adding multiple line breaks.

ADD A LINE BREAK

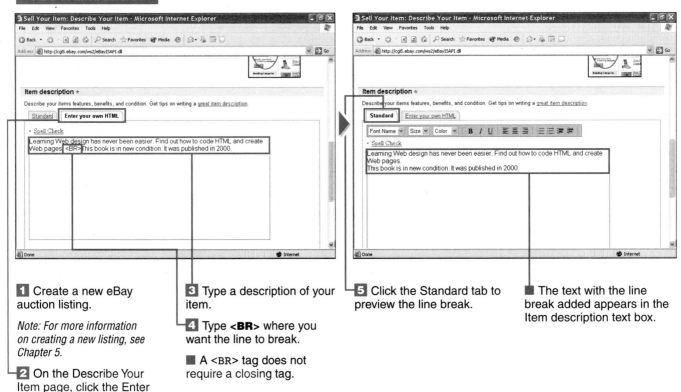

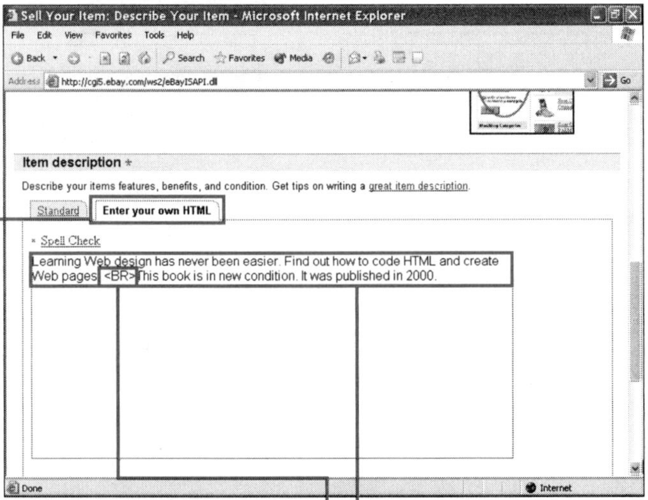

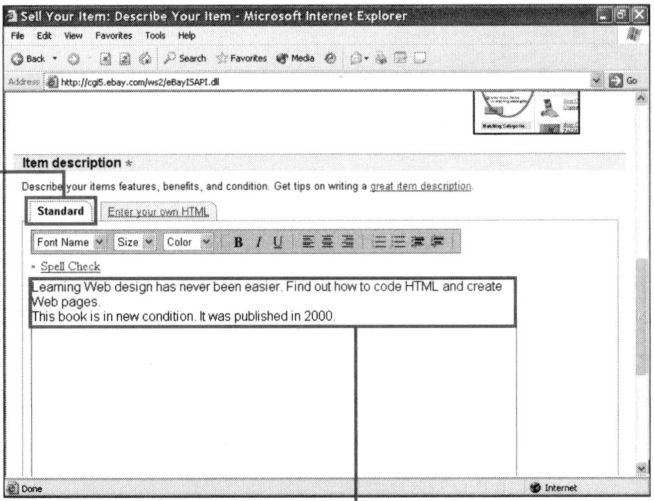

1 Create a new eBay auction listing.

Note: For more information on creating a new listing, see Chapter 5.

2 On the Describe Your Item page, click the Enter your own HTML tab.

3 Type a description of your item.

4 Type **
** where you want the line to break.

■ A <BR> tag does not require a closing tag.

5 Click the Standard tab to preview the line break.

■ The text with the line break added appears in the Item description text box.

ADD A HORIZONTAL RULE

You can use thin lines known as horizontal rules on your Web page to separate sections of content. Horizontal rules are part of the HTML standard, and it is the Web browser that produces the rules when a page loads. Although they may look like them, the rules are not separate image files. As a result, horizontal rules may appear slightly different in different types of browsers.

You can customize a horizontal rule in various ways. The default horizontal rule stretches to fill the width of the page. Alternatively, you can express the width of a rule as a number of pixels. You can also adjust the thickness of your rules.

Rules can have shading turned on, which gives them a 3-D look. Rules without shading, which have the `NOSHADE` attribute, are solid gray.

If you are not pleased with the horizontal rules that HTML gives you, you can always use an image editor to create your own wavy rules, multicolored rules, or dashed rules and insert them as images. See the section "Add a Photo Using HTML," later in this chapter.

ADD A HORIZONTAL RULE

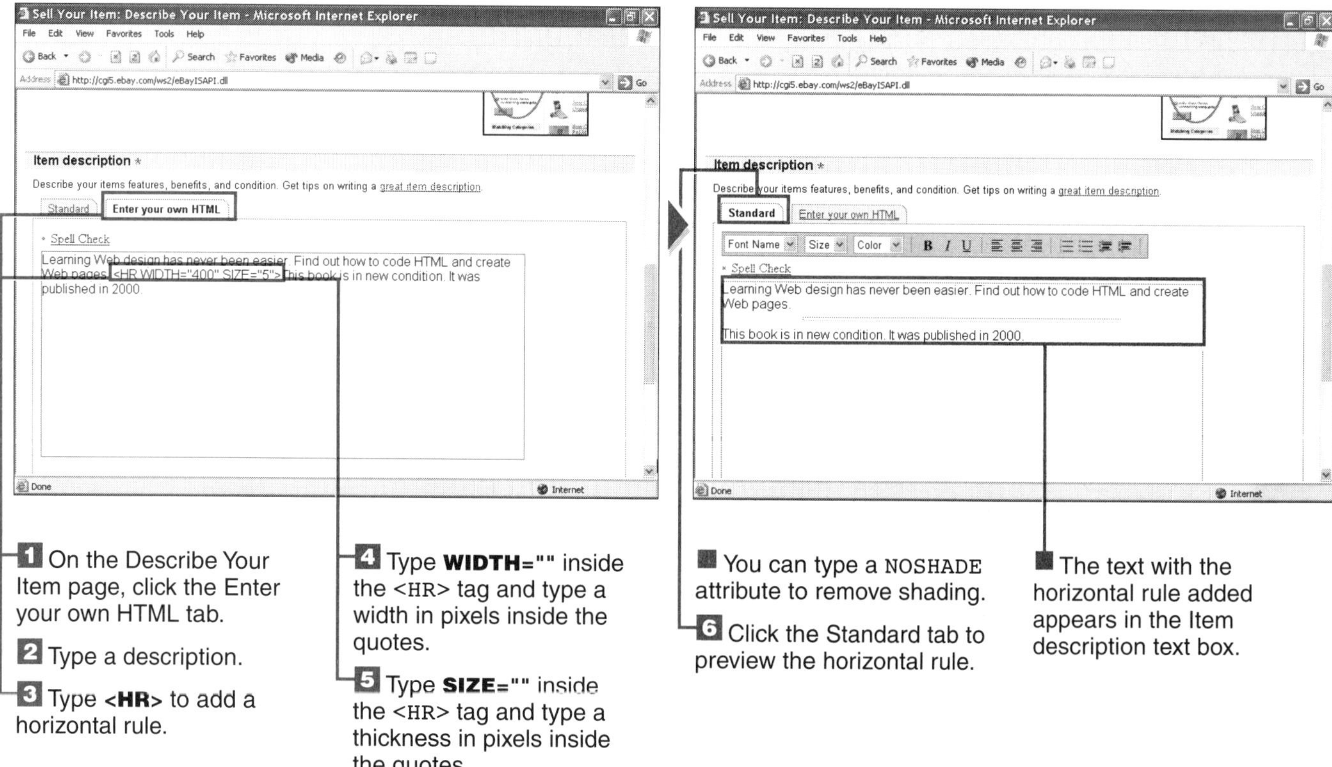

1 On the Describe Your Item page, click the Enter your own HTML tab.

2 Type a description.

3 Type **<HR>** to add a horizontal rule.

4 Type **WIDTH=""** inside the `<HR>` tag and type a width in pixels inside the quotes.

5 Type **SIZE=""** inside the `<HR>` tag and type a thickness in pixels inside the quotes.

■ You can type a `NOSHADE` attribute to remove shading.

6 Click the Standard tab to preview the horizontal rule.

■ The text with the horizontal rule added appears in the Item description text box.

CREATE A LIST

You can organize text items on your Web page into *unordered lists*, which display a set of items indented and bulleted. Unordered lists are useful for organizing elements that need to be grouped but in no particular order.

You can display step-by-step instructions on your Web page by organizing text items into an *ordered list*. Ordered lists have items that are indented and numbered. Ordered lists are useful for displaying driving directions, test questions, or recipes on your Web pages.

You can *nest* unordered and ordered lists, which means you can have a list inside another list. In such cases, Web browsers indent the inside list further and give it differently styled bullets or numbering, depending on the type of list.

Unordered lists are indicated by opening and closing `<UL>` tags, while ordered lists are indicated by opening and closing `<OL>` tags. Each item in a list is marked with an `<LI>` tag. The `<LI>` tag is used to mark list items in both types of lists.

CREATE A LIST

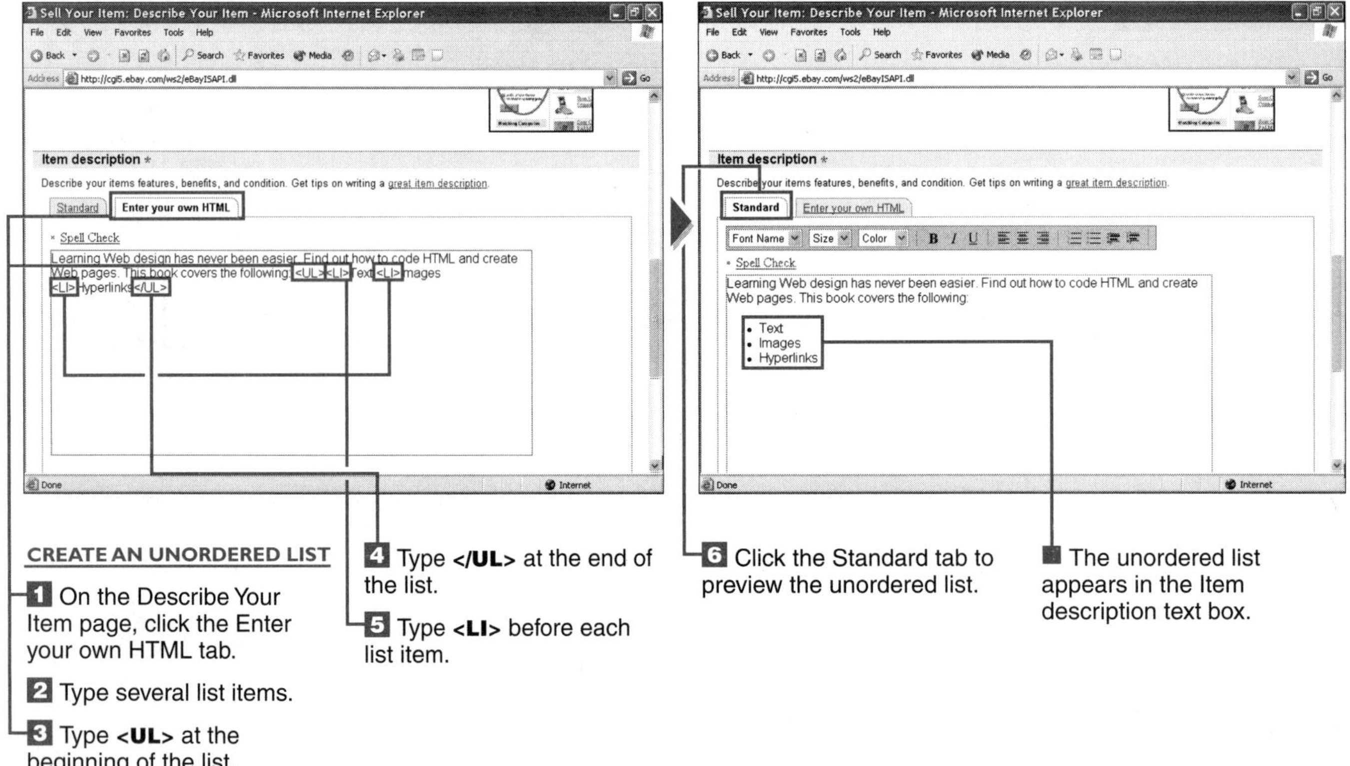

CREATE AN UNORDERED LIST

1 On the Describe Your Item page, click the Enter your own HTML tab.

2 Type several list items.

3 Type **<UL>** at the beginning of the list.

4 Type **</UL>** at the end of the list.

5 Type **<LI>** before each list item.

6 Click the Standard tab to preview the unordered list.

■ The unordered list appears in the Item description text box.

How can I customize the bullets in my unordered list?

✔ You can customize the bullets in your unordered list by adding a TYPE attribute to your <UL> tag. Setting the TYPE attribute to "Disc" will display a solid round bullet, the default. "Square" will display a solid square bullet. "Circle" will display an open round bullet. For example:

```
<UL TYPE="Square">
<LI>Item with square bullet
</UL>
```

How can I customize the bullets in my ordered list?

✔ You can also customize the starting numbers or letters in your ordered list with the TYPE attribute. Setting the TYPE attribute to 1 will display numbers in front of your items. A and a will display upper- and lowercase letters, respectively. I and i will display upper- and lowercase Roman numerals, respectively. For example:

```
<OL TYPE="a">
<LI>Item with lowercase
letter
</OL>
```

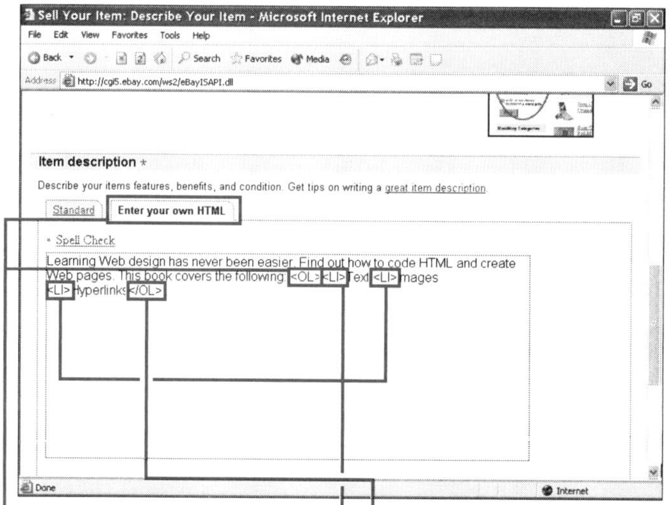

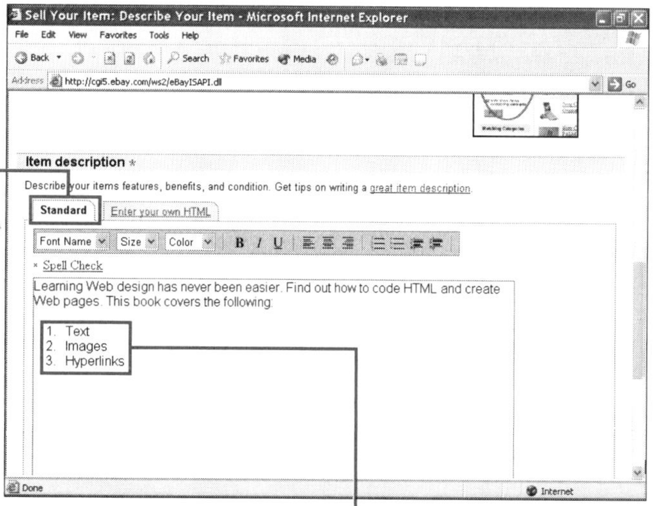

CREATE AN ORDERED LIST

1 On the Describe Your Item page, click the Enter your own HTML tab.

2 Type several list items.

3 Type **<OL>** at the beginning of the list.

4 Type **</OL>** at the end of the list.

5 Type **<LI>** before each list item.

6 Click the Standard tab to preview the ordered list.

■ The ordered list appears in the Item description text box.

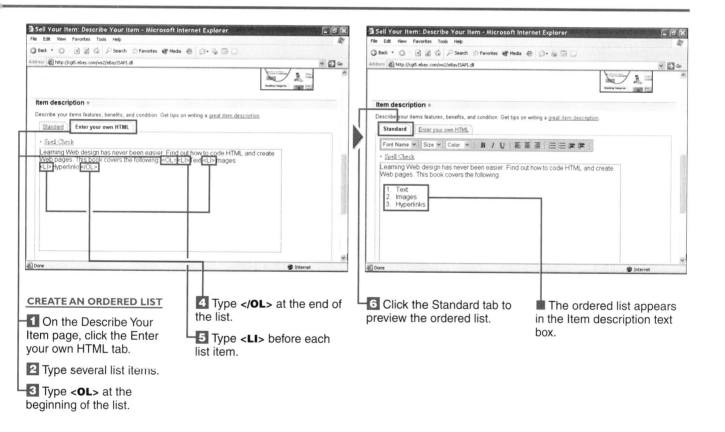

ADD A PHOTO USING HTML

You can insert different types of photos with your eBay auctions, including digital camera photos and scanned photos, using the <IMG> tag. The <IMG> tag includes an SRC attribute that specifies where the photo to be inserted is located on the Web. When a browser opens a page that includes an HTML image, it downloads the image separately from the server where it is stored and inserts it into the page.

Adding photos using HTML in your description is an alternative to using the eBay picture service to add photos. The eBay service gives you one free photo with each listing; each additional photo costs 15 cents. Adding photos using HTML <IMG> tags in your description is free, no matter how many photos you add.

If you add your photos using HTML, you will need to store your photo files on a Web server. Many Internet service providers include Web storage space with user accounts, which you can use to store your photos. You can also use many photo hosting services, many of which cater to auction customers. Search for "photo hosting" in your favorite search engine to find them.

ADD A PHOTO USING HTML

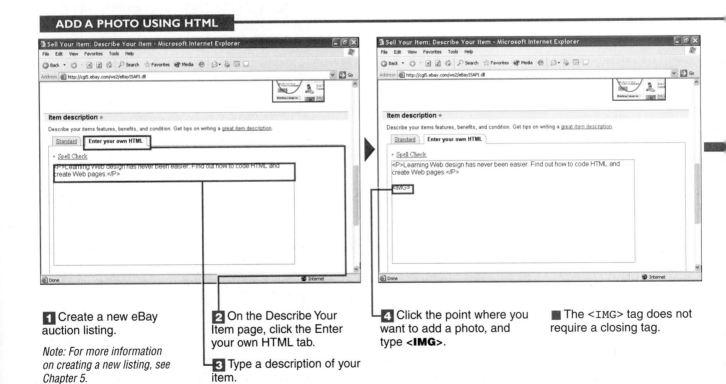

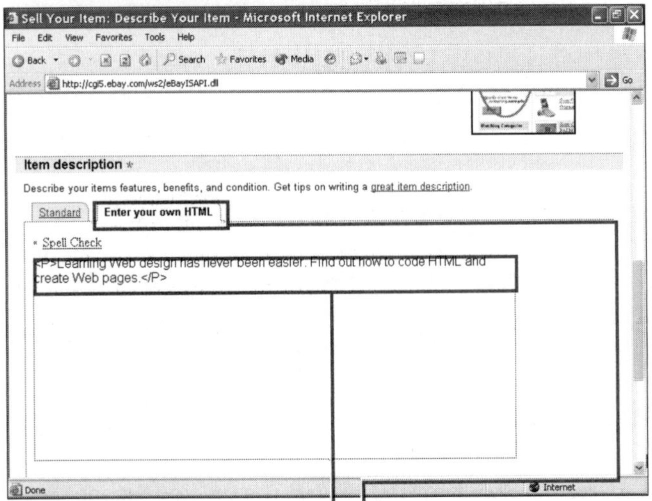

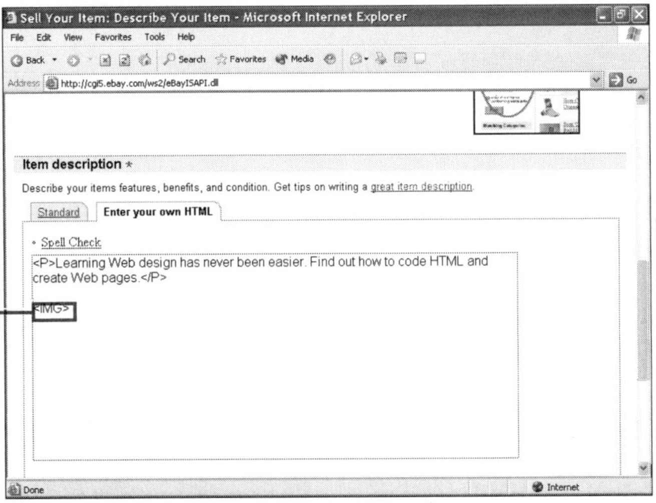

1 Create a new eBay auction listing.

Note: For more information on creating a new listing, see Chapter 5.

2 On the Describe Your Item page, click the Enter your own HTML tab.

3 Type a description of your item.

4 Click the point where you want to add a photo, and type **<IMG>**.

■ The <IMG> tag does not require a closing tag.

Can I resize a photo using HTML?

✔ Yes. You can add HEIGHT and WIDTH attributes to an <IMG> tag to specify how large your photo appears on a Web page. You specify the height and width in pixels. If the dimensions that you specify are larger or smaller than the actual dimensions of the photo, the Web browser will enlarge or shrink the photo accordingly as it displays it. For example:

```
<IMG SRC="http://www.wiley.
com/photo.jpg" HEIGHT="200"
WIDTH="300">
```

Note that it is best to resize a photo in an image editor rather than using HTML. This way, you can maximize a photo's quality. See Chapter 20 for more information about image editing.

How can I align a photo in my description?

✔ You can add an ALIGN attribute to your <IMG> tag to align your photo to the left or right of the page. Any text coming after the photo will wrap around the right or left side of the photo, respectively. For example:

```
<IMG SRC="http://www.wiley.
com/photo.jpg" ALIGN="Right">
```

Aligning your photo can enable you to fit more information in the Web browser window.

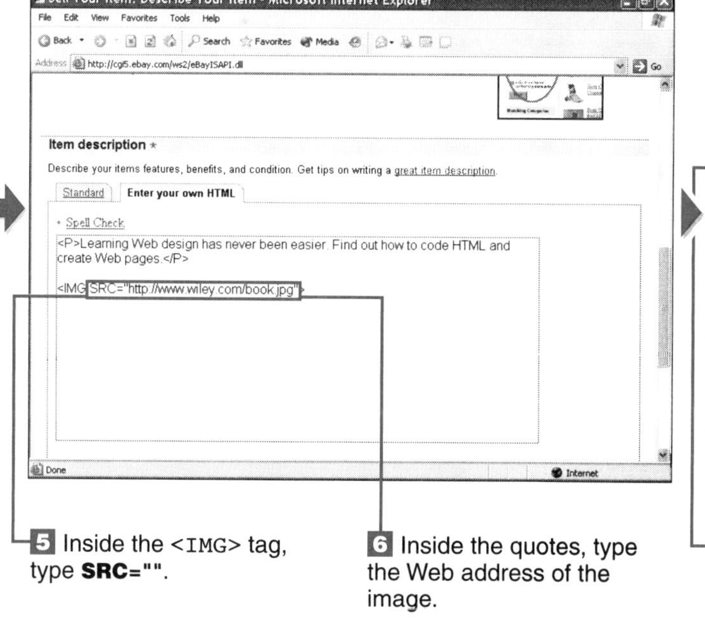

5 Inside the <IMG> tag, type **SRC=""**.

6 Inside the quotes, type the Web address of the image.

Note: Make sure you include the http:// at the beginning of the Web address.

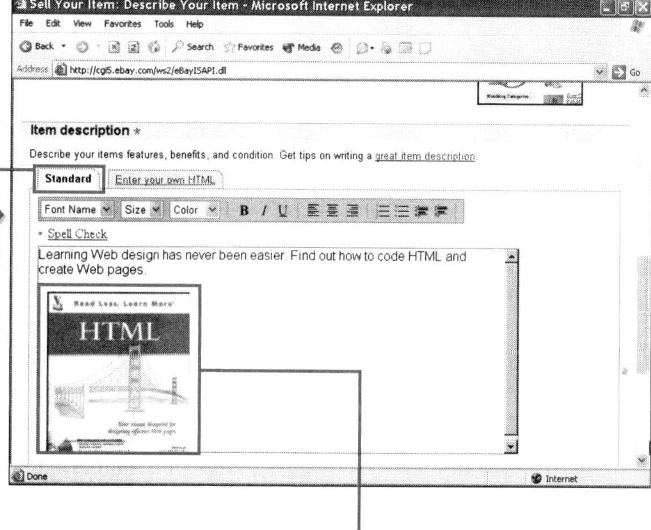

7 Click the Standard tab to preview your image.

■ The image appears in the Item description text box.

CREATE AN HTML TEMPLATE FOR YOUR LISTINGS

Odds are, after you have created a layout for your auction that you like, with text formatted and photos arranged just so, you will want to use the same layout for other auctions.

You can save a favorite layout as a template — an HTML file that you can open and copy from when creating a new listing. By saving a layout as a template, you can save yourself time and also avoid mistakes in your HTML. You can populate your template with placeholder text and images that you can replace as you create each new auction listing.

You save HTML template files as plain-text files that have a .html or .htm filename extension. You can edit them with a basic text editor, such as Notepad (Windows), SimpleText (Macintosh), or a Web editor, such as Macromedia Dreamweaver or Microsoft FrontPage.

CREATE AN HTML TEMPLATE FOR YOUR LISTINGS

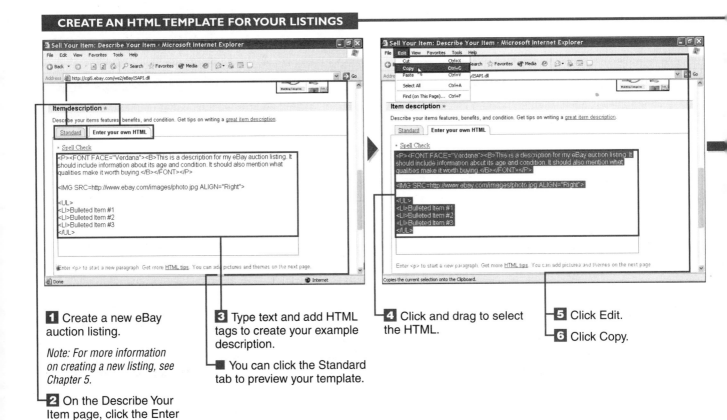

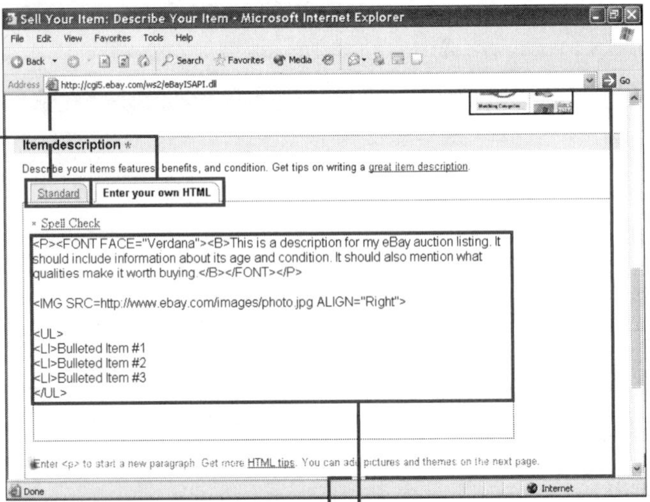

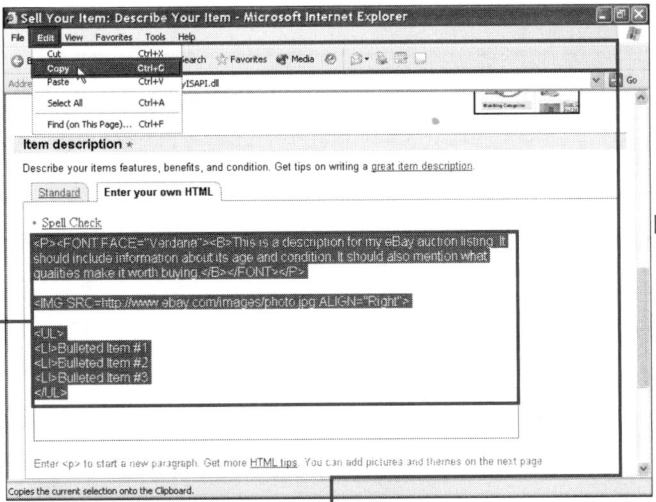

1 Create a new eBay auction listing.

Note: For more information on creating a new listing, see Chapter 5.

2 On the Describe Your Item page, click the Enter your own HTML tab.

3 Type text and add HTML tags to create your example description.

■ You can click the Standard tab to preview your template.

4 Click and drag to select the HTML.

5 Click Edit.

6 Click Copy.

How can I be sure that my HTML template is error-free?

✔ If your HTML has mistakes, your text and other content may not appear correctly in a Web browser. Mistakes can occur due to omitting closing tags or misspelling tag or attribute names. There are various free HTML validation services online, such as the one at http://validator.w3.org. Most Web editors also have built-in HTML checkers that can alert you to errors.

Where can I find premade eBay templates?

✔ The CD-ROM included with this book features a number of eBay auction templates. You can open them from the CD-ROM and use them for your auctions. The various selling tools at eBay, such as Turbo Lister and Seller's Assistant, also come with professional-looking templates that you can use to enhance your listings. See Chapters 18 and 19 for details about these eBay tools.

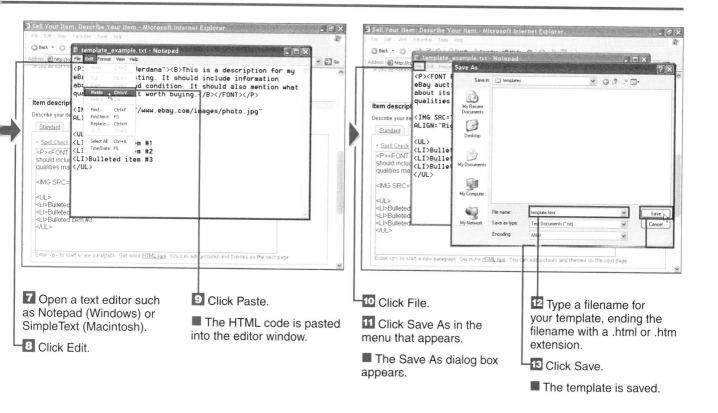

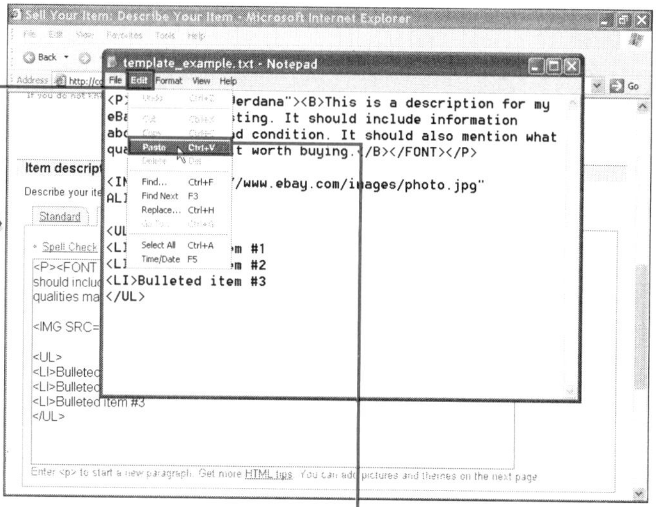

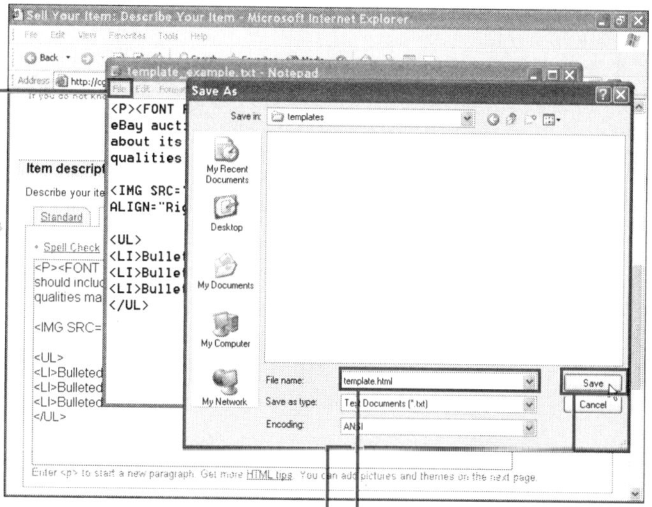

7 Open a text editor such as Notepad (Windows) or SimpleText (Macintosh).

8 Click Edit.

9 Click Paste.

■ The HTML code is pasted into the editor window.

10 Click File.

11 Click Save As in the menu that appears.

■ The Save As dialog box appears.

12 Type a filename for your template, ending the filename with a .html or .htm extension.

13 Click Save.

■ The template is saved.

ANALYZE FEEDBACK

Buyers and sellers can use GutCheck software to quickly and easily analyze an eBay user's feedback rating. The tool offers a handy alternative to viewing feedback information through the user's member profile page.

Checking the feedback ratings of users can be a good way of estimating how trustworthy and dependable they are when participating in eBay transactions.

You may want to think twice before doing business with eBay users who have many instances of negative feedback. Some users will not consider doing business with buyers or sellers with feedback ratings lower than 98%.

After you install GutCheck, you can use the software by right-clicking a User ID or feedback rating on the listing page on the eBay site. Each eBay listing displays the User ID and feedback rating of the seller and the current high bidder, if there is one. A GutCheck window appears, and the feedback information for the user is downloaded and displayed in the window. You can sort the information by clicking a table heading.

You can download the free GutCheck software here: http://www.teamredline.com/gutcheck.

ANALYZE FEEDBACK

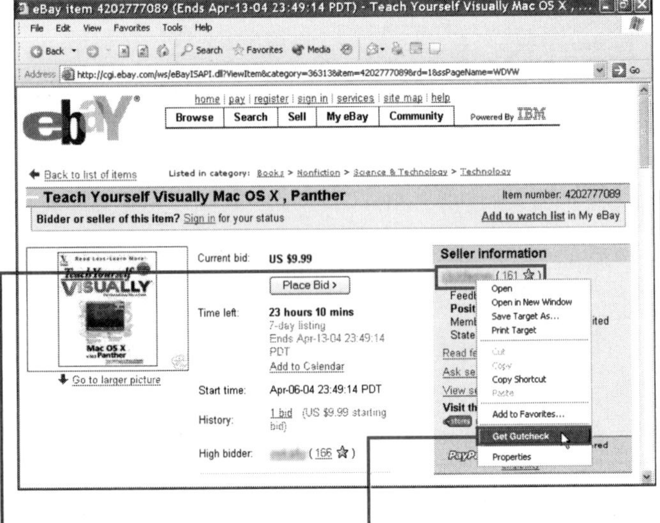

1 After installing GutCheck, view an eBay listing.

2 Right-click a User ID or feedback rating.

3 Click Get Gutcheck from the menu that appears.

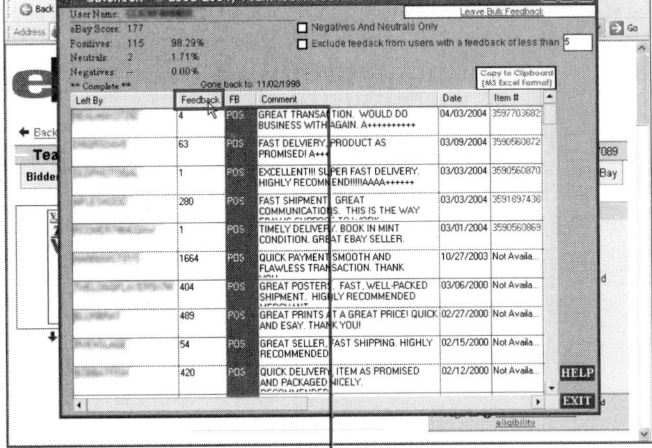

■ A GutCheck window appears, and the feedback information is downloaded.

■ For each instance of feedback, the window displays user information, feedback type, comments, date left, and item number.

4 Click a column heading.

How can I filter the feedback results in GutCheck?

✔ You will be most interested in any neutral and negative feedback that an eBay user has acquired. You can display this information on its own by clicking the Negatives and Neutrals Only option (☐ changes to ☑). You can also filter the results by clicking the Exclude Feedback option (☐ changes to ☑) and typing a threshold value. The Gutcheck window then only displays feedback only from users that have a rating above the number you chose.

How can I export the information in GutCheck?

✔ You can click the Copy to Clipboard button in the upper-right corner to copy the results to the Windows Clipboard. You can then paste the results into a word processor or spreadsheet program. The results are stored in the Clipboard in a tab-delineated format.

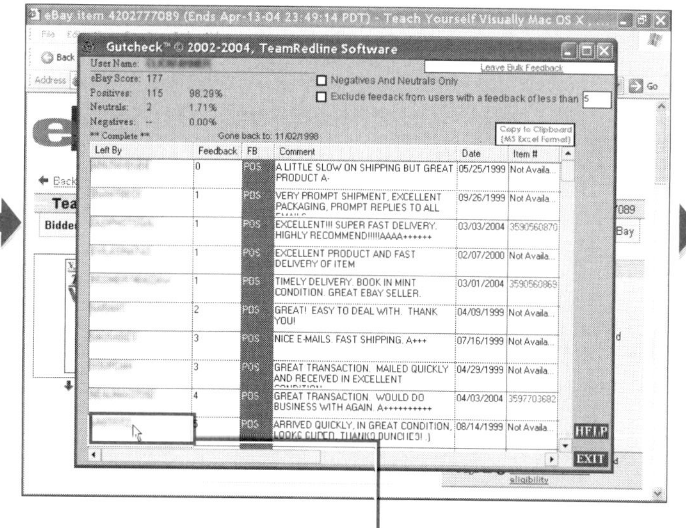

■ GutCheck sorts the feedback information by the column you clicked.

5 Double-click a user name.

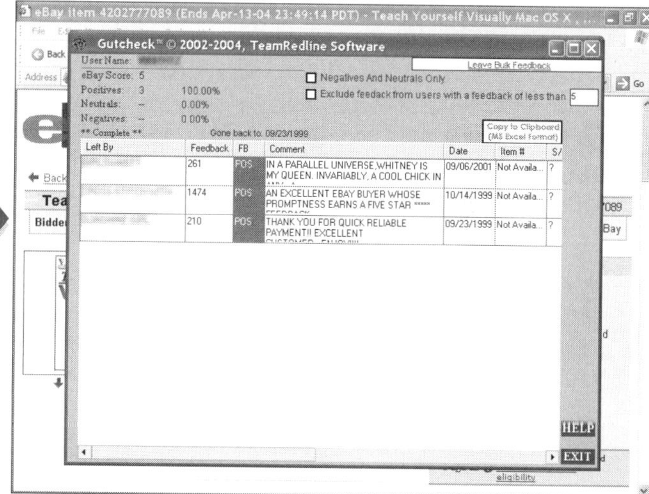

■ The feedback information for the user appears.

SNIPE AN AUCTION

Sniping is the act of placing a bid during the last seconds of an auction in order to hide your interest from other bidders. By waiting until just before an auction closes, snipers can often avoid the price escalation that can naturally occur when there are multiple parties interested in the same item.

In the early days of eBay, buyers sniped manually, staying online in front of their Web browsers until the last minute of an auction and submitting a bid through the eBay Web site. Today, there are dozens of automated services that can snipe for you.

When you sign up for a sniping service, you submit your User ID and password, so that the service can submit bids on your behalf. You then specify which auctions you are interested in and how much you are willing to pay. The sniping service submits your bid at the very end of an auction — usually seconds before it closes.

Using a sniping service keeps you from wasting time waiting for an auction to end, especially if it ends at an inconvenient time of day. Sniping services also give you better chances of winning because they do their submitting on high-speed connections using automated software.

SNIPE AN AUCTION

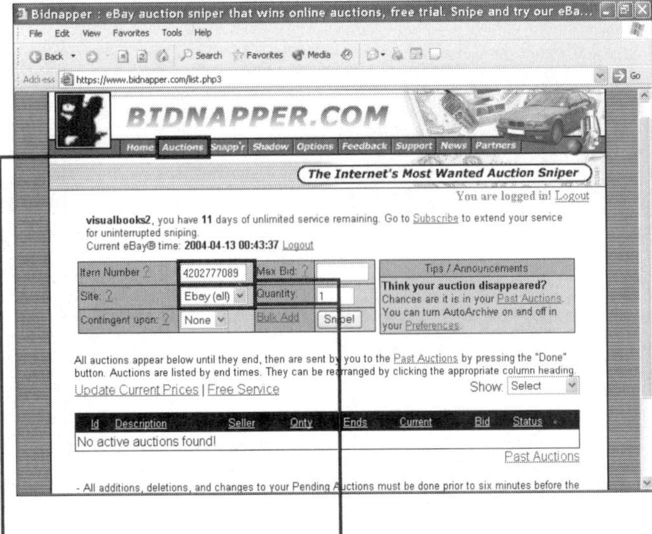

1 Visit www.bidnapper.com and sign up for the service.

Note: New users can currently use the service free for ten days.

2 Click Auctions.

3 Type the item number of the listing you want to snipe.

■ You can copy and paste the number from the auction page on the eBay site.

4 Click here and select the site where the listing is located.

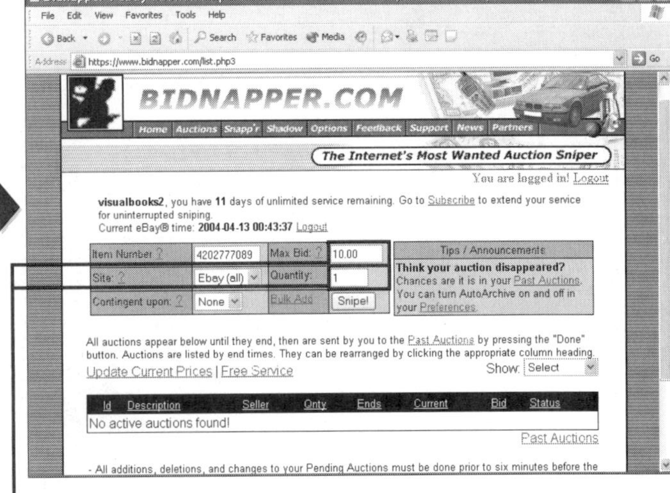

5 Type a maximum bid.

6 Type a quantity.

■ You can have Bidnapper bid on multiple items in a listing if the seller is offering more than one item.

What happens if I change my User ID or password on eBay?

✔ You will need to change your user information at any sniping services you are using. Because sniping services function independently of eBay, they have no way of knowing when you update the logon information for your eBay account. If you change your logon information only at eBay and your sniping service then tries to submit bids for you, the bid submissions will fail.

What can cause me to still be unsuccessful when using a sniping service?

✔ You may simply be outbid. Using a sniping service cannot guarantee that another buyer won't make a bid that is above your maximum.

There is also a chance that, when the sniping service is ready to bid, the difference between the current high bid and your maximum bid is less than the minimum bid increment. This situation can also prevent the sniping service from successfully submitting a bid on your behalf. For more about bid increments, see Chapter 7.

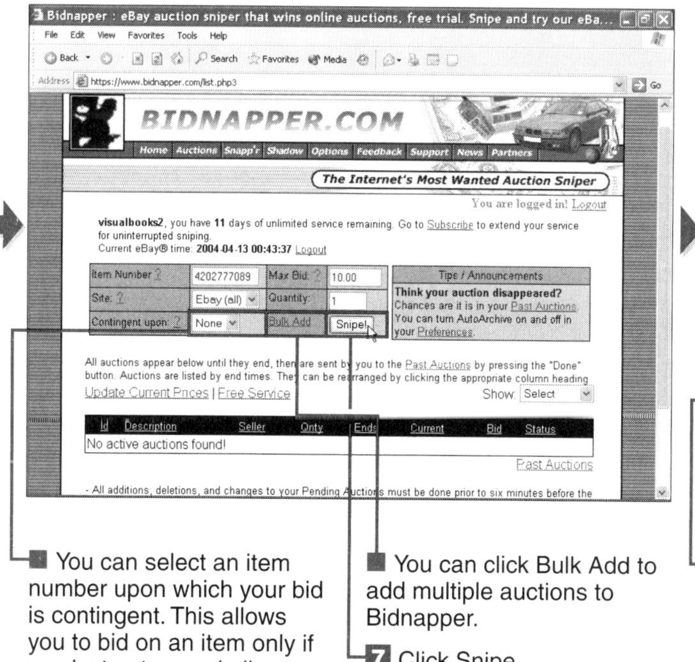

■ You can select an item number upon which your bid is contingent. This allows you to bid on an item only if you lost out on a similar item.

■ You can click Bulk Add to add multiple auctions to Bidnapper.

7 Click Snipe.

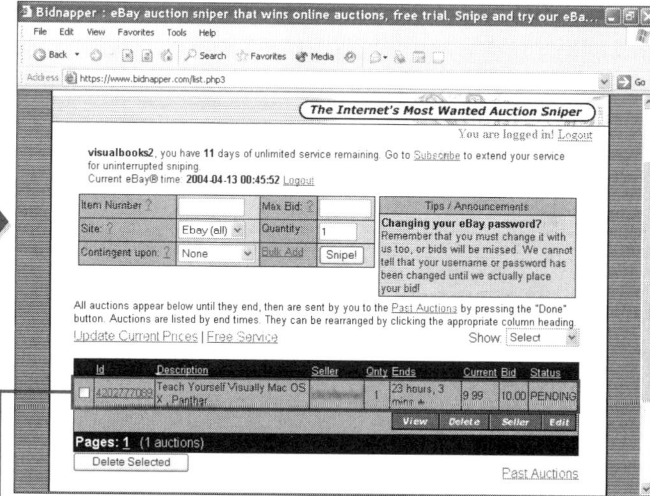

■ Bidnapper adds the listing to the list of auctions to be sniped.

■ Bidnapper sends you an e-mail after the auction ends, informing you of the sniping result.

■ You can also log on to your account in Bidnapper to view the sniping status of your auctions.

CREATE A TEMPLATE-BASED LISTING

Using professionally designed auction templates can help eBay sellers create better-looking listings with a minimum amount of work. Templates can be especially useful if you are a seller who does not know how to use HTML and does not have the time or interest to learn.

Templates typically display your auction information with stylized text, colored or textured backgrounds, and graphical border treatments. After selecting a template style and layout, you can specify your item description, payment methods, shipping options, and other auction particulars. These are then combined with the chosen template. You can copy and paste the resulting HTML into the description field when you create your listing on eBay.

Web sites such as www.nucite.com offer a limited number of free templates to use with your auctions. Often these sites offer access to a larger library of templates for a one-time fee or subscription.

If you know how to write HTML or have a Web-page editor, you can create your own templates for your eBay auctions. See Chapter 21 for details. Creating templates with HTML can help you make your listing look more interesting without having to resort to eBay upgrades, which cost money.

CREATE A TEMPLATE-BASED LISTING

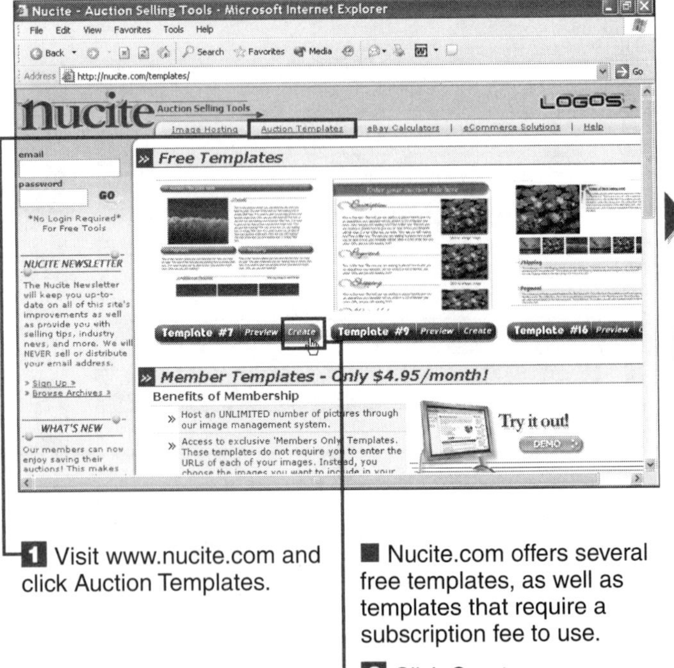

1 Visit www.nucite.com and click Auction Templates.

■ Nucite.com offers several free templates, as well as templates that require a subscription fee to use.

2 Click Create.

■ A Create Template page appears.

3 Type the title, description, and other details for your auction.

4 Type your eBay User ID.

5 Click an option to specify the links to include in your listing description.

■ Nucite uses your User ID to automatically create the links.

Who hosts the photos and graphics when I use a template service?

✔ The answer depends on the service provider. Typically, the decorative graphics that make up a template are hosted by the template service, and the listing-specific photos are hosted by you, the seller. Some template services may include photo-hosting services for your listing-specific photos.

The Nucite.com service hosts the template-specific graphics on its Web servers. You can host your listing images yourself, or you can use Nucite's hosting service, which is fee-based. For more information about photos and photo hosting, see Chapter 20.

Can I edit the HTML generated by a template-creation service?

✔ Yes. Copy the HTML into a text editor or Web-page editor. Be sure not to change the URL references for the template graphics, or the graphics might not appear correctly when you post the listing online.

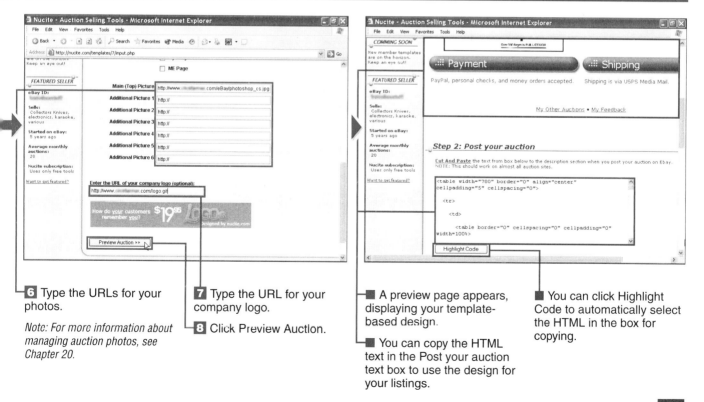

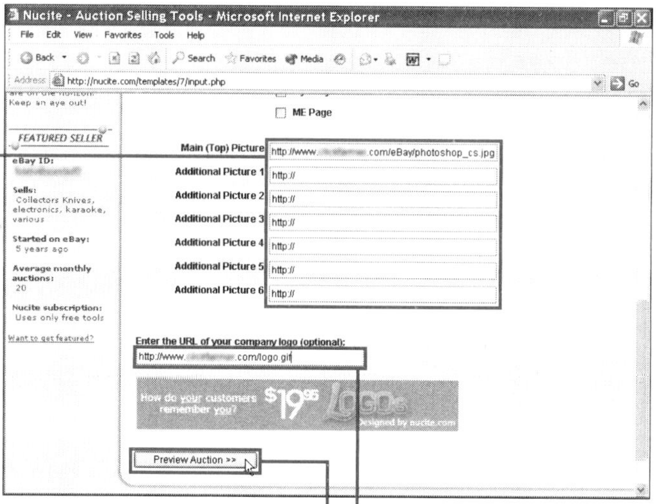

6 Type the URLs for your photos.

Note: For more information about managing auction photos, see Chapter 20.

7 Type the URL for your company logo.

8 Click Preview Auction.

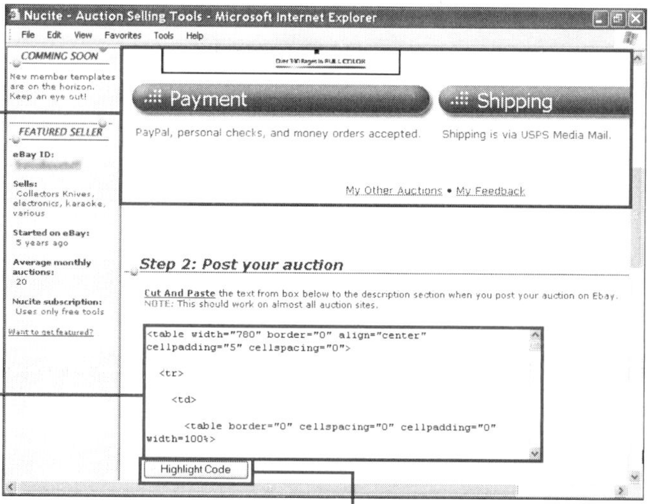

■ A preview page appears, displaying your template-based design.

■ You can copy the HTML text in the Post your auction text box to use the design for your listings.

■ You can click Highlight Code to automatically select the HTML in the box for copying.

AUTOMATICALLY NOTIFY WINNING BIDDERS

Some third-party auction management programs include the ability to automatically notify customers who have won your auctions. This can help increase the chances that you get paid for your items in a timely manner. It also helps establish good communication channels with your customers, thereby maximizing your chances of receiving positive feedback.

AuctionHelper is a Web-based auction management program that enables you to set up *auto reminders* that automatically send e-mail messages to customers if they have not submitted payment by a certain number of days after an auction closes. You can also set up auto reminders to send invoices to customers after a certain number of days.

In addition to helping you manage customer communication, AuctionHelper provides bulk submission of listings, invoicing tools, and image hosting. In this respect, it is similar to the Seller's Assistant and Selling Manager tools offered by eBay.

See Chapter 19 for more about the eBay-based sales management tools.

For a list of other third-party auction management tools, see Chapter 7.

AUTOMATICALLY NOTIFY WINNING BIDDERS

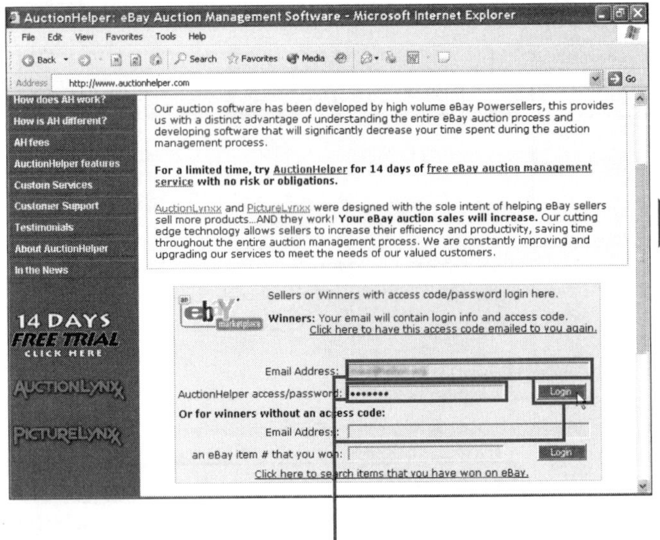

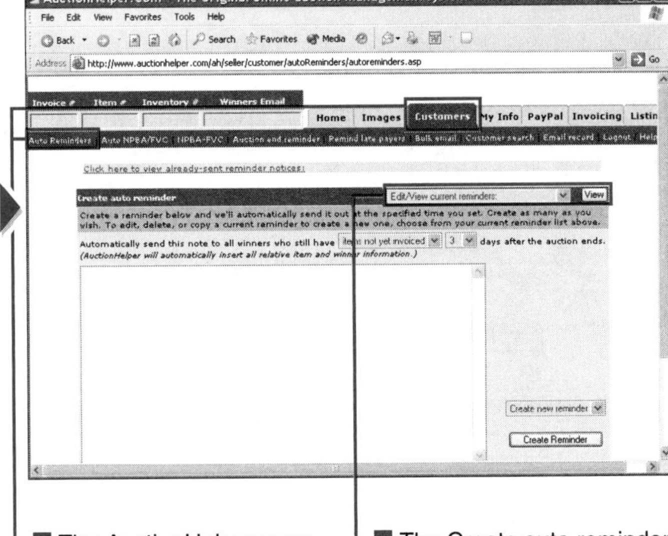

1 Visit www.auctionhelper.com and sign up for the auction management service.

■ You can use the service free for 14 days if you are a new user.

2 Type your e-mail address.

3 Type your AuctionHelper password.

4 Click Login.

■ The AuctionHelper user home page appears.

5 Click Customers.

6 Click Auto Reminders.

■ The Create auto reminder page appears.

■ You can select previous reminders and click View to view or edit them.

How can I immediately send e-mails to customers who have yet to pay?

✔ In AuctionHelper, you can do this using the Bulk E-mail feature. After logging on, click Customers and then Bulk E-mail. The tool notifies your auction winners with items or invoices not marked paid in the past 45 days, regardless of whether or not they have been invoiced. AuctionHelper sends a copy of the message to your e-mail address.

How can I look up the contact information for past customers?

✔ A handy feature offered by AuctionHelper is the ability to view the contact information for past customers. This can enable you to e-mail customers when you have posted new auctions in which they might be interested. After logging on, click Customers and then Customer Search. A search interface appears. Searching for past customers without including a search keyword returns a list of all of your past customers.

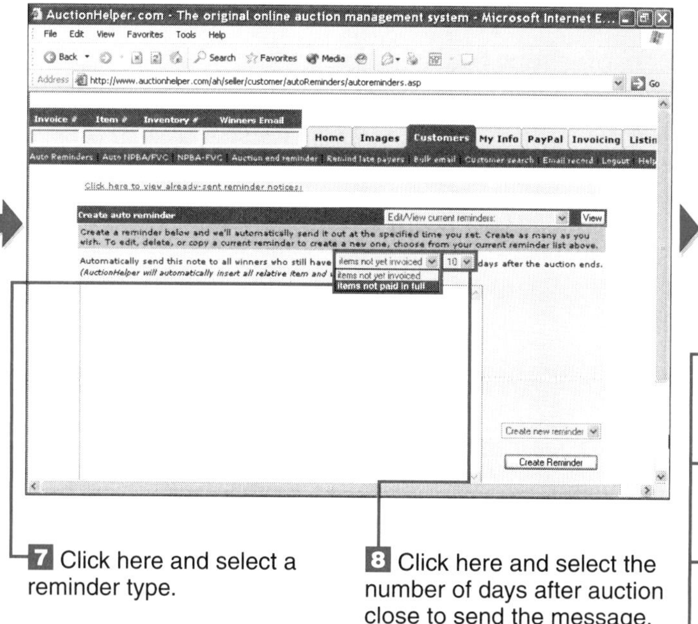

7 Click here and select a reminder type.

8 Click here and select the number of days after auction close to send the message.

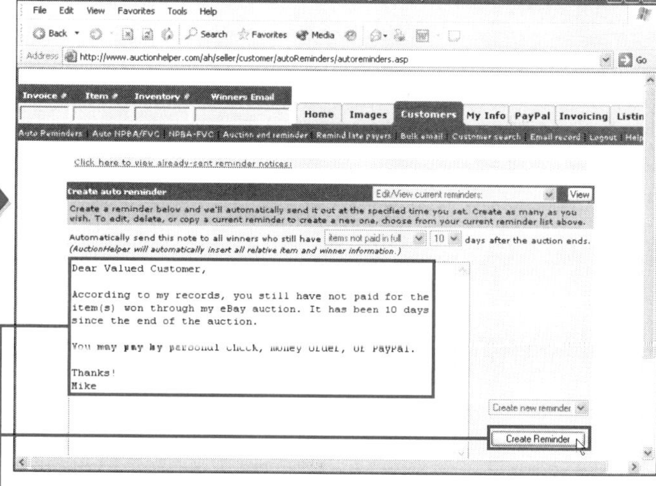

9 Type a message to be sent to the customer.

10 Click Create Reminder.

■ AuctionHelper saves the reminder information, and an e-mail is sent automatically to customers who meet the criteria you chose in steps 7 and 8.

SECTION VII

23) SET UP AN EBAY STORE

24) MARKET YOUR EBAY STORE

25) A STORE ALTERNATIVE: HALF.COM

YOUR OWN EBAY STORE

SET UP AN EBAY STORE

Sellers who have a steady inventory of for-sale items and want a more permanent presence on the eBay site can open an eBay Store.

An eBay Store gives you a set of searchable, customizable pages hosted on the eBay site where you can list your goods. You can choose a store name that is displayed on each page, select a set of custom colors for your pages, and even brand your pages with your own logo, if you have one. Buyers purchase store inventory items from your store at a fixed, Buy It Now price, without having to compete against other eBay bidders.

When you consider the multiple tasks that go into building an online Web site, setting up an eBay Store can be an economical, timesaving deal. The store format saves you from having to sign up for hosting space at an Internet service provider, and you do not have to deploy the e-commerce technology that allows people to shop and pay for items online.

You also do not have to design your own Web pages. With a store, you use eBay's templates. Buyers who are familiar with viewing and bidding on eBay auctions will find purchasing from a store easy.

eBay Store subscription fees start at $9.95 per month. The per-month fees are charged whether or not you sell anything in your store during that month. eBay currently offers new store owners a 30-day free trial before charging the subscription fees.

SET UP AN EBAY STORE

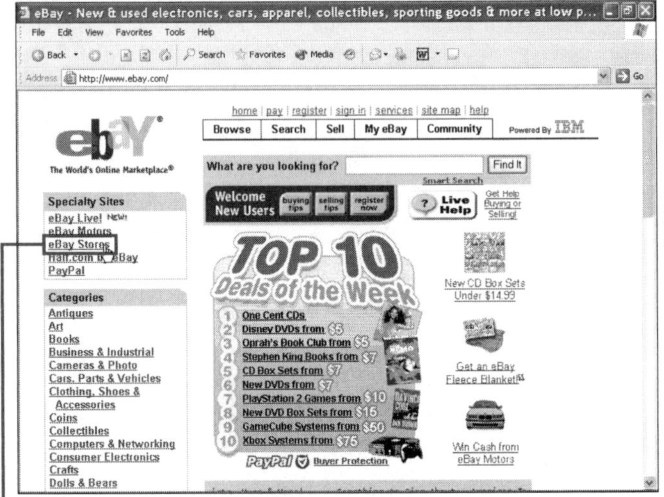

1 Click eBay Stores on the eBay home page.

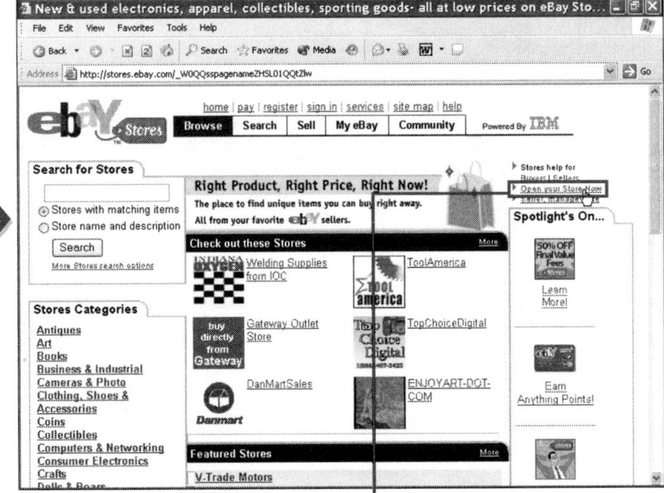

■ The eBay Stores page appears.

2 Click Open your Store Now.

What is the Web address of my store?

✔ eBay creates a unique Web address, or Uniform Resource Locator (URL), for your store using your chosen store name. To create the URL, all letters are converted to lowercase, and spaces and other special characters are removed. For example, if the name of your store is Mike's eShop, your URL will be http://stores.ebay.com/mikeseshop.

A hyphenated version of your store name, such as http://stores.ebay.com/mikes-eshop, will also work in the URL.

Using the hyphenated version when you create links to your eBay Store from other sites will make it easier for search engines to recognize keywords in your URL and associate them with your eBay Store site.

How should I describe my store?

✔ When describing your store, think of what potential customers may type if they are looking for your products, and try to include those as keywords in your desciption. At the same time, make sure your description is straightforward and grammatically correct so that your store has a professional appearance. The text in your store description is important because it will be one of the things that search engines will analyze when categorizing your store.

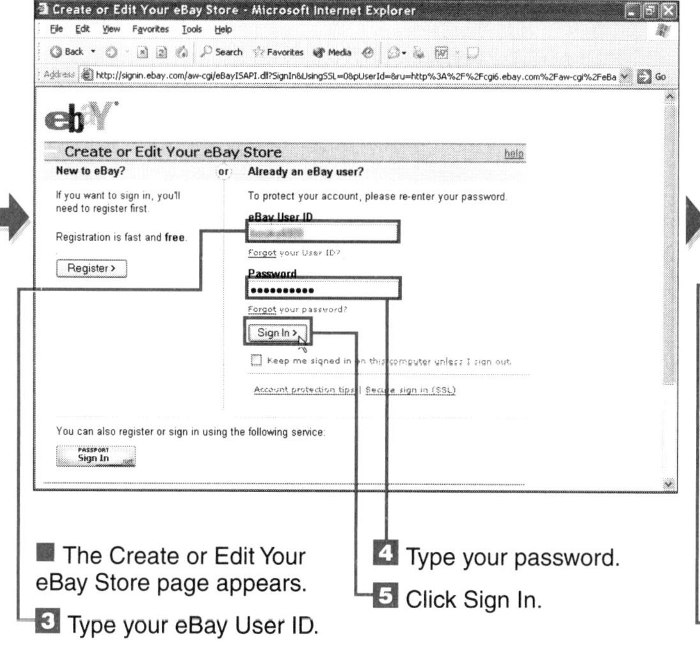

■ The Create or Edit Your eBay Store page appears.

3 Type your eBay User ID.

4 Type your password.

5 Click Sign In.

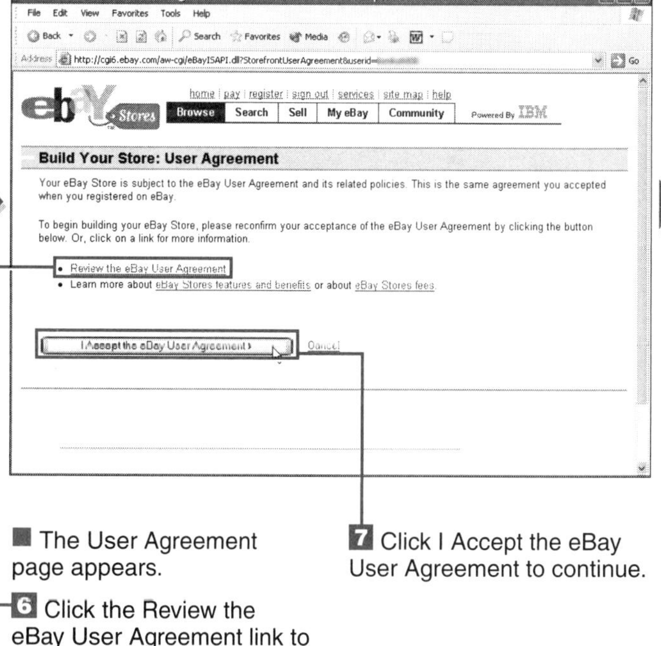

■ The User Agreement page appears.

6 Click the Review the eBay User Agreement link to read the agreement and other information.

7 Click I Accept the eBay User Agreement to continue.

CONTINUED

SET UP AN EBAY STORE (CONTINUED)

As soon as you have set up an eBay Store, customers can reach it through the Stores area of eBay. Clicking the eBay Stores link on the eBay home page takes visitors to the eBay Stores main page, where they can browse stores by category or use a search engine to find specific store items. Keep in mind that store items typically do not appear in regular eBay auction search results.

Customers can also reach your store through your regular eBay auctions. Cross-promotion tools enable you to display similar items from your store at the bottom of your listings. See Chapter 24 for more information.

There are some drawbacks to having an eBay Store, as opposed to running an online store independently. Although eBay gives you the opportunity to choose a color scheme for your store and lets you add a logo or other graphics, you are limited in how you can organize the information on your pages. You also pay fees for every item you list in your store, although the fees are lower than those for auctions.

SET UP AN EBAY STORE (CONTINUED)

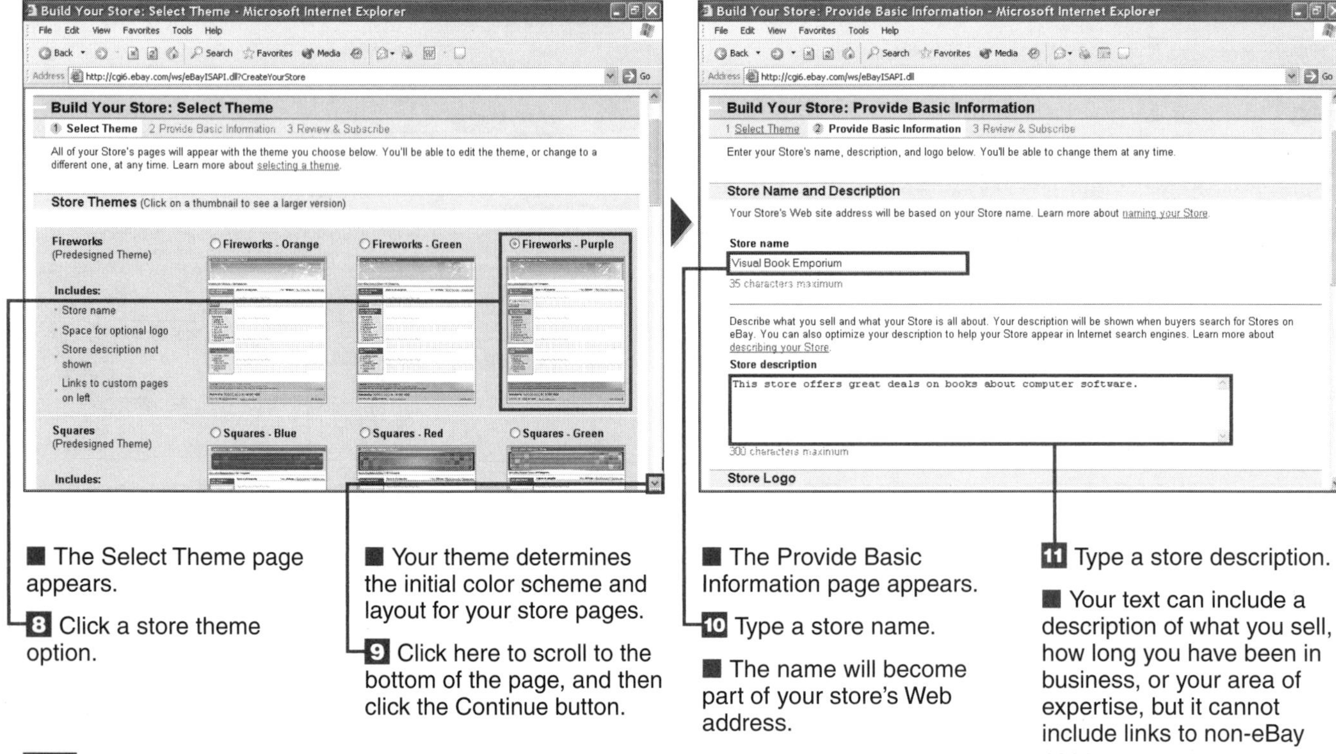

■ The Select Theme page appears.

8 Click a store theme option.

■ Your theme determines the initial color scheme and layout for your store pages.

9 Click here to scroll to the bottom of the page, and then click the Continue button.

■ The Provide Basic Information page appears.

10 Type a store name.

■ The name will become part of your store's Web address.

11 Type a store description.

■ Your text can include a description of what you sell, how long you have been in business, or your area of expertise, but it cannot include links to non-eBay pages.

How do I update the appearance of my store?

✔ You can do this by going to your store's home page, clicking the Seller, manage store link, and then clicking the Store Builder link. This enables you to update your store's name, theme, header style, and other charateristics.

Are there characters that I cannot use in my store name?

✔ eBay has a number of rules governing store names. A store name cannot start with four or more consecutive letter A's, nor can it contain www anywhere inside it. It cannot start with an e or E followed by a number. It cannot contain the characters <, >, or @. It also cannot be the username of another user on eBay.

How do I create a custom graphic for my store heading?

✔ You can create the graphic in an image-editing program such as Adobe Photoshop Elements. If your business already has a logo, you may want to use that as a starting point. Your heading graphic needs to be 310 pixels wide by 90 pixels tall. eBay resizes graphics that are not this size before they appear on your store pages.
If you want to display a custom graphic, it must be hosted on another Web server — eBay will not host it.

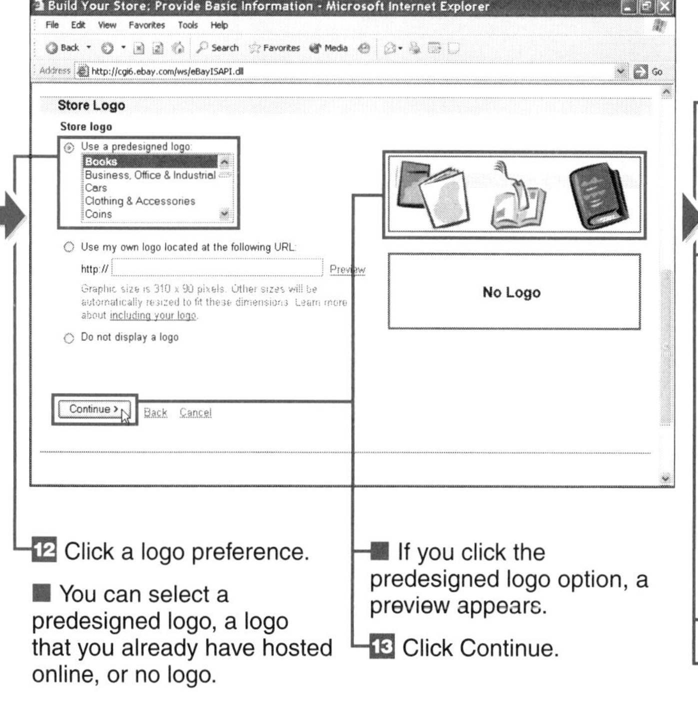

12 Click a logo preference.

■ You can select a predesigned logo, a logo that you already have hosted online, or no logo.

■ If you click the predesigned logo option, a preview appears.

13 Click Continue.

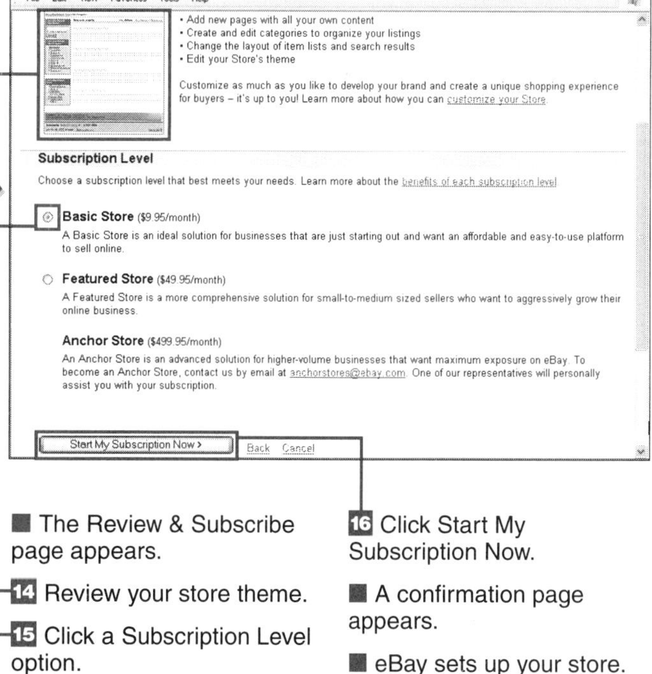

■ The Review & Subscribe page appears.

14 Review your store theme.

15 Click a Subscription Level option.

Note: To subscribe as an anchor store, see "Upgrade Your Store."

16 Click Start My Subscription Now.

■ A confirmation page appears.

■ eBay sets up your store.

ADD AN ITEM TO YOUR STORE INVENTORY

Creating a listing for your store is similar to creating a regular auction listing. Every store listing has a title, eBay category, description, and optional photos associated with it, just like regular auctions.

Unlike regular auctions, however, store inventory listings have a store-specific category associated with them, as well as a regular eBay category. You can create these store-specific categories when you create your store. They allow you to organize items within your store pages.

Store inventory items also only have a Buy It Now price. Because buyers at your eBay Store purchase items at fixed prices, you do not specify a starting price or a reserve price when you add items to your store.

Keep in mind that items that you list in your store do not normally appear in regular eBay search and browse results. Regular auctions and fixed-price listings get first priority in the regular search results. However, if a customer performs a search and there are ten or fewer auction or fixed-price results, eBay will display some relevant store listings on the results page. eBay also provides a link on the search results pages that allows viewers to display any store items that match the search.

ADD AN ITEM TO YOUR STORE INVENTORY

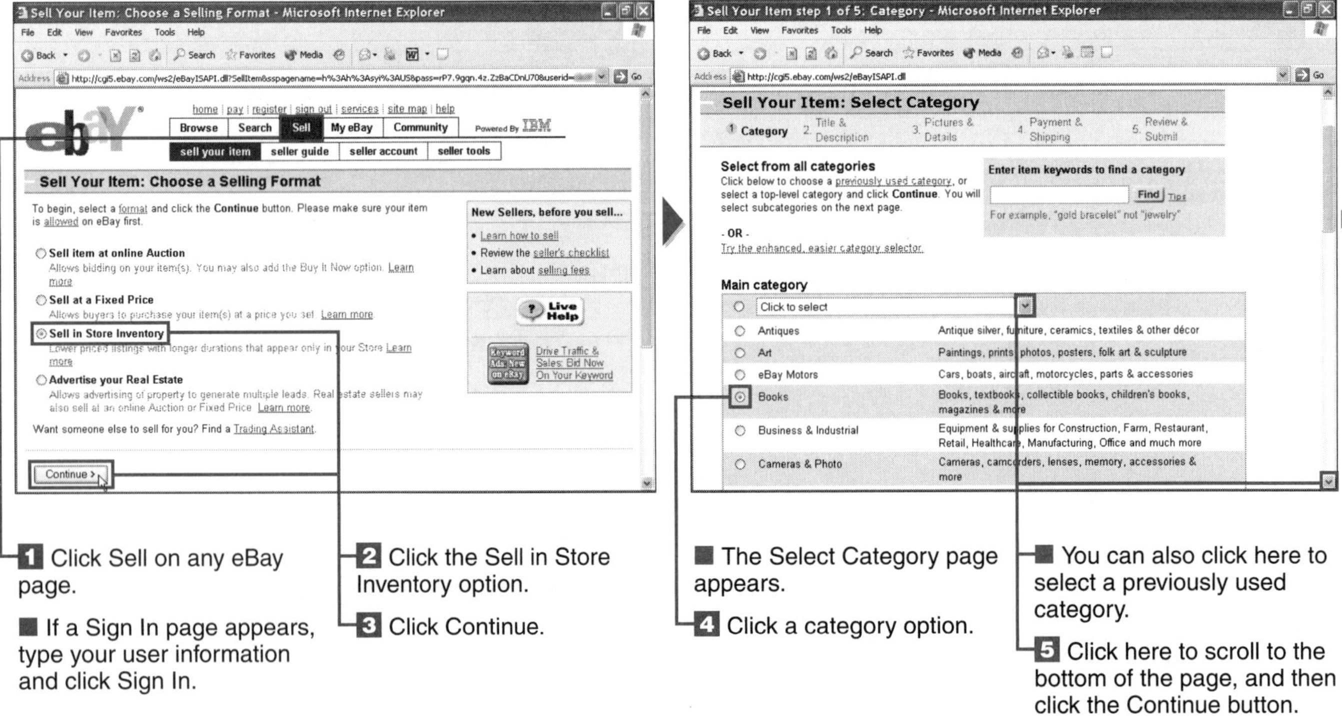

1 Click Sell on any eBay page.

■ If a Sign In page appears, type your user information and click Sign In.

2 Click the Sell in Store Inventory option.

3 Click Continue.

■ The Select Category page appears.

4 Click a category option.

■ You can also click here to select a previously used category.

5 Click here to scroll to the bottom of the page, and then click the Continue button.

How can I get customer traffic to my listings?

✔ To attract more visitors to your store listings, you can promote your store within your auctions and fixed-price listings. See Chapter 24 for more information.

You can also upgrade your store so that customers can more easily get to them through advertising on the eBay Stores main page and category pages. See the section "Upgrade Your Store," later in this chapter, for more information.

Do nonstore listings appear in my store?

✔ Yes, regular auctions and fixed-price listings appear in your store just like your store inventory items do. Potential buyers can visit your store to view and purchase everything you have listed on eBay, not just your store inventory. When your regular auctions end, those items are no longer listed in your store inventory.

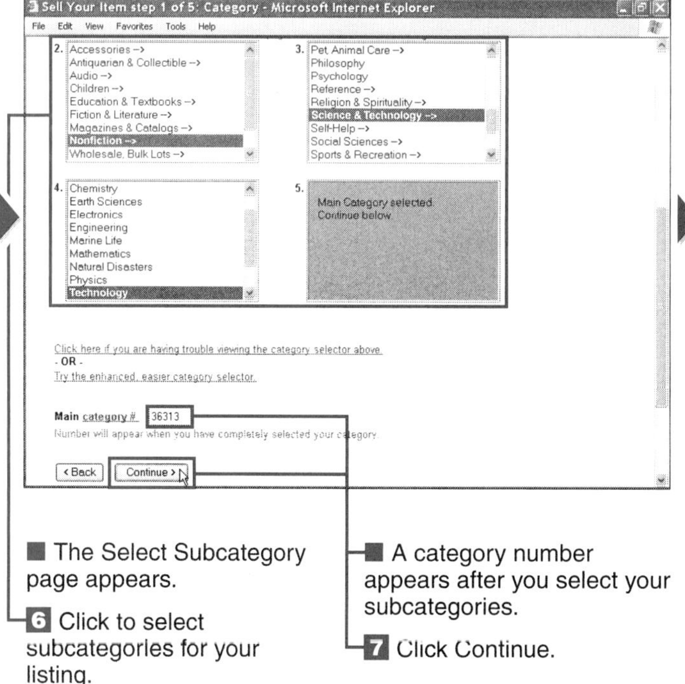

■ The Select Subcategory page appears.

6 Click to select subcategories for your listing.

■ A category number appears after you select your subcategories.

7 Click Continue.

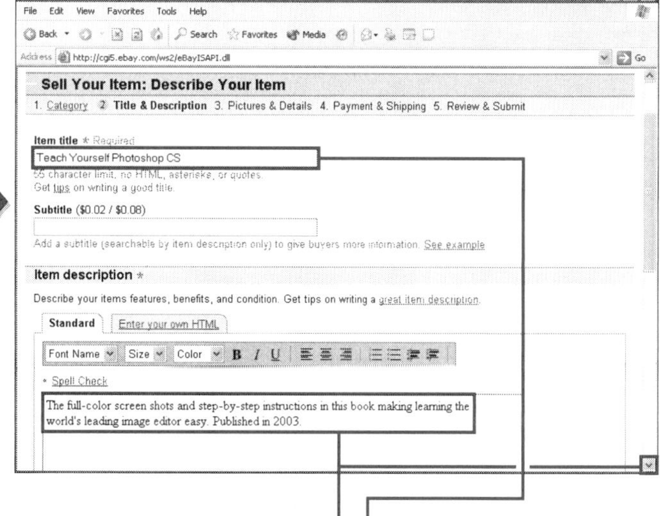

■ The Describe Your Item page, which is similar to that for creating regular eBay auctions, appears.

Note: See Chapter 5 for more information on creating eBay auctions.

8 Type a title for your item.

9 Type a description.

10 Click here to scroll down the page, and then click the Continue button.

CONTINUED

ADD AN ITEM TO YOUR STORE INVENTORY (CONTINUED)

In addition to the monthly fees you pay to keep your store running, you pay fees to eBay to list each item in your store. The good thing is, insertion fees for store items are lower than those for auction items. Insertion fees are 2 cents for every 30 days that you schedule your listing to run. Regular auction insertion fees range from 30 cents to $4.80.

You can list your store items for 30, 60, 90, or 120 days. You can also set them to appear as Good 'Til Cancelled, and the items stay for sale in your store indefinitely. You can cancel your Good 'Til Cancelled items in the Manage Your Store or My eBay areas.

If your store item sells, you pay the same final value fees as you do for regular auctions. Fees are 5.25 percent of the final selling price for items sold for up to $25, with a tiered fee structure for higher-priced items.

ADD AN ITEM TO YOUR STORE INVENTORY (CONTINUED)

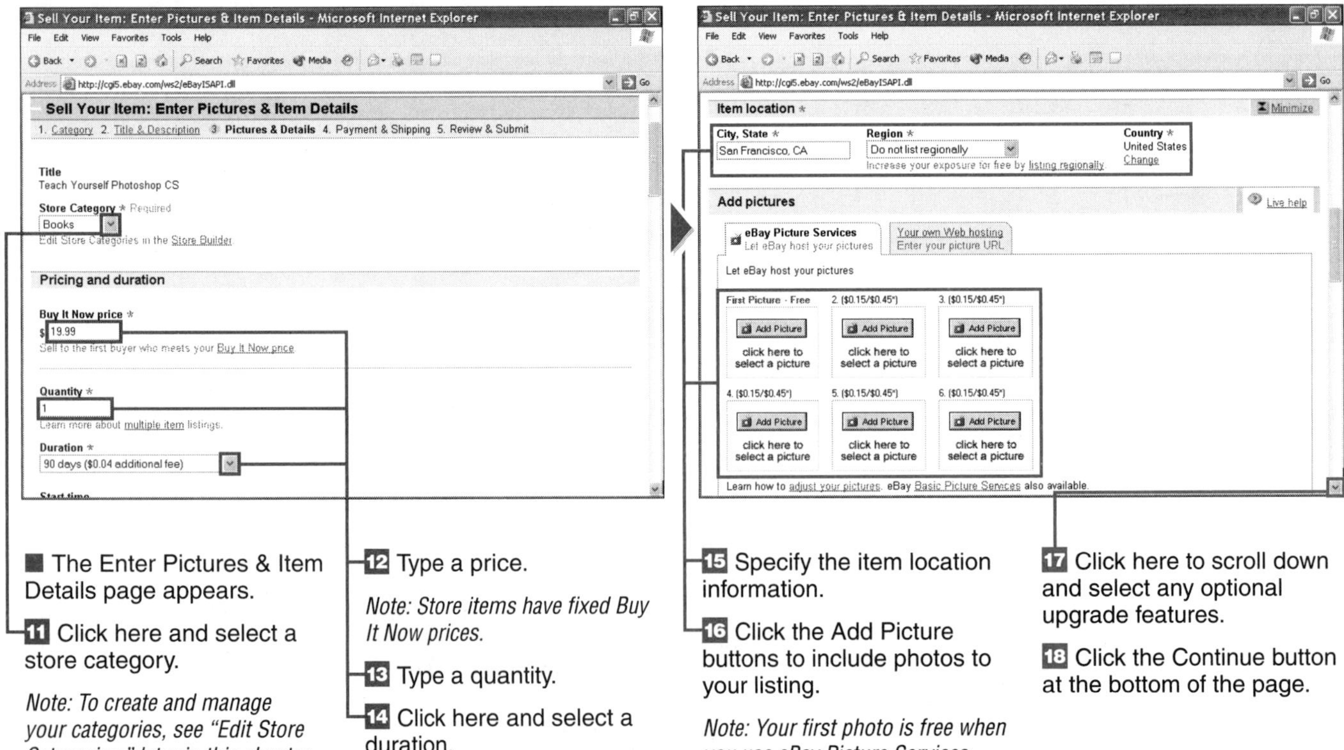

■ The Enter Pictures & Item Details page appears.

11 Click here and select a store category.

Note: To create and manage your categories, see "Edit Store Categories," later in this chapter.

12 Type a price.

Note: Store items have fixed Buy It Now prices.

13 Type a quantity.

14 Click here and select a duration.

15 Specify the item location information.

16 Click the Add Picture buttons to include photos to your listing.

Note: Your first photo is free when you use eBay Picture Services.

17 Click here to scroll down and select any optional upgrade features.

18 Click the Continue button at the bottom of the page.

Can I convert a store listing to a regular listing?

✔ No. You cannot convert the selling format of any current listing. If you want to sell a store item in a regular auction, you must create a new listing and select the different format. The easiest way is to log on to your My eBay page and click the Sell Similar link under the Manage Listings column of your current listing.

How can customers search for items within my store?

✔ Every store comes with a search engine that enables customers to search for keywords in your listings. The search form appears on the left side of your store pages, in the navigation bar. Users at your store can type a keyword in the search box and click Search to use it.

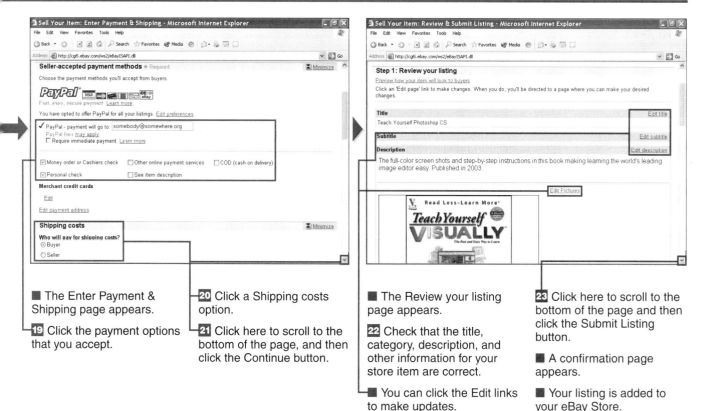

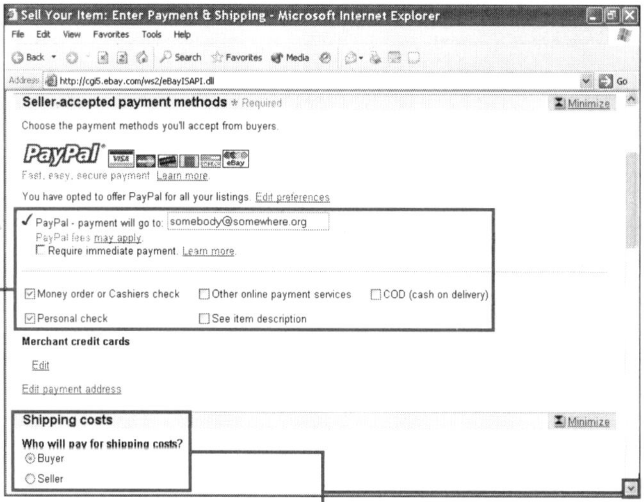

■ The Enter Payment & Shipping page appears.

19 Click the payment options that you accept.

20 Click a Shipping costs option.

21 Click here to scroll to the bottom of the page, and then click the Continue button.

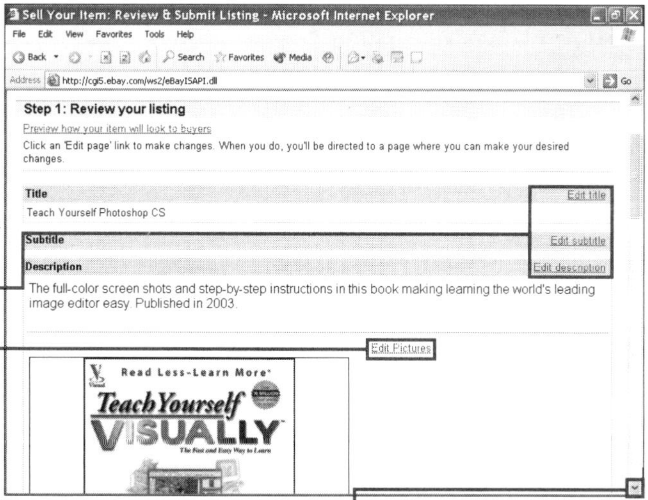

■ The Review your listing page appears.

22 Check that the title, category, description, and other information for your store item are correct.

■ You can click the Edit links to make updates.

23 Click here to scroll to the bottom of the page and then click the Submit Listing button.

■ A confirmation page appears.

■ Your listing is added to your eBay Store.

UPGRADE YOUR STORE

Subscription fees for a basic eBay Store are $9.95 per month. This level gets you a customized storefront at eBay where your store listings are displayed. You get a custom Web address that people can type into their browsers to get to your store. The Web address also lets you link to your store from other Web sites. Plus, you get access to eBay's cross-promotion tools and monthly seller reports.

To increase visibility for your store across the eBay site, you can upgrade your store subscription. For $49.95 per month, you can get a Featured eBay Store that includes priority positioning on the Shop eBay Stores section of the eBay search and browse pages; featured placement on the eBay Stores main page; and prime positioning in the top-level stores directory pages where you have items listed.

High-volume sellers who want maximum exposure can pay a fee of $499.95 per month for Anchor Store status. This gets you one million impressions per month throughout the eBay.com pages, including the eBay home page. An *impression* is counted when a visitor views an eBay page on which advertising for your store information appears. Anchor eBay Stores also get their logos displayed on the eBay Stores home page.

UPGRADE YOUR STORE

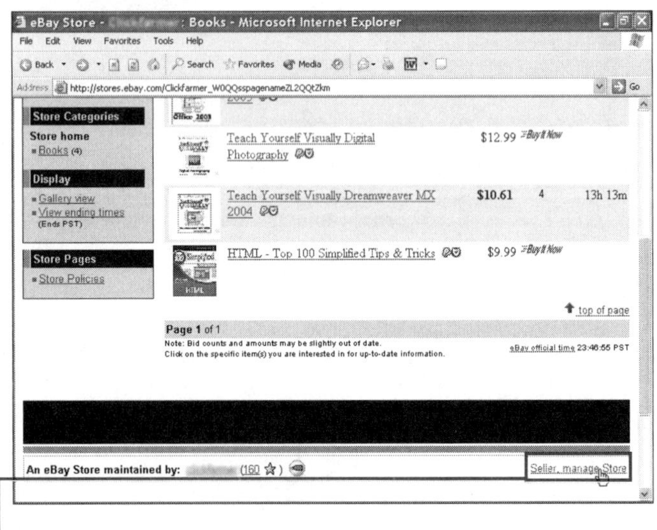

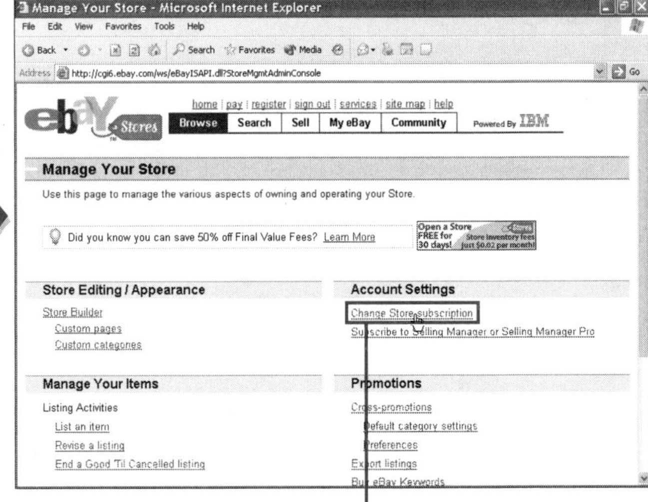

1 At the bottom of your store's home page, click Seller, manage Store.

■ The Sign In page appears.

2 Type your user information and sign in.

■ The Manage Your Store page appears.

3 Click Change Store subscription.

What requirements are there for becoming an Anchor Store?

✔ You must have a feedback score of at least 25 to set up an Anchor Store on eBay. You need a feedback rating of 20 to set up a basic or featured eBay Store.

Where are Featured Stores promoted on the eBay Stores main page?

✔ Your store name and description appear in the middle of the page beneath the Featured Stores heading and under the Anchor Stores section.

Where are Anchor Stores promoted on the eBay Stores main page?

✔ The store's name and a 64-by-64-pixel graphic appear near the top of the page under the Check out these Stores heading. When you sign up to be an anchor store, you must submit a 64-by-64-pixel graphic to eBay so that eBay can promote the store.

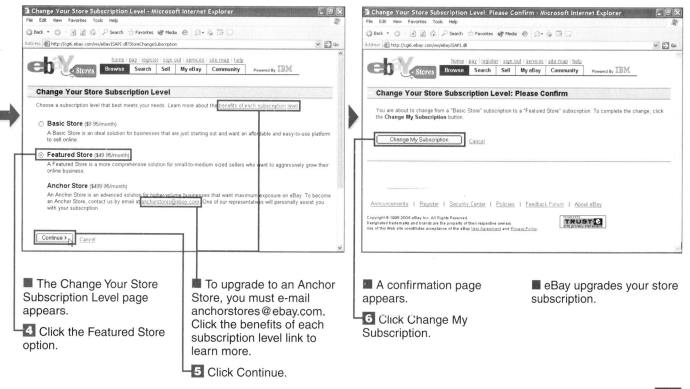

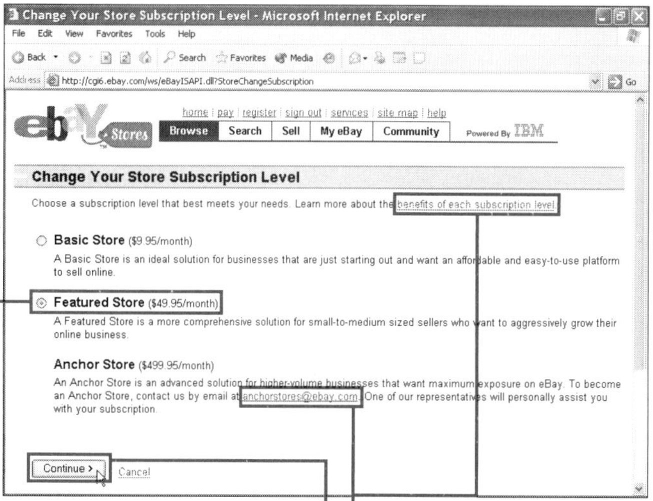

■ The Change Your Store Subscription Level page appears.

4 Click the Featured Store option.

■ To upgrade to an Anchor Store, you must e-mail anchorstores@ebay.com. Click the benefits of each subscription level link to learn more.

5 Click Continue.

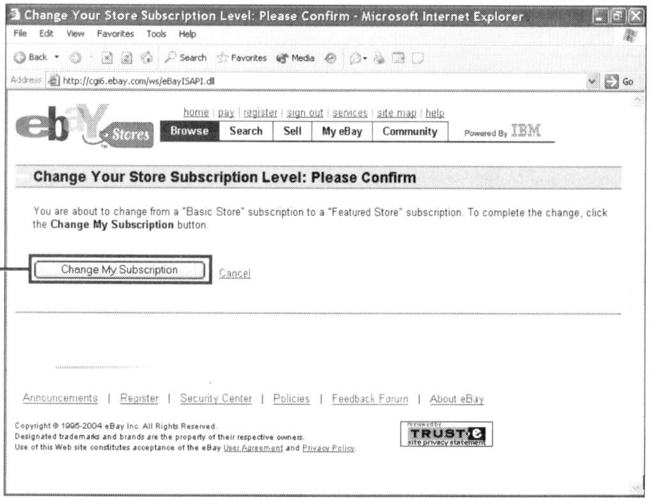

■ A confirmation page appears.

6 Click Change My Subscription.

■ eBay upgrades your store subscription.

REVISE AN INVENTORY ITEM

Because store listings can often run for months, there is a good chance you will want to revise some of them eventually. You may want to revise an item if you discover errors after you have posted it, or if it has not sold after a certain length of time. If an item is not selling, you can lower the price or add listing upgrades to make the item more attractive to customers.

If there are more than 12 hours before your listing ends, eBay allows you to revise almost everything, including the title, subtitle, description, photos, category, payment and shipping information, and even the price. If there is less than 12 hours left, you can add to the item description or add item specifics and gift services.

If someone has bid already — in a multi-item store listing, for example — you can revise price and quantity only.

An alternative to revising your listing is ending a listing early and relisting it.

REVISE AN INVENTORY ITEM

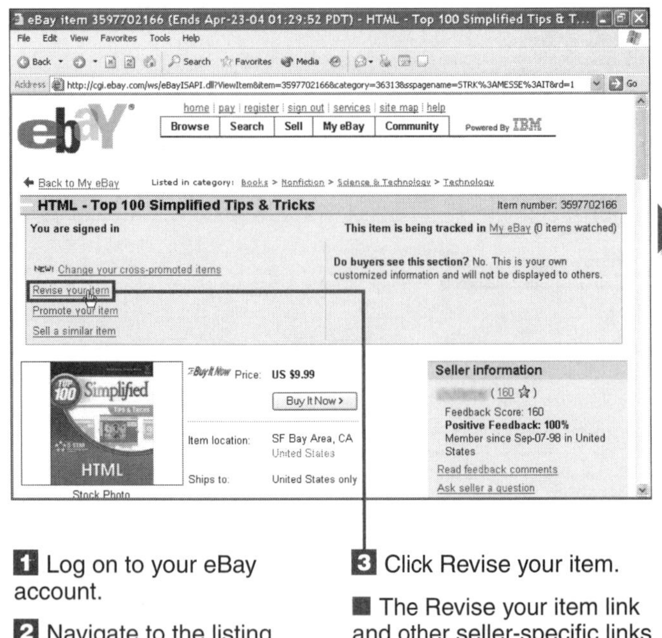

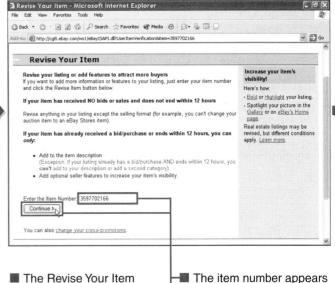

1 Log on to your eBay account.

2 Navigate to the listing page for the item.

3 Click Revise your item.

■ The Revise your item link and other seller-specific links appear only if you are logged on.

■ The Revise Your Item page appears.

■ The item number appears in the Item Number box.

4 Click Continue.

Why might I want to end my listing early?

✔ You may have listed an item in your store as Good 'Til Cancelled. You may have made a mistake when posting your listing that you cannot fix via a revision, such as a mistake in the listing format. You can also end your listing if you lose or break your item.

What fees will I incur if I revise a listing?

✔ None, unless you add upgrades to your listing during the revision process. This includes adding extra photos — eBay Picture Services charges fees after the first photo. Any additional charges appear at the bottom of the Revise Your Item page, right above the Submit Revisions button.

How do I end my store's listings early?

✔ You can end a store listing early the same way you end a regular auction early. Go to the eBay Site Map and click the End my listing link. You need to have the item number for the listing. You can also click the End your listing early link on the Revise Your Item Congratulations page. Additionally, you can end your listings via the Manage Your Store and My eBay areas.

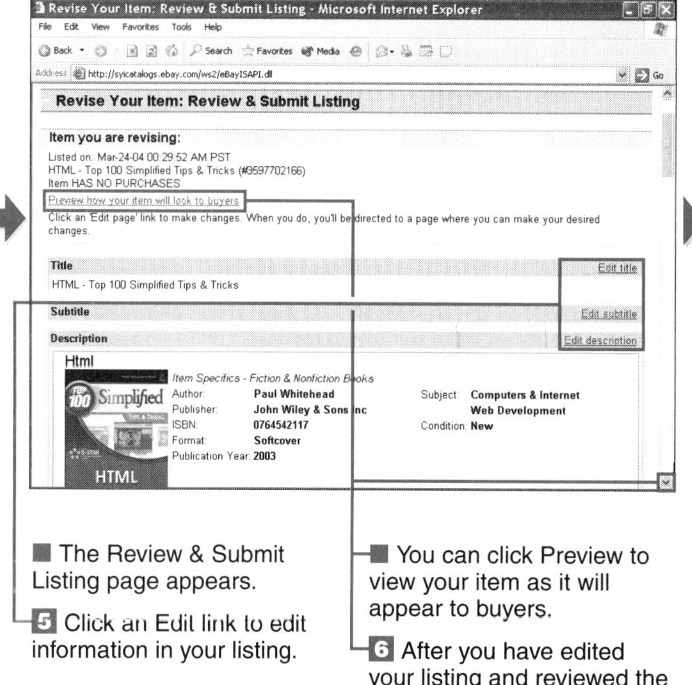

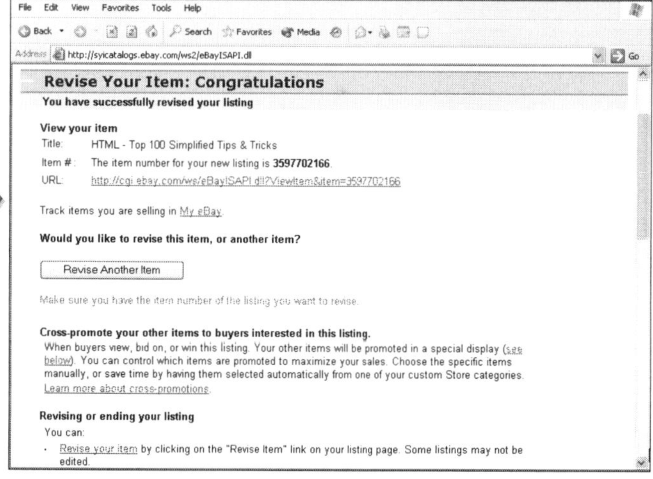

■ The Review & Submit Listing page appears.

5 Click an Edit link to edit information in your listing.

■ You can click Preview to view your item as it will appear to buyers.

6 After you have edited your listing and reviewed the updates, scroll to the bottom of the page and then click the Submit Revisions button.

■ A Congratulations page appears.

■ The store inventory item is revised.

EDIT STORE CATEGORIES

When you set up your store, you have the option of specifying up to 19 custom category names. When you create a new store item, you can specify a custom category under which to list your item in your store. Your custom categories can describe the items themselves, such as Cameras or Film, or their place in the store inventory, such as Current Specials or Closeout Deals.

The custom store categories that you define do not have to match eBay's categories, although they can.

Your custom categories appear in the navigation bar on the left side of your store pages. You can click them to view the current category listings. A number appears next to each category specifying how many store listings are currently in that category.

Categories can play an important role in driving search engine traffic to your eBay Store. Because categories appear as links on all of your eBay Store pages, search engines tend to favor them when indexing your pages. If you have keywords with which you especially want your site to be associated on search engines, be sure to include those keywords as store categories.

EDIT STORE CATEGORIES

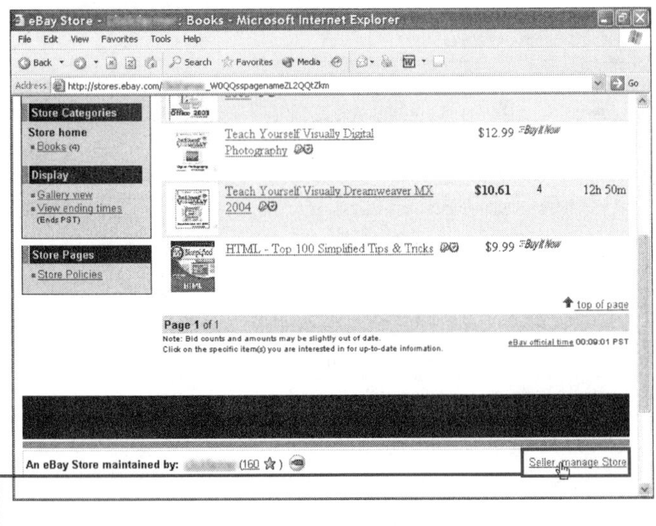

1 At the bottom of your store home page, click Seller, manage Store.

■ If you are not logged on, the Sign In page appears; type your user information and sign in.

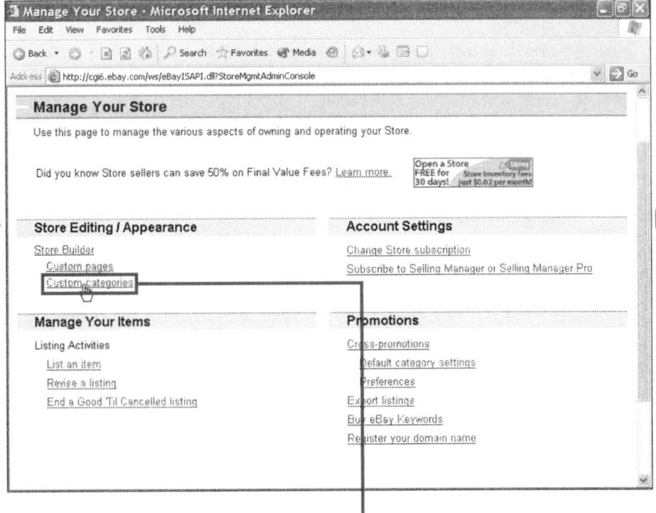

■ The Manage Your Store page appears.

2 Click Custom categories.

What happens if I do not assign a listing to a store category when I create it?

✔ If you do not assign a category to a listing, that listing will appear under the Other category for your site. The Other category is available for items whether you define the category explicitly or not.

How can I recategorize an existing listing?

✔ To assign an item to a different custom category, you can revise your listing. See the section "Revise an Inventory Item," earlier in this chapter, for more information.

Some of my store categories are not appearing. Why?

✔ The custom categories that you create for your store only appear in your store navigation bar if they have listings under them. Unpopulated categories do not appear.

What are some of the ways I can categorize my store items?

✔ You may want to categorize you items by product type, brand, price level, or condition. You may also want to create a special Sales category to highlight particularly good deals.

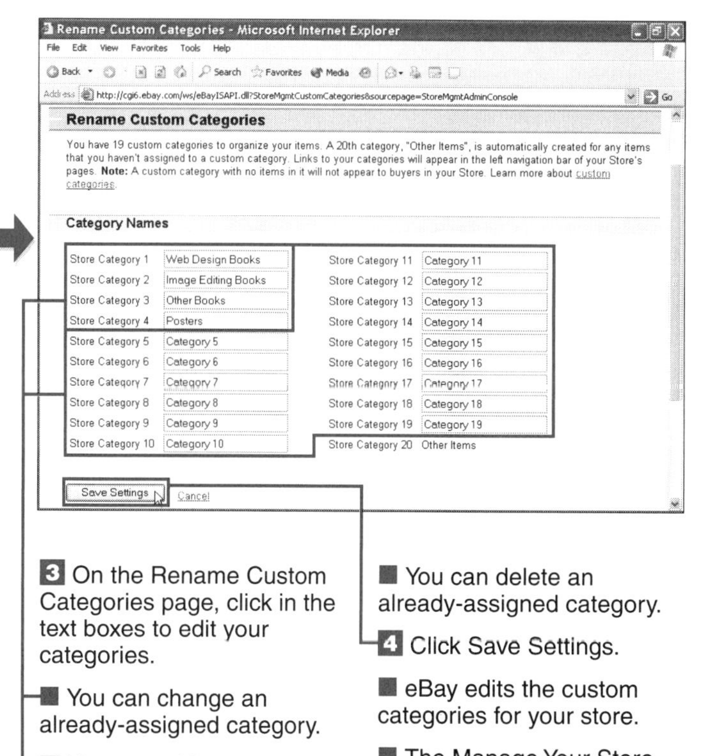

3 On the Rename Custom Categories page, click in the text boxes to edit your categories.

■ You can change an already-assigned category.

■ You can add a category.

■ You can delete an already-assigned category.

4 Click Save Settings.

■ eBay edits the custom categories for your store.

■ The Manage Your Store page reappears.

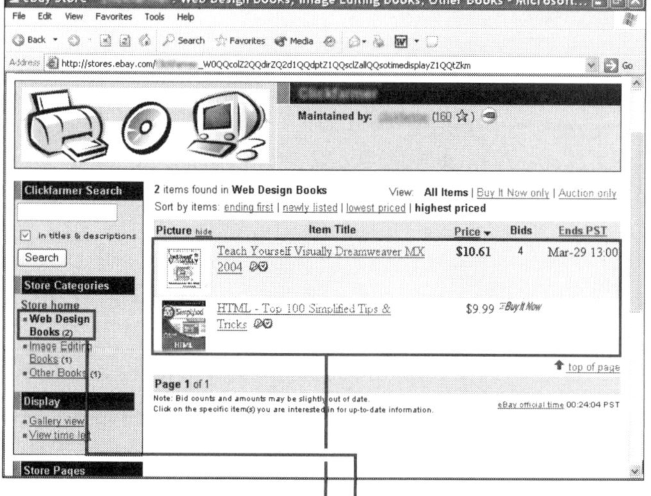

VIEW ITEMS IN A CATEGORY

1 Open your store home page.

2 On the left navigation bar, click a category.

■ The items in that category appear.

CLOSE A STORE

You may decide to close your eBay Store if the sales aren't meeting your expectations or you do not have the time to manage your store inventory. After you close a store, all of your current store inventory items end automatically. All of your current nonstore auction items remain active until their ending date is reached or they are sold.

eBay currently offers a 30-day free trial period for store owners. If you close your store before the 30-day trial ends, you will not be charged monthly store fees. You are still charged listing fees during this trial period for any items that you add to your store inventory.

Can someone use my old store name if I close my store?

✔ When you set up a store and select a store name, no one else can use that name, even if you close your store in the future. This also means that no one will ever have the same URL as your store.

CLOSE A STORE

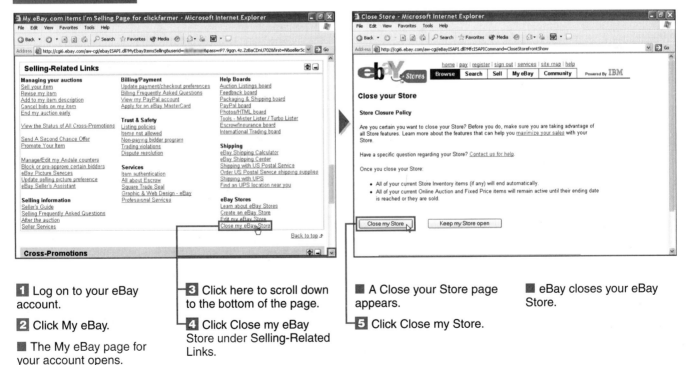

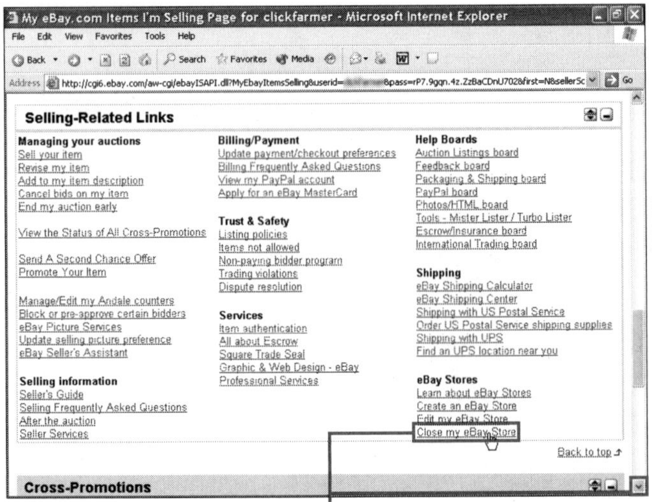

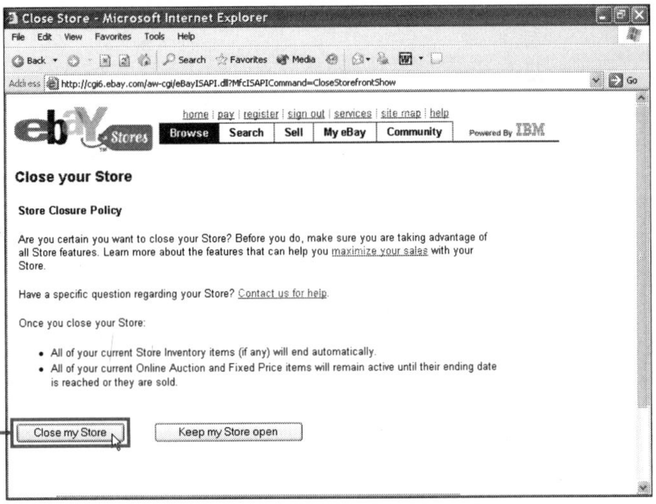

1 Log on to your eBay account.

2 Click My eBay.

■ The My eBay page for your account opens.

3 Click here to scroll down to the bottom of the page.

4 Click Close my eBay Store under Selling-Related Links.

■ A Close your Store page appears.

5 Click Close my Store.

■ eBay closes your eBay Store.

GET PROFESSIONAL DESIGN HELP

Connect with Professionals

eBay Store owners can get assistance with logo design, Web page design, copywriting, and other services through eBay's partnership with Elance. The Elance Web site matches store owners with professional service providers, including graphic designers, Web developers, and writers. With thousands of service providers registered with the company, Elance often offers an effective and economical way to expose your project to professionals around the world. You can visit the Elance page on eBay here: http://pages.ebay.com/professional_services/index.html.

Getting Bids for Projects

Buyers seeking services can post a description of their project on the Elance site, and service providers bid to do the work. Buyers select a service provider based on the amounts that the providers bid, profile information that describes the provider's experience and specialties, work samples that the providers have posted online, and feedback ratings from previous Elance buyers. Elance receives a percentage of the fees that are paid to the provider for each project.

Hire Someone Immediately

Elance also has a Buy Now option that lets you browse the profile and work samples of providers and hire them immediately without taking bids. Elance provides job-specific forms that allow you to describe the specific requirements and expectations for your project.

Communications and Billing Tools

Elance provides a messaging board that allows you to keep an accurate record of communication with your provider. There is a Work Space where you can upload and download project files and chat in real time. Elance also has a billing system that enables you to pay fees to your service provider online through the Elance Web site.

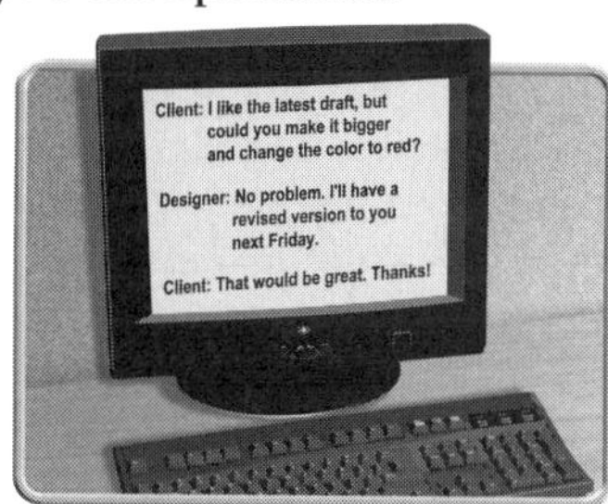

Sample Project: Logo Design

One of the most common reasons an eBay Store owner hires a professional is to have a logo designed for his or her store pages. A logo may consist of your store's name presented in interesting text, or in text combined with other graphical elements that communicate the nature of your business. With hundreds of graphics professionals registered at its Web site, Elance can help you find a logo designer who has a solid track record when it comes to creating designs for your style of store. Elance provides background information about logo design that can help you estimate how much your project should cost. It also suggests what information you should give your designer so that he or she can produce artwork that complements the types of products in your store.

SPECIFY DEFAULT CROSS-PROMOTION SETTINGS

When a buyer shows interest in your eBay listing, items from your eBay Store can be advertised in a See More Great Items box at the bottom of the page. This *cross-promotions* box displays the titles of your store items, gallery preview images, and prices. It can display up to four store inventory items. Buyers can click the titles or images to view the listings for the items.

By default, cross-promotions are automatically selected based on relationships between your custom store categories. For example, if a buyer views an item in the Sports Memorabilia category for your store, other sports memorabilia will be displayed in the cross-promotions box, if those items exist in your store.

You can change this behavior by updating the cross-promotion preferences for your different store categories. For example, you may want items from your Sports Equipment category to get first preference in the cross-promotions box for your sports memorabilia items. You can do this by changing the cross-promotion category for your sports memorabilia.

You can further customize how cross-promotions appear by determining which types of customers see which types of items. You can display one type of cross-promotions for customers who view items from ongoing listings, and another type of cross-promotions for customers who bid on or win your listings.

SPECIFY DEFAULT CROSS-PROMOTION SETTINGS

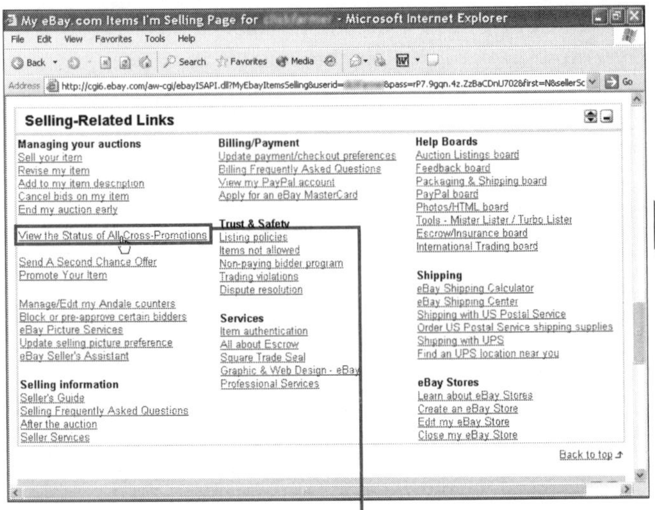

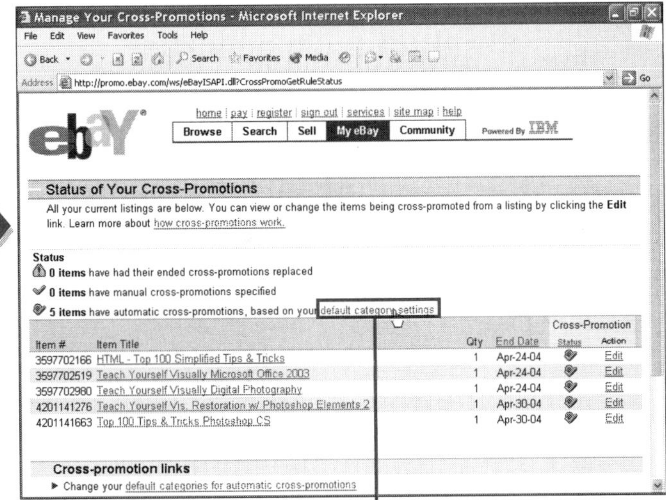

1 Log on to eBay.

2 Navigate to your My eBay page by clicking the My eBay link from the navigation area at the top of an eBay page.

3 Click the View the Status of All Cross-Promotions link in the Managing your auctions section under Selling-Related Links.

■ The Status of Your Cross-Promotions page appears.

4 Click the default category settings link.

How do I give priority to items that have a Gallery image or a Buy It Now price?

✔ On the Status of Your Cross-Promotions page, click the cross-promotion preferences link. eBay research has shown that users are more likely to make bids on listings that include photos. You can click the Show only items with Gallery images option (○ changes to ◉) to display only items that include Gallery images. Users who have just won an item are likely to be interested in other items they can purchase right away and have shipped together. You can use this to your advantage by choosing the Show items with Buy It Now first option (○ changes to ◉) under the When a user Bids on or Wins heading.

What if I have special on-sale items that I want to advertise to all my customers?

✔ If you have time-limited deals that you want all your customers to see, you can maximize the exposure of those items through the cross-promotions box. Create a sale category in your store, move the on-sale items in your store under it, and set your cross-promotion default settings to display items from the sale category.

Will eBay items from other sellers appear in my cross-promotions?

✔ No. Only items listed by you appear in the cross-promotions area for your items.

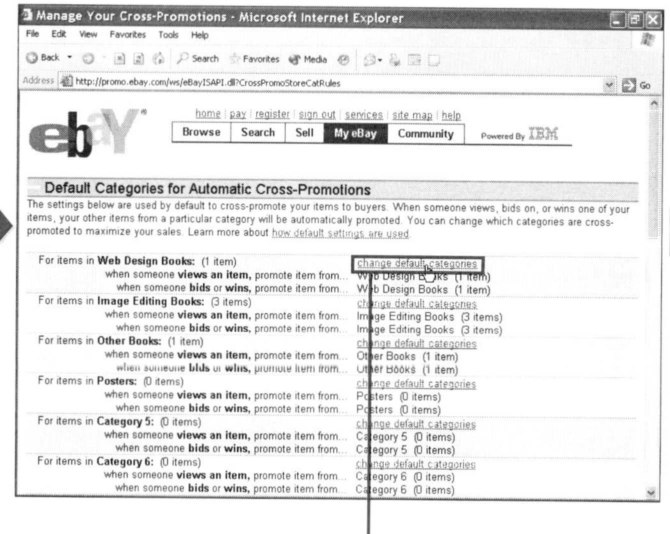

■ The Default Categories for Automatic Cross-Promotions page appears.

5 Click the change default categories link for a category.

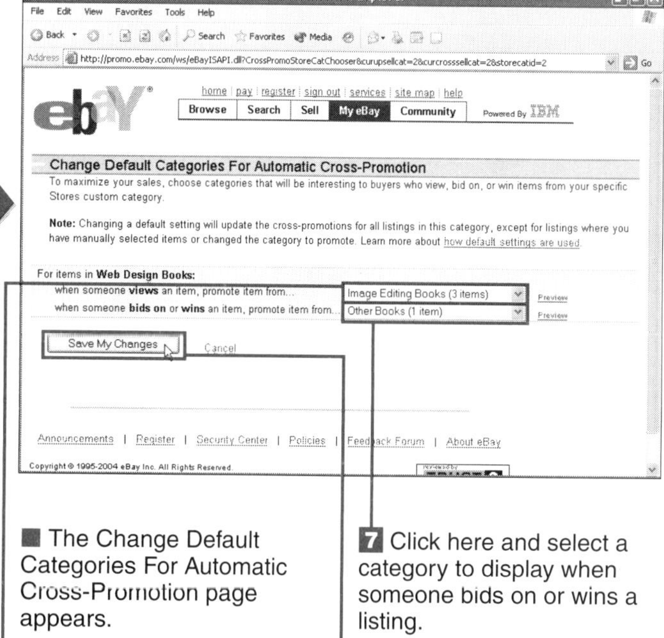

■ The Change Default Categories For Automatic Cross-Promotion page appears.

6 Click here and select a category to display when someone views a current listing.

7 Click here and select a category to display when someone bids on or wins a listing.

8 Click Save My Changes.

■ eBay saves the cross-promotion changes.

SPECIFY CROSS-PROMOTION SETTINGS FOR AN ITEM

By default, the items that are advertised in the cross-promotions box in your eBay listings are determined by the category under which they are listed. Items listed under a given category will have cross-promotion items from the same category.

You can override this behavior by specifically selecting the items to be advertised in the cross-promotions box for an item. You can specify up to four eBay items to appear in the cross-promotions box for each auction.

Customizing your cross-promotions this way can be useful if you have items that complement one another. For example, you may have created an auction for a light-blue men's dress shirt, and you want to make sure interested customers also see a store listing for a striped blue tie that matches the shirt. You can specify that the listing for the tie always appear in the cross-promotions box for the shirt listing.

After you have manually selected a specific item to cross-promote, it continues to be cross-promoted until it ends or you replace it with another item.

SPECIFY CROSS-PROMOTION SETTINGS FOR AN ITEM

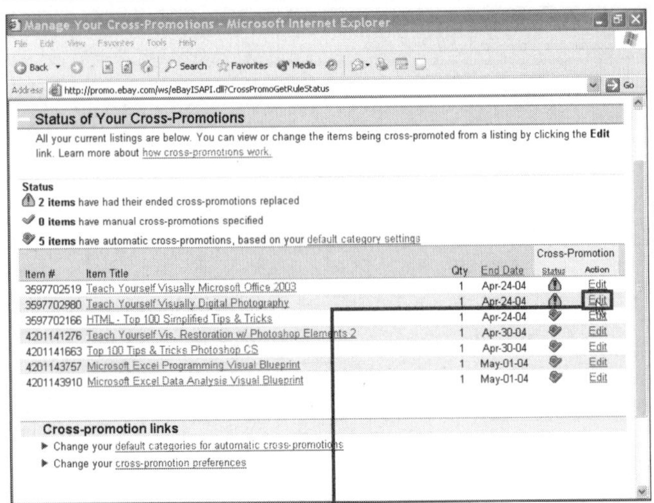

1 Log on to eBay and navigate to your My eBay page.

2 Click the View the Status of All Cross-Promotions link in the Manage your auctions section under Selling-Related Links.

■ The Status of Your Cross-Promotions page appears.

3 Click Edit to update the cross-promotions for an eBay listing.

■ The Change Your Cross-Promoted Items page appears.

■ Cross-promotions that display for the listing appear on the page.

4 Click Change Item for the cross-promotion that you want to change.

■ If Change Item buttons are not available, click the Change to a manual selection link above the cross-promotions box.

How do I turn off cross-promotions for my eBay items?

✔ On the Status of Your Cross-Promotions page, click the cross-promotion preferences link. Under Cross-Promotion Program Participation, click the Do not cross-promote my items option (○ changes to ◉), and then click the Save My Changes button. The cross-promotions box will not appear on any of your eBay listings.

How can I quickly preview the cross-promotions box that appears for a listing?

✔ You can preview the cross-promotions box for a listing by logging on, viewing that listing, and then clicking the Change your cross-promoted items link below the item title. From the preview page that appears, you can also change the cross-promotion settings for that listing.

How can I minimize the time I spend specifying cross-promotion settings?

✔ While it is useful to have the power to control your cross-promotion advertising on an item-by-item basis, specifying the cross-promotion settings for every product that you list on eBay can be time consuming. If you find yourself spending a lot of time fine-tuning your cross-promotions, you may want to consider recategorizing the items in your store so that they can be cross-promoted automatically by category. For example, if you want items from Women's Clothing and Women's Handbags automatically cross-promoted amongst one another, you can move them all to a category called Women's Clothing and Accessories.

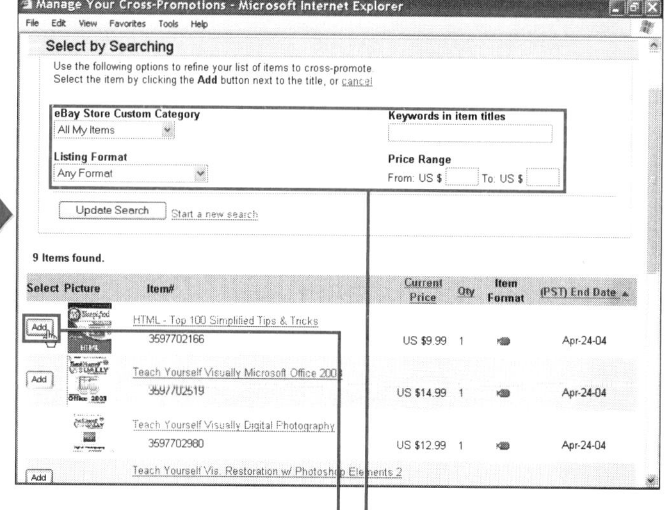

■ The Manage Your Cross-Promotions page appears.

■ The page lists your current auctions and store inventory.

■ You can filter the listings by category, listing format, keyword, or price range.

5 Click Add for the item that you want cross-promoted on your listing page.

■ The item appears in the cross-promotions box for the listing.

■ You can repeat steps 4 and 5 to cross-promote other items for that listing.

SET UP A KEYWORD ADVERTISING CAMPAIGN

Every eBay search results page has an advertising banner graphic that appears near the top, right below the eBay logo. When you click the advertising banner, you are taken to the advertiser's Web site, eBay Store, or eBay auction item.

eBay Keywords is a service that allows eBay Store owners to place custom banners in that location.

After you sign up for eBay Keywords, your banner will appear when eBay users type specific keywords in their searches. You can select the keywords when you set up your eBay Keywords advertising campaign. By picking keywords that have relevance to the items you are selling, you can attract customers to your eBay listings who are likely to make a purchase.

Your banner ad can link to your eBay Store home page, a custom category in your store, a search result within your store, a list of all your items for sale on eBay, or a single item for sale. If you are linking your eBay Keywords banner ad to a specific listing, and that listing ends, eBay will stop displaying that ad banner until you update the information in your ad campaign to point somewhere else.

SET UP A KEYWORD ADVERTISING CAMPAIGN

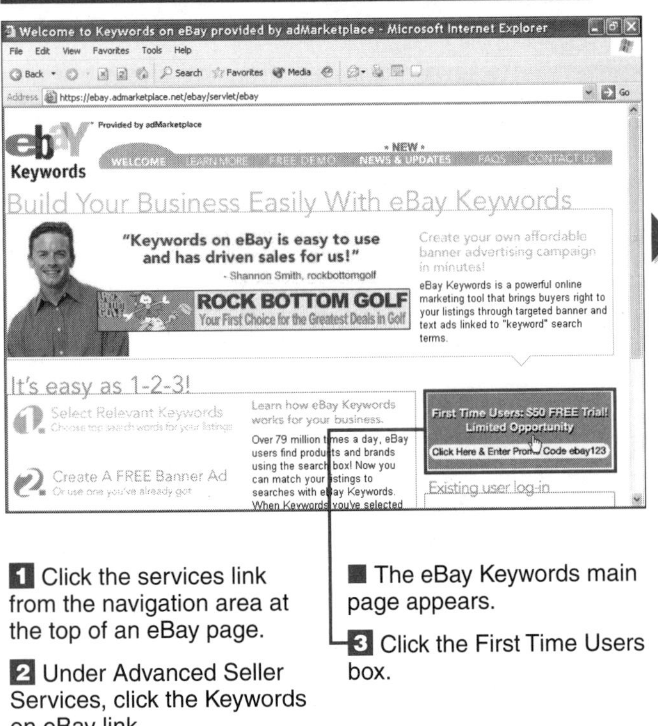

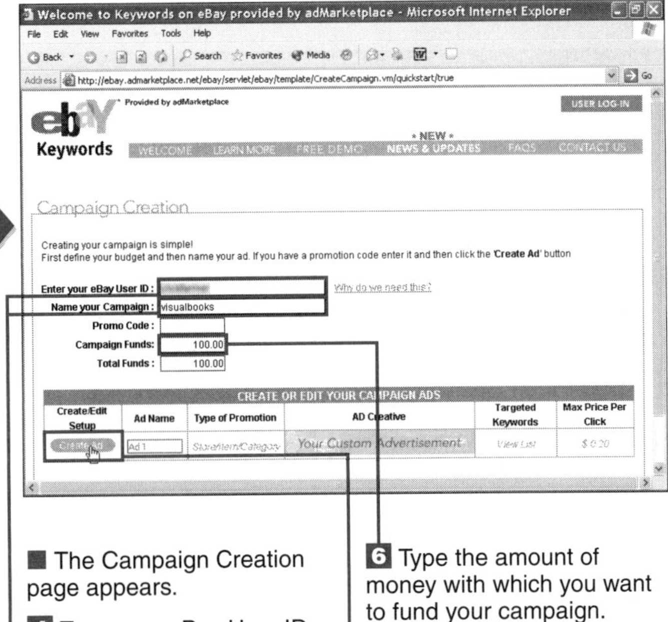

1 Click the services link from the navigation area at the top of an eBay page.

2 Under Advanced Seller Services, click the Keywords on eBay link.

■ The eBay Keywords main page appears.

3 Click the First Time Users box.

■ The Campaign Creation page appears.

4 Type your eBay User ID.

Note: The ID you use must have a store or an item currently for sale on eBay.

5 Type a name for your campaign.

6 Type the amount of money with which you want to fund your campaign.

Note: Your clickthrough fees will draw from these funds. See the tip section for more about clickthrough fees.

7 Click Create Ad.

What is the minimum amount that I can bid for a clickthrough?

✔ The minimum cost per clickthrough for an ad is 10 cents. This means that the minimum amount that can be deducted from your advertising budget when someone clicks on your banner is 10 cents.

How does my bid relate to the price I actually pay for a clickthrough?

✔ The rate you actually pay is determined by taking the next highest bid plus 1 cent. For example, if your maximum bid is $1 per click and your nearest competitor's maximum rate is 50 cents per click, you will ultimately pay 51 cents per click.

How should I select my keywords?

✔ The challenge is to select keywords that are broad enough to give you access to a large enough group of potential customers, but specific enough so that the customers who click will be likely to buy. Selecting two- and three-word phrases will get you more qualified buyers than individual keywords that are very broad. For example, if you sell computer games, CD-ROM games will probably deliver higher-quality traffic than CD, which is a very broad term. eBay recommends that you avoid selecting phrases that are four words or more because they are less likely to appear in searches.

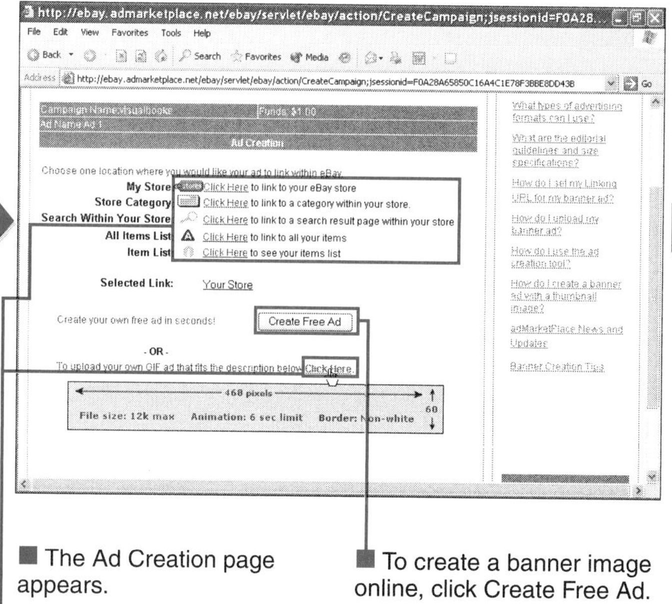

■ The Ad Creation page appears.

8 Click to specify where you want your advertising banner to link to.

9 Click to upload a banner image.

■ To create a banner image online, click Create Free Ad.

Note: See the section "Create a Keyword Advertising Banner" for more information on creating your own ad.

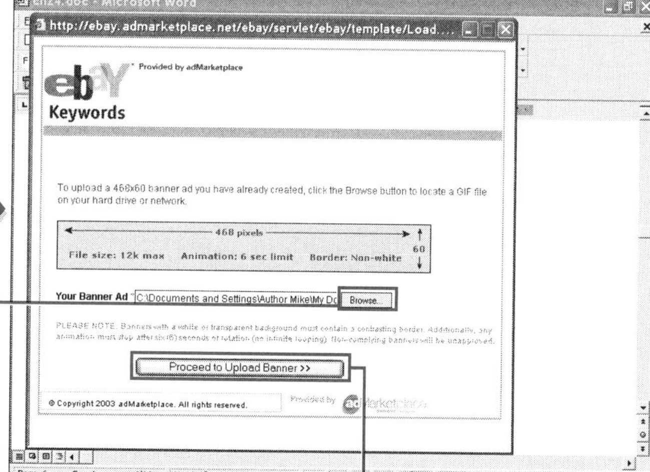

■ A new window appears, allowing you to upload a 468-by-60-pixel GIF formatted image from your computer.

10 Click Browse to select the ad banner file from your computer.

11 Click Proceed to Upload Banner.

■ A confirmation page appears showing that your banner uploaded successfully.

12 Click OK to close the window.

CONTINUED

SET UP A KEYWORD ADVERTISING CAMPAIGN (CONTINUED)

You pay for your advertising placements on the eBay site by specifying how much you are willing to pay when a customer clicks on your banner. Such an event is known as a *clickthrough*. Your bids are ranked among other advertiser bids to determine which keyword-matched banners are displayed.

Because of this competitive bidding process, keywords that are more popular with advertisers will require higher bids for advertisers to see their banners displayed. You pay only when a potential buyer clicks on your banner ad and goes to your store. Each time a customer clicks your banner, the clickthrough fee is deducted from the budget that you established when you created your advertising campaign.

When your budget runs out, your ads will stop appearing on the eBay site. You can add funds to your budget by logging on to your eBay Keywords account and using the management tools for your different campaigns. In your account, you can also view reports that show you how many times your banners were displayed, how many times they were clicked, how much you paid for the clickthroughs, and other useful information.

SET UP A KEYWORD ADVERTISING CAMPAIGN (CONTINUED)

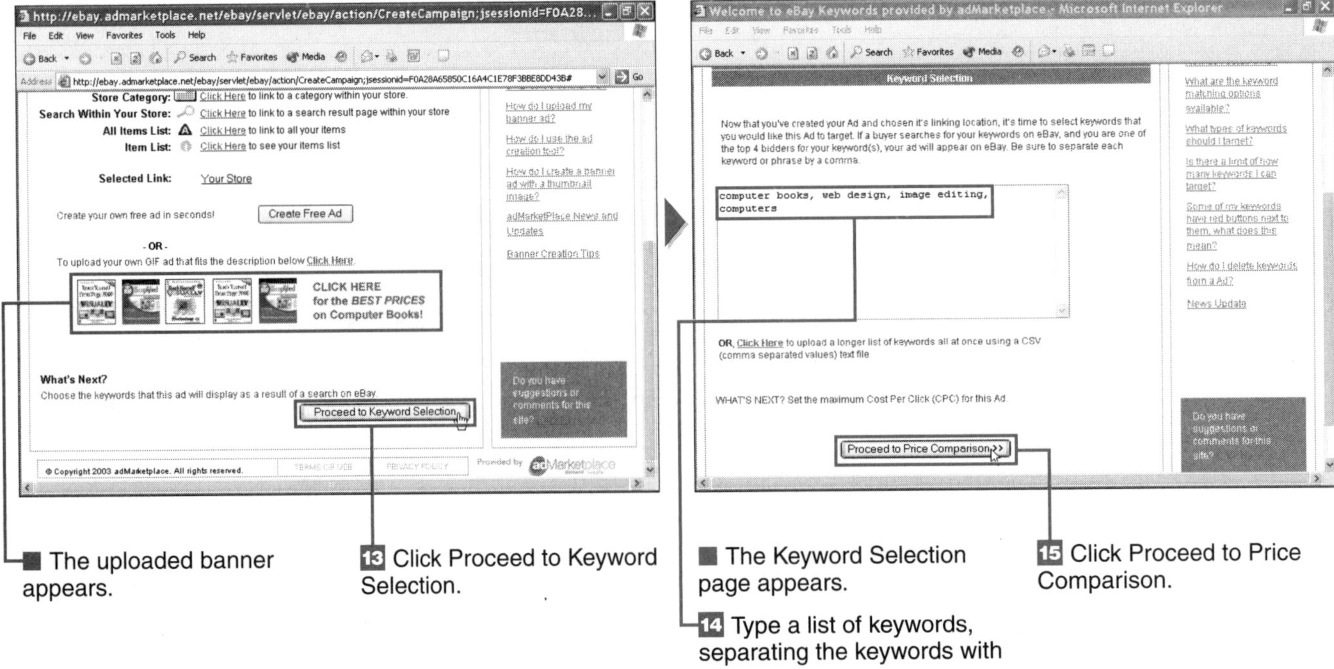

■ The uploaded banner appears.

13 Click Proceed to Keyword Selection.

■ The Keyword Selection page appears.

14 Type a list of keywords, separating the keywords with commas.

15 Click Proceed to Price Comparison.

Is there a maximum number of times a banner will appear to a customer?

✔ If a banner ad appears repeatedly to the same user, the likelihood of that user clicking on the banner decreases with each additional exposure. To keep banners fresh, the eBay Keywords program employs a technique called frequency capping. This limits the exposure of a specific ad banner over a particular time frame to customers. On the eBay site, ads are frequency capped at three exposures per user, per keyword, per 24 hours.

My clickthrough bid is ranked second for a particular keyword. Will customers ever see my ad banner?

✔ Because ad banner exposure is capped at three exposures per user, per keyword, per 24 hours, advertisers who do not submit the highest clickthrough bid can still have their ads displayed. For example, an ad for an advertiser ranked second will appear after a customer has viewed three pages for a particular keyword search on a given day. This is because the exposure of the high bidder's ad is capped after three exposures.

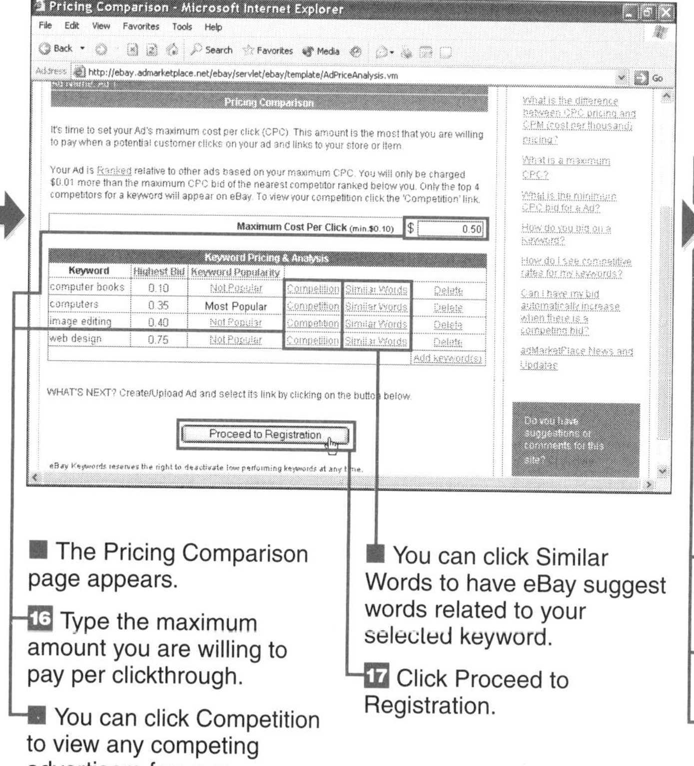

■ The Pricing Comparison page appears.

16 Type the maximum amount you are willing to pay per clickthrough.

■ You can click Competition to view any competing advertisers for your keywords.

■ You can click Similar Words to have eBay suggest words related to your selected keyword.

17 Click Proceed to Registration.

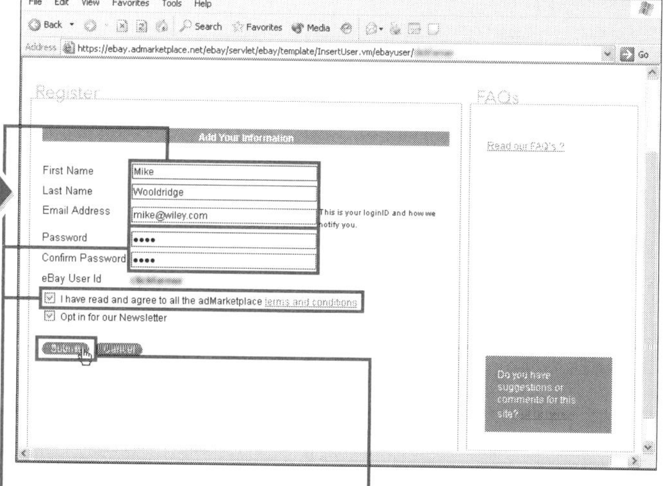

18 On the Register page, type your name and e-mail address.

19 Type a new password for the program.

20 Click this option to agree to the terms and conditions.

21 Click Submit.

■ eBay creates your keyword advertising campaign. You can click the Proceed to Payment button on the page that follows to fund your campaign.

CREATE A KEYWORD ADVERTISING BANNER

To participate in the eBay Keywords program, you need to have an advertising banner graphic that eBay can display on its pages. You can use a banner that has already been created, or if you have an image-editing program and some design skills, you can create an ad banner. (Make sure its dimensions are 468 pixels by 60 pixels and that it is no larger than 12K in file size.)

The eBay Keywords program also has a tool that lets you quickly and automatically generate an ad banner.

With the banner creation tool, you first select from one of several dozen templates. The templates have areas where you can add text that describes what you are selling, special features that your products include, and price. Many of the banners will also display the keywords for which a customer has just searched. For example, if a customer has just searched for collectible coins, the phrase Searching for collectible coins? may appear on the banner.

There are many sites on the Web that have information about creating effective advertising banners. You can type "ad banner design" into a search engine to find them.

CREATE A KEYWORD ADVERTISING BANNER

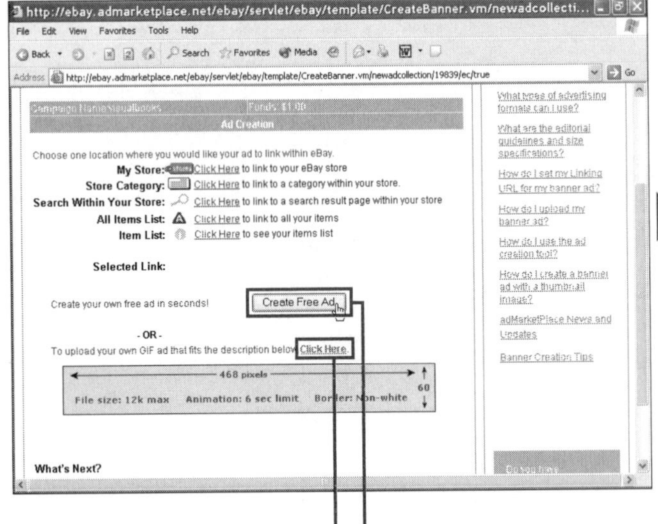

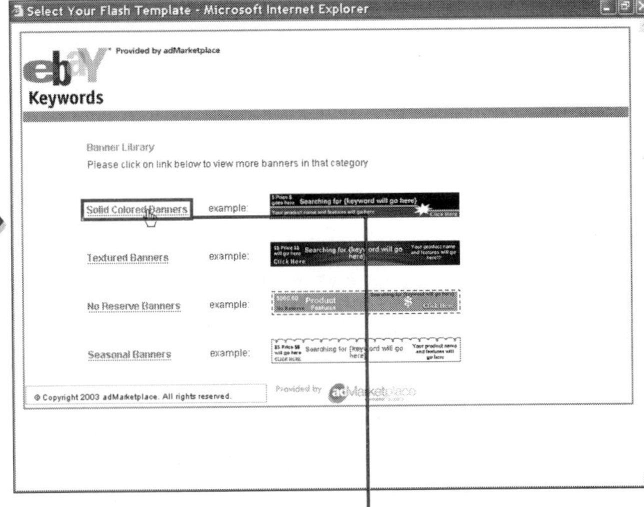

1 Create a keyword advertising campaign.

Note: For more information, see the previous section, "Set Up a Keyword Advertising Campaign."

2 On the Ad Creation page, click Create Free Ad.

■ If you already have an ad banner to use, you can click to upload it.

■ Different ad banners appear in a new window that opens.

3 Click a banner type.

Are there any simple rules that I can follow to improve my ad banners?

✔ In general, using motion in a banner can be an effective way to draw customers' attention, because if they do not notice the banner, they will never click it. You can add animation to a banner by creating an animated GIF file. Some of the templates in the creation tool also include animation. Studies also show that banners that include the phrase Click Here deliver much more traffic than those that do not.

Are there color limitations for banners?

✔ Yes, but only a few. Banners with a white background must have a contrasting border — the border cannot be white. Also, banners may not have a transparent background. These limitations help customers who view the advertisements understand that they are advertisements, and not some other Web page feature. They also help ensure that advertisements appear the same on all pages.

What are the limitations on the content that I can display in my ad banner?

✔ According to the eBay Keywords terms, banners cannot contain nude or explicit adult content, offensive language, or violent or controversial images. They cannot contain marketing for a Web address or resemble a Web address. For example, banners containing the text www., .com, and dot com are not allowed. Banners also cannot contain marketing for an e-mail address or phone number, or refer viewers away from eBay to purchase merchandise.

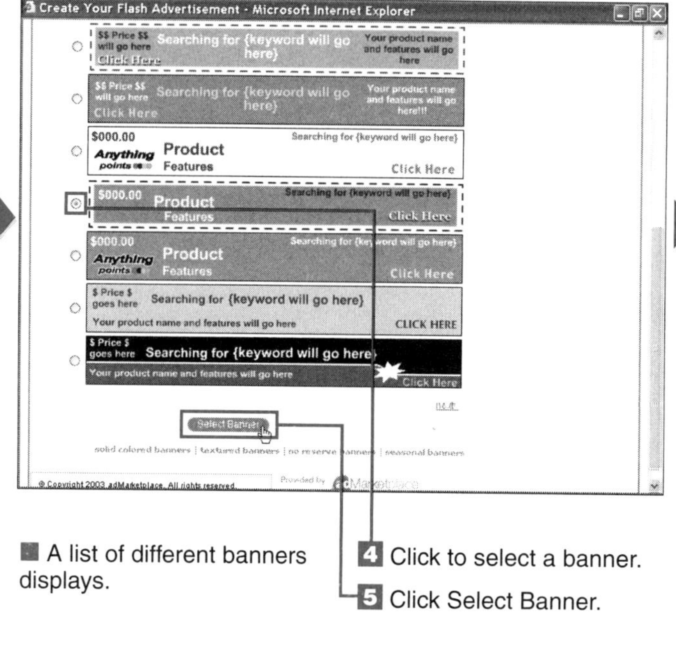

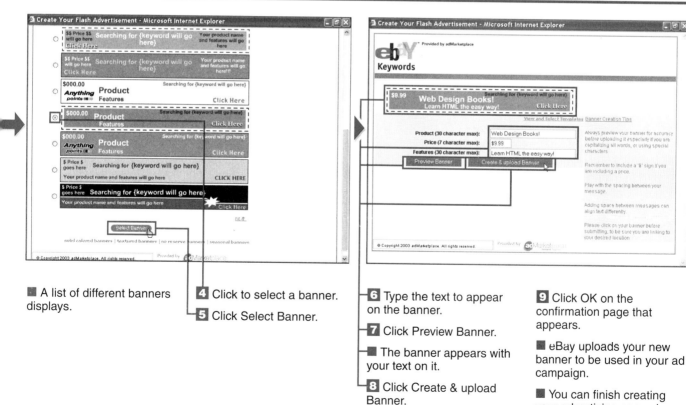

■ A list of different banners displays.

4 Click to select a banner.

5 Click Select Banner.

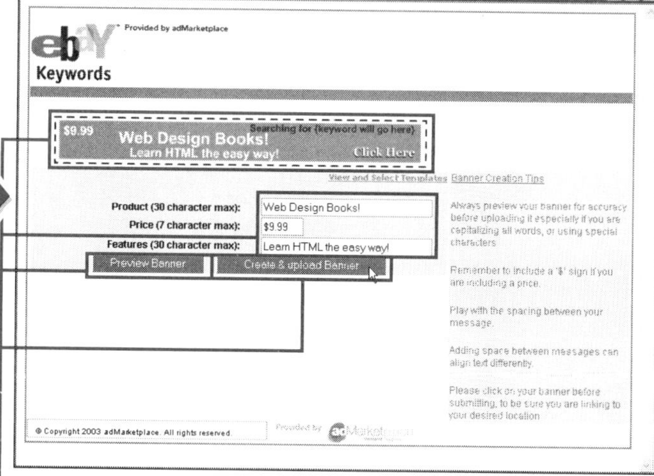

6 Type the text to appear on the banner.

7 Click Preview Banner.

■ The banner appears with your text on it.

8 Click Create & upload Banner.

9 Click OK on the confirmation page that appears.

■ eBay uploads your new banner to be used in your ad campaign.

■ You can finish creating your advertising campaign.

MAKE LISTINGS AVAILABLE FOR DOWNLOAD

You can specify that eBay make information about your store inventory listings available as a file for others to download. Some sellers set up partnerships with third parties, such as product search engines, to drive traffic to their listings. Making a file that lists your current store items available can provide these partners with up-to-date information about store listings and their URLs.

After you turn this feature on in the Manage Your Store page, eBay will make the file available within 12 hours. Information about your regular auctions and other nonstore listings, which appear in regular eBay searches and categories, are not included in this file.

The file is created as XML formatted text, a format that many search engines can easily use. The file contains the following information in the following order: item title, item description, URL of the item page, whether the item is orderable, current price, availability, item number, shipping cost (if specified in the shipping and handling field), gallery picture (if included), quantity, and price currency.

MAKE LISTINGS AVAILABLE FOR DOWNLOAD

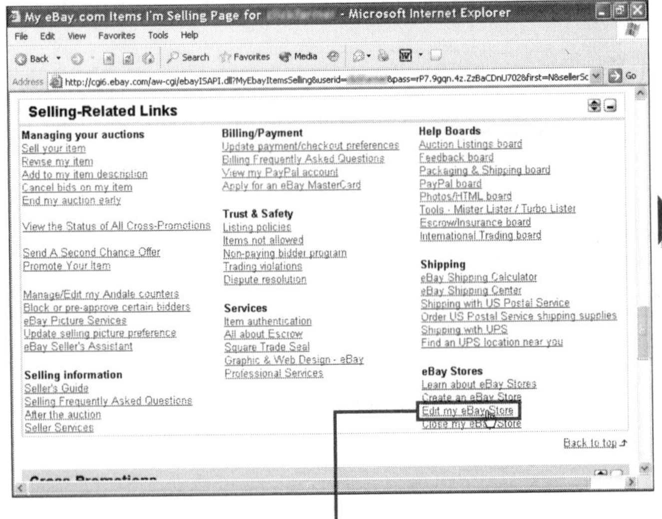

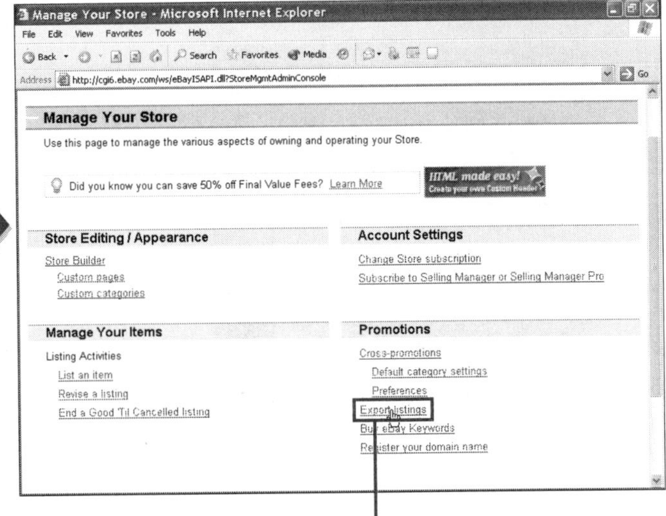

1 Log on to your eBay account and click My eBay at the top of the page.

■ Your My eBay page appears.

2 Scroll to the Selling-Related Links section.

3 In the eBay Stores section, click the Edit my eBay Store link.

■ The Manage Your Store page appears.

4 In the Promotions section, click the Export listings link.

What is the URL for my downloadable file?

✔ The URL is based on the URL of your eBay Store. For example, if your store's name is Children's Clothing, the URL will be http://esssl.ebay.com/GetListings/childrensclothing.

How long does the file stay available?

✔ Once created, it is available indefinitely. eBay will automatically keep it up to date. Whenever a third party downloads the file through the URL, the information about your store inventory is the most recent.

Is there a limit to how many times my information can be downloaded?

✔ The file can be downloaded a maximum of 50 times per day.

Is there any listing information that will not be included?

✔ Any store listings in the Mature Audiences category will not be included in the file.

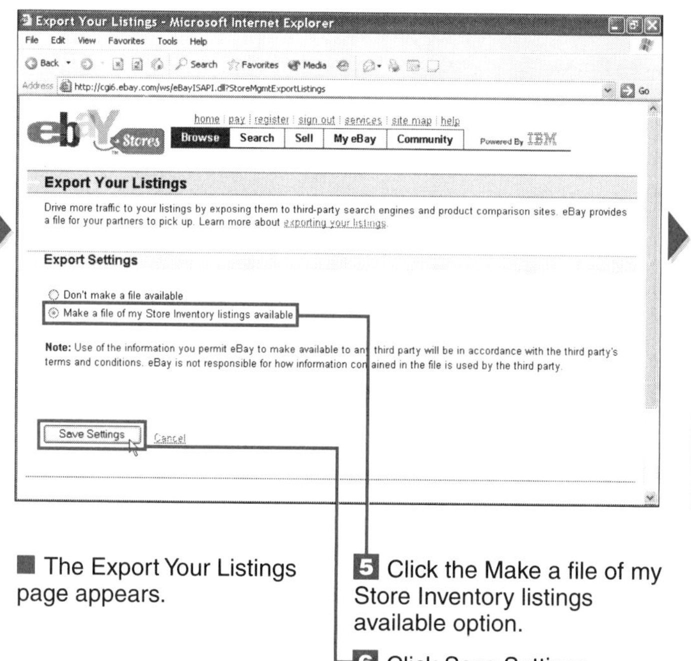

■ The Export Your Listings page appears.

5 Click the Make a file of my Store Inventory listings available option.

6 Click Save Settings.

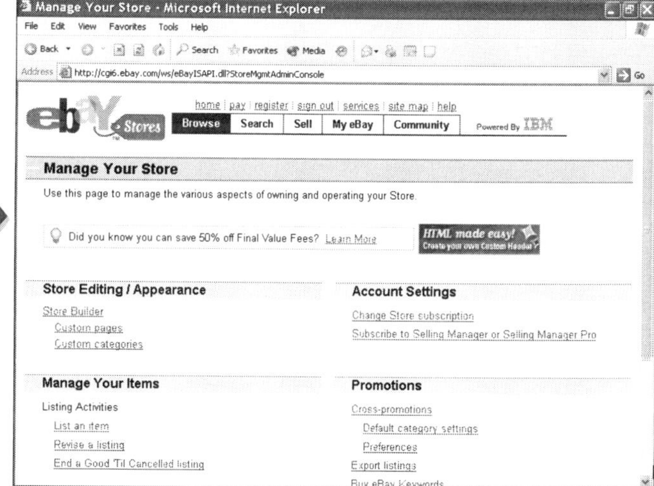

■ eBay makes your store listings available as a downloadable file.

■ The Manage Your Store page reappears.

REGISTER A DOMAIN NAME FOR YOUR STORE

Sellers who want a more personalized Web address for their store can register a custom Internet domain name. This can give your customers an easy-to-remember address to use to visit your store.

Examples of domain names include ebay.com and att.net. A domain name can be based on the name of your company or store, or on the types of products you sell. The primary limitation is that the name cannot already be registered to someone else.

Domain names come with a variety of different extensions. An extension is the last few letters of the domain name that come after the dot. The most common extensions are .com, .net, and .org, but there are dozens of others. If your first domain name choice isn't available with one extension, you can see if it is available with other extensions.

You can register a domain name through a domain name registrar. The largest domain name registrar is Network Solutions. See Appendix A for a list of other registrars.

As soon as you have registered a domain name, you can forward users who visit the domain name to your eBay Store. Usually, you set up this forwarding activity by submitting your eBay Store URL to the company that handles your domain name service. Contact your domain name registrar for details.

REGISTER A DOMAIN NAME FOR YOUR STORE

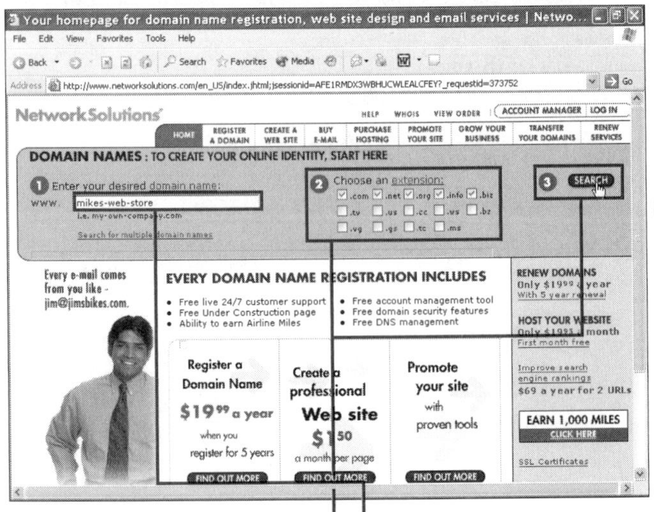

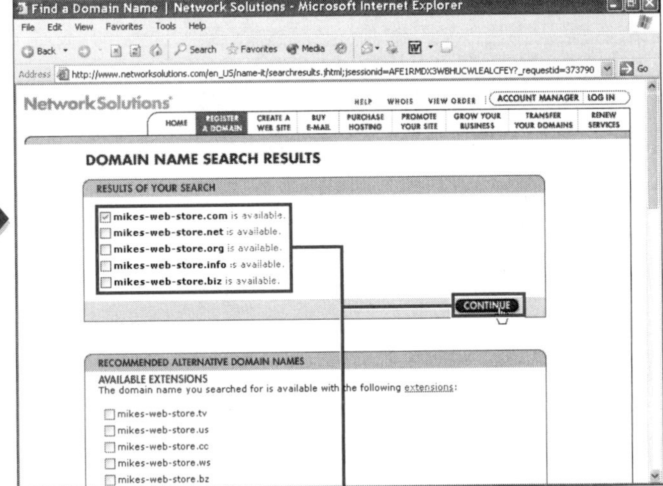

CHECK DOMAIN NAME AVAILABILITY

1 Visit the Web site of a domain name registrar.

■ In this example, the Network Solutions site at www.networksolutions.com is used.

2 Type a name into the domain name search box.

3 Select one or more extensions to search.

4 Click Search.

■ A search results page appears showing the availability of the domain names.

5 Click each domain name that you want to register.

6 Click Continue to complete the registration process.

GET SQUARETRADE VERIFIED

eBay Store owners and other sellers can instill trust in the potential buyers that view their listings by joining the SquareTrade seller verification program. When approved, sellers can display the SquareTrade seal on their auctions. The program costs $7.50 per month. Currently, it offers a 30-day free trial. Visit www.squaretrade.com for more information.

Display the Seal

By displaying a seal image on their auctions and Web sites, verified SquareTrade members show buyers that they are committed to high selling standards. Potential buyers can click the seal to view the member's SquareTrade profile page, which has details about the seller's contact information and commitment to good selling practices.

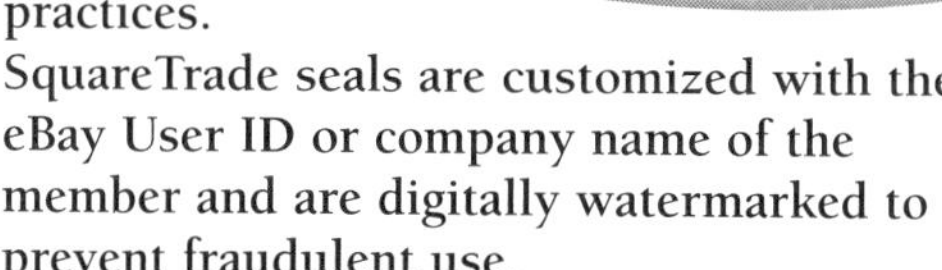

SquareTrade seals are customized with the eBay User ID or company name of the member and are digitally watermarked to prevent fraudulent use.

Become Verified

To be able to display the SquareTrade seal, sellers must be approved. This includes identity and address verification. In most cases, your identity is verified through Equifax, a third-party verification service. Your eBay history is analyzed to check if you are classified as an at-risk seller. The analysis looks at feedback quantity and quality, as well as the types of items you sell. SquareTrade also checks to see whether you have a history of resolving disputes.

In addition to initially verifying a seller, SquareTrade has a dedicated compliance team that ensures that the Seal Members continue to meet a defined set of exceptional selling standards.

Member Benefits

In addition to being able to display the SquareTrade seal, approved sellers can have SquareTrade automatically notify them if negative feedback is filed against them on eBay. If a member does receive negative feedback, SquareTrade can help the seller work with the other party to get any dispute resolved. This will oftentimes result in the buyer withdrawing the negative feedback. At the SquareTrade Web site, members can view reports that show how often and at what times buyers view their auctions. The service can help you maximize the number of buyers that see your listings.

Note that eBay offers a more limited service called ID Verify that verifies your personal information. It costs a one-time $5 fee. For more information, visit: http://pages.ebay.com/services/buyandsell/idverify-login.html.

SIGN UP FOR A HALF.COM SELLER ACCOUNT

Sellers who prefer to sell using the Buy It Now option on eBay and want to expand their online market reach can sell their items on Half.com. Similar to items in eBay Stores, items listed on Half.com sell at a fixed price. Buying at Half.com does not involve competitive bidding.

Half.com focuses on a more limited set of products than eBay — mainly books, textbooks, CDs, movies, games, computers, and electronic items. eBay bought Half.com in 2000.

Unlike eBay, Half.com charges no listing fees. It takes a commission off the selling price at the time your item sells. The commission amount varies with the selling price of the item, from 15 percent for items $50 or less to 5 percent for items that sell for more than $500.

Buyers must purchase items at Half.com with a credit card, and Half.com takes care of processing the payment. In contrast to sales on eBay, there is no need to watch the mail for checks or money orders, or manage your sales through PayPal. As a seller on Half.com, your job is simply to ship the item after it is sold.

SIGN UP FOR A HALF.COM SELLER ACCOUNT

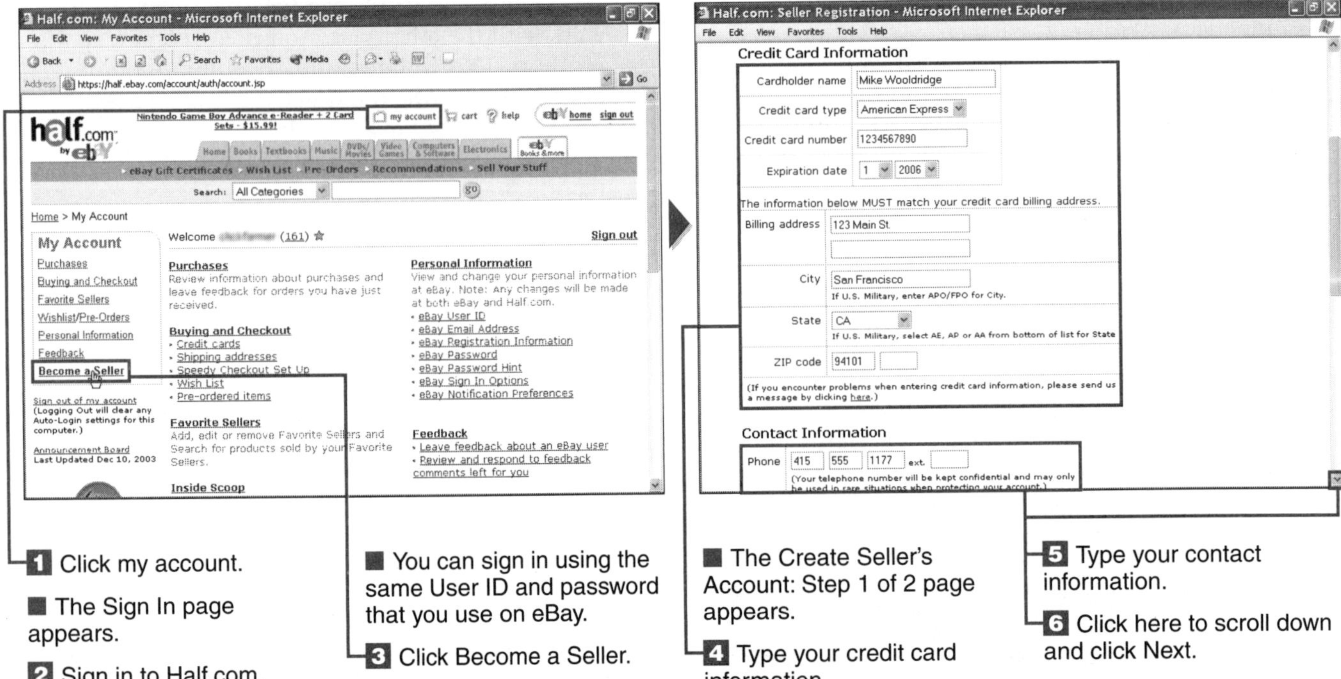

1 Click my account.

■ The Sign In page appears.

2 Sign in to Half.com.

■ You can sign in using the same User ID and password that you use on eBay.

3 Click Become a Seller.

■ The Create Seller's Account: Step 1 of 2 page appears.

4 Type your credit card information.

5 Type your contact information.

6 Click here to scroll down and click Next.

How do I get paid from Half.com?

✔ Sellers can choose to be paid one of two ways: by check or by direct deposit to a checking account. The direct deposit method offers some advantages. Payments are deposited directly into a your checking account approximately seven days earlier than you would receive a paper check. Direct deposit sellers also are paid every two weeks no matter what their seller account balance is. Check-based accounts must reach $50 for an initial check to be sent. There is also an extra $1.50 fee for each check.

I live outside the U.S. Can I use Half.com?

✔ Unlike eBay, only persons residing within the 50 United States can sell on Half.com. Buyers must live in the United States or Canada. The exception is U.S. military personnel living out of the country, who can buy or sell through an APO or FPO mailing address.

What is a Half.com shop?

✔ A Half.com shop is a place where buyers can see all the inventory offered by a seller. Half.com sellers receive a Half.com shop for free. Any time a Half.com member clicks on a seller name, he or she is taken to the seller's Half.com shop.

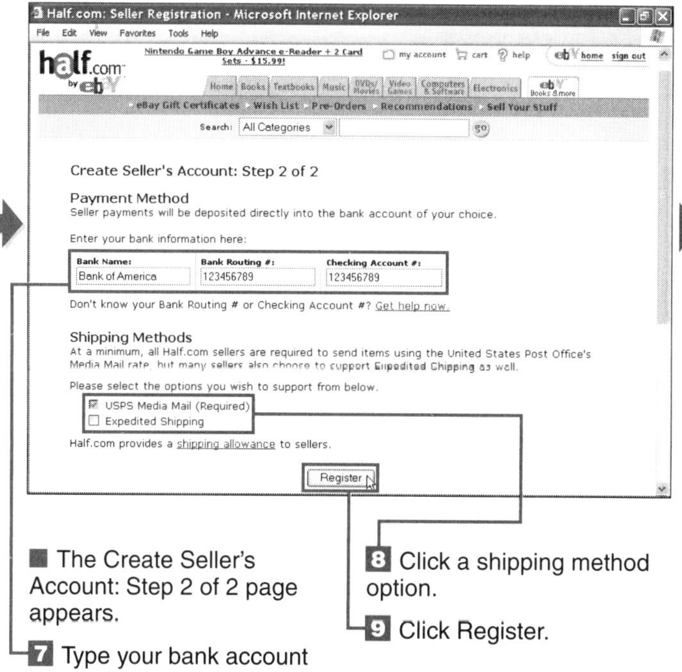

■ The Create Seller's Account: Step 2 of 2 page appears.

7 Type your bank account information.

8 Click a shipping method option.

9 Click Register.

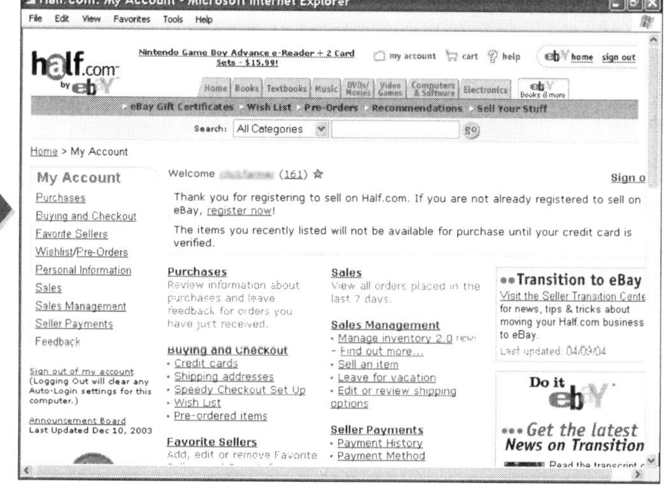

■ A My Account page appears with a confirmation message.

■ You may have to wait for Half.com to verify your credit card before you can list your items.

LIST AN ITEM

At Half.com, registered sellers can list books, textbooks, CDs, movies, games, computers, and other items. During the listing process, you categorize your product, assign it a condition, add any additional comments, and specify a price.

Many of the items that you can list on Half.com have unique product codes associated with them. Books have ISBN numbers, while music, movies, and games have UPC numbers. Half.com makes entering such numbers the first step in listing these products so it can provide the cover art, any reviews, and other product information from its extensive database.

For other products, you can select categories similar to the way you do when you list an eBay item. You also get to specify the manufacturer and other information. If your product isn't included in the Half.com database, you can add it by clicking a link on the Describe Your Item page.

On the pricing page, Half.com lists information about what your product has sold for in the past. This helps you estimate the profit you can make as well as choose a price that is competitive.

LIST AN ITEM

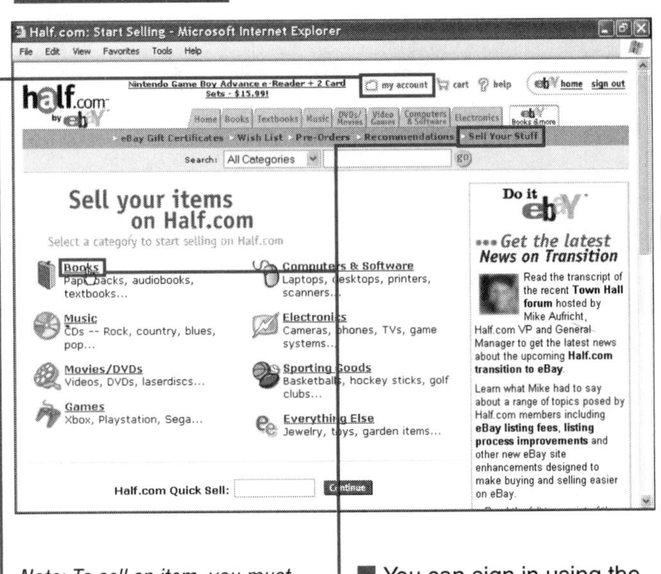

Note: To sell an item, you must have a seller's account. See "Sign Up for a Half.com Seller Account" for details.

1 Click my account and sign in to Half.com.

■ You can sign in using the same User ID and password that you use on eBay.

2 Click Sell Your Stuff.

■ The Half.com categories appear.

3 Click a top-level category for your item.

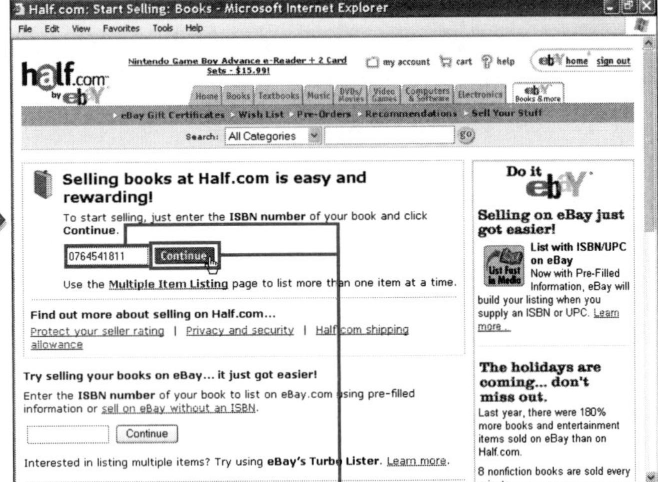

■ A page appears asking for you to describe your item; for example, if you are selling a book, type the ISBN.

■ If you are selling music, a movie, or a game, the page asks for the UPC number.

■ For other items, the pages ask you to categorize your item.

4 Type the information.

5 Click Continue.

How can I ship my sold items?

✔ All sellers listing in Half.com's Books, Music, Movies, or Games categories must use, at a minimum, U.S. Postal Service Media Mail to ship orders. Sellers in these product categories have the option of offering expedited shipping to their buyers as an upgrade. Items shipped via Media Mail usually arrive in four to 12 days from the time of shipping.

Sellers listing in the other product categories at Half.com set their own shipping costs and may choose from a variety of shipping methods.

What are the condition ratings for items?

✔ **Brand New**: New, unopened, and unused product. Original packaging and all original materials are included and in perfect condition.
Like New: Could be mistaken for being brand new or is new and still in original packaging. Shows no sign of use.
Very Good: Shows slight signs of use.
Good: Shows signs of use, but still functions as intended.
Acceptable: A well-used product.

Is there a minimum price for products on Half.com?

✔ Yes. The minimum price for products on Half.com is 75 cents.

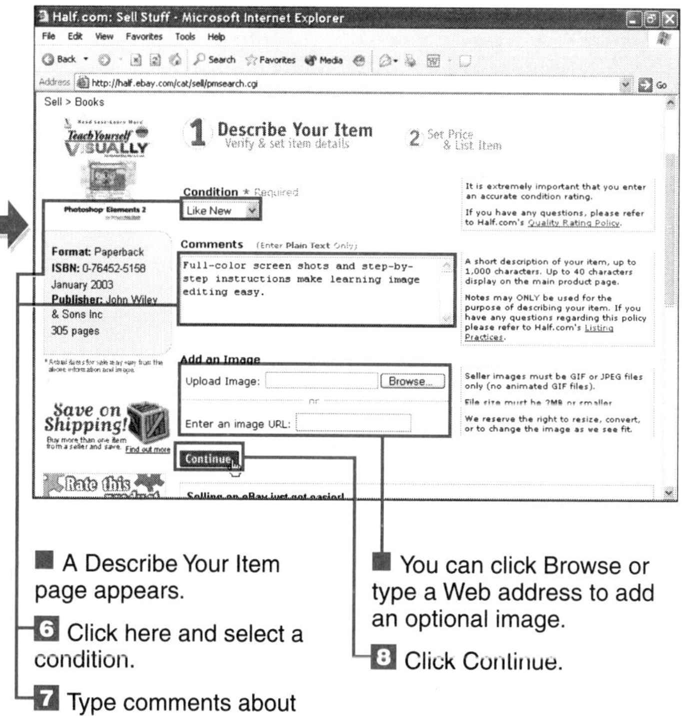

■ A Describe Your Item page appears.

6 Click here and select a condition.

7 Type comments about your item.

■ You can click Browse or type a Web address to add an optional image.

8 Click Continue.

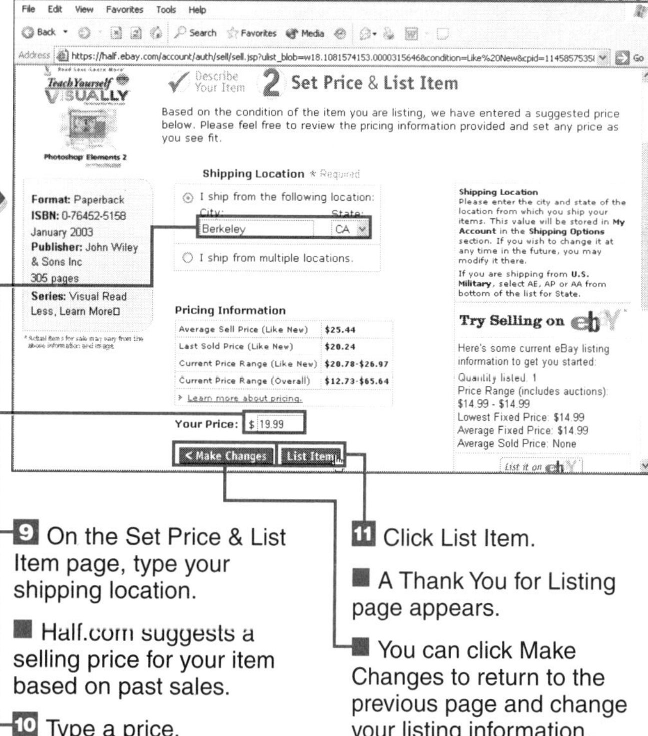

9 On the Set Price & List Item page, type your shipping location.

■ Half.com suggests a selling price for your item based on past sales.

10 Type a price.

11 Click List Item.

■ A Thank You for Listing page appears.

■ You can click Make Changes to return to the previous page and change your listing information.

LIST MULTIPLE ITEMS

For sellers listing more than one item in the Books, Music, Movies, or Games categories, Half.com offers a multiple-item interface that can help save time. On the Multiple Item Listing page, you can enter up to ten ISBN or UPC numbers. You can also specify condition ratings and add notes for each item. After submitting the information, you can set your prices one item at a time.

Sellers interested in selling large quantities of a single item can use a special bulk-listing feature if they have met certain requirements. The requirements include having sold for at least 60 days, having had at least 500 sales on Half.com, and having a feedback rating of at least 10. Sellers meeting these requirements have a quantity field presented to them during the listing process.

As soon as you list an item, the item remains listed on the site either until it is sold or until you remove it from your inventory. There are no time limits on items listed. If you sell an item outside of Half.com or if an item gets damaged, you can sign in to your Half.com account and remove the item from your inventory before someone purchases it.

LIST MULTIPLE ITEMS

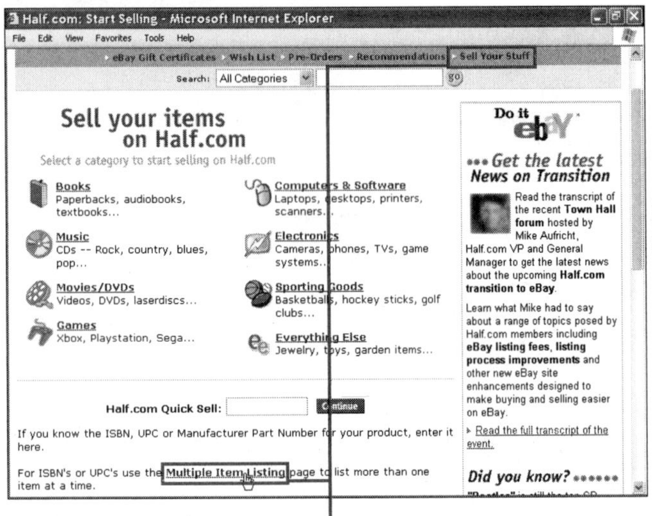

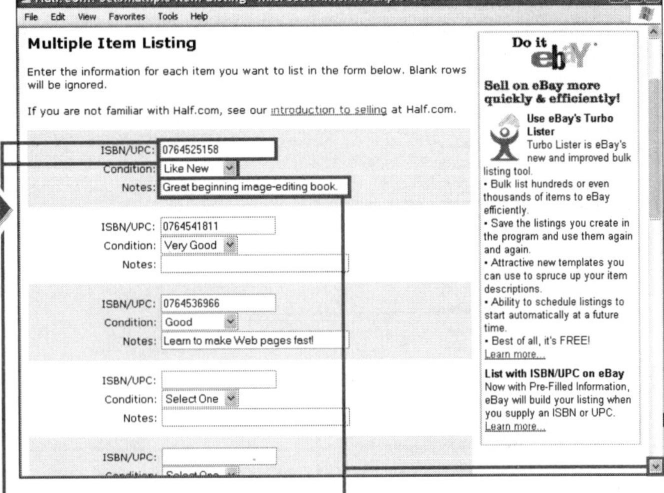

Note: To sell an item, you must have a seller's account. See "Sign Up for a Half.com Seller Account" for details.

1 Click my account and sign in to Half.com.

■ You can sign in using the same User ID and password that you use on eBay.

2 Click Sell Your Stuff.

■ The Half.com categories appear.

3 Click Multiple Item Listing.

■ The Multiple Item Listing page appears.

4 Type an ISBN or UPC number for each product.

5 Click here and select a condition rating for each item.

6 Type any optional notes for your products.

7 Click here to scroll to the bottom of the page and click Continue.

How does Half.com make its price suggestions?

✔ Half.com's suggested selling price for an item is calculated as a percentage of the best on-line retail price for a new copy of the item and depends on the quality of the item. For Like New items, the percentage is 50 percent; for Very Good, it is 45 percent; for Good, it is 40 percent; and for Acceptable, it is 35 percent.

What can I sell in the Everything Else category?

✔ According to Half.com, the following item types may be sold in the Everything Else category: Gardening, Home and Family, Jewelry, Musical Instruments, Office Equipment and Furniture, Tools, and Toys.

My book, movie, music, or game doesn't have an ISBN or UPC. Can I still list it?

✔ In many cases, yes. Use the Half.com search feature to find the item you want to sell. On the search results page, click the item you want to sell. On the item detail page, click Sell Yours Now.

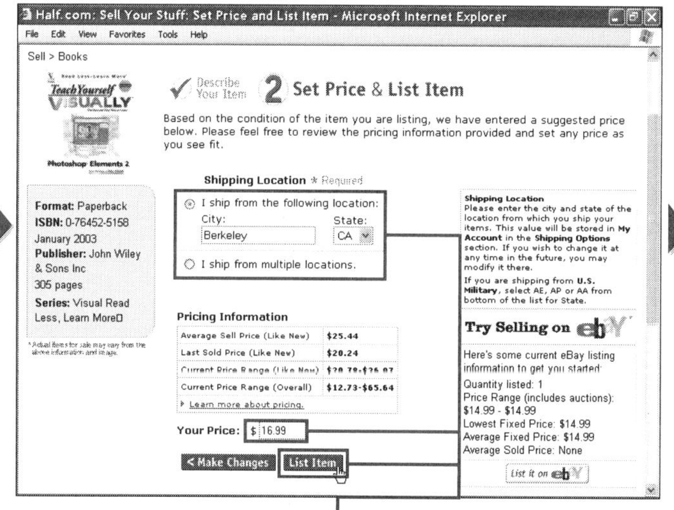

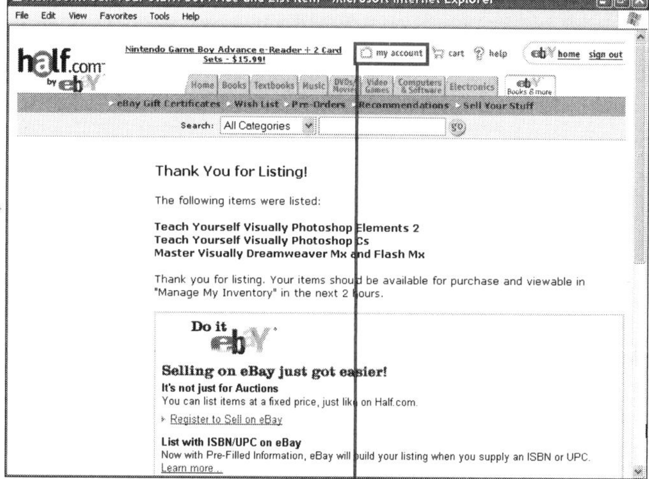

■ The Set Price & List Item page appears for your first product.

■ Half.com suggests a selling price for your item based on past sales.

8 Type your shipping information.

9 Type a price.

10 Click List Item.

■ Repeat steps 8 to 10 for each item.

■ A Thank You for Listing page appears.

■ It may take up to two hours for your listing to appear on the Half.com site.

■ You can click my account and then Manage Inventory to view or edit your listed items.

MANAGE YOUR INVENTORY

Clicking Manage Inventory on your Half.com My Account page enables you to access your entire Half.com inventory, organized by category.

You can use the inventory management buttons to edit, delete, or suspend any item you have in inventory. This lets you temporarily or permanently halt the sale of any item. You can make changes to the condition and quantity of items so that your Half.com inventory reflects what you currently have on hand. You can also update the price to make a listing more attractive to buyers, or to increase your potential for profit.

The Manage My Inventory page also includes a search feature that allows you to search for an item by its ISBN or UPC number. This can be useful when you have hundreds or thousands of items in your inventory.

Note that after you initially list an item, you will not see it for sale on the Half.com site until approximately two hours from the time you listed it. If your item does not appear two hours from the time it was listed, you should check your My Account area for a possible failed credit card alert.

MANAGE YOUR INVENTORY

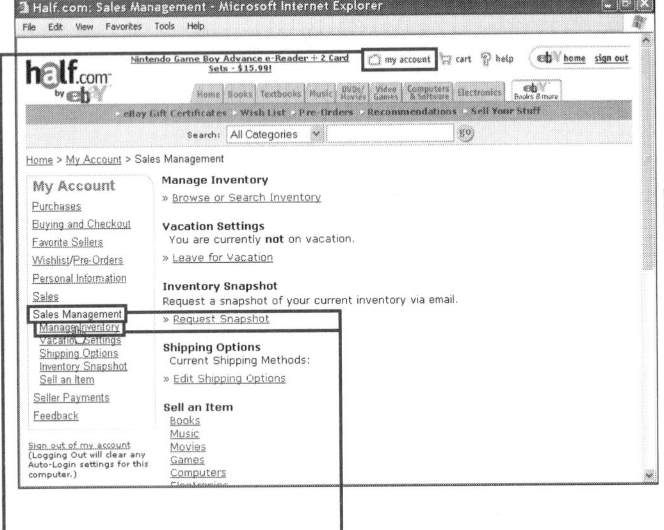

1 Click my account and sign in to Half.com.

■ You can sign in using the same User ID and password that you use on eBay.

2 Click Sales Management.

3 Click Manage Inventory.

■ The Manage My Inventory page appears.

■ The page lists the categories in which you have items listed.

4 Click a category.

What if I go on vacation and want to suspend my sales?

✔ Half.com requires sellers to confirm orders within two business days. If you go on vacation or are otherwise unable to fulfill this obligation, you can turn the vacation setting for your account to on. Your for-sale items will be suspended while you are on vacation. Click Vacation Settings in the Sales Management area of My Account to turn your vacation setting on or off.

Can I restrict where I will ship to?

✔ Half.com sellers can specify in their account settings that they will not ship to Alaska, Hawaii, or post office boxes. Click Edit Shipping Options in the Sales Management area of My Account.

What is an inventory snapshot?

✔ An inventory snapshot is a detailed list of all the current information for the items in your inventory. You can request that an inventory snapshot be e-mailed to you. Click Inventory Snapshot in the Sales Management area of My Account. A Half.com account holder can request one inventory snapshot per 24-hour period.

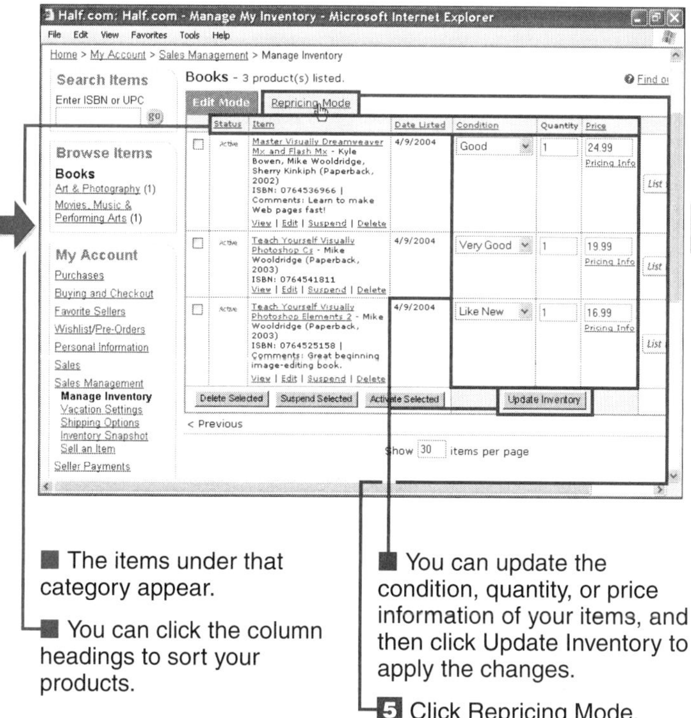

■ The items under that category appear.

■ You can click the column headings to sort your products.

■ You can update the condition, quantity, or price information of your items, and then click Update Inventory to apply the changes.

5 Click Repricing Mode.

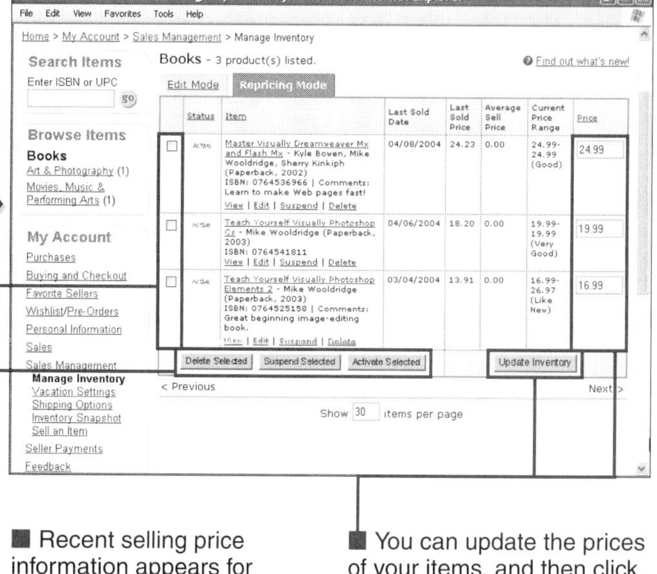

■ Recent selling price information appears for each item.

■ You can click a box by an item, and then click a button to Delete, Suspend, or Activate its listing status.

■ You can update the prices of your items, and then click Update Inventory to apply the changes.

CONFIRM AN ORDER

After a buyer purchases an item from you through Half.com, you will receive an e-mail from Half.com confirming the sale. When you receive this e-mail, you have 48 hours — excluding weekends and holidays — to confirm that you have the item and that you will ship it within 24 hours.

You can confirm the order by clicking a button in the e-mail message body, or by replying to the e-mail, making sure that the order number in the subject remains intact. You can also confirm via the Half.com Web site on your My Account page. If you do not confirm the order in time, Half.com cancels the order and you are not paid for the sale. You can also cancel an order through your My Account page.

When shipping your item after confirming, you should print the order notification e-mail from Half.com, cut off the bottom portion, and enclose that portion in your package. This serves as a reference and packaging slip. You can then ship the order according to the shipping method requested by the buyer.

CONFIRM AN ORDER

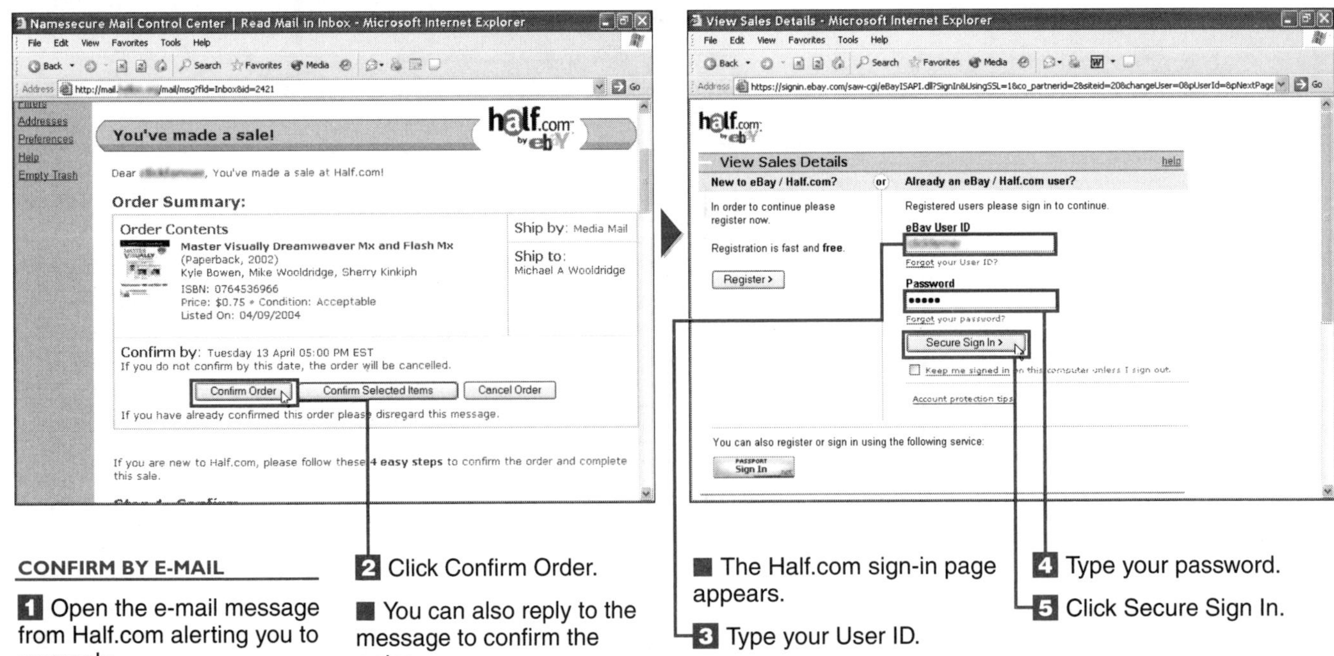

CONFIRM BY E-MAIL

1 Open the e-mail message from Half.com alerting you to your sale.

■ Half.com sends the e-mail message to the e-mail address associated with your account.

2 Click Confirm Order.

■ You can also reply to the message to confirm the order.

■ The Half.com sign-in page appears.

3 Type your User ID.

4 Type your password.

5 Click Secure Sign In.

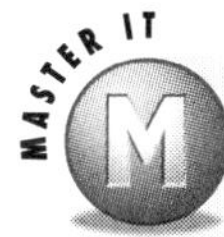

What days are considered holidays?

✔ Because sellers depend on the United States Postal Service (USPS) for most of their shipping, Half.com observes any holidays recognized by the USPS. You can find the list of holidays here: www.usps.com/communications/news/uspscalendar.htm.

Half.com does not consider any of the holidays recognized by the USPS as part of the 48 hours required for a seller to confirm an order. Weekends are also not considered part of the confirmation period.

Will I be reimbursed for shipping costs?

✔ When you sell an item on Half.com, you receive a credit to help cover the costs of shipping. The amount of the credit depends on the type of product sold. More information is available in the Half.com Help area. The shipping credit is usually sufficient to cover the cost of shipping most items. However, the allowance may not be enough to cover the cost of shipping heavier items such as multiple book sets or oversized books. In these cases, you may want to adjust the price you set for the item in order to make up for extra shipping costs.

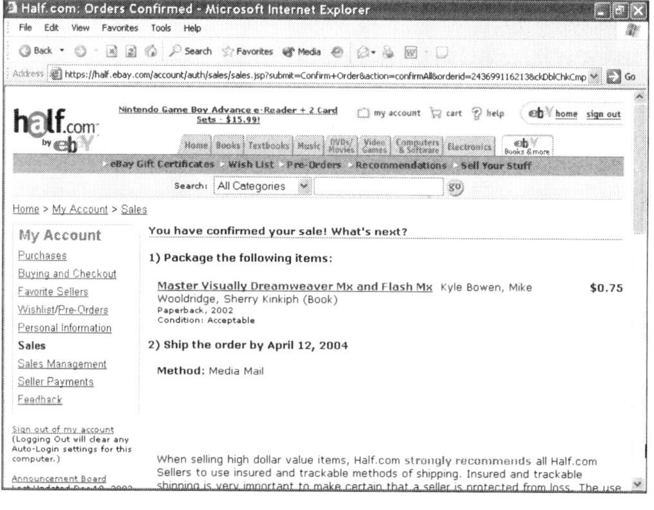

■ A confirmation page appears.

■ You must ship your package within 24 hours of confirmation.

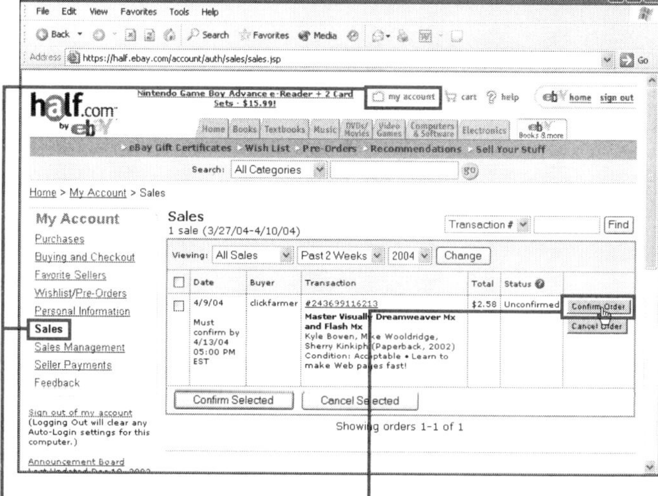

CONFIRM THROUGH YOUR MY ACCOUNT PAGE

1 Click my account and sign in to Half.com.

2 Click Sales.

3 Click Confirm Order.

■ A confirmation page appears, and Half.com confirms your order.

SECTION VIII

A) EBAY SELLER RESOURCES

B) EBAY TIME ZONES

C) HTML TAGS REFERENCE

D) WHAT'S ON THE CD-ROM

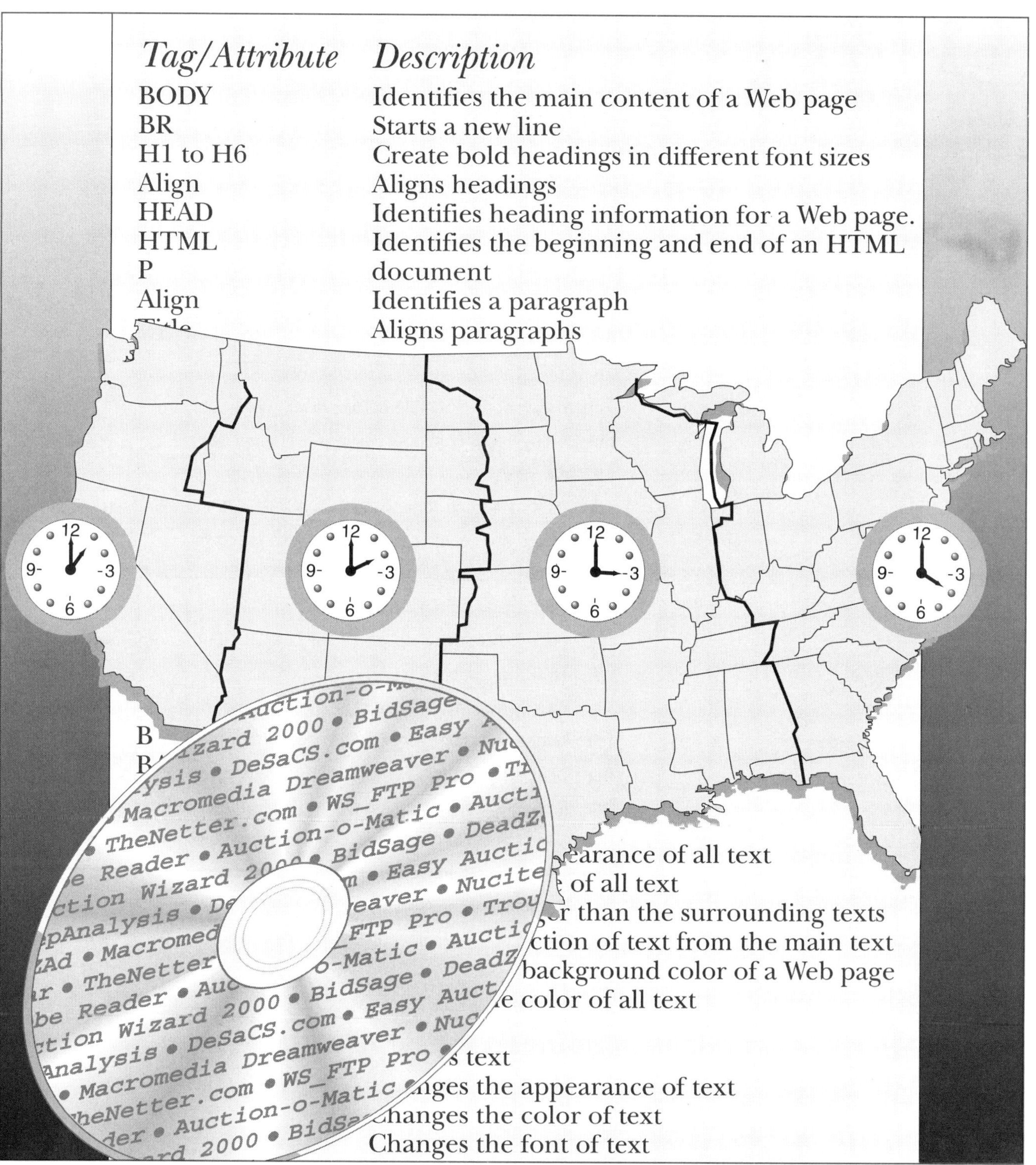
Tag/Attribute Description
BODY Identifies the main content of a Web page
BR Starts a new line
H1 to H6 Create bold headings in different font sizes
Align Aligns headings
HEAD Identifies heading information for a Web page.
HTML Identifies the beginning and end of an HTML
P document
Align Identifies a paragraph
Aligns paragraphs
12
9-
-3
6
arance of all text
of all text
r than the surrounding texts
ction of text from the main text
background color of a Web page
e color of all text
s text
nges the appearance of text
hanges the color of text
Changes the font of text
Auction Wizard 2000 • BidSage
DeSaCS.com • Easy
Macromedia Dreamweaver
TheNetter.com • WS_FTP Pro
Auction-o-Matic • BidSage • DeadZ
Reader • Auction Wizard 2000
Easy Auctio
Nucite
Trou

EBAY SELLER RESOURCES

eBay Seller Resources

Resource	*Web Location*
Site Map	http://pages.ebay.com/sitemap.html
Seller's Form	http://cgi5.ebay.com/ws2/eBayISAPI.dll?SellItem
Seller's Fees	http://pages.ebay.com/help/sellerguide/selling-fees.html
Selling Formats Page	http://pages.ebay.com/help/sell/formats.html
Seller Tools	http://pages.ebay.com/sell/tools.html
Account Billing Page	http://pages.ebay.com/sell/account.html
User Agreement	http://pages.ebay.com/help/policies/user-agreement.html
Category Overview	http://listings.ebay.com/pool1/listings/list/overview.html
System Announcements	http://www2.ebay.com/aw/announce.shtml
About Me Page Logon	http://members.ebay.com/aw-cgi/eBayISAPI.dll?AboutMeLogin
Discussion Boards	http://pages.ebay.com/community/boards/index.html
Non-Paying Bidder Alert	http://cgi3.ebay.com/aw-cgi/eBayISAPI.dll?NPBComplaintForm
Final Value Fee Credit	http://cgi3.ebay.com/aw-cgi/eBayISAPI.dll?CreditRequest
Find Members Form	http://cgi3.ebay.com/aw-cgi/eBayISAPI.dll?MemberSearchShow
Stores Home Page	http://stores.ebay.com
Current eBay Time	http://cgi3.ebay.com/aw-cgi/eBayISAPI.dll?TimeShow
Feedback Forum Page	http://pages.ebay.com/services/forum/feedback.html
Cancel Bid Login	http://offer.ebay.com/ws/eBayISAPI.dll?CancelBidShow
Bid Retraction Login	http://cgi3.ebay.com/aw-cgi/eBayISAPI.dll?RetractBidShow
Buyer Protection Page	http://pages.ebay.com/help/confidence/isgw-fraud-protection.html
Listing Upgrade Page	http://pages.ebay.com/sellercentral/tools.html
Add eBay Links Buttons	http://pages.ebay.com/services/buyandsell/link-buttons.html
eBay Security Center	http://pages.ebay.com/securitycenter/index.html
PayPal	www.paypal.com
SquareTrade	www.squaretrade.com

EBAY TIME ZONES

A part of determining start and end times for listing an auction is factoring in time zones. The eBay Web site runs on Pacific time because eBay is located in California. When considering a time of day to start and end your auction, you can consult the eBay Time Zones table to assist you in determining a time.

eBay Time Zones

eBay	*Pacific*	*Mountain*	*Central*	*Eastern*
0:00	Midnight	1:00 a.m.	2:00 a.m.	3:00 a.m.
01:00	1:00 a.m.	2:00 a.m.	3:00 a.m.	4:00 a.m.
02:00	2:00 a.m.	3:00 a.m.	4:00 a.m.	5:00 a.m.
03:00	3:00 a.m.	4:00 a.m.	5:00 a.m.	6:00 a.m.
04:00	4:00 a.m.	5:00 a.m.	6:00 a.m.	7:00 a.m.
05:00	5:00 a.m.	6:00 a.m.	7:00 a.m.	8:00 a.m.
06:00	6:00 a.m.	7:00 a.m.	8:00 a.m.	9:00 a.m.
07:00	7:00 a.m.	8:00 a.m.	9:00 a.m.	10:00 a.m.
08:00	8:00 a.m.	9:00 a.m.	10:00 a.m.	11:00 a.m.
09:00	9:00 a.m.	10:00 a.m.	11:00 a.m.	Noon
10:00	10:00 a.m.	11:00 a.m.	Noon	1:00 p.m.
11:00	11:00 a.m.	Noon	1:00 p.m.	2:00 p.m.
12:00	Noon	1:00 p.m.	2:00 p.m.	3:00 p.m.
13:00	1:00 p.m.	2:00 p.m.	3:00 p.m.	4:00 p.m.
14:00	2:00 p.m.	3:00 p.m.	4:00 p.m.	5:00 p.m.
15:00	3:00 p.m.	4:00 p.m.	5:00 p.m.	6:00 p.m.
16:00	4:00 p.m.	5:00 p.m.	6:00 p.m.	7:00 p.m.
17:00	5:00 p.m.	6:00 p.m.	7:00 p.m.	8:00 p.m.
18:00	6:00 p.m.	7:00 p.m.	8:00 p.m.	9:00 p.m.
19:00	7:00 p.m.	8:00 p.m.	9:00 p.m.	10:00 p.m.
20:00	8:00 p.m.	9:00 p.m.	10:00 p.m.	11:00 p.m.
21:00	9:00 p.m.	10:00 p.m.	11:00 p.m.	Midnight
22:00	10:00 p.m.	11:00 p.m.	Midnight	1:00 a.m.
23:00	11:00 p.m.	Midnight	1:00 a.m.	2:00 a.m.

HTML TAGS REFERENCE

Basic HTML Tags

Tag/Attribute	*Description*
BODY	Identifies the main content of a Web page
BR	Starts a new line
H1 to H6	Creates bold headings in different font sizes
Align	Aligns headings
HEAD	Identifies heading information for a Web page
HTML	Identifies the beginning and end of an HTML document
P	Identifies a paragraph
Align	Aligns paragraphs
TITLE	Creates a title in the browser title bar for a Web page

Format Text

Tag/Attribute	*Description*
B	Bolds text
BASEFONT	Changes the appearance of all text
SIZE	Changes the size of all text
BIG	Makes text larger than the surrounding texts
BLOCKQUOTE	Separates a section of text from the main text
BODY	Identifies the main content of a Web page
BGCOLOR	Changes the background color of a Web page
TEXT	Changes the color of all text
CENTER	Centers text
FONT	Changes the appearance of text
COLOR	Changes the color of text
FACE	Changes the font of text
SIZE	Changes the size of text

Tag/Attribute	Description
I	Italicizes text
PRE	Retains the spacing of text you type
SMALL	Makes text smaller than surrounding text
STRIKE	Places a line through text
SUB/SUP	Places text slightly below or above the main text
TT	Creates typewriter text
U	Underlines text

Forms

Tag/Attribute	Description
FORM	Creates a form
ACTION	Identifies the location of a CGI script for a form
METHOD	Specifies how information from a form transfers to a Web server
INPUT	Creates an item on a form
CHECKED	Selects a radio button or check box automatically
ENCTYPE	Specifies how files will transfer over the Internet
MAXLENGTH	Specifies the maximum number of characters an item will accept
NAME	Identifies an item on a form to a Web server
SIZE	Specifies the size of an item on a form
SRC	Specifies the location of the image for a graphical submit button
TYPE	Specifies the type of an item on a form
VALUE	Identifies an item on a form
OPTION	Creates a menu option
SELECTED	Selects a menu option automatically
VALUE	Identifies a menu option to a Web server
SELECT	Creates a menu on a form
NAME	Identifies a menu to a Web server
SIZE	Specifies the number of options visible in a menu
TEXTAREA	Creates a large text area on a form
COLS/ROWS	Specifies a width or height for a large text area
NAME	Identifies a large text area to a Web server

Frames

Tag/Attribute	*Description*
A	Creates a link or name anchor
HREF	Specifies the location of a linked Web page to appear in a frame
TARGET	Specifies the frame where a linked Web page will appear
BASE	Specifies information about the links on a Web page
TARGET	Specifies the frame where all linked Web pages will appear
FRAME	Specifies information for one frame
MARGINHEIGHT	Changes the top and bottom margins for a frame
MARGINWIDTH	Changes the left and right margins for a frame
NAME	Names a frame
NORESIZE	Prevents users from resizing a frame
SCROLLING	Hides or displays scroll bars for a frame
SRC	Specifies the location of a Web page that will appear in a frame
FRAMESET	Specifies the structure for frames
BORDER	Specifies a thickness for frame borders
BORDERCOLOR	Specifies the color of the borders for a frame
COLS/ROWS	Creates frames in columns or rows
NOFRAMES	Displays alternative text when frames do not appear

Image Maps

Tag/Attribute	*Description*
AREA	Specifies the information for one image area
COORDS	Specifies all the coordinates for one image area
HREF	Specifies the location of a Web page linked to an image area
SHAPE	Specifies the shape of one image area
IMG	Adds an image
USEMAP	Identifies the image map for an image
MAP	Creates an image map
NAME	Names an image map

Images

Tag/Attribute	Description
BODY	Identifies the main content of a Web page
BACKGROUND	Adds a background image to a Web page
BR	Creates a line break
CLEAR	Stops text from wrapping around an image
CENTER	Centers an image
HR	Adds a horizontal rule
ALIGN	Aligns a horizontal rule
SIZE	Changes the thickness of a horizontal rule
WIDTH	Changes the width of a horizontal rule
IMG	Adds an image
ALIGN	Aligns an image with text or wraps text around an image
BORDER	Adds a border to an image
HEIGHT/WIDTH	Specifies the height or width of an image
HSPACE	Adds space to the left and right sides of an image
SIZE	Displays alternative text when an image does not appear
SRC	Specifies the location of an image
VSPACE	Adds space above and below an image

Links

Tag/Attribute	Description
A	Creates a link
HREF	Specifies the location of a linked item
NAME	Names a Web page area displayed by selecting a link
TARGET	Specifies where linked information will appear
BODY	Identifies the main content of a Web page
LINK	Changes the color of an unvisited link
VLINK	Changes the color of a visited link

Lists

Tag/Attribute	*Description*
DD	Identifies a definition in a list
DL	Creates a list of terms with definitions
DT	Identifies a term in a list
LI	Identifies an item in an ordered or unordered list
OL	Creates an ordered list
START	Specifies a starting number
TYPE	Specifies a number style
UL	Creates an unordered list
TYPE	Specifies a bullet style

Tables

Tag/Attribute	*Description*
CAPTION	Adds a caption to a table
CENTER	Centers a table
TABLE	Creates a table
BACKGROUND	Adds a background image to a table
BGCOLOR	Adds a background color to a table
BORDER	Adds a border to a table
CELLPADDING	Changes the amount of space around the contents of cells
CELLSPACING	Changes the amount of space between cells
HEIGHT/WIDTH	Changes the height or width of a table
TD	Creates a data cell in a table
BGCOLOR	Adds a background color to a data cell
COLSPAN	Combines two or more data cells across columns
HEIGHT/WIDTH	Changes the height or width of a data cell
NOWRAP	Keeps text in a header cell on one line
ROWSPAN	Combines two or more header cells down rows

Tag/Attribute	*Description*
TR	Creates a row in a table
ALIGN	Horizontally aligns data in a table
BGCOLOR	Adds a background color to a row
VALIGN	Vertically aligns data in a table

HTML Color Codes

Color Name	*Color Code*
Aqua	#00FFFF
Black	#000000
Blue	#0000FF
Fuchsia	#FF00FF
Gray	#808080
Green	#008000
Lime	#00FF00
Maroon	#800000
Navy	#000080
Olive	#808000
Purple	#800080
Red	#FF0000
Silver	#C0C0C0
Teal	#008080
White	#FFFFFF
Yellow	#FFFF00

WHAT'S ON THE CD-ROM

The CD-ROM included in this book contains many useful files and programs. You can find a Web page providing one-click access to all the Internet links mentioned in the book, as well as several popular programs you can install and use on your computer. Before installing any of the programs on the disc, make sure a newer version of the program is not already installed on your computer. For information on installing different versions of the same program, contact the program's manufacturer.

SYSTEM REQUIREMENTS

While most programs on the CD-ROM have minimal system requirements, your computer should be equipped with the following hardware and software to use all the contents of the CD-ROM:

- A Pentium or faster processor
- Microsoft Windows 95 or later, or Macintosh OS 8 or later
- At least 32MB of RAM
- A double-speed (2x) or faster CD-ROM drive
- A monitor capable of displaying at least 256 colors or grayscale
- A modem with a speed of at least 14,400 bps
- A sound card

WEB LINKS

This CD contains a Web page that provides one-click access to all the Web pages and Internet references in the book. To use these links you must have an Internet connection and a Web browser, such as Internet Explorer, installed.

ADOBE READER VERSION

The CD-ROM contains an e-version of this book, *Master VISUALLY eBay Business Kit*, that you can view and search using Adobe Reader. As a bonus, the CD-ROM also includes an e-version of *Master VISUALLY HTML 4 and XHTML,* which you can use to enhance your auction descriptions, eBay stores, and About Me Page with HTML. You cannot print the pages or copy text from the Reader files. An evaluation version of Adobe Reader is also included on the disc.

INSTALLING AND USING THE SOFTWARE

This CD-ROM contains several useful programs.

Before installing a program from this CD, you should exit all other programs. In order to use most of the programs, you must accept the license agreement provided with the program. Make sure you read any Readme files provided with each program.

Trial, demo, and evaluation versions are usually limited either by time or functionality. For example, you may not be able to save projects using these versions.

For your convenience, the software titles on the CD are listed alphabetically.

Adobe Reader

This disc contains the free Acrobat Reader from Adobe Systems, Inc. for Windows and Macintosh. You will need this program to access the e-version of the book also included on this disc. For more information about using Adobe Reader, see the section "Use the E-Version of This Book," later in this appendix. For more information about Adobe Reader and Adobe Systems, see www.adobe.com.

Auction-o-Matic

This is a Windows trial version of an auction template maker that automatically generates HTML and JavaScript. It also lets you customize background colors and font styles, enables you to add photos and company logos (once they are hosted online), and more. For more information, see http://auction-o-matic.com.

AuctionTamer

This is a 14-day trial version of a powerful multisite auction software program for Windows that combines buying and selling management features. AuctionTamer includes complete auction-posting capabilities (with enhanced scheduling and image hosting) and works with U.S. and non-U.S. eBay sites and currencies. A tabbed browser lets you switch between eBay and related sites such as PayPal, while watch lists let you keep track of important auctions. For more information, see www.auctiontamer.com.

AuctionWizard® 2000

A Windows trial version of an auction management program you can use on your computer, AuctionWizard 2000 offers you all the tools you need to create and run your auction listings. You can automate eBay tasks, manage inventory, generate shipping labels, and more. After a 60-day free trial, the cost is $75 for the first year with a $50 renewal. For more information, see www.auctionwizard2000.com.

DeadZoom Products

ZoomPlates, Freeware version, is an auction template maker for Windows that can help you generate and organize the HTML code that you use to create your eBay listings. The DZ Table Wizard tool is a freeware version for Windows that gives you an easy-to-use interface for creating complex HTML tables. For more information, see www.deadzoom.com.

DeepAnalysis

This is a 30-day trial version of Windows software that analyzes market sectors at eBay and generates detailed market research reports. You choose an eBay category, seller, or search term, and DeepAnalysis gives you information, such as the total number of sales, sell-through rates, and average sale price per item. For more information, see www.hammertap.com/deepanalysis.

EZAd

This freeware download edition software helps you design and post your eBay auctions. The Web site also offers free image hosting and free hourly counters you can place in your ads. For more information, see www.etusa.com/auction.

Macromedia Dreamweaver

A 30-day trial version of this full-featured HTML editor and Web-site management tool, Dreamweaver includes visual layout tools, application development features, and code-editing support. You can use Dreamweaver to create professional-looking HTML templates to use with your eBay auction listings. For more information, see www.macromedia.com/dreamweaver.

Shooting Star

You can use the shareware version of this auction management program to help you track and manage multiple auctions. E-mail templates help you with your eBay communication tasks. Cost is $49.95 after a 30-day free trial. For more information, see www.foodogsoftware.com.

TheNetter.com

Included here are some of the royalty-free, downloadable Web page templates and graphics for Web designers available on TheNetter.com. eBay users can use the resources to design HTML templates for their auctions. You can download the templates and graphics online and modify them in your favorite Web editors and image editor. For more information, see www.thenetter.com.

WS_FTP Pro

An evaluation version of this Windows-based FTP (file transfer protocol) program, WS_FTP enables you to move images and other files between local and remote systems quickly and securely. You can use WS_FTP to transfer eBay auction photos to your ISP for hosting. For more information, see www.ipswitch.com.

TROUBLESHOOTING

We have tried our best to compile programs that work on most computers with the minimum system requirements. Your computer, however, may differ and some programs may not work properly for some reason.

The two most likely problems are that you do not have enough memory (RAM) for the programs you want to use or you have other programs running that are affecting the installation or running of a program. If you get error messages while trying to install or use the programs on the CD-ROM, try one or more of the following methods and then try installing or running the software again:

- Close all running programs.
- Restart your computer.
- Turn off any antivirus software.
- Close the CD-ROM interface and run demos or installations directly from Windows Explorer.
- Add more RAM to your computer.

If you still have trouble with the CD-ROM, please call the Wiley Product Technical Support phone number: 1-800-762-2974. Outside the United States, call 1-317-572-3994. You can also contact Wiley Product Technical Support through the Internet at: www.wiley.com/techsupport. Wiley Publishing will provide technical support only for installation and other general quality-control items; for technical support on the applications themselves, consult the program's vendor or author.

To place additional orders or to request information about other Wiley products, please call 1-800-225-5945.

USE THE E-VERSION OF THIS BOOK

You can view *Master VISUALLY eBay Business Kit* on your screen using the CD-ROM included at the back of this book. The CD-ROM allows you to search the contents of each chapter of the book for a specific word or phrase. The CD-ROM also provides a convenient way of keeping the book handy while traveling.

You must install Adobe Reader on your computer before you can view the book on the CD-ROM. The CD-ROM includes this program for your convenience. Adobe Reader allows you to view Portable Document Format (PDF) files, which can display books and magazines on your screen exactly as they appear in printed form.

To view the content of this book using Adobe Reader, display the contents of the CD-ROM. Double-click the PDF folder to display the contents of the folder. In the window that appears, double-click the icon for the chapter of the book you want to review.

USE THE E-VERSION OF THIS BOOK

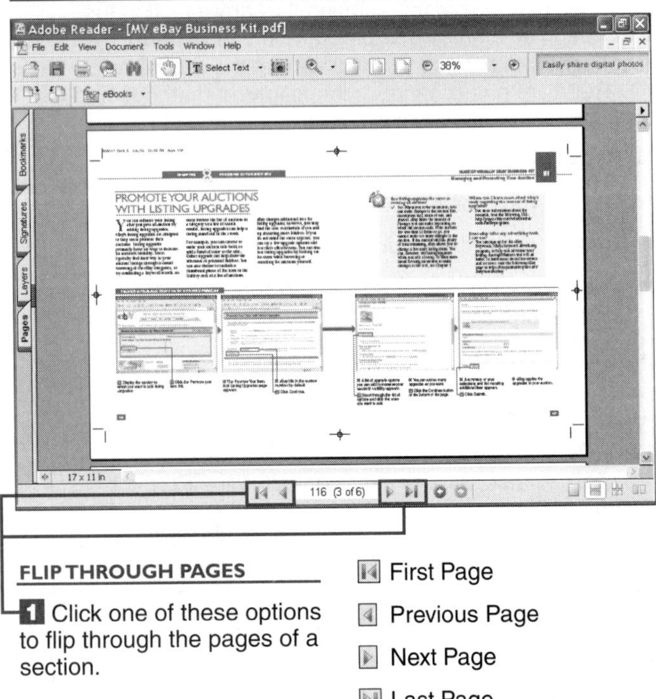

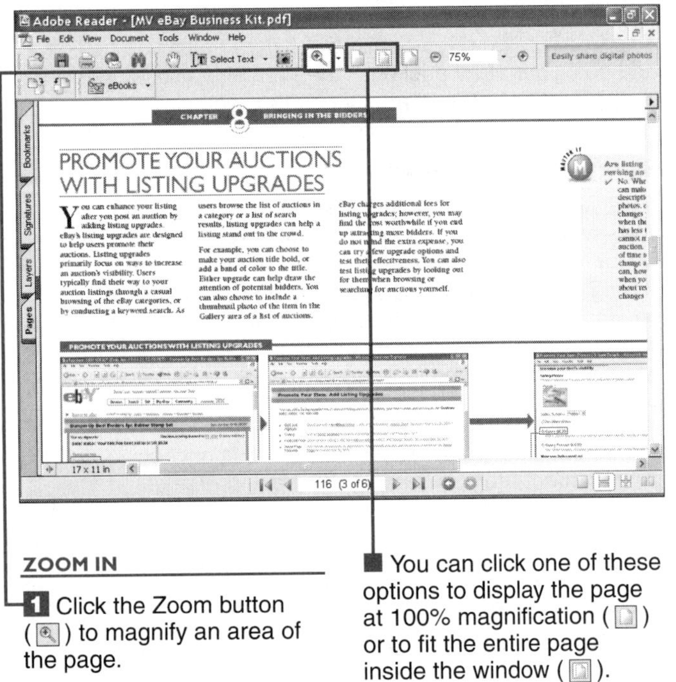

FLIP THROUGH PAGES

1 Click one of these options to flip through the pages of a section.

- First Page
- Previous Page
- Next Page
- Last Page

ZOOM IN

1 Click the Zoom button ( ) to magnify an area of the page.

2 Click the area of the page you want to magnify.

■ You can click one of these options to display the page at 100% magnification ( ) or to fit the entire page inside the window ( ).

How can I make searching the book more convenient?

✔ Copy the Reader Files folder from the CD-ROM to your hard drive. This enables you to easily access the contents of the book at any time.

Can I use Reader for anything else?

✔ Adobe Reader is a popular and useful program. There are many files available on the Web that are designed to be viewed using Adobe Reader. Look for files with the .pdf extension.

How do I install Adobe Reader?

✔ To install Reader, insert the CD-ROM into your computer's CD-ROM drive. In the screen that appears, click Software. Click Adobe Reader, and then follow the instructions on your screen to install the program.

If the CD-ROM does not load automatically, click Start and then Run. In the Run dialog box, type D:/setup.exe and click OK. If necessary, replace D with the letter of the CD-ROM drive on your computer.

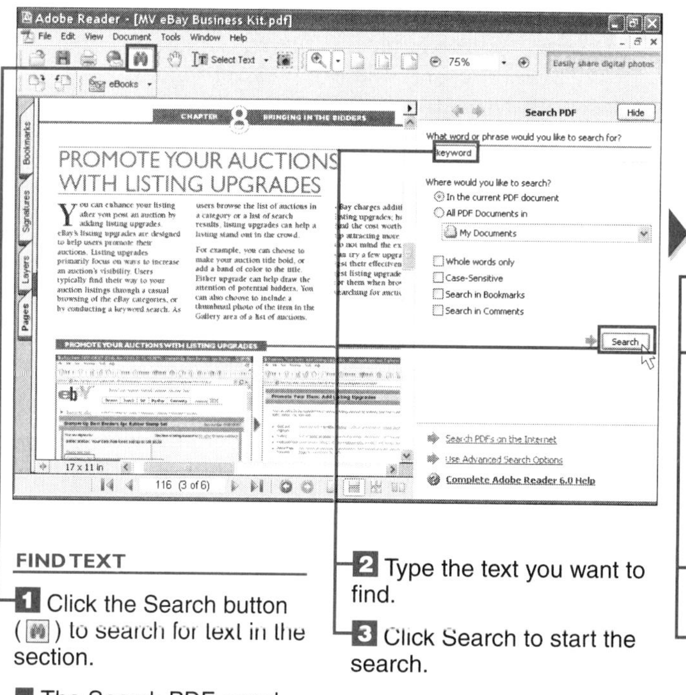

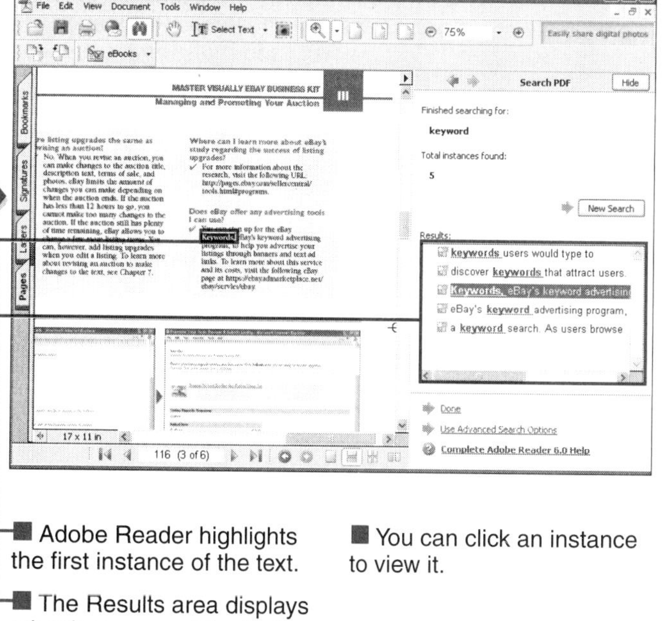

FIND TEXT

1 Click the Search button ( ) to search for text in the section.

■ The Search PDF panel appears.

2 Type the text you want to find.

3 Click Search to start the search.

■ Adobe Reader highlights the first instance of the text.

■ The Results area displays other instances of the text.

■ You can click an instance to view it.

WILEY PUBLISHING, INC. END-USER LICENSE AGREEMENT

READ THIS. You should carefully read these terms and conditions before opening the software packet(s) included with *Master VISUALLY eBay Business Kit.* This is a license agreement ("Agreement") between you and Wiley Publishing, Inc. ("WPI"). By opening the accompanying software packet(s), you acknowledge that you have read and accept the following terms and conditions. If you do not agree and do not want to be bound by such terms and conditions, promptly return the Book and the unopened software packet(s) to the place you obtained them from for a full refund.

1. **License Grant.** WPI grants to you (either an individual or entity) a nonexclusive license to use one copy of the enclosed software program(s) (collectively, the "Software") solely for your own personal or business purposes on a single computer (whether a standard computer or a workstation component of a multiuser network). The Software is in use on a computer when it is loaded into temporary memory (RAM) or installed into permanent memory (hard disk, CD-ROM, or other storage device). WPI reserves all rights not expressly granted herein.

2. **Ownership.** WPI is the owner of all right, title, and interest, including copyright, in and to the compilation of the Software recorded on the disc(s) or CD-ROM ("Software Media"). Copyright to the individual programs recorded on the Software Media is owned by the author, or other authorized copyright owner of each program. Ownership of the Software and all proprietary rights relating thereto remain with WPI and its licensers.

3. **Restrictions on Use and Transfer.**

   (a) You may only (i) make one copy of the Software for backup or archival purposes, or (ii) transfer the Software to a single hard disk, provided that you keep the original for backup or archival purposes. You may not (i) rent or lease the Software, (ii) copy or reproduce the Software through a LAN or other network system or through any computer subscriber system or bulletin-board system, or (iii) modify, adapt, or create derivative works based on the Software.

   (b) You may not reverse-engineer, decompile, or disassemble the Software. You may transfer the Software and user documentation on a permanent basis, provided that the transferee agrees to accept the terms and conditions of this Agreement and you retain no copies. If the Software is an update or has been updated, any transfer must include the most recent update and all prior versions.

4. **Restrictions on Use of Individual Programs.** You must follow the individual requirements and restrictions detailed for each individual program in Appendix D of this Book. These limitations are also contained in the individual license agreements recorded on the Software Media. These limitations may include a requirement that after using the program for a specified period of time, the user must pay a registration fee or discontinue use. By opening the Software packet(s), you will be agreeing to abide by the licenses and restrictions for these individual programs that are detailed in Appendix D and on the Software Media. None of the material on this Software Media or listed in this Book may ever be redistributed, in original or modified form, for commercial purposes.

5. **Limited Warranty.**

   (a) WPI warrants that the Software and Software Media are free from defects in materials and workmanship under normal use for a period of sixty (60) days from the date of purchase of this Book. If WPI receives notification within the warranty period of defects in materials or workmanship, WPI will replace the defective Software Media.

(b) WPI AND THE AUTHOR OF THE BOOK DISCLAIM ALL OTHER WARRANTIES, EXPRESS OR IMPLIED, INCLUDING WITHOUT LIMITATION IMPLIED WARRANTIES OF MERCHANTABILITY AND FITNESS FOR A PARTICULAR PURPOSE, WITH RESPECT TO THE SOFTWARE, THE PROGRAMS, THE SOURCE CODE CONTAINED THEREIN, AND/OR THE TECHNIQUES DESCRIBED IN THIS BOOK. WPI DOES NOT WARRANT THAT THE FUNCTIONS CONTAINED IN THE SOFTWARE WILL MEET YOUR REQUIREMENTS OR THAT THE OPERATION OF THE SOFTWARE WILL BE ERROR FREE.

(c) This limited warranty gives you specific legal rights, and you may have other rights that vary from jurisdiction to jurisdiction.

6. **Remedies.**

   (a) WPI's entire liability and your exclusive remedy for defects in materials and workmanship shall be limited to replacement of the Software Media, which may be returned to WPI with a copy of your receipt at the following address: Software Media Fulfillment Department, Attn.: *Master VISUALLY eBay Business Kit*, Wiley Publishing, Inc., 10475 Crosspoint Blvd., Indianapolis, IN 46256, or call 1-800-762-2974. Please allow four to six weeks for delivery. This Limited Warranty is void if failure of the Software Media has resulted from accident, abuse, or misapplication. Any replacement Software Media will be warranted for the remainder of the original warranty period or thirty (30) days, whichever is longer.

   (b) In no event shall WPI or the author be liable for any damages whatsoever (including without limitation damages for loss of business profits, business interruption, loss of business information, or any other pecuniary loss) arising from the use of or inability to use the Book or the Software, even if WPI has been advised of the possibility of such damages.

   (c) Because some jurisdictions do not allow the exclusion or limitation of liability for consequential or incidental damages, the above limitation or exclusion may not apply to you.

7. **U.S. Government Restricted Rights.** Use, duplication, or disclosure of the Software for or on behalf of the United States of America, its agencies and/or instrumentalities (the "U.S. Government") is subject to restrictions as stated in paragraph (c)(1)(ii) of the Rights in Technical Data and Computer Software clause of DFARS 252.227-7013, or subparagraphs (c) (1) and (2) of the Commercial Computer Software - Restricted Rights clause at FAR 52.227-19, and in similar clauses in the NASA FAR supplement, as applicable.

8. **General.** This Agreement constitutes the entire understanding of the parties and revokes and supersedes all prior agreements, oral or written, between them and may not be modified or amended except in a writing signed by both parties hereto that specifically refers to this Agreement. This Agreement shall take precedence over any other documents that may be in conflict herewith. If any one or more provisions contained in this Agreement are held by any court or tribunal to be invalid, illegal, or otherwise unenforceable, each and every other provision shall remain in full force and effect.

INDEX

Symbols

A

continued

INDEX

C

D

continued

continued

G

H

I

J

K

L

M

N

continued

Q

R

S

continued

T

U

continued

V

W

continued

X

Y

Z